MASTERING™
MICROSOFT
FRONTPAGE 97

MASTERING™
MICROSOFT®
FRONTPAGE™ 97

Susann Novalis

SYBEX®

San Francisco • Paris • Düsseldorf • Soest

Associate Publisher: Amy Romanoff
Acquisitions Manager: Kristine Plachy
Acquisitions & Developmental Editor: Melanie Spiller
Editor: Kris Vanberg-Wolff
Project Editors: Linda Good, Ben Miller
Technical Editor: David Kearns
Book Designers: Cătălin Dulfu and Patrick Dintino
Graphic Illustrator: Patrick Dintino
Electronic Publishing Specialist: Kate Kaminski
Production Coordinator: Nathan Johanson
Indexer: Ted Laux
Cover Designer: Design Site
Cover Illustrator/Photographer: Harumi Kubo and
Gene Weisskopf

Screen reproductions produced with Collage Complete.

Collage Complete is a trademark of Inner Media Inc.

SYBEX is a registered trademark of SYBEX Inc.

Mastering is a trademark of SYBEX Inc.

TRADEMARKS: SYBEX has attempted throughout this book to distinguish proprietary trademarks from descriptive terms by following the capitalization style used by the manufacturer.

Netscape Communications, the Netscape Communications logo, Netscape, and Netscape Navigator are trademarks of Netscape Communications Corporation.

The author and publisher have made their best efforts to prepare this book, and the content is based upon final release software whenever possible. Portions of the manuscript may be based upon pre-release versions supplied by software manufacturer(s). The author and the publisher make no representation or warranties of any kind with regard to the completeness or accuracy of the contents herein and accept no liability of any kind including but not limited to performance, merchantability, fitness for any particular purpose, or any losses or damages of any kind caused or alleged to be caused directly or indirectly from this book.

Photographs and illustrations used in this book have been downloaded from publicly accessible file archives and are used in this book for news reportage purposes only to demonstrate the variety of graphics resources available via electronic access. Text and images available over the Internet may be subject to copyright and other rights owned by third parties. Online availability of text and images does not imply that they may be reused without the permission of rights holders, although the Copyright Act does permit certain unauthorized reuse as fair use under 17 U.S.C. Section 107.

Library of Congress Card Number: 97-65124
ISBN: 0-7821-2027-X

Manufactured in the United States of America

10 9 8 7 6 5 4 3 2 1

*This book is dedicated
to my sons, Cameron
and Greer.*

ACKNOWLEDGMENTS

I gratefully acknowledge the contributions made by the following people:

- Leo Moll was the tour leader of the real bicycle tour to Wales and Ireland in 1991, and wrote the tour description that is the basis of the Wales-Ireland example web.
- David Walker contributed the tunes used in this book. He is the musician and Webmaster of the Internet music album, "Ain't Whistlin' Dixie" (http://mothra.nts.uci.edu/dhwalker/dixie/).
- Jeffrey L. Thomas is the author of the Castles of Wales Web site (http://www.castlewales.com/home.html). His pages and images are used in the Wales-Ireland example web.
- Joseph Rose contributed the animated GIF images and the QuickTime movie used in the Wales-Ireland example web. He is the author of the Croagh Patrick Web site (http://www.adsnet.net/rosej).

Sincere thanks to everyone who helped in the production of this book.

Thanks to James Kelley, Dean of the College of Science and Engineering, San Francisco State University, for supporting my work with Microsoft FrontPage 97.

Thanks to Microsoft for including me as a beta tester for FrontPage 97. The contributions of other members of the beta program and members of the public news group are gratefully acknowledged.

I wish to thank Melanie Spiller, Developmental and Acquisitions Editor at Sybex, for making it possible for me to write this book; and thanks to Project Editors Linda Good and Ben Miller, Editor Kris Vanberg-Wolff, and Technical Editor David Kearns. I also want to thank the production staff at Sybex for their careful work on the book, especially Nathan Johanson, Kate Kaminski, Patrick Dintino, and Molly Sharp.

Special gratitude goes to my family for their support during the trying times while I wrote this book.

Contents at a Glance

TABLE OF CONTENTS

PART II • MANAGING THE WEB

PART IV • ADVANCED TOPICS

APPENDICES

INTRODUCTION

W hen the World Wide Web started becoming extremely popular in 1995, you had to learn HTML programming in order to publish even the simplest single page on the Web. If you wanted to include any interactivity, such as collecting a comment from a user, you had to learn a programming language to write CGI programs.

What are HTML and CGI? If you aren't familiar with these terms, don't worry! I'll tell you a little (actually very little) about them in this book, but very little is all you need to know about HTML and CGI if you are building a web with FrontPage.

In the Beginning. . .

In the beginning, nonprogrammers could easily master HTML. *HTML* (*HyperText Markup Language*) is the language that you must use to prepare a text document for publishing to the Web. At first, HTML was very simple. All you could do was to change the appearance and layout of text, so the rules of the language could be summarized in a single page. But as people wanted to make their pages more interesting by displaying images and playing videos and sounds, the language became more complex. The Web and HTML continue to evolve, and now you can find entire books dedicated to HTML programming and "style."

CGI (*Common Gateway Interface*) is a set of rules you must follow when you write programs that provide interactivity to a page. Although CGI scripts themselves are easy to write, the programming languages used to write them are based on the syntax of the user-unfriendly Unix operating system, and these languages can require a great deal of effort to learn.

In a matter of months, webs changed from a few pages with simple links (text phrases marked with blue underlined font) to complex webs consisting of hundreds of pages with clickable buttons, text, and images for navigating from one page to another. These days, webs have tens of thousands of pages and often provide links to pages in dozens of other webs. How can you keep track of the pages and the links? When several authors are contributing pages to a web, how can you control who can work with it? If someone moves or removes a page and breaks a link, how can you detect the break and fix it? These web management problems have gotten more and more complex.

The Next Generation. . .

Microsoft FrontPage 97 is a tool that makes creating extraordinary web pages as easy as using a word processor, so that you can concentrate on what you want to say instead of the code you need to write to say it. FrontPage makes it possible to add searches, database queries, and data collecting as easily as setting a list of properties—so that you can concentrate on the kind of interactivity you want, instead of how to write the CGI scripts to provide it. In addition, FrontPage allows you to manage the site as a whole, so that you can see pages and links at a glance. Microsoft FrontPage 97 is the software many people have been waiting for.

Who Is This Book For?

Welcome to Mastering Microsoft FrontPage 97!

This book is for you if

- You are new to both FrontPage and to web creation. The book starts from scratch, assumes that you've never created a web page, and shows you how to use FrontPage to create an entire web.
- You have created webs, but are new to FrontPage.
- You have worked with FrontPage and want to know more about what FrontPage can do.
- You are an HTML and CGI expert and need to use your advanced skills in building a FrontPage web.

This book has two goals:

- To help you learn the basics of FrontPage in the shortest possible time
- To help you master any of the specific features of FrontPage that you want to include in your web

With these goals in mind, I organized *Mastering Microsoft FrontPage 97* as both a hands-on tutorial and as a reference.

What Do You Need?

To learn FrontPage using *Mastering FrontPage 97*, all you need in addition to the book is Microsoft Windows 95 or Windows NT and the Microsoft FrontPage 97 CD-ROM.

When you install the applications on the FrontPage 97 installation CD-ROM, as described in Appendix A, you install everything you need to get up and running on your own computer:

- The FrontPage 97 applications, including the FrontPage Editor that you use to create and edit the web pages, the FrontPage Explorer that you use to manage the web as a unit, and the FrontPage To Do List that you use to keep track of the unfinished tasks.

- A Personal Web Server that you use to display your finished web (actually, to learn all the features of FrontPage 97, you'll need to install both of the Personal Web Servers on the installation CD-ROM). If you are using Microsoft Windows NT, you'll need to install Microsoft Peer Web Services on NT 4.0 Workstation or Microsoft Internet Information Server 2.0 on NT Server.

- The Microsoft Internet Explorer 3.0 browser that you use to preview your web before "going public."

- The Microsoft Image composer that you use to create and edit images (optional).

NOTE

You do *not* need an Internet connection to create FrontPage webs or to preview the web pages and files stored on your computer's file system.

Later, when it is time to publish your work to the World Wide Web or a private company intranet, you'll need to have a connection to the Internet. You'll also need an Internet connection to preview your web if it has links to other webs on the Internet.

A Quick Look Ahead

It's time to get started learning FrontPage! Review Appendix A for installation instructions and tips on setting up your computer to work efficiently with the various components of FrontPage and the two Personal Web Servers you'll be using in this book.

Here's a quick look at what you'll learn in this book:

Part One: Overview of FrontPage introduces you to FrontPage and to web design. You'll start with a tutorial showing you the FrontPage features and how easy it is to use them. You'll learn background information on how computers and Internet applications communicate with each other, and how FrontPage fits into the Internet environment. You'll learn guidelines for designing a web and you'll explore the FrontPage wizards and templates that are available for creating web pages and entire webs.

Part Two: Managing the Web explains how to use FrontPage to manage a web. You'll learn the mechanics of working with webs, such as creating and deleting webs, importing pages and files into a web, and copying an entire web. You'll learn how to import files created in other applications and display them as part of your web, and you'll see how to use the FrontPage Explorer to view links between files, locate broken links, and update links automatically. You'll be introduced to controlling access to a web and shown how to restrict access to specific individuals and computers, and you'll also learn how to keep track of unfinished tasks.

Part Three: Creating Web Pages describes the techniques that the FrontPage Editor provides for creating and modifying Web pages. You'll learn how to create new pages from scratch and how to base new pages on existing text documents. You'll see that using the Editor to build a web page is very similar to using a word processing application: you'll format text; insert lines, images, and lists; and create lists just as you do in any word processor. You can even use drag-and-drop for most of the operations. You'll learn the Editor's special Web-related features for creating text and image links and for creating framesets. You'll learn how to use built-in programs (called bots) to automatically update changes to a Web page and to add interactivity to a page. You'll learn how to insert bots to gather information from your Web visitors, to provide text searches, and to provide a forum for online discussions. With bots, you can include features that require CGI scripts without writing any scripts yourself.

Part Four: Advanced Topics is an introduction to a few of the ways that you can enrich the content and interactive nature of your web. You'll learn how to include Microsoft Office documents (in their native formats) in your web, how to provide additional features to your pages using ActiveX Controls, and how to tie controls together using a wizard to write simple scripts. You'll see how to use the Internet Database Connector that comes with the Microsoft Personal Web server to create a live connection between your FrontPage web and a Microsoft Access database. With a live connection, the pages that display data are created and updated automatically when the database changes.

Conventions in the Book

Menu Commands   Throughout the book you'll see instructions like "Choose Insert ➤ Comment from the Editor menu bar." This means you are to open the Insert menu in the FrontPage Editor and choose the Comment command. In most cases, you'll have at least two applications, the FrontPage Explorer and the FrontPage Editor, open simultaneously, so these instructions include the name of the application.

Shortcut Key Combinations You'll see instructions like "Press Ctrl+K." This means you are to hold down the Ctrl key as you press the K key.

Text Hyperlinks This book follows the Web convention by using underlined font to indicate a text link embedded in the book's text. For example, the instruction "Click the <u>Go to Home Page</u> hyperlink" means that the underlined text phrase, Go to Home Page, is the text for a hyperlink in the page, and you are to click anywhere in the phrase.

What's on the CD-ROM?

As you work through the book, you'll participate in building example webs. The book's companion CD-ROM includes the following files needed to work through the examples:

- Files that you'll import into webs as you work are stored in the Images, PCTC Information, Sounds and Video, Wales-Ireland Manuscript and Wales-Ireland Maps, and Wales-Ireland Photos folders.

- The Webs folder on the CD-ROM includes the versions of these webs that you'll copy at the beginning of many of the chapters. For example, at the beginning of Chapter 13, you'll create a copy of the Wales-Ireland-Ch13 web. The Webs folder also includes several "answer webs"—that is, webs as they exist at the end of a chapter. For example, the answer web named Interactive is the web you create in Chapter 17.

The CD-Rom includes the Microsoft FrontPage 97 Software Development Kit. You can download updates to this software at the Microsoft Web site http://www.microsoft.com.

Endnotes

Thank you for selecting this book to help you learn Microsoft FrontPage 97. I really enjoyed writing the book and hope you enjoy using it. Please send your comments, suggestions, and corrections to me at novalis@sfsu.edu or on the World Wide Web at http://www.sybex.com.

PART—I

Overview of FrontPage

- *Create a FrontPage Web*
- *View FrontPage in the Internet Environment*
- *Design a FrontPage Web*
- *Use the FrontPage Templates and Wizards*

Chapter

1

Creating Your First FrontPage Web

Creating Your First FrontPage Web

Welcome to Microsoft FrontPage 97! Microsoft FrontPage is a group of programs for creating and managing a web. A *FrontPage web* is a set of web pages and other files that you create and manage using Microsoft FrontPage and publish on the World Wide Web or on a company intranet using a FrontPage-enabled Web server.

You use one of the FrontPage programs, called the FrontPage Explorer, to create and manage a web as a single entity. Managing a web means carrying out tasks such as creating a new web, adding content, and copying a web to another web server. In many ways, the FrontPage Explorer works just like the Windows Explorer. A second FrontPage program, called the FrontPage Editor, has tools for creating new web pages. The FrontPage Editor looks and feels very much like Microsoft Word, and you'll find that creating a web page using the FrontPage Editor is similar to creating a document using a word processor. A third FrontPage program, called the FrontPage To Do List, is used to keep track of unfinished tasks.

This chapter is a hands-on tutorial that introduces many of the features of these three FrontPage programs. We'll start at the very beginning, taking only the briefest look at how you can use FrontPage to create a web. We'll look at the easiest ways to do simple web tasks, and you'll quickly discover how easy it is to learn FrontPage. Learning FrontPage will be especially easy if you have some experience with Windows and with Microsoft Word. After you complete the six lessons of the tutorial, you won't be a FrontPage expert—that's what the rest of the book is about—but you'll have a good idea of how you can use the FrontPage Editor to create web pages, the FrontPage Explorer to understand how the pages are related, and the FrontPage To Do List to keep track of your progress.

This book assumes that you have already installed Microsoft FrontPage 97 and are using the Microsoft Personal Web Server as your Web server. It also assumes that you have installed a Web browser. Because Web browsers have different capabilities, you'll probably want to install at least two browsers to test your new FrontPage webs. We'll be using both the Microsoft Internet Explorer 3.0 and Netscape Navigator 3.0 browsers, and assume that Internet Explorer 3.0 is your default browser.

NOTE

If you haven't installed FrontPage, see Appendix A for installation instructions. If you are using another Web server, you can follow the instructions in Appendix A to change to the Microsoft Personal Web Server. If you prefer, you can continue to use another Web server that has the FrontPage Server Extensions installed, but you'll have to modify some of the steps in the lessons. Further, many of the figures will be different from your screen. You should also install all the Bonus Pack programs, including Microsoft Internet Explorer 3.0, Microsoft Image Composer, and the Microsoft Web Publishing Wizard.

A typical scenario for getting into web creation is that your company or your community group has printed information that it wants to publish on the network—and you've been assigned the task. Occasionally, the printed information is a single document prepared in a *linear* format designed to be read sequentially, one paragraph after another, like a novel. More likely, the printed information consists of several documents that can be arranged in a *nonlinear* format, like a newspaper, with sections or articles that you can read in any order. Your first task is to reorganize the printed information to take advantage of the fundamental concept of a web—hyperlinks!

A *hyperlink* is a text phrase or an image with a built-in instruction that tells the browser to jump somewhere else when you click the phrase or image (also called a *hot spot*). You can create hyperlinks that allow a visitor to your web to jump from a spot in one of your web pages to any location in your web or to a location in any other web you have access to on the World Wide Web or company intranet. A visitor to your web can use the hyperlinks on a web page to jump to another page and then jump back to the original page or jump to a new page. With hyperlinks, the web visitor is in charge. As the web author, you provide the pages and the hyperlinks, but it is the visitor who decides which pages to view and when to view them.

In this tutorial, you'll learn how to create a new FrontPage web. You'll learn how to bring existing text documents and image files into the web, how to create new pages and insert images in pages, and how to create both text and image hyperlinks. You'll see how FrontPage uses drag-and-drop techniques to copy and move objects, and you'll even use drag-and-drop to create the hyperlinks. You'll use the two views of the FrontPage Explorer to understand your web's contents and to visualize how the pages are linked. You'll use the built-in programs, called *bots*, to automate web page creation tasks, to collect data from your web's visitors, and to allow visitors to search your web.

In this tutorial, you'll create a web for a bicycle touring club. The Pacifica Cycle Touring Club (PCTC) is a fictitious club, but it has features in common with many community and social clubs. The club publishes a monthly newsletter, called The Pace Line, that includes the usual items: a calendar of club events, meeting programs, club finances, schedules of local training rides, articles of interest to club members, upcoming tour schedules, and a monthly featured tour. The club members have decided it is time to have a presence on the World Wide Web, and you've been asked to be the new webmaster. So, let's get on with it!

Lesson 1: Creating Pages in a New Web

In this lesson, you'll learn how to:

- Start up the FrontPage Explorer
- Create a new web with a home page
- Add and format text using text styles
- Create lists and nest a list within another list
- View a page in a browser
- Add a new page to the web
- Create and format a table
- Open a Word document as a web page
- Close down all components of FrontPage

Creating a Web with a Home Page

The first step in working with either a new or an existing FrontPage web is to start the FrontPage Explorer. Start the FrontPage Explorer as follows:

1. Click the Start Button on the Windows 95 taskbar, choose Programs ➤ Microsoft FrontPage ➤ FrontPage Explorer. The FrontPage Explorer window and the

Getting Started with Microsoft FrontPage dialog open (see Figure 1.1). Click the From a Wizard or Template option and click OK. Every new FrontPage web is based on one of the templates or wizards listed in the New FrontPage Web dialog (see Figure 1.2a).

FIGURE 1.1

Use the Getting Started with Microsoft FrontPage dialog to open an existing FrontPage web or create a new one.

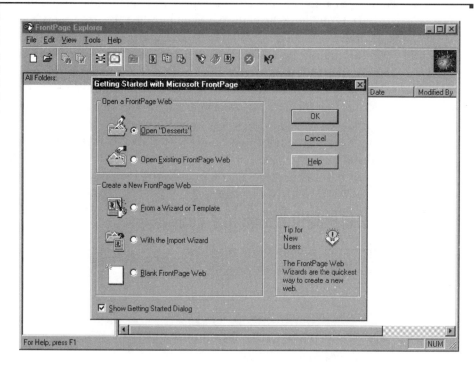

2. Click OK to accept the Normal Web template (see Figure 1.2a). The combo box in the Normal Web Template dialog shown in Figure 1.2b displays the name of your computer if you followed the installation instructions (see Appendix A for help). When you see *servername* in the book, just replace it with the name of your computer. As the figure shows, the name of my computer is pyrenees. Type **PCTC** as the name of the new web and click OK. The Explorer creates a set of folders and files for the new web.

When you create a new web using the Normal Web template, the Explorer creates a single page as the home page for the web. The *home page* is the page that the web server displays when a visitor first browses to the web. There are two ways to identify web pages. A web page has both a public *page title* that the browser displays in its title bar and a *page name* that the server uses to identify the page. When it created the web, the

Explorer assigned Home Page as the page title and default.htm as the page name. Figure 1.3 shows the new web in the FrontPage Explorer. The Explorer has two entirely different ways of displaying information about a web, called *views*. Figure 1.3 shows the view called Folder View, which looks almost exactly like the Windows Explorer. Folder View has two panes. The pane on the left, called All Folders, lists the main folder for the web, called *web folder*, and the two subfolders that the Explorer creates for every new web no matter what template or wizard you choose. You use the images folder to store image files and the _private folder to store the files and web pages that you do not want to make available to web visitors (you'll use the _private folder in Lesson 3). The pane on the right displays the contents of web folder: the two subfolders and the Home Page.

FIGURE 1.2

When you create a new web, FrontPage displays a dialog listing the wizards and templates for creating a new web (a) and a dialog for naming the new web (b).

 (a)

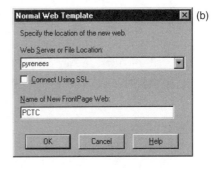 (b)

FIGURE 1.3

The Explorer's Folder View gives a hierarchical view of the web's folders in the left pane and lists the contents of a selected folder in the right pane.

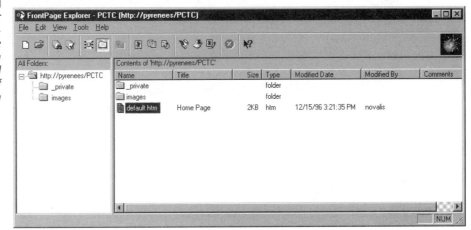

Files and Web Pages

We'll be talking a lot about a web's files and web pages. This is a good time to clarify a few basic definitions of terms we'll be using throughout the book.

A *file* is a block of information stored on a computer disk (or some other type of storage device). A file must have a name, but the filename alone isn't enough to uniquely identify a file—for that you also need to know the file's location as well. The two pieces of information are put together into the file's *path name*. The path name includes the sequence of folders that you need to traverse, starting from the main folder, or the *root folder*, of the disk. For example, C:\Webshare\wwwroot\PCTC\images\dragon.gif is the path on a C drive through a sequence of four folders to the file named dragon.gif.

The way that the information is arranged in a file is called the *file format*. Almost every application has one or more file formats of its own. The format of a file is usually included as part of the filename as a three or four letter *extension* that is appended to the end of the file's base name following a dot. For example, the name dragon.gif includes dragon as the base name and .gif as the extension. Unfortunately, applications from different vendors usually cannot process each other's files. Different types of media have vastly different file formats. The World Wide Web is a multimedia environment including text, image, sound, video, and animation file formats.

A *web page* is a file with a specific format. The format is a type of text format called HTML (HyperText Markup Language). A web page includes two kinds of text: the text information that is displayed when the page is viewed in a web browser, and special codes. The special codes may tell the browser how to display the text information, may link the page to other files, and may also include programs for the browser or the server to carry out. A web page has either .htm or .html as the file extension.

When we speak of a web's files we mean the web pages together with sound clips, image files, video clips, and files with any other file format.

We'll come back to the details of Folder View later, and we'll also take a look at the Explorer's other view, called Hyperlinks View. Right now, it's time to modify the Home Page of our new web.

Modifying the Home Page

Use the FrontPage Editor to make changes to a web page.

1. Double-click the page icon for the Home Page. The FrontPage Editor opens and displays the Home Page as an empty page with the insertion point blinking in the upper-left corner, poised for your first entry (see Figure 1.4). First, we'll give the page a new title.

PART

I

Overview of
FrontPage

FIGURE 1.4

The FrontPage Editor displays the empty home page.

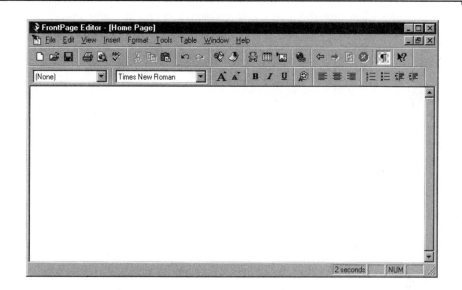

2. Choose the File ➤ Save As command from the Editor's menu, type **The Pace Line** in the Page Title text box, and click OK (see Figure 1.5). The Editor's title bar displays the new page title.

FIGURE 1.5

You can change the title of the home page in the Save As dialog.

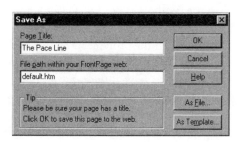

To add information to a web page, start by typing in plain text. As you go along, you add *structure* to the document by dividing text phrases into separate lines, and sentences into paragraphs. You change the appearance, or *formatting*, of text by making it bold or italic, by using a larger or smaller font for phrases or words, and by centering text or aligning text to one of the side margins. You make these structural and formatting changes in the FrontPage Editor the same way you make them in any word processing program. If you've used Microsoft Word, you'll note that many of the menu commands and toolbar buttons in FrontPage are exactly the same as in Word. If you've worked with styles in Word, you'll feel right at home; if you haven't worked with them, don't worry—you'll get plenty of practice in this book.

A *style* is a set of formatting instructions that change the look of text. There are two kinds of text styles:

- A *character style* defines the font, size, and look of selected characters (e.g. bold, italic, and underlined).

- A *paragraph style* defines the look of an entire paragraph (e.g. centering).

When you use a menu command or toolbar button to apply a style, the FrontPage Editor displays the text as it *may* appear when you view the page in a browser. However, you need to know at the outset that you don't have complete control over how your page looks in a browser. When you add structure to a page or format text, the FrontPage Editor automatically writes codes using commands of the language called the HyperText Markup Language, or HTML. HTML is the language that Web servers and browsers use to describe the structure and formatting of a text document. At the same time that you create a page in the Editor with several different fonts and paragraph alignments, behind the scenes, the Editor creates a corresponding web page in plain text and includes the structure and formatting codes also written in plain text. For example, when you format the phrase "Make me bold!" in bold font by selecting the phrase and clicking the Bold button in the toolbar, the Editor writes the following coded phrase:

<B> Make me bold! </B>

B

The symbols <B> . . . </B> are the formatting commands to the browser to display the text between the symbols as bold text. The formatting commands are called *HTML tags*. The page that you create in the Editor is an *HTML document* and has the file extension .htm. When the browser retrieves a web page from a Web server, the browser interprets the HTML tags and displays the page according to these instructions. Because browsers have different ways of interpreting the HTML tags, you don't have complete control over the way your web page will look. A web page that looks good in one browser may not look very good in another browser.

Because the Editor is doing the coding work, you never have to view the HTML coded document, but you can if you really want to.

Applying Formatting Styles

We'll use the Editor to enter some text and apply styles for the home page.

1. Type **The Pace Line** in the first line. Select Heading 1 from the Change Style combo box at the left end of the second toolbar, called the Format toolbar. The font size changes and the text is bold.

2. Click the Center button in the Format toolbar to center the paragraph, and then press Enter. Pressing Enter moves the insertion point to the next line and starts a new paragraph with the same alignment as the previous paragraph.

3. Choose View ➤ HTML from the Editor menu bar. Figure 1.6 shows the formatted text in the Editor and the View or Edit HTML window with the corresponding codes (good grief!). Click the Close button of the View or Edit HTML window.

FIGURE 1.6

The first line of formatted text in the Editor window, and the corresponding HTML-coded version.

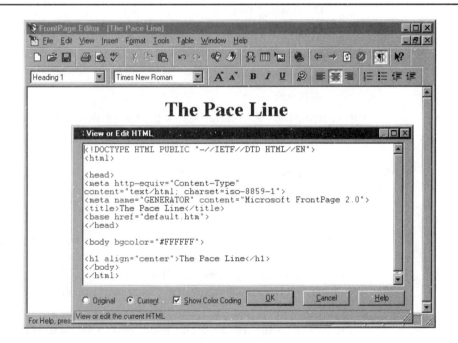

4. Type **Web of the Pacifica Cycle Touring Club** in the next line. Before you can apply a character style, you must select the text that you want to format. Hold down the left mouse button and drag to select the line of text. Click the Bold and Italic buttons in the Format toolbar.

5. Click in the next line, type **Featured Tour:** and click the Right Align button in the formatting toolbar to align the paragraph. Select the text and click the Bold button in the Format toolbar.

Creating a List

Now that the page headings are in place, we'll create a list of the main categories of information in the web. We'll use a bulleted list. In a bulleted list, each list item is preceded by a bullet and displayed as a separate paragraph.

1. Click in a new line, and click the Bulleted List button in the Format toolbar. A bullet is placed to the left of the insertion point.

2. Type each list item shown below and press Enter to start a new list item. After entering the last list item, press Ctrl+Enter to end the list.

Club Calendar

Upcoming Tours

Stories

Members Ride Statistics

Money Matters

Officers

After entering the list, you realize that the Club Calendar includes different kinds of items that you want to display as a sublist.

Nesting a List within a List

You can create a list within a list, called a *nested list*, as follows:

1. Move the insertion point to the end of the Club Calendar item, and press Enter to insert a new list item. Click the Increase Indent button in the Format toolbar, and then click the Bulleted List button to begin the nested list. The Editor indents the line and precedes the line with a bullet of a different shape (see Figure 1.7). (The actual bullet shapes vary with the browser you use.)

2. Type the items below. Press Enter after entering a sublist item to continue the list. After entering the last sublist item, press Ctrl+End to end the nested list and move the insertion point to the new line following the main list.

Meetings and Deadlines

Tour Schedule

Training Ride Schedule

FIGURE 1.7

To create a nested bulleted list, insert a new list item, indent the item, and click the Bulleted List button in the formatting toolbar.

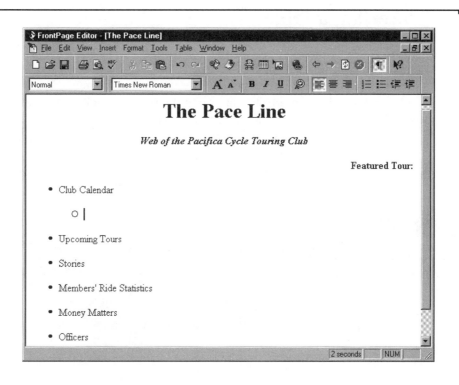

3. Click the Save button in the first toolbar, called the Standard toolbar, to save the changes to the page.

Creating a New Page

We'll create a new page for the club's meetings and deadlines schedule.

1. Click the New button in the standard toolbar to display a new blank page. Click the Save button in the Standard toolbar and type **Meetings And Deadlines** in the Page Title text box. As you enter the new page title, FrontPage automatically uses the first eight letters for the page name. (You can change the page name by typing in the text box.) Click OK to save the new page to the web.

2. Type **Meetings and Deadlines** in the first line, choose the Heading 1 style in the Change Style combo box, and click the Center button in the Format toolbar.

The information for this page includes the date, time, and location for meetings, and the date and where to send information mentioned in a deadline. This information is best displayed in a table.

Inserting a Table

Tables have cells arranged in rows and columns. You can format each cell individually just as you do when working with a table in Microsoft Word or Excel.

1. With the insertion point at the end of the Meetings and Deadlines paragraph, click the Insert Table button in the Standard toolbar and drag to create a table with five rows and four columns (see Figure 1.8). The Editor inserts a table and shows the table and cell borders as dotted lines to indicate that the border width is zero. Dotted lines are formatting marks that appear only in the FrontPage Editor and do not appear in a Web browser. To display a border in a Web browser, you have to set the border width to a number greater than zero.

FIGURE 1.8

Click the Insert Table toolbar button and drag to size the new table.

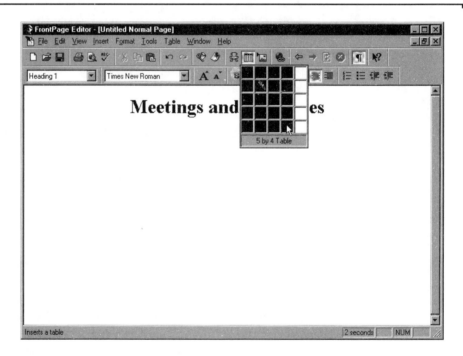

2. Choose Table ➤ Table Properties from the Editor menu bar to display the Table Properties dialog (see Figure 1.9). Type **1** in the Border Size text box and click OK.

Creating a Header Row

We'll make the cells in the first row header cells. Header cells use a bold font.

1. With the insertion point in the first table cell, choose Table ➤ Select Row from the Editor menu bar. The cells of the row are highlighted to indicate they are selected.

Overview of
FrontPage

FIGURE 1.9

*Set the border
width in the Table
Properties dialog.*

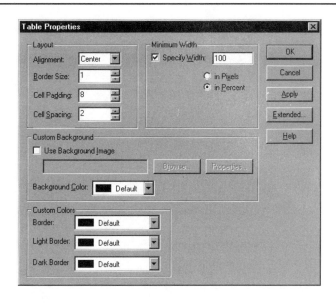

2. Choose Table ➤ Cell Properties from the Editor menu bar. Click the Header Cell
check box in the Cell Properties dialog (see Figure 1.10) and click OK.

3. Click the first cell in the table. Enter the headings shown below in the heading
cells. Press Tab to move from cell to cell.

What   When   Where   Details

4. Type the club calendar information in the cells as shown below. Include the
spelling errors (Wedesday and member). Use the Tab or the arrow keys to move
between table cells.

Club Meeting	**Wednesday, March 20 at 7:30**	**Pacifica Community Center**	**Dinner with the speaker at 6:00 at the Java Cafe next door.**
Board Meeting	**Wedesday, March 6 at 7:30**	**Pacifica Community Center**	**All club members are invited.**
Ride Listing Deadline	**Monday, March 11**	**Send April ride descriptions to Ride Coordinators**	**Any club member can lead a training ride.**
The Pace Line Deadline	**Monday, March 18**	**Send material for the April issue to the Webmaster.**	**Share your ideas and touring experiences.**

FIGURE 1.10

Use the Cell Properties dialog to create a table header row.

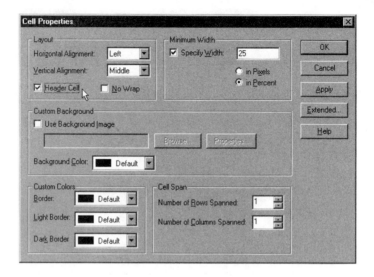

5. Click the Spell Checker button in the toolbar. The Editor spell checks the entire page and locates the first spelling error (see Figure 1.11). Click the Change All button to make the changes and locate the next error. Continue checking for errors and making changes until the Editor reports that the spelling check is complete.

FIGURE 1.11

Use the spelling checker to correct errors.

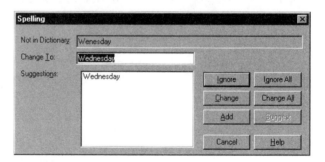

6. Select the phrase The Pace Line in the cell in the lower-left corner of the table, and click the Italic button in the toolbar. Click the Save button in the toolbar to save your work. Figure 1.12 shows the completed web page.

FIGURE 1.12

The Meetings and Deadlines web page

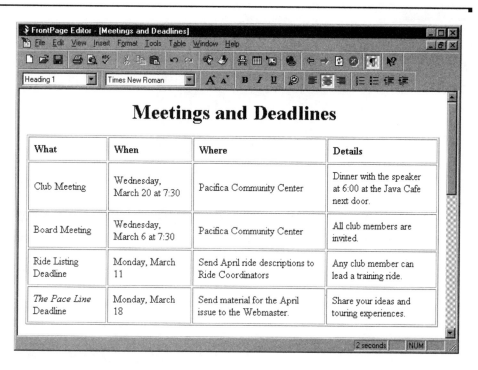

Opening a Word Document as a New Web Page

The file that the club's newsletter editor sent you includes a description of the month's featured tour to Wales and Ireland. The tour leader prepared the tour description using Microsoft Word. The file is named Wales-Ireland.doc and is on the book's CD-ROM.

1. Choose File ➤ Open from the Editor menu bar. Click the Other Location tab in the Open File dialog (see Figure 1.13a) and click the Browse button to display the Open File dialog. Use the Look in combo box to locate and open the PCTC Information folder on the book's CD-ROM. Choose All Files (*.*) in the Files of type combo box to display the files in the folder. Double-click Wales-Ireland.doc (see Figure 1.13b). The FrontPage Editor converts the Word document first to the Rich Text Format (RTF) and then to HTML, and displays the result as a web page (see Figure 1.14). In converting the Word document, the FrontPage Editor preserves the document's formatting and the images that the tour leader added.

FIGURE 1.13

Click the Browse button on the Open File dialog (a) to display the Open File dialog (b).

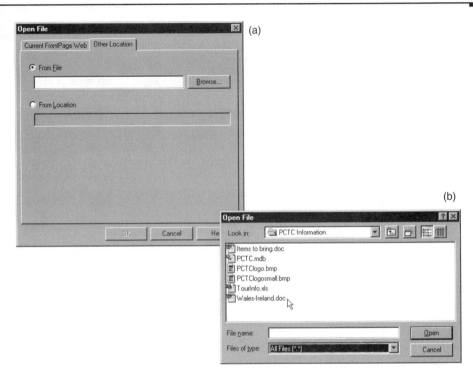

FIGURE 1.14

When you open a Word document in the Editor, FrontPage converts it to an HTML document.

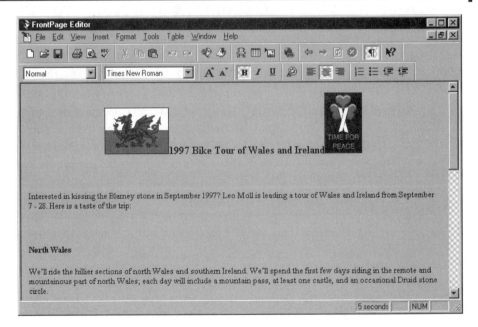

2. Click the Save button in the Standard toolbar. In the Save As dialog, type **Wales and Ireland 1997 Tour** as the page title, type **wales-ireland.htm** as the page name, and click OK. FrontPage recognizes that the page has images and displays the Save Image to FrontPage Web dialog so that you can save the images to the images folder in the web. We'll change the names of the image files to reflect what the images represent. The image on the left is the national flag of Wales and the image on the right is the peace symbol for Ireland. We'll name the images dragon and peace, respectively.

NOTE

Unlike a Word document, which can contain embedded images as part of its file, a web page is a text file and cannot contain nontext objects. In converting the Word document, the FrontPage Editor separates the text and the images into separate files and automatically creates links to the image files. To display the images in the page, you must save the image files to the web, too.

3. Change the entry in the Save as URL text box to images/dragon.gif (see Figure 1.15) and click the Yes button. FrontPage displays the dialog for the second image.

4. Change the entry in the Save as URL text box to images/peace.gif and click the Yes button.

Overview of
FrontPage

FIGURE 1.15

When you save a converted Word document that has embedded images, the Editor offers to save the images to your web.

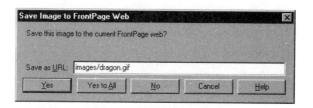

Viewing Web Pages in the Browser

It's time to see how the new web pages look in a browser. To preview a page, you don't need to be connected to a network, and if you do have a network connection, the connection doesn't have to be open. Most browsers, including Internet Explorer 3.0, work in local mode without an open network connection (see Appendix B for more information).

1. Click the Preview in Browser button in the Standard toolbar. The Internet Explorer browser opens and displays the wales-ireland.htm web page (see Figure 1.16).

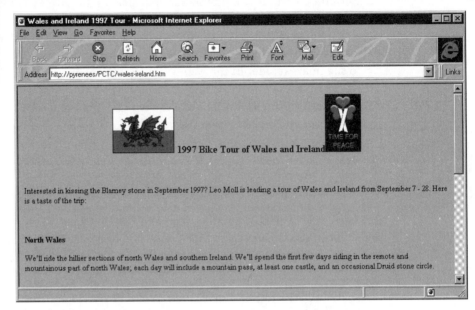

2. To preview the home page, change the browser's Address text box to **http:// *servername*/PCTC/** and press Enter. The browser displays the default.htm web page. You don't have to type the http:// part of the address because browsers assume you are using the Web protocol if you don't explicitly specify one.

3. To preview the Meetings and Deadlines page, change the Address text box to ***servername*/PCTC/meetings.htm** and press Enter.

4. Minimize the browser.

If you enter less than the last address, however, the browser or the server won't be able to find the page. For example, if you omit the computer name and enter PCTC/ meetings.htm for the address, the browser displays an error message like the one in Figure 1.17a. If you omit the .htm extension for the web page, the web server displays the 404 error shown in Figure 1.17b.

Closing Up to Take a Break

Congratulations! You've got your new FrontPage web up and running, so this is a good time to take a break. When you finish a lesson and want to take a break, save your work and exit FrontPage as follows:

1. In the FrontPage Editor, choose File ➤ Exit from the Editor menu bar. If you have an open page with unsaved changes, the Editor offers to save the changes.

Click Yes to save the changes or No to discard the changes, and close the page. After closing all open pages, the Editor closes.

2. In the FrontPage Explorer, choose Exit from the File menu, or click the window's Close button to exit from the Explorer.

PART

I

Overview of
FrontPage

FIGURE 1.17

If you omit the server name in the Address, the browser displays an error message (a). If you omit the .htm extension, the server displays an error message (b).

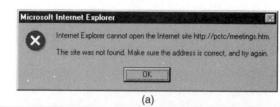

(a)

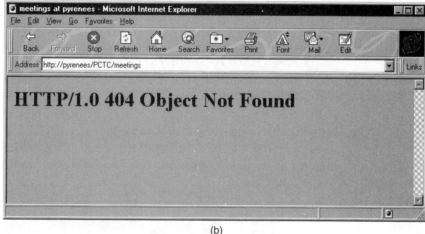

HTTP/1.0 404 Object Not Found

(b)

For More Information

Lesson 1 has shown you a few of the Editor's tools. You've learned how to create new pages and use the Editor much like a word processor to format characters and paragraphs. Chapter 10: Editor Basics completes the introduction to the Editor. Chapter 11: Working with Text and Lines covers working with text. Chapter 14: Adding Tables shows you how to use tables to display information and to lay out a web page using table cells. Chapter 15: Understanding Frames shows you a different way to lay out a web page using a special web page called a frameset that has cells called frames arranged much like the cells in a table, but with a big difference—you can use a frame cell to display an entire web page!

Lesson 2: Creating Text Links

In this lesson, you'll learn how to:

- Open an existing web
- Create a text hyperlink between pages
- Create a hyperlink to a specific location on a page
- Follow a link in a browser and in the Editor
- Create a World Wide Web link
- Create a link to a browser's e-mail program
- Change a link's colors

To begin the lesson, start up the Explorer by clicking the Windows Start button and choosing Programs ➤ Microsoft FrontPage ➤ FrontPage Explorer.

1. In the Getting Started with Microsoft FrontPage dialog, click the first option to open the web that was last opened (see Figure 1.18). The Explorer window looks pretty much the same as in Lesson 1, except the Contents pane lists the home page and the two pages you added (see Figure 1.19a). When you select a folder in the All Folders pane on the left, the pane on the right displays the folder's contents, including its subfolders and a list of its files. The list includes the file-name, title, size, file type, date, and time the file was last modified, the name of the author who modified the file, and comments about the file.

FIGURE 1.18

The Getting Started with Microsoft FrontPage dialog

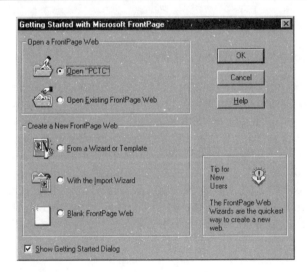

PART
1

Overview of
FrontPage

2. Click the Title heading in the right pane. The files are sorted alphabetically by title. You can sort the list by any heading just by clicking the heading.

3. Click the images folder in the left pane to view the list of image files you added (see Figure 1.19b).

4. Click the web folder in the left pane and then double-click the default.htm page icon. The FrontPage Editor opens and displays the home page.

FIGURE 1.19

The right pane of Folder View of the Explorer shows the subfolders and the files of your web folder (a). Click a folder in the left pane to display its contents in the right pane (b).

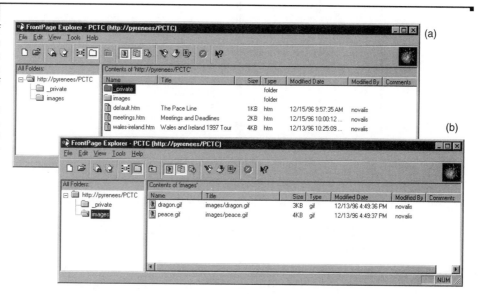

Creating a Text Link Using Drag-And-Drop

The easiest way to create links between web pages in the same web is to use drag-and-drop. To prepare for creating hyperlinks using drag-and-drop from the FrontPage Explorer, resize and rearrange the Explorer and the Editor windows as shown in Figure 1.20. (The panes of the Explorer window are decreased in width so that you can select a folder and display its contents.) Locate the start page for the link in the FrontPage Explorer and double-click the page icon to display the page in the Editor. To create a hyperlink, simply drag the target page from the FrontPage Explorer to the location in the start page where you want to create the hyperlink, and drop the page icon. FrontPage creates the hyperlink using the title of the target page as the text.

FIGURE 1.20

To prepare for creating hyperlinks using drag-and-drop from the FrontPage Explorer, resize and rearrange the Explorer and Editor windows.

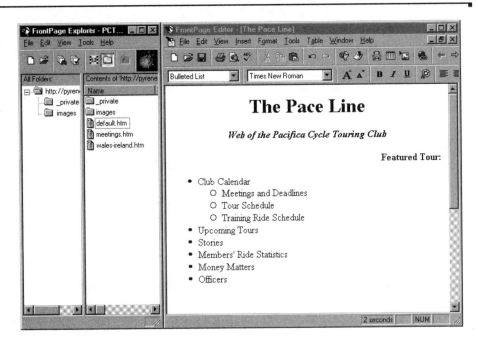

We'll create a text hyperlink to jump from the home page to the tour description page.

1. In the FrontPage Explorer, click the wales-ireland.htm page icon and hold down the left mouse button as you drag to the right of the text, Featured Tour: (see Figure 1.21). When you release the mouse button, FrontPage creates a hyperlink to the wales-ireland.htm page and inserts the page title as the text for the hyperlink. The Editor indicates a text hyperlink by underlining the text and changing the font color. The default color for a new hyperlink is blue. We'll modify the link's text in the next step.

2. Drag to select the phrase 1997 Tour and press Delete.

3. In the Explorer, click the meetings.htm page icon and drag to the Meetings and Deadlines item in the nested list. Drop the page icon to create a hyperlink to the meetings.htm page. Drag-and-drop doesn't replace the existing text in the line, so you'll have to delete the duplicate text.

4. Drag to select the duplicate phrase, Meetings and Deadlines, and press Delete.

5. Click the Save button in the toolbar.

FIGURE 1.21

Select the target page in the Explorer and drag to the location in the start page in the Editor where you want to place the hyperlink.

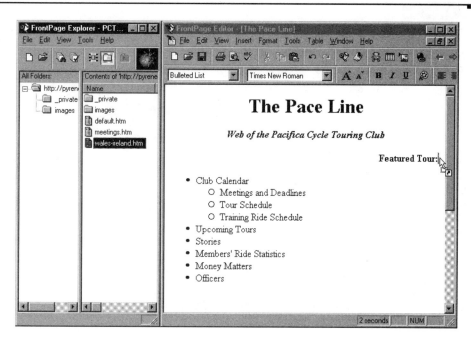

Following the Link

You can test a hyperlink by previewing the start page in a browser.

1. Click the Preview in Browser button in the Editor's Standard toolbar.

2. Click the new hyperlink with Meetings and Deadlines as the link text. The browser displays the Meetings and Deadlines page. Minimize the browser.

You can also test a hyperlink in the FrontPage Editor.

1. Click in the Editor. Press Ctrl and move the pointer to the hyperlink with Wales and Ireland as the link text. When the pointer changes shape to the follow link arrow (see Figure 1.22), click the mouse button. The Editor displays the tour description page. You can follow the link backwards from the target page to the start page using the Back command.

2. Click the Back button in the Editor's Standard toolbar. You are now back to the web's home page.

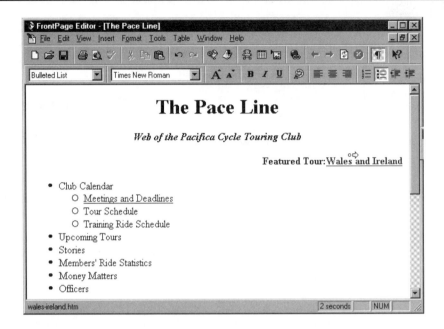

Marking a Target Location on a Page

The tour description is really interesting, but it is too long to be displayed in a single window. The last paragraph of the description explains how to sign up for the trip. To make it easier for the web user to jump to this specific location, you'll use a *bookmark* to mark the spot and a hyperlink that starts at the top of the page and has the book-marked location as its target. You'll use drag-and-drop to mark the target location and create a hyperlink in one step.

1. Click the Forward button in the Editor's Standard toolbar to display the tour description page. The Editor keeps a list of the pages you visited previously and you can use the Forward and Back toolbar buttons to cycle through the pages.

2. Scroll to the bottom of the page and select Interested as the text to mark.

3. Click and hold the right mouse button as you drag to the top of the page. To scroll to the top of the page, hold the pointer near the top edge of the window— the page scrolls automatically (see Figure 1.23a). Move the pointer to the left of the first line in the description (to the left of the word Interested) and release the mouse button. Choose Link Here in the shortcut menu (see Figure 1.23b). FrontPage marks the text at the bottom of the page as a bookmark, and creates a hyperlink at the top of the page using Interested as the link's text.

Overview of
FrontPage

FIGURE 1.23

To scroll the page while dragging the mouse pointer, hold the pointer near the page's top or bottom boundary (a). To create the hyperlink, release the mouse button and choose Link Here from the shortcut menu (b).

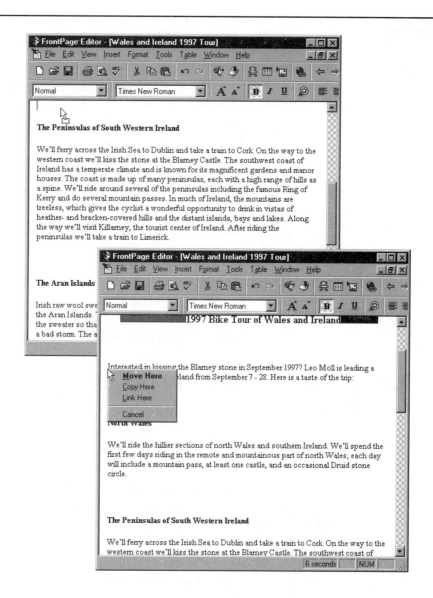

3. Select the duplicate word Interested to the right of the hyperlink, and press Delete.

4. To test the hyperlink, press Ctrl and click the hyperlink. The Editor jumps to the bookmarked location at the bottom of the page. The Editor uses a dotted under-line to indicate bookmarked text (see Figure 1.24), however, browsers do not indicate bookmarked text in any way.

FIGURE 1.24

The Editor uses a dotted underline to indicate bookmarked text.

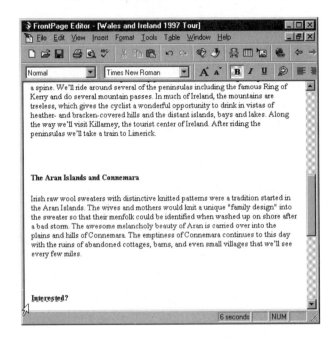

Using the Create Hyperlink Dialog to Create a Link

We need to create a link back to the home page so a visitor to the web can quickly return after reading about the tour. We'll add some new text to the top of the web page.

1. Scroll to the top of the web page, place the insertion point to the left of the Welsh flag, and press Enter. FrontPage inserts a new first line.

2. Click in the inserted line, type **[Go back to the Home Page]**, select the text you just entered, and click the Italic button in the formatting toolbar. Click the Align Right button in the formatting toolbar.

3. Click the Edit or Create Hyperlink button in the Standard toolbar. Double-click The Pace Line in the Create Hyperlink dialog as the target page of the hyperlink (see Figure 1.25a). The dialog closes and the hyperlink to the home page is created (see Figure 1.25b).

Copying a Link to Another Location

When you design navigation paths through your web, you need to think like your web visitor and try to anticipate the ways your visitor may want to travel around in your site. Right now, you've provided links from the home page to the top of the tour

FIGURE 1.25

To create a hyperlink
to another open
page, select the
page in the Create
Hyperlink dialog.

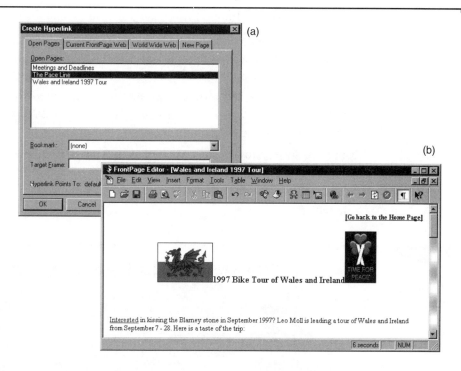

description and back to the home page from the top of the tour description. You've also provided a link from the top to the bottom of the tour description; but once the web user is at the bottom of the tour description page, there is no easy way to move somewhere else. You'll solve this problem by copying the link at the top of the tour description page to the bottom. The web visitor can then easily jump back to the home page from the top or the bottom of the tour description.

1. Drag to select the [Go back to the Home Page] text hyperlink. Right-click in the selection. Keeping the right mouse button pressed, drag to the bottom of the page (holding the pointer at the bottom of the page to force the page to scroll), and release the mouse button. Choose Copy Here from the shortcut menu. The Editor inserts a copy of the hyperlink.

2. Choose Heading 5 in the Change Style combo list and click the Align Right button in the formatting toolbar.

3. Test the hyperlink by pressing Ctrl and clicking the new hyperlink. The Editor jumps to the home page.

4. Follow the text hyperlink back to the tour description page, or click the Back button in the toolbar.

Changing Link Colors

FrontPage uses the color blue to indicate a link, and the color dark purple to indicate a link you have visited. Since most people associate the color green with Ireland, you'll change the link colors for all the text hyperlinks on the tour description web page.

1. Choose File ➤ Page Properties from the Editor menu bar and click the Background tab in the Page Properties dialog (see Figure 1.26). The tab shows the default colors for the links on the page.

2. Click the down arrow of the Hyperlink combo list and choose Green. Click the down arrows of the Visited Hyperlink combo list and choose Navy.

3. Click OK to close the Page Properties dialog box. The change takes effect immediately.

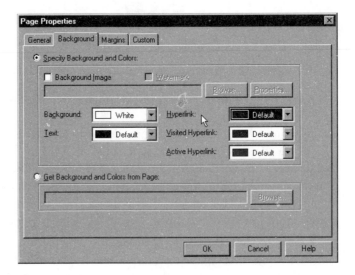

Creating Hyperlinks by Typing on the Page

It occurs to you that potential tour members might be interested in finding out more about the countries before deciding to go on the tour. You can provide hyperlinks to a few web sites on the World Wide Web. If you know the address of a web site, you can create a text hyperlink to it just by typing the address in the page. A quick phone call to the tour leader gives you a good starting site.

1. Scroll to the bottom of the tour description page, place the insertion point to the right of the question mark in the line with the text Interested?, and press Enter to insert a new line.

2. Type **Want to know more about the tour countries? Go to the Internet Travel Network at**, select the text, and click the Bold button in the formatting toolbar to remove the bold formatting.

3. Type **www.solutions.net/rec-travel/europe/** and press Enter. FrontPage recognizes you have entered a World Wide Web address and creates a hyperlink automatically.

4. Click the Save button in the standard toolbar.

5. To test the hyperlink, open your network connection. Click the Preview in Browser button in the Standard toolbar. Click the hyperlink with Interested as the link text to jump to the bottom of the page. Click the World Wide Web hyperlink. After a delay, the browser displays the home page for the Internet Travel Network in Europe.

6. Minimize the browser.

Creating an E-mail Link

You can also create a link to the visitor's mail program. You'll add the tour leader's e-mail address to the tour description page.

1. Place the insertion point at the end of the last line of the tour description page. Type **Contact Leo at moll@worldnet.att.net** and press Enter. FrontPage recognizes you have entered an e-mail address and creates a link to the browser's e-mail program automatically. Figure 1.27a shows the bottom of the tour description page with the World Wide Web link and the mail link.

2. Click the Save button and then click the Preview in browser button in the Standard toolbar. If necessary, refresh the browser.

3. Click the e-mail address. Figure 1.27b shows the mail program for Internet Explorer 3.0. Click the Close button.

NOTE

Most of the popular browsers recognize the mailto link that the Editor creates when you type an e-mail address. These browsers allow you to send e-mail messages directly from the browser. Many browsers include an e-mail program that lets the Web visitor send and receive e-mail from within the browser. In any case, the Web visitor's computer must have an Internet connection and the visitor's browser must be configured to use an e-mail program.

PART

1

Overview of
FrontPage

Closing Up and Taking a Break

You can close out of FrontPage and take a break before continuing on with the next lesson.

For More Information

In Lesson 2, you've learned how to use drag-and-drop to create a text hyperlink to another page in the web and to a specific location (a bookmark) on a web page. You've also seen that you can create text hyperlinks to World Wide Web sites and to an e-mail program just by typing on the web page. Chapter 12: Understanding Text Hyperlinks covers all the other ways to create text hyperlinks.

FIGURE 1.27

You can create text hyperlinks to a World Wide Web location and to a mail program by typing the address directly on the web page (a). The Internet Explorer 3.0 mail program (b).

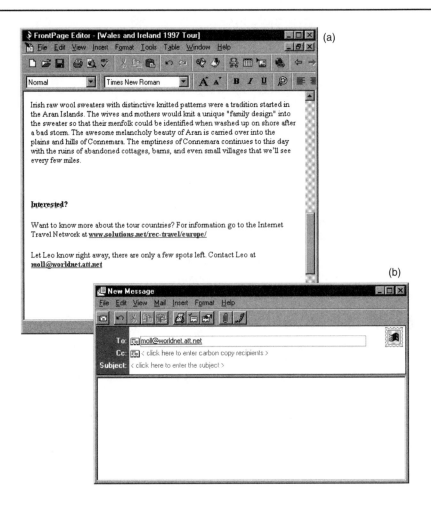

Lesson 3: Using Images

In this lesson, you'll learn how to:

- Import images from your computer's file system
- Insert an image in a page
- Insert a background image
- Make an image color transparent
- Create a clickable image hyperlink

If you closed FrontPage at the end of the last lesson, you'll need to start the FrontPage Explorer and click the first option in the Getting Started dialog to open the PCTC web. In the Explorer, double-click the home page, then the meetings.htm page, and then the wales-ireland.htm page to open all three pages in the Editor.

Importing an Image File to the Web

To make your web more attractive, you decide to add the club's logo and an image for the featured tour of the month. The book's CD-ROM contains two versions of the logo as bitmap files in the PCTC Information folder and two other images in the Images folder you'll be needing.

You can drag image files directly from your computer's file system to the Images folder in the web.

1. Open the Windows Explorer by clicking the Windows Start button and choosing Windows Explorer. Locate the CD-ROM and open the PCTC Information folder. Select the PCTClogo.bmp and the PCTClogosmall.bmp image files and drag them to the images folder in the web (see Figure 1.28). When you drop the files in the folder, the Explorer briefly displays a message that the files are being imported.

2. Open the Images folder on the CD-ROM, select the world.bmp and the vellum.jpg image files and drag them to the images folder in the web.

3. Close the Windows Explorer by clicking the window's Close button.

4. In the FrontPage Explorer, click the images folder in the pane on the left. The pane on the right displays the four image files you just imported (see the Explorer window in Figure 1.29 below). The bitmap files have been converted to the GIF image format and have the .gif extension. (You'll learn about image formats in Chapter 13.)

PART

1

Overview of
FrontPage

You can import image files by dragging from your computer's file system to the images folder in the current web.

Inserting an Image

Your new web pages look great but are lacking in visual appeal. You'll make the web more attractive by inserting the images you imported. You'll insert the club's logo and the world image on the home page using drag-and-drop.

1. Click the Back button twice in the Editor toolbar to display the home page.

2. Click the pctclogo.gif file in the Explorer and hold down the left mouse button as you drag the image to the home page. With the pointer just to the left of the page's first heading, release the mouse button. FrontPage inserts the image.

3. Repeat Step 2 to insert the world.gif image just to the left of the third line in the page. Figure 1.29 shows the home page with the inserted images.

Inserting a Background Image

You can also make your web more distinctive by displaying an image in the background. We'll use the vellum.jpg image for the background image for all the pages in the PCTC web. Although you can assign the background image individually to each page, a better solution is to create a styles page with the background image and then assign the styles page to the other pages in the web. If you later decide to change the background image, you only have to change the styles page and the other web pages are changed automatically.

1. Click the New button in the Editor's Standard toolbar to display a new blank page.

FIGURE 1.29

You can insert an image in a page by dragging the image from the Explorer and dropping it in the page in the Editor.

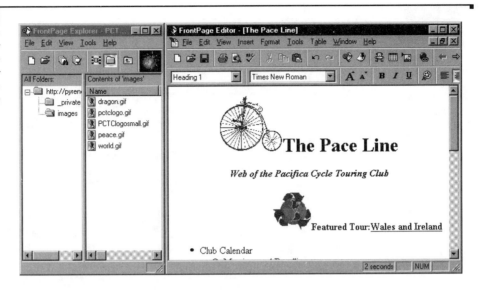

Overview of FrontPage

2. Choose File ➤ Page Properties from the Editor menu bar and click the Background tab. Click the Background Image check box (see Figure 1.30a) and then click the Browse button. Double-click the images folder in the Select Background Image dialog (see Figure 1.30b) to display the list of images. Double-click vellum.jpg in the list.

3. Click OK to close the Page Properties dialog. The background of the page is filled with the vellum.jpg image.

4. Click the Save button in the toolbar. Type **PCTC Styles** as the page title. A styles page is one of the pages that shouldn't be available to web visitors. You can hide the page by storing it in the _private folder. (Files in the _private folder are never available to web visitors even if they enter the address in a browser.) To store the page in the _private folder, type **_private/ styles.htm** as the file path to the page.

5. Choose File ➤ Close from the Editor toolbar to close the styles page.

NOTE

You can also use the Background tab in the Page Properties dialog to set custom text and link colors for the styles page.

FIGURE 1.30

You set the back-ground image for a page in the Page Properties dialog (a). Click the Browse button to display the Select Background Image dialog (b).

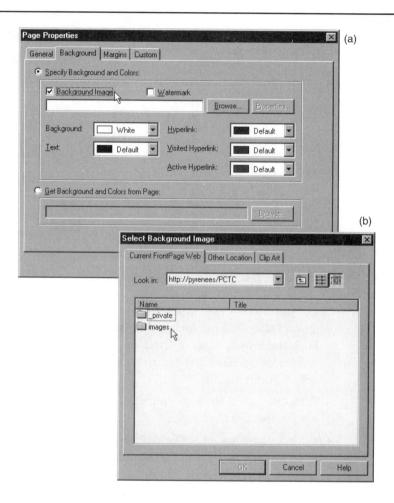

Assigning the Styles Page to Other Web Pages

You'll assign the styles page to the three web pages as follows:

1. Choose File ➤ Page Properties from the Editor menu bar and click the Background tab. Click the Get Background and Colors from Page option (see Figure 1.30a) and click the Browse button. Double-click the _private folder in the Current Web dialog (see Figure 1.31) and then double-click the styles.htm page. Click OK to close the Page Properties dialog and assign the styles page.

2. Click the Windows menu in the Editor menu bar and choose Wales and Ireland 1997 Tour from the list of open pages.

FIGURE 1.31

*Use the Page
Properties dialog to
assign another
page's colors and
background image.*

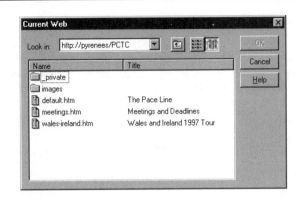

3. Repeat Step 1 to assign the styles.htm page to the wales-ireland.htm page.

4. Repeat Steps 2 and 3 to display and assign the styles.htm page to the meetings .htm page.

5. Click the Windows menu in the Editor menu bar and choose The Pace Line from the list of open pages.

When you assign a styles page, its background image and colors override the background image and colors you may have set for the original page.

Making a Color Transparent

The images in the home page don't look very good because the backgrounds of the images are white and the background of the web page is an image. You can make the background of the image transparent so that the page's background image shows through. When you make a color transparent, you see right through those parts of the image that have the transparent color to whatever color the image is underneath.

1. Click the logo. When you select an image, small selection squares appear in the corners of the image and the Image toolbar is displayed. Click the Make Transparent button in the image toolbar and move the pointer inside the image's boundary. The pointer changes to a pencil with an eraser (see Figure 1.32a).

2. Click the background of the image. The background color of the image is now transparent (see Figure 1.32b).

3. Repeat Steps 1 and 2 to make the background of the world image transparent.

4. Click the Save button in the toolbar. When you make one of the colors for an image transparent, you've changed the image. FrontPage displays the Save Image to FrontPage Web so you can save the change. Click Yes to All to save the changes to both images.

FIGURE 1.32

Making a color in an image transparent (a). The background image shows through the parts of the image with the transparent color (b).

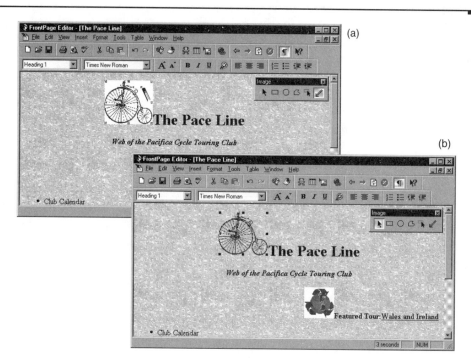

Copying and Pasting an Image

The image now looks much better. We'll copy and paste the logo with the transparent background to the Meetings and Deadlines page.

1. Click the logo to select it.

2. Click the Copy button in the toolbar to copy the image to the Clipboard.

3. Press Ctrl, and click the <u>Meetings and Deadlines</u> hyperlink. You'll paste the image just to the left of the heading at the top of the Meetings and Deadlines page.

4. Place the insertion point to the left of the text in the first line. Click the Paste button in the toolbar to paste the image. You can resize an image using the selection squares.

5. Move the pointer to one of the corners of the image. When the pointer changes to a double-arrow, press the mouse button and drag to make the image smaller (see Figure 1.33).

6. Click the Save button. Click the Back button in the toolbar to return to the home page.

FIGURE 1.33

Resize an image by dragging a resizing square.

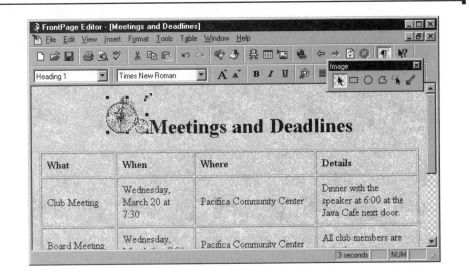

Creating a Clickable Image Link

In Lesson 2, you learned how to create text hyperlinks. If you've played around with the WWW you know that you can also create image links. We'll make the image on The Pace Line page a clickable image link that takes the visitor to the tour description page. One way to create a clickable image link is to drag the target page from the FrontPage Explorer and drop the target page on the image in the page in the Editor.

1. Click the wales-ireland.htm page icon in the Explorer window. Pressing the left mouse button, drag the icon to the world image in the Editor window.

2. Release the left mouse button to drop the page icon. The image's selection squares appear and FrontPage creates an image hyperlink to the wales-ireland.htm page. Click the Save button in the toolbar.

3. Test the link by pressing Ctrl and clicking the image. The Editor jumps to the tour description page.

This is the end of Lesson 3. You now know how to create both text and image hyperlinks. This is a good time to close up FrontPage and take a break.

For More Information

Lesson 3 has shown you how to use drag-and-drop to import an image file from your computer's file system, insert an image on a page, and create an image hyperlink. In

Chapter 6: Working with Files you'll learn other ways to import files, and in Chapter 13: Using Images and Video Clips you'll learn techniques for importing and working with images. You'll also learn how to create image maps in which different regions of an image have hyperlinks to different targets.

Lesson 4: Using the FrontPage Explorer

In this lesson, you learn how to:

- Understand links using the hierarchical representation of the Hyperlink View
- Understand a file's links using the graphical representation of the Hyperlink View
- View implicit links to embedded images
- View repeated links to the same page
- View links inside a page
- Assign an unfinished task using the To Do List

If you've been keeping track, you'll know that we've created six hyperlinks so far. In Lesson 2, we created text hyperlinks from the home page to the tour description and the meetings and deadlines pages, two text hyperlinks from the tour description page back to the home page, and a fifth text hyperlink from the top of the tour description page to a bookmark at the bottom. In Lesson 3, we added an image hyperlink from the home page to the tour description page. It isn't hard to keep track of six hyperlinks between three pages, but keep in mind that you've just started the web and there are dozens of pages that you'd need to add before publishing the web to club members. Managing the pages and hyperlinks in any but the simplest web can be a substantial undertaking. Fortunately, the FrontPage Explorer can help.

If you closed out of FrontPage at the end of Lesson 3, you'll need to start up the FrontPage Explorer and open the PCTC web. When you first open the FrontPage Explorer, its Folder View is displayed. Click the Hyperlink View button in the toolbar to display the Explorer's Hyperlink View (see in Figure 1.34).

If you see a different view, check the status of the toolbar buttons. If necessary, click to deactivate the Hyperlinks to Images, Repeated Hyperlinks, and Hyperlinks Inside Page buttons. We'll take a look at these buttons later in the lesson.

We'll look at the pane on the right later. For now, just focus on the All Hyperlinks pane on the left.

FIGURE 1.34

*The Hyperlink View
of the PCTC web
with the home page
expanded to show
its outgoing links*

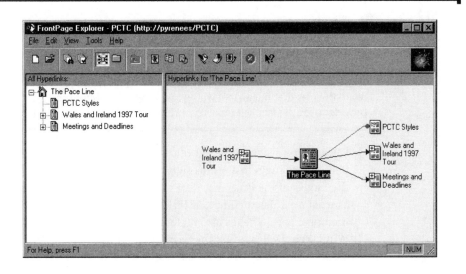

Using the All Hyperlinks Pane

The All Hyperlinks pane is a hierarchical view of the links in your web. To understand how the All Hyperlinks pane works, we'll begin by collapsing it.

1. Click the minus sign to the left of the The Pace Line icon. The All Hyperlinks pane is now in a collapsed state. The home page, indicated by the house icon, is the only item displayed. In its fully collapsed state, the All Hyperlinks pane of a web is a list of the pages and files that do not have links to each other. When a page in the collapsed list has links to other pages or files, the page has a plus sign to the left of its icon. You click a page's plus sign to expand and view links for the page.

2. Click the plus sign to the left of the home page. The plus sign changes to a minus sign to indicate that the home page is expanded to show its outgoing links to other pages and files. An *outgoing link* for a file is a link that starts in the file. In an indented list below the home page are the three pages, indicated by page icons, that are the targets of the links that start on the home page (see Figure 1.34). We created hyperlinks to the tour description and the meetings and deadlines pages in Lesson 2, and we created another kind of link, called an *implicit link*, when we assigned the styles page in Lesson 3.

NOTE

The difference between a hyperlink and an implicit link is that a Web visitor clicks a hyperlink to jump to another location, but the visitor does not click an implicit link. The visitor activates an implicit link just by browsing to the page. An implicit link is used to relate the files that make up a web page. When the visitor browses to a page, the Web browser uses the implicit links to retrieve all the files necessary to display the page.

3. Click the plus sign to the left of the Wales and Ireland 1997 Tour page icon. The plus sign changes to a minus sign and an indented list displays the files that are the targets of the links that start on the tour description page (see Figure 1.35a). The list includes the implicit link to the styles page and the hyperlink back to the home page. The list also includes the hyperlink to the location on the World Wide Web, indicated by the world icon, and the hyperlink to the e-mail program, indicated by the letter icon.

4. Click the plus sign to the left of the Meetings and Deadlines page icon. The indented list includes the implicit link to the styles page as the page's only outgoing link. Figure 1.35b shows the All Hyperlinks pane in its fully expanded state.

Next, we'll observe the additional information that becomes available when other viewing options are selected.

FIGURE 1.35

Expanding the Wales and Ireland 1997 Tour page shows its outgoing links, including an implicit link to the styles page, a hyperlink to another web page, a hyperlink to a location on the World Wide Web, and a hyperlink to an e-mail program (a). Expanding the Meetings and Deadlines page shows its single outgoing link to the styles page (b).

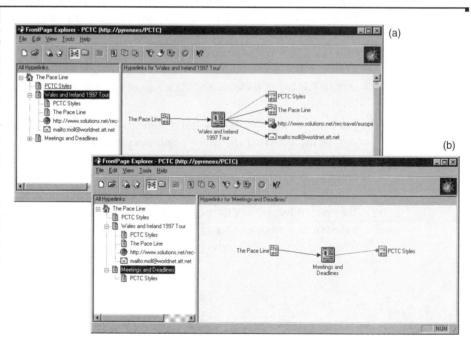

Viewing Links to Inserted Images

When you place an image on a web page, FrontPage creates an implicit link to the image. You can view the implicit links to images by clicking the Links to Images button in the toolbar. Before viewing the implicit links to images, let's collapse the All Hyperlinks pane to its fully collapsed state.

1. Click all the minus signs in the pane on the left to collapse the hierarchy and then click the Links to Images button in the toolbar. The collapsed list includes the home page and the PCTClogosmall.gif image file (see Figure 1.36a). We haven't used this image file yet, so there are no links between it and any other file in the web. Image files are indicated by a picture icon.

2. Click the plus sign to expand the home page. The indented list now includes the home page's three implicit links to the background image, the logo, and the world image (see Figure 1.36b).

FIGURE 1.36

The fully collapsed web, including its image files (a). Expanding the home page shows its implicit links to images (b).

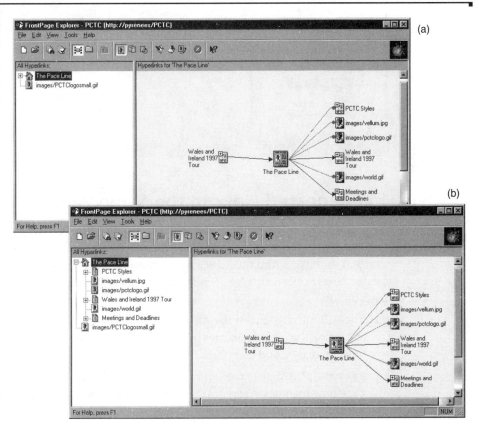

3. Click the plus sign to expand the tour description page. Its indented list now includes its three implicit links to the background image, the dragon, and the peace image.

4. Click the plus sign to expand the meetings and description page. Its indented list now includes its two implicit links to the background image and the logo. Figure 1.37 shows the left pane with both pages expanded.

FIGURE 1.37

Expanding the tour description page and the meetings and deadlines page shows the implicit links to their images.

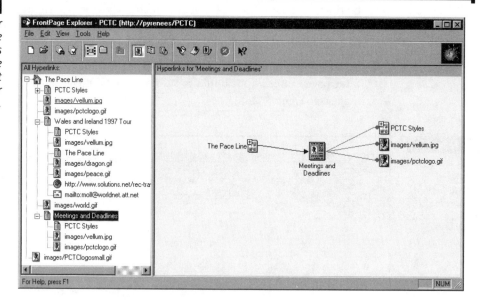

Viewing Repeated Links to the Same Page

A web page may have more than one outgoing link to a file. For example, in the PCTC web, the home page has both a text hyperlink and an image hyperlink to the tour description page. You can view a page's repeated outgoing links by clicking the Repeated Links button. First, we'll collapse the view and deactivate the Links to Images option.

1. Click all minus signs in the All Hyperlinks page to fully collapse the hierarchy. Click the Links to Images button to deactivate the button and hide the links to images, and then click the Repeated Links button in the toolbar.

2. Click the plus sign to the left of the home page icon. The list below the home page now includes Wales and Ireland 1997 Tour twice, once for the text hyperlink and once for the image hyperlink.

3. Click the plus sign to the left of the tour description page. It's list now includes The Pace Line twice, once for each text hyperlink that takes you back to the home page.

4. Click the plus sign to the left of the meetings and deadlines page. This page has no repeated links. Figure 1.38 shows the hierarchy expanded to show all repeated outgoing links.

FIGURE 1.38

Click the Repeated Links button to view all repeated outgoing links.

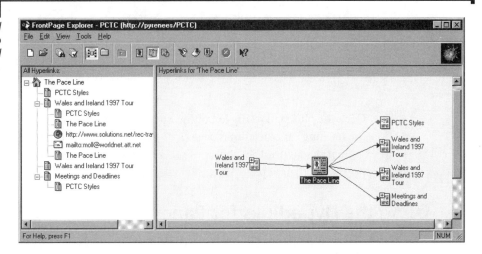

Viewing Links inside a Page

A web page can have links from one location on the page to another bookmarked location on the same page. For example, in the PCTC web, the tour description page has a text hyperlink at the top of the page to a location at the bottom of the page. You can view hyperlinks to other locations on the same page in addition to links to other files by clicking the Links Inside Page button.

First, we'll deactivate the option to view repeated links.

1. Click the Repeated Links button to deactivate the button and show outgoing links to a file only once. Click the Links Inside Page button in the toolbar.

2. Click The Pace Line page icon. The home page has no links to other locations on the home page, so the Hyperlinks pane looks the same as in Figure 1.34.

3. Click the plus sign to the left of the Wales and Ireland 1997 Tour page icon to expand the tour description page. The list below now includes the hyperlink to the bookmarked location at the bottom of the same page (see Figure 1.39).

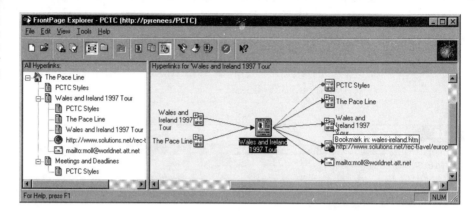

4. Click the plus sign to the left of the Meetings and Deadlines page icon to expand the meetings and deadlines page. This page has no links to other locations on the same page. Figure 1.40 shows the hierarchy expanded to show all links to locations on the same page.

Using the Hyperlinks for Pane

The All Hyperlinks pane shows a hierarchical view of the outgoing links for pages in a web. When you select an item in the All Hyperlinks pane, the pane on the right displays a graphical representation of both the incoming and the outgoing links for the selected item. An *incoming link* for a file is a link that starts on another file and ends at the file. The selected file is placed in the center of the Hyperlinks for pane with incoming links on the left and outgoing links on the right. The pane uses lines with either arrows or solid circles to indicate whether the connection is a clickable hyperlink or an implicit link, as follows:

- A blue line with an arrow indicates that there is a clickable hyperlink between the two files at either end of the line with the tip of the arrow pointing to the target of the link.

- A gray line with a solid circle indicates that there is an implicit link between the two files and that the image or page at the end with the solid circle is included or embedded inside the page at the end without the solid circle.

When you hold the pointer over an icon to the left or right of the center icon, the line connecting the icon to the center icon turns red and a small window, called a *linktip*, describes the link.

1. Click the Links Inside Page button in the toolbar to deactivate this option and show only links to other files.

2. Click either page icon for The Pace Line in the pane on the left. The pane on the right shows the links for the home page (see Figure 1.34). To the left of center is the incoming link from the tour description page and to the right of center are the two outgoing hyperlinks to the tour description and the meetings and deadline page and the implicit link to the styles page. Move the pointer to the PCTC Styles icon on the right. The line from the home page to the styles page turns red and the linktip has the following text to indicate that the link is an implicit link to the styles page

    Included Style: : _private/styles.htm

3. Click the Links to Images button in the toolbar. Figure 1.36a shows the implicit links to the background image and the two embedded images. Click the Links to Images button to deactivate this option. Hold the pointer over one of the image icons. The line from the center to the image icon turns red and the linktip has the following text to indicate that the link is an implicit link to the image:

    Embedded Image: images/world.gif

4. Click the Repeated Links button in the toolbar. Figure 1.38 shows the two repeated outgoing links to the tour description page. The Hyperlinks pane does not indicate whether a hyperlink is a text hyperlink or an image hyperlink. Click the Repeated Links button to deactivate this option.

5. Click the Hyperlinks Inside Page button in the toolbar. Click the Wales and Ireland 1997 Tour page icon in the All Hyperlinks pane. Figure 1.39 shows the hyperlink for the bookmarked location on the page. The hyperlink is shown twice: once on the left as an incoming link because the page is the target of the hyperlink and a second time on the right as an outgoing link because the page is also the start of the hyperlink.

Adding a Task to the To Do List

Although there are links from the home page to the tour description page and back to the home page, there is only a link from the home page to the meetings and deadlines page and there is no return link. We'll make a note to add a return link using another component of FrontPage, the To Do List program.

1. Click the Show To Do List button in the toolbar. You can keep track of unfinished items in the To Do List dialog (see Figure 1.40a).

2. Click Add to display the Add To Do Task dialog. Type **Add return link to home page** in the Task Name text box (see Figure 1.40b) and click OK. The task is added to the list. Click Close.

This is the end of Lesson 4. This lesson has introduced you to using the views of the Explorer to understand your web's organization. This is a good time to close up FrontPage and take a break.

FIGURE 1.40

Use the To Do List to keep track of unfinished tasks (a). Use the Add To Do Task dialog to specify the task (b).

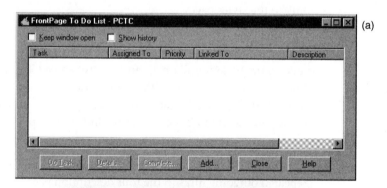

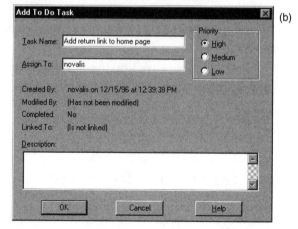

For More Information

Lesson 4 showed you how to use the FrontPage Explorer to understand how the files in a web are related with hyperlinks and implicit links. Chapter 5: Editor Basics covers additional features of the FrontPage Explorer. In Chapter 7: Managing Links, you'll learn how to manage the links in a web including how to detect and repair broken links. Chapter 8: Understanding To Do Lists covers the To Do List program. In Chapter 9: Administring a Web, you'll learn how to control access to a web and set permissions for different groups of users.

Lesson 5: Using Bots in Page Design

To give the pages of the PCTC web an identity, you decide that the pages should have a section at the bottom of the page that displays the club's name. You'll include your e-mail address and the date of your last change to the web. To provide a consistent look and feel, you decide the footer section should be the same for every page. Instead of creating a separate footer section for each page, in FrontPage you can create a single footer page and use a page design bot to include it within other pages of the web. A *bot* is an object that has a prewritten program attached. FrontPage has more than a dozen bots that provide automation and interactivity to a web. Depending on the bot, the program may be run automatically either by FrontPage when you insert the bot or save a page that has a bot or by the Web server when a visitor takes an action, such as clicking a button, to start the program.

In this lesson, you'll learn what a page design bot is, and how to:

- Create a footer page
- Use a page design bot to timestamp a page
- Use a page design bot to include a page within another page
- Use a page design bot to include a note to yourself on a page

If you closed out of FrontPage at the end of Lesson 4, start up the FrontPage Explorer and open the PCTC web.

Creating a Footer Page

First, let's create the footer as a new page.

    1. Click the Show FrontPage Editor button in the toolbar. Click the New button in the Editor's Standard toolbar. We'll use a table to lay out the information in the footer page.

Overview of FrontPage

PART

1

2. Click the Insert Table button and drag to create a table with two rows and two columns.

3. Type **The Pace Line** in the first table cell. Drag to select the text in the cell and click the Bold button in the toolbar.

4. Press the down arrow and type **Web of the Pacifica Cycle Touring Club** in the first table cell of the second row. Drag to select the text in the cell and click the Italic button and the Decrease Text Size button in the toolbar.

5. Press the right arrow and the up arrow keys, type **Send comments to webmaster @pctc.org** in the second table cell of the first row, and then press Enter. When you press Enter, FrontPage creates the e-mail hyperlink and also inserts a new line in the table cell. Press Delete to remove the extra line.

NOTE

If you have an e-mail address, you can test sending electronic mail from a FrontPage web by entering your own e-mail address instead of webmaster@pctc.org.

Adding a TimeStamp to a Page

You'll display the modification date in the last cell of the table. If you enter the data yourself, you'll have to remember to reenter the current date each time you change the web. Instead, you can automate the process using one of the page design bots in FrontPage. You insert a page design bot on a web page. When you save the page, the Web server automatically runs the bot's program and carries out the instructions. You'll insert the Timestamp bot, officially called the WebBot Timestamp Component, in the last cell of the table. The program built into the Timestamp bot instructs the Web server to read your computer's clock and display the current date and time on the web page at the spot where you inserted the bot.

1. Click in the last cell of the table, type **Last modified:**, and then click the Insert WebBot Component button in the Standard toolbar.

2. Choose the TimeStamp bot from the list in the Insert WebBot Component dialog (see Figure 1.41a), and click OK.

3. Click OK in the Timestamp Bot Properties dialog box (see Figure 1.41b) to accept the default settings. FrontPage displays the current date in the table cell.

4. Move the pointer to the date in the table cell. The pointer changes to the bot pointer shown in Figure 1.42.

FIGURE 1.41

Choose the bot you want to insert in the page (a). You can specify time and date formats in the properties dialog (b).

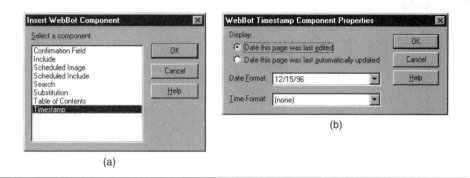

(a)

(b)

FIGURE 1.42

When you move the pointer to a bot, the pointer icon changes to the bot icon.

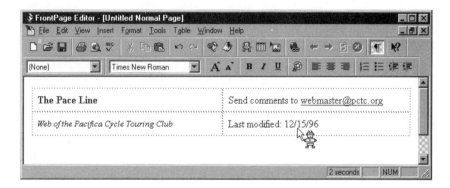

5. Choose File ➤ Close from the Editor menu bar. In the Save As dialog, type **Footer** as the page title. The footer is another page that you'll hide from the Web visitor by storing it in the _private folder. Type **_private/footer.htm** as the file path. Click OK to save the page to the _private folder.

Including the Footer in Another Page

Now you're ready to display the footer in the public pages of the web. You could copy and paste content of the footer page to the bottom of other pages. If you take this approach and later change the footer, you'll have to remember to manually update each page with the changed footer. Instead, you can automate the process using another page design bot called the Include bot (officially the WebBot Include Component) to embed the footer page in another page in the web. The program built into the Include bot instructs the Web server to automatically update the pages that contain an embedded page whenever you change the embedded page.

1. Click the Open button in the toolbar and double-click default.htm in the Open File dialog (see Figure 1.43).

FIGURE 1.43

Use the Open File dialog to open an existing page.

2. Click below the last line of text. Click the Insert WebBot Component button in the Standard toolbar, choose Include from the list in the Insert WebBot Component dialog box (see Figure 1.41a for the list of bots), and click OK.

3. Click the Browse button in the Include WebBot Properties dialog box (see Figure 1.44a), double-click the _private folder, and double-click footer.htm in the Current Web dialog (see Figure 1.44b). Click OK to close the properties dialog and insert the footer page at the bottom of the home page.

FIGURE 1.44

Use the Include bot to embed a page in another page (a). Click the Browse button to locate the other page (b).

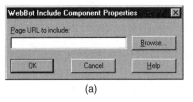

(a)

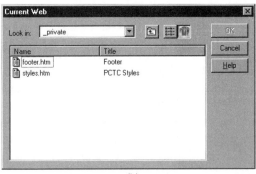

(b)

4. Move the pointer to various locations in the page. When you move the pointer to the region containing the table from the footer page, the pointer changes to the bot pointer.

5. Click the Save button in the toolbar.

When you save the page, the Web server carries out the instructions that are built into the Include bot. The server retrieves the footer page and inserts a copy of the contents of the footer page at the spot where you placed the Include bot. Figure 1.45 shows home page with the merged footer page in the Editor (a) and in the FrontPage Explorer (b).

FIGURE 1.45

The home page with the merged footer page in the Editor (a) and in the FrontPage Explorer (b).

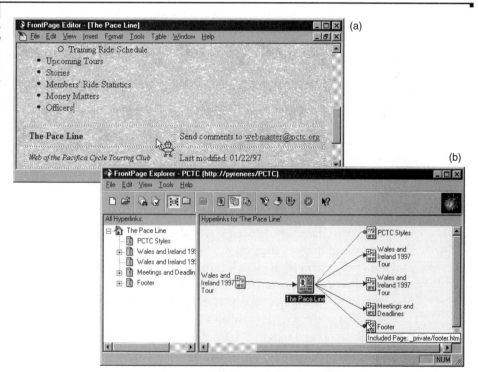

Copying the Included Page

You could repeat the steps above to embed the footer in the other pages of the web, but it is easier to copy the embedded section with the Include bot and paste it into the other pages.

1. Click anywhere in the footer section in the home page, and then click the Copy button in the toolbar.

2. Press Ctrl and click the <u>Wales and Ireland</u> text hyperlink. Click in the empty line at the bottom of the page, click the Paste button, and then click the Save button in the toolbar.

3. Press Ctrl and click the Go back to the <u>Home Page</u> text hyperlink.

4. In the home page, press Ctrl and click the <u>Meetings and Deadlines</u> text hyperlink. Click in the empty line at the bottom of the page, click the Paste button, and then click the Save button in the toolbar.

Lesson 5 has introduced you to a few of the bots that you can use to automate some of the page design tasks. This is a good time to close up FrontPage and take a break before continuing with the next, and last, lesson.

For More Information

Chapter 16: Using WebBots in Page Design covers all the page design bots. You'll learn how to use bots to create and automatically update a table of contents for the entire web or for a section of the web. You'll also earn how to collect a set of parameters such as the webmaster's e-mail address and contact information in one place, and use bots to display this information on web pages. You'll learn how to add author's comments to pages, and how to expand the capabilities of the Editor with new HTML codes.

Lesson 6: Adding Interactivity

The previous lesson introduced you to the page design bots that you can use to automate parts of the web page creation process. FrontPage has a second kind of bot called a form bot. A *form bot* is an object that has a built-in program that the Web server executes when a Web visitor takes some action to start the program, such as clicking a button in the web page. Typically, the Web visitor enters some information in a special section of the web page called a form, clicks a button to send the information to the Web server and tells the Web server to run the program inside the form bot. The program for a form bot is also called a *form handler*.

In this lesson, you'll learn how to:

- Create a search form
- Create a feedback form to collect information
- Save feedback from a Web visitor

If you closed out of FrontPage at the end of Lesson 4, start up the FrontPage Explorer and open the PCTC web.

Adding a Search

One of the features you are planning to include in the PCTC web is a description of all of the popular local training rides. To make the list more useful to the members, you need a way for members to search the ride descriptions. A club member may want to search for all rides in a particular county or all rides offered by a specific leader. In FrontPage, you can easily create a search of the pages in the web. You use the Search bot, officially the WebBot Search Component, to create a text search of the public pages—that is, all pages except the pages stored in the hidden folders such as the _private folder.

1. Double-click The Pace Line home page icon in the Contents pane in the Front-Page Explorer. Click to the right of Officers (the last item in the list) and press Ctrl+Enter to end the list and insert a new line.

2. Click the Insert WebBot Component button in the toolbar and double-click Search. Figure 1.46 shows the Search Bot Properties dialog box where you set the properties you want for the search.

You can specify options for the text search using the properties dialog.

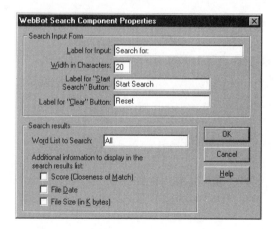

3. Click OK to accept the default choices for the properties. FrontPage creates a form and inserts a text box labeled Search For: and two push buttons with captions Start Search and Reset. The boundary of the form is indicated by dotted lines. The form boundaries are shown only in the Editor and not when you view the page in a browser. The text box and push buttons are called *form fields*. Move the insertion point anywhere between the form boundaries. The pointer icon changes to the bot pointer icon to indicate the form (see Figure 1.47).

4. Click the Save button in the toolbar.

FIGURE 1.47

The Search bot inserts a form to collect the search phrase.

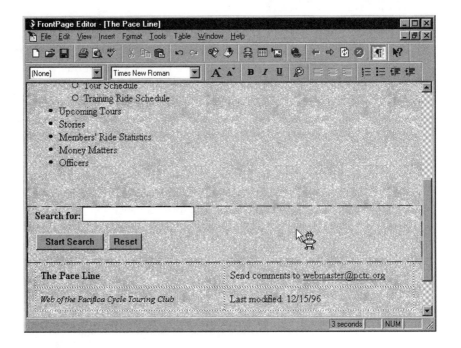

Running a Search

The search form works only when you view the page in a browser.

1. Click the Preview in Browser button in the toolbar. Scroll to the search form at the bottom of the page.

2. Type **ireland** in the Search For text box and click the Search For push button. When you click the Search For push button, the value you typed is sent to the Web server and then the Web server searches through all the public pages of the current web, looking for a match. After finding pages with matching text, the Web server generates a new temporary version of the home page that includes the results of the search and sends the modified page back to the browser. Figure 1.48 shows the home page modified to display the number of matching pages and a table with text hyperlinks to the matching pages.

3. Click the Wales and Ireland 1997 Tour hyperlink in the last table cell. After viewing the page, click the page's hyperlink to return to the home page. The browser displays the original version of the home page as it was before you ran the search.

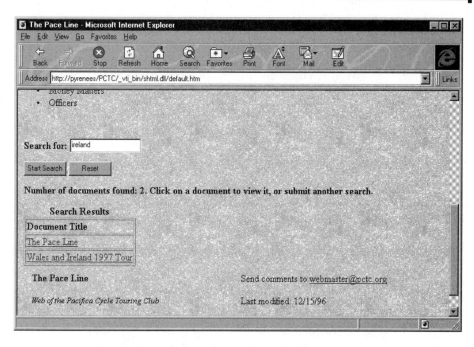

FIGURE 1.48

When you run a search in a browser, the search value is sent to the server, which locates all matching pages and creates a list of hyperlinks to the matching pages.

4. Type **ireland** in the search text box, and then click the Reset push button. The browser resets the form fields.

5. Minimize the browser.

Collecting Information from a Web User

Another feature you'll add to the PCTC web is a feedback section for the meetings. You'll solicit suggestions for speakers and discussion topics for future club meetings. To create a feedback section, you'll insert a form into the Meetings and Deadlines page.

Creating a New Form

The easiest way to create a feedback form is to use the Form Page Wizard. The wizard creates a new page with a form, but doesn't let you insert a form directly in an existing page. So after we create the new page using the wizard, we'll copy the form and paste it to the Meetings and Deadlines page.

In the feedback form, we'll include a question asking if the visitor attends meetings with a check box for the reply and a large text box for suggestions for club meeting topics and speakers.

1. Choose File ➤ New from the Editor menu bar, and double-click the Form Page Wizard in the New Page dialog (see Figure 1.49a).

2. Click Next twice. You use the third screen to create the first data entry form field (see Figure 1.49b).

3. Click the Add button. To create the check box and its label, choose boolean in the list box, type **Do you attend at least one meeting a year?** in the text box (see Figure 1.49c), and click Next.

FIGURE 1.49

Use the Form Page Wizard to create a new page that contains a data entry form (a). The wizard screen displays the requests for information that you'll add to the data entry form (b). The wizard screen for creating a request for information (c).

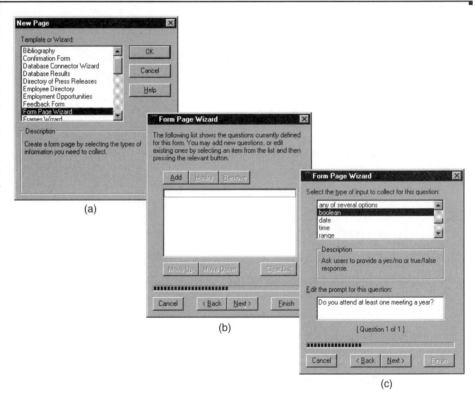

4. Click the check box option, type **Attendance** in the text box as the name for the answer, and click Next.

5. Click the Add button. Choose paragraph in the list box, type **Suggestions for club meeting topics and speakers:** in the text box (see Figure 1.50), and click Next.

6. Type **Suggestions** in the text box as the name for this answer (see Figure 1.50c), and click Next.

FIGURE 1.50

The wizard screen to specify the type of field for a boolean (yes/no) request and the name for the answer (a).Choose the paragraph item to create a request for comments (b) and name the answer in the next screen (c).

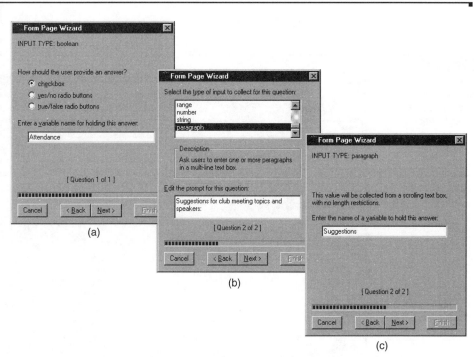

(a)

(b)

(c)

7. Click Finish. The wizard creates the new page with the form. Figure 1.51 shows the section of the new page that contains the form.

You'll copy and paste the form to the Meetings and Deadlines page and then discard the page that the wizard created.

1. Move the pointer to the left edge of the form. When the pointer changes to an arrow pointer to the upper-left, as shown in Figure 1.51, double-click to select the form. (When the form is selected, the entire region enclosed by the dotted boundary is shown in reverse video.)

2. Click the Copy button in the toolbar.

3. Click the Open button in the toolbar and double-click the Meetings and Deadlines page in the Open File dialog. Click in the last table cell and press Ctrl+Enter to insert a new line below the table. Click the Paste button in the toolbar.

4. Click the Save button in the toolbar.

5. Click the Window menu in the Editor menu bar and choose Form Page 9. This is the page the wizard created. Choose File ➤ Close in the Editor menu bar. Click No to discard the page.

FIGURE 1.51

The Form Page Wizard creates the data entry form to your specifications.

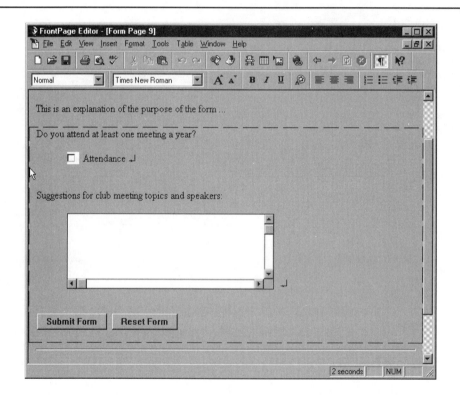

Collecting Feedback

Let's add some feedback using the new form.

1. Click the Preview in Browser button in the toolbar.

2. Click the Attendance check box, type **Tour de France** as a meeting topic, and click the Submit Form push button. When you click the Submit Form push button, the information you entered in the form's fields is sent to the Web server. The server runs form handler. As one of the instructions in the script, the server generates the confirmation page shown in Figure 1.52. Another instruction tells the server to save the information to a storage file that the Form Page Wizard created for you.

FIGURE 1.52

The confirmation page displayed after you submit the feedback form

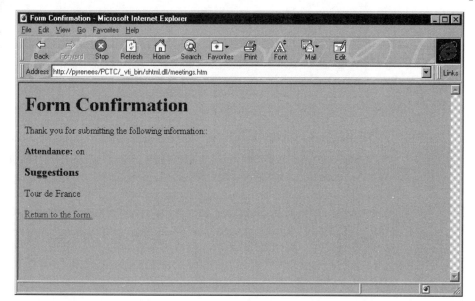

3. Minimize the browser. Click in the FrontPage Explorer and choose View ➤ Refresh from the Explorer menu bar. The Contents pane on the right displays the new storage file. The storage file has formrslt.htm as the name and Results from Form1of Page meetings.htm as the title. Since the results file has the .htm extension, it is a web page and we can view it in the Editor.

4. Double-click the formrslt.htm page icon. Figure 1.53 shows the results page with the information we entered as the first entry.

This is the end of Lesson 6. This lesson has given you a glimpse of how you can use FrontPage to add interactivity to your web. The lesson introduced you to two of the form bots that you can use to let a Web visitor communicate with your web by doing searches and by giving you information.

FIGURE 1.53

The page that stores the results of form submissions

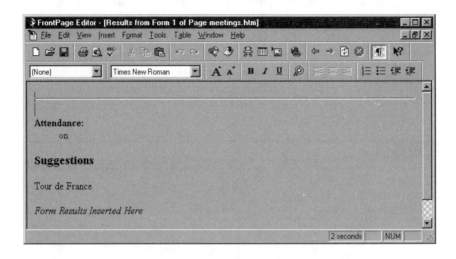

For More Information

The FrontPage form bots are powerful ways to add interactivity to a web without having to write programs for the Web server. Chapter 17: Collecting Input Data covers collecting information using a FrontPage form bot to process the data. In Chapter 18: Understanding Searches and User Registration, you'll learn more about text searches and you'll also learn how to require Web visitors to register before entering your web. In Chapter 19: Understanding Discussion Group Webs, you'll learn how to create an online discussion group as a forum for allowing your Web visitors to interact with each other.

Where to from Here?

This tutorial has given you an overview of how you can use FrontPage to create a new web. You've explored many of the basic features of FrontPage, including: how to add and format text, how to add images and tables to a page, how to create text and image hyperlinks, how to use bots to automate page creation, and how to use bots to provide interactivity. The lessons of the tutorial have shown you how easy it is to create a FrontPage web. Most of the time, you can use drag-and-drop techniques to perform web and page creation tasks. Parts II and III delve deeper into the FrontPage tools and show you techniques for using the tools efficiently.

The tutorial has only given a glimpse of FrontPage. Now that you have seen the lay of the land, it's time to move on. The rest of Part I provides background and resource information. Chapter 2: Introducing FrontPage describes how FrontPage works. You should at least browse through this chapter so that you understand how the many components work together: how a Web browser and Web server communicate and how the FrontPage Editor, Explorer, and To Do List work together with a Web server before continuing with learning more techniques for designing and creating webs.

PART

I

Overview of
FrontPage

Chapter

2

Introducing FrontPage

Introducing FrontPage

With Microsoft FrontPage, you create webs that are published by computers connected to a network and received by other computers connected to the same network. In order to understand how the components of FrontPage fit into the communication scheme, you need to understand how computers are able to talk to one another. This introduction to FrontPage begins with a nontechnical look at computer communication. Computer communication is an extremely complex, technical topic; but, fortunately, we don't have to do more than graze the surface in a few places.

Understanding How Computers Communicate

In the first years of computer history, computers worked in isolation as "stand-alones". However, it wasn't long before people wanted computers to share information with each other, and various networking schemes were developed by different computer manufacturers.

Understanding the Internet

A crucial barrier to computer communication was that the computers built by different manufacturers couldn't communicate with each other. Each computer manufacturer created its own hardware and software. Two computers built by the same manufacturer could usually talk to each other because they used the same hardware and the same language; that is, they used the same *communication protocols*. But an IBM computer couldn't talk to an NCR computer because the NCR computer used an entirely different set of communication protocols.

The solution to the hardware incompatibility problem was to agree on how the bits of information would be physically transmitted from one computer to the other and the format for the electrical signals that would carry the data. That was the easy part. You can think of transmitting a message from one computer to another like sending a letter. If the hardware between two computers is compatible, you can send electronic signals between them; this is analogous to the international postal system: you can send a letter to just about anywhere in the world. However, when you send a letter to Moscow, you won't be able to have a conversation unless you wrote the letter in Russian, or the person in Moscow reads your language. Just sending electronic signals was only the first step.

The next step was to develop a common language that any computer could use to talk with any other computer. The original simple software solution developed by the US Department of Defense in the late 1970's has evolved into a complex collection of software—the set of communication protocols that we now call TCP/IP.

Communicating Using TCP/IP

There are several layers to computer communication using TCP/IP. The first layer starts with you sitting at a computer that is connected to a network with either a full-time connection or a temporary connection using a modem that has TCP/IP software installed. If you have Windows 95 or Windows NT as your operating system, then you have TCP/IP software. (You can install TCP/IP when you install Windows or you can install it later by using the Network icon option in the Control Panel.)

Suppose you want your computer to interact to another computer, for example by sending or receiving a file from the other computer, by sending an e-mail message, or by exploring a site on the Internet. You must install the appropriate software for carrying out the task, such as ftp software to transfer files, a mail program to send and receive e-mail messages, and a Web browser to visit other Web servers connected to the Internet. The application you install is called a *client application* because you use it to make a request as a client for a service provided by another computer, such as a request to send you a file, to receive and store your mail messages, or to send a copy of one of the Web files it stores. The computer that responds to the request uses software called a *server application*, such as an ftp server, mail server, or Web server application.

You begin the communication by starting up the client application and entering your request. The client application takes your input, reformats it, and may compress or encrypt it into a standard format, and then sends the massaged input to the next software layer, called the *Transmission Control Protocol (TCP)* layer.

Transmission Control Protocol   TCP is a software program that takes the massaged input from the client application and breaks the input up into small pieces called *packets*. Each packet is limited in size to 1500 characters. The TCP program numbers each packet and places it in an envelope called a *TCP packet*. The TCP program places the TCP packet inside another envelope called an *IP envelope* and identifies the envelope with your return address and the address of the computer and the server application to which you want to send the request. Most messages are longer that 1500 characters, so your input is usually turned into several IP envelopes. The TCP program sends the IP envelopes to the next software layer, called *Internet Protocol (IP)* layer.

Internet Protocol   The job of the IP program is to handle the delivery of the IP envelopes to the other computer. Delivering the envelopes is the crucial part of the process, and I'll explain it more fully below. But for now, let's just assume that the envelopes are delivered to the other computer. Figure 2.1 depicts the TCP/IP communication.

The other computer must also have TCP/IP software installed in order to receive the IP envelopes. Its IP program receives the envelopes and sends them on to its TCP program. The TCP software on this computer has the job of collecting the IP envelopes and removing the packets. The TCP software puts the packets in order, determines if there are any missing, and determines if there are transmission errors. If there are errors or missing packets, the TCP program sends a request asking your computer to resend the message. After the TCP program reassembles the error-free packets into a complete request, it send the message to the specified server application.

FIGURE 2.1

TCP/IP communication between a client and a server application

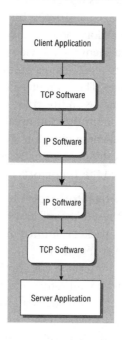

The receiving computer must have the server application software that cooperates with the client software you are using. The receiving computer may have several server applications that provide different services, such as ftp, mail, and Web server applications. Messages are addressed to a specific server application using an identification number called a *port number*. Each server type has a default port number. For example, Web server software is assigned number 80 as a port number by default. (If the computer has more than one Web server program, each must be assigned a different port number. In Appendix A, you'll learn how to assign and change port numbers.) After servicing the request, the server software sends the requested results in a standard format back to its TCP software.

NOTE

The server port is a number that is used to differentiate between different kinds of TCP/IP communication. The server port is not an actual hardware plug like a terminal, SCSI, or printer port.

The transmission process is now reversed: the TCP software on the receiving computer breaks the result into numbered TCP packets and sends each packet in an IP envelope to the network. The IP software delivers the envelopes back to you. The TCP/IP software on your computer receives the IP envelopes, assembles the TCP packets into a complete result, and returns the result to your client application. Your client application converts the result and displays it to you.

Understanding the Internet Protocol (IP)

The Internet Protocol software handles the delivery of the packets. The easiest way to understand the Internet delivery system is to think about how the postal system delivers a letter. When you mail a letter in a postal box, the postal carrier takes your letter to the local post office where is is dumped in a pile with all the other mail. Your letter's address has several parts, for example 500 Edgewater Place, Suite 500, Mariners Lagoon, San Rafael, CA 94558. Each part of the address provides information that the post office uses to decide whether to deliver the mail in its own neighborhood or to send it on to a post office substation. Mail sent on to the substation is sorted in a similar fashion and the substation decides whether to deliver the mail in its own region or send it on to another substation. The sorting and sending process is repeated again and again until your letter is delivered to its final destination.

The post office analogy is surprisingly close to the way that IP works. When you connect your computer to any network that uses the TCP/IP protocols, whether the network is a local area network, a company intranet, or the public Internet, your computer is assigned an address called an *IP address*. When you send a message to another computer on the network, the TCP software addresses the IP envelopes using your computer's IP address as the return address, and the receiving computer's IP addess and the server's port number as the forwarding address. When you send a message to another computer that is outside your local area network (if you are in one), the IP software on your computer sends the message's IP envelopes to another computer called an *IP router* that plays the role of the local post office. The IP router program sorts the envelopes using their IP addresses to decide whether to deliver the IP envelopes in its own network neighborhood or to send the envelopes on to another IP router. The IP routers are analogous to the postal substations. Each IP envelope is passed from one IP router to another until reaching its final destination. Normally, a computer has a default IP router and a list of several other IP routers that can handle the resending if the default IP router is unavailable. It is the redundancy of IP routers that gives the Internet its integrity; instead of a single chain of IP routers between your computer and the computer you are sending the message to, there is, in theory, an unlimited number of paths between the two computers. Each IP envelope can travel along a different path. At each step, the IP router software may be "smart" and able to select the optimal IP router for the next step.

IP Address

An IP address is the identification number assigned to a computer on a TCP/IP network. An IP address is also called a host address because once your computer is connected to a network, it is referred to as a host computer. Depending on how your network is administered, your computer's IP address may be permanent or temporary, and reassigned automatically by the network administrator server software. IP addresses are given as a set of four integers separated by periods. The integers range between 0 and 255; for example, the IP address of one of my computers is 130.212.16.2. The first three numbers are assigned by the Network Information Center (NIC), which controls all of the direct connections. (You can reach the NIC at hostmaster@rs.internic.net.)

If your computer has a permanent Internet connection, you can determine your computer's IP address as follows:

1. Click the Windows Start button, choose Settings ➤ Control Panel, and then double-click the Network icon to display the Network dialog.

2. Click TCP-IP in the Configuration tab of the Network dialog and then click the Properties button to display the TCP/IP Propertied dialog. The IP Address tab displays your IP address if one has been assigned.

If you access the Internet through an Internet Service Provider (ISP) using a modem, you probably don't have a permanent IP address. Instead, your ISP assigns a temporary IP address while you are connected.

When the client and server software are installed on the same computer, the two applications can communicate with each other using TCP/IP in *local mode* without opening a connection to the Internet. When you work in local mode, you computer has the default IP address 127.0.0.0.

Using Names instead of Numbers

Computers use numbers as IP addresses, but, as humans, most of us would rather use names. A name is easier to remember and can add character or personality as well as identify your computer. To satisfy the need for real names, the NIC created the Domain Naming System (DNS). In this system, Internet names have several parts or levels, separated by periods; for example, the Internet name of one of my computers is tuscany.sfsu.edu. The first name part on the left is called the host name. Each subsequent name part is called a *domain* or *subdomain,* and corresponds to a group of people that has responsibility for names within the group. Unlike IP addresses, where the hierarchy starts at the left, the name hierarchy starts at the highest level at the right.

The top-level naming domains were initially for types of organizations, such as .edu for educational institutions, .mil for military users, .gov for civilian government, .net for network providers, .com for commercial users, and .org for organizations. (More recently, top-level naming domains indicate country of origin, such as .uk for United Kingdom and .jp for Japan.) In my case, the top level is .edu, the next level is .sfsu to indicate my university's responsibility for the names of the computers connected to the Internet through the university, and tuscany is the name of my computer.

Understanding How Internet Applications Communicate

The Internet communication applications come in pairs: the client application software and server application software. The two parts communicate with each other using, you guessed it, a protocol. There are several kinds of communication applications you can use on a TCP/IP network, including telnet for logging in on another remote computer, ftp for sending and receiving files, gopher for looking up information by topic, WAIS (Wide Area Information Service) for looking up information using text searches, mailto for sending messages to and retrieving messages from a mail server, news for taking part in a discussion group, and, of course, there is the HTTP protocol for viewing files published on the World Wide Web (see the "Hypertext Transfer Protocol" section for more information on HTTP).

The World Wide Web

The World Wide Web (WWW or simply the Web) is the most recent information/ communication service on the Internet. Two of the fundamental differences between the WWW and all the other services are as follows:

- The Web is capable of presenting all media images, sounds, animations, and video in addition to text
- Web navigation is simplified—traveling to another destination on the Web requires only a mouse click on a special hotspot.

The client application you use to make requests is a Web browser, and the server application that stores files is a Web server. The WWW is based on a technology called *hypertext,* which allows documents to be linked to one another. The documents, called *Web pages* or *hypertext documents*, can link to another text, image, audio, animation, or video file. When you use your Web browser to view a document containing links, called *hyperlinks*, you can jump to the connected document or file just by clicking the hyperlink. When you click a hyperlink, you are requesting a file. Your browser sends the request to the Web server that stores the file. The Web server sends the requested file back to your browser. Normally, an author creates a set of linked hypertext documents and other files as a single entity called a *web*.

Hypertext Markup Language

You prepare a document with links to other documents and files using the commands of a language called the *Hypertext Markup Language (HTML)*. When you use the Front-Page Editor to create Web pages, the Editor writes the HTML commands for you so you don't have to learn the HTML language at all. This section gives an overview of how HTML is used to create hypertext documents so that you'll understand the document that the Editor is creating behind the scenes.

HTML is the language you use to create the hypertext links connecting to other documents or files. You also use HTML to create links to images, sound files, video clips, and other objects. HTML is the very recent invention of Tim Berners-Lee, a physicist at CERN, the European Particle Physics Laboratory. He invented HTML as a new information system that would allow researchers to exchange text information. He included the hypertext part of the language as a navigation system. The genius of hypertext is that it allows you to move freely from a document stored on a computer to a document or file stored on another computer without having to know the file-name or even which computer was storing the documents. Those details are specified by the document's author and are completely hidden from you as you simply click on a link.

A hypertext document is composed of unformatted text characters, and includes the text content (the information you want to publish in the document) and commands written in the HTML language. HTML commands have three basic purposes: to arrange or format the text content of the document, to structure the document, and to create links to other files. The basic HTML element is composed of three parts: the text you want to format and a pair of HTML codes called *tags* that enclose the text.

Formatting Elements   Suppose you want a phrase to be bold. To format the phrase, you precede the phrase with <b> as the *opening tag* and follow the phrase with </b> as the *closing tag*. The Web server sends the hypertext document with its unformatted text phrase enclosed by the formatting tags, and it is the job of the Web browser to interpret the instructions in the HTML commands. When a Web browser receives a hypertext document containing <b> Make me bold! </b>, the Web browser displays the phrase **Make me bold!** using its version of bold font. There are HTML formatting tags for changing the appearance of text char-acters and to change the layout of the text displayed in the browser window. For example, the paragraph tags <p> and </p> identify a paragraph. Most HTML tags allow you to provide additional information called *attributes* that the browser uses to carry out the command. Each attribute has a name, and you provide the information by specifying the value for the attribute. Attribute names and values are included in the opening tag using the syntax *attribute = value*. For example, to center a paragraph, you set the paragraph element's align attribute to "center" in the opening tag as follows: <p align = "center"> (text values are usually enclosed by double quotes).

Document Structuring Elements   In addition to the HTML elements for formatting text, there are HTML elements that structure the entire document. For example, all hypertext documents start with the <HTML> opening tag and end with the </HTML> closing tag.

Linking Elements   There is a special HTML element for specifying a link to another file, <A>...</A>. An important attribute of the link tag is HREF (Hypertext Reference). You set the HREF attribute to the name and location of the file that is the target of the link. For example, to set up the phrase Home Page as the text that the Web visitor clicks to travel to the page named default.htm, you create the HTML element <A HREF = "default.htm"> Home Page </A>. By default, Web browsers display the text between the link tags in blue underlined font so that the Web visitor is aware of the link.

Table 2.1 lists common HTML elements and gives examples of attributes. If you do want to learn HTML, there are many excellent references available, such as *The HTML 3.0 Sourcebook* by Ian S. Graham, John Wiley & Sons, Inc. 1996.

TABLE 2.1: COMMON HTML ELEMENTS AND ATTRIBUTES

Title	Element	Attributes	Comments
HTML document	<HTML>...</HTML>		Encloses the entire hypertext
Head	<HEAD>...</HEAD>		Encloses the head of the document
Body	<BODY>...</BODY>	background	Encloses the body of the document
Heading	<H1>...</H1>	align	Defines the formatting for a level-one heading
Paragraph	<P>...</P>	align	Defines a paragraph
Bold	<B> </B>		Bold font
Italic	<I>...</I>		Italic font
Image	<IMG>	ismap	Inserts an image in the hypertext document

Continued ▶

TABLE 2.1: COMMON HTML ELEMENTS AND ATTRIBUTES (CONTINUED)			
Title	**Element**	**Attributes**	**Comments**
Table	<TABLE>...</Table>	border, cell spacing, width	Creates a table
Table Head	<THEAD>...</THEAD>		Defines the table header cells
Form	<FORM>...</FORM>	action, method	Defines a form
Comments	<!–...–>		Creates a comment
Link	<A>...</A>	HREF, NAME	Defines a link to another file

Hypertext Transfer Protocol

Web server and Web browser (client) applications communicate with each other using the communication protocol called *Hypertext Transfer Protocol* (*HTTP*), which is designed specifically for delivering hypertext documents. But, in addition to simply delivering hypertext documents, HTTP has other features that continue to energize the communications revolution:

- The Web server can run programs and return the results to a browser.
- The Web server can receive information that you enter into a browser application and pass this information for processing by other programs stored on the server.

The programs that the Web server runs are called *gateway* programs because they often provide a gateway between the Web server and another information resource on the server's computer. In Chapter 1, you saw some examples of gateway programs. For example, the FrontPage Save Results bot uses a gateway program to process data collected from the Web visitor. The FrontPage Search bot is a more complicated example that uses a program to search through the pages of a web looking for text matches. See the "Understanding the Roles of the Web Server" section for more information on gateway programs.

Uniform Resource Locators

When you work with files on your own computer, you identify a file by specifying a name and a location. The location includes the drive letter and the sequence of folders and subfolders that you traverse to get to the file. For example, when you do a default installation of FrontPage 97, the FrontPage Editor has the path and filename C:\Program Files\Microsoft FrontPage\bin\fpeditor.exe. When you connect to the Internet, you use the *Uniform Resource Locator* (*URL*) as the Internet extension of the filename and path. A URL is an address that identifies, or points to, a specific item stored on a server application on a network. The URL also specifies the name of the server computer and the protocol that is used to retrieve the document. Typically, a URL points to a file, but a URL can also point to other items, such as a query, a table in a database, or a phrase in a text document.

To build a URL for the HTTP protocol, you arrange the three pieces of information in reverse order, starting with the protocol. Use a colon and two forward slashes (://) to separate the protocol from the name of the server computer (we'll use servername to represent the name of the server computer), and single forward slashes (/) to separate the servername from the path and the path from the filename. A typical URL for the HTTP protocol has the following syntax:

http://*servername/path/filename*

In Chapter 1, you saw examples of URLs for the HTTP protocol, such as http://*servername*/pctc/ireland.htm. When you type this URL in the browser's address text box, the browser uses the HTTP protocol to retrieve the page named ireland.htm that is in the pctc folder stored by the Web server named *servername*.

Each communication protocol may have its own URL syntax. For example, let's take a look at the mailto: protocol for e-mail. A typical URL for e-mail has the following syntax:

mailto: *e-mailaddress*

When you set up your browser application, you specify the mail application on your computer that you use to compose mail messages and mail server that your computer uses as a post office to process mail. When you type an e-mail URL into a browser's address text box or click a mailto link on a page, the browser opens the dialog box for your mail application so that you can compose an e-mail message from within the web (see Figure 2.2). The browser software automatically enters the e-mail address in the e-mail dialog box. When you click the send button in the e-mail dialog, the mail is sent by the mail program to the your computer's outgoing mail server. The mail server sends your message mail to the incoming mail server that handles mail for the recipient's computer.

FIGURE 2.2

When you click a mailto link on a page, the browser opens the specified mail program.

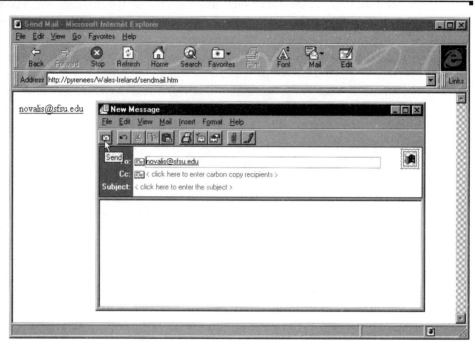

Relative URLs   When you create a web and link its files, most of the links are to other files in your own web. If you are creating a link from a page, you do not have to specify the entire URL for another file in your web. Instead, you can use a *relative URL* that gives the path and filename of the file relative to the current page. The relative path includes directions from the current page to the file, including whether to go up or down folder levels. Table 2.2 shows examples of relative URLs.

When you create a link to a file in your own web using FrontPage, the Editor normally identifies the file using a relative URL. When you use relative URLs to link files in your web, you can move the entire web to a new location without having to change the links. Normally, FrontPage takes care of the relative URLs for you. For example, if you move a file to another folder in your web, FrontPage automatically updates the relative URL with the new directions to the file. When you create a link to a file in another web on the Internet, the FrontPage Editor uses the full, or *absolute URL*.

TABLE 2.2: RELATIVE URLS	
Relative Path and Filename	**Description**
meetings.htm	meetings.htm is in the current folder (the same folder as the current page)
images/logo.gif	logo.gif is in the images folder in the current folder (one level down from the current folder)
. ./pctc.htm	pctc.htm is in the folder one level up from the current folder
images/photos/barmouth.jpg	barmouth.jpg is in the photos folder in the images folder in the current folder (two levels down from the current folder)
../../default.htm	default.htm is in the folder two levels up from the current folder

Introducing the FrontPage Client Applications

When you install Microsoft FrontPage 97, you are installing three main client applications: the FrontPage Explorer, the FrontPage Editor, and the FrontPage To Do List.

The FrontPage Explorer

The FrontPage Explorer is a tool for viewing the contents of a web and for managing the web as a unit. Here are the tasks you can carry out in the FrontPage Explorer:

- Create a new web
- Open or delete an existing web
- Open a page in the FrontPage Editor
- Create a link from a page currently open in the FrontPage Editor
- Associate editor appplications to open image, sound, video, and other files
- Copy a web from one location to another including publishing a web to another Web server
- Import an existing web (necessarily created in FrontPage) and automatically update its links

- Rename any file in a web or move it to another folder in the web and have the links update automatically
- Verify that the target files for links exist and repair broken links
- Import files with any format into a web
- Assign access permissions to other users of the web

The FrontPage Editor

The FrontPage Editor is a tool for creating, maintaining, and testing pages in a web. With the Editor, you can:

- Create a new page
- Insert text and format individual characters and entire paragraphs
- Insert images, background sounds, video clips (AVI format only)
- Insert advanced objects such as ActiveX controls, Java applets, plug-ins, and PowerPoint Animations
- Create text hyperlinks to pages and files in the web or anywhere on the WWW
- Create a clickable image and arrange for either the browser or the Web server to implement the jump to the target file
- Open a page from the WWW and save the page and its images to your web
- Add tables
- Create special pages, called framesets, that divide the browser window into sub-windows and display a separate page in each subwindow
- Insert forms to collect information from users
- Include WebBots as prewritten programs to automate web page design or to collect and handle data that the visitor supplies
- Convert the popular text formats to the HTML format and images in a variety of image formats, including BMP, TIFF, MAC, PCD, RAS, WPG, EPS, PCX, and WMF to one of the Web image formats (GIF or JPEG)

You use the Editor's tools to design the page as it would look in a typical browser. The text editing menu commands and toolbar buttons of the FrontPage Editor are nearly identical to those in Microsoft Word. The Editor has commands for creating links that start from a text phrase or an image and for inserting images and then drawing hot spots with links to other files. The Editor also has commands for inserting WebBots and other objects that contain prewritten programs.

As you create a page, the FrontPage Editor automatically translates the page into an HTML tagged version. If you know the HTML language, you can modify the objects you have inserted by including properties that the FrontPage 97 does not recognize, called *extended attributes*. You can insert HTML elements that FrontPage 97 does not recognize using HTML Markup bots. You can also view and directly edit the HTML version of the page.

The FrontPage To Do List

The FrontPage To Do List is a separate client application that you can use to keep track of unfinished and finished tasks. You can order tasks by priority and assign them to different authors.

FrontPage WebBot Components

One of the most exciting features of FrontPage is the ability to include advanced features that require programming but without having to write the programs yourself. The programming required for each feature is packaged into an object called a Front-Page WebBot Component, or simply, a *bot*. To add a feature to a page, you insert the bot and set its properties using the same kind of properties dialog that you use to set properties for any other object. There are two kinds of bots: page design bots and browse time bots.

Page Design Bots   You use page design bots to automate several design operations, such as merging pages to automatically generate a new page, or stamping a page with the time of the last edit. The programs tucked inside the page design bots are run by the FrontPage Explorer and Editor when you insert the bot or when you save a page with bots. (See Chapter 16: Using WebBots in Page Design, for more information.) Front-Page includes the software necessary to run the page design bots.

Browse Time Bots   You use browse time bots to add interactivity to a page, such as collecting information from a visitor, performing a text search of the web, or collecting and organizing replies in an online discussion (see Chapters 17, 18, and 19 for more information). The browse time bots are run by the Web server provided that the Web server is equiped with the necessary software called the FrontPage Server Extensions (see the "Server Extensions" section for more information). This book refers to a Web server that has the FrontPage Server Extensions installed as a *FrontPage-enabled Web server*.

NOTE

Only the browse time bots require FrontPage Server Extensions to be installed on your Web server. If your Web server does not have FrontPage Server Extensions installed, the page design bots in your pages are functional, but trying to run a browse time bot causes an error.

FrontPage Templates and Wizards

FrontPage includes a set of templates and wizards that you use to create new pages and entire webs. A wizard displays a series of dialogs for collecting your design input and then builds a first draft for the page or web according to your specifications. A template provides a first draft without asking any questions. Templates and wizards do much of the work for you, producing a page or web that you can customize. In most cases, you can start from scratch instead of using a template or a wizard, however, for a few FrontPage features, such as creating framesets and online discussion group webs, you must use a wizard. (See Chapter 4 for information on the templates and wizards.)

How the FrontPage Clients Communicate

When you create pages and webs using FrontPage, normally you run at least two of the clients: the FrontPage Explorer and the FrontPage Editor are open in separate windows. Adding a task to the To Do List, running a page design bot, or using a wizard activates one of the other FrontPage components. Figure 2.3 depicts the various components of FrontPage. You may be curious to know how these components communicate with each other. The FrontPage components use a communication technique called *Automation*. Automation enables applications to interact and control each other without direct input from you. For example, when you create a link between two pages using the FrontPage Editor, the link information is automatically sent to the FrontPage Explorer via Automation. When you save a page with page design bots, the page design bot engine (the software that executes the bot programs) runs the bots automatically.

FIGURE 2.3

The components of FrontPage communicate via Automation.

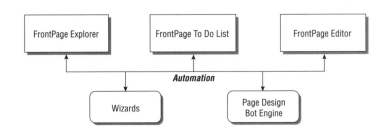

Using FrontPage without a Web Server

Normally, you use the FrontPage Explorer and Editor simultaneously, and you use the package together with a FrontPage-enabled Web server. Nevertheless, you can also use the components of FrontPage in other modes as follows:

FrontPage Editor as an HTML Editor   You can use the FrontPage Editor as a stand-alone Web page editor. You can open an HTML document from any folder in your computer's file system, edit the page, and save the changes back to the folder. You can create links; insert objects, including advanced objects such as ActiveX Controls; or write scripts. The FrontPage templates and some of the Wizards can be used to create new pages. You can insert some of the bots, but the bots may not operate unless you save the page to a web. (Other wizards and bots require that the FrontPage Explorer is running and that a web is open.)

FrontPage Editor as a Web browser   You can use the FrontPage Editor as a Web browser. Open your Internet connection, choose the File ➤ Open command in the Editor menu bar, and type the URL of a page from a web on the Internet to display the page in the Editor window. You can use the Editor's tools to edit the copy and then save the page to a folder on your computer's file system. If you are also running the FrontPage Explorer and have a web open, the page can be saved to the current web. Whether you save the page to a folder or the current web, if the page has images, the Editor prompts you to save them also.

FrontPage Explorer   You can use the FrontPage Explorer as a stand-alone application. The FrontPage Explorer has commands for importing the files of an existing web into a new FrontPage web and for managing the web. The Explorer also has commands for publishing the web to another Web server.

Creating Disk-Based Webs   You can use the FrontPage client applications without a Web server to create a web and store the web in any folder on your computer's file system. The web pages can have exactly the same features that you build into a Web server-based web. You can copy the web to any Web server for publishing to the Internet. A disk-based web can even be "published" to others on your local area network without using a Web server. However, any browse time bots in the web won't operate unless you use the FrontPage Explorer to copy the web to a FrontPage-enabled Web server.

Understanding the Roles of the Web Server

The fundamental function of a Web server is publishing information. Basically, the Web server houses documents, receives requests for documents from client applications across the TCP/IP communication channel, and returns copies of the requested documents across the channel. In support of its role in document storage and retrieval, a Web server typically includes programs for the following administrative tasks: creating a default index that is displayed when a visitor browses to a web that doesn't have a home page; controlling access to your web, for logging information about traffic; performance; changes; and problems. In addition, Web servers usually include software for remote interaction—that is, software to allow you to manage the Web server and to build and change webs on the Web server when you are working on a different computer.

Another major function of a Web server is to run programs. The ability to extend the capabilities of a Web server with additional programs is one of the most important and rapidly changing aspects of Internet communication. Web servers run external and internal programs as follows.

External Programs   The Web server can call on external programs, called *gateway programs*, to help in processing a request. Web servers use a protocol called the *Common Gateway Interface (CGI)* to communicate with gateway programs. The gateway programs are usually called *CGI programs*. The web server uses the CGI protocol to pass data to the CGI program. The CGI program may do all the processing itself or may call on other programs and files to process the request. Typically, CGI programs have the .exe file extension. An example of a CGI program is in the processing of clickable images. When a Web visitor clicks on a page that has image hyperlinks or hotspots on images, there must be a way to determine whether the pointer is inside the boundary of the image or hotspot when the mouse is clicked. Traditionally, Web servers have called on CGI programs to analyze the location of the pointer and activate the hyperlink if the pointer is within the boundary of a clickable image or hotspot. More recently, Web browsers have taken on this function. In FrontPage, you can create image hyperlinks for both server-side processing using the Web server's CGI program, and client-side image processing using the visitor's Web browser.

Internal Programs   Some Web servers include a set of programs called an Application Programming Interface (API) that extend their capabilities. Instead of being external programs that are called and run as separate programs each time they are needed, the programs of an API are loaded when the server starts and are available as dynamic link libraries (with the .dll extension). Because it works together with the internal programs of the server, an element of the server's API runs faster than an equivalent CGI program. The Microsoft Web Servers have differing versions of the Internet Server API (ISAPI), the Netscape Web servers have a Netscape Server API (NSAPI), and the WebSite Web servers have the Website API (WSAPI). (The FrontPage Personal Web Server does not include support for ISAPI and runs CGI programs as external programs.)

Server Extensions

Whether the Web server calls other programs as external CGI programs or as internal API dynamic link libraries, the programs that extend the capabilities of the server beyond the basic document storage and retrieval function are called *server extensions*.

FrontPage Server Extensions

The set of programs that must be installed with a Web server in order to provide the FrontPage features is called the FrontPage Server Extensions. Depending on the Web server, the FrontPage Server Extensions may be external programs (.exe) or internal dynamic link libraries (.dll), however, the CGI mechanism is essentially the same: data is passed from the client application to the appropriate Server Extensions program and the program returns a result in HTML format.

When you set up a Web server to run FrontPage webs, you must install the FrontPage Server Extensions on the same computer that runs the Web server. There are three main programs in the FrontPage Server Extensions:

- **Authoring support**   The program named author.exe or author.dll is responsible for functions that are required by the FrontPage Explorer, Editor, and To Do List client applications, such as storing files, updating the To Do List, and keeping track of the links between files. When you add or delete pages from the web, it is the author program that carries out the task.

- **Administrative support**   The program named admin.exe or admin.dll is responsible for providing a variety of functions, such as setting access permissions, handling clickable images, and keeping track of Web server configuration information. When you open a FrontPage web, it is the admin program that runs in order to verify your rights to browse, edit, or administer the web.

- **Browse time bots**   The program named shtml.exe or shtml.dll handles the interactive functions by running the browse time bots. When a Web visitor enters data such as a search string, a discussion article, or requested information in a data entry form and then submits the data, the shtml server extension runs the bot's program and generates an HTML page with the results.

The FrontPage Server Extensions also include the files that FrontPage uses to inventory the web's files, to keep track of finished and unfinished tasks, and to store text indexes for the HTML pages in the web.

Typically, you run the FrontPage Explorer, Editor, and To Do List client applications simultaneously to create a FrontPage web stored by a FrontPage-enabled Web Server. The client applications communicate with the Web server using the HTTP protocol on the TCP/IP channel, which in turn communicates with the FrontPage Server Extensions using CGI or one of the Web server APIs. Figure 2.4 depicts the communication among the components.

FIGURE 2.4

The FrontPage Clients use TCP/IP to communicate with the Web Server.

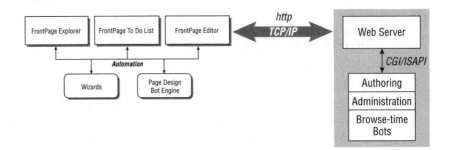

FrontPage Server Administrator   You use another FrontPage program called the FrontPage Server Administrator to install and remove the FrontPage Server Extensions. (see Appendix A for more information.)

Internet Database Connector

A new feature in FrontPage 97 is the ability to connect to a database file. The connection is based on a server extension called the Internet Database Connector, which is part of the Microsoft Web Servers (but not the FrontPage Personal Web Server). The communication process is described in Chapter 21.

Active Server Page Script Processing

A new feature called Active Server Page technology allows the Web server to run scripts that you include in a Web page. As this book is written, the popular Web browsers are able to run scripts written in VBScript and JavaScript (see Chapter 20 for more information). What is new is that the Web server will run scripts as well. The Microsoft Web Servers support the new technology as a server extension.

The FrontPage Web

When you install the FrontPage Server Extensions on a Web server, a set of FrontPage folders is placed in the Web server's content folder. The Web server's content folder is where you normally store the folders for each of the individual webs.

NOTE

You can also store individual web folders in other physical locations and then use the Web server's internal programs to map the physical location to a URL for the Web server's content folder. For example, you can map the folder with path C:\CompanyBrochure\Background\Archives\ to the URL http://*servername*/Archives/. See Appendix B for more information.

FrontPage Root Web

The Web server's content folder is also referred to as the server's *root web* folder. When you point a Web browser to the Web server by entering the URL http://*servername*/ without specifying a folder name, it is the home page stored in the server's root web that is displayed. (If the root web doesn't have a default home page, the Web server generates an index that is displayed by the browser.) You can open the Web server's root web in the FrontPage Explorer and add and edit pages in the same way you add and edit pages for any FrontPage web. In addition to the content files you may add to the root web, the root web also contains a set of FrontPage folders that are not visible in the FrontPage Explorer.

FrontPage Folders   The Web server's content folder contains a set of five FrontPage folders that have names starting with _vti_. The FrontPage folders include a folder that holds the three FrontPage Server Extension programs (_vti_bin), a folder for logging FrontPage server activity (_vti_log), a folder that contains files for keeping track of the bots used in the root web, lists of the finished and unfinished tasks on the To Do List (_vti_pvt), a folder that holds the text index for the pages in the web (_vti_txt), and a folder that holds administrative information about each file in the web (_vti_cnf).

FrontPage Web Folders

Each FrontPage web that you create in the FrontPage Explorer has its own web folder that is stored in the Web server's content folder (or mapped from another physical location). Technically, each web is a subweb of the server's root web, in the same sense that a folder has subfolders, although we won't use the term subweb. Each FrontPage web has its own content folders and files, including the pages you create in the FrontPage Editor and the files you import from other locations, that you work with in the FrontPage Explorer, Editor, and To Do List. In addition, each FrontPage web has a set of four FrontPage (vti) folders with the same names and functions as the FrontPage folders in the root web. Individual webs do not have the _vti_log folder.

NOTE

Although it appears that the root web and each individual web all have their own copies of the three FrontPage Server Extension programs author.dll, admin.dll, and shtml.dll, in fact there is only one actual copy of these programs. What is stored in the _vti_bin folder in the root web, and in each individual web are small programs called *stubs* whose only roles are to call the actual programs.

Publishing the FrontPage Web

After you have developed a FrontPage web and tested it from your local computer, it is time to publish your work. There are two basic alternatives. You can publish the web yourself using the Web server on your computer or on another computer to which you have access. Otherwise, you can use an Internet Service Provider to host your FrontPage webs.

Publishing a Web Yourself

You can publish the web yourself using any Web server, but in order to provide the interactive features based on the browse time bots, you'll need a FrontPage-enabled Web server. Here are the ways you can be your own host.

You can actually publish your FrontPage web on the Internet even if all you have is a modem and a part-time connection to the Internet through an Internet Service Provider (ISP) such as CompuServe, the Microsoft Network, or AT&T's WorldNet. Although publishing this way is possible, it isn't a very useful way to publish because you have to be online in order to make your web available, and modem connections are slow. The biggest problem with this method, however, is that many Internet Service Providers assign you a different IP address each time you log on to the service, and you may have to give the IP address to the potential visitors to your site. Even if you have an arrangement for an unlimited number of hours of connection time, typically you have to log on frequently because the connection closes automatically after a specified idle time interval (typically 20 minutes). Many Internet Service Providers offer a 24-hour service and a dedicated line with a fixed IP address. Although having a fixed IP address is more expensive than having a temporary address, you can use this method to publish your webs yourself.

Many people have a direct full-time Internet connection through their workplace. In this case, you can use any Web server to which you have access to publish your webs. While the Microsoft and the FrontPage Personal Web Servers are fine for a low volume of visitors and for nonsensitive webs, you'll probably want to move up to a more powerful server if you expect a higher volume of visitors or want the additional security and other features that a professional Web server offers.

Figure 2.5 depicts the interactions between a Web browser and a FrontPage-enabled Web server providing files from a FrontPage web.

FIGURE 2.5

The interactions between a Web browser and a FrontPage-enabled Web server providing files from a FrontPage web

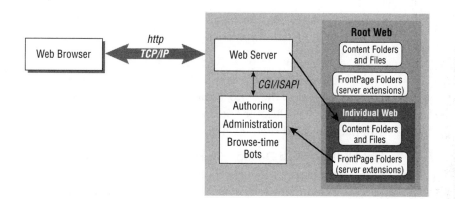

Using a Web Hosting Service

Many Internet Service Providers also offer a web hosting service. In this case, you rent disk space, transmission time, and processing time on the ISP's Web server. As a typical example, in spring 1997, you can arrange for web hosting renting 25 megabytes of storage and 1 gigabyte of transfer per month for $30 per month plus a set up fee. In order to publish a FrontPage web, the ISP must install the FrontPage Server Extensions. A growing number of ISP's can publish FrontPage webs. The Microsoft FrontPage web site as http://www.microsoft.com/frontpage/ provides a list of the ISP's that host FrontPage webs.

Using the Web Publishing Wizard

If you are use a FrontPage-enabled Web server other than the one installed on your computer, you can use the FrontPage Explorer commands to post your web to the Web server. If you are posting a web to a Web server that doesn't have FrontPage Server Extensions installed, you can use the Microsoft Web Publishing Wizard. This wizard is one of the Bonus Pack components on the FrontPage 97 CD-ROM. For more information on using the Publishing Wizard, see Appendix B.

Using FrontPage Help

FrontPage provides an online help system that is easy to use. Online help is based on the Windows 95 Help system, so you are probably familiar with the key aspects.

Context-Sensitive Help

Context-sensitive help displays a window with information relating to the specific command or operation you are trying to carry out. Here are the ways to get context-sensitive help.

Help Toolbar Button   Click the Help button at the right end of the FrontPage Explorer toolbar or the Editor's Standard toolbar. Move the help mouse pointer that appears after you click the button to the menu command or toolbar button for which you want help and click again to display a help window.

Help Button On a Dialog   Every object you insert on a page in the FrontPage Editor has a properties dialog that you use to set properties for the object. Also, nearly every operation for which additional input is required has a dialog that you use to specify the operation. Clicking the Help button that invariably appears on the right side or along the bottom of the dialog, or pressing F1, displays a help window for the dialog.

Help Topics Dialog

To obtain more extensive help, use the Help Topics dialog. Display the Help topics dialog by pressing F1 or by choosing Help ➤ Microsoft FrontPage Help from the Explorer or the Editor menu bar.

Contents Tab   The Contents tab arranges the help topics like the table of contents of a book. The major headings are displayed when you first open the dialog. Double-click the book icon to the left of a heading to expand the heading and change the closed book to an open book icon. The subheadings are displayed in an indented list. Closed book icons indicate that you can expand the topic further by double-clicking the icon. A page icon with a question mark indicates the topic is fully expanded (see Figure 2.6a). Double-clicking a page icon displays the help window for the topic. Double-click an open book icon to collapse the heading and change the icon to a closed book.

Index Tab   The index tab arranges the help topics alphabetically like the index section of a book. Type the name of the topic for which you want help in the text box at the top of the dialog. As you type letters, the list box scrolls to show the help topic that most closely matches the letters you've typed (see Figure 2.6b). Double-click an item in the list box, or select an item and click the Display button to display the help window for the topic.

FIGURE 2.6

Use the Contents tab to expand headings to display subheadings (a). Use the Index tab to locate a topic name from an alphabetical list (b).

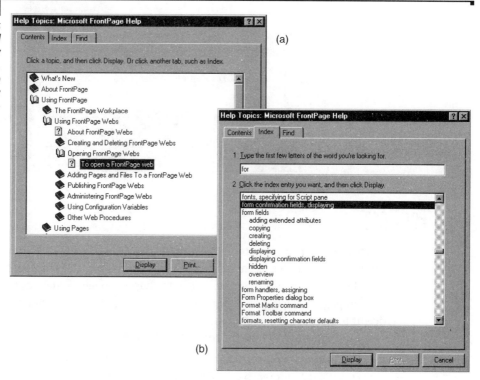

Find Tab   You can use the Find tab to search through the text of a help article. This tab is very useful when you don't know the name of a topic. In Figure 2.7 the Find tab shows the result of searching for the word publishing. The list box in the center displays the name of topics that contain the search word. Click an item in this list to narrow the search. After choosing an item, the list box at the bottom displays the matching help topics. Double-click a help topic to display the help window.

FIGURE 2.7

Use the Find tab to do a text search of the Help topics.

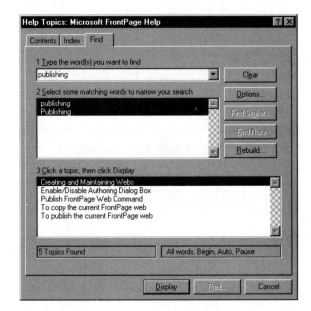

For More...

This chapter has introduced you to the basic concepts of computer communication on the Internet. You've learned how the main components of FrontPage interact with each other and with a Web server. The next chapter covers guidelines for designing webs and pages focusing on exploiting the FrontPage features to build a web that is efficient to produce and maintain.

For more information see the following chapters:

- Chapter 5: Explorer Basics shows you how to use the basic features of the FrontPage Explorer to create and manage a web.

- Chapter 8: Understanding To Do Lists describes how to use this simple but effective program to keep track of unfinished tasks.

- Chapter 10: Editor Basics shows you how to use the basic features of the FrontPage Editor to create and edit pages.
- Appendix A: Installing Frontpage 97 and the Personal Web Servers shows you how to install and FrontPage-enable the two Personal Web Servers that come with FrontPage.

PART

I

Overview of
FrontPage

Chapter

3

Designing a
FrontPage Web

FEATURING

Designing a FrontPage Web

Unless your web is going to be only a few pages, you should spend considerable time planning what you are going to display at your site. The investment of your time in planning will pay off several times over when you produce your web, and expecially later when you make changes. So shut down your computer for this chapter, and go find a comfortable reading chair. Take along a pencil and plenty of paper so you can start sketching the layout for your new web.

The purpose of this chapter is to give you plenty to think about before you start the actual production of a web. Most of the topics are quite general and apply to the design of any web. However, we'll be looking at these topics with FrontPage in mind. Remember, FrontPage is our *tool* for creating the web. As with any tool, FrontPage has particular strengths that you'll want to exploit. By being aware of the FrontPage features, you can build them into your web design right from the start.

Setting Design Goals

Creating a web can be a substantial undertaking. Yes, you can create a web with a single page, but, since you are reading this book, you probably have something more grand in mind. These days a small web site has about 100 pages and a large one has more than 10,000 pages. If you have done much exploring on the WWW, you have doubtless begun to form your own distinctive taste in webs. You find some webs are visually appealing and packed with interesting information, other webs are engaging with their coolness and enjoyment value, and some webs are repellent with too many garish colors and fancy fonts.

The purpose of this chapter is to help you to design an effective, if not a cool, web. An effective web is one that visitors come back to.

Why Are You Creating a Web?

The first question to ask yourself is why are you creating a web? You should define clearly what information you want to present and who you want to present it to. There are two major categories of webs: webs on the public Internet and those on a private company intranet.

Internet Webs

Webs destined for the public Internet will be competing with millions of other webs. The underlying theme of any Internet web is that the viewer is an active explorer. If your web doesn't present the information or doesn't present it in a way that the viewer finds satisfactory, the viewer will simply click away and probably won't come back. No matter how you design your web, it won't be effective to every viewer. You won't be able to please every Web visitor, so you need to decide who you want to attract to your web, and focus your design efforts on your target web audience.

Given that you have some information to display, the real questions are:

- What do your target visitors want to see?
- What do they want to do at your web?
- What questions do visitors have?
- What answers do they expect?

If you can think like the people who will use your web, and then design your web, or better yet, *their* web, to meet their needs, they will use it.

Many people don't browse the WWW just for fun (although there is a sizable group doing exactly that). Normally, they are looking for information when they come across your site. The first things they do at your site are to browse your pages and explore the information you are providing. You can provide the following types of information:

- Who you are and what you do
- Topics of interest related to your web's theme

- The organization's history
- The activities, services, or products you provide
- The volunteer or employment opportunities in you organization
- Schedules of upcoming activities, meetings, seminars, or product releases
- Who to contact for more information

After exploring your site for a while, visitors often want to interact in one of the following ways:

- Send their comments and opinions
- Be put on a mailing list
- Sign up for an activity, order a product, or register for a class or seminar
- Request specific information
- Search for information in your web

Intranet Webs

Webs designed for a private company intranet have a captive audience. Competition with other webs is no longer the issue. The purpose of an intranet web is more narrowly defined: the intranet web is intended as the central communication and information sharing vehicle for the organization. An effective intranet web quickly becomes the primary information sharing method in the company, making department newsletters and bulletin boards relics from the past. Nevertheless, to be effective, the intranet web must deal with many of the same design issues as its Internet cousin. In both kinds of webs, understanding the visitor is the key to success.

Make It Interactive!

Successful Internet and intranet webs invite the visitor to participate. People browse the Internet or check into the company intranet looking for opportunities to express an opinion on significant matters, become involved in online discussions with others they can learn from, get to know other people, and share their own experiences and knowledge. As the webmaster of your new web, you'll quickly learn how appreciative visitors are of opportunities to participate. You'll also see that visitors are typically very generous in offering you good ideas for expansion and suggestions for improvement. The more visitors can tell you what they want from your web, the easier it is for you to make your web more useful.

What Is Content?

This book doesn't show you how to create content; other books will show you how to create the audio, image, photo, animation, and video files that you may want to include in a web page. Instead, this book is focused on showing you how to present your content in a FrontPage web. Just what is content?

Content is information: overviews, opinions, calendars, maps, biographies, bibliographies, glossaries, product information, statistics, frequently asked questions, summaries, sounds, movies, and so on.

Content is also the relationships between information. You provide the relationships through the organization of your web and the links from one bit of information to another.

Kinds of Content   There are five kinds of content you can include:

- **Facts**   involve specific information. Facts are presented as statements and data requiring no explanation. For example, SYBEX has branch offices in San Francisco, Paris, Dusseldorf, and Soest.

- **Definitions and concepts**   explain what something is and what it is not. For example, a cache is a location in memory where a browser or web server stores copies of recently retrieved files.

- **Procedures**   are sequential steps that tell you how to do something. For example, instead of telling the visitor to "download the demo" (this statement tells the visitor *what* to do, not *how* to do it), you provide a set of simple instructions.

- **Processes**   explain how things work. Explaining how something works usually involves explaining the individual parts and how they are connected or how they interact with each other.

- **Guidelines and principles**   are general advice given by experts. For example, if you are new at planning a bicycle tour, you'll want to take advantage of the proven guidelines offered by experienced bicycle tourists.

The level of abstraction increases as you move down the list of content types. Unfortunately, the frequency of a content type's appearance in webs decreases as you proceed down the list.

Kinds of Internet Webs

As the Internet becomes a fundamental means of communication, the types of Internet webs become more varied. The Internet is unregulated and "free"—anyone who has a direct connection to the Internet or rents computer space from an Internet Service Provider can publish a web.

The general categories of Internet Webs are:

Categories	Examples
Information	news, library databases, educational sites, on-line courses, medical databases
Commerce	corporate presence sites, advertising, marketing and production information, sales of products and services
Community organizations	on-line newsletters, legislation databases
Personal	biographical webs, special interest, hobbies
Special topics	travel, sports, science, food

Once you've settled on a topic, you are free to create guided only by the rules of your organization or by your own impulses if you are creating a personal web.

Designing an Intranet Web

The main purposes of a company intranet are:

- To communicate and share information among the internal departments of the company
- To provide a sense of connectedness to the company
- To provide a sense of the interconnectedness of the parts of the company

By enhancing communication and increasing the spirit of cooperation among all company employees, the intranet offers the chance for the company to build shared visions and enrich company culture.

Design Goals for a Company Intranet   Because its intranet Web represents the company itself, the company needs to set guidelines for its Web, including defining standards for proprietary and public information, and standards for acceptable content. In addition, the company may set policy on the use of common design elements and navigational techniques, such as logos, colors, fonts, page layout, and navigation techniques that give the web its unique look and feel. The intranet web has the face and personality that the company displays to its own members. The initial decisions for the web's design and content guidelines should be made at the highest levels to be sure that the web's personality is a true reflection of the company.

Designing a Collaborative Web   To achieve the goals of the company, the intranet web needs to provide opportunities for any member to contribute. Building discussion groups into the web provides opportunities for members to participate. Focused discussion groups on topics of interest stimulate interest in the company and commitment to improving the company. For example, consider including the following types of discussion groups: the design of a new product, planning the company outing, changing the company's health services provider, the plans for a stock incentive plan, the new parking policy, and recreational activities.

Another way to achieve a collaborative web is to distribute the responsibilities for designing, creating, and maintaining the web itself. While the company needs a single Webmaster to oversee the entire web, subwebs "owned" by individual departments within the company allow several sub-Webmasters to give the necessary attention and special treatment to their individual webs. The participation of several web authors enriches the web content.

Organizing Content

Web visitors are usually in a hurry—they want to find out what your site contains and they want to move quickly to the pages that promise the specific information they are looking for. Once the visitor has traveled to a page in your web, it is up to you to lead the visitor to related information and invite the visitor to additional information in your web that may be of interest. Your organization of the content is the key to the visitor's efficient use of your web.

Arranging Content into Main Groupings

You'll start by arranging the content into several main groupings—no more than six of seven main groupings as a general rule.

Developing Patterns

The information within a main grouping can be arranged in three basic patterns: a hierarchical tree structure, a linear structure, or no structure (commonly referred to as a "web structure"). You can use one or more of the patterns in your web. Your web may include different kinds of information and, as a result, parts of your web may best be presented using different structures. The structure you use for a section of the web should follow the natural flow of information. The pages in your web may each contain a separate topic or a page may contain several related topics.

Hierarchical Tree   The hierarchical tree pattern is the familiar outline. The information is arranged in categories. The information in each category is arranged in subcategories. As appropriate, the information is each subcategory is further arranged into groupings, and so on. The natural flow of information is down and up the tree with little flow horizontally. Most webs use a hierarchical tree structure to allow the visitor to drill down from a general topic near the top to greater and greater detail.

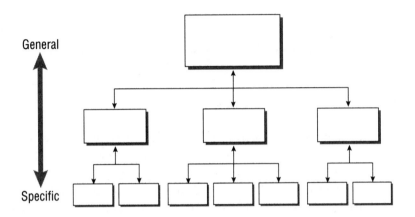

When you use a hierarchical structure, you should provide navigation paths up and down from one level to the next. All link arrows should be bi-directional. Use three or four levels at most to help in orienting your visitors. Provide a link back to the main level from all levels so that visitors can quickly return to the start without having to back track through each link of the path.

Linear Pattern   In a linear pattern, each topic has equal status, and the natural flow of information is horizontally from one topic to the next and back. Many printed documents and most works of fiction have a linear structure, as each chapter naturally follows the previous. Skipping chapters causes confusion and is not advised.

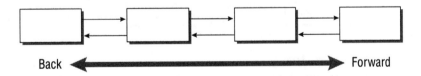

When information has a linear structure, you should provide simple navigation paths back and forth between successive documents. You should also provide paths back to the main page from each document so that visitors can return to the main page in one jump.

A linear pattern may include branching as the information digresses and then returns to the main information. For example, if you are presenting a news story, you may want to branch off to present a background story and then return to the main story.

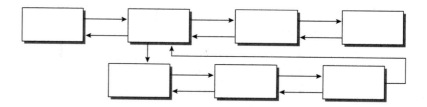

A linear pattern may be part of a hierarchy. For example, in the subsequent chapters of this book, you'll be creating a web that describes the bicycle tour of Wales and Ireland that was announced in the Pacifica Cycle Touring Club web you created in Chapter 1. The web has main sections for each country. Each section has a set of pages that describe individual days of the tour. The tour days have a natural linear structure in which day follows day. However, you can also organize the information in a hierarchy in three levels from tour introduction to tour country to individual country regions.

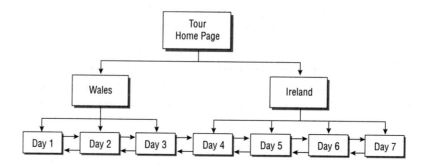

Web Structure　When there is no apparent structure to information, the relations between bits of information is free form. A bit of information may lead to another bit, which leads to another, and so on, without any overall organization or structured relationship between the information other than the designer's own sense of flow. Reading a newspaper can be a "no structure" experience. Instead of reading one article after another as they are laid out in the pages, you start with an article that catches your attention. When you are finished, or even before you are finished, an idea in the article may lead you to jump to a sidebar or a related article on the same page. In the Wales and Ireland web, we could have a free form section on regional culture with a set of topics that we link as the content we decide to include for a topic suggests. For example, a song we include in the Irish music page could lead to a page on politics, which could lead to a page on the potato famine of 1849, which could lead to a page on Dublin, which could lead to a page on gardens, and so on.

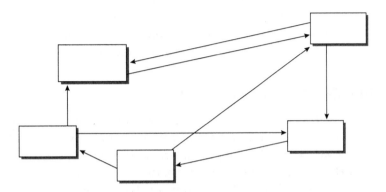

When you use the Web structure, it is easy for the visitor to get lost, since there is no intrinsic sense of where you are going or how to return to the main idea. You should provide plenty of links for returning to key locations (unless of course the point of your web is experiencing the unconnectedness of the "no structure" structure).

Developing Your Own Structure

As you arrange the topics in your web, you'll probably find that you'll be combining the three basic structures to create your own structure. Here are some basic approaches:

- Start with a highly structured hierarchy and add links to allow wandering through the structure.
- Start with an unstructured web and add a minimal structure by providing links back to a home page or a navigation bar with links to key pages.
- Start with a web that has both structured and unstructured parts.

Planning Navigation

The underlying theme of the Internet is that the viewer is an active explorer. It is the visitor who decides whether to follow a particular link. It is your job as the web designer to provide the navigation paths that make it easy to explore your web.

Navigation Guidelines

Here are some guidelines for designing the navigation through your Web:

- Make sure the viewers know where they are.
- Make sure the viewers know how to get back.
- Limit the number of clicks required to go to any page to three or four, as a general rule.
- If the hierarchical tree has more that two or three layers, provide alternate paths from higher levels directly to lower levels.

Navigation Techniques

Pay special attention to the navigation starting points you provide in the home page. The home page introduces your web and is the entry point to the main sections of the web. The paths to the main sections should be obvious. If your web uses separate webs as subwebs, the home page of the main web should contain links to the home page of each subweb. It is important to keep in mind that the visual space is limited to the visitor's computer screen and some visitor's are limited to resolutions of 640 by 480 pixels on 14 inch screens. The limitation of the visual space is compounded by the fact that many visitors don't like to scroll.

Using Tables of Contents

One way to orient your visitors to a web that has an underlying hierarchical structure is to use a hierarchical table of contents that displays the levels as indentations in the table. If each item in the table is a clickable link to the main page for the topic, then the table acts like the main switchboard for your web. You can also use a separate table of contents at the top of each page that has several topics to allow the visitor to jump quickly to other parts of the page.

Using Navigation Bars

To keep visitors oriented as they travel through your web, you should include obvious navigation paths back to the home page or to the main sections. One way to keep visitors oriented and still leave room for lots of content is to use a navigation bar which has links to the main sections, and include the navigation bar on every page. Here are some ways to include navigation bars.

Headers and Footers Include the same navigation bar in the header section of every page. You can also include the same or another navigation bar in the footer section.

Frames   If you use frames to divide the browser window into a set of subwindows, you can reserve one of the frames for a permanent navigation frame. As the visitor clicks links in the navigation frame, the target pages are displayed in another frame. The navigation frame can be in the top or bottom, or on one of the sides of the window.

Using Text Links

The start of the navigation paths should be obvious. When you use a text phrase as the start of the link, the Web browser makes the link obvious by underlining the text phrase and changing the text color. A text link is the easiest and quickest way to provide an obvious beginning to a navigation path, but it may not be the most attractive.

Using Image Links

You can start navigation links using clickable images. Although clickable images may be visually appealing, they are not always obvious. Additionally, each image you add to a page has a cost in the time to download the image. If you use image links for navigation, keep the image file small and try to reuse the image files (the browser downloads the image file only once and reuses its copy).

A Model Site: The Microsoft SiteBuilder Workshop

The Microsoft Site Builder Workshop Web is a subweb of the Microsoft site, and is a good model of efficient navigation. (The URL for the site is www.microsoft.com/workshop/default.htm.) The web uses several navigation techniques to provide paths to information and to keep the visitor oriented. As this book is being written, the site's home page uses different techniques to provide navigation to three groupings of information, as shown in Figure 3.1.

NOTE

The home page and the other pages in the Site Builder Workshop make frequent use of frames to divide the main browser window into subwindows. Each subwindow can display content from a different page (in Chapter 15, you'll learn how to create subwindows).

Navigation Bar with Buttons   Across the top of the main browser window is a navigation bar that leads the visitor to the overarching groupings of the main Microsoft Web site: the main Microsoft home page, products, search, support, shopping, and feedback. This navigation bar provides the eagle's view of the main Microsoft site.

FIGURE 3.1

*The home page of
the Microsoft Site
Builders Workshop*

Main Table of Contents Using Image Links   The main section of the browser window dominates the window's center and right. This part of the browser window is the visually interesting and colorful display of the six major content sections of the Site Builders Workshop web: authoring/editing, design/creative, programming, site administration, planning/production, and web gallery. Each content section is indicated by a graphic that has a text heading, a button, and a large multi-colored ball. Although the balls are attractive, unfortunately they don't suggest the subject they represent (except the programming ball, which has text to suggest programming code). Using icons that suggest the subject provides an additional way to orient your visitors.

Clicking any part of one of the graphics takes you to a new browser window with the home page for the subject. Figure 3.2 shows the home page for the design/creative section. The other subjects use the same page design. The page design includes an image hyperlink (with the six balls) in the upper-left corner of the browser window that takes you back to the Site Builder Workshop home page. A vertical frame along the left gives the subject's title. The horizontal frame at the top is a navigation bar that keeps you oriented by providing links to topics in both the Site Builder Workshop site and the main Microsoft site. The main area of the browser window is devoted to displaying the content. The home page of the design/creative section has a table of contents embedded in the text of the main section with text hyperlinks to subtopics. As the visitor scrolls the content frame, the other frames of the browser window remain fixed to provide permanent navigation and orientation.

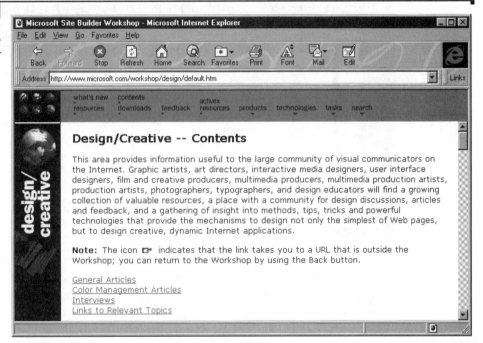

FIGURE 3.2

Clicking a ball takes you to the home page of a major content section.

Secondary Table of Contents To the left of the six content balls in the SiteBuilder Workshop home page is a table of contents as a framed page (see Figure 3.1). This table of contents is based on a different organizing principal. The list includes hyperlinks to what's new, contents, products & technologies, resources, downloads, and return to the Site Builder home page. The items in this table of contents have a small red arrow. Clicking an item changes the content displayed in the content area to the right, but leaves the other parts of the page unchanged (see Figure 3.3).

Above the table of contents in the SiteBuilder Workshop home page is the resources for web teams graphic, including an image link and a button (see Figure 3.1). Clicking the button displays a new browser window with a page design similar to the design shown in Figure 3.2.

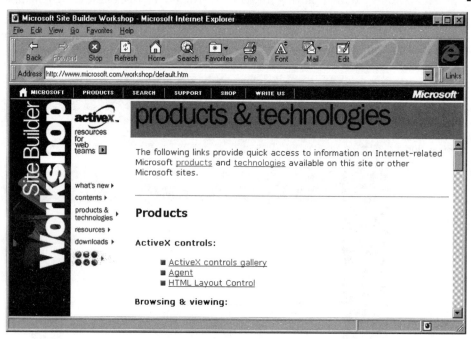

FIGURE 3.3

Clicking a list item with a red arrow changes the contents of the main frame, but leaves the rest of the browser window unchanged.

The home page for the Site Builder Workshop web manages to provide three sets of navigational links to a total of eighteen major groupings, using a visually interesting, uncluttered design.

NOTE

The Site Builder Workshop web makes frequent use of little popup windows to provide additional clues. The popup windows are created using one of the ActiveX Controls that you can download from the site and include in your own pages (see Chapter 20 for more information on ActiveX Controls).

Planning Pages

Two important limitations in web page design are:

Space   The visitor's computer screen has very limited visual space and the visitor may be unwilling to scroll.

Time   It takes a noticeable interval of time to retrieve a page and all its associated files such as images, sounds, and video files and the visitor may be unwilling to wait.

You need to plan each page carefully to balance these competing limitations of space and time with your desires to publish the most visually and aurally interesting site. The real estate at the top of the page is prime, use it wisely.

Here are some things to keep in mind as you tinker with your site:

- Keep images as small as possible, but large enough to display information and achieve the visual effect. Whenever possible, limit the image file size to 40 to 50K.

- Keep the number of images per page small so that the page downloads in an acceptable time. If necessary, you should break a page into two or more linked pages, so that each page downloads quickly.

- As a general rule, limit each page to a separate topic, but if you do include several topics on a page, include a table of contents with links to the topics at the top of the page to avoid scrolling down the page.

- Avoid long pages by using tables to lay out multi-column text and to intersperse text with images. Alternatively, use frames to lay out two or more pages in sub-windows in the browser.

Page Design Issues

If you want your visitors to return to your site and enjoy being there, remember the information you present is what keeps visitors coming back, and the page design makes their stay more pleasant. Your goal should be an effective, if not "cool" site that visitors keep coming back to. When you design a page, you have complete control over the "look" of the page. The first design decision should involve the look you are trying to achieve in your web. Do you want your web to be cool, elegant, cute, slick, bold, understated, flashy, serene, frenetic?—It's up to you.

Regardless of the look you are trying to achieve, two good design rules are:

- Keep it Simple
- Less is More

Here are some design issues to consider as you plan your site:

Common page elements   Give your web an identity by using common page elements, such as headers, footers, navigation bars, and overall page design. Although it is possible to choose a different background image or color for each page and use several fonts through a page, you'll probably want to avoid both these practices.

Text and backgrounds   Choose text and background colors that make it easy to read the text. Red and blue may be your favorite colors, but red text on a blue background (or vice versa) isn't very readable. Readability improves with greater contrast between the text and background colors, with black and white providing the very best readability. (Normally you see black text on a white background, but white text on a black background is just as good.) If you choose a background image rather than a color, keep the image design simple and choose a font size and weight so that the text is readable over the background.

Fonts Minimize the number of different fonts. Choose a readable font, and use different font sizes for emphasis instead of choosing a different font.

Planning for Efficient Production and Maintenance

An important consideration in deciding to publish a web is the need to change and to maintain the web. Static, unchanging webs do not keep visitors interest very long. Visitors expect change in both the information you publish and in the look of your web. As you plan your web, you should plan for the efficient production of your web and for the efficient implementation of the changes you will be making. This section describes some techniques you can include in your web to minimize the labor of making the inevitable changes.

Defining Common Web Data

Every web has some data that may change from time to time. Telephone and FAX numbers may change, a new web master may be appointed, a company may decide to change its name, or a club may develop a new motto. The values of some of these web parameters may be displayed on several or even all of your pages. When a value changes, you need ways to avoid having to make the changes manually each time the value appears.

FrontPage solves the problem of changing web parameters by allowing you to create a single list of the values and then by automatically updating all pages when the values change. In Chapter 16, you'll learn how to use Substitution bots to display the current values of the web parameters.

Defining Style Pages

One way to change the look of a web is to change the background color or image and to change the text and text link colors.

FrontPage makes it easy to change the look by allowing you to create one or more styles pages that lend their background and text styles to other pages. A FrontPage styles page has a background color or image and a set of text colors. When you change the background or text colors of a styles page, the other pages that borrow from the styles page are automatically updated.

Using a Table of Contents

As you add new pages and delete other pages, you need to update any tables of contents that have hyperlinks to the deleted pages or that should have hyperlinks to the new pages.

FrontPage makes it easy to update certain kinds of tables of contents. It provides a way to create a table of contents that updates automatically when you add or delete pages. In Chapter 16, you'll learn how to use the Table Of Contents bot to create self-updating contents.

Using Common Page Elements

Using common page elements has three important advantages: consistency of appearance, reduced production time, and efficient maintenance of the changing web.

When all the pages in a web or all the pages in a section of a web have common page elements, your web takes on an identity. Visitors are immediately aware when they have left your site or have traveled to another section of your web. By minimizing the number of different page designs, you can concentrate your design talents on creating one or two excellent page designs.

When you have common page elements, you save production time because you only need to design the page element once and then reuse the page element on other pages. When you design headers and footers, you can include web parameters such as the organization's motto, the webmaster's e-mail address, and the company's telephone and FAX information. Use the Substitution bots to display the web parameters. Because Substitution bots update automatically, you minimize web maintenance when the values change. Use the TimeStamp bot in the main body of the page to indicate the date that the page was last modified.

One of the strengths of FrontPage is in the maintenance of common page elements. To reuse a page element, create the element as a separate page, store it out of site in the _private folder, and then use an Include bot to merge the page element into another page. When you change a page element, the Include bot automatically locates and updates all pages that use the page element.

Using Page Elements with Limited Time Value

One way to make your web dynamic is to change the content frequently. FrontPage provides one simple way to automate the display of changed content. If you have a page or an image that you want to display for a specific time interval, such as a limited time sales promotion or the announcement of a specific event, you can use the Scheduled Include bots. These bots display the page or image for the specified time interval automatically.

Creating Custom Page and Web Templates

In Chapter 4, you'll learn about the page and web templates that are built into FrontPage. In fact, every new web and every new page must ultimately be based on a template. A template is simply a pattern for new objects. One way to deal efficiently with changing content is to create your own page template that has the design and page elements that you want to use throughout a section of the Web. Then each time you want to create a new page for the Web, you open a new page based on your template. FrontPage makes it easy to create your own page templates (see the "Saving a Page as a Template," section in Chapter 10). You can even create your own web templates without programming (see Appendix C for more information).

By investing the time up front to create page and web templates, you can really streamline the production process.

Planning the Development Process

Developing a Web is all too often a process of excessive iteration as you get your rough draft in place and begin tinkering. Often, people start creating pages with the text content first and think about the page design elements later. It is much more efficient to turn the process on end.

Analyze content   Analyze the content using paper and pencil to determine the main pages you'll need and lay out the structures you'll use for different parts of your web.

Decide on Web features   Decide on the Web features to include, such as text searches, feedback forms to collect information from visitors, and discussion groups for interaction among visitors. Then, put the content aside and concentrate for a while on the design of the web itself.

Set the Web Parameters   Make a list of the web parameters for every value that you are likely to use and reuse, including names, addresses, contact information for your company, company name, and motto. In Chapter 5, you'll learn how to make the list directly in the FrontPage Explorer.

Build the Style Pages   Create the style pages you are going to use for different sections of your web, and store them in the _private folder.

Build the Common Element Pages   Design and create the common page elements as separate pages that you can merge into other pages. Create a set of header and footer pages. Design the navigation bars to the main pages, and include a navigation bar in the header or footer pages.

Create Page Templates   Design and create the page templates with the style pages and common page elements. Use Include bots to merge page elements into other pages or use frames to display page elements in separate frames.

Build the Pages and Links   Use your custom page templates to build the pages with the content you want to publish. Add additional links to expedite travel to different locations in your site.

Testing the Web

Before going public with your Web, test it out. As you are creating your initial prototypes, do lots of off line testing on your own computer. Browsers use different colors and fonts to display the same Web page. A page that looks fine in one browser may be fairly unattractive in another browser. FrontPage makes it easy to preview your pages using different browsers and different resolutions.

When you are ready for the next test, do a trial publishing. Give trusted but critical coworkers, friends, and family the address of your site and ask them to tell you what they think. This is the tough part—after spending time with your creation, you undoubtedly think it is great, but your web isn't for you and it must be able to stand up to the critiques of others. The areas where you need feedback are:

Content design effectiveness   Is your content organized so that it is readable, easy to understand, and interesting? Do your reviewers get answers to their questions? Do they get the information they want? Do they get to interact with your Web the way *they* want?

Navigation effectiveness   Is it easy to travel around in your Web? Do your reviewers ever feel lost? Can they get to where they want to go with just a few clicks? Do your reviewers every feel they are in hyperlink jail with the only escape being to jump out of your Web altogether? Are the image hyperlinks obvious?

Aesthetic effectiveness   Are the colors pleasing? Are the pages visually interesting and appealing? Can your visitors read the text? Is the contrast with the background sufficient? Is the font size large enough? Too large? Is there enough information on a page?

Performance   Does it take too long for any of your pages to download? Solicit opinions on whether you should solve performance problems with smaller images, fewer images, or shorter pages.

When you get the opinions, solve the problems that others have told you about and then...**publish it!**

Chapter

4

Using the FrontPage Wizards and Templates

4

Using the FrontPage Wizards and Templates

In many cases, the fastest way to create a web is to use the templates and wizards that are built into FrontPage. You can use the templates and wizards to create individual web pages and entire webs.

- A *template* is a predesigned web or page that you use as a pattern for a new web or page. A template asks no questions and simply presents the web or web page for you to customize.

- A *wizard* is a tool that asks you questions about the features you want included in a new web or on a new page and then creates the web or page according to your answers. When the wizard is finished, you can customize the web or page.

FrontPage provides wizards and templates for several kinds of webs and a great variety of web pages. When you are contemplating a new web or page, check first to see if a wizard or template can create a web or page that is a reasonable approximation to the web or page you are planning. Use the wizard or template to create a first draft and then use the techniques you'll learn in the rest of the book to customize the result.

This chapter begins with an overview of the built-in wizards and templates. The second part of the chapter is a tutorial on using one of the more complex web wizards, the Corporate Presence Web Wizard. This wizard is a tour de force of many FrontPage features. With this wizard, you can create a sophisticated, professional-quality web for an organization that provides products and services. The web you create includes full text search capability, an interactive feedback form, and an online discussion group, and uses many of the design and style guidelines covered in Chapter 3.

NOTE

You'll learn how to create your own web page templates in Chapter 10: Editor Basic. The FrontPage 97 Software Development Kit (SDK) includes a utility program called Web Template Maker that you can use to create your own web templates (see Appendix D for more information). If you have programming skills, you can also use the SDK to create page and web wizards. The SDK is in the FrontPage 97 SDK folder on the book's CD-ROM.

Understanding FrontPage Web Wizards and Templates

Every new FrontPage web is based on a template or a wizard. The first step in creating a new web is selecting one of five templates or three wizards in the New FrontPage Web dialog:

Web Templates	**Web Wizards**
Empty Web	Import Web Wizard
Normal Web	Discussion Web Wizard
Personal Web	Corporate Presence Wizard
Project Web	Customer Support Web

This section describes each of these Web templates and wizards. (FrontPage also has a web template called Learning FrontPage that is used in the documentation that comes with the product.)

NOTE

Any custom Web templates and wizards you create are added to the list in the New FrontPage Web dialog.

Empty Web

When you choose the Empty Web template, FrontPage creates a new web that is "empty" in the sense that it contains no Web pages, however, the *empty web* isn't really empty. The new folder contains a folder named images that you can use to store image files, a folder named _private that you use to store the private pages and files that you want to hide from a Web visitor, and four subfolders that hold the files required by any FrontPage web (we'll call them the *_vti subfolders*). In all, an "empty" FrontPage web uses 198 KB storage space and has 9 folders containing 12 files! When you create an empty web, the FrontPage Explorer displays only the empty images and _private folders (see Figure 4.1).

PART

I

Overview of
FrontPage

FIGURE 4.1

Use the Empty Web template to create a web with no Web pages and two subfolders to hold images and private files.

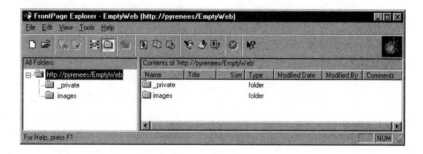

When you point your Web browser to a web folder without specifying a page in the web, the Web server looks for a page with a default name, typically default.htm or index.htm, and sends that page to the Web browser as the web's home page. If the web does not have a page with the default name, the Web server creates an index page for the web and sends it to the browser. The index page for a FrontPage web lists the two subfolders that were created for your content files, any other subfolders you create to organize content, the files and Web pages that are not stored in a subfolder, and the _vti subfolders. Figure 4.2 shows the index page for an empty FrontPage web. If you try to display the contents of one of the _vti subfolders in the browser, you won't have any success—the browser displays the message that access to the subfolder is forbidden!

The FrontPage _vti Subfolders

You don't really have to know very much about the _vti subfolders. You don't see these subfolders when you use the FrontPage Explorer to create and manage the web. However, you do see them whenever you view the contents of the web folder in the Windows Explorer, so we'll take a moment to describe the role of each _vti subfolder.

FIGURE 4.2

*The Index page
for an empty
Frontpage Web*

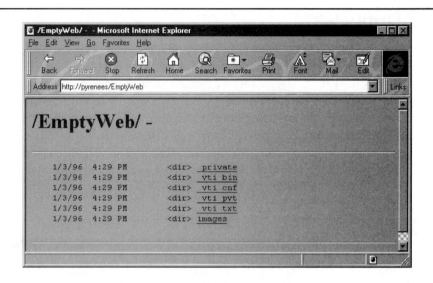

_vti subfolder	Purpose
_vti_cnf	Keeps track of the files you add to the web. For each file that you add to the web, this folder has a corresponding file with the same name, which includes information such as when the file was created and modified, and by whom, and the names of images that may be inserted.
_vti_txt	Keeps track of the text index files. There is a text index to every word you type in a public web page. If the web contains a discussion group, there is a separate text index to every word in the article and reply files that web visitors create.
_vti_pvt	Holds the lists of unfinished and completed tasks created by the FrontPage To Do List program.
_vti_bin	Holds the web's copy of FrontPage Server Extensions, including programs that handle the administrative tasks involved with controlling access to the web (admin.dll), authoring tasks such as retrieving files from the server and updating the To Do List (author.dll), and running the programs for the interactive features you include in your Web, such as searches, discussion groups, and data entry forms (shtml.dll).

Normal Web

When you choose the Normal Web template, FrontPage starts with the empty web described in the last section and adds a single blank page as the default home page for the new web. The name of the default home page depends on the Web server you are using: the Microsoft Personal Web Server names the page default.htm and the FrontPage Personal Web Server names it index.htm. You can change the default name that the Web Server assigns (see Appendix A and C for more information). When you point a Web browser to the web without specifying the name of a file, the Web server sends the default home page to the browser.

The Web you create with the Normal Web template is analogous to the blank page that a word processing program or the blank spreadsheet that a spreadsheet program displays when you create a new file in one of those programs.

Personal Web

When you choose the Personal Web template, FrontPage starts with the empty web and adds a single default home page. The home page is a template that organizes personal information into sections. You enter personal information in the designated areas of the page. The template is designed for an employment-related personal web, but you can modify the page by replacing the employment-related categories with your choice of leisure-time or other categories.

Using a Table of Contents for Page Navigation

The home page uses a simple navigation scheme that you'll see often and should plan to include in pages with several topics. The home page is divided into sections, beginning with a Contents section that lists headings for the other seven topic sections. Each item in the Contents list is a text hyperlink whose target is the heading that begins the topic; clicking a heading takes you to the topic. Each topic section contains a hyperlink back to the Contents section. These pairs of links create simple navigation paths between the Contents section and the topic sections of the page (see Figure 4.3).

The first six sections of the home page provide spaces for you to type the information you want to display and the last section contains a data entry form for collecting information from your Web visitors. The sections are as follows:

Employee Information   for information about your job and responsibilities and for linking to your department, manager, and employees who report to you.

Current Projects   for information about the projects you are currently working on.

FIGURE 4.3

The Personal Web home page uses a standard page navigation scheme: a table of page contents at the top of the page has hyperlinks to bookmarked section headings and the bottom of each section has a hyperlink back to the table of contents.

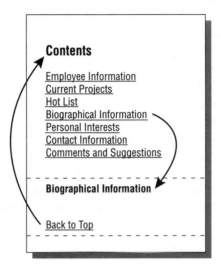

Hot List   for links to other WWW or company intranet sites to which you want to provide direct links.

Biographical Information   for listing your previous experience and personal achievements.

Personal Interests   for describing your personal interests.

Contact Information   includes a link to the browsers e-mail application so that visitors can send you e-mail directly from the browser and a link to the company's Web site.

Comments and Suggestions   for providing an opportunity for the user to give you feedback about your web page. The visitor enters comments in a fill-in form and clicks a Submit button to send comments to your Web server. The server stores the comments in a text file.

Figure 4.4 shows the Biographical Information section indicating the template text that you'll replace, the Back to Top hyperlink (blue underlined font) that takes the visitor back to the Contents section, and the bookmarked heading (blue dotted underline).

Project Web

The Project Web template is intended for creating a company intranet web that tracks a project and provides resource information about the project to others in the company. The template creates a web with standard project management features and requires only that you enter the information for the specific project. You can use the Project Web template to create a web that can be used with little modification for most projects.

FIGURE 4.4

*The Biographical
Information section
heading is marked
as a bookmark
(blue dotted under-
line) and the Back
to Top hyperlink
(blue underlined
font) takes you back
to the page's table
of contents.*

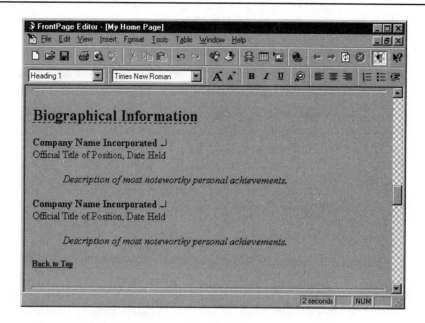

The Project Web template creates a complex web with seven main sections. Unlike the Personal Web template in which the sections are all part of a single page, the sections of the Project Web are separate pages. The main pages are as follows:

Home provides orientation to the project and lists the changes and new developments in the project.

Members contains contact information for everyone working on the project. The page begins with an alphabetical listing of the project members. Each name in the list is a text link where the target of the link is the bookmarked name at the beginning of the member's section. Each member's section has links to the browser's e-mail application and the member's URL. Each member's section also has a text hyperlink back to the bookmarked heading of the alphabetical listing.

Schedule contains a list of plans for the current and future weeks, schedule of events for the current and future weeks, and a schedule of the project's milestones and deadlines. Navigation paths between the beginning of the page and the sections are provided by text links with bookmark targets.

Status contains links to the project's status reports arranged by month or quarter, current year, and previous year. The status reports could be web pages stored in the same web or another company web, or word processing documents that are viewed in a document viewer such as Adobe Acrobat or Microsoft Word Viewer. Because of the relationship between status reports and scheduling, the Status page has a text link to the Schedule page.

Archive provides access to the project's supporting background information and archive documents. The beginning of the page contains text links to the page's several bookmarked sections. There are sections to describe the categories of people who can use the archive materials; sections with definitions of document formats; and sections with links to documents, software, and other project tools.

Discussions provides links to the two online discussion groups for the project, including a project requirements discussion and a knowledge base. In an online discussion group, a participant can propose a new topic or reply to an existing topic. Each discussion group has a set of pages as follows:

- A table of contents for the topics and replies
- A page to submit a topic or reply to an existing topic
- A page to confirm the submission
- A page to do a text search of the topics in the discussion

Each discussion group also has a folder for storing the articles and replies. The pages of a discussion group have a common header and common footer which can give the discussion group a separate identity. The header has a navigation bar with links to the discussion group's table of contents, an article submission page, a search page, and a link back to the web's main Discussions page. (See Chapter 19 for more information on dicsussion groups.)

Search provides the visitor with the ability to do a text search of the public pages in the web (including all the web's public pages except the article pages in the discussion groups). The page describes the kinds of text searches that the visitor can run.

The Project Web template uses several of the design guidelines described in Chapter 3. The main pages have a common header and a common footer. The header has a navigation bar with links to the seven pages so you can jump from any main page to any other main page. The common footer has a link to the e-mail program.

Customer Support Web

The Customer Support template creates a web that you can use for providing support services to customers. The terminology used in this web makes it particularly suitable for a software company. For example, there is a bug report page, and some of the pages refer directly to software, operating systems, patches, and work-arounds. Nevertheless, the web's design is general and you can easily adapt the web to another type of company.

The Customer Support template creates a complex web with eight main sections, each a separate page, as follows:

Welcome   gives an introduction to the support services provided.

What's New   gives a current listing of changes, including product updates, schedules for new products, and problems and solutions that may affect other customers.

Frequently Asked Questions (FAQ)   includes common questions and answers that affect all customers. Some of the answers contain tips and tricks for getting the most out of the product.

Bugs   provides a fill-in form for bug reports, and information about known problems. The beginning of this page contains text links to the page's two sections. The first section is a bug report form providing the opportunity to describe and report a bug or problem. The visitor enters the bug report and clicks a submit button to send the report to your Web server. The second is for displaying information regarding known problems with products.

Suggestions   invites customers to submit suggestions in any of several categories, including the web site, product features, customer support, the company, and marketing. This page is intended for suggestions rather than reporting problems, so the page has a text link back to the Bugs page for reporting problems.

Download   contains links to files that are available for FTP or HTTP download. The beginning of the page also contains a text link with a bookmark target to a section of the page that describes the file formats of the files you can download. The format definition section contains a text link back to the bookmark at the beginning of the page.

Discussion   includes a text link to an online customer discussion group. Customers can submit articles about problems or tips or tricks they have discovered in working with the product. Customers can also submit replies and comments to existing articles. The discussion group has a subfolder for storing the articles and replies, and has a set of web pages, as follows:

- A table of contents for the articles and replies
- A page to submit an article or reply to an existing article
- A page to confirm the submission
- A page to do a text search of the articles in the discussion

For the features of a discussion group, see the "Project Web" section in this chapter.

Search   provides the user with the ability to do a text search of the public pages in the web (but not the article pages in the discussion group). The page describes the kinds of text searches that the visitor can run.

The eight main pages of the web have a common header and common footer. The header has a navigation bar with links to the eight pages, so you can jump from any main page to any other main page. The common footer has a link to the e-mail program.

NOTE

The Customer Support template uses company information items on several pages of the web, including the CompanyName, CompanyPhone, and CompanyEmail. Since these items may change in the future, you can modify a new web based on the Customer Support Web template by defining these items as web parameters and by using Substitution bots to update the pages automatically when the values change. See Chapter 5: Explorer Basics for information on web parameters and Chapter 16: Using WebBots in Page Design for automatic updating using the Substitution bot.

Discussion Web Wizard

The Discussion Web Wizard is used to create an online discussion group as a separate web or as a component of another web. Visitors to the web can submit articles for discussion and reply to existing articles. The wizard creates the pages for the discussion web, including:

- A page for submitting articles and replies
- A page for confirming a submission
- A page for doing a text search of the articles in the discussion web
- A table of contents page for the discussion web

You can create a simple discussion group web in which each article is an independent submission or discussion group that allows replies. When you allow replies, users may reply to an existing article and subsequent users may reply to the replies, and so on. FrontPage keeps track of each of the relationships between a submission and a reply to a submission. An article together with replies to the article (the first-level replies), replies to the replies (the second-level replies), and so on, is called a *thread*. A discussion group that allows replies is called a *threaded replies discussion group*.

There are two ways you can use the wizard. In the first way, the wizard adds the discussion group pages and articles folder to another web. For example, the Customer Support Web and the Project Web templates include discussion groups as part of the webs they create. In the second way, the wizard creates a separate web. After creating a separate discussion group web, you can create links to it from your main web. Advantages of the separate web approach are that you can use separate webs to organize your files and you can easily place different restrictions on who has access to each web. In some situations, you may want to make the main web available to the public (unprotected) or a particular group of users, and restrict the discussion group to a smaller group. See Chapter 19: Understanding Discussion Group Webs for more information on using the Discussion Group Web Wizard.

Import Web Wizard

The Import Web Wizard is used to import an existing web. What you actually import is a set of files stored in any folder in your computer's file system. The folder can be a FrontPage web or a legacy web (a legacy web is a web created without using Front-Page). The folder can also be just a set of files that you want to include in a new FrontPage web. The Import Web Wizard creates a new FrontPage Web starting with the subfolders and files of an empty web, and imports copies of all the subfolders and files in the import folder. See the "Importing a Web" section in Chapter 5 for information on using the Import Web Wizard.

Corporate Presence Wizard

The Corporate Presence Wizard is used to create a web that introduces a company to visitors. The wizard displays a series of screens that let you design the features that a typical company web may have. The wizard can create a web with many of the same features that the Project Web and the Customer Support Web templates provide. The difference between this Wizard and the web templates is that you get to decide which features to include, and you get to make choices about the look and feel of the web's pages. In addition to the home page, you can choose to include any or all of five main pages. You can include the following pages:

Home Page   may have any of four page sections, including an introduction, mission statement, company profile, and contact information. There are no text links from the beginning of the page to the page sections, but you can modify the web later by creating bookmarks and hyperlinks (see Chapter 12: Understanding Text Hyperlinks).

What's New   may include any of three page sections for web changes, press releases, and articles and reviews.

Products/Services   is a summary page with text links to pages for each product and service that the company provides. You can choose to include up to five products and five services. You can make decisions about the kind of information to include for the product pages, such as product image and pricing information, and information for the services pages, such as capabilities and reference accounts. You can also choose to include an information request form for both the products and the services pages. The user requests information for a product or a service by filling out a request form and clicking a submit button.

Feedback Form   provides the opportunity for the user to submit comments. You can design the types of information you want the user to include, along with comments.

Search Form   allows the user to do a text search of the web pages. There are no design options you can choose. The wizard includes the same search form as included in the Customer Support and Project templates.

Table of Contents   provides an outline view of your web when you view the page in a Web browser. The Table of Contents page is not WYSIWYG in the Editor. The Table of Contents bot that generates the table runs when you create the page, but you can view the results only in a Web browser. Each item in the outline is a text link pointing to a page and using the page's name as the link text. (see Chapter 16: Using WebBots in Page Design for information on the features of the Table of Contents bot).

After you decide which main pages to include, and make decisions about each page, you have the opportunity to design the common headers and footers that will be part of every page in the web. In addition to a company logo and other information, you can specify whether to include a navigation bar in either the header and footer or in both. The navigation bar includes links to the main pages and provides a two-way navigation path from any main page to any other main page. Another design decision is the choice to use any of four predefined styles of page backgrounds and text colors.

The wizard requests company information including company name, address, and contact information, stores these items as web parameters, and uses Substitution bots to display these items.

We'll explore the details of creating a new Web using the Corporate Presence Wizard in the tutorial at the end of the chapter.

Understanding the FrontPage Page Wizards and Templates

FrontPage also provides a set of page templates and wizards that you can use to create the first draft of a single page. Each template creates a page with a set of instructions at the top of the page; some pages have additional instructions interspersed in the sections where you'll enter text. FrontPage uses the Comments bot to display the instructions in the Editor and then hide the instructions (and eliminate the space they occupy) when you view the page in a Web browser.

There are basically three categories of page wizards and templates: presenting information, gathering information, and general purpose. We'll start with the general purpose templates and wizards because these are the ones you'll use most often.

General Purpose

FrontPage also provides a set of templates and wizards that you use to include many of the more advanced FrontPage features.

Normal Page

You use the Normal Page template to create a new blank page.

Table of Contents

The Table of Contents template is used to create a listing of text links to pages in a web. The template uses a Table of Contents bot to create a hierarchical listing of the pages that you can reach by following links from the web's home page. The Editor displays a generic representation of the table of contents (see Figure 4.5). You must view the page in a Web browser in order to view the actual page listing. Figure 4.6 shows the Table of Contents page for the PCTC web you created in Chapter 1. See Chapter 16: Using WebBots in Page Design, for information on the Table of Contents bot.

FIGURE 4.5

The FrontPage Editor displays a generic listing for the Table of Contents bot instead of listing the actual pages.

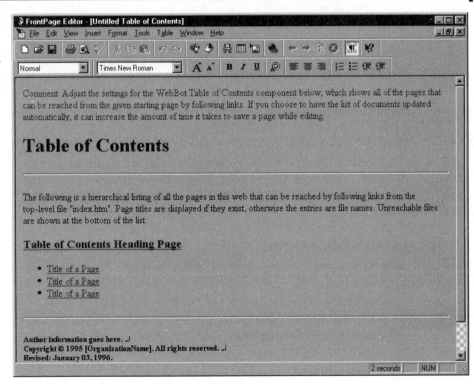

The Web browser displays the actual table of contents generated by the Table of Contents bot.

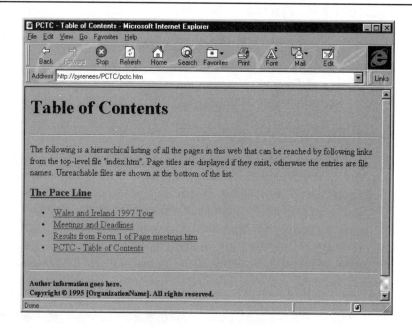

Search Page

You use the Search Page template to create a text search of the words in a Web's public pages. The pages stored in the _private folder and articles stored in the articles folder of a discussion group are not searched, although you can create a separate search of a discussion's articles. The template creates a page with two sections. The first section lets you search for a word, part of a word, or a combination of words, and the second section describes the kinds of searches you can do (see Figure 4.7). A text link at the bottom of the page points back to a bookmark at the top of the page. The template uses the Search bot to perform the search. Chapter 18: Understanding Searches and Visitor Registration describes the Search bot.

User Registration

You can use the User Registration template to create a page that lets visitors register themselves as users in a password-protected web. After the visitor registers, the server can automatically enter the visitor's name in forms. The template relies on the Registration bot to enter the information into a registration database for the web. Chapter 9: Administering a Web covers registering users and restricting access to a web, and Chapter 18: Understanding Searches and Visitor Registration describes the Registration bot.

FIGURE 4.7

The visitor specifies the search criteria in the first section of the Search Page (a). The second section describes the query language that FrontPage uses (b).

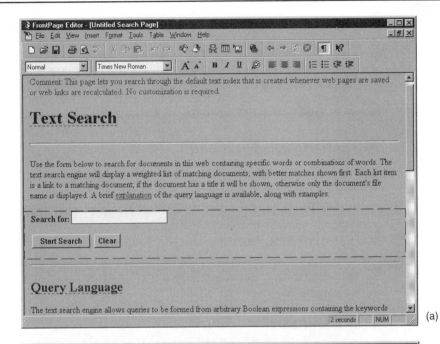

(a)

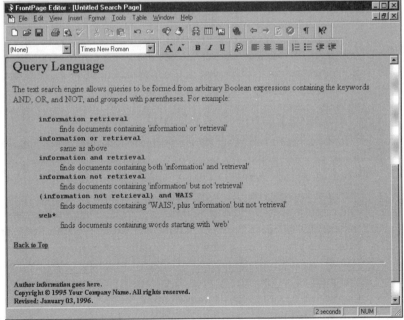

(b)

The User Registration template works only when you are using a Web server that supports security features that the Registration bot requires, such as the FrontPage Personal Web Server. The Microsoft Personal Web Server provides a different way to control access to a web and does not support the Registration bot.

Form Page Wizard

Several of the page templates include predefined fill-in forms for collecting data and submitting the input to your Web server. While you can customize the data entry form after using one of the templates, there are times when it is easier to create a new form from scratch. You can use the Form Page Wizard to create a new page that has a fill-in form. The wizard guides you through the design of the form, including entering requests for categories of information and the types of data entry controls for collecting the information. Chapter 17: Collecting Data Input explains how to use the Form Page Wizard.

Frames Wizard

Most browsers are able to display two or more web pages in the same browser window. Each page is displayed in a separate subwindow called a *frame*. A special web page called a frameset holds the frames. In FrontPage, you use the Frames Wizard to construct the frameset and create the links between the frames that allow the browser to change the pages displayed in the frames. Chapter 15: Understanding Frames covers the Frames Wizard.

Database Connector Wizard

A new feature of FrontPage 97 is the ability to connect to a database and retrieve information stored in the tables of the database. The connection to a database is made using the Internet Database Connector program that is part of the Microsoft Personal Web Server. You use the Database Connector Wizard to specify the database and create a query for database information. This wizard does not create a Web page, instead the Database Connector Wizard creates a file with the form as required by the Internet Database Connector. Conceptually, when the visitor submits the query, the Web server sends the query to the Internet Database Connector, which in turn uses the query to retrieve the requested information from the database. The Database Connector Wizard helps little in creating the file. You have to write the query yourself. See Chapter 21: Creating Dynamic Database Pages with Microsoft Access for more information on the Internet Database Connector.

Database Results

The retrieved data is returned to the Web server. You use the Database Results template to create a page in the HTX format that the Web server can use as a formatting template to lay out and generate a new page with the retrieved data. The generated page with the formatted data is returned to the browser. The Database Results template is a blank page in the HTX format. You have to write the formatting instructions yourself. Chapter 21 shows you how to write these instructions.

NOTE

The Internet Database Connector is a server extension included with the Microsoft Personal Web Server (Windows 95), the Microsoft Peer Web Server (Windows NT Workstation), and the Microsoft Internet Information Server (Windows NT Server). The FrontPage Personal Web Server does not include the Internet Database Connector.

Presenting Information

You use a template or wizard in this category to create a page with a layout that is appropriate for the kind of information you want to display.

Bibliography

The Bibliography template creates a page with the layout shown in Figure 4.8. You must arrange the references in alphabetical order yourself, enter the information for each reference, and create a bookmark to the information item that other pages refer to. This is normally the author's last name, but it could also be the title of a book, article, or web. If another page in the Web refers to an item on the list, you can create a hyperlink from that page to a bookmark on the bibliography page.

Directory of Press Releases and Press Release

You can use the Directory of Press Releases template to organize press releases by date. If there are many press releases, you can use the template's sections to group the releases. For each section, the list at the top of the page has a text link with a target that is bookmark for the section's heading (see Figure 4.9a). Each section ends with a text link whose target is the bookmark back to the top of the page.

If you want to publish individual press releases, you can use the Press Release template to create a page for each press release (see Figure 4.9b). After creating the pages, you can create a two-way navigation path by creating a link from a title in the Directory of Press Releases page to its corresponding Press Release page, and a link from the Press Release page back to the Directory page.

FIGURE 4.8

The Bibliography
page template

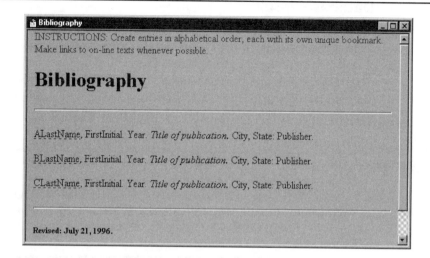

FIGURE 4.9

Use the Directory of
Press Releases tem-
plate to organize
press releases (a)
and the Press
Release template to
create a page
for each press
release (b).

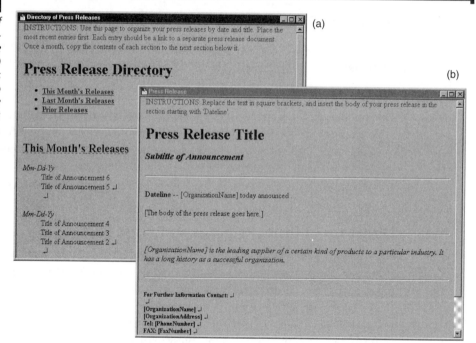

Employee Directory

Use the Employee Directory template to display a list of company employees and contact information. The page begins with an alphabetical listing of employees, which is

followed by a section for each employee (see Figure 4.10). Each employee section includes contact information, with links to the browser's e-mail program and to the employee's URL. Each section also includes a text link back to the bookmarked heading for the list. You must create the list yourself and then for each employee name, create a text link that points to the bookmark in the heading of the employee's section.

FIGURE 4.10

The Employee Directory template

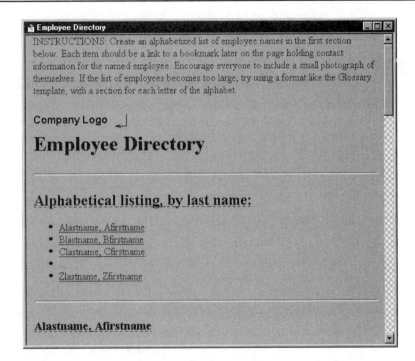

Employment Opportunities

Use the Employment Opportunities template to create a page that displays the job description, requirements, and contact information for available jobs in your company. The page uses the familiar structure of a list at the beginning of the page with text links to other page sections. Each text link points to a bookmarked section heading and the bottom of the section has a text link pointing back to the bookmarked list heading. The page also has a section for general employment inquiries.

In addition to presenting information, the Employment Opportunities page has a data entry form that a visitor can use to create and submit a personnel file. The template also creates a web page named persfile.htm for storing the submissions.

Frequently Asked Questions

A standard page in many webs is the Frequently Asked Questions, or FAQ, page. The Frequently Asked Questions template helps to organize this page with a table of contents section at the beginning and sections for each question and answer. A two-way navigation path between each question in the list and the corresponding question and answer section is provided by text links from a question in the list to a bookmarked heading of the corresponding answer section and a text link at the bottom of the section that points back to the bookmarked heading of the question list (see Figure 4.11).

FIGURE 4.11

The ubiquitous FAQ page template

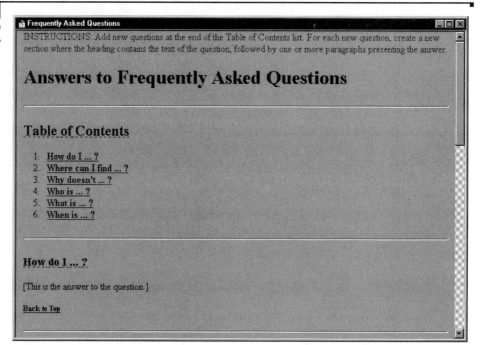

Glossary of Terms

A page that should be standard in more webs is the Glossary of Terms page. A glossary page provides definitions for all of the new or technical words used in the web. Web authors often assume that the definitions of technical terms are commonly known, but users often do not have the assumed knowledge. The Glossary of Terms template provides the structure for the page. The page begins with an index using the alphabet and a symbol such as the number sign (#) for terms that start with a digit or a symbol. Text links for each index letter or # point to the corresponding bookmarked section. Each section contains the glossary entries that begin with the section's letter; each section ends with a text link back to the alphabetical index (see Figure 4.12). You should mark each glossary term with a bookmark so that the term can be the target of links from other pages that use the term.

FIGURE 4.12

Use the Glossary template to create a glossary for your Web.

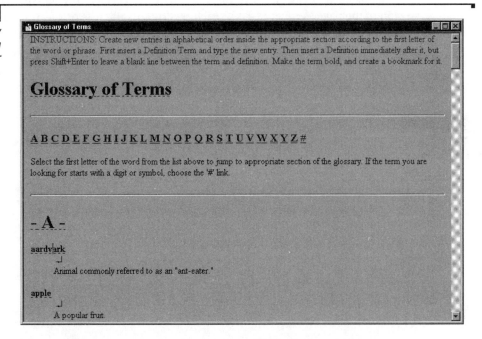

Office Directory

You can use the Office Directory template to organize the locations where your company has offices. The page begins with a list of the major geographical areas where your company has offices. Each item is a text link that points to a bookmarked section for the geographical area. Each section contains the states or regions where the company has an office with a link to a subsection that describes the office. This series of links lets the user drill down from the general categories to specific information, starting with a major geographical area, linking to a state or region, and then linking to a specific office.

Seminar Schedule, Lecture Abstract, and Meeting Agenda

Use the Seminar Schedule template to publish a conference schedule or schedule of meetings. The template creates a page that begins with a list of sessions, tracks, or meeting categories and has separate sections for each session, track or meeting category. Two-way navigation paths between each entry in the list and the corresponding section are provided by a text link from the item in the list to the bookmarked section heading and a link from the bottom of the section back to the bookmarked list at the top of the page (see Figure 4.13). Each section lists the title of a lecture or name of a meeting. You can create links from each lecture title or meeting name to separate pages describing the lecture or the meeting agenda. You can use the Lecture Abstract template (see Figure 4.14a) and the Meeting Agenda template (4.14b) to create the separate pages.

FIGURE 4.13

The Seminar Schedule template

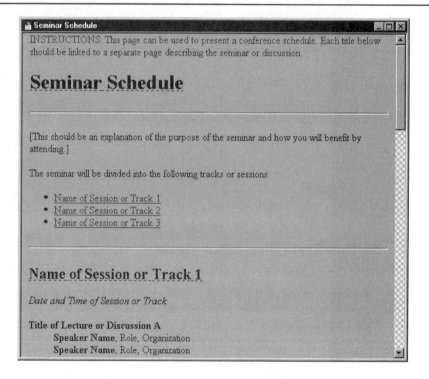

FIGURE 4.14

The Lecture Abstract (a) and Meeting Agenda (b) page templates

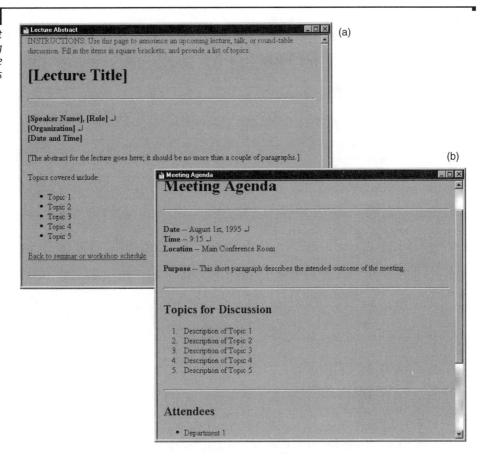

Product Description and Software Data Sheet

You can use the Product Description template to create a page for each product. The template creates a page with a list of contents at the top, and sections corresponding to each list item. The template creates the familiar two-way navigation paths from the list to individual sections for each item. Figure 4.15 shows part of the Product Description page in the Editor.

The Software Data Sheet template is a similar template specialized for the description of software products. The template creates a page with sections for an image, key benefits, key features, system requirements, and pricing and availability. The page does not include an index list to the sections with two-way navigation paths between the list and the sections, but you can create the list and the paths yourself.

FIGURE 4.15

*The Product
Description page
template*

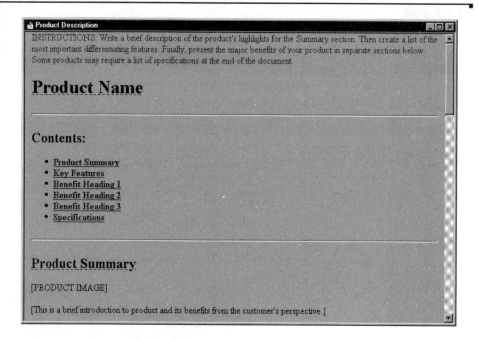

What's New

You can use the What's New template to publish the changes to your web. You enter information about the change and create a link to the page with the changed or new information (see Figure 4.16) Although the template doesn't do this, you can date stamp the page with the data of the last revision to the page using the TimeStamp bot (see Chapter 16: Using Web Bots in Page Design).

HyperDocument Page

The HyperDocument Page template helps you to organize a large manual or report. If the manual or report has several main sections, you can create a web with a home page and a table of contents for the main sections. You use the template to create a page for each main section. The top of the page has links back to the home page and the table of contents for the web.

Hot List

You use the Hot List template to organize links to other Web sites. The template creates a page that begins with a table of contents of links for each of your categories. Each link points to a bookmark in the heading of the corresponding page section. The section describes the category and lists links to teh Web sites (see Figure 4.17). The bottom of each section has a text link back to the table of contents.

FIGURE 4.16

The What's New
page template

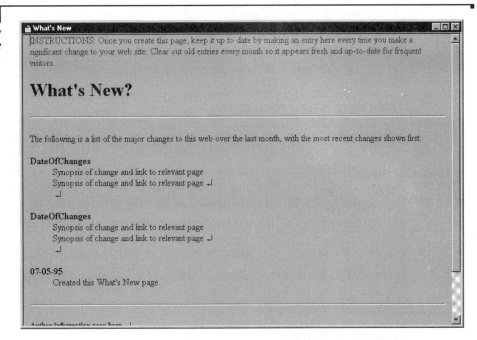

FIGURE 4.17

The Hot List page
template

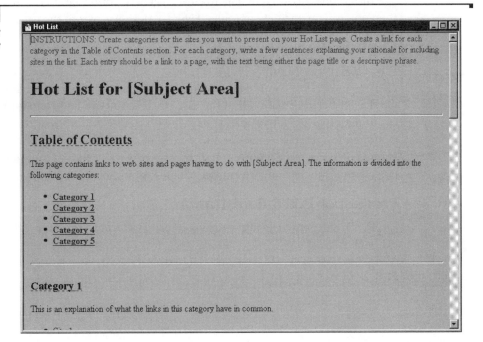

Personal Home Page Wizard

While the Personal Web template discussed in the last section creates a complete home page, the Personal Home Page Wizard lets you select the sections you want to include in your personal home page.

Gathering Information

Most of the templates in the previous section help you create pages for one-way communication: your page displays information for the user to read. FrontPage also provides ways to let visitors communicate with you. This section describes the page templates that let you collect information from a visitor. These pages contain data entry forms with text boxes for entering text information and check boxes, combo boxes and option buttons for making choices. The forms also contain submit buttons to submit the information to your Web server, and clear buttons to clear the data entry controls. When the visitor clicks the submit button, the Web server executes a program called a *form handler* that stores the information to a file or web page. The program may carry out other instructions as well. You'll learn more about forms and form handlers in Chapter 17: Collecting Input Data.

Feedback Form

Use the Feedback Form template to create a generic form that users can use to tell you their opinion for a variety of topics. Figure 4.18 shows part of the page.

Confirmation

When the visitor submits a FrontPage form, the Web server automatically creates and displays a page that confirms the submission. By default, the confirmation page displays all of the information that the user entered. You can't customize the default confirmation page, but you can replace it with a custom confirmation page. The Confirmation template provides an example of a custom confirmation page (see Figure 4.19). You use Confirmation bots to display the information submitted in specific parts of the data entry form (see Chapter 17 for more information).

Product or Event Registration

Use the Product or Event Registration template to create a form for registering a product or an event.

FIGURE 4.18

*Use a Feedback
Form page template
to create a
simple form.*

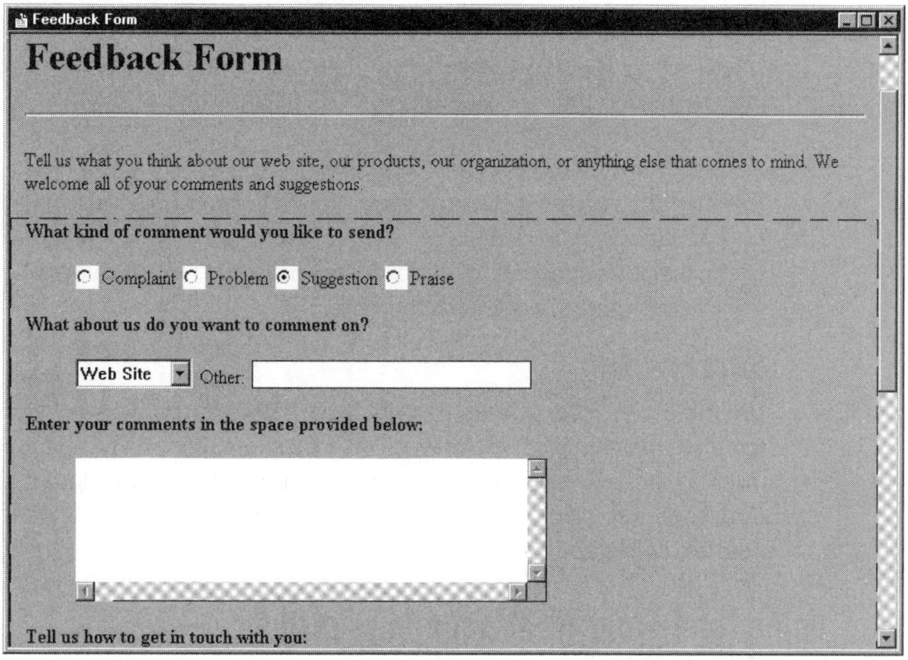

FIGURE 4.19

*The Confirmation
page template uses
Confirmation bots.*

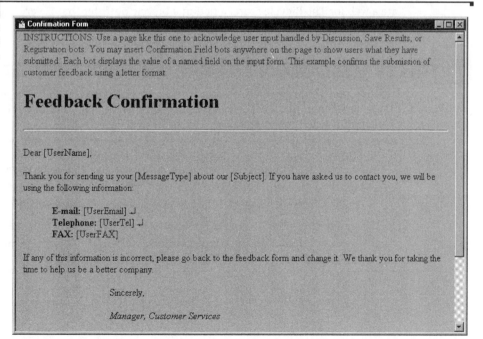

Guest Book

You can use the Guest Book template to publish the reactions of users. The template creates a page that has a form for anonymous comments and also displays the web page that stores the existing comments. The template uses the Include bot to merge the comments page into the guest book page (see Chapter 16: Using Web Bots in Page Design for information on the Include bot).

When the visitor submits the form, the Web server runs a form handler that adds the comments to the web page that stores guest comments. The visitor can view the comments just submitted by choosing the browser's refresh or reload command to retrieve the updated page from the server.

Survey Form

Use the Survey Form template as a model for designing an information survey. The template creates a page with several data entry sections and a submission section. An index at the beginning of the survey contains text links to bookmarks at the beginning of each section. Each section also has a text link that points back to the bookmark at the beginning of the list.

Using the Corporate Presence Wizard

In this section, we'll step through the screens of the Corporate Presence Wizard to create a web for The Bicycle Store, a fictional bicycle outfitter that is very popular with the members of the Pacifica Cycle Touring Club.

NOTE

If you prefer, you can create a web for your own company instead. The web you create here is not used explicitly in the rest of the book, but you can use it as an additional practice web for the book's exercises.

1. Click the Start button on the Windows task bar and choose Programs ➤ Microsoft FrontPage ➤ FrontPage Explorer. In the Getting Started dialog, click the option to create a new FrontPage Web from a Wizard or Template and click OK.

2. Double-click the Corporate Presence Wizard in the New FrontPage Web dialog (see Figure 4.20a). In the Corporate Presence Wizard dialog, type BicycleOutfitter as the name of the new web and click OK (see Figure 4.20b).

FIGURE 4.20

*Choose the
Corporate Presence
Wizard (a). Type
the name of the
new web (b).*

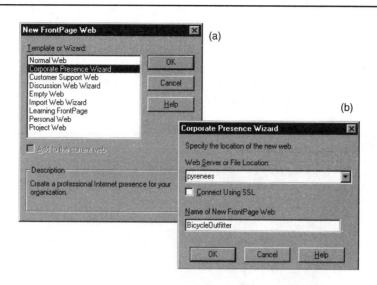

3. The first screen introduces the Wizard (see Figure 4.21a). This screen, and every screen of this wizard, has a Help button in the lower-left corner. You can obtain detailed step-by-step instructions. Click Next. Use the next screen to specify the features you want to include (see Figure 4.21b). The "Corporate Wizard Web" section earlier in the chapter describes the features.

FIGURE 4.21

*Introducing the
Corporate Presence
Web Wizard (a).
Choose the main
features (b).*

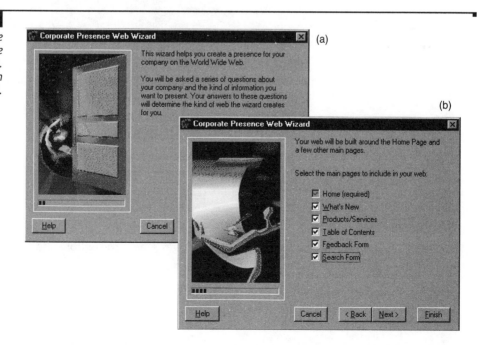

4. Check all the options and click Next. Use the next dialog to specify topics for the home page (see Figure 4.22a). Check to include an introduction and contact information and uncheck to exclude a mission statement and a company profile. Click Next.

5. Use this dialog to specify topics for your Whats New page (see Figure 4.22b). Click Next to accept the default.

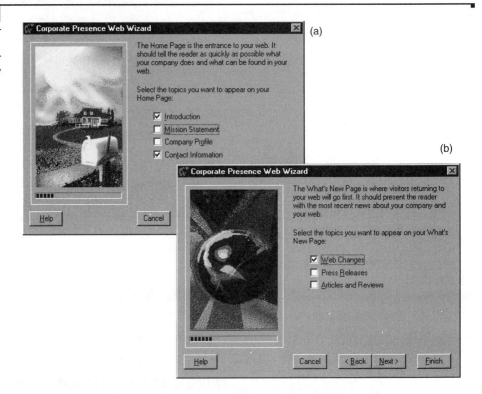

6. Use this dialog to specify the number of product and services pages you want to create (see Figure 4.23a). You can select a number between 0 and 5 for each type of page. Type **5** as the number of Product pages and **3** as the number of Services page, and click Next.

7. Use this dialog to add features to the default features described at the top of the dialog for the products and services pages. Check the options shown in Figure 4.23b and click Next.

FIGURE 4.23

Choose the numbers of product and services pages (a). Select the features of the products and services pages (b).

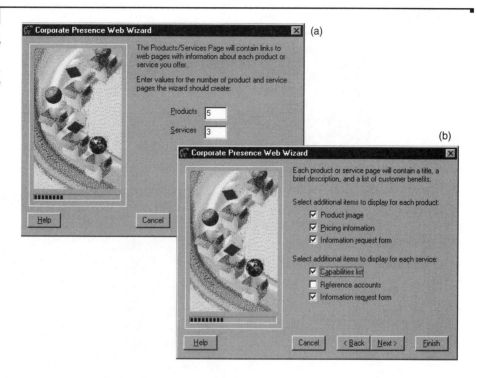

8. Use this dialog to design the Feedback form. Click the options shown in Figure 4.24a and click Next. Use this dialog to specify how you want the Web server to store the collected feedback (see Figure 4.24b). Click Next to accept the default of storing the file in a format that is compatible with database and spreadsheet programs.

9. Use this dialog to specify how you want to handle the Table of Contents page (see Figure 4.25a). Click Next to accept the default of showing only pages linked to the home page, using bullets for top-level pages, and eliminating the automatic updating option. (Although the last option sounds like a good idea, automatic updating is time-consuming. Chapter 16 describes updating alternatives.)

10. Use this dialog to specify the information in the header and footer sections (see Figure 4.25b). The important choices here are the options to include links to the main pages in the web. You'll choose to have the Wizard create the navigation links for you. Check the options shown and click Next.

FIGURE 4.24

Choose the information to collect on the Feedback Form (a) and how you want the data stored (b).

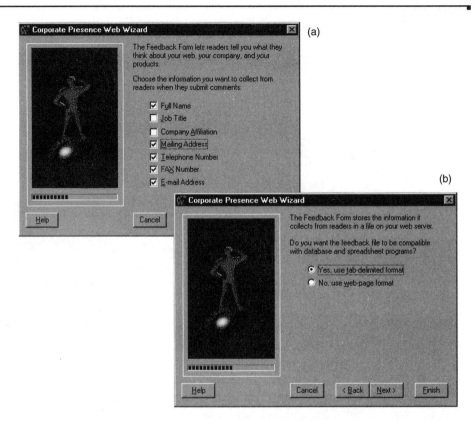

11. Use this dialog to choose one of four basic styles (see Figure 4.26a). Although the Conservative, Flashy, and Cool styles look great, we are going to choose Plain for the following reason. The Plain style uses text hyperlinks for the navigation links while the other styles use images for the hyperlinks. You can easily modify the text of a text hyperlink, but you have to create a new graphic if you want to change the "text" displayed by an image hyperlink. Click Plain and then click Next.

12. Use this dialog to choose the background pattern or color and the text and hyperlink colors (see Figure 4.26b). The choices you make here are used to create a styles page for all the pages in the web. You can modify the styles page later and the changes will be automatically reflected by the pages. You can click a color square to the right of a text category in the Text section to display the available colors and create a custom color for the text category. The graphic in the left of the screen reflects the choices you make. Choose a background pattern and click Next.

FIGURE 4.25

*Design the Table of
Contents page (a).
Design the main
page elements (b).*

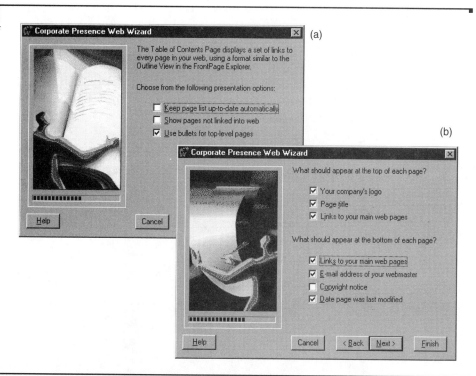

FIGURE 4.26

*Choose a graphic
page style (a) and
background pattern
and text colors (b).*

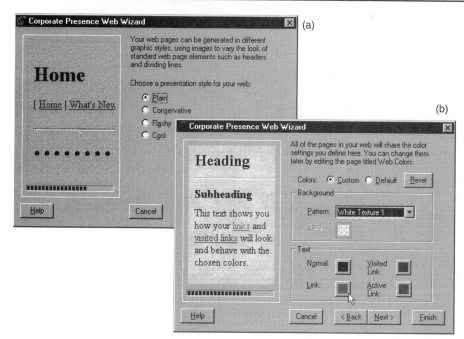

13. Use this dialog to specify whether you want to display the Under Construction image for unfinished pages (see Figure 4.27a). Click No because it is preferable to hide unfinished pages instead, and click Next.

14. Use this dialog to enter the name, short name, and address for the company (see Figure 4.27b). The Wizard creates a web parameter for each of the entries and uses Substitution bots to display the values on Web pages. Type the information shown in the figure and click Next.

FIGURE 4.27

Decide whether to mark unfinished pages (a) and start collecting web parameters (b).

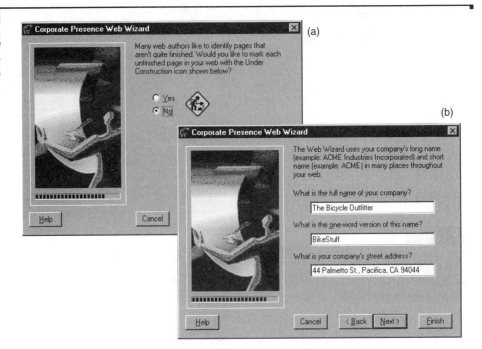

15. Use this dialog to enter additional web parameters (see Figure 4.28a). Type the information shown in the figure and click Next.

16. Use this dialog to specify whether you want the Wizard to create a To Do List (see Figure 4.28b). Because the wizard uses templates to create pages, most of the pages are in a very rough state when the Wizard creates the new web. Click Finish to have the Wizard add tasks to the To Do List.

The Wizard creates the new web according to your choices and displays the To Do List shown in Figure 4.29. You'll learn how to use the To Do List in Chapter 8. For now, just notice that the list includes the task of customizing the pages and click the Close button.

FIGURE 4.28

*Collect more web
parameters (a) and
decide whether
to start a
To Do List (b).*

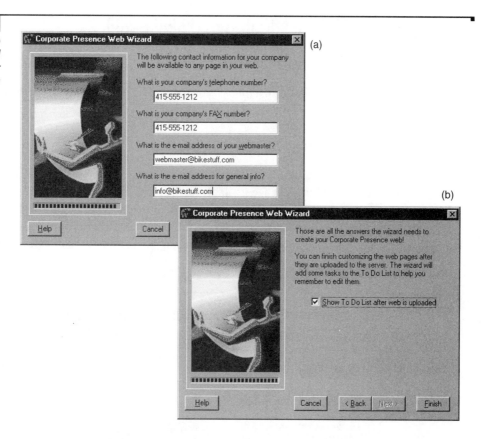

FIGURE 4.29

*The To Do List that
the Wizard creates*

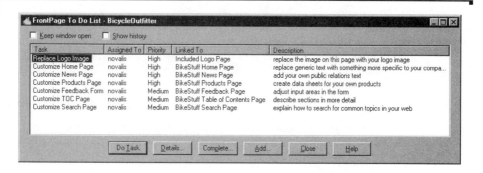

Understanding the Corporate Presence Web

In this section, we'll spend some time trying to understand the web the wizard has created. Your real purpose is discovering how the wizard implements the web design guidelines discussed in Chapter 3, so that you'll be able to use the same techniques when you build your own webs from scratch.

The Parts of the Home Page

Double-click the BikeStuff Home Page icon in the center of the pane on the left in the FrontPage Explorer (see Figure 4.30) to display the page in the FrontPage Editor. Move the pointer around the page to observe the use of bots (see Figure 4.31). In fact, it's difficult to find many regions in which the pointer icon is not the WebBot icon. You'll be learning how to create pages using bots and how to design the bots themselves in Chapter 16.

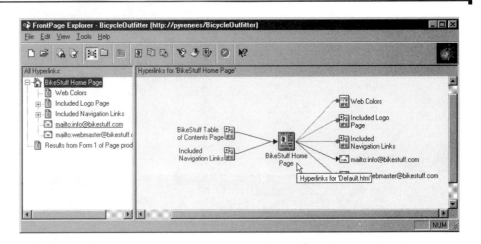

Starting from the top of the page, here is how FrontPage bots are used in this page:

Company logo   The wizard has created a separate page (logo.htm) whose only purpose is to display the company's logo. The wizard displays the logo on another page by using an Include bot to merge the logo.htm page into any other page.

FIGURE 4.31

*The Home Page in
the FrontPage Editor*

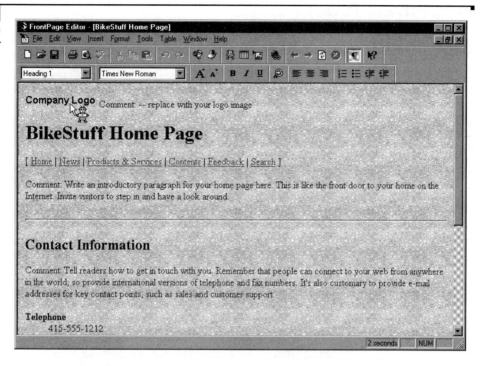

Navigation bar   The wizard has created a separate page (navbar.htm) whose only purpose is to contain hyperlinks to the main pages of the web. The wizard uses another Include bot to merge the navigation bar page into any other page that should have a navigation bar. By creating a single navigation bar page, you save yourself the time of creating separate navigation links for individual pages.

Comment   The wizard uses the Comment bot to display notes to you and other authors of the web. When the page is viewed in a Web browser, the comments are hidden and the space they occupy in the Editor is removed.

Web parameters   The wizard creates a set of web parameters based on the company information you supplied. The web parameters are stored in one location and you can easily change their values (see the "Web Parameters" section in Chapter 5). The wizard displays the values on a page using Substitution bots.

Time stamp   The wizard uses a Timestamp bot to display the date that the page was last modified.

Private Pages

In the FrontPage Explorer, click the Folder View button in the toolbar and click the _private folder in the pane on the left. The pane on the right lists the pages that are hidden from the web visitor (see Figure 4.32). Normally, you hide the pages that you use as page elements and merge into other pages using Include bots.

FIGURE 4.32

The private pages of the Corporate Presence Web

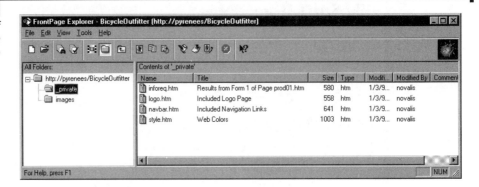

The hidden pages created by this wizard include:

inforeq.htm   The Web server uses this page to store requests for product information.

logo.htm   This page is used to display the company logo and is merged into other pages that are to display the logo using Include bots.

navbar.htm   This page includes the hyperlinks to the Web's main pages and is merged into other pages as needed using Include bots.

style.htm   This page includes the background image and stores information about the text and link colors. You can arrange for another page to borrow the background image and text colors from this page by setting a property of the other page.

If you create common header and footer pages, you can store them in the _private folder. Unfinished pages can be stored there temporarily.

The Public Pages

The Corporate Presence Web Wizard creates the public pages for all the features that you chose to include. The best way to view the public pages is in a Web browser.

In the Editor, click the Preview in Browser button in the toolbar to display the home page and spend several minutes following each of the hyperlinks in the navigation bar. Figure 4.33 shows the Table of Contents page with links to the five main pages and the second level of links from the Products Page to the individual product and services pages.

PART

I

Overview of
FrontPage

FIGURE 4.33

*The Table of
Contents page
viewed in a browser*

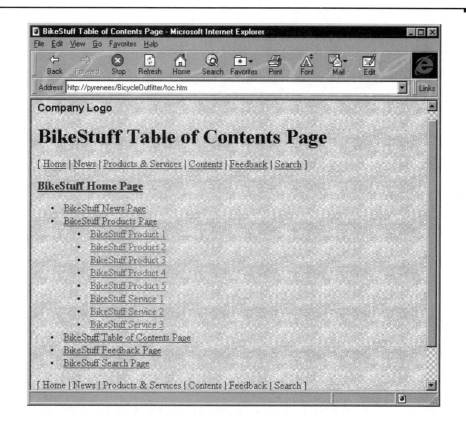

Modifying the Web . . .

The web that the wizard has created is a good first draft of the web's skeleton. The basic navigation paths are in place and pages are structured to include common elements. The next step is to enter the information about the store, the products you sell, and the services you offer into the new pages and create additional product and services pages and arrange to have them added to the table of contents. Of course, you'll want to add some photos and graphics to make your web more interesting.

Before long, you'll probably want to add new main pages and modify the navigation bar page to provide paths to the new pages. You may want to replace the generic text of the navigation bar links to reflect the personality of your site, such as replacing News with Hot Stuff, or you may want to replace the text links with interesting image links. After a while you may tire of the background image and text colors and decide it is time for a spiffier web. You may decide to add online discussion webs so that your bikie customers can discuss the pros and cons of the latest techie equipment and share touring route information.

As you tinker with the web, it will begin to reflect your tastes, but if it still lacks pizzazz, you may decide it's time to add videos of bike maintenance chores and sound clips of your favorite music and… well, there really are very few limits to what you can do with FrontPage, and there are no limits at all if you have the inclination to learn some simple programming. But, we're getting ahead of ourselves.

If you've been reading this book chapter by chapter, its time to move on. From here on out you'll probably be skipping around a lot as you learn how to create and manage webs in Part II and how to create astonishing web pages in Parts III and IV.

For More...

This chapter has introduced the many templates and wizards that are responsible for making FrontPage so powerful and also so easy to use. The following chapters provide in-depth treatment of individual wizards and templates:

- Chapter 5: Explorer Basics shows you how to use the Import Web Wizard to create new FrontPage webs based on existing files.

- Chapter 15 Understanding Frames shows you how to create and modify framesets.

- Chapter 17: Collecting Input Data shows you how to create data entry forms using the Form Page Wizard and confirmation pages using the Confirmation template.

- Chapter 18: Understanding Searches and Visitor Registration shows you how to use the Search Page template to add text searches. You also learn how to provide visitor registration based on the User Registration template.

- Chapter 19: Understanding Discussion Group Webs shows you how to use the Discussion Web Wizard.

- Chapter 21: Creating Dynamic Database Pages with Microsoft Access shows you how to create the files for connecting to an Access database using the Database Connector Wizard and the Database Results page template.

PART II

Managing
the Web

LEARN TO:

- *Work with a web in the FrontPage Explorer*
- *Work with the files and folders in a web*
- *Manage links between files*
- *Use a To Do List to keep track of tasks*
- *Control access to a web*

Chapter

5

Explorer Basics

Explorer Basics

The FrontPage Explorer is the tool you use to create and manage a FrontPage web. A *FrontPage web* is a set of folders and files. When you create a new FrontPage web, the Explorer creates a web folder and places it in the content folder of the web server that you specify. You can also store the web in any folder in your computer's file system. A FrontPage web folder contains the web pages, image, sound, video, and other files that you add to the web folder (your web's "content") and a set of subfolders that you can use to organize your content. The subfolder also contains a set of hidden subfolders (the subfolders with names that start with _vti_) that FrontPage uses behind the scenes so that your web will work as a FrontPage web. You don't work directly with the second set of subfolders. The second set is not displayed in the FrontPage Explorer, and you don't even see them until you use the Open File dialogs to locate and open a file in a web folder. (See the "Empty Web" section in Chapter 4 for more information about the _vti subfolders.)

This chapter shows you how to use the FrontPage Explorer to work with the web as a unit. You'll learn how to do the following tasks:

- Open and close an existing web
- View the list of a web's content files
- Create and delete webs
- Import a web
- Copy and move webs

Understanding the Explorer Window

To open the FrontPage Explorer, click the Windows 95 Start button and choose Programs ➤ Microsoft FrontPage ➤ FrontPage Explorer. FrontPage displays the Getting Started with Microsoft FrontPage dialog (see Figure 5.1). This dialog presents a number of useful shortcuts, but for now, just click the Cancel button to close the dialog and view the Explorer Window (see Figure 5.2).

FIGURE 5.1

The Getting Started with Microsoft FrontPage dialog

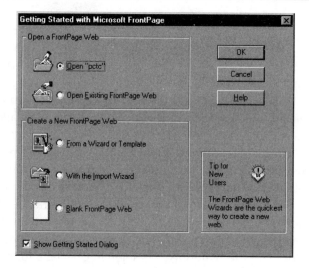

FIGURE 5.2

The FrontPage Explorer window

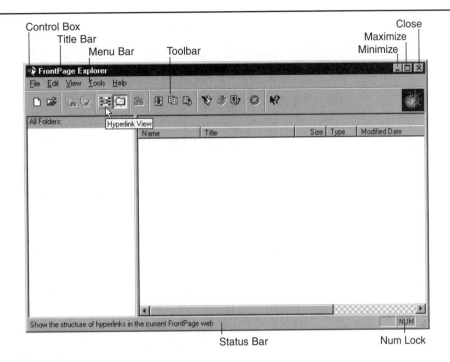

Control Box
Title Bar
Menu Bar
Toolbar
Close
Maximize
Minimize

Status Bar
Num Lock

Getting Started with Microsoft FrontPage

On opening, the FrontPage Explorer displays the Getting Started with Microsoft FrontPage dialog. This dialog has the following useful shortcuts for opening a web:

Open "*lastopenweb*"   Choose this option to open the web that was last open in the FrontPage Explorer.

Open Existing FrontPage Web   Choose this option to display the Open Web dialog that lists the existing FrontPage webs.

From a Wizard or Template   Choose this option to display the New Web dialog that lists the web wizards and templates for creating a new web.

With the Import Wizard   Choose this option to import an existing web or set of files to a new FrontPage web.

Blank FrontPage Web   Choose this option to create a new FrontPage web with no content.

The FrontPage Explorer also displays the Getting Started dialog after you close the current web. To eliminate the Getting Started dialog, click to uncheck the Show Getting Started Dialog check box at the bottom of the dialog.

The Explorer window contains the elements of the Explorer as described in Table 5.1.

TABLE 5.1: THE ELEMENTS OF THE FRONTPAGE EXPLORER WINDOW

Element	Description
Control box	Clicking the Control Box or pressing Alt+Space displays the Control menu with commands to control the window display, including Restore, Move, Size, Minimize, Maximize, and Close.
Title bar	Displays the name of the application. When a web is open, the title bar also displays the title and the name and location of the open web.
Minimize button	Clicking the Minimize button shrinks the application window to an icon placed in the Windows 95 task bar at the bottom of the screen.
Maximize button	Clicking the Maximize button expands the application window to fill the entire screen. After clicking the Maximize button, the button's icon changes to the Restore button.
Restore button	Clicking the Restore button shrinks the window from full size to its normal size. When the window is in its normal state, you can move or resize the window. To move the window, click in the title bar and drag to the new location. To resize the window, move the pointer to a corner of the window; when the pointer changes to a double-pointed arrow, press the left mouse button and drag to a new size.
Menu bar	The bar below the application title bar displays the menu categories. When you click a menu name, a drop-down menu displays the commands in the category. Commands may be available or grayed out depending on the current status of the FrontPage Explorer.
Toolbar	The bar below the menu bar displays command buttons corresponding to many of the menu commands. When you hold the pointer over a button without clicking, the button's tooltip, a brief message describing the button, is displayed.
Status bar	The bar located at the bottom of the window that displays a message and the status of various indicators. Figure 5.2 indicates that the Num Lock key is pressed.

The FrontPage Explorer Menus and Toolbar

The menus display all of the commands that you use while working in the FrontPage Explorer. Some of the menu commands have corresponding toolbar buttons. When you hold the pointer over a toolbar button, a tooltip displays the purpose of the button. Figure 5.3 shows the Explorer toolbar and Table 5.2 lists the menu commands and keyboard shortcuts. If a menu command has a corresponding toolbar button, the table shows the icon and the tooltip.

FIGURE 5.3

The FrontPage Explorer toolbar

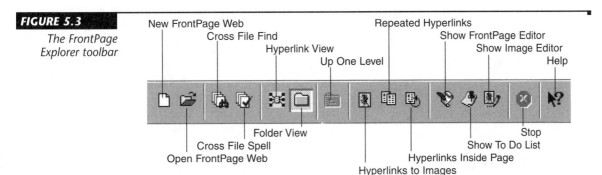

New FrontPage Web
Cross File Find
Hyperlink View
Up One Level
Repeated Hyperlinks
Show FrontPage Editor
Show Image Editor
Help

Folder View
Cross File Spell
Open FrontPage Web
Hyperlinks to Images
Hyperlinks Inside Page
Show To Do List
Stop

PART

II

Managing the Web

TABLE 5.2: THE FRONTPAGE EXPLORER MENU COMMANDS

Menu Command	Icon	Tooltip	Keyboard Shortcut	Description
File ➤ New ➤ Folder				Creates a new folder in the web
File ➤ New ➤ FrontPage Web	📄	New FrontPageWeb	Ctrl+N	Displays a list of wizards and tempates for creating a new web
File ➤ Open FrontPage Web	📂	Open FrontPageWeb		Displays a list of existing webs in the Open Front Page Web dialog
File ➤ Close FrontPage Web				Closes the current web
File ➤ Publish FrontPage Web				Copies the current web to another web server, to the same server using a different name, or to a folder

Continued ▶

TABLE 5.2: THE FRONTPAGE EXPLORER MENU COMMANDS (CONTINUED)

Menu Command	Icon	Tooltip	Keyboard Shortcut	Description
File ➤ Delete FrontPage Web				Deletes the current web
File ➤ Import				Imports one or more specified files into the current web. If no web is open, the command starts the Import Wizard.
File ➤ Export				Copies a selected file from the current web to a folder in your local file system
File ➤ Exit				Closes the Explorer and the current web if one is open
Edit ➤ Cut			Ctrl+X	Removes the selected file from the list in Folder View and places a copy on the Clipboard
Edit ➤ Copy			Ctrl+C	Places a copy of the selected files on the clipboard
Edit ➤ Paste			Ctrl+V	Pastes the files on the clipboard
Edit ➤ Delete			Del, or Delete	Deletes the selected file, breaking any links to the page
Edit ➤ Rename			F2	Changes the selected file or folder to edit mode so you can change the name (Folder View only)
Edit ➤ Open			Ctrl+O	Opens a selected page or file in the FrontPage Editor
Edit ➤ Open With				Opens the selected file using an editor that you choose from a list of available editors

Continued ▶

TABLE 5.2: THE FRONTPAGE EXPLORER MENU COMMANDS (CONTINUED)

Menu Command	Icon	Tooltip	Keyboard Shortcut	Description
Edit ➤ Add To Do Task				Adds a task to the To Do List for the current web. The task is linked to the Editor's active page.
Edit ➤ Properties			Alt+Enter	Opens the Explorer's Properties dialog for the currently selected file
View ➤ Toolbar				Displays or hides the toolbar. The toolbar is displayed when the command has a check mark.
View ➤ Status Bar				Displays or hides the status bar. The status bar is displayed when the command has a check mark.
View ➤ Hyperlink View		Hyperlink View		Displays or hides the Link view. The Link view is displayed when the command has a dot.
View ➤ Folder View		Folder View		Displays or hides the Summary view. The Summary view is displayed when the command has a dot.
View ➤ Hyperlinks to Images		Hyperlinks to Images		Displays or hides all links to images in the current web
View ➤ Repeated Hyperlinks		Repeated Hyperlinks		Displays or hides multiple links from one page to another page. By default, if a page has multiple links to another page, the Explorer shows only a single link. By checking this command, all links are displayed.

Continued ▮▶

TABLE 5.2: THE FRONTPAGE EXPLORER MENU COMMANDS (CONTINUED)

Menu Command	Icon	Tooltip	Keyboard Shortcut	Description
View ➤ Hyperlinks Inside Page		Hyperlinks Inside Page		Displays or hides the links from a page to itself
View ➤ Refresh			F5	Updates the display of all views for the current web. Views can become out-of-date when more than one person works on the web.
Tools ➤ Spelling		Cross File Spelling	F7	Use to check the spelling of selected or all pages in the current web
Tools ➤ Find		Cross File Find	Ctrl+F7	Use to search for specified text in selected or all pages in the current web
Tools ➤ Replace			Ctrl+H	Use to replace specified text with other specified text in selected or all pages in the current web
Tools ➤ Verify Hyperlinks				Use to verify internal and external links in the current web
Tools ➤ Recalculate Hyperlinks				Use to update the display of all views for the current web, to recalculate all results for the bots, and update the text index of the current web
Tools ➤ Show Editor		Show Front-Page Editor		Opens the FrontPage Editor and brings it to the top
Tools ➤ Show To Do List		Show To Do List		Opens the To Do List for the current web and brings it to the top. The command changes to display the number of items on the To Do List.

Continued ▶

TABLE 5.2: THE FRONTPAGE EXPLORER MENU COMMANDS (CONTINUED)

Menu Command	Icon	Tooltip	Keyboard Shortcut	Description
Tools ➤ Show Image Editor	🖼️	Show Image Editor		Opens the application associated with a GIF image and brings it to the top
Tools ➤ Web Settings				Displays information about the current web, including the web's name and title
Tools ➤ Permissions				Use to authorize administrators, authors, and end users
Tools ➤ Change Password				Use to change a password (Only for FrontPage Personal WebServer)
Tools ➤ Options				Use to change the FrontPage Explorer options, including configuring helper applications
Tools ➤ Microsoft GIF Animator				Use to start up the Microsoft GIF Animator (if you have the application installed)
Help ➤ Microsoft FrontPage Help	▶?	Help	F1	Displays the Help Topics dialog for FrontPage
Help ➤ Microsoft on the Web				Displays the FrontPage Support Online page if your network connection is open
Help ➤ About Microsoft FrontPage Explorer				Displays information about the Explorer and a button to initiate a network test of your TCP/IP installation

PART

II

Managing the Web

Hiding and Displaying the Status Bar

The status bar at the bottom of the Explorer window displays a brief message about the command you have selected or about the operation that is currently in progress. When you click on an Explorer menu and move the pointer to a command, the status bar describes the command. When you execute a command in the FrontPage Explorer or the FrontPage Editor, the Explorer's status bar may indicate the operation. For example, when you choose View ➤ Refresh from the Explorer menu bar, the Explorer retrieves the current versions of all the files in the current web from the web server and displays the message "Loading *webname* web" followed by the message "Opening *webname* web." When you open a Web page in the FrontPage Editor, the Explorer's status bar displays "Retrieving *pagename*..." during the time interval that the page is being retrieved.

Normally, you display the status bar. However, you can hide the status bar by choosing the Status Bar command from the Explorer's View menu. When the command is preceded by a check mark in the menu list, the status bar is displayed. Choosing the command toggles the check mark off or on.

Hiding and Displaying the Toolbar

The FrontPage Explorer's toolbar provides convenient access to several of the menu commands. Normally, you'll display the toolbar. However, when you want to maximize the size of the display area, you can hide the toolbar by choosing the Toolbar command from the Explorer's View menu. The Toolbar command in the View menu is preceded by a check mark to indicate that the toolbar is currently displayed. Choosing the command toggles the check mark off or on and hides or shows the toolbar.

Opening an Existing Web

You can open only one FrontPage web on your computer at a time. The FrontPage web you want to open can be stored by any Web server to which you have access. A FrontPage web can also be stored in any folder in your computer's file system.

 **NOTE**

> You can open the same web on two or more networked computers. Each computer must be running its own copy of FrontPage. You can run only one instance of FrontPage on a computer.

Opening an Existing Web from a Web Server

To open an existing web, click the Explorer's File menu. The File menu lists the four webs most recently opened (see Figure 5.4). If the web you want to open is shown, selecting it from this list is the fastest way to open the web.

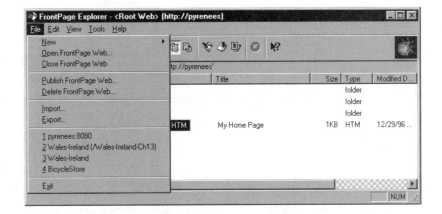

Otherwise, choose File ➤ Open FrontPage Web from the Explorer menu bar, or click the Open FrontPage Web button in the toolbar to display the Open FrontPage Web dialog. Enter the name of the Web server that stores the web you want to open, and click the List Webs button to display a list of webs stored by that server. Figure 5.5a shows the webs stored by the Web server named pyrenees. Select the web you want to open and click OK.

Whether you selected the web from the File menu list or from the Open FrontPage Web dialog, you must be authorized either as an administrator or an author to open the web. The web server may display a dialog, called an *authentication dialog*, in which you must type a user name and password in order to gain access to the web. Figure 5.5b shows the Name and Password Required dialog that the FrontPage Personal Web Server displays. If you installed the Microsoft Personal Web Server as described in Appendix A, security is not enabled, and the Web server doesn't display an authentication dialog. In Chapter 9: Administering a Web, you'll learn how to set permissions for others to use a web.

FIGURE 5.5

To open a web, specify the Web server or the name and location of the folder that stores the web (a). The authentication dialog displayed by the FrontPage Personal Web Server (b).

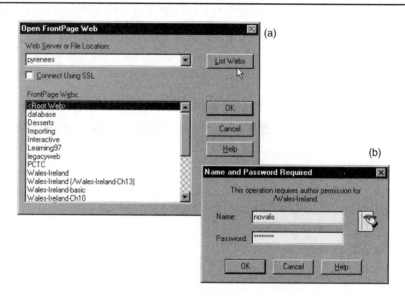

If another web is open, the FrontPage Explorer closes the existing web and opens the selected web as the current web. The *current web* is the web that is open in the FrontPage Explorer.

Opening the Root Web

The first web listed in the Open Web dialog is <Root Web>. The *root web* is the default FrontPage web that the server provides (see Chapter 2 for more information). When a visitor enters the address of the server without specifying a directory—for example, when a web visitor types http://*servername*/ in the browser's address text box—it is the home page of the server's root web that is displayed.

To open the root web in the FrontPage Explorer:

1. Choose File ➤ Open FrontPage Web from the Explorer menu bar and choose the web server whose root web you want to open.

2. Choose <Root Web> in the Open Web dialog, and click OK. If you have not previously entered your name and password for the selected Web server, the server displays its authorization dialog. If necessary, enter your user name and password and click OK. The Web server's root web opens.

To illustrate, Figure 5.6a shows a root web for the Microsoft Personal Web Server, including folders to store private files, scripts, images, and the root web's home page (default.htm). Figure 5.6b shows a root web for the FrontPage Personal Web Server (installed on port 8080 on the same computer), including similar folders, the rootweb's home page (index.htm), a page used by web visitors to register in a web named Wales-Ireland, and a text file used to hold the registration information (see Chapter 18 for information on visitor registration). (See Appendix A for more information on the two Personal Web Servers.)

FIGURE 5.6

A root web for the Microsoft Personal Web Server (a) and a root web for the FrontPage Personal Web Server installed on port 8080 on the same computer (b).

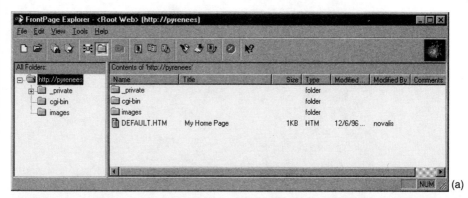

(a)

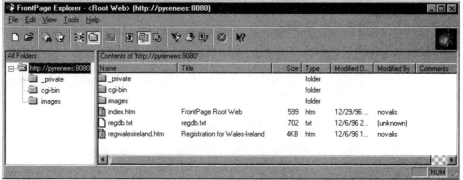

(b)

The Web server's default home page is usually a welcome page that has links to information about the server. Figure 5.7a is the default home page for the Microsoft Personal Web Server and Figure 5.7b is the default home page for the FrontPage Personal Web Server. You'll probably want to modify the Web server's default home page to give the Web visitor an overview of the webs that the server is storing, and provide links to their home pages.

FIGURE 5.7

The default home page for the Microsoft Personal Web Server (a) and the FrontPage Personal Web Server (b).

(a)

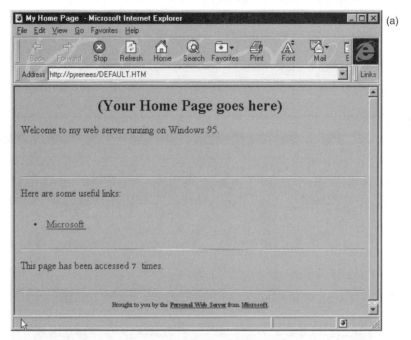

(b)

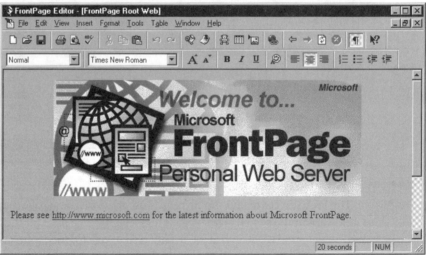

NOTE

If you restrict visitor access to a web stored by the server (see Chapter 9), the Web server displays an authentication dialog when the visitor clicks a link to enter the protected web. The FrontPage Personal Web Server provides a visitor-registration feature for a web stored by the server: in order to enter the web, the visitor must fill out a registration form stored in the server's root web. The Microsoft Personal Web Server does not provide this feature.

Opening a Web That Is Not on a Web Server

You can open a web that is stored in a folder on your computer's file system (and not on a Web server) by typing the full path and folder name in the Web Server or File Location combo box in the Open FrontPage Web dialog. For example, to open a Web stored in a folder named Webs on the book's CD-ROM, insert the disk in drive D and type **d:\Webs** (Your CD-ROM drive may use a different letter.) Click the List Webs button to view the list of webs stored in the folder. Figure 5.8 shows the root web for the Webs folder followed by the web stored in the folder.

PART

II

Managing the Web

FIGURE 5.8

To view the Webs stored in a folder of the book's CD-ROM, insert the disk and type the full path and name of the folder in the Web Server or File Location combo box.

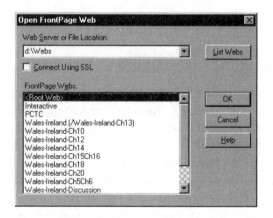

Closing a Web

When you are finished working with a web, close the web by choosing the File ➤ Close FrontPage Web from the Explorer menu bar. Before you close a web, you should first close, or at least save, the web's open pages in the Editor. After you close a web, you cannot save any page changes to it. If no web is currently open in the FrontPage Explorer when you try to save page changes, the Editor displays the message shown in Figure 5.9a. If the FrontPage Explorer is closed, the Explorer starts up and displays the Open FrontPage Web dialog so you can open a web to receive the changed page. If you open a web other than the original web and try to save the changed page, the Editor displays the message in Figure 5.9b, indicating that the page came from another web and offering you the opportunity to save the changed page to the current web.

FIGURE 5.9

You can only save a changed page to a web that is currently open in the Explorer (a). If you try to save a page to a web other than the page's parent web, the Explorer offers you the opportunity to save the page to the current web (b).

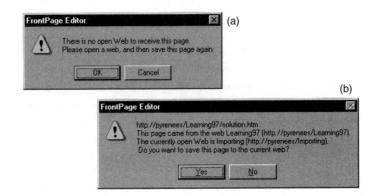

Viewing the Web's Contents

The Explorer has two views for displaying information about the files in a web: Folder View for understanding the web's contents and Hyperlink View for understanding how the web's files are linked. You can switch between the views by choosing the View ➤ Hyperlink View or View ➤ Folder View command from the Explorer menu bar or by clicking the Hyperlink View or the Folder View buttons in the toolbar. Figure 5.10a shows the Folder View and Figure 5.10b shows the Hyperlink View for the PCTC web you created in Chapter 1.

In each view, the Explorer window is divided into two panes. You can move the boundary between the panes by moving the pointer to the boundary, pressing the left mouse button when the pointer changes to a pair of vertical lines with arrows, and dragging to a new boundary location.

The two views of the Explorer provide different ways of understanding the files that are in the web and how they are related to each other. Each view gives you different information and has its own features for working with a file. You'll find yourself switching between the views to use the features. The next section describes viewing the contents of a web using Folder View. Chapter 7: Managing Links describes how to use the Hyperlinks view to understand the links that relate the files of your web.

FIGURE 5.10

The Folder View (a) and Hyperlink View (b) for the PCTC web

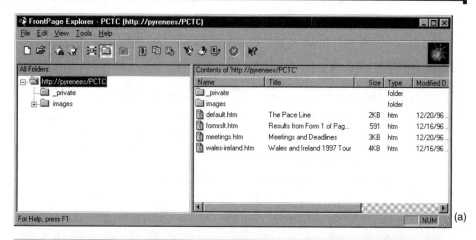

(a)

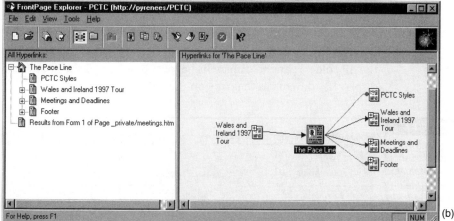

(b)

PART

II

Managing the Web

Understanding Folder View

Folder View displays the folders and files in the web. Folder View works just like the Windows Explorer.

The All Folders Pane

The All Folders pane on the left is a hierarchy of all the folders in the web. At the top is the web folder labeled with the address (absolute URL) of the web. By default, all FrontPage webs contain at least two folders. Use the _private folder to store the files you do not want to make available to web visitors and use the images folder to store image files. To organize your web's files, you can add more folders to the web and you can add folders inside other folders (see the "Working with Web Folders" section in Chapter 6). If a folder contains other folders, a plus sign is displayed to the left of the folder icon in the All Folders pane. Click the plus sign to expand the folder and display an indented list of its subfolders. After you expand a folder, the plus sign changes to a minus sign.

NOTE

The web folder for a web stored on a Web server is labeled with http: and forward slashes, such as http://pyrenees/Wales-Ireland. If the web is not on a Web server, the web folder is labeled with a drive letter and back slashes, such as D:\Webs\Wales-Ireland.

The Contents of '*foldername*' Pane

To open a folder and view its contents, click the folder icon in the All Folders pane. The folder icon changes to an open folder and the Contents of the '*foldername*' pane on the right displays the files and subfolders. In Figure 5.8a, the pane on the right displays the contents of the web folder. Figure 5.11 shows the images folder expanded in the All Folders pane to display its Logos subfolder and the Logos subfolder opened to display its contents in the pane on the right.

FIGURE 5.11

The images folder is expanded to show its subfolder in the left pane and the Logos subfolder is opened to display its contents in the right pane.

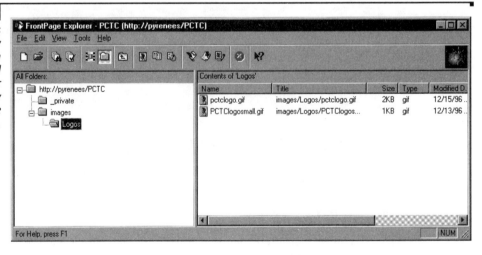

TIP

You can also open a folder by double-clicking a folder icon in the right pane of Folder View.

Creating a FrontPage Web

There are three ways to create a FrontPage web. You can create a new web using one of the FrontPage templates or wizards, and store the new web as a separate web on a Web server or in any folder in your computer's file system. You can add the pages of a new web to an existing web. You can create a new web and import files into the new web. The files you import may be from an existing FrontPage web, a web created without using FrontPage, or just a folder of files that you want to use as content in a new FrontPage web.

Creating a New FrontPage Web on a Web Server

To create a new web, choose File ➤ New ➤ FrontPage Web from the Explorer menu bar, click the New button in the toolbar, or press Ctrl+N to display the New FrontPage Web dialog (see Figure 5.12a). All FrontPage webs are based on one of the templates or wizards listed in this dialog. Chapter 4 describes the webs you can create with each of the templates and wizards listed in the dialog. After you choose a template or wizard, click OK to display the Web Template dialog (see Figure 5.12b). Specify the name of the Web server that will store the new web (or the location of a storage folder) and type the name for the new web. The web name must comply with the Web server's naming rules. For example, web names for the FrontPage Personal Web Server are case-sensitive, and may not have spaces. Click the Connect Using SSL check box to connect to a Web server that uses the Secure Socket Layer (SSL) protocol to enable secure communications between FrontPage and the Web server. (Neither of the Personal Web Servers use this security protocol.)

NOTE

You can create custom web templates and wizards using the Microsoft FrontPage 97 Software Developer's Kit on the book's CD-ROM. Appendix C shows you how to create custom web templates. Creating custom wizards requires programming skills, however, and is not covered.

FIGURE 5.12

Select a wizard or template in the New FrontPage Web dialog (a). Select a Web server or folder on your computer's file system and type the name for the new web in the Web Template dialog (b).

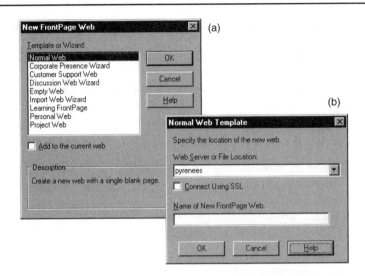

For practice, you'll create a web using the Personal Web template, as follows:

1. Click the New button in the toolbar and double-click Personal Web in the New FrontPage Web dialog to create a new web using the Personal Web Template.

2. Choose the default Web server on your computer. (If you followed Appendix A, your default Web server is the Microsoft Personal Web Server.) Your default Web server has the same name as your computer. (To view or change the name of your computer, choose Start ➤ Settings ➤ Control Panel, double-click the Network icon, and click the Identification tab in the Network dialog shown in Figure 5.13. Type the new name in the Computer name text box.)

3. Type **MyNewWeb** as the name for the new web and click OK. The Explorer creates the new web on the Web server, including the _private folder, images folder, and a default page named My Home Page. Both folders are empty. The Web server also creates the set of folders that have names starting with _vti_ . These folders are stored in the web folder, although they are not displayed by the FrontPage Explorer (see Chapter 2 for more information on _vti_ folders).

NOTE

A limitation of the FrontPage Personal Web Server is that it can store only 14 webs at a time.

FIGURE 5.13

View or change the name of your computer in the Identificatron tab of the Network dialog.

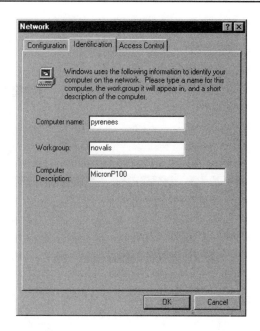

Creating a New Web Outside a Web Server

If you don't have authoring privileges to a Web server, you can create a new web and store it in a folder on your computer's file system. You can publish the web to a Web server later. To specify the location of the new web, type the full path to the folder in the Template dialog. If the folder doesn't exist, FrontPage will offer to create it.

To illustrate creating a web outside a web server, let's create a new web on a floppy disk.

1. Insert a floppy disk in drive A. Click the New button in the toolbar and double-click Learning FrontPage in the New FrontPage Web dialog.

2. Type **a:\MyWebs** in the Web Server or File Location combo box and type **Desserts** as the name of the new web (see Figure 5.14a). The FrontPage Explorer offers to create the new folder (see Figure 5.14b).

3. Click Yes. The Explorer creates the MyWebs folder, creates a root web for the folder, and then creates the Desserts web within the MyWebs folder. The next time you open an existing web, the new folder will appear in the combo list of servers and folders in the New FrontPage Web dialog.

4. Click the Open button in the toolbar and click List Webs in the Open FrontPage Web dialog. Figure 5.14c shows the new MyWebs folder on the A drive.

FIGURE 5.14

You can create a new web in any folder on your computer's hard disk (a). If the folder doesn't exist, the Explorer offers to create it (b). The folder is listed in the Open FrontPage Webs dialog (c).

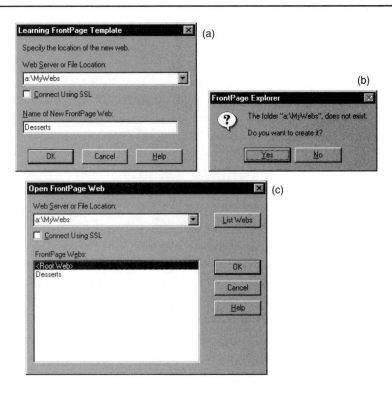

A web created outside a FrontPage-enabled Web server does not have the FrontPage Server Extension programs installed. The web does not have a text index and any browse-time bots included on pages will not function when the web is viewed in a Web browser (see Chapters 16 and 17 for information on design-time and browse-time bots). To enable these features, you must copy the web to a FrontPage-enabled Web server.

Adding Pages from a New Web to the Current Web

Instead of creating a separate new web, you can add the pages that a web template or wizard creates to the current web. To add the new pages to the current web, check the

Add to the current web option in the New Web dialog (see Figure 5.12a). The template or wizard will create a default home page with the filename default.htm and FrontPage will ask if you want to replace the existing home page with the new page (see Figure 5.15a). If you click Yes, the new home page replaces the existing home page, and if you click No, the new home page is discarded. You may want to retain both the original and the new home page. To save both pages to the current web, you'll have to change the name of the original home page—for example, to defaultold.htm—before adding the new pages. By changing the name, you can add the new default.htm page without replacing the original home page. After adding the new pages, you can rename the pages if necessary.

To illustrate, you'll add the pages from the Project Web template to the MyNewWeb web, as follows:

1. Click the File menu in the Explorer menu bar and choose MyNewWeb from the list of recently opened webs. (If MyNewWeb is not on the list, choose the Open FrontPage Web command instead.)

2. Click the default.htm filename and choose Edit ➤ Rename from the Explorer menu bar. Type **defaultpersonal.htm** as the filename and press Enter. Click Yes when the Explorer offers to update the links to this page (see Figure 5.15b).

3. Click the New FrontPage Web button in the toolbar. Select Project Web from the list, click the Add to the current web check box on the New FrontPage Web dialog, and click OK. The Explorer creates the pages for the Project web and adds them to the MyNewWeb web. Figure 5.16 shows the MyNewWeb web with the pages from the Project Web template added.

After adding the pages of a web template or wizard, the next step is to decide which home page should be the default home page for the web, change the filenames if necessary, and create links between the appropriate pages of the original web and the added web pages.

NOTE

Instead of adding pages of a new web to the current web, it is usually preferable to create a separate web. You can always create a link from one web to another so that it appears to the user as if the webs were one big web. When you create separate webs, you can have different access restrictions on them. Access controls are set for an entire web and not for individual pages in a web, so using separate webs is the only way you can have different restrictions on different pages.

FIGURE 5.15

Change the name of the default home page (a) and update the links to the page (b) before adding the default home page and the other pages of a new web.

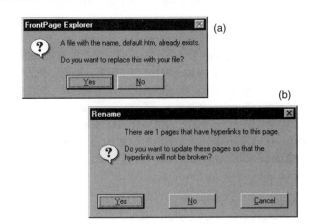

FIGURE 5.16

You can add the pages from a web template or a web wizard to an existing web.

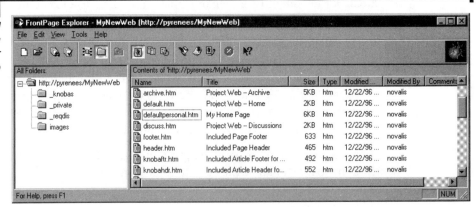

Changing a Web's Name and Title

After you create a web, you can change its name as follows:

1. Open the web in the Explorer.

2. Choose Tools ➤ Web Settings from the Explorer menu bar and click the Configuration tab in the Web Settings dialog (see Figure 5.17). A web has both a name and a title. The web name is the name of the web's folder—this is, the name that the server uses to identify your web. The webs stored by a Web server must have unique names, although you can create webs with the same name and store

them on different servers or in different folders on your computer's file system. (Creating different webs with the same name is probably not a good idea: the servers may not get confused, but you may.) You can think of the web title as the user-friendly label for a web; the title may be any length and may have spaces. When you create a new web and specify a web name, the Explorer reuses the web name as the web title by default. If you change the title so that the title and the name are different, the Explorer displays both the title and the name in the list in the Open Web dialog and in the title bar when the web is open.

FIGURE 5.17

Change the name and title of the current web in the Web Settings dialog.

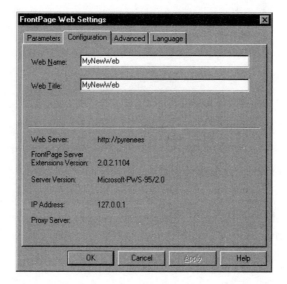

PART

II

Managing the Web

3. Change the Web Name or Web Title and then click the Apply button to save the changes to the web.

To illustrate, we'll change both the name and the title for the MyNewWeb web.

1. In the configuration tab, type **Introduction** as the web name, type **Introducing Me** as the web title, and click OK. The Explorer's title bar reflects the changes.

2. Click the Open FrontPage Web button in the toolbar. The dialog lists the title and name of the web as Introducing Me (/Introduction) (see Figure 5.18).

When the web name and title are different, the Explorer displays both the name and the title in the Open FrontPage Web list and in the application title bar.

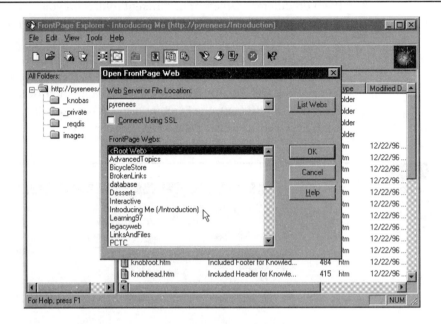

Importing a Web

Often a web has been created and exists as a folder of pages and files in your computer's file system. You may have created the web without using FrontPage (a non-FrontPage web is called a *legacy web*). Or, if the web is a FrontPage web, it may exist in a folder or may be stored by another Web server. The easiest way to import an existing web to your Web server is to use the Import Web Wizard. This Wizard creates a new FrontPage web and then copies the files from the existing web into the new web.

Start the Wizard in any of these ways:

- Close the current web in the FrontPage Explorer. Choose the With the Import Wizard option in the Getting Started with Microsoft FrontPage dialog (see Figure 5.1 at the beginning of the chapter).

- If no web is currently open, choose File ➤ Import from the Explorer menu bar and then double-click the Import Web Wizard in the New FrontPage Web dialog. (If a web is open when you choose the Import command, the Explorer offers to import files into the open web instead.)

- Choose File ➤ New ➤ FrontPage Web from the Explorer menu bar or click the New FrontPage Web button in the toolbar and then double-click the Import Web Wizard in the New FrontPage Web dialog.

To illustrate the process of importing a web, you'll create the Wales-Ireland web by importing a sample web from the book's CD-ROM. The Wales-Ireland web is the web that describes the bicycle tour of Wales and Ireland (see Chapter 3 for more information on this web). You'll be adding content to this web throughout Parts III and IV.

1. Click the New FrontPage Web button in the toolbar and double-click the Import Web Wizard. Use the Import Web Wizard dialog to specify the location and the name of the new web that the wizard creates.

2. Choose your default Web server, type **Wales-Ireland** as the name of the new web (see Figure 5.19a), and click OK. You specify the location of the folder whose files you want to import in the Choose Directory screen (see Figure 5.19b). You can either type the full path and folder name or click the Browse button to locate the folder in your computer's file system.

FIGURE 5.19

Specify the location and the name of the new web (a) and then specify the full path and name of the source folder that contains the files you want to import into the new web (b).

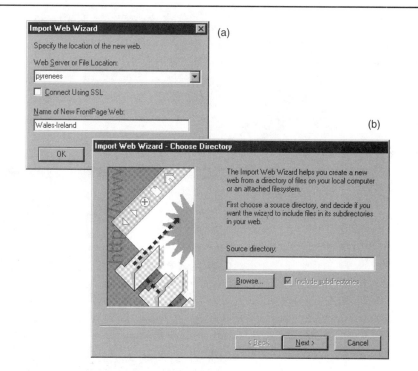

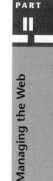

3. Click Browse and locate the Webs folder of the book's CD-ROM. Click to open the folder, click the folder named Wales-Ireland-Ch5Ch6, and click OK. By default, the Include subdirectories check box is checked so that the wizard will

copy the web's subfolders and their files. Click Next. The Edit File List dialog lists the files in the folder (see Figure 5.20a). You can import all the files or a selection. You can limit the list of files to import by selecting the files you want to exclude and clicking the Exclude button. If you change your mind after excluding files, click the Refresh button to display the complete list of files in the folder.

4. Click Next to import all of the files in the Wales-Ireland-Ch5Ch6 folder. Click the Finish button (see Figure 5.20b) to start the importing process. The Explorer creates the new Wales-Ireland web and then copies the files from the Wales-Ireland-Ch5Ch6 folder to the new web.

FIGURE 5.20

You can import all of the files or choose to exclude some files (a) and then click Finish to start the importing process (b).

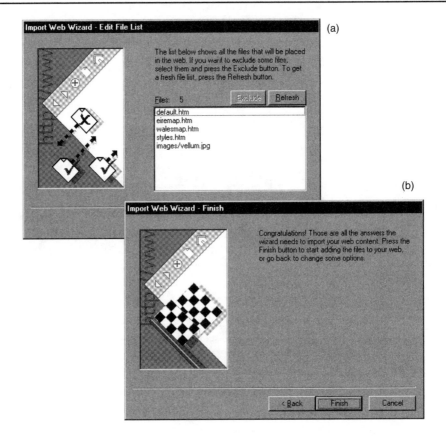

NOTE

To convert a non-FrontPage web into a FrontPage web, use the Import Web Wizard to copy the web's files into a new FrontPage web. You can then add FrontPage features to the web.

Copying and Moving a Web

A FrontPage web can be copied to another web server or to any folder in your computer's file system. A standard way to develop a FrontPage web is to create or modify the web on your computer using the Microsoft Personal Web Server or the FrontPage Personal Web Server, and then copy the web to the production web server that you use to make the web available to the World Wide Web or private intranet. FrontPage makes it easy to copy the web from your development server to the production server.

NOTE

You can copy the entire contents of a web server or folder to another web server or folder by copying the root web of the web server or folder and choosing the option to copy all of the webs contained in the root web (the *child webs*).

Use the File ➤ Publish FrontPage Web command from the Explorer menu bar to copy the open FrontPage web from its current location to a new location. Copying a web is called *publishing the web*. When you copy the current web to another web server or to a folder, the Explorer creates a new web in the location you specify and with the name you specify, and copies the current web's files into the new web.

You can also use the Publish FrontPage Web command to copy the contents of the current FrontPage web to another existing FrontPage web.

Use the Publish FrontPage Web dialog (see Figure 5.21) to specify the following information:

Destination Web Server or File Location   Specify the destination of the copied web by choosing the name of a web server from the list, by typing the location of a web server in your computer's file system, or by typing the full path and name of a folder in your computer's file system (if the folder doesn't exist, the Explorer will create it).

Connect Using SSL   If you are copying the current web to a web server that uses Secure Sockets Layer (SSL), click this check box.

Name of Destination FrontPage Web   Type the name of the new web in the destination location. To copy the the root web of a web server or a folder, type <Root Web> or leave the text box blank. To add the contents of the current web to an existing FrontPage web, type the name of the web that will be the destination of the copied content.

Copy changed pages only   Choose this option to copy only the pages that have changed since the last time you copied the FrontPage web.

Add to an existing FrontPage web   Choose this option to copy the contents of the current FrontPage web to the existing FrontPage web that you specified as the destination web in the Name text box.

Copy child webs   If you are copying the root web of a web server or folder, choose this option to copy all the FrontPage webs contained in the root web.

When you copy a FrontPage web, use the Publish Front-Page Web dialog to specify the destination and copying options.

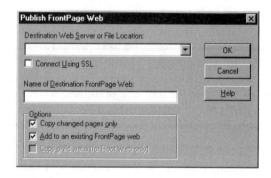

For practice, copy the Wales-Ireland web to three locations: to the root web of the MyWebs folder on a floppy disk in drive A, to the FrontPage Personal Web Server, and to an existing web stored by the Microsoft Personal Web Server.

Copying a Web to a Folder

You can copy a web to any folder in your computer's file system.

1. Choose File ➤ Publish FrontPage Web from the Explorer menu bar. Select or type a:\MyWebs in the Destination Web Server or File Location combo box.

2. Type **WalesAndIreland** in Name text box, uncheck the options, and click OK. The Explorer copies the Wales-Ireland web to the new web named WalesAndIreland in the root web of the MyWebs folder on the floppy disk.

NOTE

When the folder is not the content folder of a FrontPage-enabled Web server, the copied web does not have the FrontPage server extension programs and does not have a text index.

Copying a Web to a Web Server

You can publish a web to any FrontPage-enabled Web server using the File ➤ Publish FrontPage Web command. For practice, you'll publish the Wales-Ireland web to the FrontPage Personal Web Server.

1. Choose File ➤ Publish FrontPage Web from the Explorer menu bar. Select the FrontPage Personal Web Server you installed on port 8080 (see Appendix A for information on installing a second web server on your computer). Type **Wales-Ireland** as the name of the new web, uncheck the options, and click OK. The Explorer starts up the FrontPage Personal Web Server and displays the Name and Permission Required dialog (see Figure 5.22a).

2. Type the user name and password that you specified when you installed the Web server and click OK. The Explorer copies the Wales-Ireland web to a new web with the same name on the FrontPage Personal Web Server and displays a message that the web was successfully copied.

3. Click the FrontPage Personal Web Server icon in the Windows task bar to display the server's window (see Figure 5.22b). Click the window's Close button to stop the server.

NOTE

If you are copying a web to a company Web server or an Internet Service Provider, you'll need to obtain permission from the server administrator. If the Web server does not have FrontPage Server Extensions installed, the Web Publishing Wizard is started automatically (if installed) when FrontPage detects that the Web server is not FrontPage-enabled. See Appendix B for more information on publishing to another Web server.

PART

II

Managing the Web

FIGURE 5.22

When you copy a web to the FrontPage Personal Web Server, you must have permission to add a web (a). Close the server after copying the web (b).

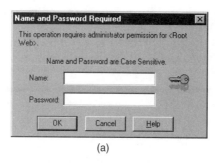

(a)

(b)

Adding a Web to an Existing FrontPage Web

You can add the files of the current web to another web as follows:

1. Choose File ➤ Publish FrontPage Web from the Explorer menu bar. Select the default web server as the destination. You'll add the Wales-Ireland web to the Introduction web you created earlier in the chapter.

2. Type **Introduction** as the name of the destination web. Click the Add to an existing FrontPage web and click OK. The Explorer copies the contents of the Wales-Ireland web to the Introduction web and displays a message that the web was copied successfully.

Copying the Root Web

To illustrate copying a root web and its contents to a new location, you'll copy the root web of the MyWebs folder on the floppy disk to your default Web server. If you choose the option to copy the child webs, the FrontPage Explorer creates a new web in the destination's root web for each child web in the root web you are copying.

1. Click the Open FrontPage Web button in the toolbar, choose a:\MyWebs in the Web Server or File Location combo list, click List Webs, and click OK to open the root web.

2. Choose File ➤ Publish FrontPage Web from the Explorer menu bar. Select the default web server as the destination. Click the Copy child webs option and clear the Copy changed pages only and Add to an existing FrontPage web check boxes. Click OK. The Explorer creates a new web in the root web of the default web server and copies into it the contents of the WalesAndIreland child web.

Deleting a Web

To delete an existing web, open the web in the FrontPage Explorer and choose File ➤ Delete FrontPage Web from the Explorer menu bar. The Explorer will ask you to confirm the deletion (see Figure 5.23). If you click Yes, the Explorer permanently deletes the web from the Web server (or from the folder storing the web). To illustrate, you'll delete the WalesAndIreland web from your default Web server and from the MyWebs folder on the floppy disk.

FIGURE 5.23

*Deleting a web is a
permanent action.*

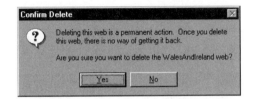

1. Click the Open FrontPage Web button in the toolbar and double-click Wales-AndIreland to open the web. Choose File ➤ Delete FrontPage Web and click Yes to delete the web.

2. Click the Open FrontPage Web button in the toolbar. Select a:\MyWebs, click the List Webs button, and double-click WalesAndIreland to open the web. Choose File ➤ Delete FrontPage Web and click Yes to delete the web. The MyWebs folder and the root web files remain on the floppy but the WalesAndIreland web has been deleted.

NOTE

You cannot delete a root web from a Web server or from a folder using the Delete FrontPage Web command in the Explorer. Use the FrontPage Server Administrator to remove a FrontPage root web from the server (see Appendix A for more information).

Understanding Web Settings

The FrontPage Explorer keeps track of several properties for each FrontPage web. You can view and change some of these properties by choosing Tools ➤ Web Settings from the

PART

II

Managing the Web

Explorer menu bar. The web properties are organized in four tabs of the Web Settings dialog as follows: Parameters, Configuration, Advanced, and Language (see Figure 5.24).

FIGURE 5.24

Web properties are organized in four tabs of the Web Settings dialog.

Web Parameters

The Parameters tab is used to create and modify the parameters that you want to use in the pages of the current web. (Web parameters are also called *configuration variables*.) Examples of typical web parameters are: the e-mail address of the webmaster, the phone and fax numbers you want to make available to Web visitors, the company or organization's name, the mailing address, the name of the contact person, and so on.

The reason you define web parameters is that FrontPage provides a way to display the values of web parameters on web pages automatically. Instead of typing each value in each location where you want the value to be displayed, you can insert a Substitution bot in each location. The Substitution bot looks up the current value of a web parameter and inserts the value directly on the page. You use the Parameters tab of the Web Settings dialog to collect in one location all of the values that characterize your web. If you change one or more of the values, you won't have to locate pages and make the changes yourself because the Substitution bot displays the current values automatically. (See Chapter 16: Using WebBots in Page Design for more information on the Substitution bot.) Figure 5.25 shows some web parameters for the Wales-Ireland web.

FIGURE 5.25

Web parameters for the Wales-Ireland web

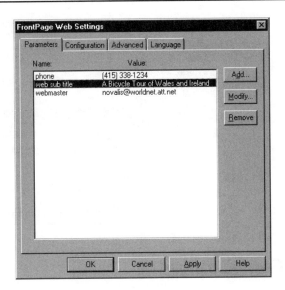

You use the Web Settings dialog to add new parameters and to modify or delete existing parameters, as follows:

- To create a new web parameter, click the Add button in the Parameters tab. Enter the parameter name and the current value in the Add Name and Value dialog (see Figure 5.26a) and click OK.

- To modify an existing web parameter, click the parameter in the list and then click the Modify button to display Modify Name and Value dialog (see Figure 5.26b). Make the changes and click OK.

- To remove a web parameter, click the parameter in the list and then click the Remove button.

After you make any changes to the list, click Apply to save the changes to the web and leave the Web Settings dialog open for further changes, or click OK to save the changes and close the dialog.

For hands-on practice with web parameters, do the following:

1. Open the Wales-Ireland web in the FrontPage Explorer. Choose Tools ➤ Web Settings from the Explorer menu bar, and click the Parameters tab.

2. Click the Add button, add the name and value of the phone parameter shown in Figure 5.25, and click OK.

3. Repeat Step 2 to add the web subtitle and the webmaster parameters. Click Apply to save the changes.

FIGURE 5.26

Clicking the Add button displays the dialog for adding a new parameter (a). Clicking the Modify button displays the dialog for changing a selected parameter (b).

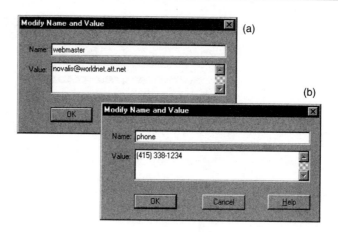

(a)

(b)

Web Configuration

The Configuration tab lists the Web Name and the Web Title (see Figure 5.27). The Web Name is the name of the current web's web folder. The Web Title is the descriptive title for the web and can have up to 31 characters or spaces. The web title is displayed in the Explorer's title bar when the web is open. You use this tab to change the web's name or title. You can change the web name only if you have administrator's permissions (see Chapter 9: Administering a Web for more information on permissions).

FIGURE 5.27

Change the web name or title in the Configuration tab.

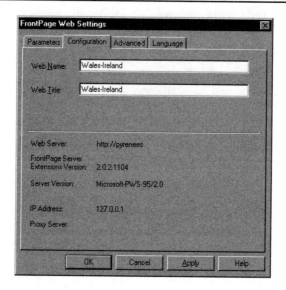

The Configuration tab also lists properties that you can't change using this dialog, including the name of the Web server, the version of the server extensions software installed on the server, the name and version of the server software you are using, the server's IP address, and the version number. (When you are working in local mode, the server name is listed as either the computer's name or as "local host," and the default IP address is 127.0.0.1).

NOTE

If you are using a Web server that recognizes Microsoft Visual SourceSafe version 5.0 or later and you have the application installed, the Configuration tab displays a Source Control Project text box below the web title text box. Microsoft Visual SourceSafe is a version control program that you can use to keep track of versions when the web has multiple authors. You can assign the current web to a Visual SourceSafe project by entering the project's name.

Advanced Settings

You can specify settings for advanced FrontPage features for the current web using the Advanced tab (see Figure 5.28), as follows:

Image Maps   Use the image map settings to specify how you want FrontPage to handle clickable image hyperlinks. To specify that the Web server process image hyperlinks, choose a server type in the Style combo box. You can choose FrontPage, NCSA, CERN, or Netscape server types. Choose <none> if you don't want the Web server to process image hyperlinks. After choosing a Web server type, enter in the Prefix text box the name and location of the program that the server will use to process the image hyperlink or accept the default program that FrontPage provides. When you choose a Web server type, FrontPage generates the HTML codes for server-side image hyperlink processing. Click the Generate client-side image maps to specify that you want FrontPage to generate the HTML codes for client-side image hyperlink processing. You can select a Web server type and click the check box to generate both types of HTML codes.

NOTE

If you are planning to publish your webs to a Web server that does not have FrontPage Server Extensions installed, choose the image map style for that Web server so that the image maps will continue to function.

PART

II

Managing the Web

Image Map Processing

A clickable image hyperlink is more complicated than a text hyperlink because you have to specify the coordinates of the clickable region, called an *image map*. When you create a clickable image hyperlink (see Chapter 13, "Using Images and Video Clips") there are two ways that the link can be processed. In the older method, called *server-side image map processing,* the Web server processes the image link. Each kind of Web server uses its own programs to determine the target of the link based on the coordinates of the pointer when the visitor clicks the image. The Style combo box lists the kinds of servers for which FrontPage has image processing programs and can create the corresponding server-side image map. In the newer method, called *client-side image map processing,* the browser uses its own programs to determine the target. In this case, the target for the hyperlink is included along with the coordinates of the clickable image. Most of the popular Web browsers are able to process images.

FIGURE 5.28

Use the Advanced tab to specify features including image map processing, validation scripting language, and showing hidden files.

Language   Specify the scripting language that you want FrontPage to use for the data validation scripts that are created automatically when you set data validation (see Chapter 17: Collecting Input Data for more information on data validation). The choices are VBScript, JavaScript, and none.

Options   Click the Show documents in hidden directories to display the contents of the web's hidden folders. This option does not affect the display of files in the web's _private folder.

Recalculate Status   The two check boxes indicate whether features of the web are out of date. Included page dependencies are out of date is checked by the Explorer if any page in the web has an Include bot that is out of date. Text index is out of date is checked by the Explorer if the web has a text index that is out of date.

Language Settings

FrontPage provides the ability to use languages other than English and character sets other than the character set used in the United States and Western Europe. Use the Language tab (see Figure 5.29) to specify the Default Web language that the Web server should use in sending error messages back to the web browser and to specify the character set you want to use for creating new pages in the FrontPage Editor.

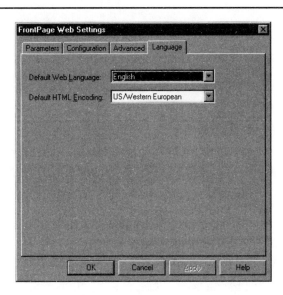

FIGURE 5.29

Use the Language tab to specify a language for error messages and a character set for creating new pages in the FrontPage Editor.

For More...

This chapter has covered the basics of working with the FrontPage web as a single entity. You've learned how to open and close existing webs, create new webs, and copy a web to a Web server or to a folder that is not in a Web server. You've also learned how to set web properties.

The following chapters provide more information about adding content to a web:

- Chapter 6: Working with Files shows you how to manage the files in your web, including how to import and export files, how to specify editors for different file types, and how to use folders to organize your files.

- Chapter 9: Administering a Web shows you how to control who can view or change a web and who can create and delete webs.

- Chapter 10: Editor Basics shows you how to create new web pages by starting from scratch, by using FrontPage templates and wizards, and by using an existing text file.

Chapter

6

Working with Files

Working with Files

Chapter 5 showed you how to work with a FrontPage web as a single entity. But we didn't pay much attention to the web's content. The *content* of a web is the set of files contained in the web folder. The primary files in a typical web are web pages. A *web page* is a file that has the HTML format. The web page is the only type of file that you can create in FrontPage. All other file types, such as image files, sound clips, video clips, text files, Microsoft Word documents, and Excel spreadsheets must be created using other applications—called *editors*—and then imported into the FrontPage web.

In this chapter, you'll learn how to use the FrontPage Explorer to work with content files. You'll learn:

- How to import and export files
- About the file types that the FrontPage Editor can display by itself
- How to assign editors to the file types that the FrontPage Editor cannot display
- How to create web folders to organize the web's content
- How to manipulate folders and files
- How to do global editing of the pages in a web

NOTE

The examples in Chapter 6 are based on the Wales-Ireland web. If you didn't create this web in Chapter 5, follow the steps in the "Importing a Web" section of Chapter 5 to create a new web named Wales-Ireland and import the files from the Wales-Ireland-Ch5Ch6 web on the book's CD-ROM.

Importing Files

There are basically two ways to add content to your web. Either you can create new web pages using the FrontPage Editor (see Chapter 10: Editor Basics), or you can import existing files into the current web. The files must be in your computer's file system, either on your computer or on another computer in your local area network. You use the FrontPage Explorer to import files and folders to the current web. When you add a folder to the import list, the FrontPage Explorer adds all the folder's files to the import list. When you import the folder, the Explorer creates the folder in the web and imports its files.

To practice importing files to the current web, you'll import files and folders from the book's CD-ROM to the Wales-Ireland web. Insert the book's CD-ROM and do the following:

1. Choose File ➤ Import from the Explorer menu bar. You use the Import File to FrontPageWeb dialog (see Figure 6.1a) to build a list of files to be imported, and then to import the files in the list.

2. Click the Add File button. You use the Add File to Import List dialog (see Figure 6.1b) to locate the folder with the files you want to import. This dialog gives you access to any file on your own computer and to any file in your local network that you have permission to use. You can add several files from a single folder to the import list at one time. Use the Look In combo box to locate the folder on your computer's file system. Use the Files of type combo box to specify the file type. The categories of file types are:

   - All Files (files with any extension *.*)
   - HTML Files (web pages with extensions *.htm, or *.html)
   - GIF and JPEG (image files with extensions *.gif, or *.jpg)
   - Microsoft Office Files (Word documents with extension *.doc, Excel files with extension *.xls, and PowerPoint files with extension *.ppt)

You'll import several Microsoft Office files.

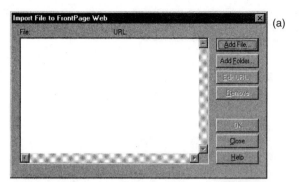
(a)

(b)

3. Locate and open the Wales-Ireland Manuscript folder on your CD-ROM drive, and choose Microsoft Office Files in the Files of Type combo box. Click to select day1.doc. To select additional files in the same folder, press Ctrl and click to select additional discontiguous files (see Figure 6.2a) or press Shift and click to select additional contiguous files. Press Ctrl and click to select day2.doc, day3.doc, day4.doc, day5.doc, and tourinfo.xls.

4. Click Open. The Add File to Import List dialog closes and the selected files are added to the list in the Import File to FrontPageWeb dialog (see Figure 6.2b). In the next step, you'll add two folders to the import list.

5. Click Add Folder. In the Browse for Folder dialog, locate and click the Sounds and Video folder (see Figure 6.3a). Click OK to close the dialog and add the contents of the folder to the list (see Figure 6.3b). Scroll the horizontal scroll bar to observe the two columns of the import list. The first column, labeled File displays the name and location of the file in your computer's file system. The second column, labeled URL, is the name and location (the relative URL) that the file will have after you import the file into the current web.

You can select one or more files from a folder (a) and click Open to add the files to the import list (b).

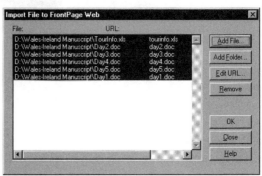

Use the Browse for Folder dialog to locate the folder (a) and click OK to add the contents of the folder to the import list (b).

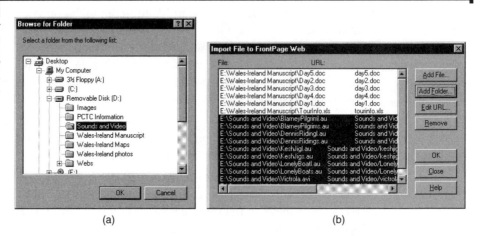

(a)   (b)

6. Repeat Step 5 to add the Images folder and its contents to the list.

You use the buttons on the Add File to FrontPage Web dialog to work with the files on the list:

Add File   Add one or more files from any folder in your computer's file system by clicking the Add File button and repeating Step 2.

Add Folder   You can add a folder to the import list. When you add a folder, you add all the files and subfolders (and all the files in the subfolders) to the import list. The Explorer creates the folder and subfolders when you import the files.

Edit URL   You can edit the name and location that the file will have after importing by selecting the file and clicking the Edit URL button. Change the file path in the Edit URL dialog (see Figure 6.4). When you change the URL, you are changing the name and location of the imported copy and the original file is not affected. You can change the name of the imported copy or you can store an imported file in a different folder in the current web. If you change the location to a folder that does not exist, the FrontPage Explorer automatically creates the folder when you import the file.

PART

II

Managing the Web

FIGURE 6.4

You can change the name and location of a file to be imported to the current web.

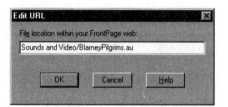

Remove   You can remove a file or a selection of files from the import list by selecting the files and clicking the Remove button.

OK   Click the OK button to import the entire list of files. While the import process is taking place, the OK button changes to a Stop button. As each selected file is imported to the current Web, the file is removed from the list. You can click the Stop button to interrupt the process and prevent the import of the remaining files. Clicking the Stop button does not reverse the process for files that have already been imported. (You'll have to delete these files if you change your mind; see the "Deleting a File or Folder" section.) If the web contains another file with the same name and location as the file you are importing, the Explorer offers to replace the existing file (see Figure 6.5). If you click No, the file is not imported, and remains on the import list.

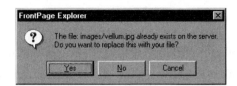

Close You can close the dialog without importing the files by clicking the Close button. FrontPage keeps track of files that you have added to the list, and displays these files the next time you display the Add File to Web dialog.

The import list for the Wales-Ireland web includes both a long and a short version for each of the sound clips (the long version has an *l* before the dot extension and the short version has an *s* before the dot extension). You'll delete the long version for now to keep the size of the practice web small. You'll also modify the names of the sound files.

1. Scroll to the files in the Sounds and Video folder. Press Ctrl and click to select the long versions of the four sound files. Click Remove to remove the selected files from the list.

2. Click the sound file named BlarneyPilgrim.au, and click the Edit URL button. In the Edit URL dialog (see Figure 6.4), change the filename to BlarneyPilgrim.au and click OK.

3. Click OK to start the import process. The Explorer displays the message in Figure 6.5 because the vellum.jpg file is already in the web. Click No. When the import process is finished, click vellum.jpg in the import list and then click Remove.

4. Click Close to close the dialog. Figure 6.6 shows the web with the imported Sounds and Videos folder and imported files.

NOTE

The four sound file in the Sounds and Video folder are from the Ain't Whistlin' Dixie Internet music album by David Walker (http://mothra.nts.uci.edu/~dhwalker/dixie/).

You can import files with any file format. When you import a file, it retains its original file format. If the original file contains embedded objects such as embedded images, the imported file contains the same embedded objects. For example, when you import a Word document (*.doc) that has embedded images, sounds, and video clips, the imported document contains the embedded objects.

FIGURE 6.6

The Wales-Ireland web after importing files and the Sounds and Video folder

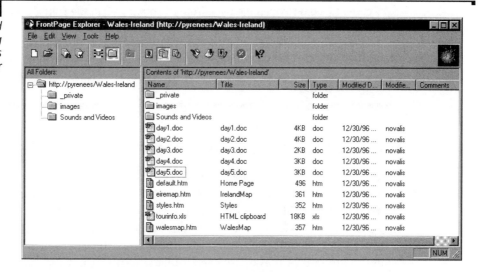

**NOTE**

You can import a file that you want to make available for downloading from your web, such as a .zip or .exe file. To make the file available to Web visitors, create a hyperlink to the file on a web page. When the visitor clicks the hyperlink in a browser, the Web browser offers to download the file.

Importing a Web Page

You can also import a web page (.htm or .html files) from another web in your computer's file system. However, when you import a page that displays objects such as images, or video clips, only the page is imported. A key difference between a Word document and an HTML page is that the Word document can contain other files as embedded files but an HTML page can contain only links to other files and does not contain the objects themselves. The imported page will have broken links to the image files. To repair the broken links to the images, you can import the image files separately and then repair the links, as explained in Chapter 7: Managing Links.

A more efficient solution for bringing a page from another FrontPage web into the current web is to open the page from the other web in the Editor. Choose File ➤ Save As from the Editor menu bar to save the page to the current web. The Editor offers to save the page's linked images and video clips to the current web. If you save the linked objects to the current web, the links are not broken. However, links to other pages are broken, including links to a styles page and pages that are merged using Include bots.

Importing Files from the Internet

You can use the File ➤ Import command from the Explorer menu bar to import only files that are stored in your computer's file system. You cannot use this command to import files directly from the World Wide Web or a private intranet to the current web. However, you can import files directly to a web folder by using the browser's commands to save copies of files from the Internet. You can use this method to import files to any web folder whether or not the web is open in the FrontPage Explorer.

For example, if you are using the Microsoft Internet Explorer 3.0, you can import an image file as follows:

1. Right-click the image you want to copy and choose the Save Picture as command in the browser's shortcut menu (see Figure 6.7).

2. Locate the web folder, or a subfolder in the web folder, in the Save As dialog (see Figure 6.8), and click Save to import a copy of the file to specified folder.

3. If you saved the file to the web folder of the web currently open in the FrontPage Explorer, choose View ➤ Refresh from the FrontPage Explorer menu bar, or press F5, to update the current web.

You can use the same technique to import the target of a hyperlink. Right-click the image or text hyperlink, choose the Save Target As command in the browser's short-cut menu (see Figure 6.7), locate the web folder in the Save As dialog, and click Save to save the target page or file to the web folder.

Before you use the files that you've saved from a World Wide Web site, make sure you have permission to use them. Check the site for permission and copyright information, and contact the site's webmaster if you have any doubts.

FIGURE 6.7

You can use the browser's commands to import a copy of an image file or a copy of the target of a hyperlink directly to a web folder.

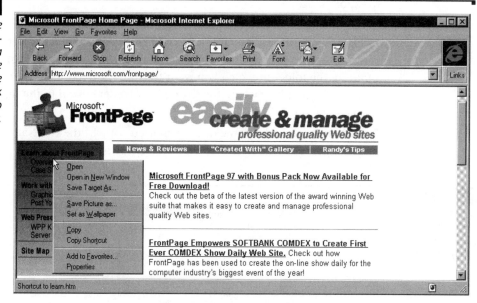

FIGURE 6.8

Use the Save As dialog to locate the web folder in your computer's file system.

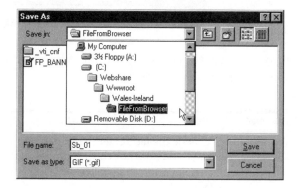

Exporting a File from a Web

You can export a file from the current web to any folder in your computer's file system that you have access to. When you export a file, the FrontPage Explorer exports a copy of the file to the folder that you specify. The original file remains in the current web. You can export only one file at a time.

To export a file:

1. Select the file in any view of the Explorer and choose File ➤ Export from the Explorer menu bar. You use the Export Selected As dialog to specify where you want to store the exported copy (see Figure 6.9). Use the Look In combo list to locate the folder in which you want to store the exported file. You can create a new subfolder by clicking the Create New Folder button to the right of the Save in combo box.

2. You can change the name of the exported copy in the File Name text box and select the file's type in the Save as type combo list.

You can export a copy of a web file to any folder in your computer's file system.

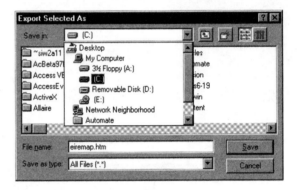

If you export a web page, only the .htm file is exported. If the page has inserted images, the image files are not exported.

NOTE

You should not change the file's extension. Changing the extension and exporting the file with a new extension does not convert the file to the new format. When you try to open the exported file using the application associated with the new extension, the results are unpredictable.

Opening a File from the Explorer

To open a file in the FrontPage Explorer, select the file in any view of the Explorer and do one of the following:

• Choose Edit ➤ Open from the Explorer menu bar

- Press Ctrl+O
- Double-click the file
- Right-click the file and choose Open from the shortcut menu.

What happens next depends on the file type, as indicated by the file's extension. If the file is a web page (.htm), the file is displayed in a window in the FrontPage Editor. An HTML file is the only type of file that you can open directly in the Editor. To open a file of any other type, you have to use another application called a *helper application.* The helper application can be a *player* (or *viewer*) such as the Microsoft Word Viewer that lets you view but not change the file, or an *editor,* such as Microsoft Word, that lets you both view and change the file.

TIP

The easiest way to open a file in the FrontPage Explorer is to double-click the file's icon in the pane on the right of either View.

Associating a File Type with an Editor

The FrontPage Explorer automatically associates players and editors with several file types. You can view the default associations by choosing Tools ➤ Options from the Explorer menu bar and then clicking the Configure Editors tab in the Options dialog (see Figure 6.10). The Configure Editors dialog lists the following editors:

- FrontPage Editor is the editor for opening .htm and html files. The FrontPage Editor is also the default editor for opening .htx files and .asp files. An .htx file is a web page that displays the results of a database query when you use the Internet Database Connector. An .asp file is the page generated by a web server using active server technology.

- FrontPage Frames Wizard is the editor for opening .frm files. A .frm file is the special type of file that FrontPage uses when you create a web page with frames (see Chapter 15: Understanding Frames).

- FrontPage Database Connection Wizard is the editor for opening .idc database query files. An .idc file is the type of file that FrontPage uses when you create a database query using the Internet Database Connector.

- Image Composer is the editor for opening .gif and .jpg image files.

- Notepad is the editor for .txt files.

FIGURE 6.10

The default associations between file types and editors used by the FrontPage Explorer

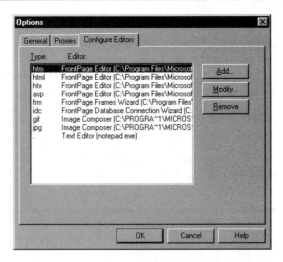

You can use the Configure Editors tab to add new associations that the FrontPage Explorer uses to open files. You can also modify or remove existing associations.

Adding a New Association

To add a new association:

1. Click the Add button. The Explorer displays the Add Editor Association dialog. Figure 6.11a shows the dialog for associating bitmap files (.bmp) with the Windows Paintbrush application.

2. Enter the filename extension in the File Type text box. For example, some QuickTime movie files have .mov extension. If you have installed QuickTime for Windows on your computer, you can associate the Movie Player with .mov files. Type **mov** in the File Type text box.

3. Enter the name of the application in the Editor Name text box and the path to the application in the Command text box. For example, type **Movie Player** as the name. Click the Browse button and locate the QuickTime Movie Player. By default, the Movie Player application is named play32.exe (for the Windows 95 32 bit version), and installs with the path C:\Windows\play32.exe. Select the application and click OK.

3. Click OK. The Add Editor Association dialog closes and the new association is added to the list in the Configure Editors dialog (see Figure 6.11b).

Changing an Association

To change the helper application for a file type, select the association you want to change in the Configure Editors tab of the Options dialog and click the Modify button. You can change the Editor Name and the path to the application in the Modify Editor Association dialog (see Figure 6.11c). You can't change the file type. If you do need to change the file type, you have to remove the association and create a new association for the new file type.

FIGURE 6.11

After you add a new association between a file type and an editor (a), the Configure Editors list displays the addition (b). You can change the editor name and location for the association (c).

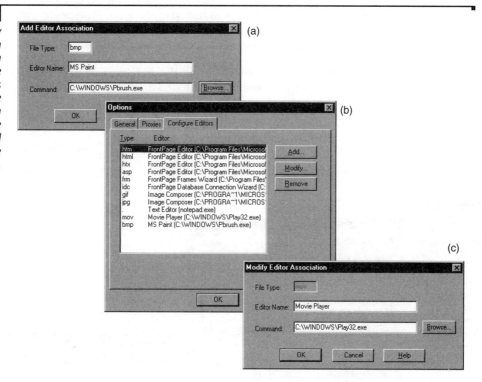

Removing an Association

To remove an association, select the association you want to remove and click the Remove button in the Configure Editors dialog.

Opening a File without a FrontPage Association

When you use the FrontPage Explorer's Open command to open a file with an extension not in the list in the Configure Editors tab, the Windows operating system starts up the editor it associates with the file extension.

NOTE

To view the editors that Windows associates with file types on your computer, start the Windows Explorer and choose View ➤ Options in the Windows menu bar. Click the File Types tab in the Options dialog to display the list of file types and associated editors (see Figure 6.12a).

You can also open a file using an editor that you select from a list of the editors in the Configure Editors tab. To select an editor, select the file in any pane of the FrontPage Explorer and do one of the following:

• Choose Edit ➤ Open With from the Explorer menu bar.

• Right-click the file and choose Open With from the shortcut menu.

Choose an editor from the Open With Editor dialog (see Figure 6.12b).

FIGURE 6.12

Use the Windows Options dialog to view the editors that your computer associates with file types (a). Use the Explorer's Open With command to specify the editor for opening the selected file (b).

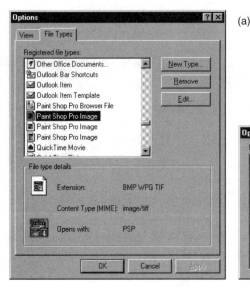

(a)

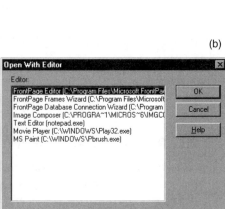

(b)

NOTE

The FrontPage Explorer uses the list of editors in the Configure Editors tab to open files while you are working in FrontPage. When you view a web in a browser, the browser has its own list of helper applications it uses to view file types.

Making a File Available to a Browser

Once a file is in the current FrontPage web, you can make the file available to Web visitors in at least one of the following three ways:

- You can display the file as part of a web page if the file is one of the file types that the FrontPage Editor is able to display.

- You can create a link from a web page to a file with any file type. When the visitor browses to a page with a link having a target that is not a web page or a .gif or .jpg image file, what happens after the link is activated depends on the visitor's browser and the additional software programs that are installed on the visitor's computer. The browser may be able to display or play the file itself, or may call on other software programs.

- You can display the file in the browser's main window if the file is an ActiveX document and the visitor's browser can display ActiveX Documents. For example, Microsoft Internet Explorer 3.0 can display a Word document, an Excel spreadsheet or a PowerPoint presentation directly in the browser's window as ActiveX documents. The FrontPage Editor is unable to display ActiveX Documents. (See the "ActiveX Documents" section in this chapter, and Chapter 20 for more information.)

The next sections provide more information about the three ways to make a file available to a web visitor.

The FrontPage File Types

When you create a web page in the FrontPage Editor, you are creating a file in the HTML file format. This is the only file type that FrontPage can create itself. All other types of files, including text, images, sounds, animation, video, and virtual reality must be created in other applications and then brought into your FrontPage web. In

PART

II

Managing the Web

addition to displaying HTML files, the FrontPage Editor can display image files with the GIF or JPG formats and video clip files with the AVI format in windows embedded into the web page. (The Editor displays the first frame of an AVI video clip as a place holder for the video clip.) The FrontPage Editor cannot display other types of files, such as Word documents, QuickTime movies, or bitmap image files; however, the FrontPage Editor can convert many other file types to one of the file types it is able to display. The FrontPage Editor can convert many text file types to HTML and many image file types to GIF or JPG. (The Editor is not able to convert any other video file types to the AVI format.)

Converting text file types to FrontPage .htm files   If the file has one of the popular text file types, including .doc, .xls, .txt, .rtf, and .htm file types, you can use the FrontPage Editor to convert the file to FrontPage HTML and either open the converted file as a new web page or insert the converted file into an existing web page. See Chapter 10 for more information on opening new pages from files and inserting files into existing pages.

Converting image file types to GIF or JPEG   If the file is an image file with any of the popular image formats, you can use the FrontPage Editor to convert the image file to either the GIF or JPEG format and display the converted image file within an existing web page. The FrontPage Editor can automatically convert image files with the following formats: GIF, JPEG, BMP, TIFF, MAC, MSP, PCD, RAS, WPG, EPS, PCX, and WMF. To display an image with another format, you'll need a helper application. See Chapter 13 for more information on image file formats.

If the file has one of the file types that the FrontPage Editor cannot convert to HTML, GIF, or JPEG, you won't be able to view the file in the Editor's window because the Editor isn't capable of displaying or playing them. Instead, you can create a link to the file.

- When you follow the link in the FrontPage Editor, the FrontPage Explorer starts the helper application specified in the Options dialogs in the FrontPage Explorer and in Windows. Normally, the helper application displays or plays the file in its own window.

- When a web visitor follows the link in a browser, it is the visitor's browser that controls which helper application is used to play the file, as well as the kinds of files that the user is able to view or hear.

NOTE

The FrontPage Editor can display the four file formats: HTML, GIF, JPEG, and AVI.

Helper Applications and Add-Ins

All Web browsers recognize the HTML file format. In addition, most browsers are capable of handling a limited number of file types, such as the GIF and JPG image file formats for displaying the images that are inserted in a web page. The list of file types that a browser can recognize and handle by itself without calling on another application is expanding rapidly as the major browser vendors compete with one another for the most capable browser.

When a visitor wants to view or play a file type that the browser doesn't recognize, the browser calls on another program to open the file. There are fundamentally two kinds of programs: helper applications and add-ins.

A *helper application* is a software program that your browser starts up as a separate application in its own window. When a web contains a link to a file that your browser can't open itself, you can direct the browser to open the file with a helper application. After the browser downloads the file to your computer, the browser starts up the helper application appropriate to the file type. The helper application decompresses the file and uses its own application window to display the text or image file or to play the sound, animation, video, or virtual reality file. After viewing the file, you close the helper application and return to the browser. Most helper applications are freeware or shareware that you can download and install on your hard disk. When you install a helper application for a browser, the browser may automatically recognize the helper application or you may have to manually instruct the browser when to use the helper application. As an example, to specify helper applications in Microsoft Internet Explorer 3.0, choose View ➤ Options from the Internet Explorer menu bar to display the Options dialog, click the Programs tab, and click the File Types button (see Figure 6.13a) to display the File Types dialog (see Figure 6.13b). To specify the helper application in the Netscape Navigator 3.0, choose Options ➤ General Preferences from the Navigator menu bar and click the Helpers tab to display the file types and helper applications (see Figure 6.14).

FIGURE 6.13

Click the File Types button in the Options dialog of the Internet Explorer 3.0 (a) to view the browser's associations between helper applications and file types (b).

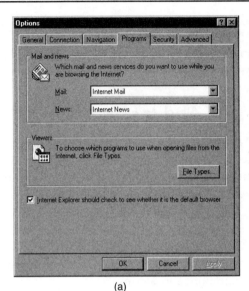

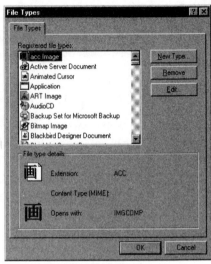

(a) (b)

FIGURE 6.14

Click the Helpers tab in the Preferences dialog of the Netscape Navigator 3.0 to view the browser's associations.

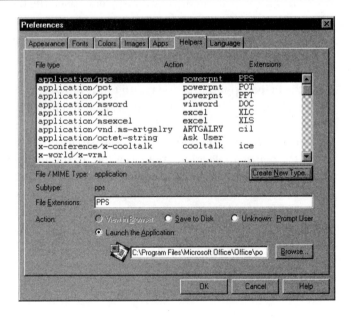

An *add-in* is a software program that is installed on the same computer as the browser and functions as an extension to the browser by adding capabilities that the browser itself doesn't have. A browser that is expanded with a set of add-ins can handle almost any file type without starting up a separate helper application. An add-in works in one of the following three ways:

- The add-in may appear to be embedded in the web page. An embedded add-in may be visible as a small rectangular window that is integrated into the web page in the same way that an embedded image is displayed. Other embedded add-ins may be visible as a push button or a familiar text box, combo box, radio buttons, or check box.

- The add-in may appear in a separate window. In some cases, the add-in may take over the current browser window.

- The add-in may be hidden without any visible elements. A hidden add-in runs in the background.

After the add-in is installed on your hard disk, the browser uses the add-in's capabilities just like another built-in browser feature. Each add-in provides a special capability, such as playing a sound or video clip or responding to a mouse click. The web page developer inserts links to add-ins in a web page. When you visit a page with a link to an add-in and you are using a web browser that supports the add-in, the browser runs the add-in program. There are two kinds of add-ins: plug-ins and ActiveX controls.

Plug-ins   Netscape pioneered the development of plug-ins as the way to bring the web to life with animation, sound, video, and interactivity. An assortment of plug-ins is included in the Netscape Navigator 3.0 browser. In addition, Netscape Navigator plug-ins developed by third parties are available for downloading from the World Wide Web. Examples of Netscape Navigator plug-ins include Macromedia Shockwave, which plays sound and animation files with a .dcr or .dir extension, and Real Audio, which plays sound files with the .ra extension. A new feature of the Microsoft Internet Explorer 3.0 is the ability to run Netscape Navigator plug-ins.

ActiveX Controls   ActiveX controls are part of the ActiveX technology that Microsoft has introduced for adding activity not only to web pages but to any application that supports ActiveX Controls. The Microsoft Internet Explorer 3.0 provides a set of ActiveX Controls. You can also download or purchase ActiveX controls and install them yourself. However, the Internet Explorer 3.0 browser has the remarkable ability to install ActiveX Controls automatically when you browse to a page that requires an ActiveX Control that is not already installed on your computer. A new ActiveX plug-in allows the Netscape Navigator 3.0 browser to run ActiveX controls. (See Chapter 20 for more information on ActiveX Controls.)

PART

II

Managing the Web

NOTE

A browser can have only one helper application, plug-in, or ActiveX control assigned to a file type. Normally, the last software program installed is the one the browser uses.

MIME Types

The protocol that browsers and servers use to communicate information about file types is called MIME, which stands for Multipurpose Internet Mail Extensions. MIME is a general method for indicating file types for any file that is transmitted on the Internet. When a browser requests a file from a server, the server retrieves the file from its file system. The server looks up the file's extension in the list of file extensions that it recognizes, and notes the MIME type that corresponds to the extension. The server sends the file's MIME type back to the browser along with the file. The browser receives the MIME type along with the retrieved file. The browser then uses its own list of MIME types and helper applications. Based on the MIME type, the browser either handles the file itself, opens the specified helper application if there is one, or asks the user what application to use.

MIME types have two parts. The first part is the general category for the file, such as text, image, audio, video, or application. The second part is the specific format, such as htm, gif, au, or mov. The two parts are separated by a slash; examples of typical MIME types are text/html, image/gif, audio/wav, video/avi, and application/postscript. Standard MIME types are the types that are registered with an organization called the Internet Assigned Numbers Authority (IANA). Types that have not been registered must have an x- preceding the specific format; examples of unregistered MIME types are audio/x-wav for sound files with the wav extension, and image/x-MS-bmp for Windows Paintbrush files.

ActiveX Documents

ActiveX Documents are another part of Microsoft's ActiveX technology for enhancing the Internet. ActiveX Documents are files that can be opened directly in either the Microsoft Internet Explorer 3.0 or the Netscape navigator (with the ActiveX plug-in installed). These browsers display ActiveX Documents in their native formats without conversion to the HTML format. ActiveX Documents are created in applications that adhere to the ActiveX standards such as Microsoft Word, Microsoft Excel, and

Microsoft PowerPoint. These documents can be embedded in a web page or opened in the full browser window. The browser's computer must have either the document's parent application, such as Microsoft Word, or the document's viewer application, such as Microsoft Word Viewer, installed. If the parent application is installed, the browser displays the application itself inside the browser window. Web visitors can use the editing tools of the parent application to edit the document and save the changed document as a file on their computer's file system (the original document stored on the web server is not altered). If a viewer is installed, the browser loads the viewer, and the viewer displays the ActiveX Document. Web visitors using a viewer cannot edit the document.

Working with Folders and Files in Folder View

You work with web folders and files in the FrontPage Explorer's Folder View using many of the same file management operations available in the Windows Explorer. Some file management operations are also available in Hyperlink View (see Chapter 7) and in the FrontPage Editor (see Chapter 10).

Creating a New Folder

When you create a new web, the FrontPage Explorer automatically creates folders for organizing the web's files. At a minimum, the Explorer creates an images folder for storing image files, and the _private folder for storing files you do not want to make available to web visitors. You can create additional folders and subfolders.

To create a new folder, do the following:

1. Switch to the Explorer's Folder View by clicking the Folder View button in the toolbar or by choosing View ➤ Folder View from the menu bar.

2. In the All Folders pane, click the folder in which you want to store the new folder, and choose File ➤ New ➤ Folder from the Explorer menu bar. The Explorer creates a new folder named New_Folder, and displays the new folder icon at the bottom of the Contents pane. The folder's name is in edit mode, so you can rename the folder.

3. Type the name for the new folder and press Enter. The Explorer displays a message that the folder is being renamed.

For practice, you'll add three folders to the Wales-Ireland web.

1. Click the web folder in the All Folders pane and choose File ➤ New ➤ Folder from the Explorer menu bar to create the new folder. Type **Manuscript** and press Enter. Figure 6.15 shows the message displayed as the Explorer renames the folder.

FIGURE 6.15

*The message dis-
played as the
Explorer renames a
folder*

2. Click the images folder in the All Folders pane and choose File ➤ New ➤ Folder from the Explorer menu bar to create the new subfolder. Type **Backgrounds** and press Enter.

3. Choose File ➤ New ➤ Folder from the Explorer menu bar to create another sub-folder for the images folder. Type **Logos** and press Enter. The plus sign to the left of the images folder in the All Folders pane indicates the presence of a subfolder (see Figure 6.16).

FIGURE 6.16

*You can create new
folders and subfold-
ers for organizing
content files.*

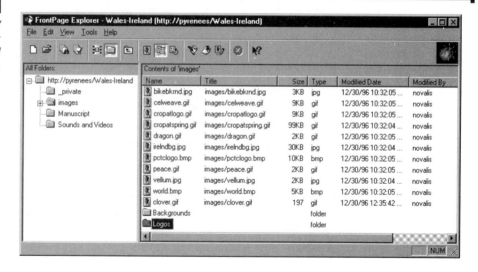

Selecting Files and Folders

To select one or more files in Folder View, open the folder that contains the files you want to select, and click the filename or file icon in the Contents pane. The filename and icon of the selected file are displayed in reversed video. To select additional files, press Ctrl and click to select each noncontiguous file, or press Shift and click a second file to add the second file and all files between the first and second files to the selection.

You can select only one folder at a time in the All Folders pane. However, you can select one or more folders in the Contents pane. You can also add both files and folders to a selection in the Contents pane by pressing Ctrl or Shift as you click additional files and folders.

You can also use the rectangle technique to select a group of files and folders. Click in the Contents pane and press either mouse button as you drag to create a selection rectangle. When you release the mouse button, all files and folders in the rectangle are selected.

NOTE

You can select files from only one folder at a time. If you try to add files from a second folder, the FrontPage Explorer forgets the selection you made in the first folder.

Changing the Name of a File or Folder

A file has both a name and a title. The Web server uses the name together with the path from the web folder to the file (the file's relative URL) to uniquely identify the file. Each file in a web must have a unique relative URL. The Title column of the Contents pane displays a file's title (by default, the title shown in the Title column is the same as the file's relative URL). You can change the name of a file or a folder in the FrontPage Explorer.

To rename a file or folder:

1. Select the file or folder in the Explorer's Folder View. Choose Edit ➤ Rename from the Explorer menu bar or click in the highlighted name. The Explorer changes to edit mode and you can change the file or folder name by typing in the name edit box.

2. Edit the name and press Enter. The Explorer displays the Rename message (for example, see Figure 6.15 earlier in the chapter) and changes the name.

NOTE

In general, you cannot change the file's title in the FrontPage Explorer. As an exception, you can change the title of an image file. See the "Understanding File Properties" section later in this chapter.

Moving and Copying a File or Folder

After you select a file or a folder or a group of files and folder you can use the familiar operations to manipulate the selection in Folder View.

You can use the Cut, Copy, and Paste commands in the Edit menu and their keyboard shortcuts. You can paste a selection to another folder in the current web, but you cannot paste the selection to another web.

The easiest way to move and copy a selection is to use the drag-and-drop techniques. To move the selection to another folder, press the left mouse button while you drag the selection to the new folder. When the the folder name is highlighted, release the mouse button. To copy the selection to another folder, press Ctrl before you release the mouse button. You can also use the right mouse button to display a shortcut menu when you drag and drop a selection. To move or copy a selection to another folder, right-click the selection and drag to the new folder. When the folder name is highlighted, release the mouse button to display a shortcut menu. Choose Move Here to move the selection, choose Copy Here to copy the selection, or choose Cancel to cancel the operation.

To explore moving files, you'll move the Word and Excel documents to the Manuscript folder. You'll also move the styles.htm page to the _private folder. The styles.htm page has the background image and text colors that you'll use throughout the web, and is not a page that should be available to web visitors.

1. Click the pointer to the right of the day1.doc file and drag to select the five Word document files. Press Ctrl and click tourinfo.xls to add the Excel file to the selection.

2. Click in the selection, drag to the manuscript folder, and release the mouse button. (You can drag to the folder in the All Folders pane or the Contents pane.) The Explorer displays the Rename dialog for each file as it is moved to the folder (see Figure 6.17).

FIGURE 6.17

When you move a file to another folder in the web, the Explorer automatically updates the file's name and location.

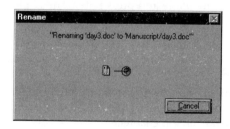

3. Click the styles.htm page, drag to the _private folder, and release the mouse button. The Explorer renames and moves the page.

To create a copy of a file in the same folder, press the left mouse button and press Ctrl as you move the pointer away from the highlighted file. When you release the mouse button, the Explorer creates a copy of the file and appends _copy(n) to the base name of the original file, where n is an integer. For example, if the filename is world.bmp, the first copy is named world_copy(1).bmp, and the second copy is named world_copy(2).bmp, and so on. You can create a copy of a folder and its contents by selecting the folder in the Contents pane and using the same technique. The Explorer creates a copy of the folder and all of its contents. The Explorer names the new folder by appending _copy(n) to the name of the original folder, but does not rename the copied contents.

NOTE

When you move a file to another folder in the current web, you are changing the file's path in the web. If the file you are moving is the target of any links, these links are broken during the move. An important feature of the FrontPage Explorer is the ability to update the file's incoming links automatically. You'll learn how this works in Chapter 7.

Deleting a File or Folder

To delete a selection of files and folders, do the following:

1. Click the file or folder you want to delete. Press Ctrl or Shift as you click additional files or folders in the Contents pane.

2. Press Delete. The Explorer displays a confirmation message.

The confirmation message lists the selected file folders in the Items to delete box (see Figure 6.18) and provides the following choices:

- If you click Yes, the Explorer deletes the first item and displays the confirmation message if there are additional items.

- If you click Yes to All, the Explorer deletes all the items.

- If you click No, the Explorer cancels the deletion of the first item and displays the confirmation message if there are additional items.

- If you click Cancel, the Explorer cancels further deletions. Any files you may have deleted before clicking Cancel remain deleted.

You can delete the first item, all the items, cancel the deletion of the first item, or cancel further deletions.

When you delete a folder, you delete all of its contents.

To illustrate, you'll delete the clover.gif file in the images folder and the Backgrounds and Logos folders.

1. Click the Logos folder in the Contents pane. Press Ctrl and click the Backgrounds folder.

2. Press Delete. Click Yes to All to delete both folders.

3. Click the images folder in the All Folders pane. Click clover.gif and press Delete. Click Yes to delete the file.

Understanding Folder and File Properties

The Explorer keeps track of several properties for each folder and for each file in the web. To view the properties of a folder or file, do any of the following:

- Click the folder or file in either pane of Folder View and choose Edit ➤ Properties from the Explorer menu bar.

- Right-click the folder and choose Properties in the shortcut menu.

- Click the folder and press Alt+Enter.

Folder Properties

The Properties dialog (see Figure 6.19) for a folder has a single tab with the following properties:

Property	Description
Name	The name of the folder
Type	All folders have the folder type

Location	The full address of the folder
Contains	A tally of the number of files and subfolders contained in the folder
Allow scripts or programs to be run	Check this option if the folder cotains programs that you want the server to run

You can change only the last property.

FIGURE 6.19

*The Folder
Properties dialog*

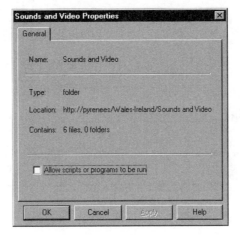

File Properties

The Properties dialog for a file has tabs for displaying General and Summary properties.

General   The General tab (see Figure 6.20a) includes the Name, Title, Type, Size in kilobytes, and the Location. The Location is the file's full address (absolute URL). For most file types, you can't change any of the properties in the General tab. As an exception, if the file is an image file, the Title text box is editable, and you can change the title and the relative path.

Summary   The Summary tab (see Figure 6.20b) displays properties including the date and time that the file was created, the name of the author who created the file, the date and time that the file was last modified, and the name of the author who made the last modification. Each time you save a new or changed file, FrontPage reads the computer's clock to determine the date and time of the save operation. FrontPage knows the author who created the file or made the change because the author has to log in each time the web is opened. You can't change any of these properties. The Summary tab also includes the

PART

II

Managing the Web

Comments property. The Comments property is the only property that you can change in this dialog.

After making a change, click the Apply button to save the changes and leave the dialog open, or click OK to save the changes and close the dialog.

The General tab (a)
and the Summary
tab (b) of the File
Properties dialog

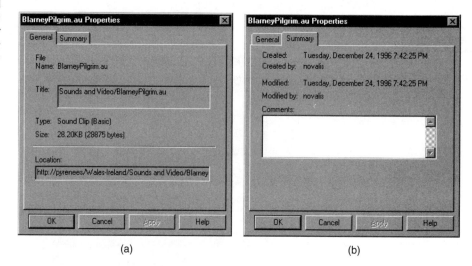

(a)   (b)

Global Editing of a Web

When you create web pages in the FrontPage Editor, the Explorer keeps an index of every word you type in the page. The Explorer uses the text index to provide the ability to spell check the pages in the current web and the ability to find and replace selected text. You can use these features with a selection of pages, or you can apply these features to all the pages in the web.

Spell Checker

To run the spell checker, choose Tools ➤ Spelling from the Explorer menu bar, click the Cross File Spelling button in the toolbar, or press F7. The Spelling dialog (see Figure 6.21a) provides the option to check the spelling of all pages in the web or selected pages. The Selected pages option is available only if you selected a set of pages before opening the Spelling dialog. Click the check box to postpone the corrections and add the pages with misspellings to the To Do List (see Chapter 8 for more information on using the To Do List).

To explore, run the Spell Checker for all the pages in the Wales-Ireland web.

1. Click the Cross File Spelling button in the toolbar. Click the All pages option, click the check box to add the spelling correction to the To Do List, and click Start. The Explorer checks each page in the web and displays a status message (see Figure 6.21b). After checking all the pages, the Explorer adds the task to the To Do List and displays the message shown in Figure 6.21c.

FIGURE 6.21

Use the Cross File Spelling feature to spell check one or more pages (a). The Spell Checker displays a status message (b) and then reports the number of tasks added to the To Do List (c).

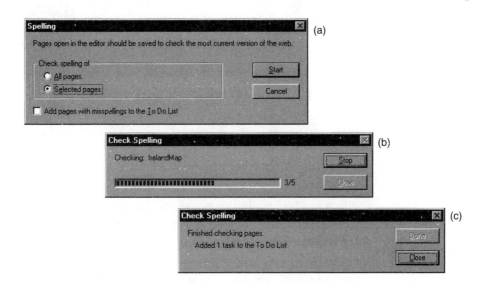

PART

II

Managing the Web

2. Click Close. In the next step, you'll spell check the web again and make the spelling correction.

3. Click the Cross File Spelling button in the toolbar. Click the All pages option and click Start. The Explorer checks the pages and reports the results in the Check Spelling dialog (see Figure 6.22).

In our example, there is only one spelling error on a single page. More generally, there will be errors on several pages. You can choose to correct the errors on every page, postpone the corrections by adding tasks to the To Do List for one or more pages, or you can ignore the errors.

FIGURE 6.22

Use the Check Spelling dialog to display the pages that have words that are not in the dictionary.

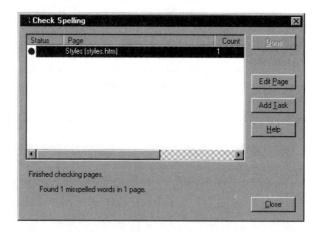

To correct the errors on the styles.htm page:

1. Click Edit Page. The page is displayed in the FrontPage Editor with the first occurrence of the misspelled word highlighted. The Spell Checker has found the image file extension jpg as a "word" that is not in the dictionary. The Spelling dialog displays jpg in the Not in Dictionary text box and a list of suggestions (see Figure 6.23a). (Chapter 11 explains the options available in the Spelling dialog.) You'll add jpg to the dictionary.

2. Click Add. The "word" is added to the Dictionary and the Spell Checker searches for additional occurrences of jpg on the styles.htm page. Click OK in the Finished checking documents dialog (see Figure 6.23b) to close the dialog and the page. Click Close to close the Check Spelling dialog.

Find and Replace

To find a specified text phrase in selected pages or in all pages of the current web, choose Tools ➤ Find in the Explorer menu bar, click the Cross File Find button in the toolbar, or press Ctrl+F. Type the text phrase you want to find in the Find What text box. You can click the options to match the entire phrase and to match the case. You can choose to search in all pages or in the selected pages. Figure 6.24a shows the Find dialog with options to search all the pages in the Wales-Ireland web for the word Wales, matching the case. After you click OK to start the search, the Explorer searches the pages and displays the Find occurrences dialog, reporting two matches on the

Home Page and one match on the Styles page (see Figure 6.24b). You can view the occurrences of the phrase by selecting a page in the list and clicking Edit Page.

FIGURE 6.23

The Spelling dialog displays the options for each item that is not in the dictionary (a) After checking the selected page, the Spell Checker displays this message (b).

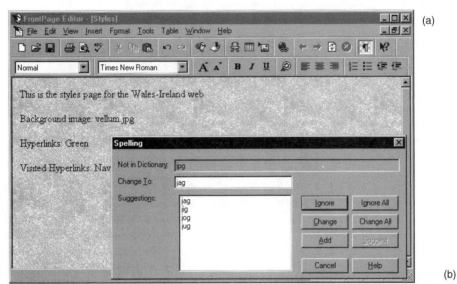
(a)

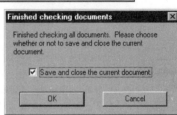
(b)

To find a specified text phrase and replace it with another text phrase, choose Tools ➤ Replace in the Explorer menu bar, or press Ctrl+H. Type the text phrase you want to find in the Find What text box, and type the replacement phrase in the Replace with text box in the Replace in FrontPage Web dialog (see Figure 6.24c). You can click the options to match the entire phrase and to match the case. You can choose to search in all pages or in the selected pages. Figure 6.24c shows the Replace dialog with options to search all the pages in the Wales-Ireland web for the word style matching the case and the whole word and replacing it with Style.

PART

II

Managing the Web

FIGURE 6.24

Use the Cross File Find feature to search the selected pages for a text phrase (a). The Find occurrences dialog displays the pages that have the text phrase (b). Use the Cross File Find and Replace feature to replace a text phrase with another text phrase in selected pages (c).

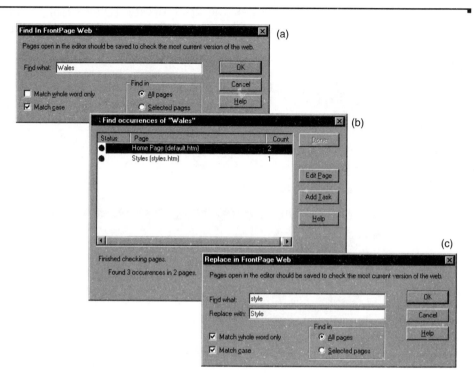

NOTE

The Spell Checker and Find and Replace features work only with the pages (HTML files) in the web and do not work with other text files you have imported, such as Word documents or Excel spreadsheets. These features search only the words you have typed directly on a web page and do not search in a page's name or title, or in pages you have inserted using Include bots.

For More...

In this chapter, you've learned how to add content to a web by importing files. You learned how to associate editors with file types, so that the Explorer can start up the appropriate editor for viewing or playing a file, and how to work with folders and files, including creating new folders, and moving, copying, and deleting files and folders. You've seen that the Explorer provides the ability to spell check, find specified text, and replace specified text in all the pages (HTML) of the web in a selection of pages.

These chapters provide more information about working with the web's content:

- Chapter 10: Editor Basics describes how to open a text file as a page, including the conversion to the HTML format.

- Chapter 11: Working with Text and Lines shows you how to add text information to a page, including how to use the spell checker and the find and replace features for a single page.

- Chapter 13: Using Images and Video Clips describes the image formats that the FrontPage Editor can display, and how to insert image files in a page.

PART

II

Managing the Web

Chapter

7

Managing Links

FEATURING

Managing Links

Links are the keys to the success of the Internet. The idea is really so simple—a *link* is an instruction to a Web browser to retrieve a file. The instruction is inserted in a web file, which then becomes the *start* of the link. The file to be retrieved is the *target* of the link. Links are also called hyperlinks.

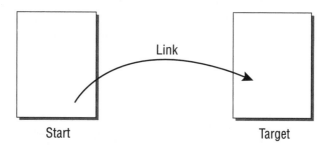

Start   Target

In this chapter, you'll learn about the different ways to characterize and categorize links. Understanding the characteristics of a link helps you to understand why links break, how to avoid link breakage, and how to repair broken links. A link is broken when the the target no longer exists. A web is complete as long as none of its links are broken.

Managing links in a web means performing the checks and maintenance activities to make sure that all the targets exist. You won't be learning much about creating links in this chapter. You learn how to create links in Chapter 12: Understanding Text Hyperlinks and in Chapter 13: Using Images and Video Clips. Instead, in this chapter, you'll learn how to use the FrontPage Explorer to automate much of the labor required to manage the links in a web.

NOTE

To work through the examples in this chapter, you need to replace the Wales-Ireland web you may have saved to your computer in the previous chapters with a modified version of the web on the book's CD-ROM. Open your Wales-Ireland web and choose File ➤ Delete FrontPage Web from the Explorer menu bar to delete the web. Then choose File ➤ Import and use the Import Web Wizard to create a new web named Wales-Ireland and to import all the files from the web named Wales-Ireland-final on the book's CD-ROM.

Link Taxonomy

You can characterize a link according to whether it starts or ends on a file, whether its target file is in the same web as the start, and whether the Web visitor needs to take some action other than browsing to the file in order to activate the link. This section describes each way to categorize links.

Outgoing and Incoming Links

A link has a direction—it begins at the start location and ends at the target location. A file can be the start of some links, which are called the file's *outgoing links*, and the target of other links, which are called the file's *incoming links*.

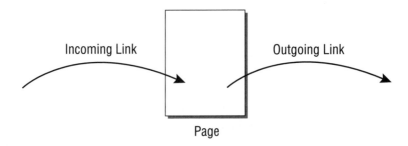

Internal and External Links

The target of a link can be another file in the same web as the start file, and can even be another location in the start file. Links that start and end on files in the same web are called *internal links*. Links that start in a web and have targets outside the web are called *external links*. Figure 7.1 depicts internal and external links. External links can have targets of different kinds. The figure shows examples of targets that are pages in other webs, applications such as an e-mail program, and ActiveX Controls.

FIGURE 7.1

Links with targets in the same web as the start file are internal links and links with targets outside the web are external links.

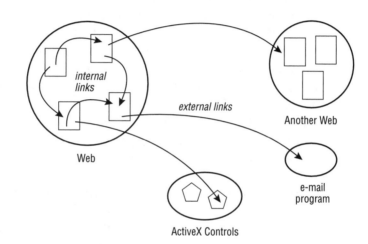

PART

II

Managing the Web

Explicit and Implicit Links

A link can be characterized according to how the link is activated. A link is *activated* when the browser is given the instruction to retrieve the target. If the Web visitor must do something to activate the link (something other than browsing to the page), we'll call the link extrinsic. Otherwise, if the mere act of browsing to the page is all that is needed to activate the link, we'll call the link implicit.

   Explicit and implicit links are often called clickable and nonclickable links, respectively, because the Web visitor activates most explicit links by clicking a text phrase or an image, whereas the Web visitor does not click anything to activate an implicit link. The terms clickable and nonclickable are no longer accurate categories because web programming has enriched the visitor's interactions with the browser. When a page is enhanced with scripts, visitor actions other than clicking can activate the link, such as moving the pointer over an image or pressing a key. As Web programming continues to give more control over the Web environment to the Web developer, some of the distinctions that are useful now will become blurred, and possibly inaccurate.

Explicit Links

In FrontPage, you work with two basic varieties of explicit links: text hyperlinks and image hyperlinks. Text hyperlinks start at a text phrase in a page. The browser indicates a text hyperlink by underlining the link text, and displaying the link text and underlining in a different color than the default text on the page (see Chapter 12 for information on creating text hyperlinks). Image hyperlinks start in an image displayed in a page. Either the entire image or a specific part can be used as the start of the link (see Chapter 13 for information on creating image hyperlinks). The target of a hyperlink can be any of the following:

Another Web page If the target is the name of another Web page, activating the link replaces the start page with the target page. The browser displays the beginning of the target page.

A specified location in another Web page If the target is the name of a location, called a bookmark, in another Web page, activating the link replaces the start page with the target page with the bookmarked location at the top of the browser window.

An ActiveX Document or a specified location in an ActiveX Document The Microsoft Internet Explorer 3.0 is able to display a Microsoft Word, Excel, or PowerPoint document in its native format in the browser using ActiveX technology (see Chapter 20 for more information). These applications allow you to bookmark locations. These documents can both start and target files for text hyperlinks.

A file with another format If the target is a file in a format such as an image file, sound clip, or video clip, the browser may display the file itself or call on a helper application or an add-in to display the file.

An application If the target is an application, such as a mail program or a file transfer program, activating the link starts the application.

Implicit Links

Implicit links are usually created when you "insert" some kind of object in a Web page. When you insert an object such as an image, an AVI video clip, or an object called an ActiveX Control, the FrontPage Editor creates an implicit link to the file. After insertion, the FrontPage Editor and a Web browser normally display some visual representation of the inserted object, although many inserted objects have no visual representation. For example, inserting an image file displays the image in a small window inside the page, but inserting a background sound displays nothing. Most ActiveX Controls have a visual representation, such as the text box, that is displayed when you insert a text box ActiveX Control, however, there are other ActiveX Controls that have no visual representation.

You create an implicit link to another Web page when you use a FrontPage Include bot to insert a Web page and merge the inserted page into the original page. You also create implicit links to a Web page when you allow that page to lend its styles (background image and text colors) to other pages.

An implicit link is activated when the Web visitor browses to the page. Automatically, the Web browser begins to retrieve the targets of the implicit links on the page. The browser first checks its own cache to see if the target has been retrieved recently and then, if necessary, sends a request to the Web server specified in the target address. As target files are retrieved, the browser updates the window display. A background sound file may be played, and images, AVI videos, and ActiveX Controls may be displayed one after another until all the targets have been retrieved.

Viewing Links in the FrontPage Explorer

Understanding how the files in your web are linked can be an awesome task—even a small web with a few dozen pages normally has tens or hundreds of links. Links add up fast:

- Every image displayed on a page is the target of a link that starts on the page.
- A page may have dozens of clickable hyperlinks to other locations.
- A well-designed navigation scheme anticipates the preferences of Web visitors as they travel to different places in your web and to other Web sites that have related information. A well-designed web provides many alternative paths to web locations.
- To make navigation as obvious as possible to different visitors, pages often include several image and hyperlinks to the same target.

The FrontPage Explorer helps you to understand how the pages and files of your Web are related. The Explorer's Hyperlink View has two panes to provide different ways to understand links. Figure 7.2 shows Hyperlink View for the Wales-Ireland web (the figure shows a version of the web at the completion of the book). The All Hyperlinks pane on the left provides a hierarchical view of outgoing links for all the files in the web. The Hyperlinks for 'filename' pane gives a graphical view of both incoming and outgoing links for the selected file. Lesson 4 of Chapter 1 showed you how to use Hyperlink View to understand the links in a very simple web. In that lesson, you used Hyperlink View of links you had created yourself. Here, you'll see how to use Hyperlink View to help in understanding the links in a more complex web that you didn't create (yet).

FIGURE 7.2

The left pane of Hyperlinks View gives a hierarchical view of all the outgoing links and the right pane gives a graphical view of both incoming and outgoing links for a file.

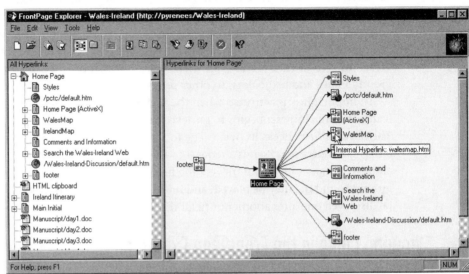

The FrontPage Explorer helps you to make sense of links by providing ways to limit which links are displayed. Figure 7.2 gives the most restricted view of the links for the Home Page: this figure displays no images files (that is, no files that FrontPage recognizes as image files), no repeated links to the same target, and no links to bookmarks in the Home Page. Let's see what Hyperlink View can tell us about the links for this page.

The All Hyperlinks Pane

The All Hyperlinks pane on the left of the Explorer's Hyperlink View is a hierachical list of the links in the web. If a file has outgoing links, a plus sign is displayed to the left of the file's icon. Click the plus sign to display the list of the file's outgoing links. After expanding, the plus sign changes to a minus sign and the file's outgoing links are displayed in an indented list. Hyperlink View uses different icons to represent files. The common file icons are:

- The house icon is used to indicate the web's home page.
- The page icon is used to indicate web pages, sound files, and video files.
- The picture icon is used to indicate image files.
- The world icon is used to indicate a location on the World Wide Web or a private intranet.

- The letter icon is used to represent an e-mail link to the visitor's mail program.
- The page icon with the symbol for Microsoft Word or Excel indicates an ActiveX document

In Figure 7.2, the All Hyperlinks pane lists nine outgoing links for the Home Page, including two external links to locations on the World Wide Web. Neither Internet address includes a protocol such as http:// for another web site, because they are both links to other webs on the same Web server. The other seven links are internal links to other files in the same web. The filenames suggest that the Home Page gets its styles from a Styles page and has a footer section based on a footer page.

You can trace a sequence of links by expanding files with plus signs to show more outgoing links. As an example, click the plus sign to expand the WalesMap page (see Figure 7.3). The WalesMap page is linked to the same Styles and footer pages and has five additional links to the day pages that describe the Wales part of the tour.

PART

II

Managing the Web

FIGURE 7.3

Click a plus sign to the left of a file icon to display the file's outgoing links.

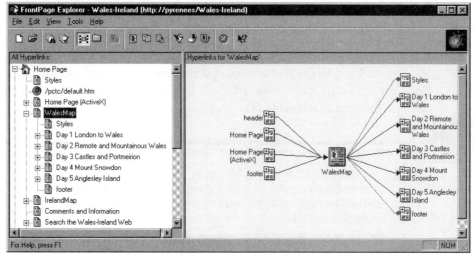

Click the plus sign to expand the Day 1 page (see Figure 7.4) to show its links to the same Styles and footer pages and a link to a header page. The Day 1 page has a link to a sound file, a link to the Day 2 page, and an external link to a Web site.

Expanding links in the All Hyperlinks pane allows you to trace a path of outgoing links starting from any file in the list. However, this pane does not easily reveal the incoming links for a page and does not reveal whether links are explicit or implicit. The pane on the right provides this information.

FIGURE 7.4

You can trace a path in the All Hyperlinks pane by expanding a sequence of files with outgoing links.

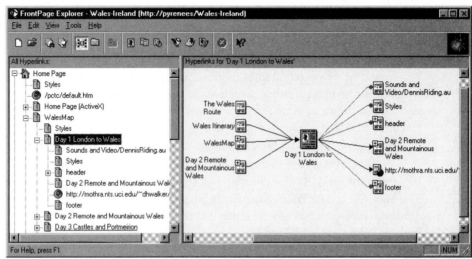

The Hyperlinks for *'filename'* Pane

To view the links for a file, click the filename or the file's icon in the All Hyperlinks pane. The selected filename is highlighted and the Hyperlinks for *'filename'* pane on the right displays the selected file in the center of the pane, the file's outgoing links to the right of center, and the file's incoming links to the left of center.

NOTE

You can view the links for a file displayed in Folder View. Right-click the filename or file icon in the right pane of Folder View and choose Show Hyperlinks from the shortcut menu. The Explorer switches to Hyperlinks view with the selected file centered in the pane on the right.

A clickable hyperlink is shown as a blue line with an arrow at one end. The tip of the arrow points to the link's target. A nonclickable implicit link is shown as a gray line with a solid circle at one end. The circle is at the target end of the link. To get more information about a link, place the pointer over the icon to the left or to the right of center. The link color changes to red, and a link tip provides information about the type of link and the filename of the target. In Figure 7.2, the hyperlink from the Home Page to the WalesMap page has the link tip Internal Hyperlink: walesmap.htm, which indicates that the link is a hyperlink to a file in the current web and that the target is the walesmap.htm page. Other examples of link tips for the Wales-Ireland web are:

- Included Style: _private/styles.htm indicates that the link from the Home Page to the Styles page is an implicit link. In this case, the link is defined when you set a page property so that the Home Page page gets its background image and text colors from the styles.htm page.

- Included Page: _private.footer.htm indicates that the link from the Home Page to the footer page is an implicit link. In this case, the link is defined when you use an Include bot to merge the footer page into the Home Page.

- mailto Hyperlink: mailto:novalis@worldnet.att.net indicates an external hyperlink from the footer page to the mail program on the visitor's computer.

- Embedded Image: images/peace.gif indicates that the link from the Home Page to the peace.gif image file is an implicit link defined when you insert or embed the image file in the page. (Select the Links to Images option to view this link.)

- External Hyperlink: http://mothra.nts.uci.edu/~dhwalker/dixie/ indicates that the link from the Day 1 page to the World Wide Web site is a hyperlink to a location outside the current web.

- Bookmark in: day1.htm indicates an internal hyperlink from one location in the day1.htm page to a bookmark on the same page.

- CLSID Hyperlink: CLSID: *ActiveX identification string* indicates a link from the Home Page (ActiveX) page to an ActiveX control stored on the browser's computer (or automatically downloaded and then stored on the browser's computer).

NOTE

The FrontPage Explorer uses the blue hyperlink line and arrow to represent a link to an ActiveX Control. However, the link is actually an implicit link in the sense that the link is activated automatically when the visitor browses to the page. The ActiveX control is retrieved from the browser's computer and displayed on the page without further action by the visitor.

Figure 7.2 earlier in the chapter shows that the Home Page is the target of only one link, a link from the footer page. The footer page icon appears on both the left and right of the Home Page: the icon on the right represents the implicit link from the Home Page to the footer as merged page and the icon on the left indicates that there is a hyperlink in the footer page that points to the Home Page. Typically, a footer page includes navigation links to all the main pages in a web, including the Home Page. Figure 7.5 shows the Home Page, and identifies the nine links.

PART

II

Managing the Web

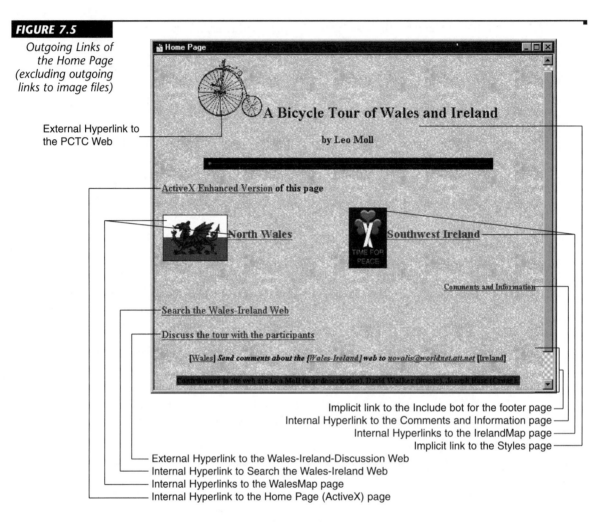

FIGURE 7.5

Outgoing Links of the Home Page (excluding outgoing links to image files)

If a target file to the right of center in the Hyperlinks pane has a plus sign in the upper-left corner of the icon, you can click the plus sign to display the outgoing links to the right of the target file—that is, the targets of the target file. You can then click the plus sign in the icon for one of its target files to display the targets of the selected file. In this manner, you can continue to trace out a sequence of links. Figure 7.6 shows one such sequence of links: the first link starts on the Home Page and ends on the WalesMap page; the second link is hyperlinkto the Day 1 page, a third link is an implicit link to the styles.htm. In a similar way, you can trace a sequence of incoming links by clicking the plus sign of a file icon to the left of the center.

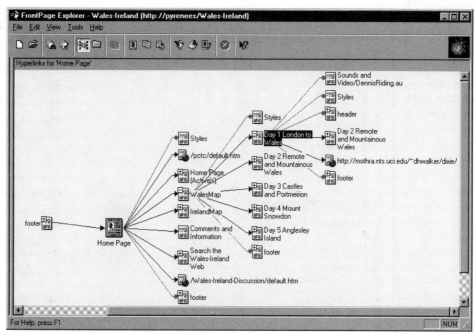

FIGURE 7.6

You can trace a sequence of outgoing links by clicking the plus sign in a target file icon to display its outgoing links.

PART

II

Managing the Web

Adding More Links to the Hyperlink View

The three options for displaying additional links are:

Hyperlinks to Images   Select this option to display links that have targets that are image files. Image files can be the start of clickable image hyperlinks and can be the targets of both clickable hyperlinks and implicit links to inserted images. To select the option, click the Hyperlinks to Images button in the toolbar, or choose View ➤ Hyperlinks to Images from the Explorer menu bar.

Figure 7.7 shows the Hyperlink View for the Home Page with the Hyperlinks To Images option turned on. The figure displays five additional implicit links to the images that are inserted in the page and a link to the background image.

Repeated Hyperlinks   Select this option to display each repeated link as a separate link. *Repeated links* are links that have the same start file and the same target. By default, when a file has more than one link to another file, the link is shown only once. To display repeated links, click the Repeated Hyperlinks button in the toolbar or choose choose View ➤ Repeated Hyperlinks from the Explorer menu bar.

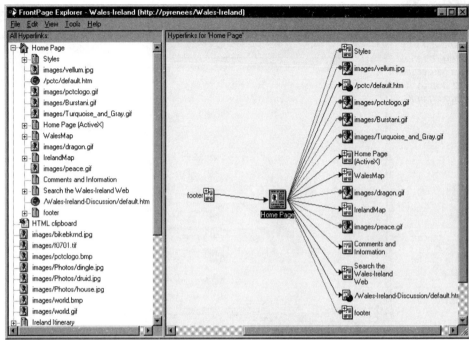

When the Hyperlinks to Images option is turned on, the Hyperlinks pane includes the links that have image files as targets.

Figure 7.8 shows the Home Page with only the Repeated Hyperlinks option turned on. The WalesMap and the IrelandMap pages are each the target of two internal hyperlinks.

Hyperlinks Inside Page   Select this option to display each hyperlink from a start location on a page to a target location on the same page. By default, hyperlinks between locations on a page are not shown. To select this option, click the Hyperlinks Inside Page button in the toolbar, or choose View ➤ Hyperlinks Inside Page from the Explorer menu bar.

Turning the Hyperlinks Inside Page option on has no effect on the display of Hyperlink View for the Home Page because the Home Page has no links that start and end on the page. Figure 7.9 shows the Hyperlink View for the Day 1 London to Wales page. There is an internal hyperlink to the same page. If you turn on the Repeated Hyperlinks option as well, you'll see that this hyperlink is a repeated link and that there are five hyperlinks to bookmarks in the Day 1 London to Wales page.

FIGURE 7.8

When the Repeated Hyperlinks option is turned on, each hyperlink to a location outside the start file is shown as a separate link.

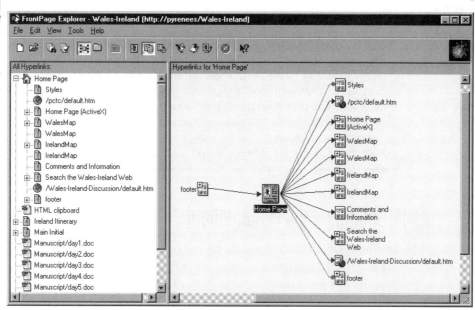

FIGURE 7.9

When the Hyperlinks Inside Page option is turned on, hyperlinks that start and end at bookmarks in the same file are shown.

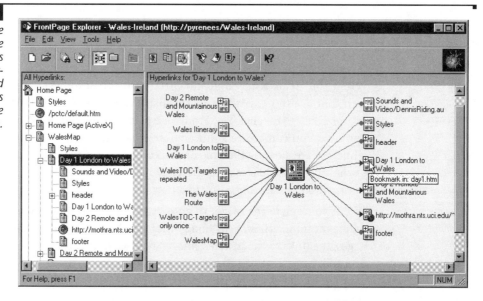

NOTE

The panes of Hyperlink View provide a modest amount of help in trying to understand the links in a web. These views provide little in the way of link analysis, however. Suppose you are interested in knowing whether there is a path of links from one particular page to another. FrontPage provides no easy way to determine the answer to the question "Can I get there from here?" Another feature that would be very helpful would be a printable analysis of a page, including the text hyperlinks and link text, the image hyperlinks and image file, and the targets for all outgoing hyperlinks, implicit links and targets for all outgoing implicit links, and similar information for all incoming links.

Understanding Link Management

One of the main tasks in managing a web is verifying that all the links point to existing targets. If the target of a link doesn't exist, the link is broken. The FrontPage Explorer displays a broken link in both panes of Hyperlink View using the broken page icon. Figure 7.10 shows broken links to the comments.htm page and the Burstani.gif image. The All Hyperlinks pane shows the broken links as broken page icons and the Hyperlinks for 'Home Page' pane show the broken links as broken lines from the Home page to the target files.

How Links Break

Here are some ways to break a link.

- When you create a new link and specify the target to be a page in the current web that doesn't exist, the Editor displays the error message box shown in Figure 7.11. If you click Yes, FrontPage creates a broken link. To avoid the broken link, you can create a link to a new page and either create the new page while you are creating the link, or you can have FrontPage add a new blank page to the web and add a task to the To Do List automatically (see Chapter 12 for information on creating a link to a new page).

- When you delete the target of an existing internal link. For example, if you delete an image file for an image that you had inserted in one or more web pages, the links to the inserted image are broken. If you delete a multimedia file or a web page, links to those files are broken the instant you delete the file. Figure 7.10 shows the result of deleting the two target files.

- When the target file for an existing external link is deleted or the name of the file is changed, the external link is broken.

PART

II

Managing the Web

FIGURE 7.10

Broken links are shown as broken file icons in the All Hyperlinks pane and as broken lines in the Hyperlinks for 'filename' pane.

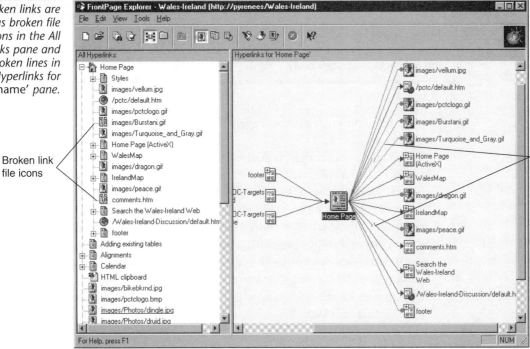

Broken link file icons

Broken link lines

FIGURE 7.11

When you create a new internal hyperlink to a nonexistent file, you create a broken link.

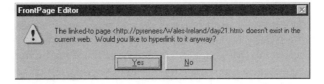

- When you import a web page that has links to other files or images, FrontPage does not prompt you to save any of the links. All of the links are broken, including implicit links to inserted images, sounds, and videos, hyperlinks to other pages and files, and links to included pages and styles pages. However, if the current web has files with the same names and locations as the page's target files, then FrontPage will automatically substitute the files in the current web and eliminate the broken links. For example, if you import a page that has a link to an image file named dragon.gif to a web that also has an image file named dragon.gif, the link is not broken. (The two dragon.gif files may be different images, but if the file name and location in the two webs is identical, the link is not broken.).

NOTE

If the current web has files with the same names and locations as an imported page's target files, then FrontPage will automatically substitute the files in the current web and eliminate the page's broken links.

- When you open a page from another web in the FrontPage Editor and save the page to the current web, FrontPage offers you the opportunity to save the inserted images, sounds and video files to the current web. If you choose not to save the images to the current web, the implicit links to these files are broken. If the current web has files with the same names and locations as the missing target files, FrontPage substitutes the current web's files and automatically repairs the links. If the page has merged pages that were inserted using Include bots, the links to these pages are broken when you save the page to the current web. If the current web has pages with the same name and location as the merged pages, FrontPage substitutes the current web's pages and the links are automatically repaired. However, a link to a styles page is not automatically reset if the current web has a styles page with the same name and location as the styles page in the other Web.

WARNING

If a page that is opened from another web borrows its styles from another page in that web, the link to the styles page requires special handling for the following reason. Even if the current web has a styles page with the same name and location as the styles page in the other web, when you save the page to the current web, the link to the styles page in the current web will not be made. The page will continue to be linked to the styles page in the other web, which causes an error because a page can borrow its styles only from another page in the same web. The error is indicated by a red triangle in the All Hyperlinks view (see Figure 7.12). You can avoid the error by resetting the styles page to the current web. In the Background tab of the Page Properties dialog, click the Specify Background and Colors option and click OK to close the dialog and sever the setting to the styles page in the other web. Reopen the Page Properties dialog, click the Get Background and Colors from Page option, specify the styles page in the current web, and click OK. Save the corrected setting, and the error is eliminated.

Automatic Updating of Internal Links

FrontPage automatically updates links, and prevents and mends broken links in the following cases:

- When you change the name or location of an inserted image, sound, or video file in the current web that is the target of one or more implicit links in the current web, FrontPage renames the file and updates the internal links automatically.

FIGURE 7.12

The red triangle indicates the error that occurs when you save a page to the current web that is linked to a styles page in another web and the link to the styles page doesn't reset to the styles page in the current web with the same name and location.

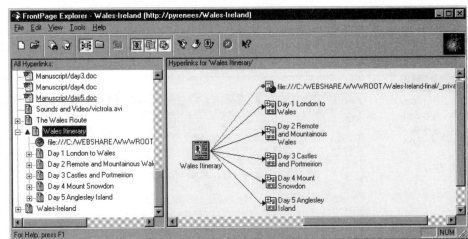

FIGURE 7.13

When you change the name or location of a target of one or more hyperlinks in the current web, FrontPage offers to update the links.

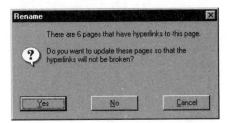

- When you change the name or location of a page or file in the current web that is the target of one or more hyperlinks in the current web, FrontPage displays the message indicating the number of links that have hyperlinks to the page and asking if you want to update the links (see Figure 7.13). Click Yes to have FrontPage update the links automatically. If you click No, you break the links.

- When you add a page, image, or file to the current web that has the same name and location as the target of a broken link, FrontPage automatically updates the broken link using the page, image, or file as the target of the link. For example, if you import a page with broken links to other pages or images, and later import the other pages and images, the links are mended automatically.

Verifying and Repairing Links

Both explicit and implicit links can be broken.

When you view a page with a broken implicit link to an image, the Editor displays the broken implicit link with the broken image icon shown in Figure 7.14.

FIGURE 7.14

The FrontPage Editor shows a broken implicit link as a broken picture icon.

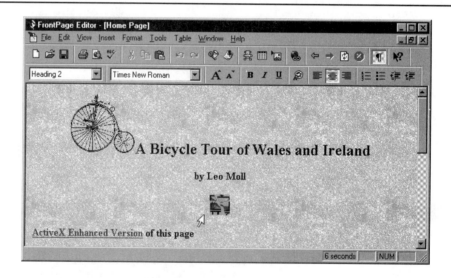

Browsers have their own way to display a broken implicit link; for example, Figures 7.15a and 7.15b show the broken implicit link in the Internet Explorer 3.0 and the Netscape Navigator 3.0.

When a page has a broken explicit link, you don't know about the break until you click the link. If you try to follow a broken hyperlink in the Editor, the Editor displays a similar error message (see Figure 7.16a). In a Web browser, clicking a broken hyperlink causes the error with the error number 404 (see Figure 7.16b).

Verifying Links

It is possible to verify that all internal links have targets by manually expanding all of the pages in the FrontPage Explorer. It is also possible to verify that all external links

FIGURE 7.15

The broken implicit link in the Internet Explorer 3.0 (a) and in the Netscape Navigator (b)

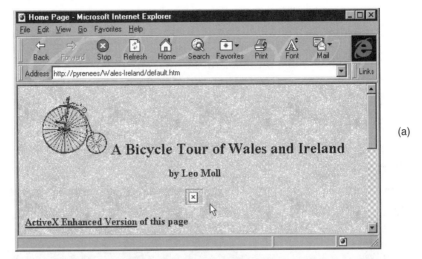

(a)

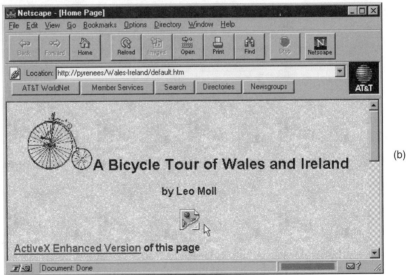

(b)

have targets by trying to follow each external link. While the manual approach is possible, it certainly isn't practical. One of the most useful features of the FrontPage Explorer is that the Explorer automates the process of verifying links. You use theTools ➤ Verify Hyperlinks command in the Explorer menu bar to verify the targets and report broken links. When you execute the Verify Hyperlinks command, the FrontPage Explorer checks all internal links, postpones the check of external links, and displays the Verify Hyperlinks dialog. Figure 7.17 shows the Verify Hyperlinks dialog for the Wales-Ireland web after deleting the comments.htm page and the burstani.gif image file. The first column of the Verify Hyperlinks dialog displays a colored circle and indicates the status of the link. A red circle followed by the word Broken indicates that the link is broken, a yellow circle followed by a question mark indicates that the link is an external link and has not been verified yet, and a green circle followed by OK indicates that the link has a valid target. The second column labeled URL lists the name and location of the target. The third column labeled Linked From indicates the file in the current web that is the start of the link. You can resize the Verify Hyperlinks dialog by dragging a border.

FIGURE 7.16

The error message when you try to follow a broken hyperlink in the FrontPage Editor (a) and in a Web browser (b)

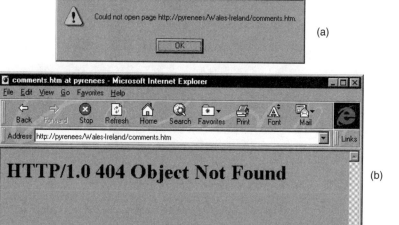

Figure 7.17 displays the two broken hyperlinks to the missing comments.htm page and the two broken implicit links to the missing burstani.gif image file. The figure also lists the thirteen external links with unknown status.

To verify external links, click the Verify button. FrontPage can verify external links only if your network connection is open. If your network connection is closed, FrontPage reports that all external links are broken. If your network connection is open, FrontPage checks the external links and reports each link as either broken if the target URL can't be found or as OK if the target URL can be found. FrontPage uses a green circle to indicate a good link (see Figure 7.18). Verifying external links can take a long time if there are many external links. You can stop the verification by clicking the Stop button (the Verify button changes to a Stop button while FrontPage is checking the external links). If the Web server that stores the target of one of the current web's external links is not turned on, the link will be reported as broken.

PART

II

Managing the Web

FIGURE 7.17

The Verify Hyperlinks dialog lists broken internal links and lists all external links.

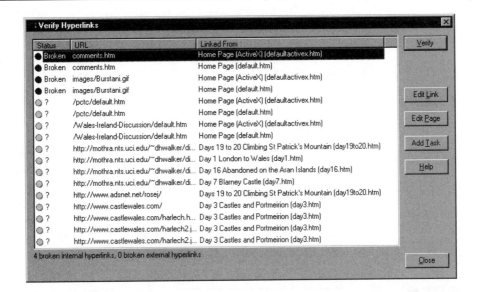

FIGURE 7.18

Click Verify to verify the web's external links. If the target can be located, the link is reported as OK.

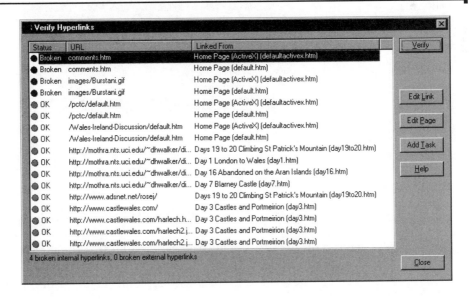

Repairing a Broken Link

When an internal link is broken because you have deleted the target file from the current web, you can repair the broken link in two ways:

- You can add a target file with the same name and location as the deleted file. The added file doesn't have to be the same file as the one you deleted, but it must have the same name and location.

- You can redirect the link to a new target page, image, or file.

If you know the name and address of the new target, you can redirect the link as follows:

1. Select the link you want to edit in the Verify Hyperlinks dialog and then click the Edit Link button in the Verify Hyperlinks dialog.

2. Type the name and location of the new target in the With text box in the Edit Link dialog (see Figure 7.19). In the figure, the links to the burstani.gif image file are redirected to the turquoise_and_gray.gif image file. If you click the Browse button, the Internet Explorer 3.0 opens and directs you to locate the page. If you are creating a link to a page on the World Wide Web, browse to the page. If you are creating a link to a page in your computer's file system, choose File ➤ Open from the browser menu bar and locate the file.

FIGURE 7.19

To redirect links to a missing file, enter the name and location of the new target in the Edit Link dialog.

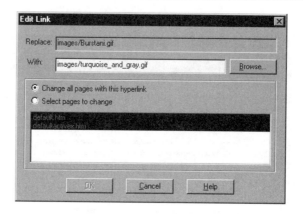

3. You can choose to redirect all of the links to the missing file or redirect only a selection of links. To redirect all links to the missing file to the same new target, choose the option to Change all pages with this link. To redirect only some of the links to the missing file to this target, click the option to Select pages to change. The text box in the lower part of the Edit Link dialog displays a list of

pages with links to the same missing file. Select the links you want to redirect and click OK to redirect the links on the selected pages to the new target.

If you don't know the name and location of the new target, or if you prefer to edit the link directly on the page, select the link you want to edit in the Verify Hyperlinks dialog and then click the Edit Page button. The selected page is displayed in the Editor and you can edit or remove the link using the techniques described in Chapters 12 and 13.

You can also defer repairing the link to another time and add the repair task to the To Do list by selecting the broken link in the Verify Hyperlinks dialog and clicking the Add Task button. After clicking the Add Task button, the status of the broken link changes to To Do list and the task is added to the list (see Figure 7.20). In the figure, the repair of the two links to the comments.htm page have been added to the To Do List.

FIGURE 7.20

You can add the task of repairing a broken link to the To Do List.

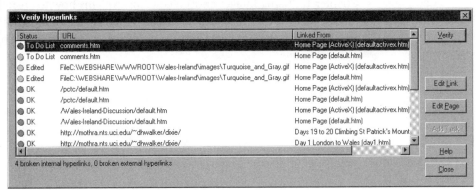

PART

II

Managing the Web

Recalculating Links

Normally, FrontPage updates the FrontPage Explorer automatically when you make changes. However, if there are other authors working on the web at the same time, you won't see their changes until the next time you open the web, unless you happen to open a page after they saved their changes or ask FrontPage to update all views in the Explorer. You request the update of the web by choosing the Tools ➤ Recalculate Links command in the Explorer menu bar. FrontPage updates the entire web by stepping through the links, executing the scripts for the bots you inserted in designing web pages (see Chapter 16 for information on the page design bots), and updating the text index that the server creates to keep track of the text you entered in the pages. When you execute the Recalculate Links command, the Explorer's Status bar displays the message "Updating hyperlinks and text indices...". The process may take a few minutes. You can click the Stop button in the Explorer toolbar to end the process.

For More...

This chapter has explained how to characterize links and how to use the Hyperlink View of the FrontPage Explorer to help you to understand how the files in a web are related with links. The two important link management features of FrontPage are the ability to update internal links automatically when you rename or change the location of a file in the web and the ability to verify both internal and external links and then present a list of links with missing targets.

The following chapters provide more information on links:

- Chapter 12: Understanding Text Hyperlinks shows you how to create text hyperlinks and edit hyperlinks. You'll also learn how to work with hyperlinks, including copying and moving links to new locations.

- Chapter 13: Using Images and Video Clips explains how to create image hyperlinks. You'll learn how to create a single hyperlink for an image and how to create regions in the image and use each region as the start of a hyperlink to a different target.

Chapter

8

Understanding
To Do Lists

FEATURING

Understanding To Do Lists

An important chore in creating a web is keeping track of unfinished tasks. This is especially inportant when there are several authors working on a web. FrontPage provides the To Do List program so that you can easily manage tasks. You can use the To Do List program to add unfinished tasks, assign tasks to authors, assign task priority, and keep a history of completed tasks. The To Do List for a web is available to all web authors, so that everyone working on the web is aware of the status of tasks.

NOTE

To work through the examples in this chapter, you need to replace your Wales-Ireland web with a modified version on the book's CD-ROM. Open the Wales-Ireland web you created in previous chapters and choose File ➤ Delete FrontPage Web from the Explorer menu bar to delete the web. Then choose File ➤ Import and use the Import Web Wizard to create a new web named Wales-Ireland and to import all the files from the web named Wales-Ireland-final on the book's CD-ROM.

Opening and Closing the To Do List

You can open the To Do List from both the FrontPage Explorer and the Editor. To view the To Do List, do one of the following:

- Choose Tools ➤ Show To Do List from either the Explorer or the Editor menu bar. The command in the Explorer menu changes to show the number of unfinished tasks.

- Click the Show To Do List button in the Explorer or Editor menu bar.

The FrontPage To Do List window displays a current list of unfinished tasks (see Figure 8.1a). The list includes the name of the task, the author assigned to complete the task, the priority assigned to the task, the page the task is linked to, if any, and a description of the chore.

When you first open the To Do List, the list is arranged in the order that the task was added. Click any of the column headings to sort the list alphabetically by the information in the heading. For example, to sort the list to determine the chores assigned to a specific author, click the Assigned To heading; to determine the tasks linked to a page, click the Linked To heading. To resize a column, drag the right edge of the column heading. Changes to the sort order and column sizes are not saved when you close the To Do List.

You can resize the window by dragging a window boundary in the usual way, and you can click the Maximize button to maximize the window.

Close the To Do List by clicking the Close button or the window's Close button. If the task is linked to a file, the To Do List window closes automatically when you click the Do Task button. Clicking the Do Task button opens the editor for the file, so you can carry out the task. You can keep the To Do List window open while you carry out the task by clicking the Keep window open check box before clicking the Do Task button.

The To Do List program keeps track of the completed tasks in a separate list. Click the Show history check box to display the Completed column and merge the completed tasks into the list (see Figure 8.1b).

NOTE

When you copy the current web using the File ➤ Publish FrontPage Web command, the To Do List items are copied to the new web. However, when you import a web using the Import Wizard, the To Do List items are not imported to the new web.

FIGURE 8.1

Click a column heading to sort the FrontPage To Do List (a). Click the Show History check box to include the completed tasks in the list (b).

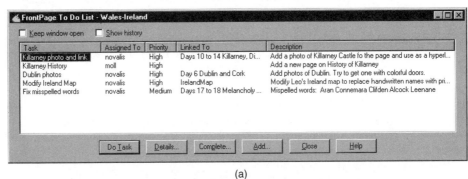

(a)

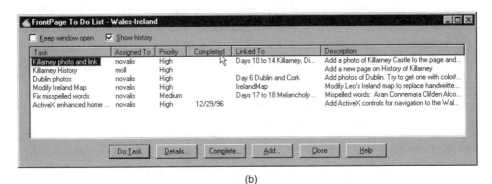

(b)

PART

II

Managing the Web

Adding and Deleting Tasks

Tasks can be linked to a specific file or unlinked.

Adding a Linked Task

To add a new task that is linked to a file, click the file in any pane of the FrontPage Explorer and choose Edit ➤ Add To Do Task from the Explorer menu bar. If the file is a web page, you can also create a new task linked to the page by opening the page in the FrontPage Editor and choosing Edit ➤ Add To Do Task from the Editor menu bar. You specify the linked task in the Add To Do Task dialog (see Figure 8.2a).

To practice adding a linked task, do the following:

1. Click the comments.htm page in the Explorer and choose Edit ➤ Add To Do Task from the Explorer menu bar.

2. Type **Add comment entry form** in the Task Name text box, click Medium as the task priority, assign the task to Cameron, and type **Add a form to collect comments** as the Description.

3. Click OK to add the task and close the dialog.

Adding an Unlinked Task

Sometimes a task is not linked to a specific page. For example, you can add a task to spell check all the pages in the current web.

To add an unlinked task, display the To Do List and click the Add button.

To practice adding an unlinked task, do the following:

1. Click the Show To Do List button in the Explorer toolbar and click the Add button.

2. Type **Spell-check the Web** in the Task Name text box (see Figure 8.2b) and click OK to add the task.

FIGURE 8.2

You can add a task that is linked to a file in the web (a) or a task that is not linked (b).

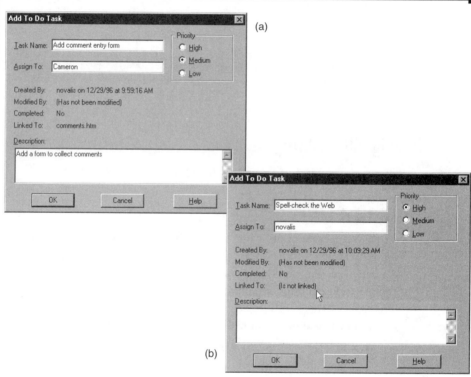

Adding Linked Tasks in the Spell Checker

When you use the Spell Checker in the FrontPage Explorer to spell check one or more pages in the current web, you can postpone the spelling corrections by adding the tasks to the To Do List.

- To add all pages with misspellings, click the check box in the Spelling dialog that is displayed before the spell check takes place (see Figure 8.3a).

- To add a selected page with misspellings, run the spell check, click the page in the Check Spelling list (see Figure 8.3b), and click the Add Task button to add the page to the To Do List.

PART

II

Managing the Web

FIGURE 8.3

When you spell check the pages of a web in the Explorer, you can add all pages with misspellings to the To Do List (a) or add a task for a selected page (b).

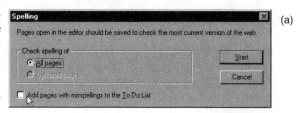

(a)

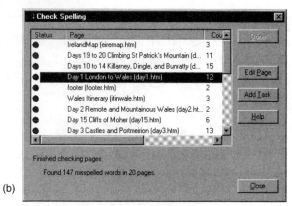

(b)

Adding a Linked Task for a New Hyperlink Target Page

When you create a hyperlink to a page that doesn't exist yet in the current web, the Editor creates the new page automatically. You have the option to edit the new page immediately, or add the new page to the To Do List for editing at a later time (see Figure 8.4).

When you create a hyperlink to a new page, you can add the page's editing to the To Do List.

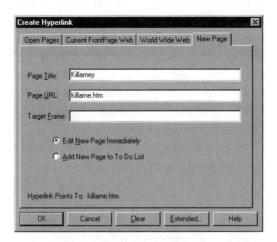

Adding Tasks Using the Corporate Presence Wizard

When you create a new web using the Corporate Presence Wizard, you can use the last dialog to request that the wizard add a set of tasks to the To Do List (see Figure 8.5).

You can ask the Corporate Presence Web Wizard to create a To Do List (a) and the wizard adds some tasks to the list (b).

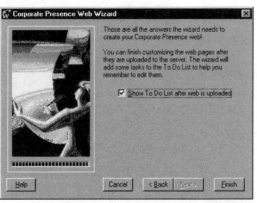

Working with Tasks

After adding a task to the To Do List, you can modify the task, mark it as completed, and remove the task from the list of unfinished tasks or from the list of completed tasks.

Modifying a Task

To modify a task, display the To Do List and click the Details button in the FrontPage To Do List window. Make the changes in the Task Details dialog (see Figure 8.6).

To explore changing a task, do the following:

1. Click the Show To Do List button in the Explorer toolbar, click the Fix misspelled words item, and click the Details button.

2. Assign the task to Cameron and change Misspelled words: to **Add place names to dictionary:** in the Description. Click OK to make the change.

FIGURE 8.6

Use the Task details dialog to modify a task.

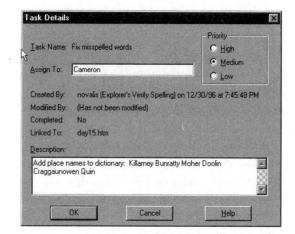

NOTE

You cannot modify the task name or linking for an existing task. To change the task name or the linking, you need to delete the task and create a new task.

Marking a Task as Completed

After completing a task, you can mark the task as completed and store the completed task in the history list. To mark a task as completed, display the To Do List, click the task, and then click the Complete button. The Complete Task dialog (see Figure 8.7) has an option to mark the task as completed and add the completed task to the history list, and another option to delete the task from the To Do List without adding the task to the history list.

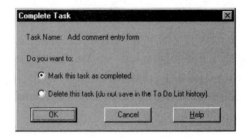

If a task is linked to a file in the current web and the task can be completed using the file's editor, you can start the file's editor by clicking the task in the To Do List and clicking the Do Task button. If the task is not linked, the Do Task button is grayed out and unavailable.

To explore completing a task, do the following:

1. Click the Show To Do List button in the Explorer toolbar, click the option to Keep window open, click the Fix misspelled words item, and click the Do Task button. The FrontPage Editor opens, displays the Day 15 page in the FrontPage Editor, and displays the Spelling dialog (see Figure 8.8).

2. Click the Add button in the Spelling dialog as each place name is displayed to add the name to the dictionary. Click OK when the Editor reports that the spelling check is complete. Close the FrontPage Editor.

3. Click the Complete button in the To Do List window and click OK to mark this task as completed. The completion date is shown in the To Do List.

Viewing a Completed Task

To view a completed task:

1. Display the To Do List and click the Show history check box to display the completed tasks.

2. Click the completed task and then click the Details button. The Task Details dialog shows the completed task (see Figure 8.9). You can change the description of a completed task, but you can't change any other information.

PART

II

Managing the Web

FIGURE 8.8

Completing the task of adding place names to the dictionary

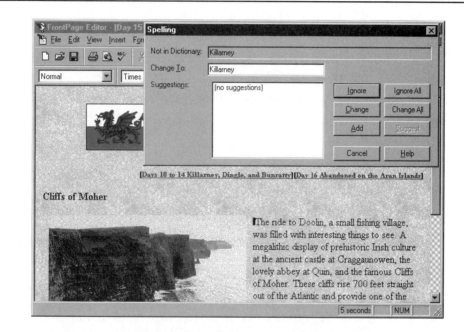

FIGURE 8.9

You can change the description of a completed task.

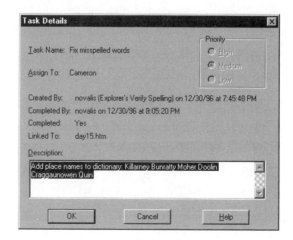

Deleting a Task

To delete an uncompleted task from the To Do List:

1. Display the To Do List, click the task you want to delete, and click the Complete button.

2. Click the option to Delete this task and click OK.

To delete a completed task from the history list:

1. Display the To Do List and click the Show history check box to show the completed tasks.

2. Click the task you want to delete and then click the Remove button. When you click a completed task, the caption of the Complete button changes to Remove. The item is removed from the history list.

Printing the To Do List and the Completed Task History List

FrontPage doesn't provide a command for printing the lists of completed and uncompleted tasks. However, both lists are stored as pages in the current web so you can open the pages in the FrontPage Editor and print them out. The lists are stored in the web's _vti_pvt folder with the page names _x_todo.htm and _x_todoh.htm, respectively.

To practice printing a list:

1. If necessary, click the Show FrontPage Editor button in the Explorer toolbar. Click the Open button in the Editor toolbar. Click the Other Location tab in the Open File dialog and then click the Browse button.

2. Locate the web folder and double-click the _vti_pvt folder (see Figure 8.10a). Double-click the page you want to open (see Figure 8.10b).

3. Choose File ➤ Page Setup from the Editor menu bar to set up the page for printing, and then choose File ➤ Print or press Ctrl+P to print the page.

Figure 8.11 shows portions of the Active To Do List of uncompleted tasks and To Do List History. The columns provide the following information for each task:

Heading	Description
Number	The number order of the item
Task	The name of the task

Priority	The priority assigned to the task
Author	The name of the author who created the task
Created By Tool	The tool used, if any. Examples of tools are Explorer's Verify Spelling and Verify Hyperlinks.
Created On, Modified On	The date and time the task was created or modified
Completed	Y if the task was completed and N otherwise
Modified By	The name of the author who modified the task
Assigned To	The name of the person the task is assigned to
Link To	The filename of the page the task is linked to, if any
Magic	The URL of the link's target file
Description	The description of the task

FIGURE 8.10

The web's _vti_pvt folder (a) stores pages for the To Do List and the History list (b).

(a)

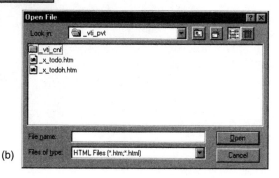

(b)

FIGURE 8.11

You can print the To Do List (_x_todo.htm) (a) and the To Do List History (_x_todoh.htm) (b).

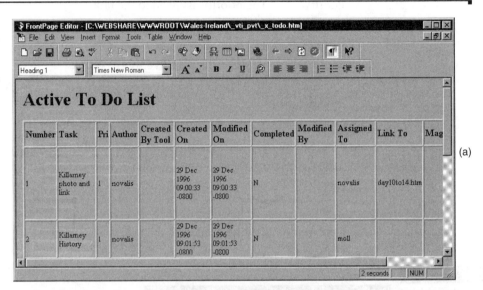

(a)

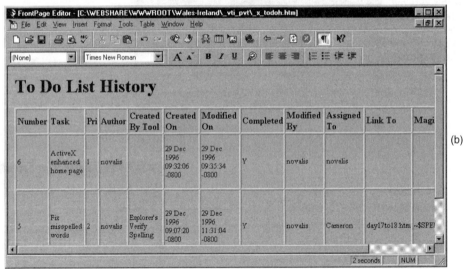

(b)

For More...

In this chapter, you've learned how to add tasks to the To Do List in the Explorer and the Editor.

The following chapters show you examples of adding tasks to the list perform other web creation tasks:

- Chapter 6: Working with Files shows you how to add items to the To Do List when you spell check a web.

- Chapter 12: Understanding Text Hyperlinks shows you how to add target page editing to the list when you create a hyperlink to a new page.

PART

II

Managing the Web

Chapter

9

Administering a Web

Administering a Web

One of the most important tasks in administering a web is managing security—that is, controlling who can view and make changes to the web. There are basically two aspects to managing security: controlling access to the Web server itself and controlling the content of an individual web.

Access to the Web Server

Access to the Web server is handled by the computer's operating system. When a Web server is run from the UNIX operating system or from the Windows NT operating system, security is a critical issue because these operating systems allow users on other computers to log on to the computer that houses the Web server. With the Web server accessible to other computers on the Internet, system administrators and Web administrators must take precautions against unauthorized outsiders entering their systems. The security features provided by these operating systems are complex. Running a Web server from the Windows 95 operating system is less of a security risk because Windows 95 doesn't permit you to log on from another computer over the Internet. The Windows 95 operating system is, therefore, ideal for running a Web server for a small public or educational web site. However, Windows 95 doesn't have many of the networking and security features that make UNIX or Windows NT the preferred choice for running a Web server for any private intranet and for any Web site that handles sensitive information.

Controlling Web Content

Controlling the content of a Web means making sure that its published web content correctly reflects the intent of the organization, is inoffensive, and does not violate copyright laws. In a private intranet, controlling Web content means that authors are restricted to authoring their own web and cannot make changes in someone else's web. In one sense, controlling content means controlling who has the right to modify web content files. However, there is a second aspect to content control. In both the World Wide Web and private intranets, controlling content also means controlling who can view pages in a Web browser. For example, a company with a World Wide Web site may wish to restrict an online discussion web to its customers. The same company may also have a private intranet and use controlled departmental webs as a principal means of communication among co-workers in departments. Each department may have a private web for its own use and one or more nonprivate webs for publishing information to others in the company.

Each Web server has its own techniques for controlling access to webs. In this chapter, you'll learn the access control features of the FrontPage Personal Web Server. You'll learn how to authorize individuals to use a web and assign each user one of three access levels. You'll also learn how to password-protect a web. The access control provided by the FrontPage Personal Web Server is easy to learn and to set up. In learning how to control access with the FrontPage Personal Web Server, you become familiar with some of the fundamental concepts involved in the more complicated and more powerful control systems offered by Web servers such as the Microsoft Personal Web Server.

WARNING

When you use the access control feature of the FrontPage Personal Web Server, you must also be sure that you have used the security features of your operating system to restrict access rights to the web folder. See online Help for Windows 95 or Windows NT for more information.

NOTE

To work through the examples in this chapter, you must have the FrontPage Personal Web Server installed on your computer (see Appendix A for installing the server on port 8080) and a web named Wales-Ireland stored by this server. If necessary, create the web as follows: In the FrontPage Explorer, close the current web, choose File ➤ Import and use the Import Web Wizard to create a new web named Wales-Ireland on the FrontPage Personal Web Server and to import all the files from the web named Wales-Ireland-Ch5Ch6 in the Webs folder on the book's CD-ROM. (See Chapter 5: Explorer Basics for more information.)

Controlling Access in the FrontPage Personal Web Server

The fundamental concepts of controlling access to Webs stored in the FrontPage Personal Web Server are:

- Permissions to use a web are granted to individuals and to computers.

- Permissions are set for a web as an entity and not for individual pages or folders in a Web.

- Access is controlled by *user authentication*—users must prove that they are allowed to enter a web by typing a name and password in an authentication dialog.

Permission Levels

There are three levels of permissions, also called access rights, that you can assign: end-user, author, and administrator permissions.

End-User Access Rights   End-user access rights include permission to browse the public pages of a web in a Web browser. End-users cannot view the web in the FrontPage Explorer.

Author Access Rights   Author access rights include permission to make changes to a web using FrontPage as well as all end-user permissions to browse the public pages of the web in a Web browser. Author access rights include permission to create and modify pages, import and export files, create and delete folders, verify links, and recalculate links. Authors can change their own passwords, configure editors, and register a proxy server for the local network.

Administrator Access Rights   Administrator access rights include permission to give others permission to use a web, as well as all author permissions to make changes using FrontPage, and all end-user permissions to browse the public pages of the web in a Web browser. Administrator access rights also include permission to create new webs, import webs, delete existing webs, and publish a web to the FrontPage Personal Web Server.

Setting Administrative Access Rights to the Web Server

When you installed the FrontPage Personal Web Server, one of the dialogs requested that you enter a name and a password (see Figure 9.1). In providing the information, you were defining yourself as the Webmaster for the entire Web site; you were giving yourself full permissions as the administrator of the FrontPage Personal Web Server.

FIGURE 9.1

When you install the FrontPage Personal Web Server, you define an administrator for the entire Web site.

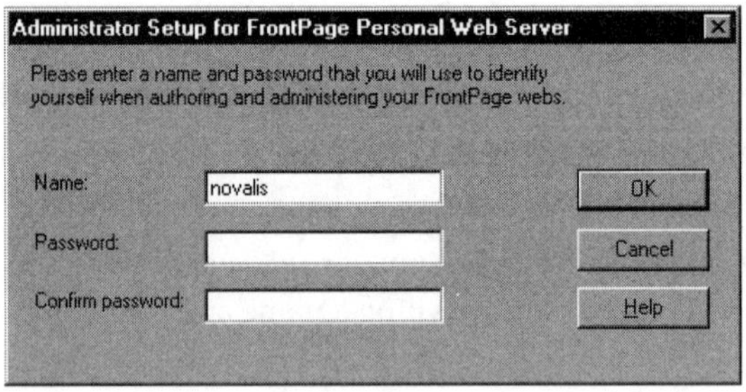

You can use the FrontPage Server Administrator to change your administrator password, define additional administrators for the entire Web server, and define administrators for individual webs stored by the server. Start the FrontPage Server Administrator as follows:

1. Click the Start button on the Windows 95 taskbar, choose Programs ➤ Microsoft FrontPage ➤ FrontPage Server Administrator. The FrontPage Server Administrator dialog lists the ports on your computer that currently have FrontPage Server Extensions installed (see Figure 9.2). If you followed the installation procedures described in Appendix A, you have installed the Microsoft Personal Web Server on port 80 (the default port for Web servers) and the FrontPage Personal Web Server on port 8080. (See Appendix A for more information on the features of the FrontPage Server Administrator.)

2. Click 8080 in the Select port number list box and then click the Security button. The Administrator name and password dialog displays <RootWeb> as the Web

server's default web and the name you entered during installation (see Figure 9.3a). The Password field is blank. To change your password, type the new password in the Password text box, retype the same password in the Confirm password, and click OK.

FIGURE 9.2

Use the FrontPage Server Administrator to define administrators for the entire Web site or for an individual Web.

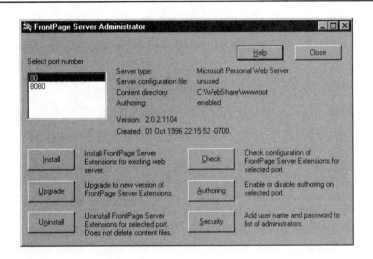

Adding a Web Administrator

You can use the Administrator name and password dialog to define new administrators for the server's root web or for an individual web stored by the Web server. Type the name of the web in the Web name text box. To define a new administrator for the Web server, type <Root Web>, and to define a new administrator for a web stored by the server, type the name of the web. You must type the name exactly, as there is no combo list of the webs stored by the server. Type the name and password for the new administrator and then confirm the password by retyping in the Confirm password text box. When you click OK, you authorize a new administrator for the specified web and limit access for this web to anyone who knows the name and password you've entered. An authorized administrator has the complete set of permissions as an author and as an end-user of the web, so an authorized administrator for a web is also an authorized author and an authorized end-user for the web.

For practice, let's add an administrator for the Wales-Ireland Web.

1. In the Administrator name and password dialog, type **Wales-Ireland** as the web name, type **cameron** as the name and **surfsup** as the password. Retype the password and click OK. The server confirms the new administrator (see Figure 9.3b).

FIGURE 9.3

Use the Administrator name and password dialog to add a new administrator for a web or change an administrator's password (a). The message displayed after you add an administrator for a web (b).

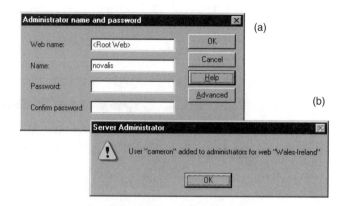

Controlling Access by Computer   You can also control access by limiting the computer that the person is using. Click the Advanced button in the Administrator name and password dialog to display the Internet address restriction dialog (see Figure 9.4). By default, the Internet address (IP number) is *.*.*.* and, because each asterisk represents any integer from 1 to 255, the administrator can access the web from any IP address. Type the Internet address (the IP number) you want to use for the restriction. You can use an asterisk as a wild card for any of the four integer parts of the IP address. For example, you can provide access for a web to the group of computers that have IP addresses beginning with 130.255.124.*

NOTE

The Name and Password you type in the Administrator name and password text boxes are case-sensitive.

Understanding the FrontPage Authentication Process

When you start the FrontPage Explorer and attempt to open the root web or an individual web stored by the FrontPage Personal Web Server, the server runs the FrontPage authentication process. The first step in the authentication process is the display of the authentication dialog (see Figure 9.5). When you click OK, the server checks the name and password you entered against the lists of authorized administrators and authors, and determines the access rights you have.

FIGURE 9.4

You can restrict the administrator's access to a specified Internet address.

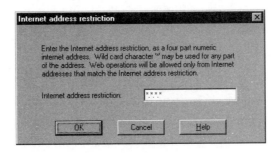

FIGURE 9.5

The FrontPage Explorer displays the FrontPage authentication dialog when you attempt to open the server's root web.

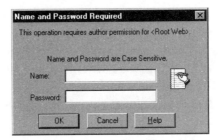

If you enter a name and password of an authorized administrator or author for the web, the web opens; otherwise, the authentication dialog is displayed again and the web does not open. The FrontPage Explorer keeps track of the permission level it used when it opened the web. After the FrontPage Explorer opens a web with the specified access rights, if you close and reopen the same web while the FrontPage Explorer is running, the Explorer reopens the web with the same access rights without redisplaying the authentication dialog. When you shut down the FrontPage Explorer, all permissions granted during the session are discarded.

For practice with these concepts, do the following:

1. Start the FrontPage Explorer, choose File ➤ Open FrontPage Web, choose the FrontPage Personal Web Server, and click the List Webs button. Click OK to initiate opening the root web. Type **cameron** and **surfsup** in the author authentication dialog and click OK. The authentication process fails because this name-password pair has no permissions for the root web. Click Cancel.

2. Click the Open FrontPage Web button in the toolbar, click List Webs in the Open FrontPage Web dialog, choose Wales-Ireland, and click OK. Type **cameron** and

surfsup in the authentication dialog and click OK. (The process of entering a name and password and being authenticated to enter is called *logging on*.) The Wales-Ireland web opens because this name-password pair has administrator permissions for the Wales-Ireland web.

3. Choose File ➤ Close FrontPage Web from the Explorer menu bar. Repeat Step 2 to initiate opening the Wales-Ireland web. An authentication dialog is not displayed and the Wales-Ireland web opens with administrator access rights.

4. Click the Open FrontPage Web button in the toolbar, click List Webs in the Open FrontPage Web dialog, choose any other individual web stored by the server, and click OK. Type **cameron** and **surfsup** in the authentication dialog and click OK. The authentication process fails because this name-password has no permissions for any web except the Wales-Ireland web.

5. Click the Open FrontPage Web button in the toolbar, click List Webs in the Open FrontPage Web dialog, choose the root web, and click OK. Type your server administrator name and password in the authentication dialog and click OK. The server notes that you have entered the root web with administrator permissions and opens the root web. You can now open any web stored by the server without the server displaying the authentication dialog.

NOTE

Once you open the root web with administrator permissions, you have unlimited access as an administrator to all the webs stored by the server.

Authorizing Access to the Root Web

Once you have opened the root web as an administrator, you can change your password and set permissions for other users of the root web.

Changing Your Password

Choose Tools ➤ Change Password from the Explorer menu bar to display the Change Password for *name* dialog (see Figure 9.6). The name you used to open the web is listed in the title bar. Type the old password and the new password, and then confirm the new password and click OK.

FIGURE 9.6

After logging on to a web in the FrontPage Explorer, you can change your password.

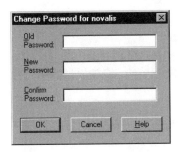

Viewing and Changing Access Rights

You can create new administrators, authors, and end-users for the root web. To view and change access permissions for the root web, choose Tools ➤ Permissions from the Explorer menu bar. The Permissions dialog has two tabs: Users and Computers.

Authorizing Users   The Users tab (see Figure 9.7a) lists the names and access rights of all those authorized to use the current web, and has the following features:

Add   Click the Add button to display the Add Users dialog (see Figure 9.7b). Enter the name and password for the new user and click an option to assign rights to browse the current web (end-user access rights); to author and browse the current web (author access rights); or to administer, author, and browse the current web (administrator access rights).

Edit   Select a user from the list and click the Edit button to display the Edit Users dialog (see Figure 9.7c). Click an option to change the access rights of the selected user.

Remove   Select a user from the list and click the Remove button to remove the user from the list. No confirmation message is displayed.

Browse access   Click the first option, Everyone has browse access, to grant end-user access to everyone who browses to the web. Click the second option, Only registered users have browse access, to restrict browse access only to entries in the permission list. When you click the second option, the web is called *protected*, or *password protected*. (see Chapter 18 for information on allowing web visitors to self-register in a web).

After making changes in the Users tab, click the Apply button to save the changes and leave the Permissions dialog open, click OK to save the changes and close the dialog, or click Cancel to close the dialog without saving any changes.

The Users tab lists the authorized users for the current web and indicates whether the web is password-protected (a). You can authorize new users (b) and change the access rights of an existing user (c).

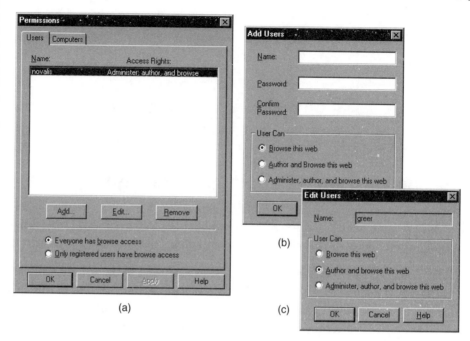

(a) (b) (c)

NOTE

If you publish your webs to the World Wide Web, one security strategy is the permissive strategy that allows everyone to have browse access to the root web and then control access to individual webs stored by the server. Another is the restrictive strategy in which you give no access to the root web and only controlled access to individual webs.

Authorizing Computers   The Computers tab is used to define restrictions in addition to the restrictions you defined in the Users tab. The Computers tab (see Figure 9.8a) lists the Internet addresses and access rights for all the computers authorized to use the current web. By default, all IP addresses, listed as *.*.*.*, have full access, and the authorized users in the Users tab can access the web from any computer.

You restrict access by computer as follows:

> **Add**   Click the Add button to display the Add Computer dialog (see Figure 9.8b) to specify access rights to a computer or a group of computers. Type the IP address of the group of computers and click an option to specify the access rights.

Edit   Select an IP address and click the Edit button to display the Edit Computer dialog (see Figure 9.8c) to change the access rights of the computers with the selected IP address.

Remove   Select an IP address and click the Remove button to remove access rights for the selected IP address.

An authorized administrator for a web who is using a computer with browse access rights can only browse the web.

FIGURE 9.8

The Computers tab lists the access rights assigned to computers by IP address (a). You can add a new computer and assign permissions (b), and you can modify permissions assigned to an existing computer (c).

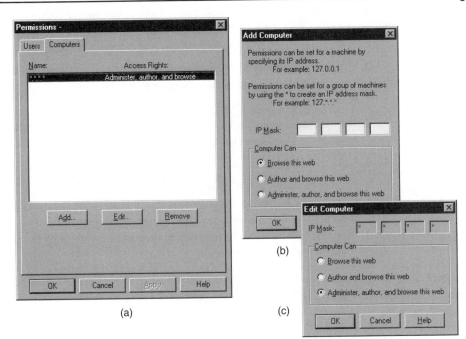

(a)

(b)

(c)

Authorizing Access to an Individual Web

If you have administrator access rights to one of the individual webs stored in the root web, also called a *subweb*, you can change your password and control access to the web by opening the web in the FrontPage Explorer and using procedures similar to those described in the previous section for the root web. There is one important difference: the Permissions dialog has an additional tab, the Settings tab that you use to specify whether the sub-web has the same permissions that have been set for the root web, or has its own set of permissions (see Figure 9.9a).

PART

II

Managing the Web

Setting Unique Permissions for a Subweb

If you choose the first option, Use same permissions as root web, the Users and Computers tabs are unavailable because the users and computers authorized to use the current web are the same as those authorized to use the root web. If you choose the second option, Use unique permissions for this web, you can use the Users and Computers tabs to add users and computers and change or remove access rights for the subweb as described in the "Viewing and Changing Access Rights" section.

To practice this, let's set permissions for the Wales-Ireland web:

1. Open the Wales-Ireland web and log on to the web as cameron, with surfsup as the password. Choose Tools ➤ Permissions, and click the option to use unique permissions for the Wales-Ireland web. Click the Users tab.

2. Click the Add button. Type **greer** as the name, and **gnarly** as the password. Retype to confirm the password, click the option to give author access rights to the new user, and click OK.

3. Repeat Step 2 to authorize a user named **rich** with password **wheelsdown,** and assign end-user access rights.

4. In the Permissions dialog, click the option to give browse access only to registered users (see Figure 9.9b). Click OK to save the changes and close the dialog.

5. Choose File ➤ Exit to shut down the FrontPage Explorer and discard the access rights granted in the session. The Wales-Ireland web now has four authorized users, including two administrators, one author, and one end-user. In addition, the web is password-protected.

Internal and External Authentication

Let's test the authentication process. There are actually two authentication processes: FrontPage starts an internal authentication process whenever someone tries to open a web in the FrontPage Explorer, and the web server starts an external authentication process whenever anyone tries to browse to the web in a Web browser.

To test the processes, do the following:

1. Start the FrontPage Explorer, and click OK in the Getting Started dialog to initiate opening the Wales-Ireland web. The FrontPage authentication process begins. The Name and Password Required dialog displays the name of the person who last logged on to the Wales-Ireland web during the previous session. Type **rich** as the name, and **wheelsdown** as the password, and click OK. Access is denied because rich has browsing rights only, and cannot open the web in the FrontPage Explorer.

Managing the Web

FIGURE 9.9

Use the Settings tab to specify whether a subweb has its own permissions or inherits the permissions of the root web (a). To password-protect a web, choose the option Only registered users have browse access (b).

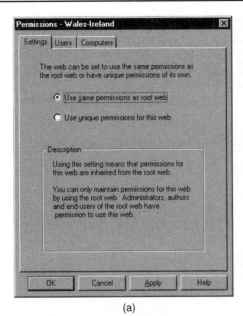

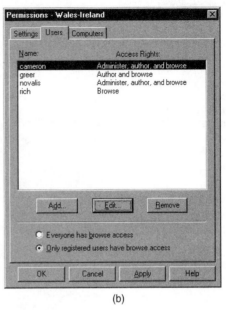

(a)   (b)

2. Type **greer** as the name, and **gnarly** as the password, and click OK. The web opens because greer has author access rights. As an author, greer can change his password and make changes to the files using the commands in the FrontPage Editor and the Explorer.

3. Choose Tools ➤ Permissions. Because greer has author access rights only, the FrontPage authentication dialog is displayed, indicating that administrator permissions are required to change permissions. Click Cancel.

4. Double-click the home page (default.htm) to display the page in the FrontPage Editor. Click Preview in Browser in the Editor toolbar. Whenever someone tries to access a web using a Web browser, the Web server's authentication process starts. In a password-protected web, the Web server instructs the browser to display its authentication dialog. Figure 9.10a is the authentication dialog for the Microsoft Internet Explorer 3.0. If you fail to enter the name and password of an authorized user, the browser displays its failure message. The Internet Explorer 3.0 browser redisplays the authentication dialog so you can try again. Click Cancel. The browser displays the message shown in Figure 9.10b.

5. Click the Refresh button in the browser. The browser displays the authentication dialog again. Type the name and password of any of the four authorized users and click OK. The browser displays the home page of the Wales-Ireland web.

When a visitor browses to a password-protected web, the Web server instructs the browser to display an authentication dialog (a). If the authentication fails, the browser displays this message (b).

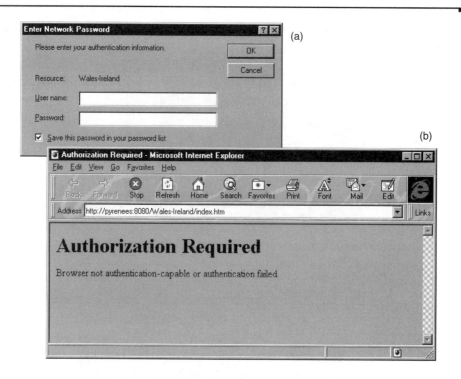

NOTE

You cannot set permissions for a disk-based web stored in a folder in your computer's file system.

For More...

In this chapter, you've learned how to control access to a web stored by the FrontPage Personal Web Server. This security system is a model of the many of the security features that other Web servers provide.

For more information about the topics in this chapter, see the following:

- Chapter 18: Understanding Searches and Visitor Registration shows you how to set up visitor registration for a passsword-protected Web.

- Appendix A: Installing FrontPage and Personal Web Servers shows you how to run both the Microsoft Personal Web Server and the FrontPage Personal Web Server on your computer.

- Appendix C: Microsoft Personal Web Server introduces you to administering webs stored on this server.

PART III

Creating Web pages

LEARN TO:

- Work with a page in the Editor
- Lay out a page with text, lists, and lines
- Create text links
- Add images, image links, and video clips to a page
- Lay out a page using tables
- Divide the browser window into frames
- Automate page design with WebBots
- Add data entry forms to collect information
- Add a text search
- Create an online discussion group

Chapter

10

Editor Basics

Chapter

10

Editor Basics

The FrontPage Editor is the tool you use for creating and modifying web pages. The Editor is a WYSIWYG (What You See Is What You Get) tool, at least for the text and images you add to a page. As you type in text or add a table or an image, the Editor displays a browser version of the page. Keep in mind that the visitor's Web browser has the final say in how the page looks, so what you see in the FrontPage Editor is just one version of the page. Behind the scenes, the Editor automatically creates the HTML coding for each element of your page.

 NOTE

The FrontPage Editor isn't completely WYSIWYG. In the chapters in the second half of Part III, you'll learn about page items that the Editor can't display accurately. These items, such as frames and data entry forms, require a full-featured browser such as Microsoft Internet Explorer 3.0 or Netscape Navigator 3.0.

In the Editor, you work with individual pages. In subsequent chapters, you'll learn how to add content to a page, but you also have to know how to work with the page as a file. This chapter covers the simple housekeeping chores, such as:

- Opening and closing a page and creating a new page
- Renaming a page

- Moving a page to another folder, and hiding or deleting a page
- Setting page properties
- Saving a page and printing a page
- Adding a page task to the To Do List

Understanding the Editor Window

There are two ways you can work with the Editor, depending on whether a web is currently open in the FrontPage Explorer. If there is no web open in the FrontPage Explorer, the Editor acts like a stand-alone page editor; you can create and edit a page and then save the page to any folder in your computer's file system. You can also save the page as a template and use it as the basis for new pages. If there is a web open in the FrontPage Explorer, you can also save the page to the current web.

Opening and Closing the Editor

To open the Editor, do any of the following:

- Click the Windows 95 Start button, choose Programs, choose Microsoft Front-Page, and then choose FrontPage Editor from the flyout menu. The FrontPage Editor opens and displays a new page based on the Normal Page template (see Figure 10.1a).

- If the Explorer is already open, click the Show FrontPage Editor button on the Explorer toolbar, or choose Tools ➤ Show FrontPage Editor from the Explorer menu bar. The FrontPage Editor opens with a blank window (see Figure 10.1b).
- If a web is open in the Explorer, double-click a page icon in the right pane of either Folder View or Hyperlink View. The FrontPage Editor opens and displays the page you selected.

To close the Editor, do either of the following:

- Click the Close button in the upper-right corner of the Editor window (see Figure 10.2).
- Choose File ➤ Exit from the Editor menu bar.

If a page is open and you've made any changes, the Editor prompts you to save the changes before closing the page and exiting.

Elements of the Editor Window

The Editor window contains the elements shown in Figure 10.2 and described in Table 10.1.

FIGURE 10.1

Opening the Editor from Windows displays a new blank page (a). Opening the Editor by clicking the Show FrontPage Editor toolbar button in the Explorer displays an empty window (b).

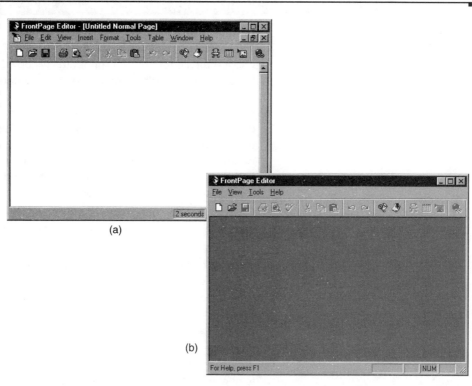

(a)

(b)

TABLE 10.1: THE ELEMENTS OF THE EDITOR WINDOW	
Element	**Description**
Control Box	Clicking the Control Box or pressing Alt+Space displays the window control menu with commands to control the window display, including Restore, Move, Size, Minimize, Maximize, and Close.
Title Bar	Displays the name of the application and the title of the active page.
Minimize button	Clicking the Minimize button shrinks the application window to an icon placed in the Windows 95 task bar at the bottom of the screen.
Maximize button	Clicking the Maximize button expands the application window to fill the entire screen. After clicking the Maximize button, the button's icon changes to the Restore button.

Continued ▶

PART

III

Creating Web Pages

TABLE 10.1: THE ELEMENTS OF THE EDITOR WINDOW (CONTINUED)	
Element	**Description**
Restore button	Clicking the Restore button shrinks the window from full size to its normal size. When the window is in its normal state, you can move or resize the window. To move the window, click in the title bar and drag to the new location. To resize the window, move the pointer to a corner of the window; when the pointer changes to a double-pointed arrow, press the left mouse button and drag to a new size. (In Figure 10.3, the Editor's window displays a Maximize button and the page's window displays a Restore button.)
Close button	Clicking the Close button closes the open pages (after prompting you to save changes) and then closes the Editor.
Menu Bar	The bar below the application title bar displays the menu categories. When you click a menu name, a drop-down menu displays the commands in the category. Commands may be available or grayed out, depending on the current status of the Editor.
Toolbar	The bar below the menu bar displays command buttons corresponding to many of the menu commands. When you hold the pointer over a button without clicking, the button's tooltip, a brief message describing the button, is displayed.
Status Bar	The bar located at the bottom of the window. The left end of the status bar displays a message, and the right end displays the status of various indicators.
Download Indicator	The first status bar indicator gives the estimated time to download the page at 28.8 Kbs.
NumLocks Indicator	The second status bar indicator displays NUM after you press the NumLocks key to activate the number pad portion of your keyboard.

Editor Menu Choices and Toolbar Buttons

Before you open a page, the Editor window is empty, the Editor menu bar contains only a few menus, and most of the toolbar buttons are grayed out and unavailable (see Figure 10.1b). After you open a page, the Editor menu bar contains a full set of menus and most of the toolbar buttons become available (see Figure 10.2). The menus display all the commands that are available in the Editor (see Figure 10.3). You'll learn about the individual menu commands as we need them in this chapter and the chapters that follow.

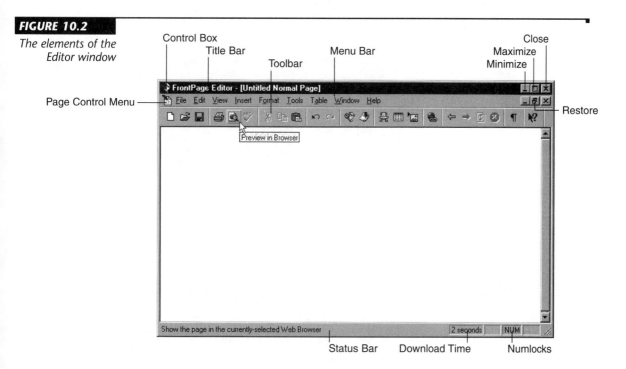

FIGURE 10.2

The elements of the Editor window

To get help on a menu command or toolbar button, click the Help button at the right end of the toolbar (the cursor changes to a question mark), and then click the menu command or toolbar button. FrontPage displays online help for the selected item.

The Editor toolbar buttons are arranged into five toolbars:

Standard toolbar   contains buttons as shortcuts to menu choices for manipulating and editing pages. This chapter covers most of the buttons on the Standard toolbar. (The Standard toolbar is the only toolbar shown in Figure 10.2.)

PART

III

Creating Web Pages

FIGURE 10.3

The Editor's menus

Page Control menu

Restore
Move
Size
Minimize
Maximize

Close   Ctrl+F4

Next   Ctrl+F6

File menu

New...   Ctrl+N
Open...   Ctrl+O
Close

Save   Ctrl+S
Save As...
Save All

Page Properties...

Preview in Browser...
Page Setup...
Print Preview
Print...   Ctrl+P

Send...

1 http://localhost/Desserts/my.htm
2 http://localhost/Desserts/lesson4.htm
3 C:\Program Files\Microsoft FrontPage97\pages\saveto.tem\saveto.htm
4 C:\FrontPage Webs\Content\Desserts97\saveto.htm

Exit

Edit menu

Undo Insert   Ctrl+Z
Can't Redo

Cut   Ctrl+X
Copy   Ctrl+C
Paste   Ctrl+V
Clear   Del
Select All   Ctrl+A

Find...   Ctrl+F
Replace...   Ctrl+H
Add To Do Task...
Bookmark...
Database   ▶
Hyperlink...   Ctrl+K
Unlink

Font Properties   Alt+Enter

View menu

✓ Standard Toolbar
Format Toolbar
Image Toolbar
Forms Toolbar
Advanced Toolbar
✓ Status Bar
✓ Format Marks

Refresh
HTML...

Insert menu

Break...
Horizontal Line
Symbol...
Comment...

Image...
Video...
Background Sound...

File...
WebBot Component...
Other Components   ▶
Form Field   ▶

Marquee...
HTML Markup...
Script...

Hyperlink...   Ctrl+K

Format menu

Font...
Paragraph...
Bullets and Numbering...

Background...
Remove Formatting

Tools menu

Spelling...   F7

Forward
Back
Follow Hyperlink

Show FrontPage Explorer
Show To Do List
Show Image Editor

Font Options...

Table menu

Insert Table...
Insert Rows or Columns...
Insert Cell
Insert Caption
Merge Cells
Split Cells...

Select Cell
Select Row
Select Column
Select Table

Caption Properties...
Cell Properties...
Table Properties...

Window menu

Cascade
Tile
Arrange Icons

✓ 1 Untitled Normal Page

Help menu

Microsoft FrontPage Help   F1
Microsoft on the Web...

About Microsoft FrontPage Editor

Format toolbar   contains buttons that are shortcuts for text formatting options, such as color and size, and paragraph formatting, including alignment. Chapter 11 covers the formatting toolbar.

Images toolbar   contains buttons as shortcuts for manipulating images, such as creating hotspots and making colors transparent. Chapter 14 covers the images toolbar.

Forms toolbar   contains buttons as shortcuts for inserting fields into form sections on pages. Chapter 17 covers the Form Fields toolbar.

Advanced toolbar   contains buttons as shortcuts for inserting advanced items such as ActiveX Controls and scripts. Chapter 20 covers the Advanced toolbar.

The Standard Toolbar Buttons and Menu Choices

Table 10.2 describes the purpose for each Standard toolbar button, the corresponding menu command, and the keyboard shortcut, if one exists.

TABLE 10.2: STANDARD TOOLBAR BUTTONS IN THE EDITOR

Button	Tooltip	Function	Menu Command	Keyboard Shortcut
▢	New	Opens a new blank page based on the Normal Page template	File ➤ New and then choose the Normal Page in the New Page dialog	Ctrl+N
🗁	Open	Displays a dialog for opening a page from the current web, from a file, or from a URL	File ➤ Open	Ctrl+O

Continued ▌▶

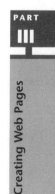

TABLE 10.2: STANDARD TOOLBAR BUTTONS IN THE EDITOR (CONTINUED)

Button	Tooltip	Function	Menu Command	Keyboard Shortcut
	Save	Saves the active page in HTML format to the current web if the page was opened from the web, or back to the file, if the page was opened from a file. Start the Save As dialog for a new page.	File ➤ Save	Ctrl+S
	Print	Prints the active page to a printer or file	File ➤ Print	Ctrl+P
	Preview in Browser	Displays the current version of the active page in the selected browser	File ➤ Preview in Browser	
	Check Spelling	Checks the spelling in the active page, but not in any included pages	Tools ➤ Spelling	F7
	Cut	Removes the selected items from the page and copies them to the Clipboard	Edit ➤ Cut	Ctrl+X
	Copy	Copies the selected items from the page onto the Clipboard	Edit ➤ Copy	Ctrl+C
	Paste	Pastes the contents of the Clipboard at the insertion point and replaces the current selection.	Edit ➤ Paste	Ctrl+V
	Undo	Reverses the last change you made to the page.	Edit ➤ Undo Typing or Edit ➤Undo Insert	Ctrl+Z
	Redo	Reverses the effect of the last Undo	Edit ➤ Redo Typing or Edit ➤ Redo Insert	Ctrl+Y

Continued

		TABLE 10.2: STANDARD TOOLBAR BUTTONS IN THE EDITOR (CONTINUED)		
Button	**Tooltip**	**Function**	**Menu Command**	**Keyboard Shortcut**
	Show FrontPage Explorer	Use to open the Explorer or to bring the Explorer window to the top of the desktop, if the Explorer is already open	Tools ➤ Show FrontPage Explorer	
	Show To Do List	Opens the To Do list for the current web, or brings the To Do List window to the top of the desktop if the To Do List is already open	Tools ➤ Show To Do List	
	Insert WebBot Component	Use to insert a WebBot component	Insert ➤ WebBot Component	
	Insert Table	Use to create and insert a new table at the insertion point	Table ➤ Insert Table	
	Insert Image	Use to insert an existing image from the current web, from a file, from a URL, or from the Clip Art library	Insert ➤ Image	
	Create or Edit Hyperlink	Use to create or edit a text link based on the selected text	Edit ➤ Hyperlink or Insert ➤ Hyperlink	Ctrl+K
	Back	Displays the previously displayed page	Tools ➤ Back	Alt+←
	Forward	Displays the next page in the Editor's page list	Tools ➤ Forward	Alt+→
	Refresh	Displays the version of the active page that was last saved, and prompts you to save a new page if it hasn't been saved	View ➤ Refresh	

Continued ▶

PART

III

Creating Web Pages

TABLE 10.2: STANDARD TOOLBAR BUTTONS IN THE EDITOR (CONTINUED)

Button	Tooltip	Function	Menu Command	Keyboard Shortcut
	Stop	Use to stop the Editor's progress in following a link	Tools ➤ Stop	
¶	Show/Hide	Shows or hides hard line returns, bookmarks, and form outlines	View ➤ Format Marks	
	Help	Use to display information about the on-screen item that you click after clicking this button	Help ➤ Microsoft FrontPage Help	

Opening an Existing Page

When you work with the FrontPage Editor, you are working with web pages in HTML format.

Opening a Page in the Current Web

If the page you want to open is in the current FrontPage web, you can open the page starting either from the Editor or from the FrontPage Explorer.

Opening a Page from the Editor   To open a page from the Editor:

1. Choose File ➤ Open from the Editor menu bar, or click the Open button in the toolbar to display the Open File dialog. The Current FrontPage Web tab displays the folders and all the web pages that are saved to the current web (see Figure 10.4). The list includes only web pages, that is only files with the HTM extension and does not include files with other formats, such as image files or Office 97 files. (Non-HTML files are listed in the Other Location tab.) The pages are listed by Name and Title. The Name is the filename of the page, for example lesson2.htm or feedback.htm, and the Title is the the page identifier that is shown in the FrontPage title bar and in some browsers when the page is displayed. Click the headings to sort by Name or by Title. Click a folder to display its web pages. Use the Look in combo box and the Up one level button to locate a page. Click the display buttons to toggle between displaying only icons and displaying details.

FIGURE 10.4

The Current FrontPage Web tab of the Open File dialog lists the pages stored in the open web.

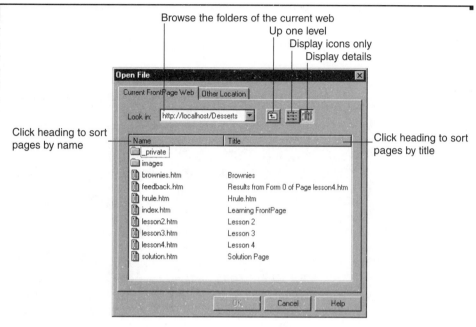

Browse the folders of the current web
Up one level
Display icons only
Display details

Click heading to sort pages by name

Click heading to sort pages by title

2. To open a page, double-click the page in the list, or select the page and then click the OK button.

Viewing Pages in the Editor   By default, the Editor opens a web page in a maximized window that fills the entire Editor window so you can view only one page at a time. If you prefer, you can work with page windows that are not maximized; click the Restore button to shrink the open page windows to normal size. You can view the list of open pages using the Window menu (see Figure 10.5a); the active page is the one with the check mark in front of its name.

The commands in the Windows menu provide familiar ways to view the windows:

- Use the Cascade command to resize the windows of all open pages and display them in a staggered cascade, as in Figure 10.5a.

- Use the Tile command to resize the windows and arrange them in rows and columns, as in Figure 10.5b.

- Minimize windows and use the Arrange Icons command to arrange the minimized icons at the bottom of the Editor window.

Opening a Page from the Explorer   There are two ways you can open a page starting from the FrontPage Explorer:

- In the right pane of either Hyperlink View or Folder View, double-click the page icon, select the page icon, and press Enter; or right-click the page icon and

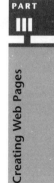

PART

III

Creating Web Pages

choose Open from the shortcut menu. (You can open any page displayed in Hyperlink View—not just the page in the center of the Hyperlinks pane.) FrontPage opens the Editor, if it is not already open, and displays the page.

FIGURE 10.5

Use the commands in the Windows menu to cascade (a) or tile the open windows (b).

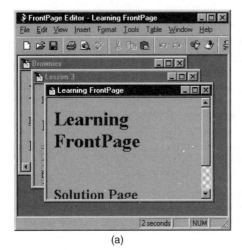

(a)

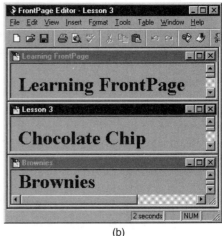

(b)

- If the Editor is already open and you have arranged the Explorer and Editor windows to display both windows, you can use drag-and-drop to open a page. Select the page in either pane of Hyperlink View or in the right pane of Folder View, and drag it to the Editor window. You can drop the page on any part of the Editor window except on an open page (see Figure 10.6). If you drop the page you want to open on an open page in the Editor, FrontPage inserts a text hyperlink to the dropped page instead of opening the page).

Opening a Page from a File or a URL

Often information that you want to include in your web exists in one of the following ways:

- As a non-HTML file in the current web, such as an Excel or Word file
- As a file anywhere in your computer's file system
- As a web page or a non-HTML file on the World Wide Web or on your intranet

You can open one of these files if the file has any of the formats that the Editor is able to convert. When you open the file, the Editor converts the contents of the file to the HTML format and displays a new web page with the converted contents. If the file contains images, the Editor converts the images to the GIF or JPG format. You'll learn more about image formats in Chapter 13.

PART

III

Creating Web Pages

FIGURE 10.6

To open a page by drag-and-drop, select the page icon in any pane of the Explorer except the All Folders pane, and drag to a region in the Editor outside all open pages and release the mouse button.

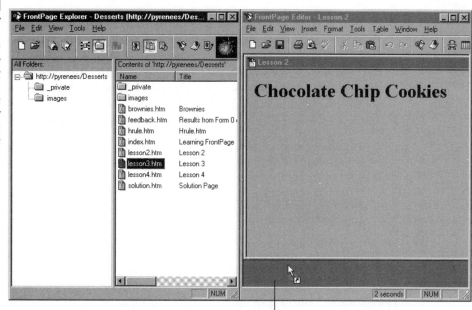

Drop the page icon outside any open page

Table 10.3 lists the common file types that the Editor can convert to HTML.

TABLE 10.3: THE FILE TYPES THAT THE EDITOR CONVERTS TO HTML

File Type	Description
Text (.txt)	The basic format for text documents without formatting
Rich text (.rtf)	Rich text format is a method of encoding a text document's structure and formatting using the ASCII character set
HTML (.htm or .html)	The format for documents that use the HTML tags to encode the document's structure and formatting
Microsoft Word (.doc)	The format for documents created in Microsoft Word 2.0, 6.0, 95, 97, and Word 6.0 for MS-DOS
Microsoft Excel (.xls)	The format for spreadsheets created in Microsoft Excel 4.0, 5.0, 95, and 97
Lotus	The format for spreadsheets created in Lotus 1-2-3 2.x-4.x
WordPerfect	The format for documents created in WordPerfect 5.x-7.x

NOTE

When you open a file with the HTML format that has been created in another web editor, the file may contain HTML tags that FrontPage doesn't recognize. In this case, the FrontPage Editor converts the file to the FrontPage HTML format. In the conversion, unrecognized HTML tags are replaced with WebBot components called HTML Markup WebBots. See Chapter 16 for more information.

There are two ways you can use a file with one of these file types, depending on whether you want to open a new page or use the file contents in an existing page as follows:

- You can use File ➤ Open from the Editor menu bar to open the file and display its converted contents in a new page, or

- You can use Insert ➤ File from the Editor menu bar to open the file and insert its converted contents into an existing page

Displaying a File in a New Page   To open a file in a new web page, choose File ➤ Open from the Editor menu bar to display the Open File dialog and click the Other Location tab (see Figure 10.7a). To open a file on your computer, including a non-HTML file in the current web, click the From File option, and click the Browse button to select the file in the Open File location dialog (see Figure 10.7b). Use the Files of type combo list to choose a file type, select the file, and click Open.

When you open a file with one of the formats in Table 10.3, FrontPage converts the contents of the file to an HTML document and displays a new page with the converted contents. The conversion process depends on the file type.

- If you open a Word or WordPerfect document or an Excel or Lotus spreadsheet, FrontPage first converts the file to the Rich Text format and then to the HTML format. In converting the file, some of the formatting is preserved and some is lost, as follows:

    Bulleted and numbered lists are preserved, although the numbering style may be lost.

    Heading styles 1 through 6 are preserved and translated to FrontPage heading styles. Other heading styles are lost.

    Graphics in the file are converted to GIF files. FrontPage automatically creates links to the GIF files.

    Bold and italic fonts are preserved.

    Footnotes are placed at the end of the page. FrontPage automatically creates links from the footnote references to the footnote.

FIGURE 10.7

Click the Other Location tab in the Open File dialog to open a non-HTML file in the current web, a file in the computer's file system, or a file on the World Wide Web or on your intranet (a). To locate a file on your computer, click the Browse button to display the Open File location dialog (b).

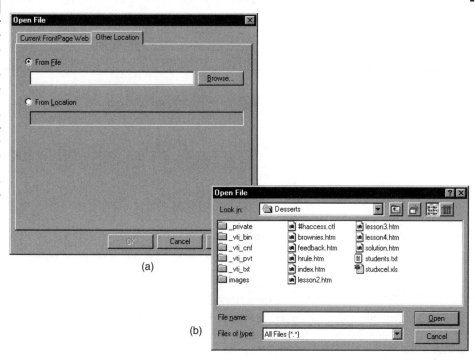

(a)

(b)

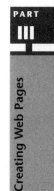

- If you open a .txt file, FrontPage displays a dialog in which you specify the FrontPage paragraph style you want to use (see Figure 10.8). The following are the four options for converting a .txt file:

    One formatted paragraph   converts the text in the file to formatted text (*formatted text* has white spaces for the spaces and tabs), preserves the line endings in the .txt file by inserting line breaks, as in the .txt document, and treats the entire text as a single paragraph. The text is displayed in typewriter font (*typewriter font* is the text style that looks like typewritten text with each character having the same width). The result is that the new page looks like the .txt document.

    Formatted paragraphs   converts the text in the file, as in the first option, except that each paragraph in the .txt file is a separate paragraph in the new page.

    Normal paragraphs   converts each paragraph in the file to the default paragraph style, called the Normal style. The text in the normal style is displayed in a proportional font, with characters having varying widths.

PART

III

Creating Web Pages

Normal paragraphs with line breaks   converts each paragraph in the file to the default paragraph style and preserves the line endings in the .txt file by inserting line breaks.

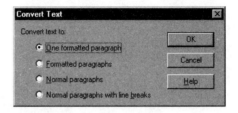

• If you open an .htm or .html file, FrontPage reviews the HTML tags in the file. Each HTML tag that FrontPage doesn't recognize is automatically replaced by an HTML Markup WebBot containing the unrecognized HTML.

Exploring the .txt Conversion Options   To explore the conversion options for a .txt file, we'll open a .txt file using each of the conversion options shown in Figure 10.8. Open the Wales-Ireland web in the FrontPage Explorer.

NOTE

If you did not create the Wales-Ireland web in the earlier chapters of the book, import the web now following the steps in Chapter 5. Use the Import Web Wizard to create a new web named Wales-Ireland, and import the contents of the folder on the CD-ROM named Wales-Ireland-Ch10.

1. Choose File ➤ Open from the Editor menu bar, click the Other Location tab in the Open File dialog, click the Browse button to locate the Day8.txt file Wales-Ireland Manuscript folder on the book's CD-ROM, and click Open. Choose the One formatted paragraph option in the Convert Text dialog and click OK. The Editor converts the contents and displays the contents in the new page shown in Figure 10.9. Note that the white space is preserved.

2. If the Formatting toolbar is not displayed, choose View ➤ Format Toolbar from the Editor menu bar. With the insertion point anywhere in the text, click the Center button in the toolbar. Note that all lines in the page are aligned to the center. When you choose the one formatted paragraph option, the entire text is treated as a single paragraph (see Figure 10.10).

FIGURE 10.9

When you convert a text file using the One formatted paragraph option, the page looks like the text document.

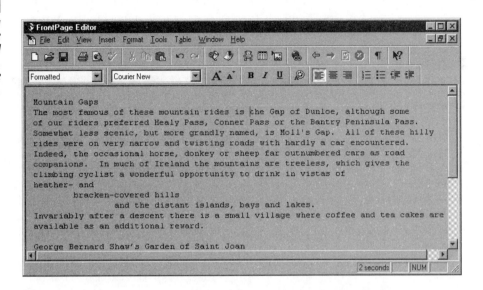

FIGURE 10.10

Because the entire page is a single paragraph, aligning any part of the page aligns the entire page.

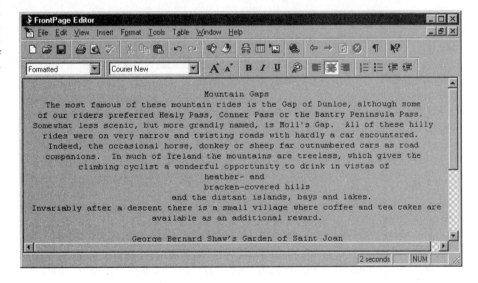

PART

III

Creating Web Pages

3. Choose File ➤ Close from the Editor menu bar and click No to close the page without saving it.

4. Repeat Step 1 to open the Day8.txt file again and choose the Formatted paragraphs option. The new page looks identical to Figure 10.11. Place the insertion

point in the first paragraph and click the Center button in the Formatting tool-bar. Note that only the first paragraph is aligned to the center.

FIGURE 10.11

When you convert a text file using the Formatted para-graphs option, each paragraph in the text file is a sepa-rate paragraph in the web page. You can center one paragraph without centering the other paragraphs.

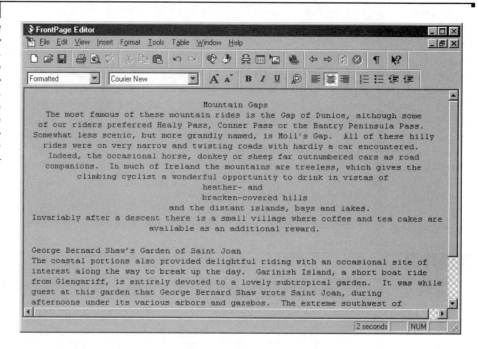

5. Repeat Step 3 to close the page without saving it.

6. Repeat Step 1 to open the Day8.txt file again and choose the Normal paragraphs option. The Editor converts the contents and displays the contents in the new page. Note the proportional font, that the white space is not preserved, and that there are no line breaks. Place the insertion point in the first paragraph, and click the Center or Align Right button in the toolbar (see Figure 10.12a). Note that each paragraph is treated separately.

7. Repeat Step 3 to close the page without saving it.

8. Repeat Step 1 to open the Day8.txt file again and choose the Normal para-graphs with line breaks option. Note the proportional font, and that the white space is not preserved, but that there are line breaks. With the insertion point anywhere in the text, click the Center or Align Right button in the toolbar (see Figure 10.12b). Note that each paragraph is treated separately.

FIGURE 10.12

Converting a .txt file to the Normal paragraphs without line breaks (a) and with line breaks (b).

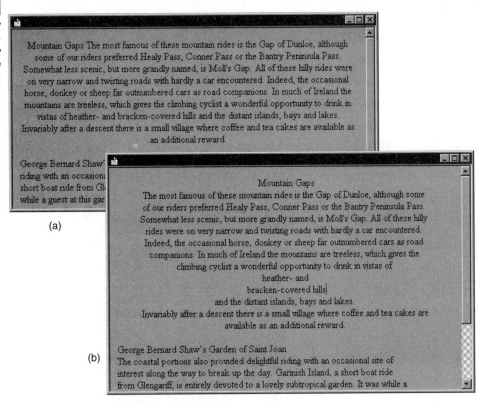

(a)

(b)

Opening a Page From a URL   You can open a page or a file from the World Wide Web or from your intranet. Choose File ➤ Open from the Editor menu bar, click the Other Location tab in the Open File dialog, and click the From Location option. You must enter the full URL of the file you want to open (see Figure 10.13). The easiest way to get the full URL is to browse to the file on the Web or on your intranet, copy the URL from the address text box in the browser, and paste the URL in the From Location text box.

Inserting a File into an Existing Page

You use the Insert ➤ File command from the Editor menu bar to insert a file from your computer's file system into the active page. If the file has one of the formats that FrontPage knows how to convert, the Editor converts the contents of the file as

PART

III

Creating Web Pages

described in the last section and inserts the converted contents at the location of the insertion point in the active page.

Here are the steps:

1. Place the insertion point in the active page where you want to insert the file, and choose Insert ➤ File from the Editor menu bar.

2. Using the Look in combo box in the Select a File dialog, locate the folder that contains the file you want to open (see Figure 10.14).

FIGURE 10.13

To open a page on a file from the World Wide Web or from your intranet, enter the absolute URL in the From Location text box.

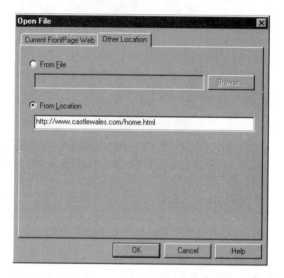

FIGURE 10.14

Use the Select a File dialog to select a file from your computer's file system for insertion into an existing web page.

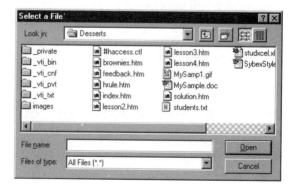

3. Choose the file type from the Files of Type combo box, select the file, and click OK. If the file is a Word or WordPerfect document, or an Excel or Lotus spreadsheet, or if the file has the rich text file format, FrontPage converts the file automatically and inserts the converted file in the page. If the file has the .htm (or .html) format, the Editor converts the file to FrontPage HTML and inserts HTML Markup WebBot components in place of any unrecognized HTML. If the file has the text format, FrontPage offers to convert the document, and displays the Convert File dialog shown in Figure 10.8. Select an option and click OK.

As an example, we'll insert a file into an existing page in the Wales-Ireland web. If the web is not open, open it now.

1. In the Editor, click the Open button in the toolbar, and choose the Days 10 to 14 Killarney, Dingle, and Bunratty page in the Open File dialog.

2. Scroll to the bottom of the page and place the insertion point in the line below the last with text (see Figure 10.15a).

3. Choose the Insert ➤ File command from the Editor menu bar and choose Rich Text Format in the Files of Type combo box in the Select a File dialog. Locate the Bunratty.rtf file in the Wales-Ireland Manuscript folder on the book's CD-ROM and click Open. The Editor converts the file to HTML and inserts the converted contents at the location of the insertion point and moves the insertion point to the end of the inserted text. (See Figure 10.15b.)

FIGURE 10.15

Place the insertion point where you want to insert the file (a). The Editor inserts the converted contents of the file and moves the insertion point to the end of the inserted text (b).

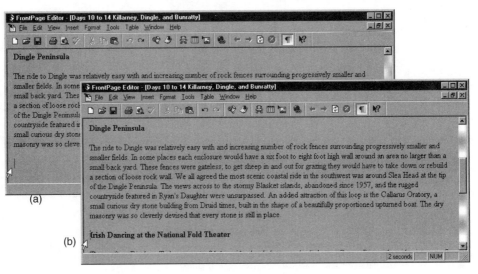

PART

III

Creating Web Pages

If the file you are inserting contains images, the Editor automatically converts them to the GIF or JPEG formats depending on the number of colors and displays the converted images in the Editor. When you save the page with the inserted file, you have the option of saving its images also. Chapter 14: Using Images and Video Clips explains saving images.

Viewing a Page in a Browser

You can view the active page in any browser installed on your computer. Choose File ➤ Preview in Browser from the Editor menu bar. FrontPage displays the Preview in Browser dialog (see Figure 10.16a). FrontPage automatically detects the browsers installed on your computer. You can add another browser to the list by clicking the Add button to display the Add Browser dialog (see Figure 10.16b) and you can delete a browser you have added by selecting the added browser and clicking the Delete button. (You can only remove browsers you have added to the list and you cannot remove the browsers that FrontPage detects.)

FIGURE 10.16

Choose the browser and window size in the Preview in Browser dialog (a). Click the Add button to add another browser to the list (b).

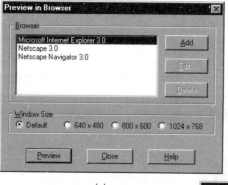

(a)

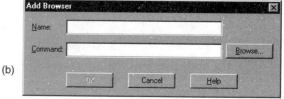

(b)

Select the browser and window size you want to use and click OK. FrontPage opens the browser and displays the active page.

After you have selected a browser, you can preview a page by clicking the Preview in Browser button on the toolbar. FrontPage opens the previously selected browser. Your Internet connection does not need to be open in order to preview a page in a browser. You can create and test pages on a computer that doesn't have a network connection.

NOTE

Clicking the Preview in Browser toolbar button opens the previously selected browser and does not display the Preview in Browser dialog. To change the browser, choose the File ➤ Preview in Browser command in the Editor menu bar instead.

Saving a Page

The FrontPage Editor saves pages in HTML format. You can save a page to the current web, or you can save the page to an .htm file in any directory. You can also save a page as a template and use the template as the pattern for creating new pages.

Saving a New Page to the Current Web

If you are creating a new page from scratch or opening a new page based on an existing page or file from the World Wide Web or your intranet, use the File ➤ Save command from the Editor menu bar or click the Save button in the toolbar to save the active page to the current Web. If you are opening a new page from an existing file in your computer's file system, using the File ➤ Save command only saves any changes you have made back to the original file, so you must use the File ➤ Save As command from the Editor menu bar to save the active page to the current web.

The Editor displays the Save As dialog (see Figure 10.17). You enter a Page Title in the first text box. The Title is the public name that the page goes by. The Title is displayed in the title bar of the browser, and in the title bar of the Editor, and is used in the Explorer to identify the page. As the page's public name, the Title should be descriptive of the page and may contain spaces and symbols. You should avoid cryptic abbreviations that have no meaning to most users.

As you type in the Title, the Editor automatically enters several characters, up to a maximum of eight characters, in the second text box as the File path within your FrontPage web, which is also called the Page URL. (In deciding which characters to include, the Editor omits the adjectives the, a, and an; recognizes spaces, and makes a best guess at a reasonable filename.) Although the Editor suggests filenames of no more than eight characters, you can change the filename to more than eight. Normally the file path within your web is just the filename, such as castles.htm or index.htm, but if the file is contained within a folder, the file path must include the name of the folder. For example, if the web has a folder named Wales, you can save the castles.htm file in the Wales folder by entering Wales/castles.htm in the second text box.

FIGURE 10.17

*Use the Save As dia-
log box to specify
the Page Title
and URL.*

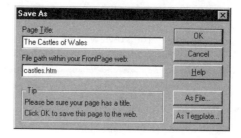

The entry in the second text box is the name that FrontPage uses to identify the page. When you create links to the page, the Editor uses the file path within the web to identify the target of the link. If you move a page to another folder in the web, the Explorer updates the new file path and updates the broken links. The file path within the web must be unique; no two pages in a web can have the same file path. By contrast, the Page Title doesn't have to be unique; you can have two pages with the same Page Title in a web, as long as they have a different file path (Page URL). If you try to save a page and another page in the web has the same file path, the Editor displays the message shown in Figure 10.18, offering the option to replace the other page with the new page.

FIGURE 10.18

*The message
displayed when you
try to save a page
with the same file
path in the web
(Page URL) as
another page in
the current web*

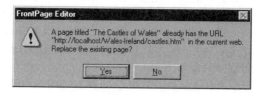

After entering a Page Title and File path, click OK to save the page to the current web. If the page has inserted images, FrontPage displays the Save Image to FrontPage Web dialog that provides options for saving the images also (see Figure 10.19). Chapter 13: Using Images and Video Clips explains saving images and the options shown in the dialog. The next sections describe the As File and the As Template buttons.

PART

III

FIGURE 10.19

Use the Save Image to web to add inserted images to the current web.

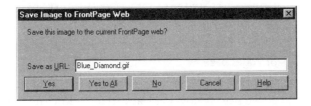

As an example, we'll save two of the new pages opened earlier in the chapter. If you've been working along in this chapter, you should have four pages open in the Editor, including the home page; the new page we opened from the Day8.rtf file; the page with the title Days 10 to 14 Killarney, Dingle, and Bunratty that has the inserted file; and the page with the title The Castles of Wales that we opened from the World Wide Web.

1. Click the Window menu to view the list of open pages. The active page has a check mark in front of it (see Figure 10.20). Choose the page without a title; this is the new page opened from the day8.rtf file.

FIGURE 10.20

The Window menu lists the open pages with a check mark in front of the active page.

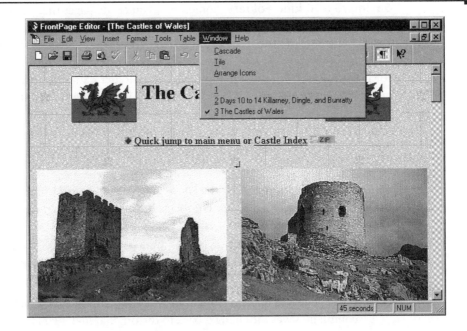
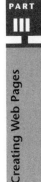

2. Choose File ➤ Save As from the Editor menu bar. Enter **Day 8 Mountain Gaps and Gardens** in the Page Title text box. The Editor proposes the file path day8.htm. Click OK to save the page to the web.

3. Choose File ➤ Close to close the active page. The active page is now the Castles of Wales page.

4. Choose File ➤ Close to close the page without saving it to the current web. The active page is now the Days 10 to 14 Killarney, Dingle, and Bunratty page with the inserted file.

Saving Changes to an Existing Page   If the page has been saved before, choosing the Save command from the File menu or clicking the Save button on the toolbar saves the changes to the page. If you inserted images since the last time you saved the page, FrontPage displays the Save Image to Web dialog that provides options of saving the images also. Chapter 13: Using Images and Video Clips explains saving images.

As an example, let's save the Days 10 to 14 Killarney, Dingle, and Bunratty page with the inserted file:

1. Choose File ➤ Save from the Editor menu bar to save the changes to the page.

2. Choose File ➤ Close from the Editor menu bar to close the page.

Saving to a Hidden Folder   Sometimes, you create pages that you don't want to be available to a browser. For example, you may have special header and footer pages that you include in other pages, or style pages that you use to set the colors for pages in the web, or you may have pages that are under development that are not ready for publication. You can store these pages in a folder named _private that FrontPage creates for each new web for this specific purpose. To save a page to the hidden folder, enter the Page Title as before, and modify the file path within the web (Page URL) by inserting _private/ in front of the default file path; for example, if the file path is header.htm, then hide the page by changing the filename within the web to _private/header.htm.

Saving All Open Pages   Use the File ➤ Save All command from the Editor menu bar to save all of the open pages. FrontPage looks at each open page to determine the appropriate save process as follows:

- If the page was opened from the current web, the Save All command saves the page to the web; if you inserted any images that are not already in the web, the Editor displays the Save Image to FrontPage Web dialog (see Figure 10.19).

- If the page was opened from a file in your computer's file system, the Save All command saves the changes back to the original file. If you inserted any images, the Editor displays the Save Image to File dialog so that you can save the image to the same folder as the original file.

- If the page is new to your computer's file system (created from scratch or opened from a file on the World Wide Web or on your intranet), the Save All command displays the Save As dialog. If the page has images, the Editor prompts you to save the images to the current web.

Saving a Page to a File

The File ➤ Save As command in the Editor menu bar is used when you want to save the active page as a file to any folder on your computer's file system. Click the As File button in the Save As dialog (see Figure 10.21a) to display the Save As File dialog shown in Figure 10.21b. Use the Save In combo list to locate the folder you want to save the file in, or click the Create New Folder button to create a new folder. Enter the name for the file in the File name text box. Choose the file type in the Save As Type combo box; by default, a web page has the .htm extension.

FIGURE 10.21

Click the As File button in the Save As dialog (a) to display the Save As File dialog (b). You can save a page as a file to any folder on your file system.

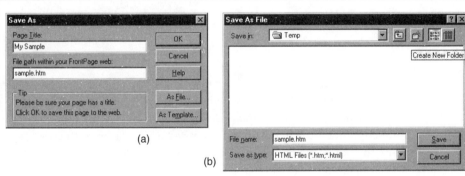

(a)

(b)

If the page has images, the Editor displays the Save Image to File dialog so that you can save the image along with the page.

Saving a Page as a Template

One way to achieve consistency among pages in your web is to create your own page templates. A page template can contain the information and page elements that are common to pages in your web. By basing new pages on your own template, you don't have to recreate the common elements for each new page. For example, in the Wales-Ireland web, we'll save the page shown in Figure 10.22a as a template for new pages with miscellaneous information about touring in Wales. The page template you create is listed in the New Page dialog along with the built-in FrontPage templates (see Figure 10.22b).

PART

III

Creating Web Pages

FIGURE 10.22

Create a page with the information and elements you want to include in new pages (a). The page template you create is listed in the New Page dialog (b).

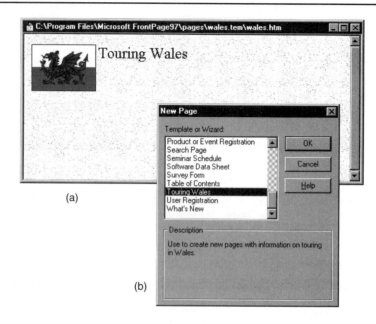

(a)

(b)

You use the File ➤ Save As command from the Editor menu bar to save the active page as a template. Click the As Template button in the Save As Dialog (see Figure 10.23a) to display the Save As Template dialog (see Figure 10.23b). Enter a template title and a description for the template; these entries are displayed in the New Page dialog. You use the Name text box to specify the template's filename that FrontPage needs to keep track of the template.

FIGURE 10.23

Click the As Template button in the Save As dialog (a) to save the active page as a new page template. Specify the template's title, file-name, and description in the Save As Template dialog (b).

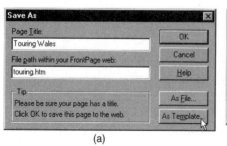

(a)

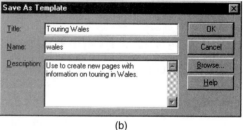

(b)

When you create a new template, you are actually creating both a template file and a template folder with the same name as the file to hold the template file. FrontPage stores your custom template together with all the built-in FrontPage page templates. If you installed FrontPage using the default installation, the page templates are in the Program Files\Microsoft FrontPage\Pages folder. You use the Name text box in the Save As Template dialog to specify the name of the template file (and the template folder). FrontPage creates a template file appending .htm to the name and a template folder appending .tem to the end of the name; for example, if you enter wales in the Name text box, FrontPage places a new template file named wales.htm inside a new template folder named wales.tem, and then stores the folder in the Program Files\Microsoft FrontPage\Pages folder.

If the active page contains images that you have added or modified for the template, the Save Image to File dialog box is displayed for each new or changed image, providing the option to save the new or changed images in the new template folder.

NOTE

You can also create a page template that contains pages that are merged together using Include bots. See the "Creating a Template Using Included Pages" section in Chapter 16.

Replacing a Page Template   You can replace an existing template with a new template based on the active page. To illustrate, suppose you want to replace the Touring Wales template with the page shown in Figure 10.24a. Here are the steps:

1. Choose File ➤ Save As from the Editor menu bar and click the As Template button in the Save As dialog (see Figure 10.24b). If you know the title, name, and description of the template you want to replace, you can type the information into the text boxes in the Save As Template dialog (see Figure 10.24c). Instead, you can click the Browse button to display the list of existing page templates in the Pages folder.

2. Click the Browse button in the Save As Template dialog to display the existing templates (see Figure 25a). Click the template you want to replace, click OK to close the template list, and click OK in the Save As Template dialog to replace the selected template with the active page. Click Yes in the confirmation message (see Figure 10.25b).

PART

III

Creating Web Pages

FIGURE 10.24

Replace an existing template with the active page (a) by saving the page as a template (b). Click the Browse button to display the existing templates(c).

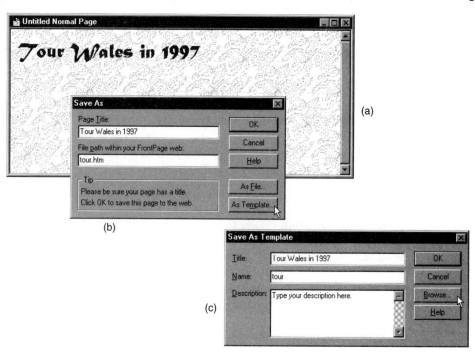

(a)

(b)

(c)

FIGURE 10.25

Choose the template you want to replace (a). After closing the dialogs, click Yes in the confirmation message (b) to replace the template.

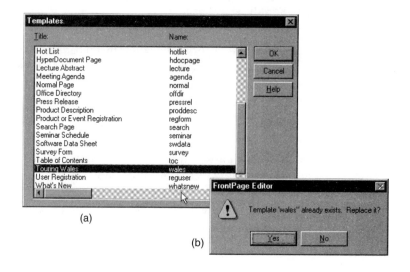

(a)

(b)

Deleting a Page Template   There appears to be no way to delete a template from the list using the template dialogs. One way to delete an existing template is to locate the template folder in your computer's file system and delete the file. Here are the steps:

1. Choose File ➤ Open from the Editor menu bar, click the Open Location tab in the Open File dialog (see Figure 10.26a), and click the Browse button to display the Open File location dialog (see Figure 10.26b).

2. Click the template folder you want to delete and press the Delete key to delete the folder.

Reloading a Page

After you make changes to a page, you may change your mind and decide to discard the changes. You can use the View ➤ Refresh command from the Editor menu bar or click the Refresh button in the toolbar to return to the saved version of the page. If you did make changes to the page, FrontPage displays a confirmation message (see Figure 10.27). Click No to discard the changes and reload the saved version, and click Yes to save the changes before reloading the page.

FIGURE 10.26

To locate an existing template, use the Open command to display the Open File dialog (a) and browse to locate the template folder in the Pages folder in your computer's file system (b).

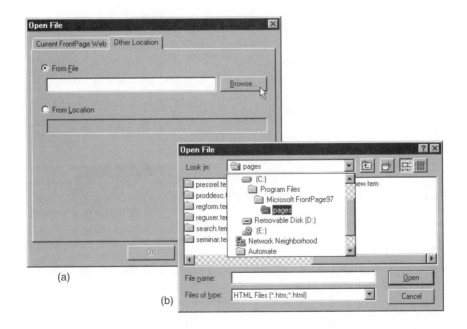

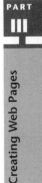

PART

III

Creating Web Pages

If you make changes to a page and click the Refresh button, the Editor asks for confirmation to save the changes before refreshing the display.

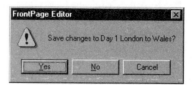

 NOTE

If others in your network have author permissions to the web, another author may modify another copy of the same page and save the changes during the time you are working with the page. FrontPage saves the other author's changes without notifying you. You can view the changes made by someone else by reloading the page from the server.

Closing a Page

To close the active page, choose File ➤ Close from the Editor menu bar or click the Close button in the upper-right corner of the page's window. (If the page window is maximized, the page window Close button is located at the right end of the menu bar just below the FrontPage Close button.) If you made no changes to the page, the Editor closes the page. If you changed the page, the Editor displays a message asking if you want to save the changes (see Figure 10.28).

When you try to close a page with changes, FrontPage displays a message asking if you want to save the changes.

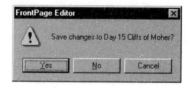

If you click No, the Editor closes the page and discards the changes. If you click Yes, what happens next depends on how you opened the page and your actions after opening the page. Here are the alternatives:

- If you opened a new page in the current web, the Editor displays the Save As dialog. You can save the new page to the current web, to a file, or as a template.

If you click OK, the Editor saves the page in the current web and closes the new page.

- If you made changes to an existing page in the current web, the Editor saves the changes to the current web and closes the page.

- If a web is open and you opened a page from a file or another web (using the Open File command), the Editor saves the changes to the file and then closes the page. The file is not saved as a page in the current web unless you choose File ➤ Save As from the Editor menu bar.

- If no web was open when you opened and changed an existing page, the Editor saves the changes to the file and then closes the page.

- If no web was open when you created a new page, the Editor displays the Save As dialog. You can save the new page to a file or as a template. To save the page to a web, you must first open the web.

- If you opened the page from a web and then closed the web, the Editor displays the message shown in Figure 10.29a, prompting you to open the web before saving the changes. A web must be open before you can save changes to one of its pages.

- If you opened the page from a web, then closed the first web and opened a second web, the Editor displays the message shown in Figure 10.29b. You can save the changed page to the second web or you can discard the changes to the page; you cannot save the changes to the first web unless you close the second web and reopen the first.

FIGURE 10.29

The message when you try to save changes to a page but the web is not open (a). The message when you try to save changes to a page stored in a web, but a different web is open (b).

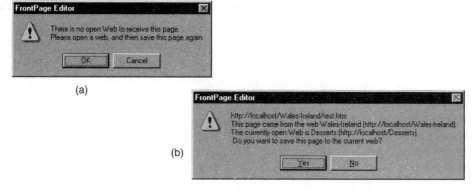

(a)

(b)

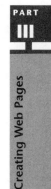

Creating a New Page

You use the New command in the File menu to create a new page. Each page you create in the Editor is based on a template. Even the blank page that you start with when you want to create a page from scratch is based on a template called the Normal Page. There are basically two ways to create a new page: you can use the Normal Page to start from scratch or you can use one of the other page templates or wizards. FrontPage provides a set of predesigned templates, and you can also create your own templates (see Chapter 4 for a description of the built-in page templates).

Starting from Scratch

To start with a blank page, choose the File ➤ New command in the Editor menu bar or press Ctrl+N. Click OK in the New Page dialog to use the Normal Page template (see Figure 10.30a). You can avoid displaying the New Page dialog by clicking the New button in the toolbar. A new blank page with the default title Untitled Normal Page is displayed (see Figure 10.30b).

FIGURE 10.30

To display a new blank page, choose the Normal Page template (a). A new blank page based on the Normal Page template (b).

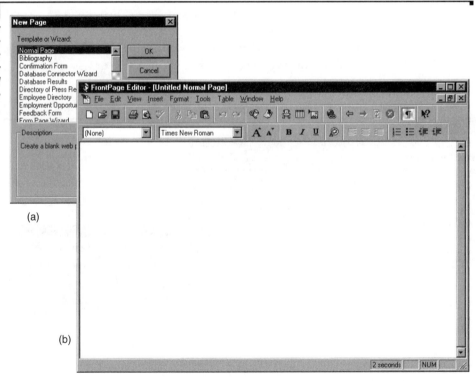

(a)

(b)

Using Templates and Wizards

To create a new page using a template or a wizard do the following:

1. Choose the File ➤ New command from the Editor menu bar and select the template or wizard from the list in the New Page dialog box. The Description in the lower pane of the dialog box gives a brief description of the selected template or wizard.

2. Click OK to display a new page based on the selected template. If you selected one of the page wizards instead of a template, the Editor displays the screens for the wizard that collect the information needed to build the page; after you supply the needed information, the wizard builds the page. We'll look at the Frames Wizard in Chapter 15: Understanding Frames, the Form Page Wizard in Chapter 17: Collecting Input Data, and the Database Connector Wizard in Chapter 21: Creating Dynamic Database Pages with Microsoft Access.

The new page based on a template contains directions for finishing the page. The directions are included as comments on the new page and are visible only when you view the page in the Editor. If you move the cursor over the comment paragraph, the shape changes to the WebBot pointer, indicating that the comment is created as a WebBot component. Figure 10.31 shows a new page based on the Bibliography page template. (If you create this page and move the cursor over the date at the bottom of the page, the cursor changes to the WebBot pointer, indicating that the current date is created using a WebBot component.) See Chapter 16 for information on using WebBots in page design.

FIGURE 10.31

The new page based on the Bibliography template includes comments with directions for completing the page. The comments are invisible when you view the page in a Web browser.

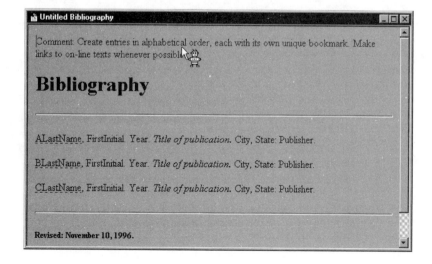

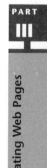

PART

III

Creating Web Pages

Setting Page Properties

Each page has a set of characteristics such as its title, name, background color, hyperlink colors, creation date, and so on. Each of these characteristics is called a property of the page. The same is true for every item you work with in FrontPage; each image, text paragraph, table, or WebBot component that you insert in a page has a set of properties. FrontPage displays the properties of an item in a property sheet. Some items, such as pages, have more than one property sheet.

Each page has two different property sheets. The first property sheet, called Page Properties, displays the design specifications, such as background image and hyperlink information, that you set when you are working with the page in the Editor. The second property sheet, called Properties, displays the administrative information, such as when the page was created or modified, that you set when you are working with the page in the Explorer. In this section, you'll learn how to display and set properties in both kinds of property sheets.

Viewing Page Properties in the Editor

To view the Page Properties for a page, open the page in the Editor and choose File ➤ Page Properties from the Editor menu bar. A quicker way to display the properties is to right-click on the page and choose the Page Properties command in the shortcut menu (see Figure 10.32).

FIGURE 10.32

Right-click in the page to display the shortcut menu, and choose Page Properties to display the Page Properties dialog.

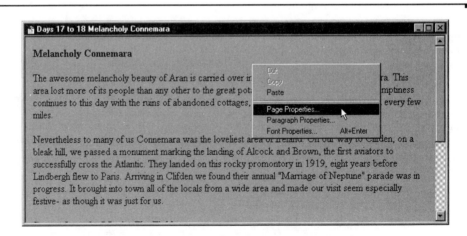

The Page Properties dialog arranges the properties in four tabs: General, Background, Margins, and Custom (see Figure 10.33).

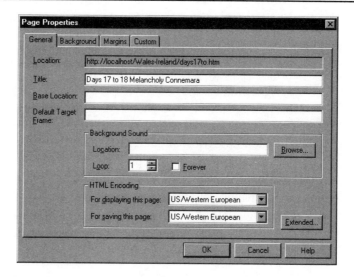

FIGURE 10.33

The General tab of the Page Properties

Understanding the General Properties

The General tab of the Page Properties dialog includes the following properties:

Location   is the complete or absolute URL for the page, including a protocol, server name, directory name, and filename, such as http://pyrenees.sfsu.edu/ Wales-Ireland/eiremap.htm. If the page was opened from a file, the Location is the word file followed by the full path to the file, such as file:///C:/FrontPage Webs/Content/Desserts/lesson2.htm. Each page in the web must have a unique Location. You cannot change the Location using the Page Properties dialog. When you move a page to another folder in the FrontPage Explorer, FrontPage changes the Location automatically.

Title   is the public name that the page goes by. The Title is displayed in the title bar of the Editor and the title bar of some browsers. As the page's public name, the Title should be descriptive of the page and may contain spaces and symbols. The page Title doesn't have to be unique, and several pages in the web can have the same Title. Avoid cryptic abbreviations that have no meaning to most users. The first time you save a page, you specify the Title in the Save As dialog box. You change the Title in the Page Properties dialog.

Base Location   is the URL that is used to convert a page URL into an absolute URL. For example, if a page URL is index.htm and the absolute URL is http:// granite.sfsu.edu/Wales-Ireland/index.htm, then the Base URL is http://granite .sfsu.edu/Wales-Ireland/, where the trailing slash must be included.

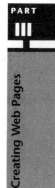

PART

III

Creating Web Pages

Default Target Frame   When you create a frame set on a page, you can create links to specific frames within the frame set. In addition, you can designate one of the frames as the default target frame; in this case, links to the page that do not specify a frame will point to the default target frame. (See Chapter 15 for more information on frame sets.)

Background Sound   You can specify a sound file that a Web browser plays when the page is displayed, and you can specify the Location of the sound file as a file in the current web or in your computer's file system. Click the Browse button to locate the sound file. If the sound file is not in the current web, when you save the page, the Editor prompts you to save the sound file in the current web. You can specify the number of loops for repeating the sound file or check to have the file repeated as long as the page is displayed.

HTML Encoding   You can create pages in specific languages that use other characters. By default, FrontPage uses the character set for Western European languages.

Understanding Extended Attributes

The General tab of the Page Properties dialog has a button with the caption Extended... (see Figure 10.33). Clicking this button displays the Extended Attributes dialog (see Figure 10.34). As you work through the chapters of Part III, you'll observe that the property sheet for nearly every item has an Extended Attributes dialog.

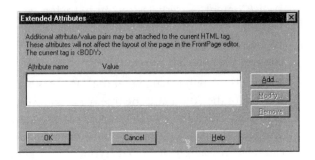

FIGURE 10.34

Use the Extended Attributes dialog to include kinds of information (attributes) for a page item that FrontPage doesn't recognize.

Understanding the Background Properties

The Background tab includes properties that affect the appearance of the page (see Figure 10.35).

There are two options for setting background images and colors for a page: You can specify unique background images and colors for the page, or you can use the background images and colors from another page. The background images and color and the text and link colors are called the *styles* of the page.

Extended Attributes

The purpose of the Extended Attributes dialogs is to allow you to extend the capability of FrontPage. When you create new pages and insert content, the Editor translates your page and content specifications into HTML tags. For example, the <BODY> and </BODY> tags enclose all the content of the page. Most tags have additional information that you can specify about the item that the tags define. The additional features are called *attributes* of the tag. As examples, some of the attributes for the <BODY> tag are the background color (BGCOLOR), background image (BACKGROUND), the text color for all text that isn't a hyperlink (TEXT), and the text color of the text hyperlinks that haven't been followed yet (LINK). You specify an attribute by including the attribute name and the value for the attribute inside the opening tag using the syntax attributename=value, called a *name-value pair*. For example, the opening tag <BODY BACKGROUND= "images/paper.jpg"> specifies that the page uses the paper.jpg image file stored in the images folder as the background image.

In FrontPage, you set the values of attributes using the property dialogs. Although Front-Page recognizes most of the attributes of HTML tags, HTML is constantly evolving, and new attributes are added. The purpose of the Extended Attributes dialog is to allow you to include new attributes that FrontPage doesn't recognize. You use the Extended Attributes dialog to enter the new attribute and the value you want to set. Some of the new features in FrontPage 97 are the attributes that weren't recognized in FrontPage 1.1, such as background sound (BGSOUND), which was an extended attribute of the page's header tag <HEAD> in FrontPage 1.1, but is a recognized attribute in FrontPage 97.

The addition of new attributes is only one of the ways that HTML is evolving. Another way is the definition of new HTML tags. FrontPage also allows you to include new HTML tags that FrontPage doesn't recognize. You use the HTMLMarkup WebBot component to include a new HTML tag.

PART

III

Creating Web Pages

Background Image You can select an image file that the Editor uses to create a tiled background for the page. The Editor lays copies of the image side by side and row by row to fill the page. You can specify that the tiled background scrolls as you scroll through the page or remains fixed as you scroll the contents of the page over the background. To specify a background image, click the Background Image check box and click the Browse button to display the Select Background Image dialog. You can select an image in these ways:

From the current web The Current FrontPage Web tab lists all the image files stored in the current web (see Figure 10.36a).

FIGURE 10.35

The Background tab includes properties that affect the appearance of the page.

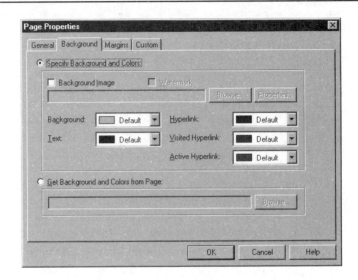

From a file in your computer's file system Click the From File option in the Other Location tab (see Figure 10.36b). Click the Browse button to locate any image file in your computer's file system. When you save the page, the Editor prompts you to save the file to the current web.

From the FrontPage Clip Art library Click the Clip Art tab to display the available images in the FrontPage Clip Art library (see Figure 10.36c). Choose a category in the combo list and click an image to select it.

From the World Wide Web or your intranet Click the From Location in the Other Location tab. You must enter the absolute URL of the image file. The easiest way to enter the absolute URL is to browse to the location on the Web or your intranet that has the image you want to use. If your browser is the Microsoft Internet Explorer, right-click on the image and choose the Properties command in the shortcut menu to display the Properties dialog for the image (see Figure 10.37). Copy the address from the Properties dialog, close the browser, and paste the URL in the From Location text box. When you save the page, the Editor does not prompt you to save the image to the current web.

You can explore background images and watermarks as follows:

1. If necessary, open the Wales-Ireland web and open the page Days 10 to 14 Killarney, Dingle, and Bunratty in the Editor. Right-click anywhere in the page to display the Page Properties dialog. Click the Background tab and then click the Background Image check box.

FIGURE 10.36

You can select a background image from an image in the current web (a), from any file in your file system, the World Wide Web, or your intranet (b), or from the FrontPage Clip Art library (c).

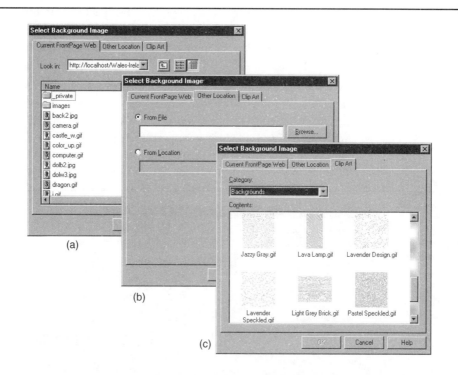

(a)

(b)

(c)

FIGURE 10.37

Determine the URL of an image on the World Wide Web or your intranet by right-clicking on the image in the Microsoft Internet Explorer 3.0 browser to display the Properties sheet for the image.

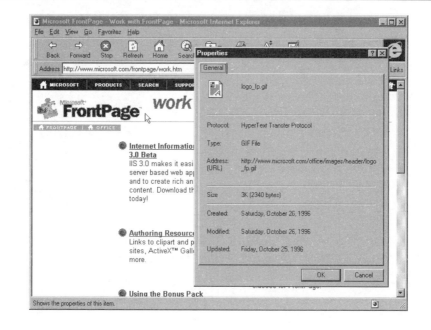

2. Click the Browse button to display the Select Background Image dialog. Double-click the images folder and double-click the irelndbg.jpg file. Click the Properties button on the Page Properties dialog to view the properties of the image (see Figure 10.38a).

3. Click the Edit button on the Image Properties dialog (see Figure 10.38b) to open the Microsoft Image Composer and display the image (see Figure 10.39). (If you haven't installed the Image Composer, whatever image editor you have associated with GIF and JPEG images opens instead.) You can edit the image, save the changes to the current web, and then close the Editor.

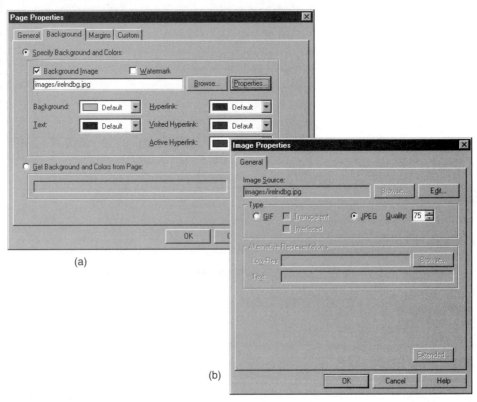

4. Click OK to close the Page Properties dialog and click the Save button in the toolbar to save the changes to the page. Click Yes when FrontPage prompts you to save the background image in the current web. The Editor creates a tiled background and displays the result (see Figure 10.40). The image covers so large a region that only two tiles are needed to cover the page.

FIGURE 10.39

Use the Microsoft Image Composer to edit the background image.

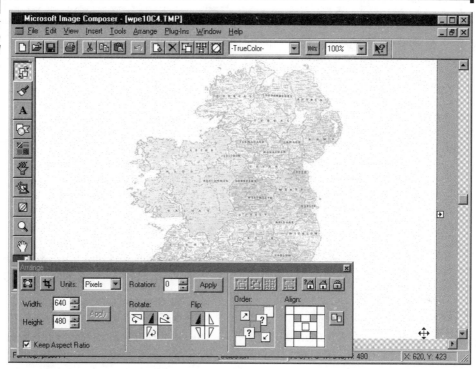

5. Scroll through the page. The background image scrolls with the text. In the next step, you fix the image by making it a watermark.

6. Right-click in the page to display the Page Properties dialog. Click the Background tab and check the Watermark check box. Click OK to close the dialog.

7. Click the Save button in the toolbar to save the change. Click Yes when FrontPage prompts you to save the background image. You cannot observe Watermark property in the Editor and must preview the page in a Web browser to see the effect.

8. Click the Preview in browser button in the toolbar. Scroll the page in the Web browser. The background stays fixed as the text scrolls by.

PART

III

Creating Web Pages

FIGURE 10.40

When you specify a background image, the Editor creates a tiled background to fill the page.

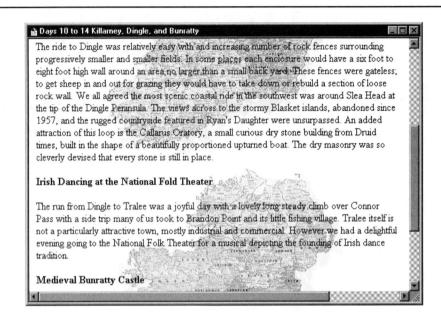

Colors   To set any of the color styles, select a color from one of the combo lists in the Background tab of the Page Properties dialog (see Figure 10.35). You can specify color styles for the following:

Style	Description
Background	The color that is displayed if you haven't selected a background image. If you have selected a background image, then the background color will be displayed in place of any color in the background image that is transparent. (See Chapter 13: Using Images and Video Clips to learn how to make a color transparent.)
Text	The color of all the text on the page except the text hyperlinks
Hyperlink	The color of the links on the page that haven't been visited
Visited Hyperklink	The color of all of the links on the page that have been selected in the browser
Active Hyperlink	The color of the active link. An active link is the link that is currently selected in the browser

Basing a Page's Styles on Another Page

You can base the styles for the current page on the styles you have set for another page. Click the Get Background Colors From Page option button and then click the Browse button to display a list of the pages in the current web. When you select a page from the list, FrontPage applies the colors and background image of the selected page to the current page. When you select this option, you automatically set all the styles for the current page, so the check boxes for the remaining styles are grayed out and unavailable; this means that either you choose to base a page on the complete set of styles from another page, or you make all of these decisions for the current page; you can't mix and match.

One of the steps in planning a web is choosing the styles for the entire web or for parts of the web. A key to efficient web design is creating styles pages with the settings you want to use, and then basing other pages on the style pages. If you make a change in a styles page, FrontPage automatically updates the styles of all of the pages based on the page.

A styles page is one of the pages that isn't really part of your public web; FrontPage has a way to hide these pages from the public. When you create a new web, Front-Page automatically creates a folder named _private for all of the pages you want to keep private. You can save a new page to the _private folder by including the folder name in the file path. To move an existing page to the _private folder, switch to the FrontPage Explorer, select the page icon and drag the icon to the _private folder. As an example, we'll use the Styles page in the Wales-Ireland web as the basis for the background and colors for another page in the Web.

1. Open the Home Page in the Editor. Right-click in the page and choose the Page Properties command from the shortcut menu.

2. Click the Get Background and Colors from Page option box, and then click the Browse button. Double-click the _private folder and then double-click styles.htm. After you base a page's styles on another page, the check boxes and combo lists in the upper section of the dialog are grayed out and unavailable (see Figure 10.41).

3. Click OK to close the Page Properties dialog. The Editor retrieves the styles and displays the background image. Click the Save button in the toolbar to save the changes to the page.

4. Repeat Steps 1,2, and 3 to set the page styles for the WalesMap and the IrelandMap page.

PART

III

Creating Web Pages

FIGURE 10.41

You can base the background and color styles on the styles of another page.

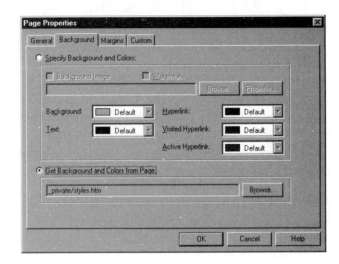

Understanding the Margins and Custom Page Properties

Use set page margins in the Margins tab of the Page Properties dialog (see Figure 10.42a). To set a top or left margin, click the check box and specify the size of the margin as the number of pixels.

Use the Custom tab of the Page Properties dialog to view the meta tags for the page (see Figure 10.42b). A *meta tag* is an HTML tag that supplies information about the page but does not affect its display. A meta tag can only be located in the header portion of the page denoted by the HTML <HEAD> </HEAD> tags. As an example, Figure 10.42 displays the Generator meta tag which refers to the editor that was used to create the page. The Generator meta tag has the value Microsoft FrontPage 2.0.

Viewing Page Properties in the FrontPage Explorer

The Editor keeps track of a page's design properties and the FrontPage Explorer keeps track of the page's administrative properties, such as creation and modification dates. To view the administrative and web-related properties for a page:

1. Select the page in any of the views of the FrontPage Explorer.

2. Choose the Edit ➤ Properties command from the Explorer menu bar, or right-click the page and choose Properties from the shortcut menu.

The Properties dialog has two tabbed panes. The General pane shown in Figure 10.43a displays the File name, the Title, the file Type and Size, and the Location of the file. The Location is the file's absolute URL. The Summary pane shown in Figure 10.43b displays dates and names of the authors who created and modified the page;

FIGURE 10.42

The Margins and the Custom tabs of the Page Properties dialog

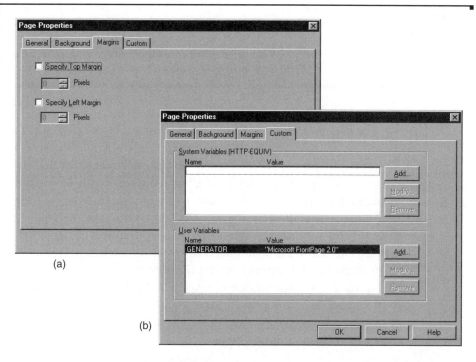

(a)

(b)

FIGURE 10.43

The Explorer has a Properties dialog for each file in the current Web.

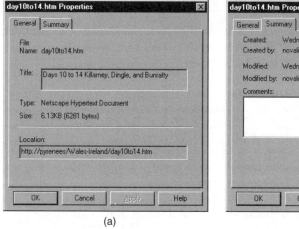

(a)

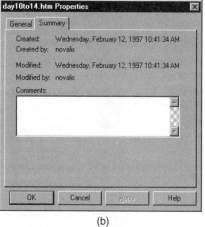

(b)

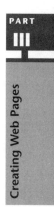

FrontPage handles this administrative information automatically by reading the computer's system clock to get the date and time, and recording the name of the author when the author logs in. You can use the Comments section in the Summary pane to record comments.

NOTE

The contents of the Comments list box in the Summary tab can be displayed on a page using a Substitution bot (see Chapter 16 for more information).

Printing a Page

A printed web page is not the same as the page that you see in the Editor or a Web browser. Links and images are printed as they appear in the Editor; however, form fields do not appear when you print a web page, and background images are not printed. Another difference is that when you print a page, the Editor breaks the web page into the required number of printed pages and assigns page numbers to the printed pages. The Editor automatically places the web Page Title at the top and the page number at the bottom of each printed page.

Use the File ➤ Print Preview command in the Editor menu bar to view how the web page will appear as printed pages. Figure 10.44 shows Print Preview for the Days 10 to 14 Killarney, Dingle, and Bunratty page. Use the File ➤ Print command in the Editor menu bar to print the pages.

FIGURE 10.44

When you print a web page, the Editor breaks the web page into a number of printed pages and assigns page numbers to the printed pages.

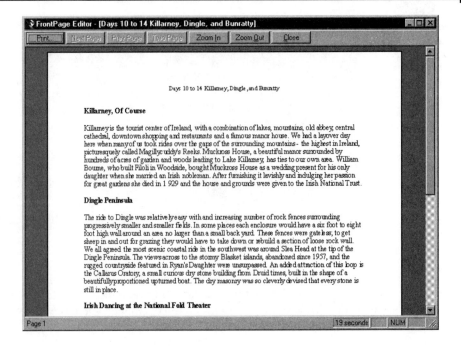

Viewing HTML

You can use the View ➤ HTML command from the Editor menu to view the HTML codes that the Editor generates for a page.

As an example, we'll view the HTML code for a new page based on the Bibiography template.

1. Choose File ➤ New from the Editor menu bar. Select Bibliography from the New Page template list and click OK. Click the Save button in the toolbar to save the new page. Figure 10.45a shows the new page.

2. Choose the View ➤ HTML command from the Editor menu bar (see Figure 10.45b).

A page based on the Bibliography template (a) and the HTML for the page (b)

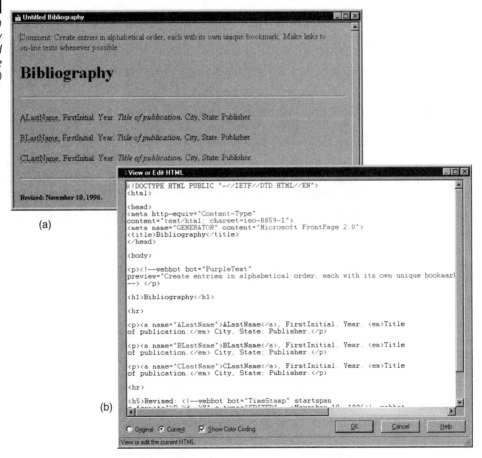

(a)

(b)

You can use the View or Edit HTML window to display two versions of the HTML codes: the original version for the page when you first opened it, and the current version for the page that the Editor generates when you make any changes after opening the page. The Editor creates a new current version if you edit the page or if you only resize the page window. When you open the View or Edit HTML window, it displays the current version by default. You can edit the current display using the usual cut, copy, and paste commands and keyboard shortcuts.

1. Click in the View or Edit HTML window and change Bibliography to Bibliographies. Toggle between the Original and Current option buttons.

2. Click OK to close the View or Edit HTML window. The Untitled Bibliography page displays the change you made.

3. Close the page without saving the change.

Page Mechanics

This section describes several ways to manipulate a page.

Changing a Page Title

You change the title for a page by setting the Title property in the Editor.

1. Choose File ➤ Open from the Editor menu bar, and select the page whose title you want to change. You can select a page in the current web or any web page in your computer's file system.

2. Choose File ➤ Page Properties from the Editor menu bar, or right-click in the page and choose Page Properties from the shortcut menu.

3. Modify the page title in the Title text box and click OK.

4. Click the Save button in the toolbar. If the page is in the current web, the FrontPage Explorer displays the changed page title immediately.

Changing a Page Location

The page Location is changed by moving the page in the FrontPage Explorer.

1. Select the page in the Contents pane of Folder View in the FrontPage Explorer.

2. Hold down the left mouse button, drag the page icon to the destination folder, and release the mouse button. The Explorer displays a message that the file is renamed. If the relocation would cause links to break, the Explorer displays a dialog that gives you the opportunity to update the links.

3. Click Yes to update the links and No to break the links.

NOTE

You can't change a page's location in the Editor except by choosing File ➤ Save As and saving a copy of the current page to a new location.

Deleting a Page from a Web

You delete a page or several pages from the current web using the FrontPage Explorer. See the "Deleting a File or Folder" section in Chapter 6.

WARNING

There is no way to reverse a deletion. Once you delete a web page, it is gone forever.

Exporting and Importing a Page

You can export a page in the current web to a new .htm file in any folder in your file system. You use the FrontPage Explorer to export a page. See the "Exporting a File from a Web" section in Chapter 6.

TIP

You can export a page from the current web to another web in your file system by exporting the page to the other web's content directory. When you open the other web, the new page is included in the web automatically.

You can import a page to the current web from another web or from any "text" file (with one of the formats in Table 10.3) in your file system using the FrontPage Explorer. See the "Importing Files" section in Chapter 6.

When you import a page from another web in your file system, you may break the links that the page has to other files. As an example, Figure 10.46 shows the broken links that are the result of importing the meetings.htm page from the PCTC web to the Wales-Ireland web. The broken links occur because the meetings.htm page has links to the meeting.htm, training.htm, and footer.htm pages in the PCTC web. Chapter 7: Managing Links describes the options for dealing with broken links.

Importing a page from another web may result in broken links.

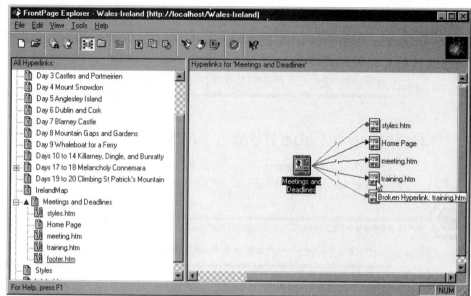

NOTE

When you import a file using the Import command in the FrontPage Explorer, the file's format is not changed; for example, you can import a .txt or a .bmp file directly into the web. It is only when you try to open the .txt file in the Editor (using the Editor's File ➤ Open command) or when you try to insert the image in a page (using the Editor's Insert ➤ Image command) that the Editor converts the contents of the file.

Adding a Page Task to the To Do List

When you are working in the Editor, you may want to delay the completion of a task for the page you are working with. For example, you may want to add links to another section of the web you haven't created yet or assign page design tasks to someone in the graphics department.

Add a task that is linked to the active page to the To Do List, as follows:

1. Choose the Edit ➤ Add To Do Task command from the Editor menu bar.

2. Enter the task name and description in the Add To Do Task dialog (see Figure 10.47a) and click OK. The task is added to the To Do list. You can view the To Do list when you are working in either the Editor or the Explorer.

3. To view the To Do list, choose the Tools ➤ Show To Do List command in the Editor or the Explorer menu bar or click the To Do List button in the Editor or the Explorer toolbar (see Figure 10.47b).

Chapter 8: Understanding To Do Lists explains how to use the To Do List.

FIGURE 10.47

You can add a task to the To Do list for the active page in the Editor (a). You can view the To Do List (b) from the Explorer or the Editor.

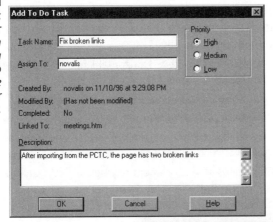

(a)

(b)

What Goes into a Page?

In this chapter, you've learned how to work with pages as entities without looking at what goes into a page. You've learned how to manipulate pages: how to open, save and close them; how to move, delete and export them; and how to set their properties. The next several chapters deal with the contents of pages.

Table 10.4 lists the kinds of elements you can insert into a page and where you can learn more about these page elements.

PART

III

Creating Web Pages

TABLE 10.4: WEB PAGE OBJECTS

Object	Descriptions	Where to Look for Information
"text" files	Choose Insert ➤ File to insert a file if it has one of several common formats. The FrontPage Editor converts the file to HTML and inserts the converted contents into the page.	Chapter 10
Horizontal Lines	Insert Choose Insert ➤ Horizontal Line to insert a horizontal line.	Chapter 11
Text	Type, format, and edit text and paragraphs directly using the Editor's tools.	Chapter 11
Symbols	Choose Insert ➤ Symbol to insert a special character.	Chapter 11
Comments	Choose Insert ➤ Comment to insert a comment that is invisible when the page is viewed in a Web browser.	Chapter 11
Marquees	Choose Insert ➤ Marquee to insert animated text, called a marquee.	Chapter 11
Hyperlinks	Choose Insert ➤ Hyperlink to create a text hyperlink.	Chapter 13 covers creating text hyperlinks and Chapter 14 covers image hyperlinks.
Image files	Choose Insert ➤ Image to insert an Image in a wide variety of image formats. FrontPage converts the image file to GIF or JPEG and inserts the converted contents.	Chapter 14 covers inserting images and creating image links.
Video files	Choose Insert ➤ Video to insert a Video for Windows (.avi) file directly on a page for viewing in a Web browser.	Chapter 13
Background sound files	Choose Insert ➤ Background Sound to embed a sound clip in many of the popular sound formats for playing in a Web browser.	Chapter 13

Continued ▶

Object	Descriptions	Where to Look for Information
	TABLE 10.4: WEB PAGE OBJECTS (CONTINUED)	
Tables	Choose Table ➤ Insert Table to insert and configure a table.	Chapter 15
Frames	Choose File ➤ New to create a new page with frames using the Frames Wizard.	Chapter 16
Forms	Choose Insert ➤ Form Field to insert a form field in an existing form for gathering information from a Web visitor.	Chapter 17
WebBots	Choose Insert ➤ WebBot Component to insert and configure a WebBot component.	Chapter 16 covers using WebBots in page design, and Chapters 17, 18, and 19 cover using WebBots to create interactive pages.
HTML elements	Choose Insert ➤ HTML Markup to insert an HTML element that FrontPage does not recognize.	Chapter 11
Scripts	Choose Insert ➤ Script to insert a script.	Chapter 20
ActiveX Controls, Plug-ins, Java applets, and Powerpoint animations	Choose Insert ➤ Other Components to insert objects that extend the range of interactive and multimedia capabilities for a page.	Chapter 20
Dynamic data values from a database	Choose Edit ➤ Database to insert placeholders for parameters and data values.	Chapter 21

Dealing with Multimedia Files

In addition to inserting multimedia files directly into a FrontPage page, you can also create a hyperlink on a page to open the file. For example, you can embed a sound file as a background sound that plays as soon as the Web visitor browses to the page or you can create a hyperlink to the sound file so that the sound plays only when the visitor clicks the hyperlink.

In order to open a multimedia file, the computer needs to know which helper application or add-in to start.

PART

III

Creating Web Pages

While you are developing a web, you can tell FrontPage which helper application to use. Chapter 6: Working with Files explains how to associate a helper application using the FrontPage Explorer. After associating a helper application for the file's type, when you follow the link in the Editor, FrontPage opens the helper application. For example, if you use the Media Player to play a .wav file, following the link opens the Media Player with the file ready to play; you have to click the Play button yourself and close the Media Player after the file has been played.

When you publish a web, the Web visitor's browser must also know how to open the file. If the visitor's browser cannot play the file itself and is not configured to start a helper application or an add-in for the file's type, the file won't run properly.

Keyboard Shortcuts for Working with Pages

Table 10.5 lists keyboard shortcuts for working with pages in the Editor, including shortcuts for navigating in a page; navigating between pages; and opening, saving and printing a page. See Tables 11.2 and 11.3 in Chapter 11 for keyboard shortcuts for editing objects you add to a page.

TABLE 10.5: KEYBOARD SHORTCUTS FOR WORKING WITH PAGES

Keyboard Shortcut	Description
Home	Move to the beginning of the line
End	Move to the end of the line
Ctrl+Home	Move to the top of the page
Ctrl+End	Move to the bottom of the page
Page Up, Page Down	Move through the page a screen at a time
Up Arrow, Down Arrow	Move through the page a line at a time
Ctrl+F6	Move forward through open pages
Shift+Ctrl+F6	Move backward through open pages
Ctrl+N	Display the New Page dialog
Ctrl+O	Display the Open File dialog
Ctrl+S	Save the active page
Ctrl+P	Print the active page

Manipulating Page Elements

The chapters ahead cover techniques for working with each type of page element. There are some operations that are common to most objects that you can insert in a page. This section describes the common operations.

Selecting Objects   Before you can manipulate an object, you must first select it. Different objects have their own selection rules that will be described in the upcoming chapters; however, as a general rule, you can select all the objects embedded in a line by clicking the mouse in the first column in the page. This unmarked column in the left margin is reserved for selecting lines and is called the *selector bar*. You can select all objects in contiguous lines by clicking in the selector bar of the first line, holding down the left mouse button, and dragging to the last line you want to select. You can drag towards the top or towards the bottom of the page. You can also select contiguous lines by clicking the selector bar of the first line, and then pressing the Shift key while you click the selector bar of the last line. You cannot select discontiguous lines. Selected objects are highlighted (displayed in reversed video).

Moving Objects by Drag-and-Drop   You can move selected objects using the drag-and-drop technique. To move a selected object, left-click the object, hold down the left mouse button as you drag the selection to a new location, and release the left mouse button to drop the selected object at the new location. You can move a single object or a selection of objects. You can move the selection to a new location on the active page or to a location on another open page in the Editor.

Copying Objects   Choose Edit ➤ Copy from the Editor menu bar, click the Copy button in the toolbar, or press Ctrl+C to copy selected objects to the Clipboard. The Clipboard can hold only one selection at a time. Copying a selection replaces the Clipboard's current contents. You can copy just about any object, including text, images, links, bookmarks, bots, forms, or tables. When you copy the object, you are copying the HTML coding as well. If you paste the contents of the Clipboard into a FrontPage Editor page, the HTML coding is pasted also. If you paste the contents to another application, only the text is pasted.

Pasting Objects   Choose Edit ➤ Paste from the Editor menu bar, click the Paste button in the toolbar, or press Ctrl+V to paste the contents of the Clipboard at the insertion point. After pasting, the Clipboard continues to hold a copy of the selection. If you selected objects before pasting, the selected objects are overwritten.

Copying and Pasting Objects by Drag-and-Drop   You can copy selected objects and paste the selection to a new location in one operation. Right-click in the selection and hold down the right mouse button as you drag the selection to a new location. When you release the right mouse button, a shortcut menu appears at the insertion point. Choose the Move Here command to move the selection or the Copy Here command to paste a copy of the selection.

You can use drag-and-drop for a single object or a selection of objects. You can drag-and-drop the selection to a new location on the active page or to a location on another open page.

Cutting Objects   Choose Edit ➤ Cut from the Editor menu bar, click the Cut button in the toolbar, or press Ctrl+X to remove selected objects from the page and place a copy of the selected objects in the Clipboard.

Deleting Objects   Choose Edit ➤ Clear from the Editor menu bar, or press the Delete or Backspace key to remove selected objects from the page without placing a copy of the selected objects in the Clipboard.

 Undoing and Redoing Actions   After you make a change to a page, you can reverse the change by choosing Edit ➤ Undo from the Editor menu bar, clicking the Undo button in the toolbar, or pressing Ctrl+Z to reverse the change. After undoing a change, you can redo the change by choosing Edit ➤ Redo from the Editor menu bar, clicking the Redo button in the toolbar, or pressing Ctrl+Y. You can undo and redo the last 30 changes you made. The Undo and Redo commands in the Edit menu change to reflect the specific action you made. For example, after you type characters, the Undo Typing command is displayed in the Edit menu and after pasting a selection, the Undo Paste command is displayed instead.

For More...

This chapter has shown you how to work with a web page as a file. The other chapters in Part III show you how to embed or insert objects for displaying and laying out content in a page. Table 10.4 lists the types of objects that you'll learn to insert and the chapter that covers each type of object. The "Manipulating Page Elements" section describes general techniques for working with an inserted object.

Chapter

11

Working with Text and Lines

Working with
Text and Lines

There are many ways to include text in a web page. You can:

- Open a new web page based on a "text" file
- Insert a "text" file into an existing web page
- Type characters directly
- Paste text copied to the Clipboard in another document

Chapter 10 covered the first two methods, and this chapter explains the last two. Once the text is on the page, you often need to manipulate the text by changing how the characters look, including their color, size, boldness, and underlining, and how paragraphs look, including alignment and indentation. This chapter covers the techniques that the FrontPage Editor provides for manipulating text. You'll quickly discover that most of the techniques are the same as those in word processing applications. In particular, if you have experience with Microsoft Word, you already know most of the menu commands and keyboard shortcuts. This chapter also explains how to animate text and how to use horizontal lines to embellish a page.

For hands-on experience working with text, create a new FrontPage web as follows:

1. In the Explorer, choose File ➤ New FrontPage webfrom the Explorer menu bar, or press Ctrl+N. Click OK in the New FrontPage web dialog to create a new web with a single blank page (see Figure 11.1a). In the Normal web Template dialog, type **TextAndLines** as the name of the new web (see Figure 11.1b).

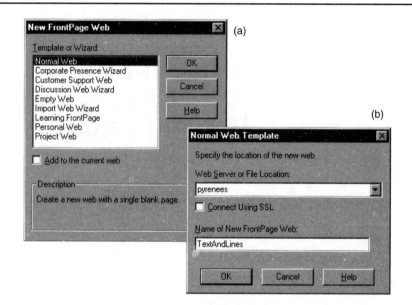

2. Click the Show FrontPage Editor button in the Explorer toolbar. So that we have some text to work with, we'll create a new page by opening an existing Word document in the Editor.

3. In the Editor, choose File ➤ Open, click the Other Location tab in the Open File dialog (see Figure 11.2a), and then click the Browse button to display the Open File dialog. Choose All Files (*.*) in the Files of type combo box, locate the Wales-Ireland Manuscript folder on the book's CD-ROM, and double-click to open the folder. Click the Day1.doc file on the book's CD-ROM, and then click Open (see Figure 11.2b). Click OK in the Open File As dialog. The Editor converts the file first to the RTF format and then to the HTML format, and displays the converted contents in a new page (see Figure 11.3a).

FIGURE 11.2

Click From File in the Other Location tab to open a page on a file in your computer's file system (a). Click Browse to display the files in your computer's file system (b).

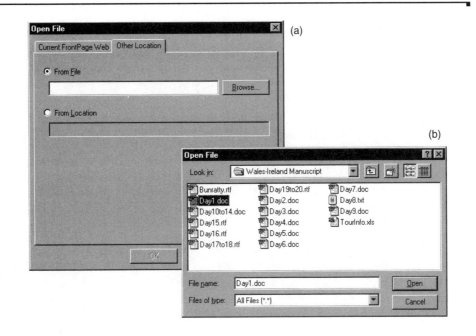

(a)

(b)

4. Choose File ➤ Save As from the Editor menu bar and click OK to save the page to the current web using the title and name that the Editor suggests. The Editor suggests a title based on the first several words of the page and extracts up to eight characters of the title as the name (see Figure 11.3b).

The Format Toolbar and Keyboard Shortcuts

When you change the appearance and layout of text, you are changing the text's format. You can format either characters or paragraphs. The Editor provides a set of menu commands and toolbar buttons for changing the format of selected text. Figure 11.4 shows the Format toolbar. You can display the Format toolbar by choosing View ➤ Format Toolbar from the Editor menu bar.

PART

III

Creating Web Pages

A Word document is converted automatically to HTML and displayed as a new page (a). When you save the document to the web, the Editor suggests a title and name (b).

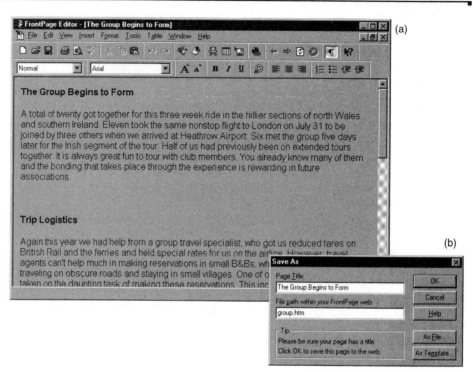

The Format Toolbar

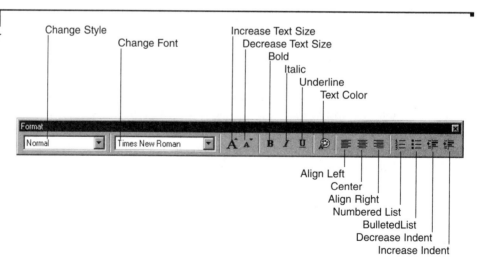

Table 11.1 lists the formatting buttons, the corresponding menu command, and keyboard shortcut.

TABLE 11.1: FORMAT TOOLBAR BUTTONS AND KEYBOARD SHORTCUTS				
Button	**Tooltip**	**Function**	**Menu Command**	**Keyboard Shortcut**
Normal	Change Style	Changes the paragraph style of the selected paragraph	Format ➤ Paragraphs and Format ➤ Bullets and Numbering	
Times New Roman	Change Font	Changes the font of the selected characters	Format ➤ Font	
A	Increase Text Size	Increases the font size by one level	Format ➤ Font	Shift+Ctrl+>
A	Decrease Text Size	Decreases the font size by one level	Format ➤ Font	Shift+Ctrl+<
B	Bold	Toggles the font style from regular to bold	Format ➤ Font	Ctrl+B
I	Italic	Toggles the font style from regular to italic	Format ➤ Font	Ctrl+I
U	Underlined	Toggles the character style to underlined	Format ➤ Font	Ctrl+U
	Text Color	Displays the Color dialog for changing text color	Format ➤ Font	
	Align Left	Aligns the paragraph to the left margin	Format ➤ Paragraph	
	Center	Aligns the paragraph about the center	Format ➤ Paragraph	

Continued ▶

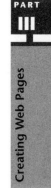

PART

III

Creating Web Pages

TABLE 11.1: FORMAT TOOLBAR BUTTONS AND KEYBOARD SHORTCUTS (CONTINUED)

Button	Tooltip	Function	Menu Command	Keyboard Shortcut
	Align Right	Aligns the paragraph to the right margin	Format ➤ Paragraph	
	Numbered List	Reformats the currently selected paragraphs as a numbered list	Format ➤ Bullets and Numbering	
	Bulleted List	Reformats the currently selected paragraphs as a bulleted list	Format ➤ Bullets and Numbering	
	Decrease Indent	Remove the indentation of the selected paragraph		Shift+ Ctrl+M
	Increase Indent	Indent the selected paragraph		Ctrl+M

Text Mechanics

For the most part, typing text in a web page is similar to typing text using any word processing application, such as Microsoft Word. The FrontPage Editor has many of the familiar text editing techniques.

Selecting Text

In most cases, you must select the text before you can manipulate it. Selected text is highlighted (displayed in reversed video).

To select a line of text, click in the selector bar in the left margin of the page. The selector bar is not marked, but when you move the pointer into the selector bar, the pointer changes to a white arrow.

To select all text in contiguous lines, click in the selector bar of the first line and hold down the left mouse button, as you drag the mouse to the last line you want to select. You can drag towards the top or towards the bottom of the page. You can also select contiguous lines by clicking the selector bar of the first line, and pressing the Shift key while you click the selector bar of the last line. You cannot select discontiguous lines.

To select a group of characters, click to place the insertion point at the beginning of the text you want to select, hold down the left mouse button, and drag to include the last character. You can drag to the left or right, and you can drag to include characters from contiguous lines.

1. Move the pointer to the selector bar of the first line in the page, and click to select the entire line. The Editor places the blinking insertion point at the end of the selected text. Figure 11.5 shows highlighting of the selected line and shows the pointer as an arrow indicating that the pointer is in the selector bar.

Select an entire line by clicking in the left margin. The pointer changes to an arrow and the selected text is highlighted (displayed in reversed video).

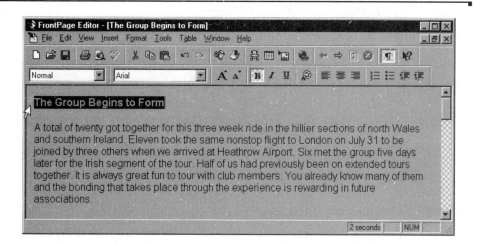

2. Click in the selector bar in the first line of the page. Holding down the left mouse button and drag to select four lines.

3. Click in the selector bar in the first line of the page. Press Shift and click in the selector bar of the fourth line.

4. Click to the left of the word Group in the first line of the page. Hold down the left mouse button and drag to select the first four letters.

5. Double-click anywhere in the word Begin to select the entire word.

PART

III

Creating Web Pages

Copying and Pasting Text

You can use the familiar methods to copy and paste text. This section covers the menu commands and the next section describes the drag-and-drop technique.

To copy selected text to the Clipboard, choose Edit ➤ Copy from the Editor menu bar, click the Copy button in the toolbar, or press Ctrl+C. When you copy a text selection to the Clipboard, you also copy its formatting.

To paste the contents of the Clipboard at the insertion point, choose Edit ➤ Paste from the Editor menu bar, click the Paste button in the toolbar, or press Ctrl+V. If you selected objects before pasting, the selected objects are overwritten.

When you paste text from one web page into another web page, the FrontPage Editor may change the text's formatting. If you paste a text selection from a web page into a document of another application, the formatting is lost and only unformatted text is pasted. If you paste text from a document in another application to a web page, the original formatting is lost.

To observe formatting changes when you paste text selections, do the following:

1. Scroll down the page and click in the selector bar of the line starting Bus to Machynlleth, Wales. Press Ctrl+C to copy the selection. Click in the line below the last line of text and press Ctrl+V to paste the selection.

2. Click in the selector bar of the line you pasted to select the line. Change the format by clicking the following sequence of toolbar buttons: Increase Text Size, Italics, and Center (see Figure 11.6a). Press Ctrl+C to copy the text, click in the next line, and press Ctrl+V to paste the selection. The pasted selection retains the text size and bold style, but loses is centered alignment.

3. Press Ctrl+Z to undo the last paste.

4. Start up Microsoft Word, or another word processing application, and open a new document. Press Ctrl+V to paste the contents of the Clipboard to the document. All of the formatting is lost (see Figure 11.6b).

5. Select the text in the Word document, and change the format by clicking the following sequence of toolbar buttons in Word: Bold, Italic, and Center. Press Ctrl+C to copy the text, click in the next blank line in the page in the Editor, and press Ctrl+V to paste the selection. The Editor converts the selection to HTML and pastes it at the insertion point. The selection pasted from Word retains the text size and bold italic style, but loses is centered alignment.

6. Close Word without saving the document.

When you copy text with formatting in a web page (a) and paste to a Microsoft Word document, the formatting is lost (b).

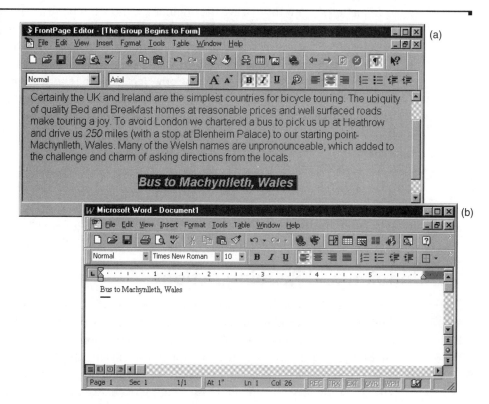

Cutting and Deleting Text

To cut text, choose Edit ➤ Cut from the Editor menu bar, click the Cut button in the toolbar, or press Ctrl+X to remove selected text from the page and place a copy of the selection in the Clipboard.

To delete text, use the Delete or Backspace key to remove selected text from the page without placing a copy of the selected objects in the Clipboard.

Using Drag-and-Drop to Move or Copy Text

The easiest way to move selected text is to use the drag-and-drop method. Select the text that you want to move. Click in the selection, hold down the left mouse button as you drag the selection to the new location, and then release the mouse button. The selection is moved to the new location—that is, the original selection is cut to the Clipboard and pasted at the new location in one step. You can use drag-and-drop to move a selection to another location on the same page to a location on another open page.

PART

III

Creating Web Pages

Sometimes you want to leave the original selection and paste a copy to a new location. You can use drag-and-drop to copy the selection to a new location in one step. To copy instead of move, select the text that you want to copy, right-click in the selection, hold down the right mouse button as you drag the selection to the new location, and release the mouse button. Choose Copy Here from the shortcut menu to copy the selection to the new location—that is, the original selection is copied to the Clipboard and pasted at the new location in one step.

You can use the drag-and-drop technique to move or copy a selection to another location on the same page or to a location on another open page.

Undoing and Redoing Actions

After you make a change to a page, you can reverse the change by choosing Edit ➤ Undo from the Editor menu bar, clicking the Undo button in the toolbar, or pressing Ctrl+Z to reverse the change. After undoing a change, you can redo the change by choosing Edit ➤ Redo from the Editor menu bar, clicking the Redo button in the toolbar, or pressing Ctrl+Y. You can undo and redo the last 30 changes you have made. The Undo and Redo commands in the Edit menu change to reflect the specific action you made; for example, after you type characters, the Undo Typing command is displayed in the Edit menu and after pasting a selection, the Undo Paste command is displayed instead.

To explore these techniques:

1. Select the text you pasted from Word and click the Cut button in the toolbar. The text is copied to the Clipboard and removed from the page.

2. Click the Undo button in the toolbar. The cut is reversed and the text is displayed.

3. Click the Redo button in the toolbar. The last action is reversed and the text is removed.

4. Select the last two lines of text (the lines you pasted earlier), and press Delete.

Finding and Replacing Text in a Page

To find a text phrase, use the Edit ➤ Find command in the Editor menu bar to display the Find dialog (see Figure 11.7a). Enter the text phrase you want to locate in the Find

What text box. You can choose to find the whole word and to match the case. You can also choose the direction of the search, searching down towards the end of the page or up towards the beginning of the page.

To illustrate finding text:

1. Choose Edit ➤ Find in the Editor menu bar, or press Ctrl+F. Type **ireland** in the Find What text box, and click the Find Next button. The first occurrence of the word is selected and highlighted. Click the Find Next button repeatedly and locate three additional occurrences. After all occurrences have been found, the Editor displays the message shown in Figure 11.7b.

FIGURE 11.7

Use the Find dialog to specify the text search (a). After searching the entire page, the Editor displays a message (b).

(a)

(b)

2. With "ireland" as the search text, click the Match case check box and then click the Find Next button. The Editor displays the message shown in Figure 11.7b without finding any matches. Click OK to close the message.

3. Type **tour** as the search text and click to uncheck the Match case check box. Click the Find Next button repeatedly to locate the text in the following words: tour, tours, tourist, and touring. Click OK to close the message.

4. With tour as the search text, click Match whole word only and then click the Find Next button repeatedly. The Editor locates the two occurrences of the word tour before terminating the search. Click OK to close the message.

To replace a specified text phrase with another text phrase, use the Replace command in the Edit menu to display the Replace dialog (see Figure 11.8). Specify the text you want to replace in the Find What text box and specify its replacement in the Replace with text box. As with the Find dialog, you can choose to match the whole word and to match the case of the search text. Click the Find Next button to locate the next occurrence of the search text and click the Replace button to replace the

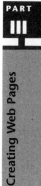

PART

III

Creating Web Pages

occurrence with the replacement text. Alternatively, you can click the Replace All button to replace all occurrences of the search text at once. When you click the Replace All button, the Editor begins the search at the top of the page.

Use the Replace dialog to find and replace specified text in the active page.

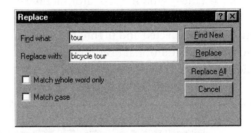

To practice finding and replacing text:

1. With the insertion point at the beginning of the page, choose Edit ➤ Replace command from the Editor menu bar or press Ctrl+H. Type **tour** in the Find What text box and **bicycle tour** in the Replace with text box.

2. Click the Find Next button. The Editor finds the first occurrence. Without replacing the first occurrence, click the Find Next button to find the second occurrence, and click Replace to replace the text.

3. Click the Replace All button. The Editor replaces all occurrences of the search text and leaves the insertion point at the location of the last replacement. Because the Editor starts at the top of the page, the second occurrence that we replaced in Step 2 is replaced again. Click Cancel to close the Replace dialog.

4. Click the Undo button in the toolbar repeatedly to undo the replacements.

NOTE

When you include another file in a page using the Include WebBot component, the Find and Replace commands do not search for the specified text in the included file. To find and replace specified text in an included file, you must open the file and search it separately.

When you are working in the Editor, you can find and replace specified text on the active page only. A new feature in FrontPage 97 is that you can use the Tools ➤ Find

and Tools ➤ Replace commands in the Explorer menu bar to find and replace specified text in all pages or in a selection of pages in the current web. See the "Global
Editing of a Web" section in Chapter 6.

Checking the Spelling

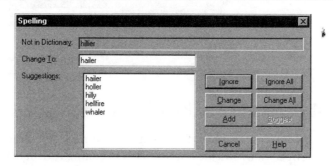

Use the Tools ➤ Spelling command from the Editor menu bar, click the Check Spelling
button in the toolbar, or press F7, to check the spelling of the active page. When a
word that is not in the dictionary is found, the Editor displays the Spelling dialog with
the word shown in the Not in Dictionary text box (Figure 11.9). The dialog suggests a
correction in the Change to text box and lists additional suggestions. Click a word in
the list to select it and place it in the Change To text box. The buttons in the dialog
indicate the choices:

Ignore	Ignore the suggestions and leave the word as is for the current word or all occurrences of the word. You can click Ignore All to ignore all suggestions.
Change	Change the word to the text in the Change To text box for the current word or all occurrences of the word. You can click Change All to change all words that the Spell Checker locates to the words that the Checker suggests.
Add	Add the current word to the dictionary and leave the word as is.
Cancel	Cancel the spell check of the rest of the page.

Unless you click Cancel to end the spell check, after you take action on the current
word, the Editor locates the next word that is not in the dictionary.

PART

III

Creating Web Pages

FIGURE 11.9

*Using the Spell
checker*

NOTE

FrontPage maintains a custom dictionary. When you click the Add button, the word is added to the dictionary.

NOTE

When you include another file in a page using the Include WebBot component, the Spelling command does not search for misspelled words in the included file. To check for spelling errors in an included file, you must open the file and check it separately.

When you are working in the Editor, you can check the spelling on the active page only. A new feature in FrontPage 97 is that you can use the Tools ➤ Spelling command in the Explorer menu bar to check for spelling errors in all pages or a selection of pages in the current web. See the "Global Editing of a Web" section in Chapter 6.

Using the Thesaurus

Use the Tools ➤ Thesaurus command from the Editor menu bar, or press Shift+F7, to find alternatives for the selected word. The Thesaurus dialog lists the possible meanings for the selected word (see Figure 11.10). You can select a meaning and display possible synomyns, and choose to replace the selected word with a synonym.

FIGURE 11.10

Use the Thesaurus dialog to display possible synonyms for the selected word.

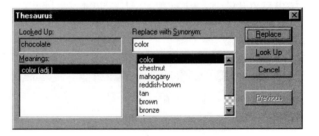

Keyboard Shortcuts for Editing Pages

Table 11.2 lists keyboard shortcuts for editing. These shortcuts apply to general editing operations and are not restricted to editing text. Table 11.3 lists keyboard shortcuts for editing text. See Table 10.5 in Chapter 10 for a list of keyboard techniques for working with pages.

TABLE 11.2: KEYBOARD SHORTCUTS FOR EDITING

Key Combination	Description
Ctrl+C or Ctrl+Insert	Copy selected item to the Clipboard
Ctrl+X or Shift+Delete	Copy selected item to the Clipboard and remove the selection from the page
Ctrl+V or Shift+Insert	Paste Clipboard contents and replace the current selection on the page
Ctrl+Z or Alt+Backspace	Undo the last action
Ctrl+Y	Redo the last undone action
Ctrl+A	Select all items on the page
Shift+Enter	Insert a line break
Shift+Space	Insert a nonbreaking space
Shift+Ctrl+Space	Insert a hard space
Delete	Delete selected item
Alt+Enter	Display the properties dialog for the selected item

TABLE 11.3: KEYBOARD SHORTCUTS FOR EDITING TEXT

Key Combination	Description
Ctrl+F	Display dialog to find selected text
Ctrl+H	Display dialog to replace selected text
Ctrl+B	Toggle bold for selected text
Ctrl+I	Toggle italic for selected text
Ctrl+U	ToggleUnderline of selected text
Shift+Ctrl+>	Increase font size of selected text
Shift+Ctrl+<	Decrease font size of selected text
Ctrl+M	Indent the selected paragraph
Shift+Ctrl+M	Outdent the selected paragraph
Ctrl+Space or Shift+Ctrl+Z	Reset text formatting to normal
Ctrl+=	Increase subscript level of selected text
Shift+Ctrl+=	Increase superscript level of selected text
Ctrl+Enter	End a list
F7	Spell-check the page

PART

III

Creating Web Pages

Understanding Formatting and Styles

Text formatting in a web page means specifying the appearance and arrangement of the text on the page. There are two kinds of text formats: *character formats* and *paragraph formats*. In FrontPage, formatting characters means selecting between the default font and typewriter font, selecting the font size and style (such as bold or underlined), the color of characters, and the vertical position of characters (for superscripts and subscripts). Formatting paragraphs means positioning lines by selecting alignments and indentations.

A *style* is a collection of formatting selections that change the appearance of the text. There are two kinds of styles: *character styles* that define the appearance of selected characters within a paragraph, and *paragraph styles* that define the appearance of lines and the text in the paragraph. When you start creating a web page, FrontPage uses a predefined style for paragraphs called the Normal style.

The Normal style includes Times New Roman font, black text color, and text size 12 and lines aligned with the left margin and without indentations. FrontPage provides a set of paragraph styles you can apply to individual paragraphs or to all the paragraphs on the page. Click the arrow of the Change Styles combo list in the format toolbar to view the list of paragraph styles (see Figure 11.11). FrontPage also provides a set of character styles you can apply to selected text within paragraphs.

FIGURE 11.11

Click the arrow of the Change Styles combo box in the format toolbar to display the list of paragraph styles. The format toolbar has buttons for many of the character styles.

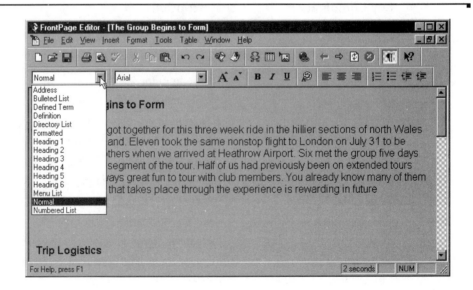

NOTE

The character style you apply to a piece of text within a paragraph overrides the paragraph style you may have applied to the paragraph.

Character Formats and Styles

You can change the format of a text phrase by selecting it and clicking buttons in the Format toolbar (see Table 11.1 for a description of the buttons). Although clicking toolbar buttons is the fastest way to change a format, the buttons provide only a few of the available format choices. The full set of character styles is displayed in the Font dialog. Display the Font dialog by doing any of the following:

- Choose Format ➤ Font from the Editor menu bar.
- Right-click the selected text and choose Font Properties in the shortcut menu.
- Press Alt+Enter.

The character formats and styles are arranged in the two tabs of the Font dialog, as shown in Figure 11.12.

Understanding the Regular Character Styles

The Font tab of the Font dialog displays the standard choices for formatting characters (See Figure 11.12a). You can choose from a large selection of fonts, font styles, font sizes, and effects, as follows:

Font   The default font is Times New Roman. Change the font by choosing a font name from the list.

Font Style   The default is Regular. You can change the font style to italic, bold, or bold italic.

Size   The default text size is 12 points, called the Normal size. You can change the font size by selecting another size in the Size list box. In addition to the normal size, there are seven sizes, as follows: 8 pt, 10 pt, 12 pt, 14 pt, 18 pt, 24 pt, and 36 pt.

Effects   You can underline, strikethrough, and change to typewriter font. Typewriter font is a special font that has identical spacing for every letter or character.

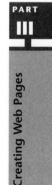

FIGURE 11.12

Use the Font dialog to change the format of selected text using regular styles (a) and special styles (b).

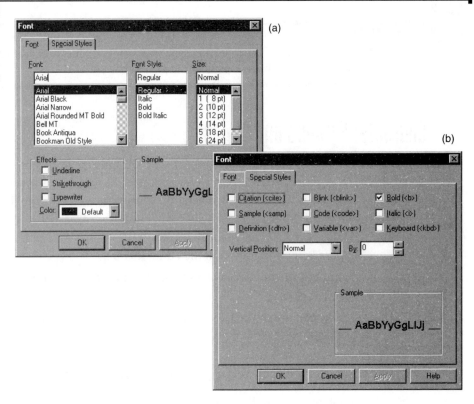

Color   The default is black. Change the text color by choosing a color from the list. Click Custom, the last item in the list, to create additional colors using the Color dialog (see Figure 11.13b below).

As you make choices in the Font tab, the Sample rectangle reflects your choices. Click Apply to apply the choices to the selected text in the page while the Font dialog is still open. Click OK to apply the choices to the selected text in the page and close the Font dialog.

If you click the Text Color toolbar button to change the color, you can choose the color from the Color dialog (see Figure 11.13a). Click the Define Custom Colors at the bottom of the Color dialog to display the expanded version (see Figure 11.13b).

To define a custom color:

1. Click the Text Color toolbar button and click Define Custom Colors.

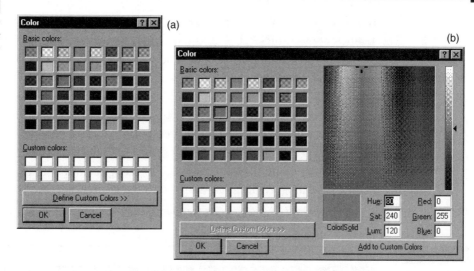

FIGURE 11.13

Use the Color dialog to select a basic color (a) or create a custom color (b).

2. Click in the custom color rectangle and move the pointer around in the rectangle. As the pointer moves to each spot in the rectangle, the numical values for the color's hue, saturation, and luminosity, and the numerical values for the color's red, green,and blue components are displayed.

3. Select a color and click Add to Custom Colors. The color you selected is placed in an available custom color box below the basic color boxes. Click OK to close the dialog and save the custom color.

Understanding the Special Styles

In addition to the regular character styles available in the Font tab, the Special Styles tab of the Font dialog displays a set of Special Styles (see Figure 11.12b). The Special Styles are available in HTML coding and may appear when you open .htm pages created in other applications or when you open a file that FrontPage converts to HTML. The FrontPage Editor may not be able to display a special style, such as Blink.

Creating Subscripts and Superscripts   You can create subscripts and superscripts by changing the vertical position of the selected characters relative to the other characters in the line. Select superscript or subscript from the Vertical Position combo box in the Special Styles tab and choose a number for the vertical shift.

PART

III

Creating Web Pages

To explore character fonts:

1. Select the text "twenty got together" in the paragraph below the first heading and choose Format ➤ Font from the Editor menu bar, or press Alt+Enter.

2. In the Font tab, choose the bold italic font style, choose 4 (14pt) as the font size, click the Underlined check box, and choose red in the Color combo list.

3. Click the Special Styles tab. Choose Superscript in the Vertical Position combo box and set the vertical shift to 4. As you click the arrows to adjust the vertical shift, the black lines in the Sample rectangle that indicate the bottom of the text line shift to indicate the magnitude of the vertical shift.

4. Click OK to apply the character style to the selected text in the page and close the Font dialog. Figure 11.14 shows the changed format.

5. Click the Undo button in the toolbar to undo the format change.

FIGURE 11.14

Create subscripts and superscripts in the Special Styles tab of the Font dialog.

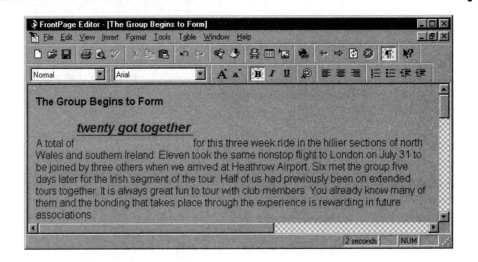

Resetting to the Normal Format

To reset the text format to the default Normal style, select the text and choose Format ➤ Remove Formatting from the Editor menu bar or press Ctrl+Space.

Inserting a Symbol

To insert a symbol at the insertion point:

1. Choose the Insert ➤ Symbol command from the Editor menu bar. Choose from the available characters in the Symbol dialog (see Figure 11.15). The selected character is displayed next to the Insert button.

2. Click the Insert button to insert the selected character. The Symbol dialog remains open and you can select another symbol.

3. Click the Close button to close the dialog.

FIGURE 11.15

You can insert one or more symbols using the Symbol dialog.

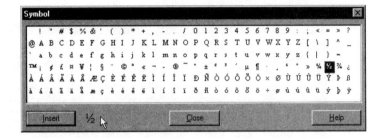

Inserting a Line Break

When you are working in a page and you press Enter, the Editor inserts a new line below, moves the text to the right of the insertion point to a new line, places the insertion point at the left of the new line, and begins a new paragraph. (The Editor does not display the paragraph symbol at the end of a paragraph, so clicking the Show/Hide ¶ does not have the effect you might expect from the ¶ symbol on the button.) You can start a new line without starting a new paragraph by inserting a line break.

To insert a line break at the insertion point:

1. Choose Insert ➤ Break from the Editor menu bar, or press Shift+Enter.

2. Click OK in the Break dialog to insert a normal line break (see Figure 11.16a). The other options in the Break dialog are used to insert line breaks when an image has been inserted in a page margin; these options are explained in Chapter 13. The Editor inserts a line break symbol at the insertion point and

PART

III

Creating Web Pages

moves the text to the right of the insertion point to a new line. (See Figure 11.16b). By default, FrontPage shows all line breaks.

3. You can hide the line breaks by selecting and unchecking View ➤ Format Marks from the Editor menu bar menu or by clicking the Show/Hide ¶ toolbar button.

FIGURE 11.16

Use the Break dialog (a) to insert a line break that forces a new line without starting a new paragraph. Click the Show/Hide ¶ toolbar button to view the line breaks (b).

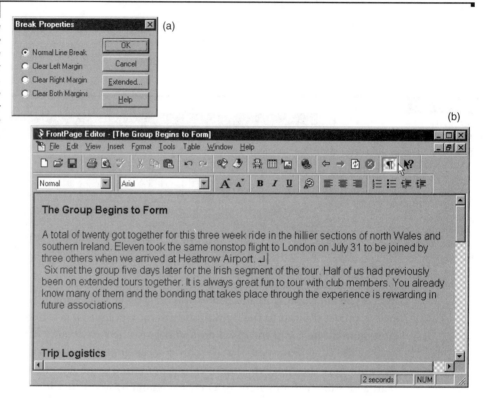

Paragraph Formats and Styles

The real difference between the FrontPage Editor and a word processing application is apparent in paragraph formatting. In a word processing application such as Word, you can use paragraph formats to control line length, the alignment of lines at the left and right boundaries or in the center, the amount of space between lines, the amount of space above and below a paragraph, and the horizontal placement of text using indentations and tab stops. In an HTML editor, such as the FrontPage Editor, there is no need to control line length because the line length adjusts automatically when you resize the page's window either in the Editor or in a web browser. In the Editor, you can align or indent paragraphs, but you can't adjust the vertical spacing between lines or paragraphs.

NOTE

When you use the Normal font, pressing the Tab key or the Space bar produces a single space between characters and subsequent key presses have no effect. To insert additional spaces, press Ctrl+Shift+Space. The Tab key is useful only if you are using the Formatted Text paragraph style.

Understanding Paragraph Properties

The FrontPage Editor provides a set of paragraph properties, including a set of built-in paragraph styles, alignment to the left or right margin or about the center, and indentation and outdentation. (In addition to these formats, the Editor includes styles for creating lists. List styles are described in the "Understanding Lists" section later in the chapter.)

Choose Format ➤ Paragraph to display the Paragraph Properties dialog (see Figure 11.17). The Paragraph Properties dialog displays the properties you can set for the paragraph, including the paragraph format and alignment.

FIGURE 11.17

The Paragraph Properties dialog lists built-in paragraph formats.

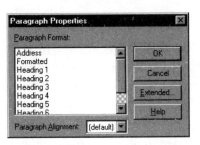

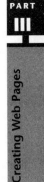

NOTE

Like other property sheets in the Editor, the Paragraph Properties dialog has an Extended button. You click this button to display a dialog for specifying attributes for the paragraph that FrontPage doesn't recognize. See the "Understanding Extended Attributes" section in Chapter 10 for more information.

Changing a Paragraph's Style   Each built-in paragraph style in the list has the default text format listed in Table 11.4. In the built-in styles, the text is aligned to the left margin and there are no indents.

TABLE 11.4: THE FRONTPAGE PARAGRAPH STYLES

Style Name	Text formatting
Normal style	Normal font (Times New Roman font, regular style, black), 12 pt
Formatted style	Typewriter font in 12 pt. You can use the Space bar and the Tab key to control the horizontal placement of text.
Address style	Italic text
Heading 1	Normal font, 24 pt
Heading 2	Normal font, 18 pt
Heading 3	Normal font, 16 pt
Heading 4	Normal font, 12 pt
Heading 5	Normal font, 10 pt
Heading 6	Normal font, 8 pt

You can change a paragraph's style by placing the insertion point anywhere within the paragraph and choosing Format ➤ Paragraph from the Editor menu bar and then choosing the style from the list in the Paragraph Properties dialog. Alternatively, choose a new style from the Change Style combo list in the Format toolbar.

Changing a Paragraph's Alignment   Change the alignment of a paragraph by placing the insertion point anywhere within the paragraph and clicking the Left

Align, Center, or Right Align button in the Format toolbar. You can also use the Paragraph Properties dialog. Select Left, Center, or Right in the Paragraph Alignment combo list (see Figure 11.17).

Changing a Paragraph's Indentation   Change the indentation of a paragraph by placing the insertion point anywhere in the paragraph and clicking the Increase Indent button in the Format toolbar, or pressing Ctrl+M. You can remove the indentation by clicking the Decrease Indent button in the Format toolbar, or by pressing Shift+Ctrl+M.

Creating a New Paragraph

You create a new paragraph on a new page just by starting to type. To begin a new paragraph with the same paragraph style, press Enter. The Editor does not display the paragraph symbol to mark the end of a paragraph, so the only way to determine the boundaries of a paragraph is to apply one of the paragraph styles and observe the lines that are affected by the new style.

You can insert a new paragraph at the location of the insertion inside a paragraph by pressing Enter. The Editor moves the insertion point and the text to the right of the insertion point to a new line and creates a new paragraph with the same paragraph style.

To create a new paragraph with a different paragraph format or style, press Enter to create the new paragraph and then select a new style in the Change Style combo list in the Format toolbar, or choose Format ➤ Paragraph from the Editor menu bar to define a new paragraph style using the Paragraph Properties dialog.

To explore creating new paragraphs:

1. If necessary, open the page with the title The Group Begins to Form.

2. Press Ctrl+End to move to the end of the page. Place the insertion point at the end of the last paragraph and press Enter. The Editor moves the insertion point to the next line and starts a new paragraph with the same (Normal) style.

3. Place the insertion point at the end of the first sentence in the last paragraph and then press Enter. The Editor splits the paragraph and places the insertion point at the beginning of the new second paragraph. (See Figure 11.18a.)

4. Select Heading 2 in the Change Style combo list. The paragraph style of the new paragraph changes to Heading 4 (see Figure 11.18b).

5. Press Ctrl+Z to undo the style change. Press Ctrl+Z a second time to undo the paragraph split.

FIGURE 11.18

Press Enter to create a new paragraph with the same paragraph style as the previous paragraph (a). Select a new paragraph style for the new paragraph using the Change Style combo list in the toolbar (b).

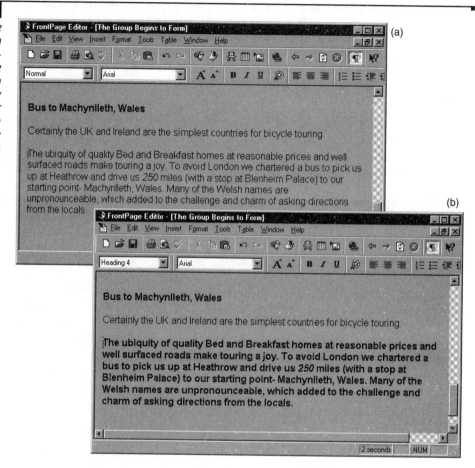

Understanding Lists

Lists are a good way to organize and display information. FrontPage provides five kinds of lists:

Bulleted or unordered list   Each item in the list is preceded by a bullet (the shape of the bullet is determined by the browser) and starts a new paragraph.

Numbered or ordered list   Each item in the list is automatically numbered and starts a new paragraph.

Definition or glossary list   Each item in the list consists of a pair of paragraphs, a term, and a definition (usually indented). Definition lists don't have bullets or numbers.

Menu list   Each item is a short paragraph.

Directory list   Each item is a short paragraph. Depending on the browser, a Directory list may be arranged vertically or horizontally.

The appearance of a list depends on the browser. Many browsers ignore the Menu and Directory list styles. The most common types of lists are the bulleted and numbered lists. (In most browsers, the display of Directory and Menu lists is identical to Bulleted lists.)

Choose Format ➤ Bullets and Numbering from the Editor menu bar to display the List Properties dialog. The dialog has a tab for both types of lists (see Figure 11.19).

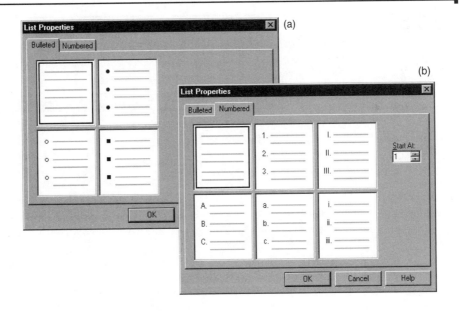

Use the Bulleted tab to change or apply one of the bulleted list styles. Use the Numbered tab to change or apply one of the numbered list styles; you can specify the first number you want the Editor to use.

Creating a Bulleted List

In a bulleted list, the items can appear in any order. To begin a new bulleted list, place the insertion point in the line where you want to start the list. (If you've already entered the first item, place the insertion point in the item.) Click the Bulleted List button in the Format toolbar, or select a bulleted list style by choosing Format ➤ Bullets and Numbering from the Editor menu bar.

To explore creating lists, open a new Normal Page in the Wales-Ireland web and do the following:

1. Click the Bulleted List button in the Format toolbar to begin a new list.

2. Type **The First Day of the Trip** as the first item in the list.

3. Choose Format ➤ Bullets and Numbering from the Editor menu bar. The Bulleted tab indicates the list style is currently applied (see Figure 11.20a). A new Other tab appears in the List Properties dialog and indicates the list type (see Figure 11.20b).

FIGURE 11.20

Use the Bulleted tab to view or change a bulleted list style (a). The Other tab indicates the list type (b).

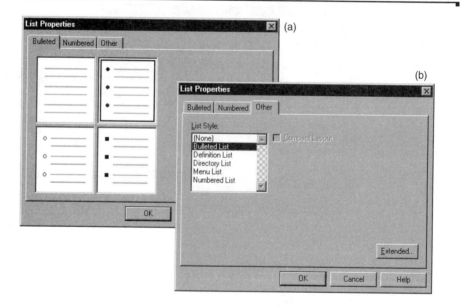

4. Type the items in the list as shown in Figure 11.21a. Press Enter after each item to start a new bulleted item in the list. After the last item, press Ctrl+Enter to end the list. In the next step, you'll change the bullet style.

5. Place the insertion point in any of the list items. Choose Format ➤ Bullets and Numbering from the Editor menu bar. Change the list style by choosing the style in the lower-left of the Bulleted tab. Click OK. Figure 11.21b shows the new style.

After you enter the last item in the list, press Ctrl+Enter to end the list.

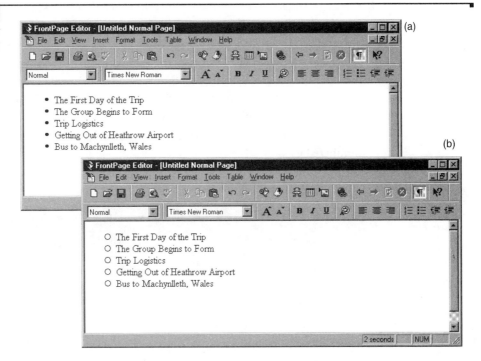

Place the insertion point at the end of any list item and press Ctrl+Enter to insert a new line below the list and move the insertion point to the new line. Place the insertion point at the beginning of any list item and press Ctrl+Enter to insert a new line above the list and move the insertion point to the new line.

Creating a Numbered List

You use a numbered list when you want to specify a particular order for the items. To start a new numbered list, click in a new line where you want to begin the list (or if you've typed in the first item, click in the item) and click the Numbered List button in the Format toolbar. Alternatively, select a numbered list style by choosing Format ➤ Bullets and Numbering from the Editor menu bar and clicking the Numbered tab to display the numbered list styles.

You can easily convert one list type to another.

1. Click in the selector bar in the left margin to select the first bulleted list item and drag to select the entire list. Left-click the selection and press Ctrl as you drag the selection to the line below the list. Release the left mouse button to copy the list.

2. Click the Numbered List button in the Format toolbar to change the bulleted list to a numbered list. To change the style of the list, you choose Format ➤ Bullets and Numbering from the Editor menu bar, click the Numbered tab, select one of the numbered list styles (see Figure 11.19b), and click OK.

3. Press Ctrl+Enter to end the list. Figure 11.22 shows examples of bulleted and numbered lists.

FIGURE 11.22

Bulleted and numbered lists

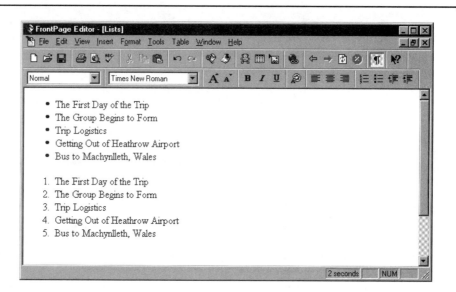

Creating a Definition List

To create a definition list, you must create pairs of paragraphs: the first paragraph is the term you want to define and the second paragraph is the definition. To create a definition list

1. Enter the first term you want to define.

2. Choose Defined Term in the Change Style combo list in the Format toolbar, and then press Enter. The insertion point moves to the next line; the Editor automatically indents the line.

3. Type the definition of the term and press Enter. The insertion point moves to the beginning of the next line.

4. Repeat Steps 1, 2, and 3 for each item you want to define.

5. After entering the last defintion, press Ctrl+End to end the Defintion list.

To practice creating a definition list, do the following:

1. With the insertion point at the beginning of a new line, create a Definition list with the terms and definitions shown below. Figure 11.23 shows the Definition list.

Term	**Definition**
Style	A collection of formatting instructions that changes the look of text or a paragraph.
Template	A set of formats and styles for text and images for a page that you use as a pattern to create new pages.

2. Save the page with the title Lists.

3. Click the Preview in Browser button in the toolbar to view the page in the browser. Both Netscape Navigator and Internet Explorer display the Bulleted, Numbered, and Definition lists the same ways that the Editor displays the lists, except that the bullet styles vary with the browser.

FIGURE 11.23

In a definition list, the term and its definition are on separate lines.

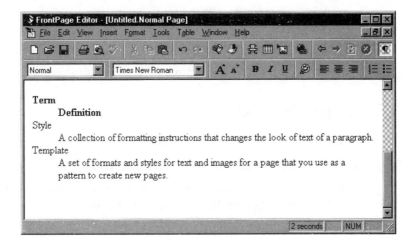

Inserting and Deleting List Items

You can insert and delete items in the list. The Editor keeps the list style you specified. When you insert or delete items in a numbered list, the Editor automatically adjusts the numbers for the other items in the list.

Inserting a New Item

To insert an item in a bulleted or numbered list, place the insertion point at the end of an item in the list and press Enter. The Editor inserts a new list item below the insertion point and moves the insertion point to the beginning of the new item. If the list is a Numbered list, the Editor automatically renumbers the remaining list items. To add an item to the end of the list, place the insertion point at the end of the last item and press Enter.

1. In the numbered list in the Lists page, place the insertion point at the end of the fourth item and press Enter. Figure 11.24a shows the new item with the last item renumbered.

2. Type **Stopping at Blenheim**.

3. Place the insertion point at the end of the last item and press Enter. Figure 11.24b shows the new last item.

4. Press Ctrl+Z to undo the last addition to the list.

Deleting an Item

To delete an item in a list:

1. Place the pointer directly over the number or bullet of the item you want to delete. The pointer will change to an arrow.

2. Double-click to select both the text and the bullet or number (see Figure 11.25).

3. Press Delete to delete. The Editor deletes the item. If the list is a numbered list, the Editor automatically renumbers the remaining items.

Changing the List

After creating a list you can change its type.

Changing a List Type   To change a list's type:

1. Right-click anywhere in the list and choose List Properties in the shortcut menu. The Editor displays the List Properties dialog.

FIGURE 11.24

Insert a new list item within a list (a) and at the end of the list (b) by placing the insertion point at the end of an item and pressing Enter.

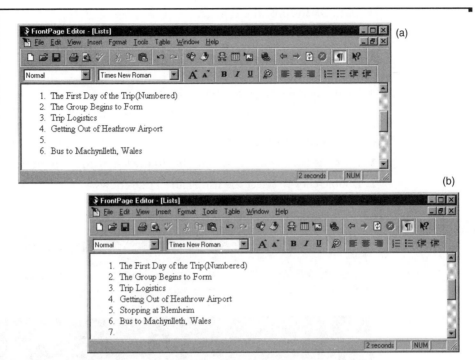

FIGURE 11.25

Double-click the list number or bullet to select the number or bullet and the item text.

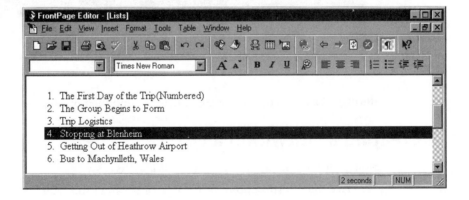

2. Click the Other tab and choose the new list type in the List Properties dialog (see Figure 11.20b). If you select the Bulleted list or the Numbered list, you can click the Bulleted or Numbered tab to select a list style.

PART

III

Creating Web Pages

3. Click OK to apply the change.

To change a list's type to a numbered or bulleted list:

1. Click anywhere in the list and then click the Numbered List or Bulleted List button in the Formatting toolbar.

2. To change the list style, right-click and choose List Properties in the Shortcut menu. Select a list style and click OK to apply the style.

Selecting a List   To select a list:

1. Place the pointer in the selector bar to the left of any item in the list.

2. Double-click to select the list. Figure 11.26 shows a selected list.

FIGURE 11.26

Double-click in the selector bar to select the entire list.

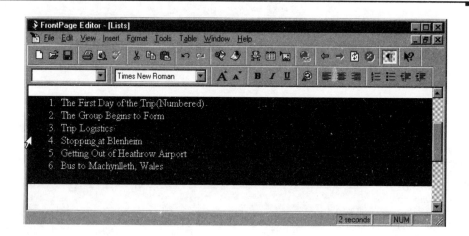

Deleting a List   To delete a list, first select it, and then press Delete.

Creating a List within a List

Creating a list within another list, or a *nested list,* is easy.

1. Place the insertion point at the end of the item that you want to precede the nested list.

2. Press Enter to create a new list item. Click the Increase Indent button on the Format toolbar. The Editor indents the item and starts the nested list.

3. Type the first item in the nested list. Click the Bulleted List or the Numbered List button in the Format toolbar.

4. Enter additional sublist items and press Enter after each item.

5. To end the nested list and begin the next item in the primary list, press Ctrl+Enter and then click the Decrease Indent button on the Format toolbar.

To illustrate, let's insert a nested list to the Getting Out of Heathrow Airport item in the bulleted list.

1. Place the insertion point at the end of the Getting Out of Heathrow Airport list item.

2. Press Enter and click the Increase Indent toolbar button (see Figure 11.27a).

3. Enter the nested list items below (see Figure 11.27b):

Finding the Bus Operator

Loading in the Bikes - Under, Over, and Everywhere

4. Press Ctrl+End to end the nested list and jump out of both lists to the end of the page. Alternatively, place the insertion point at the end of the Bus to Machynlleth, Wales item and press Ctrl+Enter to jump out of the primary list.

FIGURE 11.27

To create a nested list, insert a new item and press Increase Indent in the Format toolbar to change to a nested list (a). To jump out of both lists, press Ctrl+End (b).

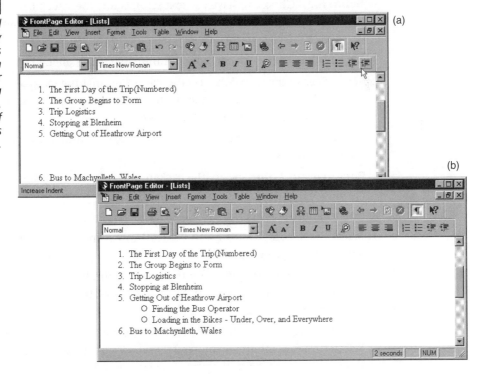

PART

III

Creating Web Pages

Adding a Marquee

A marquee is a region on a web page that displays scrolling text. Because the text scrolls automatically without input from the Web user, the text is called animated text. A marquee is a good way to get the user's attention. FrontPage 97 allows text to scroll only horizontally, but you can include vertically scrolling text as an extended attribute. The Editor is unable to display the animation, so you must preview the page in a browser that can display a marquee.

To animate text on a page, choose Insert ➤ Marquee from the Editor menu bar. The Marquee Properties dialog (see Figure 11.28) shows the properties you can set as follows:

Text Enter the text you want to animate. If you selected text before choosing the Marquee command, the selected text is displayed.

Direction Choose to have the text move to the right or to the left.

Movement Speed Specify the delay in milliseconds before the text begins to move.

Behavior Choose to have the text scroll across the screen like a ticker tape, slide into place and remain stationary on the page, or slide back and forth from one end of the page to the other.

Align with Text Specify how the animated text is aligned with normal text.

Size Specify the size of the rectangular region that the marquee occupies. By default, the width of the marquee is the width of the page but you can specify the width and height in percent or pixels.

Repeat Specify whether the animation repeats continuously or a definite number of times.

Background Color Specify the background color that fills the marquee region.

To explore animated text:

1. Select the heading Getting Out of Heathrow Airport in the page with the title The Group Begins to Form.

2. Choose Insert ➤ Marquee from the Editor menu bar. Set the marquee proper-ties,as shown in Figure 11.28. With these settings, the heading will scroll contin-uously from left to right across the page.

3. Save the page. Choose File ➤ Preview in Browser from the Editor menu bar. Select Microsoft Internet Explorer 3.0 as the Web browser and click OK. The Web browser displays the scrolling text (see Figure 11.29).

FIGURE 11.28

*Design the ani-
mated text using
the Marquee
Properties dialog*

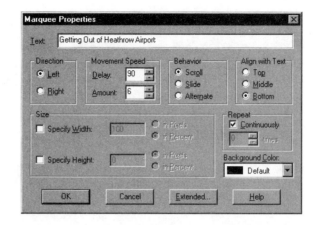

FIGURE 11.29

*A snapshot of the
animated heading as
it travels to the right
across the page.*

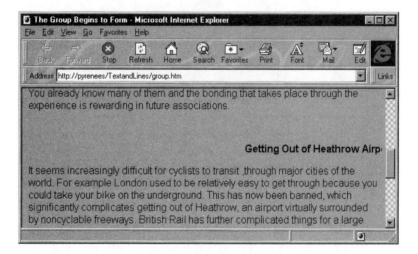

4. Click in the Editor, right-click on the marquee, and select Marquee properties. Change the Text to Heathrow Airport and the Behavior to Alternate. Click the Specify Width check box, enter 50, and make sure the in Percent option is selected. Select yellow as the Background color. The marquee region is reduced to half the page width and the text slides back and forth across the yellow background.

5. Place the insertion point at the left of the marquee region and type **Getting Out Of** (see Figure 11.30a).

6. Save the page. Click in the browser and then click the Refresh button in the toolbar. Figure 11.30b shows the new marquee style.

PART

III

Creating Web Pages

FIGURE 11.30

You can design the marquee region so that only part of the heading is animated(a). A snapshot of the moving animated text (b).

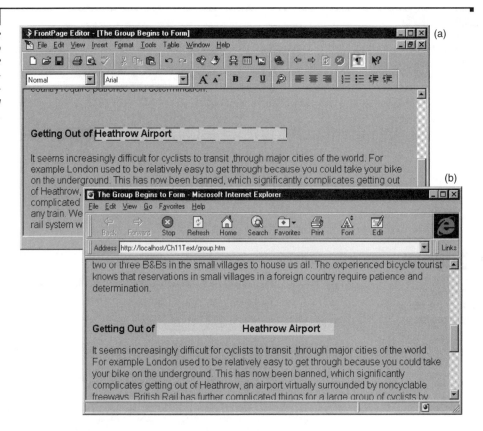

Horizontal Lines

Horizontal lines are a good way to separate parts of a page or to separate a list from paragraphs of text.

Inserting a Horizontal Line

To insert a horizontal line:

1. Place the insertion point where you want the line.

2. Choose the Insert ➤ Horizontal Line command from the Editor menu bar. By default, the Editor inserts a line the width of the page at the insertion point and 2 pixels in height.

Understanding Horizontal Line Properties

Right-click on the line and choose Horizontal Line Properties from the shortcut menu or press Alt+Enter. The Horizontal Line Properties dialog (see Figure 11.31) displays the properties you can set as follows:

Width   Specify the line width as a percent of the page width of in pixels.

Height   Specify the height of the line in pixels.

Alignment   When the line does not span the width of the page, you can align the line to the left, center, or to the right.

Color   Specify the line color. By default, the line has no color and appears sunken. You can shade the line or specify no shading.

FIGURE 11.31

The Horizontal Line Properties dialog

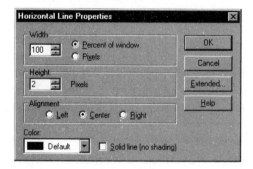

NOTE

Like other property sheets in the Editor, the Horizontal Line Properties dialog has an Extended button. Click this button to display a dialog for specifying attributes for the line that FrontPage doesn't recognize. See the "Understanding Extended Attributes" section in Chapter 10 for more information.

For practice, we'll place a horizontal line below the first list in the Lists page, and change its properties.

1. Choose the Windows command in the Editor menu bar and select the Lists page.

2. Place the insertion point at the end of the last item in the first bulleted list and choose Insert ➤ Horizontal from the Editor menu bar (see Figure 11.32a).

3. Right-click on the line and set the line width to 50 per cent, click to align Left, and click the Solid line check box. Click OK. Figure 11.32b shows the new line.

4. Click the Save button in the toolbar and click the Close button to close the page.

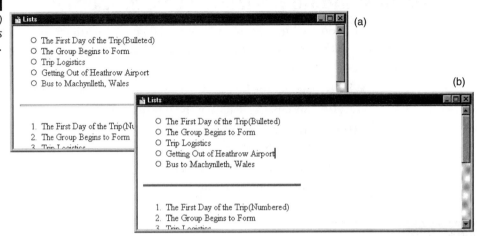

FIGURE 11.32

Inserting a line (a) and changing its properties (b).

Selecting a Horizontal Line

You can change a line's properties, but you must first select the line. To select the line, place the pointer anywhere over the line and double-click. Alternatively, place the insertion point anywhere in the line, and then click and drag past the right end of the line.

Deleting a Horizontal Line

To delete a horizontal line, select the line and press Delete.

Adding a Comment

You can add a comment to a web page as a note to yourself or to other authors. Comments are visible only in the Editor and are invisible in all Web browsers. To add a comment, place the insertion point where you want the comment and choose Insert ➤ Comment from the Editor menu bar. Type the comment in the Comment dialog (see Figure 11.33a) and click OK to insert the comment.

To practice adding a comment:

1. Press Ctrl+Home to move the insertion point to the top of the page. Press Enter to insert a new line at the top of the page. Press Ctrl+Home to move the insertion point to the new line.

2. Choose Insert ➤ Comment from the Editor menu bar. Type the following comment **Ask Leo if he has a photo of loading the bikes into the bus at the airport** and click OK.

3. The comment is inserted in the line. Move the insertion point to the comment. The pointer changes to the WebBot symbol to indicate that the ability of the comment to be visible in the Editor and invisible in Web browsers is due to a bit of programming tucked inside the WebBot.

FIGURE 11.33

Enter notes to yourself or to other Web authors in the Comment dialog (a). The ability of the comment to be visible in the Editor and invisible in Web browsers is due to a bit of programming tucked inside a WebBot (b).

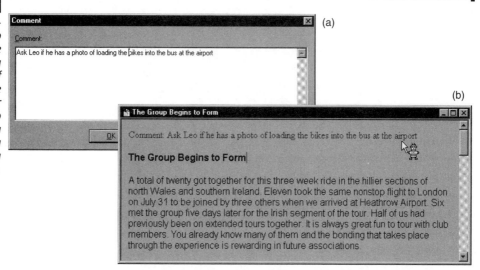

For More...

In this chapter you've learned how to change the appearance of text in a web page. For the most part, formatting text in the FrontPage Editor is very similar to formatting text in a word processing application such as Microsoft Word.

These chapters provide more information on working with text:

- Chapter 12: Understanding Text Hyperlinks shows you how to use a text phrase as the start of a hyperlink.

- Chapter 13: Using Images and Video Clips shows you how to align text and images including how to wrap text to one side of an image.

- Chapter 14: Adding Tables shows you how to use tables to create multi-column text layouts.

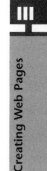

PART

III

Creating Web Pages

Chapter

12

Understanding Text Hyperlinks

Understanding Text Hyperlinks

The last two chapters have shown you how to create Web pages using the FrontPage Editor. This chapter explains how to link a page to another Web page or to any file.

A *link* is a way to navigate from a location on one page to a location on another page. You need only specify the *start* and the *target* of the link and FrontPage writes the HTML codes that make the link work.

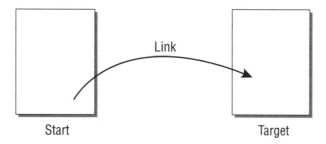

Start   Target

A page can be the start of some links, called *outgoing links*, and the target of other links, called *incoming links*.

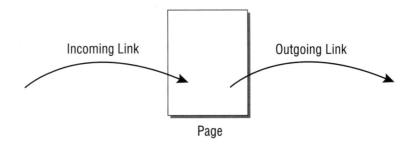

There are two basic kinds of links: hyperlinks and implicit links.

- A *hyperlink* is a link that a Web visitor clicks in order to make the jump from the start to the target. When a Web visitor clicks on the text or image that marks the start of the hyperlink, the browser sends the target information to the Web server that stores the target. The server locates the target file and sends it back to the browser.

- An *implicit link* is a link that the Web visitor does not activate except by browsing to the page. For example, FrontPage creates implicit links when you insert an image on a page or specify a background sound. When a Web visitor points a browser to a page with embedded images or files, the browser reads the implicit link information, sends requests for the included files to the server that stores the files, and then displays the retrieved images and files automatically.

This chapter covers creating text hyperlinks. In a *text hyperlink*, the start of the hyperlink is a text phrase. Chapter 13: Using Images and Video Clips shows you how to create image hyperlinks in which the start of the hyperlink is an image or part of an image, and how the Editor automatically creates intrinsic links when you embed an image or video clip.

Both the FrontPage Editor and Explorer have methods for creating text hyperlinks. The easiest and fastest way to create text hyperlinks is with the drag-and-drop method. However, drag-and-drop techniques are limited to creating text hyperlinks between existing pages and files in the current web, so this chapter also covers ways to create text hyperlinks to new target pages you haven't created yet, and to targets on the World Wide Web and on your intranet.

NOTE

To work through the examples in this chapter, you must replace your Wales-Ireland web with a modified version on the book's CD-ROM. Open the Wales-Ireland web you created in previous chapters and choose File ➤ Delete FrontPage Web from the Explorer menu bar to delete the web. Then choose File ➤ Import and use the Import Web Wizard to create a new web named Wales-Ireland and to import all the files from the web named Wales-Ireland-Ch12 on the book's CD-ROM.

Creating Text Hyperlinks in the Editor

You can create a text hyperlink to another page or file in the current web or to any page or file stored by any Web server to which you have access. This means you can create links from your web to any file available to you either on the company's intranet or on the World Wide Web. All you need to know is the location (URL) of the target file.

To create a text hyperlink in the Editor, open the start page (the page that you want to use as the start of the hyperlink), select the text phrase for the link, and choose Insert ➤ Hyperlink from the Editor menu bar, click the Create or Edit Hyperlink button in the Standard toolbar, or press Ctrl+K. The Create Hyperlink dialog (see Figure 12.1) has tabs for four ways to create text hyperlinks, as follows:

Open Pages   to create a text hyperlink to a page that is currently open in the Editor. You can even create a text hyperlink to another text phrase on the same page.

Current FrontPage Web   to create a text hyperlink to another page or file in the current web.

World Wide Web   to create a text hyperlink to a page or file on the World Wide Web or on your intranet.

New Page   to create a new page in the current Web and a text hyperlink to the new page.

NOTE

The Create Hyperlink dialog has an Extended button. Click this button to display a dialog for specifying attributes for the hyperlink that FrontPage doesn't recognize. See the section "Understanding Extended Attributes" in Chapter 10 for more information.

PART

III

Creating Web Pages

To display the Create Hyperlink dialog, open the start page and choose Insert ➤ Hyperlink from the Editor menu bar, click the Create or Edit Hyperlink button in the Standard toolbar, or press Ctrl+K.

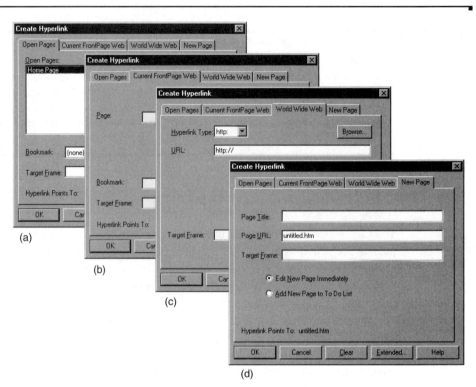

(a)

(b)

(c)

(d)

The easiest way to create a text hyperlink when the target is in the current web is to use drag-and-drop. For details, see this chapter's drag-and-drop sections: "Creating a Text Hyperlink by Dragging from the Explorer," "Using Drag-and-Drop to Create a Text Hyperlink to a Bookmark," and "Using Drag-and-Drop to Move or Copy a Text Hyperlink."

To explore the four ways to create text hyperlinks, we'll carry out a few of the navigation plans we looked at in Chapter 3 for the Wales-Ireland web. We'll start by creating a text hyperlink from the Home Page to the Wales page.

1. Open the Wales-Ireland web in the Explorer. In Folder View, double-click the WalesMap in the pane on the right. The Editor displays the WalesMap page.

2. In the Editor, click the Open button in the toolbar or press Ctrl+O to display the Open File dialog. Double-click on Home Page. The Open File dialog closes and the Editor displays the home page.

Creating a Text Hyperlink to an Open Page

To create a text link that starts with a text phrase, called the *link text*, on the active page in the Editor and ends on another page that is also currently open in the Editor, do the following:

1. Select the text for the link. Choose Insert ➤ Hyperlink from the Editor menu bar, click the Create or Edit Hyperlink button in the toolbar, or press Ctrl+K. The Open Pages tab of the Create Hyperlink dialog displays a list of open pages with the active page highlighted (see Figure 12.2).

2. Select the target page in the list of open pages and click OK. The Editor creates the text hyperlink. The Editor underlines and changes the text color of the selected text to indicate the text hyperlink.

FIGURE 12.2

To create a text hyperlink to an open page, select the target page from the list of open pages and click OK.

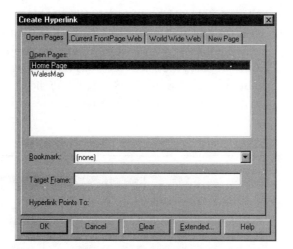

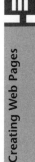

You can also create the link without selecting any text on the active page. In this case, the Editor creates a link to the target page you select in the Create Hyperlink dialog, and inserts the underlined and colored title of the target page at the insertion point.

The lower part of the Open Pages tab has two text boxes. You'll learn about the Bookmark text box in the "Understanding Bookmarks" section later in this chapter and about the Target Frame text box in Chapter 15: Understanding Frames.

As an example, create the link from the Home Page to the WalesMap page.

1. With Home Page as the active page, select the text "North Wales,"click the Create or Edit Hyperlink button in the toolbar, and then click the Open Pages tab.

2. Select the WalesMap page in the Create Hyperlink dialog. The dialog displays walesmap.htm to the right of Hyperlink Points To: at the bottom of the dialog. Click OK to create the link. The selected text is displayed in dark green and is underlined to indicate the start of the link. To test the link, we'll preview the Home Page in a browser.

3. Click the Preview in Browser button in the toolbar. Click the new hyperlink. The browser displays the WalesMap page.

4. Close or minimize the browser.

Creating a Text Hyperlink to a New Page

You can create a text hyperlink that starts with a text phrase on the active page in the Editor and ends at a new page that you haven't created yet. In setting up the link, you must specify the Page Title and URL for the new page. You can create the new page immediately or you can add the task to the To Do List.

1. Select the text for the link and then click the Create or Edit Hyperlink button in the toolbar or press Ctrl+K. Click the New Page tab (see Figure 12.3). The Editor proposes the selected text as the Page Title and up to eight characters of the selected text as the Page URL. If you didn't select text before displaying the Create Hyperlink dialog, the Page Title text box is blank and the Page URL is untitled.htm.

FIGURE 12.3

Use the New Page tab to create a hyperlink to a new page in the current web.

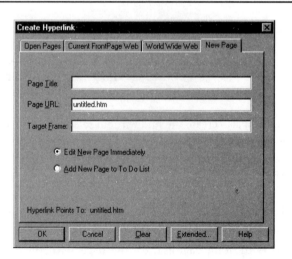

2. If necessary, enter the Page Title and the Page URL for the new page. Choose an option to create the new page now or add the task to the To Do List and click OK. The Editor displays the New Page dialog.

3. Choose a template or wizard for creating the page. If you selected the option to edit the page immediately, the Editor displays the page; otherwise, the Editor creates the page, saves it to the current web, and adds the page to the To Do list.

To illustrate, we'll create a text hyperlink on the Home Page to a new page that we'll use for gathering input from web users.

1. Place the insertion point in a new line in the Home Page, choose Heading 5 from the Change Style combo box in the Format toolbar, and type **Comments and Information.** Click the Align Right button in the Format toolbar. We'll use this text as the start of a link to a new page.

2. Select the text, click the Create or Edit Hyperlink button in the toolbar, and then click the New Page tab. The Page Title and Page URL are filled in using the selected text (see Figure 12.4a).

3. Click the Add New Page to To Do List option and click OK.

4. Click OK in the New Page dialog. The Editor creates the new page using the Normal Page template. The Editor creates the link from the Home Page to the new page (see Figure 12.4b). Press Ctrl+S to save the changes.

FIGURE 12.4

The Editor suggests the Page Title and Page URL based on the selected link text (a). After creating the new page, the Editor creates the link (b).

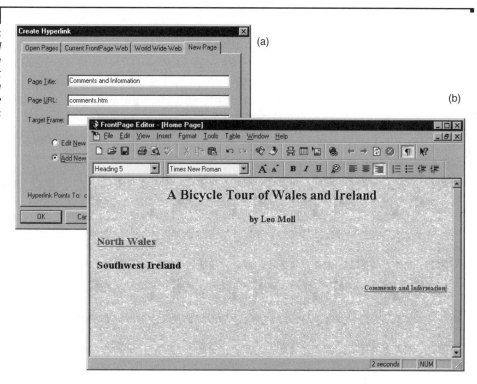

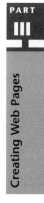

PART

III

Creating Web Pages

5. Click the Show To Do List button in the toolbar. The To Do List includes the new page (see Figure 12.5). Click Close.

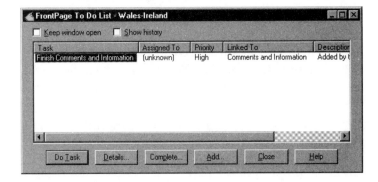

6. To test the new hyperlink, click the Preview in Browser button in the toolbar. If necessary, click the browser's Refresh button to reload the new version of the page. Click the new hyperlink. The browser displays the new blank page. Close or minimize the browser.

Creating a Text Hyperlink to any Page or File in the Current Web

To create a text hyperlink that starts with a text phrase on the active page in the Editor and ends on any page or file in the current web:

1. Select the text for the link and choose Insert ➤ Hyperlink from the Editor menu bar, click the Create or Edit Hyperlink button in the toolbar, or press Ctrl+K. Click the Current FrontPage Web tab in the Create Hyperlink dialog (see Figure 12.6a). This tab also has Bookmark and Target Frame text boxes that you'll learn about later in this chapter.

2. Enter the page URL in the Page text box. If you don't know the URL, click the Browse button to display the Current Web dialog (see Figure 12.6b) to review the list of the pages and files stored in the current web.

3. Click OK. The Editor creates the hyperlink. If you didn't select link text before opening the Create Hyperlink dialog, the Editor inserts the page's title at the insertion point as the link text. If you are creating a hyperlink to a file instead of a Web page, the Editor inserts the filename as the link text.

FIGURE 12.6

Use the Current FrontPage Web tab to create a hyperlink to any page or file in the current web (a). Click the Browse button to display the contents of the current web (b).

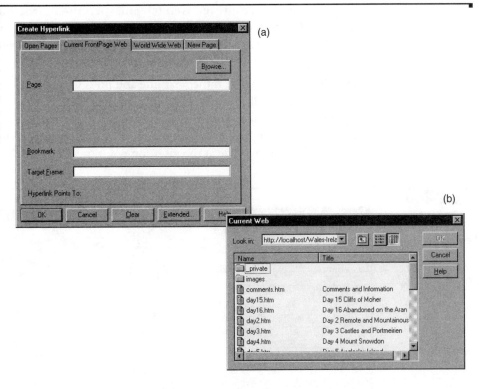

NOTE

Whether the target is a page or a file, the process of creating the hyperlink is the same. The difference between the two kinds of hyperlinks occurs when a Web visitor clicks the link. If the target is a file, clicking the link in the Web browser requires the browser to start up a helper application for the file type and open the file within the helper application. For example, suppose you import a .doc Word file to the web and create a link to the file. When the Web visitor clicks the link, the visitor's browser opens the particular helper application on the visitor's computer that is associated with the .doc extension and displays the file.

We'll create text hyperlinks from the WalesMap page to the pages that describe the first two days of the tour.

1. Click the Windows menu and select WalesMap from the list of open pages.

2. Place the insertion point in a new line and type **Day 1 London to Wales.** Click in the selector bar to select the text and click the Create or Edit Hyperlink button in the toolbar.

PART

III

Creating Web Pages

3. Click the Current FrontPage Web tab and then the Browse button. In the Current Web dialog, double-click the Day 1 London to Wales page. The day1.htm is displayed in the Page text box and to the right of Hyperlink Points To: at the bottom of the dialog. Click OK to create the hyperlink.

4. Place the insertion point in the next line and press Ctrl+K to display the Create Hyperlink dialog. Click the Browse button in the Current FrontPage Web tab. In the Current Web dialog, double-click the Day 2 Remote and Mountainous Wales page. The day2.htm Page URL is displayed. Click OK to create the hyperlink. The Editor inserts the page title at the insertion point (see Figure 12.7).

FIGURE 12.7

Create text hyper-links to other pages in the current web based on link text you type on the page or on the title of the target page.

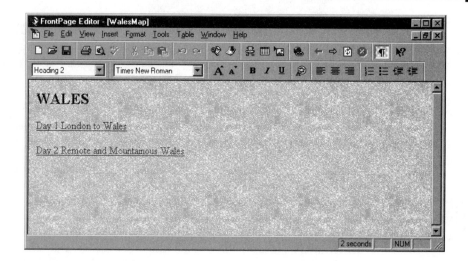

5. Press Ctrl+S to save the changes.

6. Click the Preview in Browser button in the toolbar. If necessary, refresh the browser to display the new version of the page. Click to test the new links and then minimize the browser.

To illustrate creating a text hyperlink to a file in the current web, we'll create a link to a sound file.

1. Click the Open button in the toolbar or press Ctrl+O. Double-click Day 7 Blarney Castle in the Open File dialog.

2. Place the insertion point at the end of the first heading and press Enter to insert a new line. Type **Listen to the Blarney Pilgrim Irish reel** and click the Align Right button in the toolbar.

3. Select Blarney Pilgrim as the link text and click the Create or Edit Hyperlink button in the toolbar.

4. Click the Current FrontPage Web tab and then click the Browse button. In the Current Web dialog, double-click the Sounds and Videos folder and then double-click blarneypilgrim.au. Click OK to create the hyperlink.

5. Press Ctrl+S to save the changes.

6. Click the Preview in Browser button in the toolbar. Click the new hyperlink. What happens next depends on the Web browser. For example, if you are previewing the page in Netscape navigator, a small window with sound player controls appears and the sound file plays (see Figure 12.8). To hear the sound file again, click the play button in the window. Click the window's Close button and minimize the browser.

FIGURE 12.8

When you click a hyperlink to a sound file in Netscape Navigator 3.0, a sound player window appears and the browser plays the file.

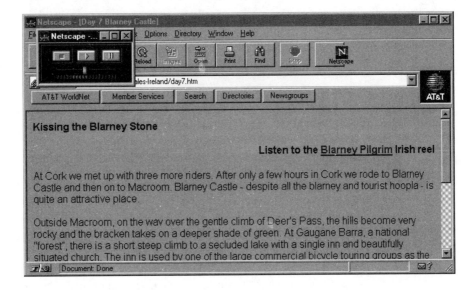

You can add multimedia effects to a FrontPage Web. After importing a multimedia file to the web, create a link to open and play the file. The Web visitor's browser must be configured to start the helper application required to play the file. See Chapter 6: Adding Content to a Web for information on associating helper applications with files.

PART

III

Creating Web Pages

Creating a Link to a File on the Internet

You can create a text hyperlink that starts with a text phrase on the active page in the Editor and ends on any page, file, or other resouce available to you on the World Wide Web or on your intranet. Clicking the hyperlink in a browser takes the Web visitor to the site you've linked to. To create the link, do the following:

1. Select the text for the link in the active page and choose Insert ➤ Hyperlink from the Editor menu bar. Click the Create or Edit Hyperlink button in the toolbar or press Ctrl+K. Then click the World Wide Web tab in the Create Hyperlink dialog (see Figure 12.9).

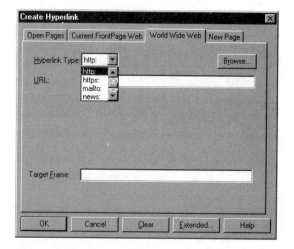

2. Select the type of hyperlink you want to use. The Editor enters the protocol portion in the URL text box. By default, the Hyperlink Type text box displays http, the hyperlink type for the World Wide Web. The combo box lists the other hyperlink types that FrontPage recognizes, including: file, ftp, gopher, mailto, https, news, telnet, and wais. If you create a link to a file using one of these protocols, the Web visitor's computer must have the appropriate client application installed. Without the client application, the Web browser can't open the file (see Chapter 2 for more information).

3. Click in the URL text box and enter the address (absolute URL) of the page or file. If you know the URL, you can type the address; otherwise, open your browser and browse to the page (or locate the file), copy the address in the browser, and then paste the address in the URL text box. Click OK to create the hyperlink.

NOTE

If you have a browser running and your network connection is open, the URL text box in the World Wide Web tab automatically displays the absolute URL of the page currently displayed in the browser.

To illustrate, we'll create a link from the Day 3 Castles and Portmeirion page to the Web named The Castles of Wales on the World Wide Web. This site (http://www.castlewales.com) is an excellent example of an educational site.

1. Click the Open button in the toolbar and double-click the day3.htm page in the Open File dialog.

2. Click in the line below the text and choose Insert ➤ Horizontal Line from the Editor menu bar. At the insertion point, type **Wales is home to many outstanding examples of medieval castle building. Learn about more than 170 Welsh castles at The Castles of Wales, by Jeff Thomas.**

3. Select The Castles of Wales as the link text, click the Create or Edit Hyperlink button in the toolbar, and click the World Wide Web tab.

4. Type **www.castlewales.com** as the URL and click OK to create the link.

We'll also create a link to the browser's e-mail program, as follows:

1. Place the insertion point in a new line, and choose Address from the Change Style combo box in the Format toolbar.

2. Type **Send comments about this Web to its Webmaster: Jeff Thomas jltbalt@worldnet.att.net** and press Enter. The Editor recognizes you've typed in an e-mail address and creates the link automatically. Let's investigate the link.

3. Place the insertion point anywhere in the e-mail address and click the Create or Edit Hyperlink button in the toolbar. The Edit Hyperlink dialog indicates that a link with the mailto Hyperlink Type has been created. The URL is mailto: jltbalt@worldnet.att.net.

4. Click the Save button in the toolbar.

5. To test the links, click the Preview in Browser button in the toolbar. Figure 12.10 shows the page in Netscape Navigator 3.0. Click The Castles of Wales hyperlink. Figure 12.11 shows the home page for the site (that is, the home page at the time I wrote the book). Plan to spend some time at this site for an education on both Welsh castles and on designing a Web site. Click the e-mail address. Figure 12.12 shows the e-mail window.

FIGURE 12.10

The first hyperlink on the day3.htm page takes you to another Web site on the World Wide Web and the second takes you to e-mail.

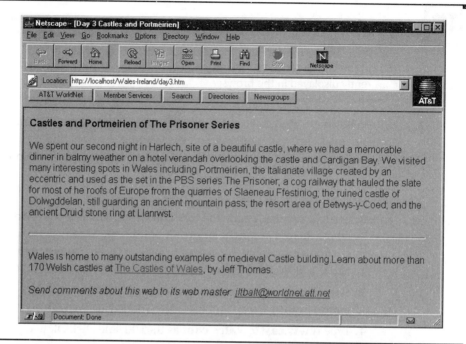

FIGURE 12.11

The home page of The Castles of Wales Web site

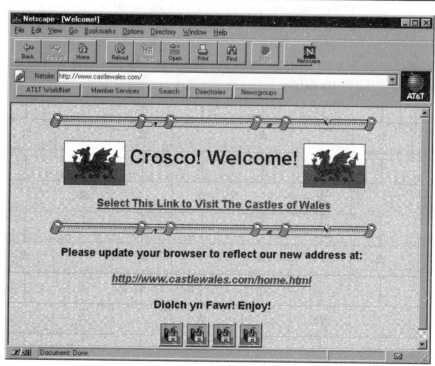

FIGURE 12.12

The e-mail window in Netscape Navigator 3.0

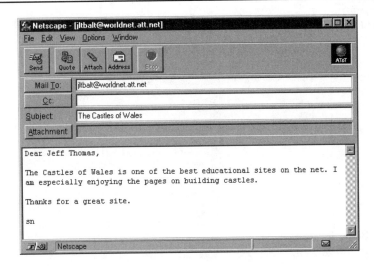

FIGURE 12.12

The e-mail window in Netscape Navigator 3.0

Creating a Text Hyperlink by Typing on the Page

You can also create a hyperlink to a World Wide Web site just by typing the absolute URL directly on the page. To illustrate, we'll create a hyperlink to another page in Thomas's Web site.

1. Place the insertion point in a new line and type **See what Jeff has to say about Harlech castle at http://www.castlewales.com/harlech.html.** After you press the Space bar or press Enter, the Editor automatically creates a text hyperlink to the URL and colors and underlines the URL.

2. Press Ctrl+S to save the changes to the page. You can test the link by previewing the page in your Web browser.

Creating a Text Hyperlink by Dragging from the Explorer

You can also create a text hyperlink by dragging and dropping from the Explorer to the Editor. The drag-and-drop technique is very fast and efficient when you create several text hyperlinks at one time. You create a text hyperlink by dragging the target page or file in the Explorer and dropping it on a line of the start page in the Editor. FrontPage inserts the title of the target page as the link text.

To create a text hyperlink with the drag-and-drop method:

1. Resize the Explorer and Editor windows and arrange them side by side on the screen (see Figure 12.13).

2. In the Editor, open the start page for the link you want to create.

FIGURE 12.13

Drag the target page or file from the Explorer and drop it on the start page to create a text hyperlink.

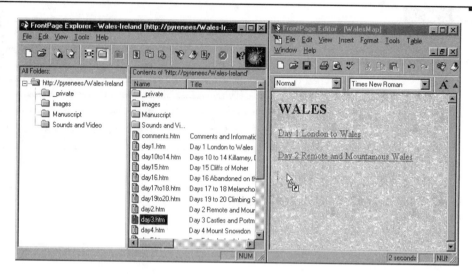

3. In either view of the Explorer, click the target page for the link. Holding down the left mouse button, drag to the start page in the Editor. The shape of the pointer changes to indicate a link is in process. Release the left mouse button in the line where you want the new link. The Editor inserts the title of the target page at the drop location and creates a text hyperlink.

We'll use the drag-and-drop technique to create text links to the other three pages that describe the Wales part of the Wales-Ireland Web.

1. Resize the Explorer and Editor windows as shown in Figure 12.13.

2. In the Editor, click the Windows menu and select WalesMap in the list of open pages.

3. In the Explorer, click the day3.htm page icon. Holding down the left mouse button, drag the pointer to a line below the Day 2 line and release the mouse button.

4. Repeat Step 3 to drag the day4.htm and day5.htm page icons to new lines in the WalesMap page and create new text hyperlinks. In the next step, we'll change the heading style and paragraph format.

5. With the pointer in the selector bar, drag to select the five text hyperlinks. Choose Heading 3 from the Change Style combo box in the Formatting toolbar and then click the Bulleted List button in the Format toolbar. Figure 12.14 shows the new links.

6. Click the Save button in the toolbar. Test the links by clicking the Preview in Browser button in the toolbar and then clicking the hyperlinks.

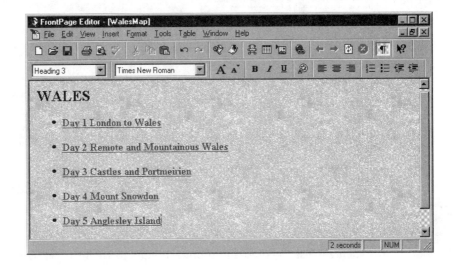

The drag-and-drop technique is particularly useful in creating hyperlinks for the linear navigation between sequential pages. In the Wales-Ireland Web, the day pages are intended to be read sequentially so you can create text hyperlinks to the next and previous pages in the story. In the steps below, you'll create the hyperlinks for the Day 16 page.

1. In the Explorer, double-click day16.htm to open the page in the Editor. In the Editor, place the insertion point in the beginning of the first line and press Enter to insert a new first line.

2. In the Explorer, click day15.htm, drag the page icon and drop it in the first line in the Editor. Type square brackets to enclose the link text.

3. In the Explorer, click day17to18.htm, drag the page icon, and drop it in the first line to the right of the Day 15 hyperlink. Type square brackets to enclose the link text.

4. Click in the selector bar for the line, choose Heading 5 in the Change Style combo list, and click the Align Right button in the Formatting toolbar. Figure 12.15 shows the new hyperlinks.

Use the drag-and-drop technique to create text hyperlinks to the next and the previous page of sequential pages.

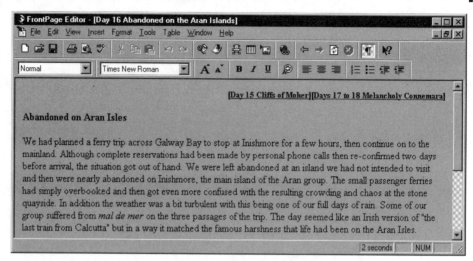

When you use the drag-and-drop technique to create a text hyperlink, the target page's title is used for the link text. After creating the hyperlink, you can change the link text (see the "Changing the Link's Text" section later in this chapter).

Following a Hyperlink in the Editor

The last few sections have shown you how to create the different kinds of text hyperlinks using the Editor and the Explorer. In each case, we tested the hyperlink by previewing the page in a Web browser and clicking the link text to follow the link to its target. FrontPage provides a way to follow most links while you are working in the Editor. While you are developing links between pages, following links in the Editor is often the most convenient way to test links.

Follow a Text Hyperlink Forward

To follow a link starting on the active page in the Editor, do one of the following:

- Place the insertion point anywhere in the text containing the link, and choose the Tools ➤ Follow Link command in the Editor menu bar.

- Press Ctrl and then click the hyperlink you want to follow. With the Ctrl key pressed, when you move the pointer to a hyperlink, the pointer's shape changes to the "link arrow" shown in Figure 12.16.

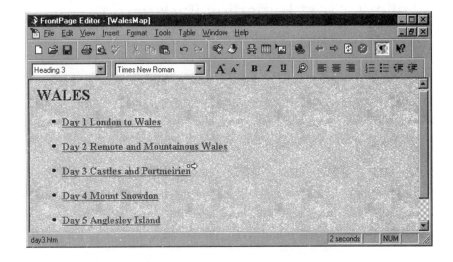

If the target of the link is a page in the current web, the Editor opens the target page (if it is not already open) and makes it the active page. If the target of the link is a file in the current web, FrontPage opens the helper application and directs the helper to open the file. If the target is not in the current web, and your network connection is open, the Editor opens the target page. If you try to follow a link to a URL on another computer and your network connection is closed, the Editor and Explorer display error messages (see Figure 12.17 a and b).

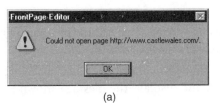

(a)

(b)

PART

III

Creating Web Pages

Stop Following a Link

Following a link may take longer than you are willing to wait. You can stop following the link in the Editor by clicking the Stop button in the toolbar.

Follow a Text Hyperlink Backward

The Editor keeps a list of the pages you have visited in your visiting order. After you have followed a hyperlink, you can reverse the direction and follow the hyperlink backwards by clicking the Back button in the toolbar or by choosing the Tools ➤ Back command in the Editor menu bar. After following a hyperlink backwards, you can click the Forward button in the toolbar to move forward again.

Testing the Example Hyperlinks

We'll use the Editor to test the hyperlinks we created for the Wales-Ireland Web. To prepare for the test, close all of the open pages except the Home Page.

1. Display the Home Page in the Editor.

2. Press Ctrl and click the North Wales link. The WalesMap page opens as the active window.

3. Press Ctrl and click the Day 1 link. The Day 1 page opens as the active window.

4. Click the Back button in the toolbar.

5. Place the pointer in the Day 3 Castles and Portmeirion link. Choose Tools ➤ Follow Link from the Editor menu bar. The Day 3 page is displayed.

Testing Links to Other Computers

If your network connection is closed, trying to follow the links on this page gives the error messages shown in Figures 12.17. If your network connection to the WWW is open, do the following:

1. Press Ctrl and click The Castles of Wales hyperlink. The home page for the Web site is retrieved and displayed as a new page in the Editor.

2. Press Ctrl, move the pointer to the e-mail address, and click. The Editor is unable to open the e-mail window, and displays the message shown in Figure 12.18.

The message displayed when you try to follow a mailto link in the Editor

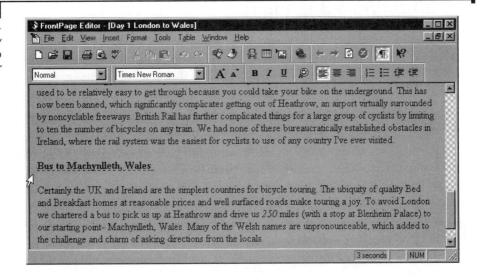

Understanding Bookmarks

The links to target Web pages that we've created so far have been links to the top of the page. Often you want to create a link to a specific location within the target page. The specific location on the target page that you want to use as the target of the link is called a *bookmark*.

NOTE

You can define a bookmark only for a text phrase on a page. You cannot define a bookmark for images or other items you insert in the page.

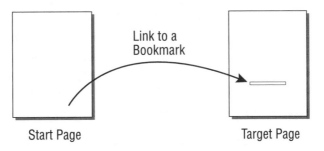

Link to a
Bookmark

Start Page   Target Page

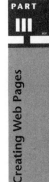

Creating a Bookmark

To create a bookmark on a target page in the Editor:

1. Click the Open button in the toolbar, select the target page in the Open File dialog, and click OK. Select the text that you want to use as the bookmark.

2. Choose the Edit ➤ Bookmark command from the Editor menu bar. FrontPage suggests the selected text as the bookmark's name in the Bookmark dialog (see Figure 12.19a).

3. Accept the suggested name or enter a new name and click OK. The Editor inserts a dotted, colored underline to mark the selected text as a bookmark (see Figure 12.19b).

FIGURE 12.19

To mark a specific location on a page as the target of a hyperlink, use the Bookmark dialog (a). The Editor inserts a dotted underline below the marked text to indicate a bookmark (b).

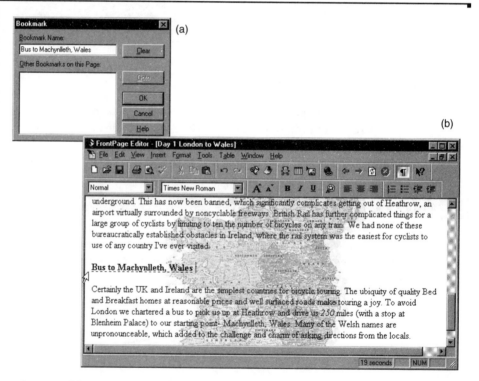

Creating a Text Hyperlink to a Bookmark

You create a text hyperlink to a bookmark on an open Web page by specifying the bookmark's name in the Bookmark text box in the Create Link dialog (see Figure 12.20a). If the target page is not open, specify the bookmark in the Current FrontPage Web tab (see Figure 12.20b). A bookmark is indicated using a number symbol (#) in front of the bookmark name; for example, the page URL of the bookmark shown in Figure 12.20 is day1.htm#Bus to Machynlleth, Wales.

FIGURE 12.20

Specify the bookmark when you create or edit a text hyperlink to an open page (a) or any page in the current web (b).

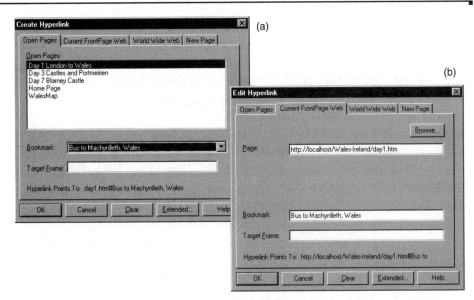

To illustrate jumping to a bookmark, we'll modify the first text hyperlink on the WalesMap page to link to a bookmark on the day1.htm page.

1. Click the Windows menu and select Day 1 London to Wales from the list of open pages. Scroll down the page and select the heading Bus to Machynlleth, Wales.

2. Choose Edit ➤ Bookmark from the Editor menu bar. Click OK in the Bookmark dialog to accept the selected text as the bookmark name and create the bookmark (see Figure 12.19). Now you'll modify the hyperlink to the Day 1 page.

3. Click the Windows menu and select the WalesMap page. Place the insertion point in the <u>Day 1 London to Wales</u> hyperlink and press Ctrl+K or choose the Create or Edit Hyperlink button in the toolbar.

4. Choose the Day 1 London to Wales page in the Open Pages tab of the Edit Hyperlink dialog. Click the down arrow of the Bookmark combo list and choose Bus to Machynlleth, Wales (see Figure 12.20a). Click OK to change the hyperlink's target to the bookmarked heading.

5. To follow the new hyperlink, press Ctrl and click in the Day 1 London to Wales hyperlink. The Editor displays the Day 1 page and jumps directly to the bookmark.

6. Click the Back button in the toolbar to return to the WalesMap page. Click the Undo button in the toolbar to undo the change in the hyperlink.

PART

III

Creating Web Pages

Although you can only create new bookmarks on your own Web pages, you can create a link to an existing bookmark on a page on the WWW or an internal intranet. Enter the absolute URL of the bookmark in the World Wide Web tab of the Create Hyperlink dialog. The home of the Castles of Wales web site has a bookmark named Please Select. To use this bookmark as the target of a link, enter the URL http://www.castlewales.com/home.html Please Select.

Using Drag-and-Drop to Create a Text Hyperlink to a Bookmark

The easiest and fastest way to create a text hyperlink to a bookmark is to create both the bookmark and the link at the same time using drag-and-drop. When you create a text hyperlink to a bookmark with drag-and-drop, the link and the bookmark can be on the same page or on different pages.

To create a bookmark and a text hyperlink simultaneously:

1. In the Editor, select the text you want to use as the bookmark.

2. Right-click in the selected text and drag to the line where you want the text hyperlink. The Editor displays a gray line at the location in the line where you can drop the selected text (see Figure 12.21a).

3. Release the mouse button and select Link Here from the shortcut menu (see Figure 12.21b). The Editor marks the selected text as a bookmark with a dotted underline, inserts a copy of the selected text at the spot where you dropped the text, and uses the text to create a text hyperlink (see Figure 12.21c).

Using Bookmarks to Create a Table of Contents

Bookmarks are very useful in creating a table of contents for a long page. When a page is more than one or two browser window heights in length, it is a good idea to save the visitor from having to scroll through the page by creating a page table of contents at the top of the page. Each item in the table of contents is a hyperlink to a bookmark on the page.

To illustrate, we'll create a table of contents for the Day 1 London to Wales page. We'll drag a copy of each paragraph heading and drop it in a list at the top of the page, as follows:

1. Click the Windows menu and choose the Day 1 London to Wales page.

FIGURE 12.21

You can create a text hyperlink and a bookmark simultaneously using drag-and-drop in the Editor.

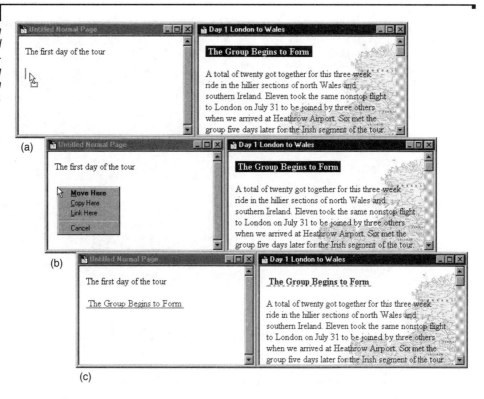

2. Press Ctrl+Home to move to the top of the page. Press Enter four times to insert four lines.

3. Select the first paragraph heading. Right-click and drag to the first line in the page. Release the mouse button and choose Link Here from the shortcut menu. The Editor inserts a copy of the heading, creates a text hyperlink to the selected heading, and marks the selected heading as a bookmark.

4. Scroll to the next paragraph heading. Select the heading, and then right-click and drag to the first empty line at the top of the page. Release the mouse button and choose Link Here from the shortcut menu. To force the page to scroll to the top, hold the pointer near the top edge of the page window.

5. Repeat Step 4 for the third and fourth paragraph headings. Figure 12.22 shows the new list of text hyperlinks as a table of contents for the page.

PART

III

Creating Web Pages

FIGURE 12.22

Use drag-and-drop to create the hyperlinks and bookmarks for a table of contents.

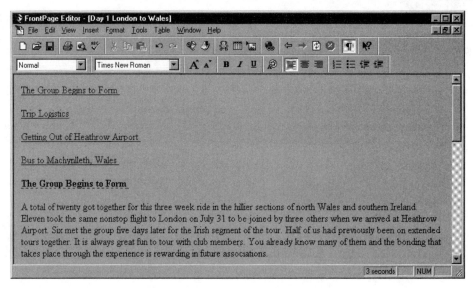

Visiting a Bookmark on the Active Page

You can review the list of bookmarks on the active page by choosing Edit ➤ Bookmark from the Editor menu bar to display the Bookmark dialog. Figure 12.23 shows the list of bookmarks for the Day 1 London to Wales page. You can jump to a bookmark on the active page by selecting the bookmark and clicking the GoTo button on the dialog. The Editor jumps to the selected bookmark and the dialog remains open. Click OK to close the dialog.

FIGURE 12.23

Use the Bookmark dialog to visit any bookmark on the active page.

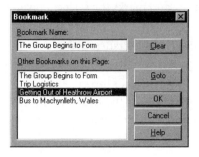

NOTE

You can use the Bookmark dialog to visit bookmarks on an active page only. You can jump a bookmark on another page only if you have created a link to the bookmark. In this case you "visit" the bookmark by following the link.

Deleting a Bookmark

To delete a bookmark:

1. Place the insertion point in the text and choose Edit ➤ Bookmark from the Editor menu bar.

2. Click the Clear button in the Bookmark dialog. The bookmark is deleted.

NOTE

If the bookmark you deleted is the target of a link, deleting the bookmark doesn't break the link to the page; when you click the link, you jump to the top of the page.

Text Hyperlink Mechanics

After you create a link, you may want to modify it by changing its colors or its target, or by moving, copying, or deleting it. This section describes the ways you can work with a link.

Selecting a Hyperlink

There are two parts to a text hyperlink: the text characters and the hyperlink information. When you create a text hyperlink, the hyperlink information is connected to each individual character in the link text. You can display the Edit Hyperlink dialog by clicking any character of the link text and then taking an action to display the dialog, such as pressing Ctrl+K. By contrast, if you want to copy or move the text characters and the hyperlink information, you must select all the text characters you want to copy or move.

Cutting, Copying, and Pasting a Hyperlink

When you cut or copy one or more text characters of a link, you are also copying the hyperlink information to the Clipboard. You can paste the characters and the hyperlink information to another location on the same page, or to another page in the Editor. You can use the Cut, Copy, and Paste commands in the usual way, but it is usually faster to use the Editor's drag-and-drop capability. You can drag-and-drop a text hyperlink to a new location on the active page or to another open page in the Editor.

NOTE

If you paste the contents of the Clipboard to another application such as Microsoft Word, only the text is pasted and the link information is discarded.

To explore these concepts, open the WalesMap page in the Editor and do the following:

1. Select only the word London of the Day 1 hyperlink.

2. Right-click and drag to the line below the Day 5 hyperlink. Release the mouse button and choose Move Here in the shortcut menu. The Editor moves the letters of the word London along with their attached hyperlink to the new location. Click the Undo button in the toolbar.

3. Select the phrase London to Wales, right-click, and drag to the line below the Day 5 hyperlink. Release the mouse button and choose Copy Here in the shortcut menu. The Editor copies the text phrase and its attached hyperlink and pastes it to the new location. Click the Undo button in the toolbar.

Changing the Link's Text

You can change the text associated with a link without changing the hyperlink information. You can select and edit any character of the link text except the first or last character. If you try to edit the first or last character, FrontPage deletes the hyperlink information for the character.

To explore these concepts, open the WalesMap page in the Editor and do the following:

1. In the Day 1 hyperlink, select the word London and type **England** over the selected text. The link text is changed, but the hyperlink information is unchanged. Click the Undo button in the toolbar.

2. In the <u>Day 1</u> hyperlink, select the word Wales and type **Dublin** over the selected text. Because you've edited a selection that includes the last character, the link information for the edited selection is discarded. The link text is changed and Dublin is not part of the link. Click the Undo button in the toolbar.

Changing the Target

To change the target of a link:

1. Click anywhere in the link and do any of the following to display the Edit Hyperlink dialog:

- Click the Create or Edit Hyperlink button in the toolbar.
- Choose Edit ➤ Hyperlink from the Editor menu bar.
- Press Ctrl+K.
- Right-click and choose the Properties command in the shortcut menu.

2. Choose a tab and edit the link information as described in the "Creating Text Links" section.

Deleting a Text Hyperlink

You can delete the hyperlink information without deleting the text associated with the link. Use the Edit ➤ Unlink command from the Editor menu bar to delete the hyperlink information associated with a selection of characters without deleting the text.

- To delete the hyperlink information associated with the entire link text, click anywhere in the link and choose Edit ➤ Unlink from the Editor menu bar.
- To delete the hyperlink information associated with one or more characters associated with the link, select the characters you want to unlink, and choose Edit ➤ Unlink from the Editor menu bar.
- To delete the text and the hyperlink information, select the characters you want to delete and press Delete.

Changing Text Hyperlink Colors

You can change the link colors of all the text hyperlinks on a page. By default, the Editor and browsers display the hyperlinks on a page in a color different from the

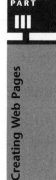

PART

III

Creating Web Pages

normal text color. After you visit a link, the Editor and Web browsers change the color to a second color called the visited hyperlink color. You specify text hyperlink colors for all the hyperlinks on a page; you cannot specify unique text colors for an individual hyperlink. To change the text hyperlink colors in the Page Properties dialog, see the "Understanding the Background Properties" section in Chapter 5.

Keep in mind that most browsers let the Web visitor set default color preferences which override the colors you choose in the Editor.

Adding Extended Attributes for a Hyperlink

FrontPage provides the ability to set additional HTML attributes for the hyperlink. To add HTML attributes that FrontPage doesn't provide directly, click the Extended button on the Edit Hyperlink dialog (see Figure 12.22). Enter the attribute name and value in the Extended Attributes dialog (see Figure 12.27). See the "Understanding Extended Attributes" section in Chapter 10 for more information.

Keyboard Shortcuts for Hyperlinks

Table 12.1 lists keyboard shortcuts for working with hyperlinks. See Tables 11.2 and 11.3 in Chapter 11 for keyboard shortcuts for editing.

TABLE 12.1: KEYBOARD SHORTCUTS FOR HYPERLINKS

Keyboard combination	Description
Ctrl+K	Display the Create Hyperlink or Edit Hyperlink dialog
Alt+→	Follow the link history forward
Alt+←	Follow the link history backward
Ctrl+left mouse button	Follow a link

For More...

In this chapter, you've learned how to create text hyperlinks to other pages and files using drag-and-drop techniques and using the Create Hyperlink dialogs in the Editor. The target of a hyperlink can be a specific location on a page (marked as a bookmark), or a page or a file in your web, or in any web available to you on the World Wide Web or private intranet. You've learned how to follow a link and how to modify both the link text and the hyperlink information.

The following chapters provide additional information about hyperlinks:

- Chapter 3: Designing a FrontPage Web discusses ways to organize content and plan navigation in your Web.

- Chapter 7: Managing Links shows you how the Explorer handles links, including the automatic update of internal links and how to repair broken links.

- Chapter 13: Using Images and Video Clips shows you how to embellish a web with images and video clips. You'll also learn how to create image hyperlinks.

Chapter

13

Using Images and Video Clips

Chapter

13

Using Images and Video Clips

I mages and video clips bring life to your Web site. You'll surely want to use images for decorating and drawing attention to your pages in addition to providing information. The images you select help to project a personality for your Web.

In many ways, working with images and video clips in FrontPage is similar to working with text, so you'll be able to leverage much of what you've learned about text in the previous two chapters. You can import image and video files, insert images on Web pages, and align images with each other and with text. In the world of text, the Editor displays text in the HTML format and converts text files to HTML. In the world of images, the Editor displays images in either of two Web image formats (GIF and JPEG) and converts image files to one of these formats. In the world of video clips, the Editor recognizes only one video format (AVI) and is not able to convert other types of video formats.

 NOTE

Graphics Interchange Format (GIF) is the most popular image format on the Web. GIF images use up to 256 colors. Joint Photographic Expert Group (JPEG) is the second most popular Web image format. JPEG images use more than 256 colors, so their color quality is superior to GIF images. Because of the additional color information, JPEG files are larger than GIF files. See "GIF and JPEG File Formats" for information on the advantages and disadvantages of each format.

Working with Images

The biggest difference between working with text and images in the FrontPage Editor is that while you create text by typing characters on the page, the FrontPage Editor provides no tools for creating or editing images.

NOTE

The Bonus Pack that comes with FrontPage 97 includes an outstanding image editor called the Microsoft Image Composer. Appendix B provides a brief introduction to using the Image Composer; covering the application in any depth would be another book.

You can add image files to a Web in two ways: you can import an image file using the Explorer and store the file in its original format in the Web, or you can insert an image in a page using the Editor. Chapter 6: Adding Content to a Web covers importing image files to the Web. While you can import images with the popular image formats and store them in their original formats, the Editor and most Web browsers can display only images with the GIF and JPEG formats. Browsers must call on helper applications to display images in the other formats; for example, a browser may call on MSPaint to display a bitmap (.bmp) image in its own application window. Normally, you want to display an image as an integral part of a Web page (called an *inline image*) instead of in a separate window (called an *external image*).

NOTE

Web browsers can handle two kinds of images: inline images and external images. An *inline image* is an image that you have inserted in a page; the Web browser requests the image from the server when it requests the page and displays the image in the page's window. An *external image* is not requested along with a page and displayed in a page's window. Instead, the Web visitor requests the external image separately, normally by clicking a link on a page; in response, the Web browser requests the image file and displays the file in a separate window. Depending on the browser you are using and how you have configured it, the Web browser may call on a helper application to display the external image or may open another one of its own browser windows to display the image.

You display an image in a page (as an inline image) by inserting the image file in the page. When you insert an image file, FrontPage automatically converts the format to either the GIF or JPEG format and inserts the converted contents of the image file.

In this chapter, you'll learn techniques for inserting images on pages, working with images after you insert them, and creating image hyperlinks. Because image files are typically large, performance is an important issue. We'll look at guidelines and tips for achieving good performance and while using images for information and decoration.

NOTE

When you create a new Web, FrontPage automatically creates a folder named Images. You don't have to store the image files in this folder, but using the Images folder is a good way to organize your files.

NOTE

To work through the examples in this chapter, you'll need to replace your Wales-Ireland web with a modified version on the book's CD-ROM. Open the Wales-Ireland web you created in previous chapters and choose File ➤ Delete FrontPage Web from the Explorer menu bar to delete the web. Then choose File ➤ Import and use the Import Web Wizard to create a new web named Wales-Ireland and import all the files from the web named Wales-Ireland-Ch13 in the Webs folder on the book's CD-ROM.

Inserting an Image on a Page

To display an image as part of a page, you insert the image file. You can insert image files in all of the popular image formats to a FrontPage Web page, including GIF, JPEG, BMP, TIFF, MAC, MSP, PCD, RAS, WPG, EPS, and PCX. When you insert an image file in a page, the Editor carries out two tasks:

- It converts the contents of the image file and creates a new image file with the GIF format if the image has 256 or fewer colors, or with the JPEG format if the image has more than 256 colors.
- It creates an intrinsic link to the new image file.

NOTE

The phrase "inserting an image" really means "creating an implicit link to a GIF or JPEG image file." We'll continue to use the first phrase because everybody else does, but keep in mind that when you insert an image you are creating a link.

PART

III

Creating Web Pages

Inserted images are also called embedded images. When you display a page with embedded images, the Web browser requests the image files using the implicit link information.

Inserting an Image

To insert an image in a page, open the page, place the insertion point at the spot where you want the image to be displayed, and choose Insert ➤ Image from the Editor menu bar or click the Insert Image button in the toolbar. The Image dialog (see Figure 13.1) has tabs for three ways to insert the image, as follows:

Current FrontPage Web to insert an image that has already been saved to the current Web. The image can have any of the image formats that FrontPage recognizes.

Other Location to insert an image from a file in your computer's file system or from a page on the World Wide Web or your intranet.

Clip Art to insert an image from the FrontPage clip art library.

FIGURE 13.1

To display the Image dialog, open a page in the Editor and choose Insert ➤ Image from the Editor menu bar or click the Insert Image button in the toolbar.

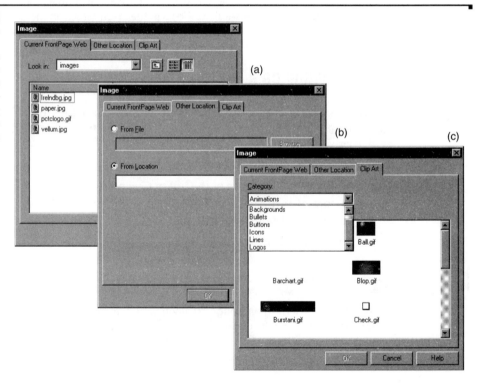

TIP

The easiest way to insert an image stored in the current Web is to use drag-and-drop techniques. For details, see the chapter's drag-and-drop sections: "Inserting an Image by Dragging from the Explorer" and "Using Drag-and-Drop to Move or Copy an Image".

Inserting an Image Stored in the Current Web

To insert an image that is stored in the current Web:

1. Place the insertion point in the active page where you want to display the image, and choose Insert ➤ Image from the Editor menu bar or click the Insert Image button in the toolbar. The Current FrontPage Web tab displays the image files in the current Web (see Figure 13.2).

2. Select the image from the list and click OK. If the selected file is not a GIF or JPEG file, the Editor converts the contents of the file to a new GIF or JPEG file. The Editor creates an implicit link to the file and displays the image at the insertion point.

FIGURE 13.2

The Current FrontPage Web tab displays the GIF and JPEG image files in the current Web.

PART

III

Creating Web Pages

To illustrate, we'll insert the celweave.gif in the WalesMap page as follows:

1. Click the Open button in the toolbar, and double-click WalesMap in the Open File dialog. Place the insertion point in the first line just to the right of Wales.

2. Click the Insert Image button in the Standard toolbar. Double-click the Images folder to display the images stored in the current Web (see Figure 13.2). Double-click celweave.gif. The Celtic weave image is inserted (see Figure 13.3).

3. Click the Save button in the toolbar. The implicit link to the image file is saved.

FIGURE 13.3

When you save the page, the Editor saves the link to the Celtic weave image file.

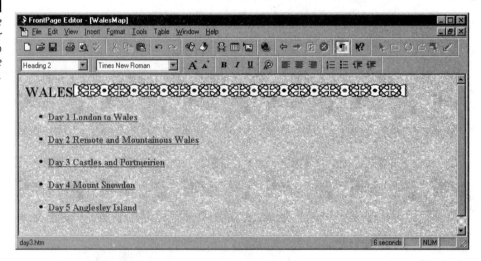

Inserting an Animated GIF

An easy way to add motion to a page is to insert an animated GIF image. An animated GIF is a simple animated graphic composed of several GIF images welded together into a single file. A modified GIF file format handles the display of one image after another. Any browser that suppports the modified GIF format, such as Microsoft Internet Explorer 3.0 and Netscape Navigator 3.0, can display the animation without an additional helper application or add-in. You insert an animated GIF image in a Web page exactly as if it were a regular image.

For practice, you'll insert an animated GIF file in one of the pages of the Wales-Ireland web.

1. Click the Open button in the toolbar and double-click the day19to20.htm page in the OpenFile dialog.

2. Place the insertion point at the end of the paragraph describing Saint Patrick's Mountain and press Enter to insert a new line. Click the Insert Image button in the Standard toolbar, double-click the images folder, and double-click cropat-spring.gif. The picture of a spring at the base of the mountain is displayed. The Editor can't display the animation, so we'll have to view the page in a browser.

3. Type **The spring at Mt. Patrick (called Croagh Patrick in Ireland)**, select the text, and click the Italic, Bold, and Decrease Text Size buttons in the Format toolbar.

4. Click the Save and Preview in Browser buttons in the Standard toolbar. The spring water tumbles down and the clouds roll by (see Figure 13.4).

FIGURE 13.4

Use animated GIF images to give motion to your Web pages.

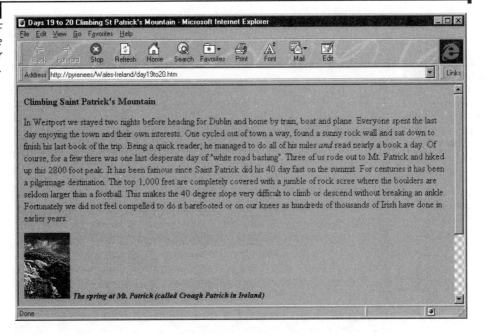

NOTE

It's easy to make your own animated GIF image files from a series of images. Download the Microsoft GIF Animator from the Microsoft Web site at www.microsoft.com.

Inserting an Image by Dragging from the Explorer

A faster way to insert any kind of image file stored in the current Web is to drag the file from the Explorer to the active page in the Editor. To illustrate, we'll insert the pctclogo.bmp bitmap file in the Home Page page, as follows:

1. Click the Open button in the toolbar and double-click the Home Page in the Open File dialog. Place the insertion point in the first line just to the left of the text.

2. Resize and rearrange the Explorer and Editor windows as shown in Figure 13.5. Open the Images folder. Click the pctclogo.bmp icon, hold down the left mouse, drag to the left of the first line of text, and release the mouse button. The Editor creates a new GIF file based on the bitmap file, creates the implicit link, and displays the converted file (see Figure 13.6).

3. Click the Save button in the toolbar. The implicit link to the image file is saved.

FIGURE 13.5

The fastest way to insert any kind of image file stored in the current Web is to drag from the Explorer to the page in the Editor.

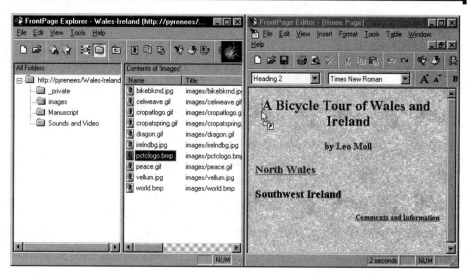

Saving the Inserted Image

When you attempt to save the page after inserting images from your computer's file system, the Editor reviews the status of each image you inserted since the last time you saved the page. If a newly inserted image is a GIF or JPEG file already stored in the current Web, the Editor need only save the implicit link to the file. For each newly inserted image that is not already stored in the current Web as a GIF or JPEG file, the Editor displays the Save Image to FrontPage Web dialog (see Figure 13.7a). You can change the URL by editing the Save as URL text box. Here are the options for saving the GIF or JPEG image file:

Yes to save the GIF or JPEG image file in the current Web

Yes to All to save all of the newly inserted GIF or JPEG images in the Web

No to not save the GIF or JPEG image file in the current Web

Cancel to close the dialog box without saving the image file displayed in the dialog box and without displaying the dialog box for the remaining images. Images you already saved before clicking Cancel have been saved.

FIGURE 13.6

When you insert a bitmap (.bmp) image file, the Editor creates a new GIF file based on the image file, creates an implicit link, and displays the converted file.

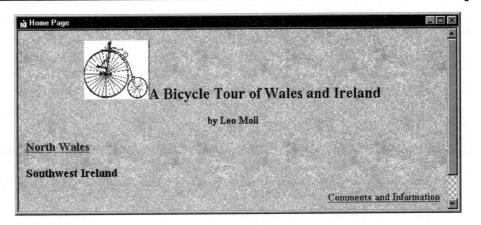

If the newly inserted image has the same name as a GIF or JPEG image previously saved to the current Web, the Editor displays a slightly different version of the Save Image to FrontPage Web dialog with the options shown in Figure 13.7b. Click Replace to replace the previously saved image with the new GIF or JPEG image or click Use Existing to keep the previously saved image.

If you click No in either version dialog, the image is not saved to the current Web as a GIF or JPEG image. If you save the page without saving the GIF or JPEG image, you are saving the link information to a file that doesn't exist in the current Web; when you next open the page in the Editor or in a Web browser, a broken image icon appears in place of the image (see Figure 13.8a). The Explorer displays the link as a broken page icon and a broken link in Hyperlink View (see Figure 13.8b).

FIGURE 13.7

When you save a page with a newly embedded image, the Editor prompts you to save the image to the current Web as a GIF or JPEG image file.

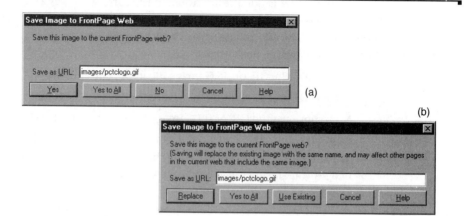

FIGURE 13.8

The Editor or Web browser displays a "broken image" when the implicit link to the image is broken (a). The Explorer displays the link as a broken page icon and a broken link in Hyperlink view (b).

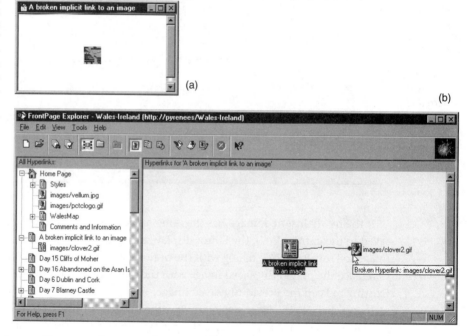

Inserting an Image from a File Not in the Current Web

To insert an image from any image file in your computer's file system but not stored in the current Web:

1. Place the insertion point in the active page where you want to insert the image and choose Insert ➤ Image from the Editor menu bar or click the Insert

Image button in the toolbar. Click the Other Location tab in the Image dialog. Click the Browse button to display the Insert dialog. Use the Look in combo box to locate the file and the Files of Type combo box to specify the format of the image file you want to insert.

2. Click Open. If you are inserting a non-GIF, non-JPEG file, the Editor must convert the contents and create a new GIF or JPEG image file. Then, the Editor creates an implicit link to the GIF or JPEG image file and displays the image at the insertion point.

As an example, we'll insert the clover.gif image from the book's CD-ROM to the IrelandMap page. Because the image we are inserting is a GIF file, the Editor won't need to do the conversion step.

1. Click the Open button in the toolbar, select the EireMap page in the Open File dialog and click OK. Place the insertion point to the right of the text in the first line and click the Insert Image button in the toolbar.

2. Click the Other Location tag in the Image dialog, click the Browse button, and locate the Images folder on the CD-ROM. Double-click the clover.gif file. The Editor creates an implicit link to the GIF file and displays the file at the insertion point (see Figure 13.9a).

3. Click the Save button in the toolbar. Click to the left of the text in the URL text box and type **Images/**to save the file to the Images folder in the current Web (see Figure 13.9b). Click Yes to save the GIF file to the current Web.

FIGURE 13.9

The clover image is inserted from a folder not in the current Web (a). When you save the page, the Editor prompts you to save the file in the current Web (b).

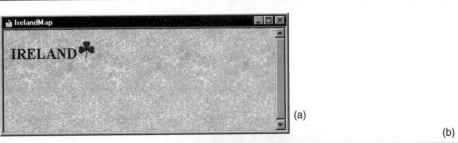

(a)

(b)

PART

III

Creating Web Pages

Inserting an Image from the World Wide Web or your Intranet

You can insert an image from the World Wide Web or your intranet. The Editor handles the insertion in a way that is quite different from the insertion of an image file from your own computer's file system. When you insert an image from the World Wide Web or your intranet, the Editor creates an implicit link to the image file stored on the other Web server and does not offer to save the image file to the current Web. To insert the image, you need to know the file's absolute URL; the easiest way to get the URL is to browse to the Web site, locate the image, and copy its absolute URL.

1. Place the insertion point in the active page where you want to insert the image and choose Insert ➤ Image from the Editor menu bar. Click the Other Location tab.

2. Enter the absolute URL of the image file and click OK. If your network connection is open, FrontPage retrieves the image file and displays the image at the insertion point. If the network connection is closed, the Explorer displays the error message shown in Figure 13.10a and displays the broken image icon shown in Figure 13.10b in place of a target image. Whether or not the network connection is open, FrontPage creates the image link to the file.

FIGURE 13.10

The error message displayed when you create a link to the WWW or intranet and your network connection is closed (a). The Editor uses the "broken image" to represent the image (b).

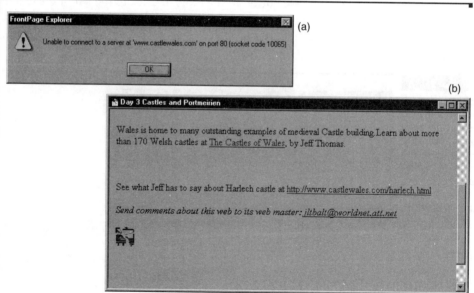

3. Click the Save button in the toolbar. When you save the page, you are saving the link to the WWW or intranet image file. FrontPage creates the link to the external WWW or intranet file and lists the link in the Outline view in the Explorer using the world icon.

WARNING

When you insert an image from the World Wide Web or your intranet, the Editor creates an implicit link to the image file stored on the other Web server and does not offer to save the image file to the current Web. You can retrieve a copy of an image from the Internet using the commands in your browser to import the copy to your web folder (see the "Importing Files from the Internet" section in Chapter 6).

Let's create a link on the Day 3 Castles and Portmeirion page to an image on The Castles of Wales site.

1. Click the Open button on the toolbar, and double-click the day3.htm page in the Open File dialog.

2. Scroll to the link to the harlech.html page.

3. With Microsoft Internet Explorer 3.0 as the current browser, click the Preview in Browser button on the toolbar. Click the text hyperlink to the harlech.html page in the Web site. Scroll to a photo on the page. Right click in the photo and choose Properties in the shortcut menu (see Figure 13.11a). Drag to select the address and press Ctrl+C to copy.

4. Minimize the browser. Place the insertion point in the line below the text. Click the Insert Image button in the toolbar, click the Other Location tab, and click the From Location option. Click in the text box and paste the image URL (see Figure 13.11b).

5. Click OK to create the link to the image on The Castles of Wales Web site. The Editor displays the image in the day3.htm page (see Figure 13.12).

If you close your Internet connection and try to view the day3.htm page in the Editor, FrontPage displays the message shown in Figure 13.10a when the Explorer tries to make the connection specified in the image link. The Editor displays the broken image shown in Figure 13.10b. If your Internet connection is open, but Jeff's server is not, the Editor won't be able to retrieve the image and the broken image is displayed.

Creating Web Pages

FIGURE 13.11

You can obtain the absolute URL of the image from your Web browser (a) and paste the URL to create the implicit link to an image on the World Wide Web or on your intranet (b).

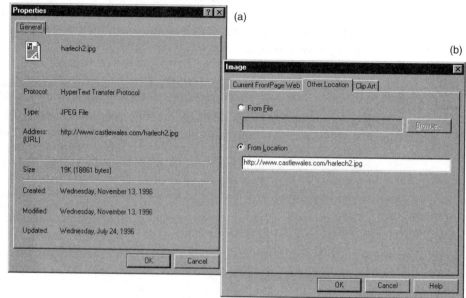

FIGURE 13.12

The photo is retrieved using a link to The Castle of Wales Web site.

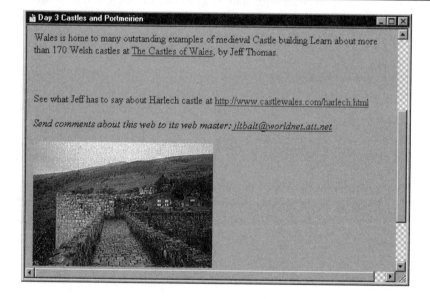

Inserting a Clip Art Image

To insert an image from the FrontPage clip art library:

1. Place the insertion point in the active page where you want to insert the image and choose Insert ➤ Image from the Editor menu bar or click the Insert Image button in the toolbar. Click the Clip Art tab. The Category combo list includes animations, backgrounds, buttons, icons, lines, and logos (see Figure 13.13).

2. Select a category and double-click an item in a collection. The Editor inserts the image at the insertion point.

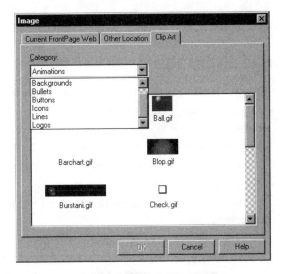

Let's add a colored line to the Home Page.

1. Click the Windows menu in the Editor menu bar and select Home Page. Place the insertion point to the right of the author's name in the second line, and press Enter to insert a new line.

2. Click the Insert Image button in the toolbar and click the Clip Art tab. Choose the Lines category and double-click on the turquoise and gray.gif. The Editor inserts the line (see Figure 13.14).

3. Click the Save button in the toolbar, modify the URL to images/turquoise_ and_gray.gif, and click Yes to save the image to the current Web.

Selecting an Image

There are two ways to select an image in the active page in the Editor:

- Move the pointer to the right or left boundary of the image, click the left mouse button, and drag. The selected image is shown in reverse video (see Figure 13.15a). Another way to select an image is to click in the selector bar of the line containing the image; this method selects all of the text and images in the line.

- Click the image. When you click the image, the Editor displays small rectangles in the corners of the image (see Figure 13.15b), but the image is not shown in reverse video.

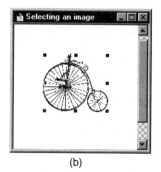

(a)   (b)

For many operations, you can use either method of selecting an image. The difference between the two methods is that clicking an image activates the Image toolbar while displaying the image in reverse video does not activate the Image toolbar. You use the Image toolbar to make a color transparent and to define hotspots as areas within the image for creating hyperlinks. (See the "Making a Color Transparent" and "Understanding Image Maps" sections.)

Copying and Pasting an Image

You can use the familiar commands to copy and paste a selected image:

- **To copy the selected image**   Choose Edit ➤ Copy from the Editor menu bar, right-click the image and choose Copy from the shortcut menu, or press Ctrl+C. When you copy an image, you also copy the implicit link to the image.

- **To paste a copied image**   Place the insertion point at the location where you want to paste the image and choose Edit ➤Paste from the Editor menu bar, or press Ctrl+V, or right-click where you want to paste the image and choose Paste from the shortcut menu. The Editor pastes the image and the implicit link at the insertion point and displays the image.

- **To copy and paste the selected image in one step**   Right-click the selected image and drag to the new location; the pointer changes shape and a short vertical bar indicates the new location (see Figure 13.16a). Release the mouse button and choose Copy Here from the shortcut menu (see Figure 13.16b). The Editor pastes the image (see Figure 13.16c).

FIGURE 13.16

To copy and paste in one step, right-click a selected image, drag to a new location (a), and choose Copy Here from the shortcut menu (b). The copy is pushed (c).

(a)

(b)

(c)

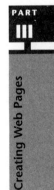

Creating Web Pages

Cutting or Deleting an Image

To cut an image   Select the image and choose Edit ➤ Cut from the Editor menu bar, right-click the image and choose Cut from the shortcut menu, or press Ctrl+X. When you cut an image, you remove the image from the page and place a copy of the image and its implicit link on the Clipboard.

To delete an image   Select the image and press Delete.

Using Drag-and-Drop to Move or Copy an Image

The easiest way to move or copy an image to a new location is to use drag-and-drop. To move or copy the selected image to a new location, right-click the image and drag to the new location; the pointer changes shape and a short vertical bar indicates the new location (see Figure 13.17a). Release the mouse button. Choose Move Here from the shortcut menu (see Figure 13.17b) to move the image. The Editor cuts and pastes the image and its link information to the new location (see Figure 13.17c). If you choose Copy Here from the shortcut menu, the Editor copies the image to the new location and leaves the original image in its place.

FIGURE 13.17

To move an image, right-click a selected image, drag it to a new location (a), and choose Move Here from the short-cut menu (b). The image is moved (c).

(a)   (b)   (c)

**TIP**

The easiest way to move a selected image is to press the left mouse button instead of the right button while you click the selected image and drag to the new location. Release the button to move the image.

Image Properties

To view the properties of an inserted image, click the image and choose the Edit ➤ Image Properties command from the Editor menu bar, or press Alt+Enter, or right-click the image and choose Image Properties from the shortcut menu. The Image

Properties dialog displays the properties for the selected image in three tabs (see Figure 13.18), as follows:

General to specify image source, formats, alternate representations, and hyperlink information

Video to specify video source and play options (see the section "Inserting a Video" for a discussion of the properties on the Video tab)

Appearance to specify the layout and size of the image

FIGURE 13.18

The Image Properties dialog

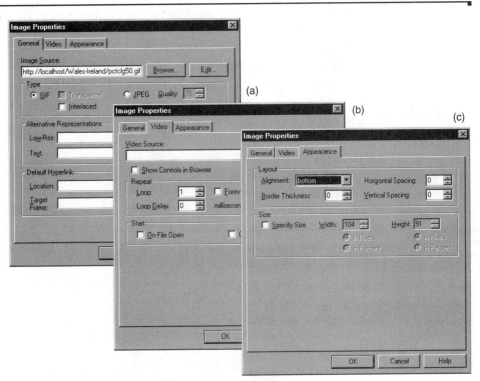

Understanding the General Image Properties

The General tab (see Figure 13.19) include the following properties:

- **Image Source**   The Image Source text box displays the URL for the image. If you have saved the image as an inline image in the Web, the image source is the page URL—for example, images/world.gif. If the image hasn't been saved,

PART

III

Creating Web Pages

the image source is File: followed by the path to the image file in your file system, or the URL to the file on the WWW or the internal intranet. You can edit the image source by typing, but it is usually easier to click the Browse button to display the Image dialog so you can select an image file (see Figure 13.1 at the beginning of the chapter). Click the Edit button to start the Microsoft Image Composer for editing the image.

- **Type**   All inserted images are converted automatically to a compressed image format, either the GIF or JPEG format, depending on the number of colors in the image. Both formats use compression schemes to reduce the size of the file. You can convert an image from GIF to JPEG or from JPEG to GIF by clicking the Option button. When you convert the format, you must increase or decrease the number of colors required in the format. Each format has advantages, as explained in the next section.

- **Alternate Representations**   You can display a smaller image while a larger image is loading from the server. For browsers that don't display images, you can specify an alternate text message. See the "Using Alternate Representations" section for more information.

- **Default Hyperlink**   You can specify hyperlink information for the image (see the "Understanding Image Links" section in this chapter and Chapter 15: Understanding Frames).

FIGURE 13.19

Use the General tab to specify the image source, image format, alternate representations, and image hyperlink information.

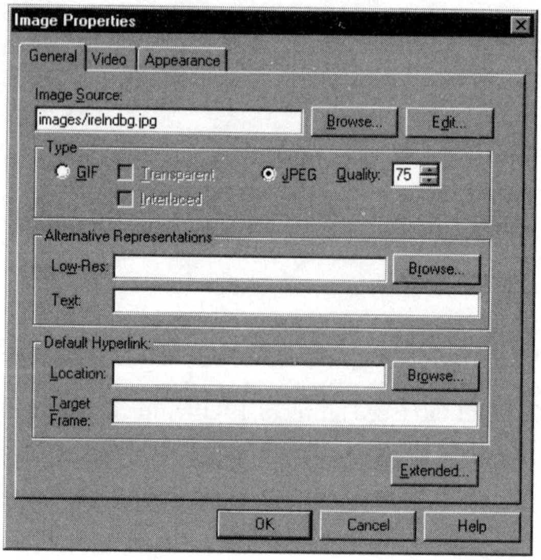

NOTE

Like all property sheets in the Editor, the Image Properties dialog has an Extended button. Click the Extended button on the General tab to display a dialog for specifying attributes for the image that FrontPage doesn't recognize. See the section "Understanding Extended Attributes" In Chapter 10 for more information.

GIF and JPEG File Formats

GIF   The GIF format is the most popular image format on the Web. If a browser can display images at all, it can display GIF images. The GIF format uses a smaller number of colors (256 or fewer), so the color quality may be inferior to the JPEG version. However, there are two special features that are available only for GIF images.

- **Transparency**   The *transparency* feature lets you specify one color that is tranparent when the GIF file is loaded into a Web page. The background colors show through those parts of the image with the transparent color. When an image has a tranparent color, the Transparent check box in the Image Properties dialog is checked. You can uncheck the Transparent check box to return the color to its nontransparent state. You can use the Editor to specify the transparent color as discussed in the "Making a Color Transparent" section.

- **Interlacing**   The *interlacing* feature allows a GIF file to be stored in a special way that makes the image appear to load faster in a browser. The image information in a noninterlaced file is stored in rows from top to bottom; when the file loads in a browser, the rows are displayed in groups, one group after another from top to bottom. In an interlaced file, alternating rows of pixels are stored (first, third, fifth, and so on) first, followed by the remaining rows (second, fourth, sixth, and so on). When an interlaced file is loaded, the typical browser displays the lines in the order they are stored, so the browser displays a "rough draft" of the image first and then fills in the details. You can't create an interlaced image using FrontPage. The Image Properties dialog indicates whether the image is Interlaced of not. To save a file as an interlaced GIF image, you need to use a graphics editor such as Paint Shop Pro.

JPEG   The JPEG format uses a more efficient compression scheme than the GIF format, so JPEG image files are usually smaller than GIF files. Because JPEG images use more than 256 colors, their color quality is usually superior to a GIF

PART

III

Creating Web Pages

image. There is a trade-off between compression and image quality: as the compression increases and the file becomes smaller, the image quality decreases. You can decide on how much compression you want to use. When you save an image in the JPEG format, the Image Properties dialog displays a Quality field that you use to specify an integer from 1 to 99 (see Figure 13.19). The higher the number, the higher the image quality, but the larger the file size because there is less compression. The default for Quality is 75.

NOTE

How much an image can be compressed depends on the image. Compression schemes are based on complex mathematical formulas that consider the patterns in the image as well as its size and resolution. An image with a completely random set of pixels won't compress at all, while a solid color image compresses to less than 1K, regardless of its size. GIF images normally compress to about one-fourth the original size, and JPEG images manage to squeeze images to an even smaller size. The compression scheme that is used in the GIF and JPEG formats is called *lossy* because when you convert an image to the GIF or JPEG format, the compression scheme discards some data. The compressed and decompressed image is no longer identical to the original image (the difference is negligible, however).

Understanding Transparency

You can make a single color transparent. When you make a color transparent, the background color, and background image if there is one, shows through for each pixel in the image that has the transparent color. This technique is particularly useful when the background of the image is a different color than the background color of the page and you want the image to appear to be floating on the page. The Transparent check box on the General tab of the Image Properties dialog indicates whether the image contains a transparent color. You use the Image toolbar to make a color transparent. If the Image toolbar is not displayed, choose View ➤ Image Toolbar from the Editor menu bar to display the toolbar. Use the Make Transparent button to change the transparency of a color (see Figure 13.20). The other buttons on the Image toolbar are explained in the "Understanding Image Links" section.

FIGURE 13.20

Use the Image toolbar to make a color transparent.

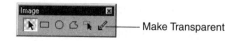

Making a Color Transparent   For practice in making a color transparent, we'll make the background of the pctclogo.gif image transparent:

1. Click the Window menu and choose Home page from the list of open pages. Click the bicycle image. The Image toolbar becomes active.

2. Click the Make Transparent button in the Image toolbar and then move the pointer to the image. The pointer icon changes to the Make Transparent pencil eraser (see Figure 13.21a).

3. Click on the color you want to make transparent. Deselect the image by clicking in another location on the page. Figure 13.21b shows the result of making the background transparent for the embedded bicycle image; notice that the page's background image displays through the transparent background of the image.

4. Click the Save button. FrontPage displays the Save Image to FrontPage Web dialog because making a color transparent affects the image. Click Replace to replace the original image file.

5. Click the image and press Alt+Enter to display the Image Properties. The Transparent check box is checked.

FIGURE 13.21

Click the Make Transparent button and click on the image to make a single color transparent (a). The background color or image displays through the transparent color (b).

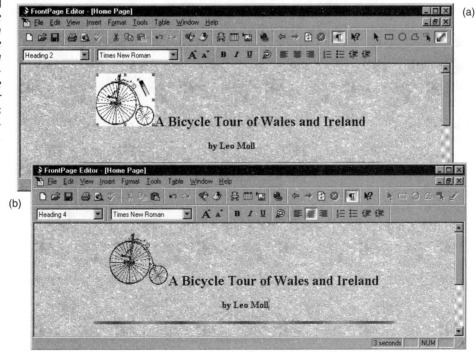

PART

III

Creating Web Pages

Making a Color NonTransparent   To change a transparent color to its original color:

1. Click the image that has a transparent color.

2. Click the Make Transparent button in the Image toolbar and then move the pointer to the image. When the pointer icon changes to the Make Transparent pencil eraser, click to return the transparent color to the original color.

NOTE

Only one color can be transparent at one time; if you try to make a second color transparent, the first transparent color returns to its original color.

Only GIF images have the transparency feature; if you try to make a color transparent for a JPEG image, FrontPage offers you the option of converting the image to a GIF file. GIF images use a smaller number of colors, so converting to a GIF file in order to make a color transparent may result in an image with poorer color quality.

Understanding the Appearance Properties

Use the Appearance tab of the Image Properties dialog to align the image with text, create a border, and resize the image (see Figure 13.22).

FIGURE 13.22

Use the Appearance tab to align the image with text, create a border, and resize the image.

Aligning an Image

When you insert an image in a line in the page, there are two ways you can align the image:

- Use the alignment buttons in the Format toolbar to align the entire contents of a line.
- Use the layout properties in the Appearance tab of the Image Properties dialog to align an image and text on the page.

To explore both kinds of alignment, let's create a new page:

1. Click the New button in the toolbar to display a new blank page. Right-click in the page and choose Page Properties from the shortcut menu. Click the Background tab and choose Default as the Background color.

2. Click the Insert Image button in the toolbar, double-click the images folder, and double-click the world.bmp image file.

3. Type **with text** and choose Heading 6 in the Change Style combo list in the Format toolbar. The image and the text you entered should be on the same line (see Figure 13.23).

4. Click the Save button in the toolbar and save the page with the title Alignments and the file path alignments.htm. Change the URL to Images/world.gif and click Yes to save the converted image file to the current Web.

FIGURE 13.23

Prepare the Alignments page for exploring aligning the contents of a line and aligning an image with text.

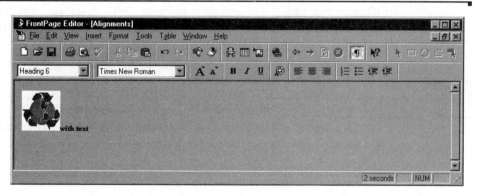

 Aligning an Image on the Page   Use the Left Align, Center, and Right Align buttons in the Format toolbar to align the contents of a line with respect to the left margin, the center, and the right margin respectively. Figure 13.24 shows the three alignments when there is a single image and some text on the line.

PART

III

Creating Web Pages

FIGURE 13.24

Use the alignment buttons on the Format toolbar to align the contents of a line.

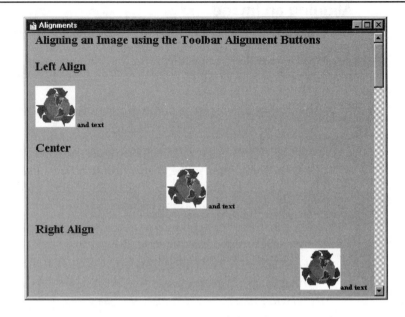

Aligning an Image with Text   If you have text and images on the same line, you can specify how an image is aligned with respect to its neighboring text by setting layout properties in the Image Properties dialog. The choices in the Alignment combo list in the Appearance tab allow you to align the bottom, top, or middle of the image with the current line of text, as shown in Figure 13.25. The absbottom, absmiddle, texttop, and baseline choices allow finer adjustments to the alignments shown in the figure. With any of these choices, the image is aligned with the first line of the text and the remaining lines of text in the paragraph are displayed below the image.

NOTE

> For the examples of aligning an image with text, open the Days 17 to 18 Melancholy Connemara page, copy the first two paragraphs of text, and paste to the Alignments page.

Wrapping Text around an Image   You can also wrap the text in the paragraph to the left or right side of the image. You use the left and right choices in the Alignment combo list in the Appearance tab to place the image in the left or right margin and wrap the text down the right or left side of the image, as shown in Figure 13.26.

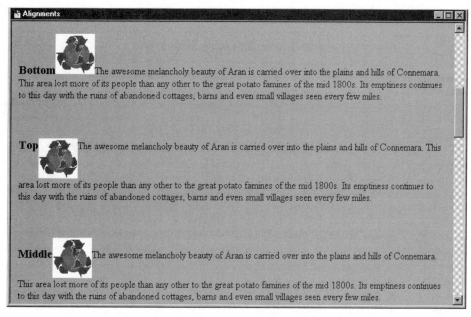

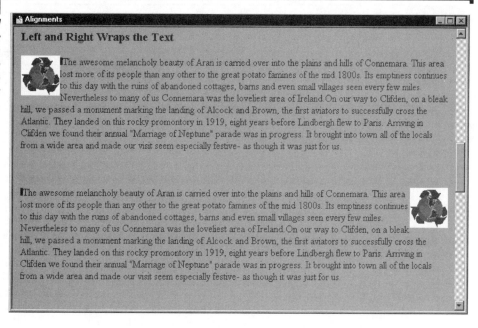

PART

III

Creating Web Pages

Horizontal and Vertical Spacing   You can specify the horizontal spacing between an image and the nearest text or image on the same line by entering the number of pixels in the Horizontal Spacing text box in the Appearance tab. Figure 13.27 shows examples of spacings from 1 to 50 pixels.

FIGURE 13.27

Use the Horizontal Spacing property in the Appearance tab to set the horizontal spacing between the image and the nearest text or image.

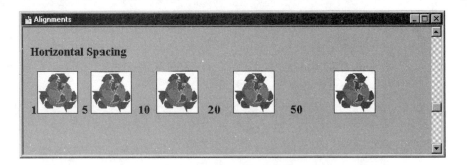

You can specify the vertical spacing between an image and the nearest text or image in the line above or below the current line by entering the number of pixels in the Vertical Spacing text box in the Appearance tab. Figure 13.28 shows examples for spacings of 5 and 50 pixels.

FIGURE 13.28

Use the Vertical Spacing property in the Appearance tab to set the vertical spacing between the image and the nearest text or image in the line above or below the current line.

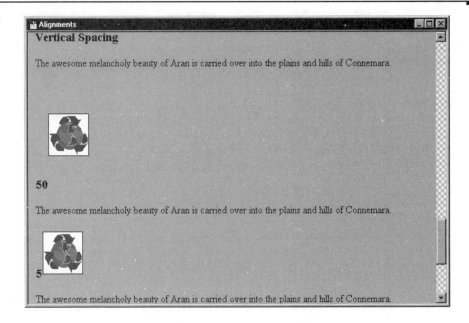

To move an inserted image to the beginning of a new line, place the insertion point to the left of the image and press Enter. To end a line with an inserted image, place the insertion point to the right of the image and press Enter.

Creating a Border

You can create a black border for the selected image by setting the Border Thickness property in the Appearance tab to the number of pixels you want for the thickness. Figure 13.29 shows examples of border thicknesses of 1 to 20 pixels.

FIGURE 13.29

Use the Border Thickness property in the Appearance tab to create a black border.

Changing the Size

There are two ways to resize an image: using the Image Properties dialog or resizing the image directly on the page.

You can change the size of an image using the properties in the Appearance tab. Click the Specify Size check box and change the Width and Height properties by entering the number of pixels or the percentage of the page for each property.

A faster way to resize an image is to work directly with the image in the active page in the Editor. Click the image in the active page and move the pointer to one of the resizing squares. When the pointer shape changes to a double arrow (see Figure 13.30a), hold down the left mouse button and drag the resizing square to the new size (see Figure 13.30b).

PART

III

Creating Web Pages

To resize an image, click the image and drag one of the resizing squares.

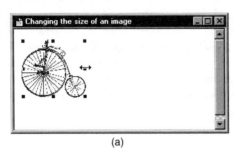
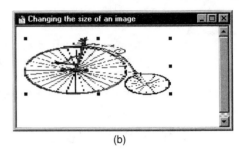

(a)   (b)

Understanding Image Hyperlinks

FrontPage provides two ways that you can create clickable image hyperlinks. You can create a single hyperlink for the entire image so that clicking anywhere on the image activates the link. Alternatively, you can create separate hyperlinks for different parts of the image. Clicking in a part of the image that has a link, called a *hotspot*, activates the link. An image with hotspots is called an *image map*. When you create one or more hotspots for an image, you can also create a default link for the parts of the image that are not hotspots.

You can create image hyperlinks with exactly the same types of targets as you create for text hyperlinks, including pages, bookmarks on pages, and files. As you create an image hyperlink, the Editor displays the identical Create Hyperlink dialog (see Figure 13.31) to specify the target of both text and image hyperlinks. This chapter describes only creating the starting end of the image hyperlink and you can learn about creating the target end in Chapter 12: Understanding Text Hyperlinks.

The easiest way to create an image hyperlink to a page or file in the current Web is to drag the target page or file from the Explorer and drop the page or file on the image in the start page in the Editor. You cannot use drag-and-drop between pages in the Editor to create an image hyperlink to a bookmark.

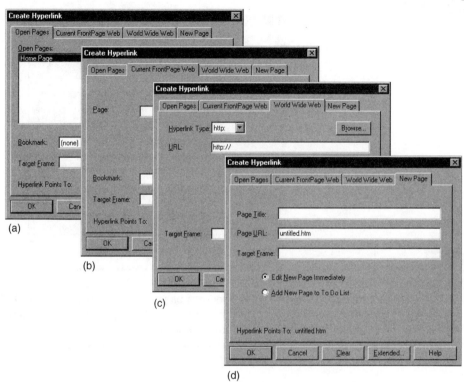

FIGURE 13.31

Use the Create Hyperlink dialog to specify the target end of an image hyperlink.

Creating a Single Hyperlink for an Image

To create a single hyperlink for an image:

1. Click the image and then click the Create or Edit Hyperlink button in the Standard toolbar, choose the Edit ➤ Hyperlink command from the Editor menu bar, or press Ctrl+K.

2. Specify the target of the link using the appropriate tab of the Create Hyperlink dialog, and click OK to create the link.

To practice this, create a single hyperlink from the PCTC logo image on the Home Page of the Wales-Ireland Web to the home page of the PCTC Web. Figure 13.32 shows the dialog for creating the link. Save the page and preview the page in a Web browser.

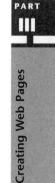

PART

III

Creating Web Pages

Use the World Wide
Web tab to create
an image hyperlink
to another location
on the World Wide
Web or your
intranet.

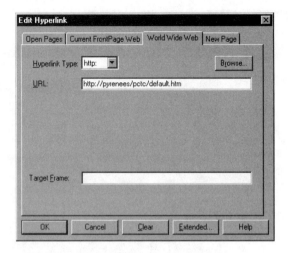

When the target is a bookmark on a page, you must use the Create Hyperlink or Edit
Hyperlink dialogs to specify the bookmark. You cannot create the image hyperlink by
dragging the bookmark text to the image.

Using Drag-and-Drop from the Explorer to Create an Image Hyperlink

When the target of the image hyperlink is a page or file in the current Web, you can
create an image hyperlink with drag-and-drop.

1. Open the start page in the Editor and insert the image you want to use for the
   image hyperlink.

2. Resize and rearrange the Explorer and Editor windows as shown in Figure 13.33.

3. Select the target page or file icon in any view of the Explorer, drag to the start
   page, and drop the file icon on the image. The Editor creates an image hyperlink
   to the target file.

Let's add the Wales map image and the Irish peace image to the Home Page and
create hyperlinks with drag-and-drop.

1. Click Open in the toolbar and double-click the Home Page in the Open File dialog.

FIGURE 13.33

Create an image hyperlink by dragging the target page or file to the image in the start page.

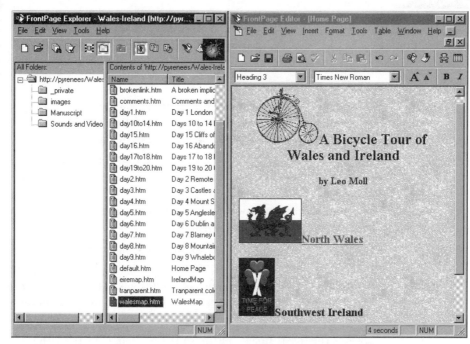

2. In the FrontPage Explorer, click to open the images folder. Click dragon.gif in the Contents pane, and drag-and-drop to the left of North Wales in the Home Page. Click peace.gif in the Contents pane, drag-and-drop to the left of Southwest Ireland in the Home Page. Now that the Wales map and the Irish peace images are in place, we'll create the image hyperlinks.

3. In the FrontPage Explorer, click the web folder, click walesmap.htm in the Contents pane, and drag-and-drop it on the Wales map image. Click eiremap.htm in the Contents pane, and drag-and-drop it on the Irish peace image.

4. Click the Save button in the Editor toolbar to save the image hyperlinks.

Creating and Editing a HotSpot on a Image

You use the Image toolbar to create hotspots.

The Image Toolbar

The Editor has a special toolbar, called the Image toolbar, that you use for creating hotspots on images (see Figure 13. 34).

PART

III

Creating Web Pages

FIGURE 13.34

Use the drawing tools on the Image toolbar to create a hotspot on an image.

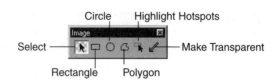

You activate the Images toolbar by clicking the image. To draw a hotspot on an image, use the drawing tools on the Images toolbar. After dragging a drawing tool to define the area for the hotspot and releasing the left mouse button, the Editor displays the Create Hyperlink dialog. You use the tabs of the Create Hyperlink dialog to specify the target of the hotspot and click OK to close the dialog and create the hyperlink.

To explore creating hotspots, we'll create a new page and insert the map that Leo drew for the Wales portion of the trip.

1. Click the New button in the toolbar to display a new blank page. Right-click in the page and choose Page Properties from the shortcut menu. Click the Background tab, click the Background image check box, click the Browse button, double-click the Images folder in the current Web, choose vellum.jpg, and then click OK.

2. Click the Insert Image button in the toolbar, click the Other Location tab, and then click the Browse button. Locate the walesmap.gif image file in the Leo's Maps folder on the book's CD-ROM and click Open to insert the image.

3. Click the Save button in the toolbar and save the page with the title The Wales Route and the filename walesrte.htm. Click Yes to save the image file (see Figure 13.35).

Creating a Rectangular Hotspot

To create a rectangular hotspot on an image in the active page:

1. Click the image and then click the Rectangle button in the Image toolbar.

2. Move the pointer inside the image. The pointer icon changes to a pencil.

3. Move the pointer to any corner of the rectangular hotspot you want to create. Press the left mouse button and drag to create a rectangle. When you release the left mouse button, the Editor displays the Edit Link dialog box.

4. Choose the tab and specify the target of the link.

5. Click OK to create the link.

FIGURE 13.35

The Wales Route page is marked with the geometric areas that we'll use as hotspots and the target pages for the hyperlinks.

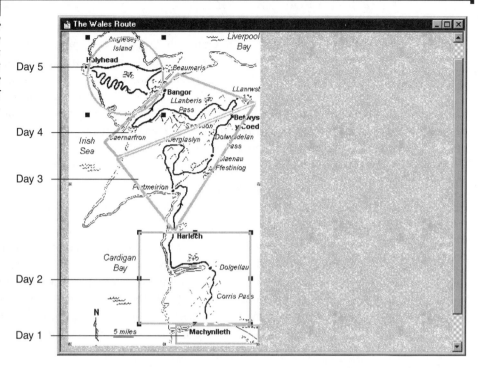

For example, click in the walesmap image. Using Figure 13.35 as a guide, create the rectangular hotspot for Day 1 and create a hyperlink to the day1.htm page in the current Web. Then create the rectangular hotspot for Day 2 and create a hyperlink to the day2.htm page in the current Web.

Creating a Circular Hotspot

To create a circular hotspot on an image in the active page:

1. Click the image and then click the Circle button in the Image toolbar.

2. Move the pointer inside the image. The pointer icon changes to a pencil.

3. Move the pointer to the center of the circular hotspot you want to create. Press the left mouse button and drag to create a circle. When you release the left mouse button, the Editor displays the Edit Link dialog box.

4. Choose the tab and specify the target of the link.

5. Click OK to create the link.

For example, click in the walesmap image. Using Figure 13.35 as a guide, create the circular hotspot for Day 5 and create a hyperlink to the day5.htm page in the current Web.

PART

III

Creating Web Pages

Creating a Polygonal Hotspot

When you want to create a hotspot with an irregular boundary, you can use the Polygon tool to define the hotspot region. You use the tool to create each side of the polygon by clicking on a corner, releasing the mouse, and then clicking on the next corner. The Editor automatically draws the side between two consecutive clicks. Continue in this fashion to define the corners of the polygon and have FrontPage draw the lines between consecutive corners. To create the last corner, double-click the left mouse button to open the Create Hyperlink dialog and then draw the last side after you specify the link's target.

To create a polygonal hotspot on an image in the active page:

1. Click the image and then click the Polygon button in the Image toolbar.

2. Move the pointer inside the image. The pointer icon changes to a pencil.

3. Move the pointer to the first corner of the polygonal hotspot you want to create. Click the left mouse button to create the first corner. Release the mouse button and move the pointer. As you move the pointer within the image, the Editor displays a line between the corner and the pointer. Move the pointer to the second corner and click and then release the left mouse button to create the second corner. The Editor draws the side between the corners. Continue in this fashion to create the corners of the polygon. Double-click to create the last corner. The Editor displays the Create Hyperlink dialog box.

4. Choose the tab and specify the target of the link.

5. Click OK to create the link. The Editor draws the last side of the polygon.

If the polygon you created isn't what you intended, press Delete and start again.

As an example, click in the walesmap image. Using Figure 13.35 as a guide, create the triangular hotspot for Day 3 and create a hyperlink to the day3.htm page in the current Web. Then create the four-sided polygonal hotspot for Day 4 and create a hyperlink to the day4.htm page in the current Web. Click the Save button in the toolbar.

Hotspot Mechanics

When the image is not selected, the hotspots are not visible. The Editor provides ways to make the hotspot boundaries visible so that you can edit the boundaries.

Selecting a Hotspot   You can select a hotspot as follows:

1. Click on the image. The Editor displays the boundaries of the hotspots superimposed on the selected image.

2. Move the pointer to the hotspot you want to select and click the left mouse button. Selection squares appear at the corners of the hotspot. (If the hotspot is a

circle, the selection squares appear at the corners of an invisible square around the circle. Alternatively, press the Tab key to cycle through the hotspots, selecting one hotspot at a time in a generally clockwise direction; pressing the Shift key while you press the Tab key selects one hotspot at a time in a counterclockwise direction.

Selecting Multiple Hotspots in an Image   You can select multiple hotspots on one image by clicking the image and doing one of the following:

- Hold down the Shift key as you click the left mouse button to select each hot spot.
- Click the left mouse button, hold down the button, and drag to create a selection rectangle. Every hotspot with part of its boundary enclosed by the selection rectangle is selected when you release the left mouse button.

Figure 13.36 shows the five hotspots for The Wales Route page with the hotspots for Day 2 and Day 5 selected.

FIGURE 13.36

The five hotspots for The Wales Route page with the hotspots for Day 2 and Day 5 selected

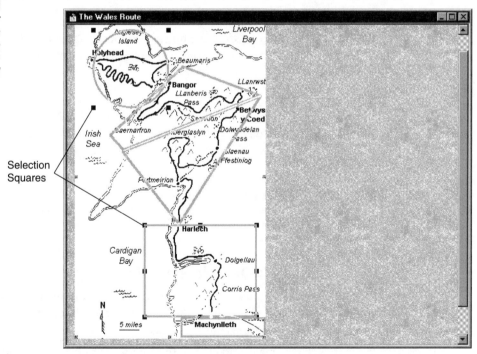

PART

III

Creating Web Pages

Moving a Hotspot   You can move a hotspot to a new location within the image. To move a hotspot:

1. Select the hotspot or hotspots you want to move.

2. Click the left mouse button and drag the hotspot to a new location within the image. If you try to drag a hotspot past the boundary of the image, the hotspot stays at the boundary.

Resizing a Hotspot   You can resize an existing hotspot. To resize a hotspot:

1. Select the hotspot you want to resize.

2. Move the pointer to one of the selection handles. For the rectangular and circular hotspots, the pointer changes shape to a double-pointed arrow indicating the direction you can drag the handle to resize the hotspot. For the polygonal hotspot, you can drag the handle in any direction.

Overlapping Hotspots   If you move a hotspot to a new location or resize a hotspot so that two or more hotspots overlap, the hotspot that controls the overlap area is the hotspot you created most recently. When you click in the overlap region, the controlling hotspot is selected.

Highlighting a Hotspot   Often the hotspot boundaries are difficult to see. FrontPage provides a way to display only the hotspots. To display the hotspots but not the image:

1. Click the image.

2. Click the Highlight hotspots button in the Image toolbar. The Highlight Hotspots button is a toggle button; click the button a second time to display the image. Figure 13.37 shows the highlighted hotspots for the image in The Wales Route page.

Deleting a Hotspot   To delete a hotspot:

1. Select the hotspot or hotspots you want to delete.

2. Press the Delete key.

Setting an Image's Default Hyperlink

After creating hotspots for an image, you can create a default hyperlink for the image. When the Web user clicks in a part of the image without a hotspot, the default hyperlink is activated. To define a default hyperlink:

1. Right-click the image and choose Image Properties from the shortcut menu, or click the image and choose the Edit ➤ Image Properties from the Editor menu bar or press Alt+Enter.

FIGURE 13.37

Click the image and then click the Highlight Hotspots button in the Image toolbar to display the hotspots but not the image.

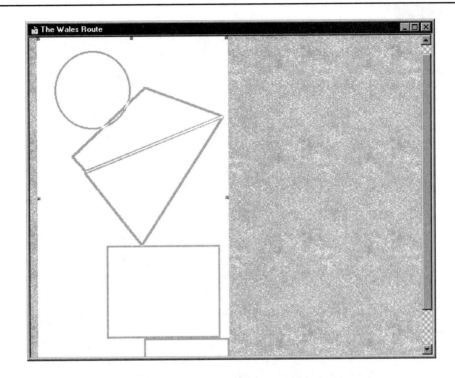

2. In the Default Hyperlink rectangle of the Image Properties dialog (see Figure 13.38), click the Browse button to display the Create Hyperlink dialog.

3. Specify the hyperlink target and click OK to create the default hyperlink.

Alternatively, click in the image in an area where there are no hotspots defined and then click the Create or Edit Hyperlink button in the toolbar. The Editor displays the Edit Hyperlink dialog and you can define the default hyperlink's target and click OK to create the default link.

Editing an Image Hyperlink

To edit an image hyperlink, click the image and then click the Create or Edit Hyperlink button in the toolbar or press Ctrl+K. The Editor displays the Edit Hyperlink dialog for the image's link or for the image's default link if the image has hotspots and you clicked in a region without hotspots.

To edit a hotspot, click on the image, select the hotspot, and then click the Create or Edit Hyperlink button in the toolbar or press Ctrl+K. Alternatively, you can display the Edit Hyperlink dialog for a hotspot by selecting the hotspot and then double-clicking.

Modify the link in the Edit Hyperlink dialog and click OK to create the new hyperlink.

Use the Default Hyperlink section of the Image Properties dialog to specify the hyperlink for a part of an image map that isn't a hotspot.

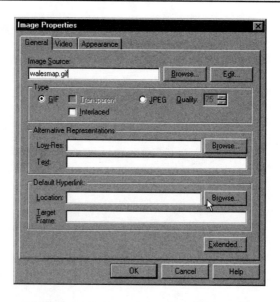

TIP

Although double-clicking a selected hotspot displays the Edit Hyperlink dialog, this technique does not work for the image itself. If you select and double-click an image, the Microsoft Image Composer starts and displays the image in its window.

Deleting an Image Hyperlink

You use the Edit ➤ Unlink command from the Editor menu bar to delete the hyperlink information from an image, a hotspot on an image, or the default hyperlink.

To delete a hyperlink for an image or a hotspot   Click the image or select a hotspot in an image and choose Edit ➤ Unlink from the Editor menu bar.

To delete the default hyperlink for an image with hotspots   Click on the image in a region where there are no hotspots and then choose Edit ➤ Unlink from the Editor menu bar.

Testing Image Hyperlinks

You can test image hyperlinks in exactly the same way that you test text hyperlinks.

To choose a Web browser and preview the page, choose the File ➤ Preview in Browser command from the Editor menu bar. Or click the Preview in Browser button in the Standard toolbar to preview the page in the currently selected Web browser.

Alternatively, you can follow an image hyperlink forward to its target or backwards to its start. See the "Following a Hyperlink in the Editor" section in Chapter 12 for more information.

Inserting a Video Clip on a Page

To display a video as part of a page, you insert the video file. You can insert video files only in Video for Windows format (.avi). When you insert an AVI video clip in a page, the Editor creates an implicit link to the video file. When you display a page with inserted video clips, the Web browser requests the video files using the implicit link information.

NOTE

The phrase "inserting an AVI video" really means "creating an implicit link to an AVI video file." We'll continue to use the first phrase because everybody else does, but keep in mind that when you insert an image you are creating a link.

NOTE

To include a video file in another format such as a Macromedia Director or QuickTime movie, insert a plug-in or an ActiveX Control to play the corresponding video file (see Chapter 20 for information).

Inserting an AVI Video Clip

To insert an AVI video clip in a page, open the page, place the insertion point at the spot where you want the image to be displayed, and choose Insert ➤ Video from the Editor menu bar. The Video dialog (see Figure 13.39) has tabs for two ways to insert the video clip as follows:

Current FrontPage Web to insert an AVI video clip that has already been saved to the current Web

Other Location to insert an AVI video clip from a file in your computer's file system or from a page on the World Wide Web or your intranet

FIGURE 13.39

To display the Video dialog, open a page in the Editor and choose Insert ➤ Video from the Editor menu bar.

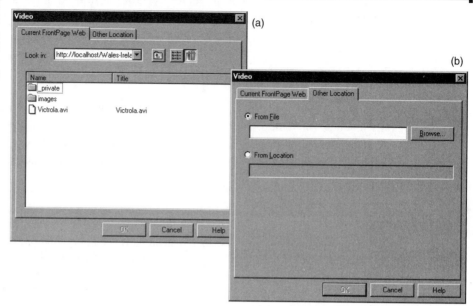

Inserting a Video Clip from the Current Web

To insert an AVI video clip stored in the current Web:

1. Place the insertion point in the active page where you want to display the video and choose Insert ➤ Video from the Editor menu bar. The Current FrontPage Web tab displays the AVI video files in the current Web. Video files in other image formats, such as .mov or .qt, are not displayed (see Figure 13.39a).

2. Select the video clip from the list and click OK. FrontPage creates an implicit link to the file and displays the first frame of the video clip at the insertion point.

3. Click the Save button in the toolbar to save the page. The Editor saves the link to the video file in the current Web.

Inserting a Video Clip from a File Not in the Current Web

To insert an AVI video clip from any AVI video file in your computer's file system, but not stored in the current Web:

1. Place the insertion point in the active page where you want to insert the video and choose Insert ➤ Video from the Editor menu bar. Click the Other Location

tab in the Video dialog. Click the Browse button to display the Video location dialog (see Figure 13.40a). Use the Look in combo box to locate the file.

2. Click Open. The Editor creates an implicit link to the video file and displays the first frame of the video clip at the insertion point.

3. Click the Save button in the toolbar. The Editor displays the Save File to Web dialog (see Figure 13.40b). Click Yes to save the file to the current Web. If you click No, the file is not saved to the Web and the implicit link to the video file is broken.

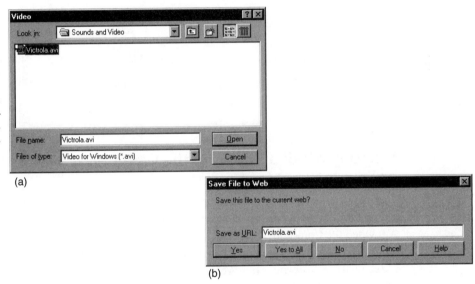

(a)

(b)

To illustrate, we'll insert the victrola.avi video clip from the web's Sounds and Video folder on a new page.

1. Click the New button in the toolbar. Choose Insert ➤ Video from the Editor menu bar.

2. Double-click the Sounds and Video folder and double-click the victrola.avi file. The Editor creates an implicit link to the AVI file and displays the first frame of the file at the insertion point (see Figure 13.41).

3. Click the Save button in the toolbar.

FIGURE 13.41

When you insert an AVI video clip in a page, the Editor displays the first frame.

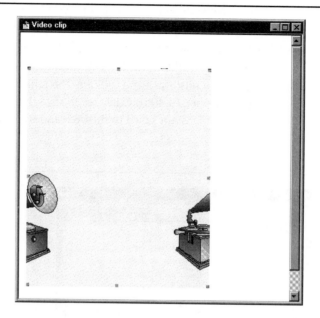

Inserting a Video Clip from the World Wide Web or Your Intranet

You can insert an AVI video clip from the World Wide Web or your intranet. The Editor handles the insertion in a way that is quite different from the insertion of an AVI video file from your own computer's file system. When you insert a video file from the World Wide Web or your intranet, the Editor creates an implicit link to the video file stored on the other Web server and does not offer to save the video clip file to the current Web. To insert the video clip, you need to know the file's absolute URL; the easiest way to get the URL is to browse to the Web site, locate the video clip, and copy its absolute URL.

1. Place the insertion point in the active page where you want to insert the video clip and choose Insert ➤ Image from the Editor menu bar. Click the Other Location tab.

2. Enter the absolute URL of the video clip file and click OK. If your network connection is open, FrontPage retrieves the video clip file and displays the first frame of the video clip at the insertion point. If the network connection is closed, the Explorer displays an error message and displays an empty square in place of the video clip. Whether or not the network connection is open, FrontPage creates the link to the file.

3. Click the Save button in the toolbar. When you save the page, you are saving the link to the WWW or intranet video clip file. FrontPage creates the link to the WWW or intranet file and lists the link in the Outline view in the Explorer using the world icon.

If you close your Internet connection and try to view the page in the Editor, FrontPage displays an error message and the Editor displays the empty square. If your Internet connection is open, but the server that stores the video clip is not, the Editor won't be able to retrieve the image and the empty square is displayed.

NOTE

You can also retrieve a copy of a video file from the Internet and save the copy directly to the web folder. See the "Importing Files from the Internet" section in Chapter 6.

Understanding Video Properties

To view the properties of an inserted video clip, click the image and choose the Edit ➤ Image Properties command from the Editor menu bar, or press Alt+Enter, or right-click the image and choose Image properties from the shortcut menu. The Image Properties dialog displays the Video tab (see Figure 13.42).

FIGURE 13.42

You can set the properties for a video clip in the Video tab.

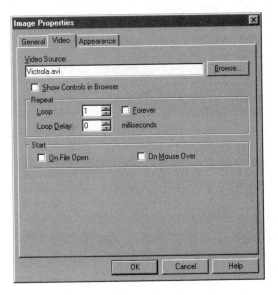

PART

III

Creating Web Pages

- **Player controls** Click the Show Controls in the Browser check box to show player control along the bottom of the video (see Figure 13.43).

- **Repeat** You can specify the number of loops or click the Forever check box to have the video clip repeat endlessly. You can specify the number of milliseconds delay between the next repeat of the video clip.

- **Start** Specify that the video clip starts playing when the Web visitor opens the page by checking the On File Open check box. You can click the On Mouse Over check box to have the video clip start to play when the Web visitor moves the mouse pointer over the video clip.

FIGURE 13.43

Preview a video clip in a Web browser that is able to play AVI video files.

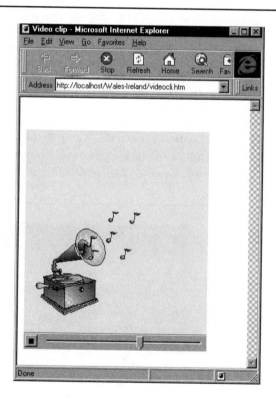

Viewing an AVI Video Clip

The Editor is not able to play the AVI video clip inserted in a page. To view the clip, click the Preview in Browser button in the toolbar. Not all Web browsers can play AVI video clips, so make sure to select a browser such as Microsoft Internet Explorer 3.0. When the Web browser opens, the video clip plays according to the properties you set.

As an example,

1. Right-click the victrola.avi video clip, and click all four check boxes in the Video tab of the Image Properties dialog.

2. Click the Save button in the toolbar.

3. Click the Review in Browser button in the toolbar. The Web browser displays the first frame of the video. Move the mouse over the video clip. The video clip starts to play (see Figure 13.43).

Creating a Link to a QuickTime Movie

A simple way to include a non-AVI video clip is to create a hyperlink to the video file. When the Web visitor clicks the hyperlink, the visitor's browser may be configured to play the video. To illustrate, we'll create a link to an Apple QuickTime movie.

1. Click the Open button in the toolbar and double-click day19to20 in the open File dialog.

2. Insert a line above the heading "Our Last Meal Together" and type **Join us on the hike (QuickTime movie)**.

3. Select the entire line of text and create a text hyperlink to the cropatpath.mov file in the Sounds and Video folder (see Figure 13.44). See Chapter 12 for help on creating a text hyperlink.

4. Click the Save button and then click the Preview in Browser button in the toolbar.

5. In the browser, click the new hyperlink. What happens next depends on your browser. For example, if you are using the Microsoft Internet Explorer 3.0 with the ActiveMovie ActiveX Control installed (you download Active Movie when you download the Internet Explorer 3.0), the browser plays the QuickTime movie in a small window in the center of the browser window (see Figure 13.45).

Performance Considerations

While images and video clips add visual interest to a Web page, they do take time to load into the browser. The larger the image or video clip file, the longer it takes to load. Performance is a critical issue in designing a Web site. A Web site with many graphic enhancements, exciting video clips, background sounds, and gorgeous photo graphic may not hold a Web visitor's attention for more than a few seconds if your pages take too long to load. This section describes a few of the ways you can improve the performance of your Web site.

PART

III

Creating Web Pages

FIGURE 13.44

You can include a non-AVI video clip by creating a hyper-link to the file.

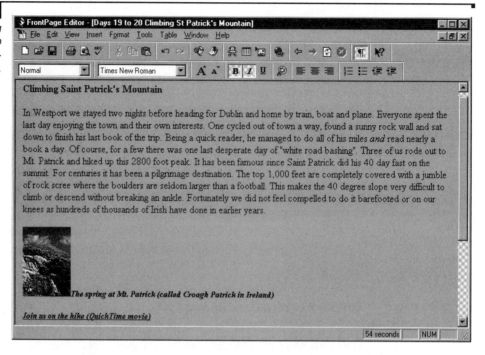

FIGURE 13.45

The ActiveMovie add-in for Microsoft Internet Explorer 3.0 plays a QuickTime movie in a small window in the center of the browser window.

Using Alternate Representations

There are two alternate representations for an image or video clip: an alternate text message and an alternate image. To specify an alternative, right-click on the image and choose Image Properties from the Shortcut menu, or click on the image and choose Edit ➤ Image Properties from the Editor menu bar to display the Image Properties dialog. The Alternate Representation properties are on the General tab (see Figure 13.46).

Specifying an Image's Alternate Text

Not all browsers display images. You can provide a text message that the browser can display if it is unable to display the image. To create a text message:

1. Right-click on the image and choose Image Properties from the shortcut menu, or click on the image and choose Edit ➤ Image Properties from the Editor menu bar.

2. Enter the alternate text message in the Text text box in the Alternate Representation section of the Image Properties dialog. Click OK to close the dialog.

Some Web browsers, including Microsoft Internet Explorer 3.0, display the alternate text message while the image or video clip is loading.

PART

III

Creating Web Pages

Providing an Image's Alternate Low-Resolution Image

Large images and video clips may take several seconds to load in a browser. While a large file loads, you can display a small image in its place by specifying the small image in the Low Res text box in the Alternate Representation section of the Image Properties dialog. Click the Browse button to select the alternate image. You can choose a GIF of JPEG image saved in the current Web, or you can click the From URL button in the Insert Image dialog to display the Open Location dialog and specify the URL of an image from the WWW or intranet.

Reusing Images

When a Web browser loads a Web page, the browser first sends a request for the page itself to the server and displays the page. The browser reads the page and determines if additional files are needed. Each additional file may mean a separate request back to the browser. As the Web browser receives responses from the server, the responses are temporarily stored in the browser's cache. Before issuing a request to a Web server, the browser first looks for the requested file in its cache; if the file is in the cache, the browser uses its own copy and doesn't send the request to the server. The browser is able to use information stored in its cache more quickly because it doesn't have to wait while the request goes to the server. The server finds the files, and sends a copy back to the browser.

You can take advantage of the caching behavior and make your images display more rapidly by reusing images in your Web. When you reuse an image file in several places in your Web, the browser needs to take the time to retrieve the image file only if it is not already in the cache. Normally, this means the browser retrieves the image file the first time the user opens a page in your Web that requires the image. If the image is used several times on the same page, the browser uses its own cache copy to display the remaining images. If the Web visitor jumps to another page that uses the same image, the browser continues to use its own cache copy.

Avoiding Large Bitmaps

The first time a page needs an image file, the browser must retrieve the file from a server. Even with the current image compression schemes used in the GIF and JPEG formats, large files take time to load. Unless the Web server is fast, a large image may take longer to load than the visitor is willing to wait. One solution is to avoid large images altogether. Another solution is to display a small version of the image on the page along with a text hyperlink to the full-size version; the text can indicate the size of the full-size version so that the Web visitor has the choice to wait while the full-size version opens.

Tiling Bitmaps

When you specify an image as a background image, the browser automatically displays copies, or *tiles*, of the same file in rows and columns to completely fill the background of the page. Since a single image file is used, the time to display the tiled background is only a moment longer than the time to retrieve and display a single tile.

You can use the same idea to cover a large part of a page with small tiles of one or a few different images. Figure 13.47 shows the result of creating a design with tiles; multiple copies of the clover.gif image are placed side-by-side to create a banner for the Ireland Map page.

FIGURE 13.47

Using tiled images to create a banner

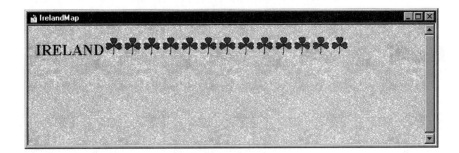

Client-Side versus Server-Side Clickable Images

By default, when you create clickable images, FrontPage automatically includes the hyperlink's target URL in the HTML coding for the page. This type of coding of a clickable image hyperlink is called a *client-side image link* because it requires that the browser knows how to process the HTML coding. In fact, most of the popular browsers know how to process client-side clickable images. Client-side image processing is the newer way to handle clickable images. Previously, the server had to do all the processing. Clickable images that are processed by a server require a different kind of coding that includes the coordinates of each image and the coordinates of each hotspot and are called *server-side clickable images*. FrontPage provides the ability to create both kinds of clickable images.

PART

III

Creating Web Pages

Setting the Clickable Image Style

You set the clickable image style for the current Web in the Explorer. Choose the Tools ➤ Web Setting command from the Explorer menu bar and click the Advanced tab. By default the Generate client-side image maps check box is checked (see Figure 13.48).

The Style combo box lists the major server types including FrontPage, NSCA, CERN, Netscape. If you select a server type, FrontPage automatically creates the HTML coding so that servers of that type can process the clickable image using server-side processing. If you select <none>, FrontPage does not generate the HTML coding for server-side processing of clickable images.

By choosing a server style and clicking the Generate client-side image maps check box, FrontPage generates the HTML coding for both client-side and server-side clickable image processing.

FIGURE 13.48

Specify whether to have the browser or the Web server process image hyperlinks in the Explorer's Web Settings dialog.

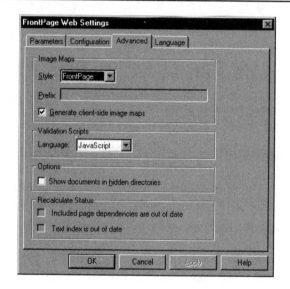

For More...

This chapter has shown you how to insert image files and video clips. You've learned how to create image hyperlinks and image maps, and to distinguish which regions in an image have links to different targets.

The following chapters provide more information on the topics covered in this chapter:

- Chapter 6: Working with Files shows you how to import files with any format into the open web in the FrontPage Explorer, and how to import files from the Internet into the web folder.

- Chapter 14: Adding Tables shows you how to use tables to lay out images.

- Chapter 16: Using WebBots in Page Design shows you how to include an image for a specific time interval.

Chapter

14

Adding Tables

Adding Tables

Tables have two very different purposes in a web: for organizing information into rows and columns, and
for laying out a page. Tables are an excellent way to organize and display large
amounts of information. A table is particularly useful when the information consists
of a set of elements and the elements have common categories; you can arrange the
information into a table with the elements as rows and the categories as columns.
Figure 14.1 shows the first three days of the itinerary of the bicycle tour in North
Wales arranged as a table; each element (row) of the table is a day, and the information categories (columns) are the number of the day, the destination for the day, the
miles and feet of climb for the day, and comments about the day's journey.

In FrontPage, tables are also a great way to lay out a page. The previous chapters
have covered a few simple page layout techniques. In Chapter 11, you learned techniques for laying out the text on a page, including alignment of paragraphs and lists.
In Chapter 13, you learned techniques for aligning images on the page and aligning
an image with a paragraph of text. However, the layout techniques you learned about
are limited: you haven't learned how to display a page with more than one column of
text, how to place a border around a paragraph, or how to create grids of images and
text. You can do these layout tasks with tables. Tables give you great control over

placing text and images on a page. The Editor also provides table formatting tools that you can use to make your tables more attractive.

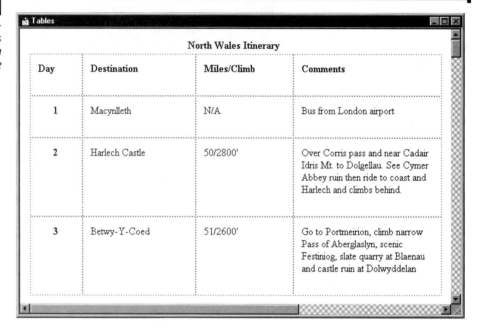

North Wales Itinerary			
Day	Destination	Miles/Climb	Comments
1	Macynlleth	N/A	Bus from London airport
2	Harlech Castle	50/2800'	Over Corris pass and near Cadair Idris Mt. to Dolgellau. See Cymer Abbey ruin then ride to coast and Harlech and climbs behind.
3	Betwy-Y-Coed	51/2600'	Go to Portmeirion, climb narrow Pass of Aberglaslyn, scenic Festiniog, slate quarry at Blaenau and castle ruin at Dolwyddelan

This chapter covers the parts of a table, how to insert tables, how to insert content into a table, and how to use tables for page layout. You'll learn how to modify table elements after you've created the table: how to work with the content in the table, and how to insert and delete table parts.

NOTE

To work through the examples in this chapter, you'll need to replace the Wales-Ireland web you created in previous chapters with a modified version on the book's CD-ROM. Open your existing Wales-Ireland web and choose File ➤ Delete FrontPage Web from the Explorer menu bar to delete the web. Then choose File ➤ Import and use the Import Web Wizard to create a new web named Wales-Ireland and to import all the files from the web named Wales-Ireland-Ch14 stored in the Webs folder on the book's CD-ROM.

Understanding the Parts of a Table

Tables have many parts, so we'll start with some table terminology.

A table is a rectangular arrangement of horizontal *rows* and vertical *columns*. The intersection of a row and a column is the individual rectangle called a *table cell*. A table may also have a *caption* which describes the table's contents; the caption can be placed at the top or bottom of the table. Figure 14.2 shows the parts of a table.

FIGURE 14.2

The parts of a table

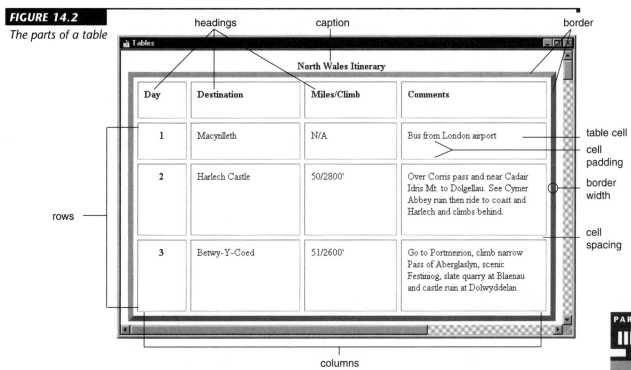

Table *headings* label the columns and the rows; the font of a header cell is usually displayed in a bold font. The table may be enclosed by a *border* with a *border width* you can specify.

There are two cell dimensions you can specify. The *cell padding* is the distance from the inside edge of a cell to the cell contents. You can think of the cell padding as the cell's margin. The *cell spacing* is the distance between cells. You can think of the cell spacing as the cell's border between it and other cells. In Figure 14.2, the cell spacing is displayed as the width of the strips between the cells.

PART

III

Creating Web Pages

Adding an Existing Table to a Page

In many cases, you've already created a table in another program and want to include the table in a page. The other Microsoft Office applications, including Word, Excel, and Access, all have techniques superior to those in FrontPage for manipulating the information in a table. For example, in these applications, you can sort the rows of a table alphabetically by columns, or columns alphabetically by rows, and you can do calculations based on the numerical contents of cells. By contrast, FrontPage has excellent formatting techniques for changing the appearance of the table.

You can add the contents of an existing table created in another Microsoft Office application (and in most other applications that allow tables) to the active page in the Editor, as follows:

1. Open the file in the other application.

2. Select the table or table cells and copy them to the Clipboard using the application's copy commands.

3. Click in the Web page where you want to place the table cells and paste the selection.

You can also use drag-and-drop techniques.

When you copy a table in another application, you also copy that application's formatting instructions. Pasting the table in a Web page also pastes the formatting. After pasting the table in the page, you can use the formatting techniques described in this chapter to modify the table's appearance.

To illustrate, we'll create a new page and add existing tables from Word, Excel, and Access.

1. Click the New button in the toolbar.

2. Locate the Word document named ItemsToBring.doc in the PCTC Information folder on the book's CD-ROM. Double-click to open the document using Microsoft Word. Resize the Word and FrontPage Editor windows and arrange them side by side.

3. Select the table in Word. Hold down the left mouse button, drag to the page in the Editor, and release the mouse button. The Editor converts the table to HTML and displays the results (see Figure 14.3). The formatting of the Word table is retained: the row heading is bold and the second column is centered. Close Microsoft Word.

FIGURE 14.3

You can add a
table from
Microsoft Word.

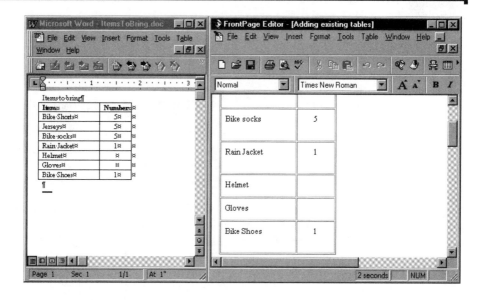

4. Locate the TourInfo.xls Excel workbook in the Manuscript folder in the current web. Double-click to open the workbook using Microsoft Excel (see Figure 14.4a). The workbook contains two spreadsheets: Itinerary and Travelers.

5. Select the first four rows and columns of the Itinerary spreadsheet and press Ctrl+C. Click in the page in the Editor, place the insertion point in the line below the previous table, press Enter to insert a new row, and press Ctrl+V to paste the table. The formatting of the Excel spreadsheet is retained: the row heading is bold and the first column is centered (see Figure 14.4b). Close Microsoft Excel.

6. Locate the PCTC.mdb Access database in the PCTC Information folder on the book's CD-ROM. Double-click the Members table in the Database window to open the datasheet (see Figure 14.5a).

7. Click the square in the upper-left corner of the datasheet to select the row headings and the rows of the datasheet. Choose Edit ➤ Copy from the Access menu bar. Click in the page in the Editor, place the insertion point in the line below the previous table, press Enter to insert a new row, and choose Edit ➤ Copy from the Editor menu bar to paste the table. The Access table formatting is quite different from the formatting of the Word or Excel tables (see Figure 14.5b). Close Microsoft Access.

FIGURE 14.4

You can copy a table from Microsoft Excel (a) and paste it in a Web page (b).

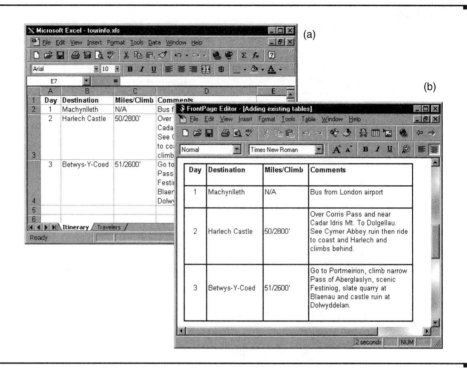

FIGURE 14.5

You can copy a datasheet from Microsoft Access (a) and paste it in a Web page (b).

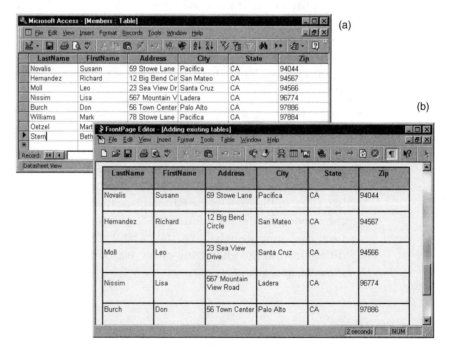

8. Click the Save button in the toolbar. Save the page with the title Adding an existing table, and with the filename officetables.htm.

Creating a New Table

There are two ways to create a new table. Place the insertion point in a new line in the active page and do one of the following:

- Click the Insert Table button in the Standard toolbar and drag to select the number of rows and columns you want (see Figure 14.6a). When you release the mouse button, the Editor creates the table (see Figure 14.6b).

FIGURE 14.6

Use the Insert Table toolbar button to create a new table with a specified number of rows and columns(a). When you release the mouse button, the table is inserted in the page (b).

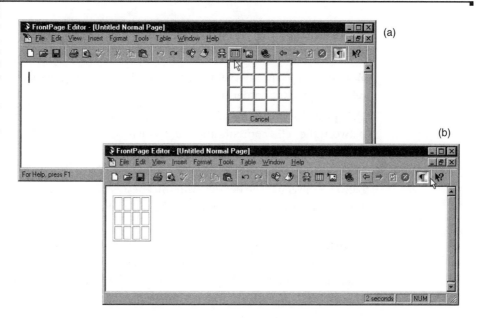

- Choose the Table ➤ Insert Table command from the Editor menu bar. The Insert Table dialog (see Figure 14.7) shows the properties you can set when you create the table.

You can set the following table properties:

Size   Specify the number of horizontal rows and vertical columns.

Alignment   Use the alignment combo box to position the table on the page. You can choose left, right, or center to position the table on the left or right side of the page or in the center of the page.

FIGURE 14.7

Use the Insert Table dialog to create the table.

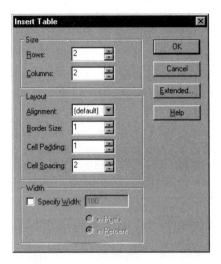

Border Size   Specify the number of pixels for the border that surrounds the table. The default border size is one.

Cell padding   Specify the number of pixels to set the closest distance between the cell's contents and the inside border of the cell. The default padding size is one pixel.

Cell spacing   Specify the number of pixels to set the thickness of the strips between the cells. The default strip thickness is two pixels. The strips between the cells are visible only when the Border Size is a number greater than zero and are invisible otherwise.

Width   Click the Specify Width check box to specify the width of the table. You can specify either a percentage of the width of the browser's window or a fixed number of pixels. The default width is 100 percent of the page window.

- **In Percent**   When you specify the table's width as a percentage, the width adjusts as the browser window is resized. When you specify the table width as a percentage, by default you also specify the widths of every column with a percentage width. For example, if you specify a table width of 80 percent and use percent widths for the columns, the table and column widths adjust so that the table spans 80 percent of the browser window.

- **In Pixels**   When you specify the table's width as a number of pixels, the width is fixed and doesn't adjust as the browser window is resized. If the table is wider than the window, you have to scroll horizontally to view parts of the table.

NOTE

The Insert Table dialog has an Extended button. You click this button to display a dialog for specifying attributes for the table that FrontPage doesn't recognize. See the section "Understanding Extended Attributes" in Chapter 10 for more information.

Figures 14. 8 and 14.9 show different settings for the same table. The settings in Figure 14.8a are the default values for alignment, border size, cell padding, cell spacing, and width; and the table in Figure 14.8b is aligned to the right, has a border size of 10 pixels, a cell padding of 15 pixels, a cell spacing of 3 pixels, and a table width of 90 percent of the window. The tables in Figure 14.9 have the default values, except the border size is zero. When you set the border size as zero, the Editor displays both the borders for the table and for the cells as dotted lines (see Figure 14.9a). The dotted line is a format mark which you can hide by choosing the Format Marks command in the View menu; Figure 14.9b shows the same table with the Format Marks turned off, which is the way a Web browser would display the table.

FIGURE 14.8

The default settings (a) and modified settings (b) for the same table.

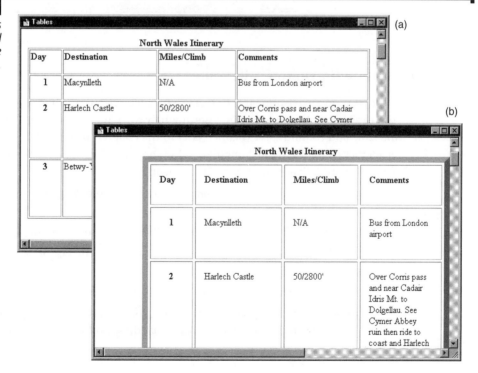

PART

III

Creating Web Pages

FIGURE 14.9

With a border size of zero pixels, the Editor displays the table and cell borders as dotted lines (a). Web browsers display the table with no borders (b).

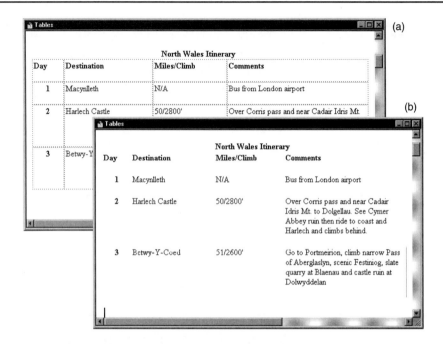

Understanding Table Properties

After you add an existing table or create a new table, you can change its properties. You can change the table size by inserting new rows and columns and deleting existing rows and columns, as explained later in the chapter. You can change all other properties using the Table Properties dialog shown in Figure 14.10. To display the Table Properties dialog, do any of the following:

- Right-click anywhere in the table and choose Table Properties from the shortcut menu.

- Click in the table and choose Table ➤ Table Properties from the Editor menu bar.

- Double-click in the margin selector bar to select the entire table (and caption) and press Alt+Enter.

The Table Properties you can set in Figure 14.10 include:

Layout   You can specify the alignment of the table on the page, the size of the border surrounding the table, the cell padding, and the cell spacing as described in the previous section.

FIGURE 14.10

Use the Table Properties dialog to modify an existing table.

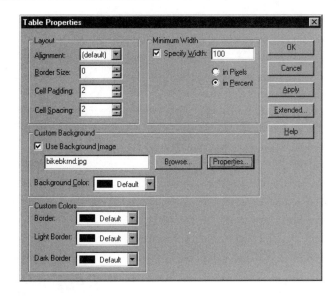

Minimum Width   You can specify the width of the table as a fixed number of pixels or as a percentage of the page width, as described in the previous section.

Custom Background   You can specify a background for the area covered by the table and its caption. To specify a background image, click the Use Background Image check box and enter the location of the image you want to display. If you don't know the URL, click the Browse button to display the Select Background Image dialog (see Figure 14.11a) and click OK to insert the image. To change the properties of the background image, click the Properties button on the Table Properties dialog to display the Image Properties dialog (see Figure 14.11b); you can start the Microsoft Image Composer to edit the image by clicking the Edit button. To specify a background color, choose a color in the Background Color combo list. Figure 14.12 shows a page with a background image for a table and a different background image for the page.

Custom Colors   You can specify a single color for the table border and cell borders. To create a three-dimensional effect, you can specify two colors as follows: the Light Border color is used in the upper-left sections of the table and the lower-right sections of the cell borders, and the Dark Border color is used in the remaining sections.

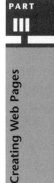

PART

III

Creating Web Pages

FIGURE 14.11

Click the Browse button on the Table Properties dialog to select a background image (a). Click the Properties button on the Table Properties dialog to view the properties of the selected background image (b).

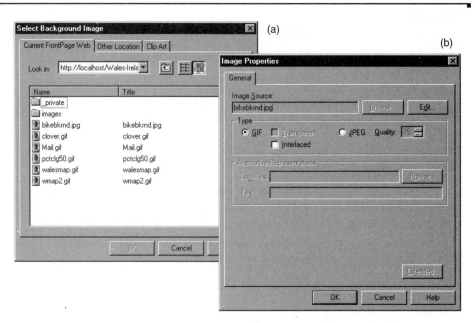

FIGURE 14.12

The background image for the table and its caption override the background image for the page.

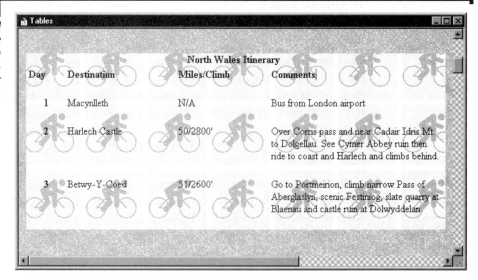

NOTE

The Table Properties dialog remembers the settings you specify for a table and uses these settings the next time you create a table.

NOTE

Like all property sheets in the Editor, the Table Properties dialog has an Extended button. You click this button to display a dialog for specifying attributes for the table that FrontPage doesn't recognize. See the "Understanding Extended Attributes" section in Chapter 10 for more information.

Inserting a Table Caption

A table caption is the title for the table, and is considered to be one of the parts of the table. To insert a caption, place the insertion point in any table cell and choose the Table ➤ Insert Caption command from the Editor menu bar. The Editor moves the insertion point to the center of the table just above the first row. Type in the caption text; after you have entered the text, move the pointer to another location and click. If you want to modify the caption text, just click in the caption text to edit, and click out when you are finished editing.

Inserting Text and Objects in Table Cells

To insert text, place the insertion point in the table cell and type the characters. To insert any of the objects listed in the Editor's Insert menu into a table cell, place the insertion point in the table cell and choose the object from the menu list. The objects you can insert include line breaks, horizontal lines, symbols, comments, images, video clips, files, WebBot components, advanced components (Java Applets, ActiveX controls, plug-ins and PowerPoint animations), forms, marquees, hyperlinks, and bookmarks. You can also insert other tables as nested tables. Figure 14.13 shows examples of most of the types of objects you can insert in a table cell.

NOTE

Note that you cannot insert another web page in a table cell. In Chapter 16: Understanding Frames, you'll learn how to display two or more Web pages inside a another special web page called a frameset.

After typing text in a table cell, you edit the text using the same text editing and formatting techniques you learned about in Chapter 11. After inserting an object, you can change the object's properties using the formatting and editing tools that the Editor provides for the object. Typically, to edit an object, right-click the object in the

PART

III

Creating Web Pages

table cell and choose the object's Properties command in the shortcut menu, or press Alt+Enter to display the properties sheet. Refer to the chapter that corresponds to an object to learn more about working with the object.

FIGURE 14.13

This table contains example of the types of objects you can insert in table cells.

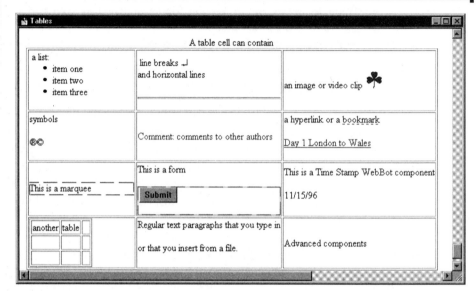

Using Tables for Page Layout

An important use of tables is for laying out a page. This section shows you how to:

- Use tables to lay out images and text
- Create multi-column text
- Use a one-cell table to create a text or image frame

Laying Out Images and Text   In Chapter 13: Using Images and Video Clips, you learned how to align an image and text on the same line. Often you need other types of alignment that only tables can provide. In Chapter 12 you created a set of text hyperlinks on the WalesMap page to the five pages of the Wales section of the Wales-Ireland trip (see Figure 14.14a), and in Chapter 13·you created an image map with hotspots for the same five days (see Figure 14.14b).

FIGURE 14.14

The WalesMap page with hyperlinks to five pages (a) and The Wales Route page with a map for the pages (b).

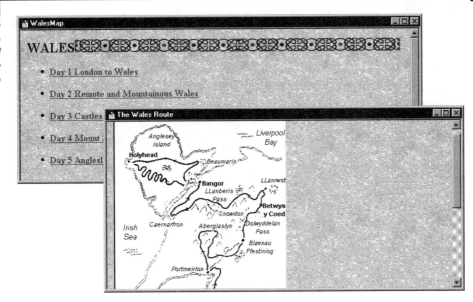

Using a table, you can display the map and the list side by side, as follows:

1. Click Open in the toolbar and double-click the WalesMap page in the Open File dialog. Click the Open button again and double-click The Wales Route page. Click the page window's Restore button to restore both page windows to normal size so that you'll be able to drag from one page to the other.

2. In the WalesMap page, click in the line below the list, and choose Table ➤ Insert Table from the Editor menu bar.

3. Set the number of rows to 1, the number of columns to 2, the alignment to Center, the border size to 2, and the cell padding to 5. Click the Specify Width check box, and enter 90 as the table width in percent. Click OK.

4. Double-click in the selector bar of the list to select the entire list. Click in the list, hold the left mouse button down, and drag to the table cell on the left. Release the left mouse button. The Editor moves the entire list to the table cell.

5. In The Wales Route page, click in the selector bar to select the image. Right-click in the image, hold the right mouse button down, and drag to the table cell on the right. Release the mouse button and choose Copy Here in the shortcut menu. The Editor moves a copy of the image to the table cell (see Figure 14.15).

6. Click in WalesMap page and press Ctrl+S to save the page. Close both pages.

FIGURE 14.15

The Wales map page uses a table to lay out the list of text hyperlinks and the clickable image map of Wales side by side.

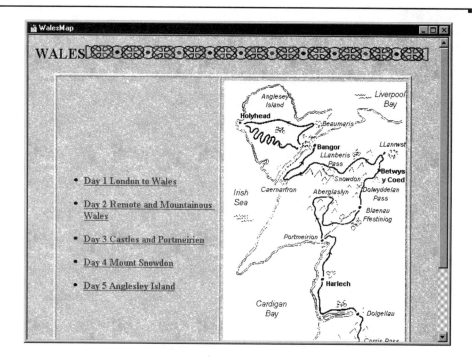

Multi-column Text   You can use a table to create pages with several columns of text. As an example, in the Wales-Ireland web, the page Day 4 Mount Snowdon has paragraphs (see Figure 14.16a). We'll insert three photographs to make the page more interesting, and then use a table to lay out the paragraphs and photos in two columns and three rows.

1. Click the Open button in the toolbar and double-click the day4.htm page. Click to the left of the first heading and press Enter to insert a new first line.

2. Click in the new line, and choose Table ➤ Insert Table from the Editor menu bar. Create a table with three rows and two columns, set the border size and the cell padding to zero, and set the table width to 100 percent.

3. Select the first heading and all but the last sentence of the first paragraph. Click in the selection, hold down the left mouse button, and drag to the table cell in the first row and first column. Release the mouse button. Place the insertion point in the empty first line of the cell and press Delete. Place the insertion point to the right of the heading and press Delete twice to run the heading and the text together, and then press Space.

4. Select the remaining sentence of the paragraph. Click in the selection, hold down the left mouse button, and drag to the table cell in the second row and second column. Release the mouse button.

5. Select the last paragraph and its heading. Click in the selection, hold down the left mouse button, and drag to the table cell in the third row and first column. Release the mouse button. Place the insertion point in the empty first line of the cell, and press Delete. Place the insertion point to the right of the heading, and press Delete twice to run the heading and the text together, and then press Space. Figure 14.16b shows the page. Now we'll insert images in the three empty cells.

FIGURE 14.16

Use a table to change the layout of text from regular paragraphs (a) to two columns (b).

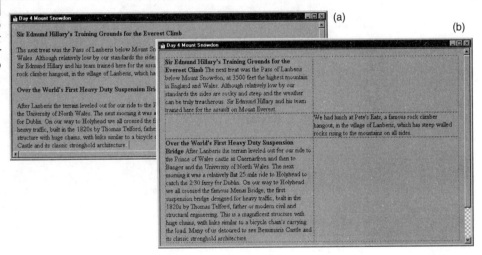

6. Click in the empty cell in the first row and then click the Insert Image button in the toolbar. Following the techniques explained in Chapter 13, insert the image file lanberis.jpg from the Wales-Ireland Photos folder on the book's CD-ROM. In the next step, you'll insert two other photos from the same folder.

7. Repeat Step 6 to insert the image file petes.jpg in the empty cell in the second row and repeat Step 6 once more to insert the image file bridge.jpg in the empty cell in the third row. Figure 14.17 shows the page with the Format Marks turned off.

8. Press Ctrl+S to save the page. Click Yes to All to save the three images to the current Web. In the next step, you'll create a new folder to store the photos.

9. In the FrontPage Explorer, create a new folder named Photos as a subfolder of the Images folder and move the three photos to the new folder (see Chapter 6 for more information).

PART

III

Creating Web Pages

NOTE

You cannot use the Save Images to FrontPage Web dialog to create a new folder by modifying the URL.

FIGURE 14.17

FIGURE 14.17

Intersperse images and text in a table for a more attractive page.

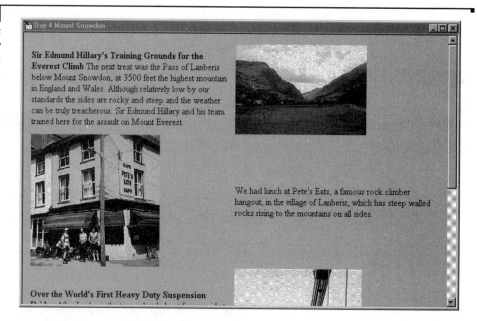

Using a One Cell Table

You can use a one-cell table to create a border for a piece of text or to create a picture frame for an image or a video clip. For example, in the Wales-Ireland web, the bottom of page Day 3 Castles and Portmeirion includes the text hyperlink to the The Castles of Wales Web site on the World Wide Web, the e-mail link to the author of the site, and the link to a photo from the Web site (see Figure 14.18). We'll use a one-cell table to create a border for the text and another one-cell table to create a picture frame for the image. If necessary, open your Internet connection so that you'll be able to retrieve the image.

Creating a Border for Text Paragraphs   To create a border for text paragraphs:

1. Click Open in the toolbar and double-click the day3.htm page.

FIGURE 14.18

The Day 3 page with links to The Castles of Wales web site.

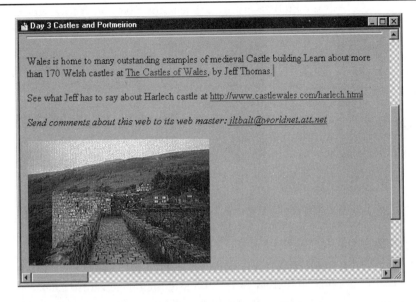

2. Click in the line below the last line of text and choose Table ➤ Insert Table from the Editor menu bar. Create a table with one row and one column, set the alignment to Center, the border size to 2, the cell padding to 5, and the width to 80 percent.

3. Select the three paragraphs with the text hyperlinks and the mailto link. Left-click in the selection, drag to the table cell, and release the mouse. The paragraphs are moved to the table cell.

4. Place the insertion point in the empty first line in the cell and press Delete. Figure 14.19 shows the text border.

FIGURE 14.19

Use a one-cell table to create a border for text.

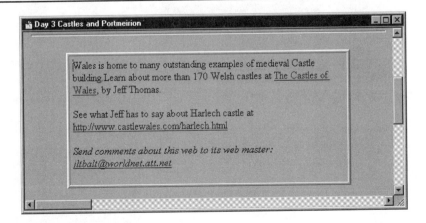

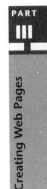

PART

III

Creating Web Pages

Creating a Picture Frame   The hardest part of creating a picture frame for an image is getting the correct size. You can determine the size of the image in pixels and use this information to create the table.

1. Click in the line below the image. Click the Insert Table button in the toolbar and create a table with one row and one column.

2. Click in the margin selector bar to the left of the image to select the image. Left-click the selected image, drag the image to the cell, and release the left mouse button. The image is moved to the table. The height of the cell matches the height of the image, but the table width needs to be adjusted (see Figure 14.20a). Unfortunately, the Editor does not allow resizing of tables by dragging a table boundary.

3. Right-click the image, select Image Properties from the shortcut menu, and click the Appearance tab (see Figure 14.20b). Select the width, press Ctrl+C, and click OK to close the dialog.

4. Right-click in the table, choose Table Properties, click in the Specify Width text box, and press Ctrl+V to paste the image width. Click the In Pixels option and click OK to close the dialog. Figure 14.21 shows the picture frame.

FIGURE 14.20

After dragging an image to the table cell (a), right-click the image, choose Image Properties, and click the Appearance tab to determine the width of the image (b).

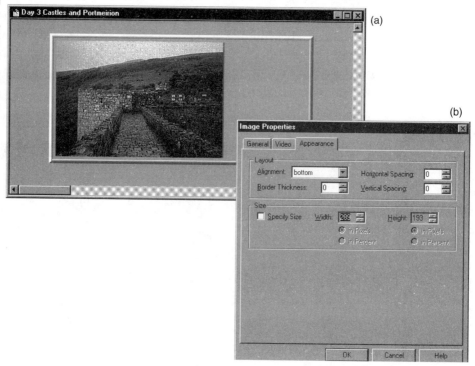

FIGURE 14.21

Use a one-cell table to create a picture frame for an image or a video clip.

Selecting and Changing Table Elements

After creating a table, you may need to modify it. The general rule is that you must first select the table part that you want to modify, display the property sheet for the part, and then make the changes in the property sheet.

Selecting the Table

You can select a table in one of two ways:

- Click anywhere in the table cells or caption and choose Table ➤ Select Table from the Editor menu bar, or
- Move the pointer to the selection bar to the left of the table, and when the pointer icon changes to a white arrow, double-click to select the table.

The selected table is displayed in a band of reverse video (see Figure 14.22a).

To select multiple tables on the same page, select the first table using one of the methods described, then press the Shift key while you move the pointer and double-click in the selector bar for the other tables (see Figure 14.22b).

Changing Table Properties

With the table selected, use any of these methods to display the Table Properties dialog:

- Press Alt+Enter.
- Right-click anywhere in the selection and choose Table Properties in the short-cut menu.
- Choose the Table ➤ Table Properties command from the Editor menu bar.

FIGURE 14.22

Select a table by double-clicking the the selector bar to the right of the table (a). Press Shift and repeat the process to select additional tables (b).

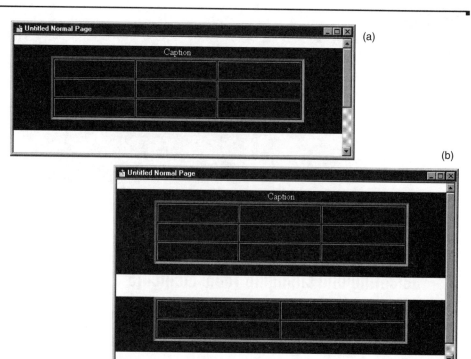

You can use the Table Properties dialog to change any of the table properties except the number of rows and columns in the table. You change the table size by inserting or deleting rows or columns as explained in the "Cutting and Deleting Cells" and "Adding Cells" sections.

You can set properties for multiple tables. Select multiple tables as described in the last section, press Alt+Enter, or right-click in any selected table and choose Properties in the shortcut menu. When you set properties in the dialog, all of the selected tables are affected.

Selecting and Editing the Table Caption

To select the table caption, move the pointer to the left of the caption; when the pointer icon changes to a white arrow, double-click. The selected caption is displayed in a reverse video line that spans the table (see Figure 14.23a).

Displaying Caption Properties With the table caption selected, press Alt+Enter, right-click anywhere in the caption line, and choose Caption Properties in the Shortcut menu or choose Table ➤ Caption Properties to display the Caption Properties dialog (see Figure 14.23b). You can use this dialog to move the caption to the bottom or the top of the table.

Editing the Caption Edit the caption by placing the insertion point in the caption's text and editing and formatting the text using most of the editing and character formatting tools you learned in Chapter 11. You can change the size and color of the characters and make the characters bold, italic, or underlined. You select the caption text by double-clicking in the text. Use the toolbar buttons in the Format toolbar or press Alt+Enter to display the Font Properties dialog and make the changes in the dialog.

You cannot use paragraph formatting or styles. You can use the alignment buttons in the formatting toolbar to align the caption to the left or right of the table, but these alignments are displayed only in the Editor and not in most browsers.

FIGURE 14.23

With the pointer to the left of the caption text, double-click to select the Caption (a). Press Alt+Enter to display the Caption Properties dialog (b).

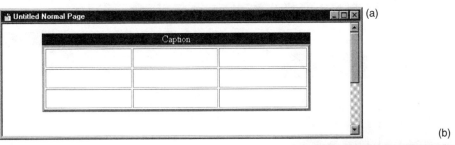

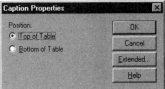

NOTE

You can use the caption's text to create a text hyperlink. Select the text you want to use for the hyperlink, click the Create or Edit Hyperlink button in the toolbar, and then specify the link's target as explained in Chapter 12.

PART

III

Creating Web Pages

Selecting Cells and Cell Content

Often you need to modify the properties of a single cell or a selection of cells. The rule is the same as before: first select the cell or cells, display the property dialog for cells, and make the changes in the property dialog. Note that there is a difference between the cell and the contents of the cell. To change a cell, you must select the cell, and to change the contents, you must select the contents.

Selecting a Single Cell   You can use either of the following methods to select a cell:

- Click anywhere in the cell and choose Table ➤ Select Cell from the Editor menu bar.

- Move the pointer to the left edge of the cell; when the pointer changes to a white selection arrow, double-click to select the cell (14.24a). A single click selects text or the object inserted in the cell, but does not select the cell itself (14.24b).

FIGURE 14.24

When the pointer is just inside the left edge of the cell, double-click to select the cell (a). A single click selects text or the object in the cell but does not select the cell (b).

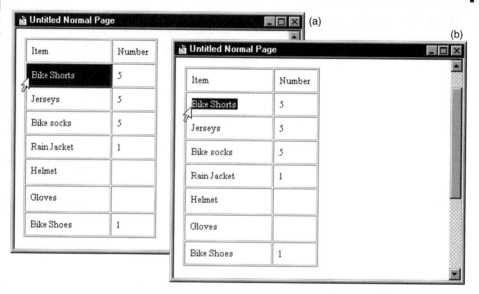

Selecting the Content of a Single Cell   When you select a cell, you select both the cell and the cell's contents. You can also select only the contents of a cell. To select the contents of a cell but not the cell itself, move the pointer to the left side of the cell; when the pointer icon changes to the white selection icon pointing to the right, hold down the left mouse button and drag to select the cell's entire contents. You can also select an individual object using the object's selection techniques.

After selecting all or part of the contents of a cell, you can use the familiar commands to cut, copy, or paste the selection, and you can use drag-and-drop to copy or move the selection. You can delete the selection without deleting the cell by pressing the Delete key or choosing the Clear command from the Edit menu.

Figure 14.25 illustrates the difference between selecting a cell and selecting the contents of a cell. In Figure 14.25a, contents of the cell are selected, copied, and pasted in the first cell of the second table. In Figure 14.25b, the cell is selected, copied, and pasted in the first cell of the second table.

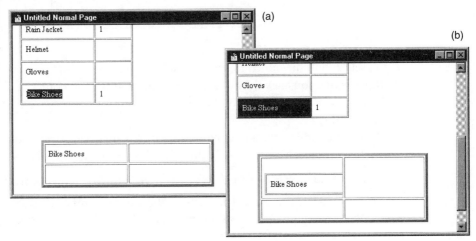

FIGURE 14.25

You can select and copy just the contents of a cell (a), or the cell and its contents (b).

Selecting Multiple Cells   To select multiple cells, select the first cell as described above and then press the Shift key while you drag to select neighboring cells or click in each noncontiguous cell that you want to add to the selection (see Figure 14.26). This is the only way to select noncontiguous cells.

Selecting a Column or Multiple Columns   To select a column, do either of the following:

- Move the pointer to the top border of the column you want to select; when the pointer icon changes to a black selection arrow, click the top border (see Figure 14.27a).
- Place the insertion point anywhere in the column and choose Table ➤ Select Column from the Editor menu bar.

FIGURE 14.26

To select multiple cells, select the first cell and then press Shift while you drag or click to add additional cells to the selection.

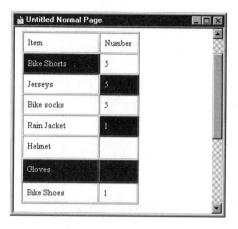

To select multiple noncontiguous columns, select a column and then press the Shift key while you click the black selection arrow at the top border of the additional columns you want to select. You can select columns from the same table or columns from several tables.

To select multiple contiguous columns in the same table, select a column and hold down the left mouse button as you drag left or right to select additional columns.

Selecting a Row or Multiple Rows   To select a row, do either of the following:

- Move the pointer to the left border of the row you want to select; when the pointer icon changes to a black selection arrow, click the left border (see Figure 14.27b).

FIGURE 14.27

Select a column by moving the pointer to the top border and clicking when the pointer changes to a black selection arrow (a). Select a row by moving the pointer to the left border and clicking when the pointer changes to a black selection arrow (b).

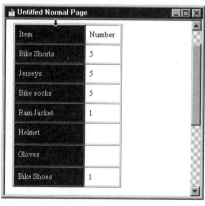

(a)

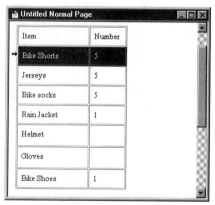

(b)

- Place the insertion point anywhere in the row and choose Table ➤ Select Row from the Editor menu bar.

To select multiple noncontiguous rows, select a row and then press the Shift key while you click the black selection arrow at the left border of the additional rows you want to select. You can select rows from the same table or rows from several tables.

To select multiple contiguous rows in the same table, select a row and hold down the left mouse button as you drag up or down to select additional rows.

Displaying Cell Properties

To change the properties of a single cell, right-click in the cell and right-click in any cell in the selection, and then choose Cell Properties from the shortcut menu or choose Table ➤ Cell Properties from the Editor menu bar.

To change the properties of a selection of cells, select the cells as described above and choose Table ➤ Cell Properties from the Editor menu bar or right-click in any cell in the selection and choose Cell Properties from the shortcut menu.

The Cell Properties dialog (see Figure 14.28) shows the properties you can change for the selection as follows:

Layout You can change the horizontal and vertical alignment of the contents of the cell by selecting from the combo lists. Align the contents horizontally to the left, center, or right of the cell and vertically to the top, middle, or bottom of the cell. After you set the horizontal alignment in the Cell Properties dialog, you can override the setting by selecting the cell's contents and clicking an alignment button in the formatting toolbar. Click the Header Cell check box to apply header formatting (bold font) to the selected cells. By default, web browsers wrap the contents of a cell; click the No wrap check box to not wrap the contents.

Minimum Width You can specify the width of cells by clicking the Specify Width check box and entering either the number of pixels or the percentage width of the table. If a cell spans a single column, setting the width to a number of pixels of percentage larger than the width of other cells in the column increases the displayed width of all of the entire column. Setting the width of a cell or cells in a row to be larger than the width of the table gives unpredictable results.

Custom Background A cell can have a background image or a background color that is different from the table and the page. Click the Use Background Image check box and enter the location of the image you want to use or click the Browse button and locate the image using the Select Background Image dialog. Select a background color from the Background Color combo list.

FIGURE 14.28

Use the Cell Properties dialog to modify one or more cells.

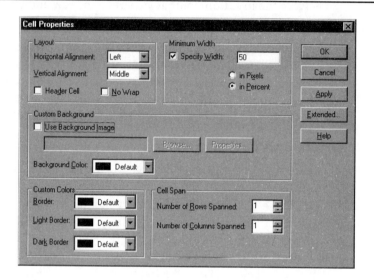

Custom colors   If the table has a border—that is, if the table's Border Size property is greater than zero—then the cells have borders also. You can choose a single color for all four parts of the cell border, or you can choose two colors for a three-dimensional effect. If you choose two colors, the Dark Border color is used for the top and left borders, and the Light Border color is used for the right and bottom borders of the cell. (The locations of the Light and Dark Borders for a cell are the opposite of the colored border locations for a table.)

Cell Span   You can specify the number of rows or columns that a cell spans. When you increase the column span of a cell, the cells to its right and in the same row are shifted to the right. To illustrate, if you increase the column span of the cell in the third row and third column of the table in Figure 14.29, the cell in the third row and the fourth column is shifted to the right (see Figure 14.30). Decreasing the column span of a cell shifts the cells to its right and in the same row to the left. Increasing the row span of a cell affects the cells in the rows below: cells in subsequent rows to the right of the changed cell are shifted to the right. For example, if you increase the row span of the cell in the third row and the third column of the table in Figure 14.29, the cells in the fourth row in the third and fourth columns are shifted to the right to make room (see Figure 14.31). Decreasing the row span of a cell shifts cells in subsequent rows to the left.

FIGURE 14.29

The North Wales
Itinerary table

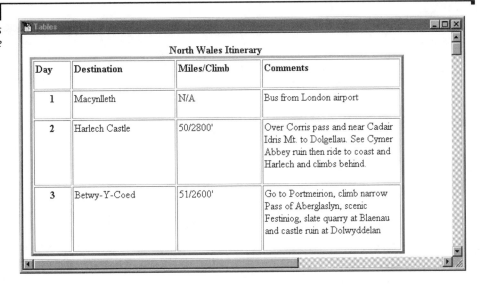

FIGURE 14.30

When you increase
the column span of
a cell, the cells to its
right are shifted to
the right.

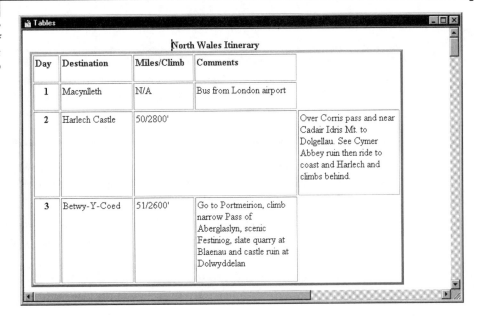

PART

III

Creating Web Pages

When you increase the row span of a cell, the cells below it are shifted to the right.

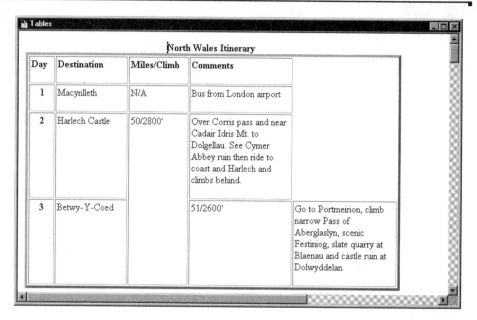

NOTE

Like all property sheets in the Editor, the Cell Properties dialog has an Extended button. You click this button to display a dialog for specifying attributes for the cell that FrontPage doesn't recognize. See the "Understanding Extended Attributes" section in Chapter 10 for more information.

To illustrate setting cell properties, we'll realign the three images we inserted in the Day 4 Mount Snowdon page. If necessary, click the Open button in the toolbar and double-click the day4.htm page in the Open File dialog.

1. Click the image in the first row and choose Table ➤ Select Cell from the Editor menu bar. Press Shift, click the image in the second row, and click the image in the third row.

2. Press Alt+Enter to display the Cell Properties dialog. Set the Horizontal Alignment to Center, and click OK to close the dialog and center the images in the cells.

3. Save the changes to the page.

Cell Mechanics

You can manipulate a cell or a selection of cells using the familiar editing tools, including cut, copy, and paste. Keep in mind that you are working with cells (including their content) and not just the content.

Copying and Pasting Cells   You can copy a single table cell and in most cases, you can also copy a selection of cells in a single table to the Clipboard. For example, you can copy one or more rows and one or more columns; the rows or columns do not have to be contiguous. When the selection cannot be copied, the Copy command in the Edit menu is grayed out and unavailable; pressing Ctrl+C does not give an error message, but the selection is not copied.

When you paste, any currently selected items are overwritten.

When you paste a selection of table cells to other table cells, the shape of currently selected table cells must be the same as the selection on the Clipboard; if the shape is different, the Editor displays an error message.

When you click in a table cell and paste a selection of table cells, you insert the selection as a table within the table cell. Figure 14.32 shows an example of pasting a selection to a single table cell.

When you move the insertion point outside a table, you create a new table by pasting the selection. Figure 14.33 shows an example of pasting a selection outside a table.

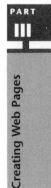

FIGURE 14.32

The first row of one table is pasted in the first cell of a second table.

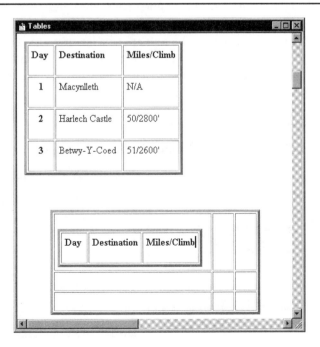

FIGURE 14.33

The first row of a table is pasted to a location outside a table.

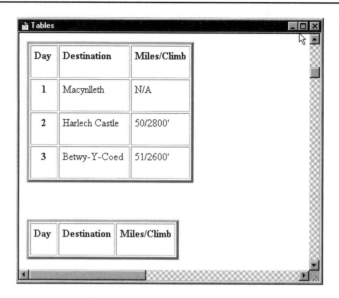

Cutting and Deleting Cells

You can cut a single cell and in most cases, you can also cut a selection of cells from a single table to the Clipboard. When the selection cannot be cut, the Cut command in the Edit menu is grayed out and unavailable; pressing Ctrl+X does not give an error message, but the selection is not copied.

When you cut cells, the cells are removed from the table and the cells to the right and in the same rows as the cut cells shift to the left to fill in the empty spaces. For example, when you cut the selection shown in reverse video in Figure 14.34a, the cells shift as shown in Figure 14.34b.

FIGURE 14.34

After cutting the selected cells in (a), the table has the empty spaces shown in (b).

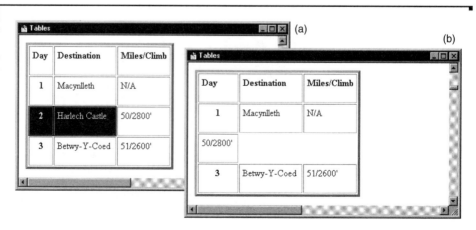

To delete a cell or a selection of cells, choose Edit ➤ Clear command from the Edit or menu bar or press Delete. The selection to be deleted may include cells from more than one table.

NOTE

To cut or delete the contents of a cell without cutting or deleting the cell, select the cell contents and choose the Cut or Clear command from the Edit menu.

Inserting Cells

You can insert individual cells, entire rows, or entire columns.

Inserting a Cell   To insert an individual cell, place the insertion point in a cell or select a cell, row, or column, and choose the Table ➤ Insert Cell command from the Editor menu bar.

- If you place the insertion point in a cell, the new cell is inserted at the location of the insertion point and the other cells in the row to the right of the new cell are shifted to the right. If the insertion point was in the middle of the cell contents, the original cell may be split into two cells, with the new cell inserted between them. For example, Figure 14.35 shows the splitting of a cell to insert the new cell.

- If you select a cell, the new cell is inserted to the left of the selected cell and the other cells in the row to the right of the selected cell are shifted to the right.

- If you select a row, the new cell is inserted to the left of the last cell in the selected row. If you select a column, the new cell is inserted as the new bottom cell in the selected column and the cells to its right are shifted to the right.

Inserting a Row or Column   To insert one or more rows or columns in a table, place the insertion point in a cell or select a cell, row, or column, and then choose the Table ➤ Insert Rows or Columns command from the Editor menu bar. Use the Insert Rows or Columns dialog (see Figure 14.36a) to specify whether to insert rows or columns, the number of rows or columns, and the location of the new rows or columns. You can insert rows above or below the cell with the insertion point or the selected cell, row, or column. You can insert columns to the left or right of the cell with the insertion point or the selected cell, row, or column. Figure 14.36b shows one row inserted below the cell shown in reverse video.

PART

III

Creating Web Pages

FIGURE 14.35

If the insertion point is in the middle of the cell contents, inserting a cell splits the original cell into two and places the new cell between them.

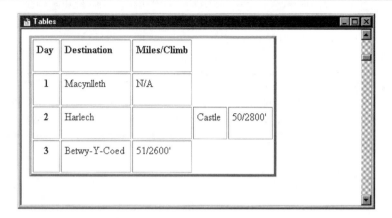

FIGURE 14.36

Use the Insert Row or Column dialog to specify the number of rows or columns to insert (a). In this case, we've inserted a single row below a cell (b).

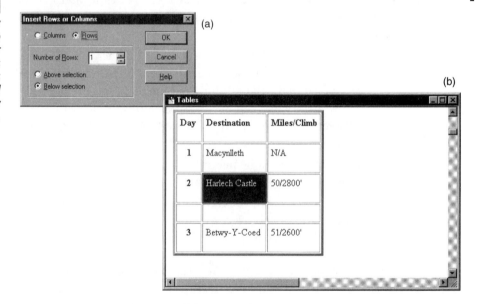

If you select multiple cells, you can insert rows above the top cell or below the bottom cell in the selection and you can insert columns to the left of the left-most cell or to the right of the right-most cell in the selection.

Inserting a Line above or below a Table

You can insert a line below a table by placing the insertion point at the end of the contents of any cell and pressing Ctrl+Enter. The Editor inserts a new line below the table and places the insertion point in the inserted row.

You can insert a line above a table by placing the insertion point at the beginning of the contents of any cell and pressing Ctrl + Enter. The Editor inserts a new line above the table and places the insertion point in the inserted row.

Splitting and Merging Cells

To divide a cell into two or more rows or columns, place the insertion point in the cell or select the cell and then choose the Split Cells command in the Table menu. Use the Split Cells dialog (see Figure 14.37a) to specify whether to split the cell in rows or columns and the number of cells after the split. The graphic in the dialog indicates how the cell looks after splitting.

After splitting a cell into two or more columns, the contents of the original cell are placed in one cell and the additional cells are placed to the right, as shown in Figure 14.37b. When you split a cell into columns, the column spans of other cells in the original column are affected. For example, after splitting the cell in the Destination column into two columns as shown in Figure 14.37b, the other cells in the Destination column span two cells.

Use the Split Cells dialog (a) to split a cell into a specified number of columns (b) or rows (c).

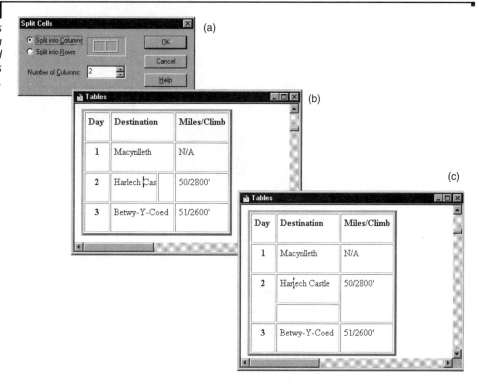

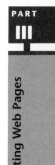

When you split a cell into two or more rows, the contents of the cell are placed in one cell and the additional cells are placed below it, as shown in Figure 14.37c. The row spans of the other cells in the original row are affected; in Figure 14.37c, the other cells in the Day 2 row span two rows.

If the cell you want to split spans more than one column, there are limitations on your ability to split the cell. You can split the cell into any number of rows, but you can only split the cell into the number of spanned columns. For example, in Figure 14.38a, the selected cell spans three columns; the Split Cells dialog indicates the column span automatically, and you cannot change the number in the Number of Columns text box; you can split the cell only into three columns. You can split the cell into any number of rows, as shown in Figure 14.38b.

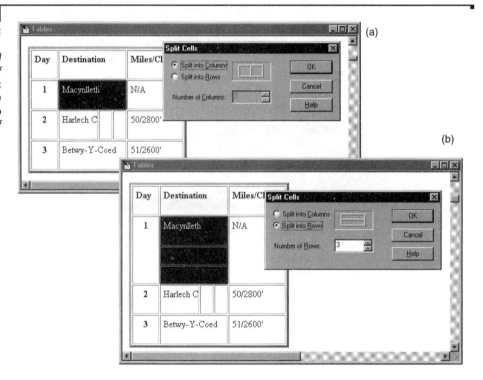

FIGURE 14.38

When a cell spans several columns, you can split the cell into the number of spanned columns (a), and you can split the cell into any number of rows (b).

Similarly, if a cell spans more than one row, you can only split the cell into the same number of rows already spanned, but you can split the cell into any number of columns.

Two or more cells can be merged into a single cell. The cells must be contiguous and the selection must be in the shape of a rectangle. To merge the selection into a single cell, choose the Merge Cells command from the Table menu. The contents of the original cells are placed in the merged cell; text paragraphs in original cells are merged as separate paragraphs. Figure 14.39 shows the selection before and after the merger.

FIGURE 14.39

Merging a rectangular selection of cells (a) into a single cell (b).

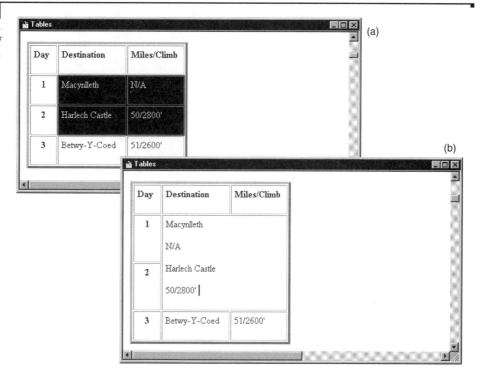

(a)

(b)

For More . . .

This chapter has described how to use tables to display "tabular" information and how to use tables to lay out a page. You've learned how to insert a table and change its properties. You've learned how to work with individual table cells including setting cell properties, inserting, deleting, splitting, and merging cells.

The following chapters provide more information about laying out pages:

- Chapter 16: Understanding Frames shows you how to create a special page with cells, called frames, that can contain other pages.

- Chapter 17: Collecting Input Data shows you how to create a data entry form on a page. You'll learn how to use tables to improve the layout of the form.

PART

III

Creating Web Pages

Chapter

15

Understanding
Frames

Understanding Frames

In the last chapter, you learned how to use tables to organize information and lay out objects on a web page. While tables are a great way to display information, frames are even better! You can divide the browser window into several subwindows and display a different page in each subwindow. The subwindows are called *frames* and the special Web page that divides the browser window into subwindows is called a *frameset*. Figure 15.1 shows an example of a frameset that displays content from four different web pages. In the figure, each frame has a border, so it's easy to distinguish the header and footer frames at the top and bottom, the table of contents frame at the left, and the main content frame on the right. You'll create this frameset later in the chapter.

Using frames, you can view several documents at once, create slide presentations, or collect information from the visitor in one frame and then display the results in another. You can dedicate a frame to a permanent table of contents to keep visitors oriented to your Web. Other frames can be dedicated to fixed headers and footers with navigation bars. Frames are an excellent way to use the browser window efficiently. The best way to understand how framesets work is to create a few of them.

FIGURE 15.1

Use a frameset to
divide the browser
window into regions
that display content
from different
web pages.

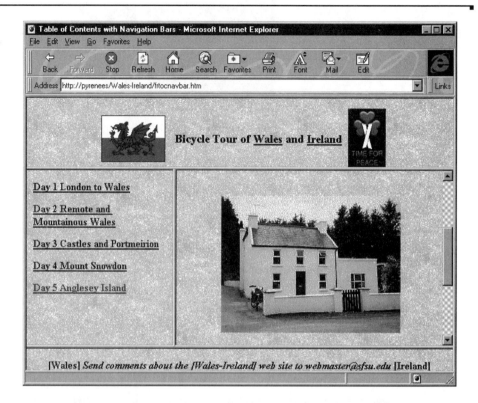

NOTE

To work through the examples in this chapter, you'll need to replace your Wales-Ireland web with a modified version on the book's CD-ROM. Open the Wales-Ireland web you created in previous chapters and choose File ➤ Delete FrontPage Web from the Explorer menu bar to delete the web. Then choose File ➤ Import and use the Import Web Wizard to create a new web named Wales-Ireland and to import all the files from the web named Wales-Ireland-Ch15Ch16 on the book's CD-ROM.

Creating a Frameset

FrontPage provides a Frames Wizard for creating framesets. Framesets are more complicated than simple web pages, so we'll begin by creating two simple examples. In the first example, we'll create a frameset that displays web pages in two unlinked frames. When frames are not linked, each frame is independent of the other. In the second example, we'll create a frameset that displays web pages in two linked frames.

When frames are linked, changing the content in one frame can affect the content displayed in another frame.

Understanding Unlinked Frames

To get started, we'll use the Frames Wizard to create the simplest possible frameset that displays two web pages side-by-side in unlinked frames. We'll display two of the day pages in the Wales-Ireland web.

1. Choose File ➤ New from the Editor menu bar. Choose the Frames Wizard from the list of new page templates and wizards, and click OK. In the first wizard screen, you specify whether you want to use a template or create your own grid (see Figure 15.2a). We'll look at the templates later in the chapter.

2. Choose the Make a custom grid option and click Next. In the Edit Frameset Grid screen, you specify how you want to divide the browser window into sub-windows by entering the number of rows and columns you want in the frameset (see Figure 15.2b). The intersection of a row and a column is a subwindow. When you change the numbers of rows and columns, the graphic changes to illustrate your choice.

FIGURE 15.2

Choose to use a template or make your own grid (a). Specify the number of rows and columns in the Edit Frameset Grid dialog (b)

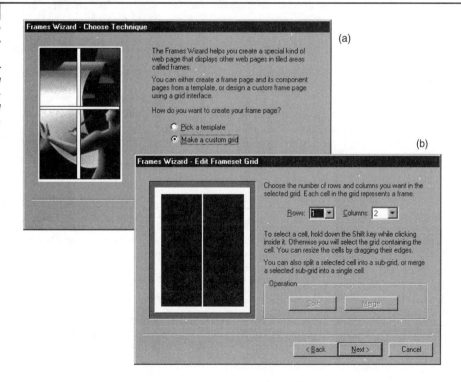

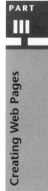

3. Choose one row and two columns and click Next. You use the Edit Frame Attributes screen to name each frame and specify the URL of the page you want to display in the frame. After you click a frame in the graphic on the left, the text boxes on the right become active (see Figure 15.3a). In the frame on the left, we'll display the Day 1 page and in the frame on the right, we'll display the Day 6 page. We'll name the frames left and right.

Click to select a frame in the graphic in the Edit Frame Attributes dialog (a). Click the Browse button to display the Choose Source URL dialog (b).

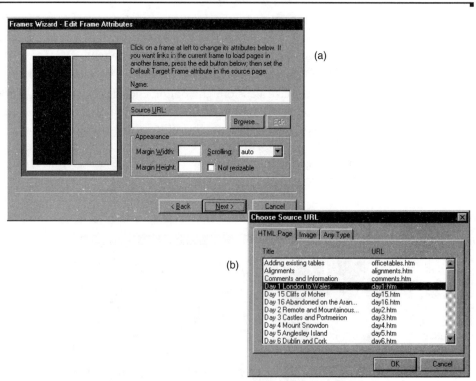

4. Click the frame on the left, type **left** in the Name text box, and click the Browse button to the right of the Source URL text box to display the Choose Source URL dialog (see Figure 15.3b). Double-click the Day 1 London to Wales page to select the page and close the dialog.

5. Click in the frame on the right, type **right** in the Name text box, and then click the Browse button. Double-click the Day 6 Dublin and Cork page.

6. Click Next. You use the Choose Alternate Content dialog to specify an alternative web page in case the user's browser doesn't know how to display frames (see

Figure 15.4a). The popular browsers are able to display frames, but it's a good idea to specify an alternative if you are creating a web for the World Wide Web.

7. Click Next. In this dialog you specify the Title and URL for the new frameset page (see Figure 15.4b). Type **Trip Days** as the title and **frTripDays.htm** as the page URL. Click Finish.

FIGURE 15.4

Specify an alternate page in the current web to be displayed by a browser that can't display frames (a). Enter a title and URL for the frameset (b).

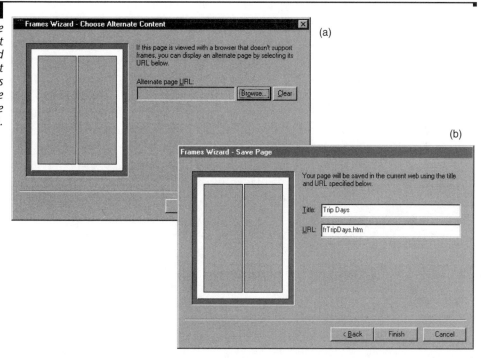

Because frameset pages are special purpose pages that do not display their own content, you may wish to distinguish them from the content pages in your Web. For example, I identify a frameset page by starting its name with the prefix fr.

FrontPage creates the new frameset and closes the last wizard screen.

Viewing a Frameset Page

FrontPage is not able to display a frameset page in the Editor. When you choose a frameset in the Open File dialog in the Editor, or if you double-click the page icon in the the Contents or Hyperlinks pane in the FrontPage Explorer, the Frames Wizard starts. You can only view the frameset page in a Web browser that recognizes frames. We'll create a link to the new frameset on the web's home page.

1. In the Editor, click the Open button in the toolbar and double-click the Home Page in the Open File dialog.

2. In either view of the Explorer, click theTrip Days page icon. Drag the page icon to the Home Page and drop the page icon to create a text hyperlink below the last line of text.

3. Click the Save button and then click the Preview in Browser button in the toolbar. Click the Trip Days text hyperlink (the background sound of the Day 1 page plays.) Figure 15.5 shows the frameset in the Internet Explorer 3.0 browser. You can scroll the page in each frame separately. You can also resize the frames. To resize, move the pointer to the boundary between the frames; when the pointer icon changes to a double arrow, hold down the left mouse button and drag to resize.

4. Click the text hyperlink to the Day 2 page at the top of the left frame. The Day 2 target page is displayed in the left frame and the frame on the right is not affected. Click the text hyperlink at the top of the left frame to display the Day 3 page and click again to display the Day 4 page. The browser automatically displays a horizontal scroll bar to allow you to view the images on the Day 4 page.

5. Click the text hyperlink at the top of the right frame. The Day 7 target page is displayed in the frame on the right. The frame on the left is not affected.

Viewing the Alternate Page

When you create a frameset page, you can specify an alternate page to be displayed by Web browsers that don't know how to display frames (see Figure 15.4a). If you don't select an alternate page, the Editor creates a default alternate page. You can view the alternate page in the Editor as follows:

1. Right-click a frameset page in the FrontPage Explorer and choose Open With from the shortcut menu to display the Open With Editor (see Figure 15.6).

2. Click the FrontPage Editor and click OK.

Choosing the FrontPage Editor displays the alternate page that will be displayed by a Web browser that doesn't know how to display frames. If you did not specify an alternate page when you created the frameset, the Editor displays the default alternate page (see Figure 15.7a). If you specified an alternate page, FrontPage creates a new page based on the page you specified; in this case, the FrontPage Editor displays the message that the page is being retrieved from the server (see Figure 15.7b).

FIGURE 15.5

The Trip Days frame-set displays a page about Wales in the left frame and a page about Ireland in the right frame. The frames are unlinked, so the tar-get of a hyperlink in a framed page is dis-played in the same frame as the page.

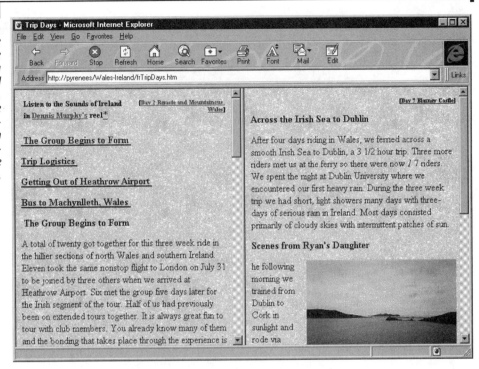

FIGURE 15.6

Choose the FrontPage Editor in the Open With Editor dialog to view the alternate page.

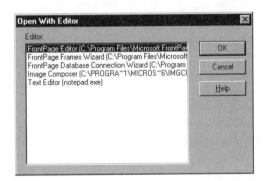

If you click the Preview in Browser button in the toolbar when the Editor displays the alternate page, the Web browser displays either the frameset or the alternate page depending on the browser's capabilities.

The Editor displays a default alternate page if you didn't specify an alternate page (a) or a message that that the specified page is being retrieved (b).

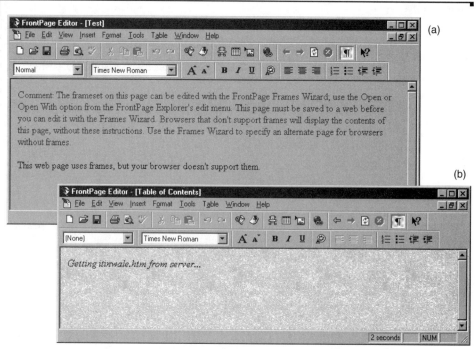

A fast way to preview a frameset in a Web browser is to right-click the frameset in the FrontPage Explorer, choose the Open With command in the shortcut menu to display the alternate frameless page in the Editor, and then click the Preview in Browser button in the Editor toolbar.

Linking the Frames

Let's look at a table of contents frameset as a more complicated example. We'll create a new frameset with two frames. The frame on the left is named contents, and holds the table of contents page. A table of contents page contains a list of topics and each item in the list is a hyperlink to a topic page. The frame on the right is named main, and displays one of the topic pages. We'll design the frameset so that when you click on a hyperlink in the contents frame, the main frame displays the target of the hyperlink.

To illustrate, let's display the Wales Itinerary page as the table of contents page. This page has hyperlinks to the pages for each day of the Wales part of the trip.

1. Choose the File ➤ New command from the Editor menu bar, choose the Frames Wizard in the New Page dialog, and click OK.

2. Click the Make a custom grid option and click Next. In the Edit Frameset Grid dialog change change the number of rows to one, leave the number of columns as two, and click Next.

3. Click the left frame in the graphic, set the Name of the frame to contents, click the Browse button, and double-click the Wales Itinerary page (- itinwales.htm). We need to specify that the targets of the hyperlinks on this page are to be displayed in the frame on the right.

4. Click the Edit button to the right of the Browse button on the Edit Frame Attributes dialog. The Editor displays the Wales Itinerary page. The next step is to tell FrontPage where to display the targets of the links on this page.

Specifying the Target Frame

There are two ways to tell FrontPage where to display the target frame of a link: you can specify an individual target frame for each hyperlink and you can specify a default target frame for any hyperlink on the page for which you haven't specified an individual target frame.

To specify an individual target frame for a link, click the text or image link and click the Create or Edit Link button in the toolbar, or press Ctrl+K, to display the Edit Hyperlink dialog. In the Target Frame text box type the name of the frame that you want to use to display the target of the link. Figure 15.8b shows the Edit Hyperlink dialog for the first hyperlink on the Wales Itinerary page.

FIGURE 15.8

To specify a target frame for a specific hyperlink (a), set the Target Frame in the hyperlink's Edit Hyperlink dialog (b).

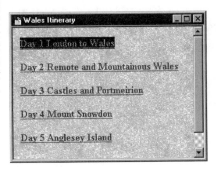

(a)

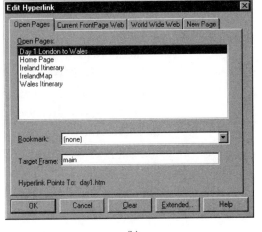

(b)

PART

III

Creating Web Pages

To specify a default target frame for all the hyperlinks on a page that don't have individual target frames defined, choose the Page Properties command from the File menu to display the Page Properties dialog (see Figure 15.9).

Enter the name of the frame you want to use as the default in the Default Target Frame text box.

FIGURE 15.9

To specify a default target frame for the hyperlinks on a page that don't have individual target frames defined, set the Default Target Frame in the Page Properties dialog.

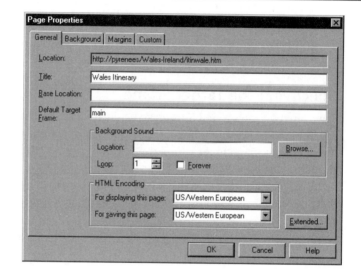

In our example, we want all the hyperlink targets to be displayed in the main frame. We can set all the targets at once by setting the default target frame for the page.

1. Right-click in the Wales Itinerary page and choose the Properties command in the shortcut menu.

2. Type **main** in the Default Target Frame text box and click OK. Click the Save button in the toolbar.To return to the wizard screen, click the Minimize button in the upper-right corner of the Editor's window.

3. Click in the right frame and type **main** in the Name text box. We'll be displaying the target pages in this frame. To avoid a blank frame when you browse to the frameset, we'll display the first day page as the initial page. Click the Browse button and choose the Day 1 page (day1.htm).

Understanding the Appearance Properties

You use the Appearance properties in the Edit Frame Attributes dialog to design the layout of the frameset as follows:

- **Resizing the frames**   Resize the frames using the graphic on the left of the dialog. Move the pointer to a boundary between two frames; when the pointer icon changes to a double arrow, press the left mouse button and drag to move the boundary to set the initial size that the browser displays (see Figure 15.10). By default, the web visitor can resize the frames. To prevent resizing of a frame, click the frame in the graphic and then click the Not resizable check box.

- **Frame margins**   You can specify the margins for each frame. The margin is the distance between the edge of the frame and the content. Click in the graphic to select a frame and enter the number of pixels for the Margin Width (the width of the vertical margins) and the Margin Height (the width of the horizontal margins).

- **Scrollbars**   You can specify whether a frame displays a vertical scroll bar. Choose auto in the Scrolling combo box to allow the browser to display a vertical scroll bar if necessary, yes to display a vertical scroll bar at all times, and no to prevent scrolling. You can't specify whether the frame displays a horizontal scroll bar; the Editor adjusts the width of the content, if possible, and displays a horizontal scroll bar only if the content cannot be adjusted to the width of the frame.

FIGURE 15.10

To resize frames, move the pointer to a boundary between two frames in the graphic. When the pointer icon changes to a double arrow, press the left mouse button and drag to move the boundary.

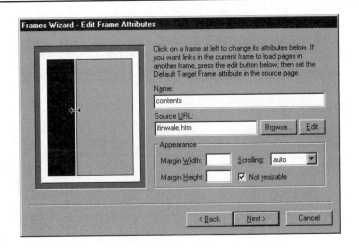

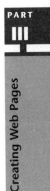

To change the layout, do the following:

1. Drag the boundary between the two frames in the graphic of the Edit Frame Attributes dialog so that the left frame is one third of the page.

2. Click the contents frame in the graphic, set the Margin Width to 5, set Scrolling to No, and click the Not resizable check box.

3. Click the Next button. We'll set the Wales Itinerary page as the alternate page displayed by a browser that doesn't recognize frames.

4. Click the Browse button, choose the Wales Itinerary page in the Choose Source URL dialog, and click OK. Click Next.

5. Type **Table of Contents** as the frameset Title and **frtocsimple.htm** as the URL. Click Finish. FrontPage creates the frameset and closes the wizard. Next, we'll create a text hyperlink to the frameset in the Home Page.

6. Click the Window menu from the Editor menu bar and choose Home Page from the list of open pages. In the Explorer, click the frtocsimple.htm page icon, drag to the bottom of the Home Page, and drop the page icon to create a text hyperlink.

7. Click the Save button and then click the Preview in Browser button in the toolbar. Click the Table of Contents hyperlink. Click the Day 3 hyperlink in the table of contents to view the target page in the frame on the right (see Figure 15.11).

FIGURE 15.11

When the frames are linked, the target of a hyperlink that starts on a framed page can be displayed in another frame.

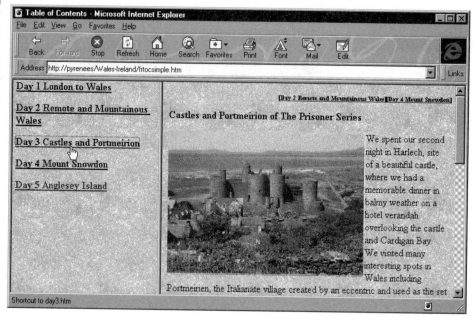

Editing a Frameset

After creating a frameset, you may need to edit the frameset or one of its source pages. The easiest way to view the structure of a frameset and its source pages is to right-click the frameset in the Contents pane in the FrontPage Explorer and choose Show Hyperlinks in the shortcut menu. The Explorer switches to Hyperlink View and the Hyperlinks pane displays the frameset with implicit links to the source pages. Figure 15.12 shows the Hyperlink view of the Table of Contents frameset with implicit links to the pages that are displayed initially in the two frames. (The figure also shows the hyperlink from the home page.)

- To edit a source page, double-click the page icon in the Hyperlink pane of the Explorer. FrontPage opens the page in the Editor.

- To edit the frameset, double-click the frameset page icon in the Hyperlink pane of the Explorer. FrontPage opens the Frames Wizard in editing mode, starting with the Edit Frameset Grid dialog. You can change frameset properties and properties of individual pages using the wizard's dialogs.

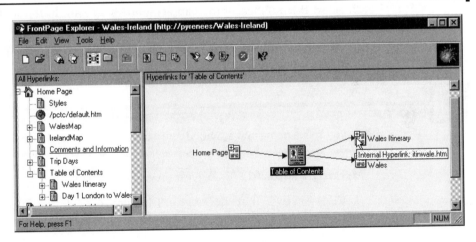

Changing the Grid

You use the Edit Frameset Grid dialog to edit the grid by changing the number of frames and resizing the frames. You can also split a frame into a subgrid of additional frames and you can merge a subgrid into a single frame.

Changing the number of rows and columns   When you increase the number of rows and columns in an existing frameset, the additional rows are

PART

III

Creating Web Pages

placed below the existing frames and the additional columns are placed to the right of the existing frames. The original frames are not affected. The graphic in the left of the dialog displays the additional frames. If you decrease the number of rows or columns, the wizard discards the frames in rows starting from the bottom and columns starting from the right.

Resizing a frame   To resize frames, move the pointer to the boundary between any two frames in the graphic in the left of the dialog. When the pointer icon changes to a double arrow, press the left mouse button and drag in the direction of the arrows to resize the frames.

Selecting a frame   The wizard highlights each selected frame in the graphic. When you first open the Frames Wizard to edit the frameset, all of the frames are selected and highlighted. To select an individual frame, press Shift and click in the frame. To select a subgrid, click in any frame in the subgrid.

Splitting a frame into a subgrid   To split a frame into subframes:

1. Press Shift, click in the frame you want to split, and then click the Split button. The wizard splits the selected frame into two rows and two columns by default (see Figure 15.13).

2. Select the numbers of rows and columns you want in the subgrid using the Rows and Columns combo boxes.

3. Use the Edit Frame Attributes dialog to specify the new settings for each frame in the subgrid.

NOTE

When you split a frame into a subgrid, the wizard discards the original frame.

Merging a subgrid   To merge a subgrid into a single frame:

1. Click in any cell of the subgrid. Clicking in a cell of a subgrid selects the entire subgrid and makes the Merge button available.

2. Click the Merge button.

NOTE

You can only merge the frames of a subgrid that you created previously by splitting a frame.

FIGURE 15.13

You can split a frame into a subgrid of frames.

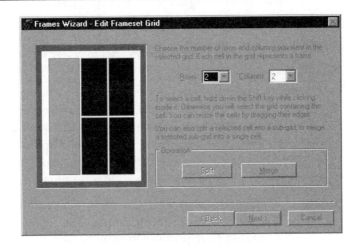

Changing the Properties of a Frame

After changing the frameset grid, click the Next button to display the Edit Frame Attributes. Click a frame in the graphic on the left to select the frame (see Figure 15.14).

FIGURE 15.14

Use the Edit Frame Attributes dialog to change the properties of a frame.

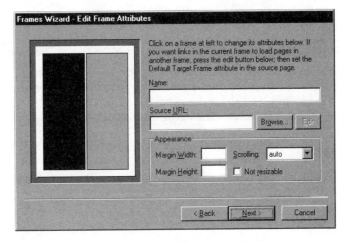

You use the Edit Frameset Attributes dialog to change the following properties of the frame cell:

Name   Specify the name of the frame cell.

Source URL   Specify the location of the file you want displayed in the frame. You can specify any file stored in the current web. Type the URL or click the

Browse button to display the web's files. The files are arranged in three categories: the HTML Page tab lists the web pages, the Image tab lists the image files, and the Any Type tab lists all of the files in the current web. If you select a sound file or a video clip, the browser may starts a helper application or plug-in to play the file.

Edit the source page   If the source file is a page, you can click the Edit button to display the page in the Editor. (If the source file is not an HTML page, the Edit button is dimmed and is not available.) If the page has hyperlinks, you can specify where the targets of the links will be displayed. If you don't specify a target frame, the target is displayed in the same frame as the page. To specify that the target of a hyperlink be displayed in another frame in the frameset, do the following:

- **Target of an individual hyperlink**   Click the hyperlink and click the Create or Edit Hyperlink button in the toolbar. Set the Target Frame in the Edit Hyperlink dialog to the name of a frame where you want the target to be displayed.

- **Default target of hyperlinks**   Right-click in the page and choose Page Properties in the shortcut menu. In the General tab, set the Default Target Frame to the name of the frame in the frameset where you want to display the targets of the hyperlinks for which you haven't specified individual target frames.

NOTE

If you set the Target Frame for a hyperlink or the Default Target Frame for a page to a value that is not the name of a frame in the frameset, the browser opens a separate browser window for displaying the target page.

- **Appearance**   Specify the margin widths, whether a frame has a vertical scroll bar, and whether the web visitor can resize the frame. (See the "Understanding the Appearance Properties" section for more information.)

Specifying an Alternate Page

After you modify the individual frames, click Next to display the Choose Alternate Content dialog (see Figure 15.4a in the "Understanding Unlinked Frames" section). You can specify another web page in the current web as the page that will be displayed when a Web visitor points to the frameset with a Web browser that is not able to display framesets.

Saving the Changes

After you modify the frameset, the Save Page dialog (see Figure 15.4b) gives you the opportunity to save the modified frameset as a new page with a different URL. If you click Finish without changing the URL, the Editor displays the message shown in Figure 15.15. Click Yes to save the changes to the frameset.

FIGURE 15.15

To save changes to a frameset, click Yes to overwrite the original frameset.

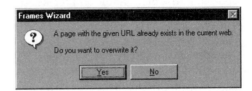

Understanding the Frameset Templates

Now that you understand how framesets work, it is easier to understand how to use the frameset templates. FrontPage includes a set of templates for six useful layouts of linked frames. For each template, the Frames Wizard creates a frameset page and names each of the frames in the frameset. The wizard also creates a new template page for each frame and creates any links between the frames that the template requires. If the template intends a page to be the start page for hyperlinks to another frame, the wizard sets the page's Default Target Frame to the name of the target frame. After the wizard is finished, you can modify the template pages or replace them with your own pages.

Exploring the Six Layouts

Let's explore the layouts using the Wales-Ireland web as an illustration:

Banner with Nested Table of Contents

The wizard creates a frameset page with a banner frame at the top, a table of contents frame on the left, and a main frame on the right (see Figure 15.16a). This layout is useful when your web contains a set of major topics and each major topic has a set of subtopics. For example, the Wales-Ireland web has two major topics: the tour through Wales and the tour through Ireland, and each tour has a set of days as subtopics. The banners' hyperlinks are directed to the table of contents frame, so you create a navigation bar in the banner page that includes hyperlinks to the Wales and the Ireland

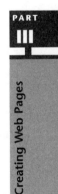

PART

III

Creating Web Pages

portions. When the Web visitor clicks a hyperlink in the navigation bar of the banner, the table of contents frame displays a page for either the Wales or the Ireland portion of the tour. The hyperlinks in the table of contents frame are directed to the main frame, so you include hyperlinks to the days for each tour. When the Web visitor clicks a link in a table of contents page, the browser loads the page describing the day into the main frame. The main frame does not direct its hyperlinks to another frame. If the Web visitor clicks a hyperlink on a page describing a day in the main frame, the target page is displayed in the main frame and replaces the existing page.

Main Document Plus Footnotes

The wizard creates a frameset page with a main frame at the top and a footnotes frame at the bottom (see Figure 15.16b). This layout is useful when a document in your Web contains pages with footnotes. The hyperlinks in the main frame are directed to the footnote section. When the Web visitor clicks a hyperlink in the main document, the corresponding footnote is displayed in the scrolling footnote frame. The footnote frame does not direct its hyperlinks to another frame. For example, an expanded version of the Wales-Ireland web may include footnotes with historical or cultural information for the pages describing the days of the tour.

FIGURE 15.16

The Banner with nested Table of Contents template (a). The Main document plus footnotes template (b).

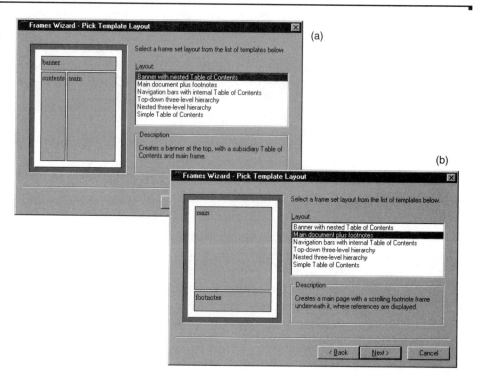

Navigation Bars with Internal Table of Contents

The wizard creates a frameset page with navigation bars as the top and bottom frames, a table of contents frame at the left, and a main frame at the right (see Figure 15.17a). This layout is similar to the Banner with nested Table of Contents except that it has a second navigation bar in the bottom frame. The hyperlinks in the top and bottom frames are directed to the table of contents frame and the hyperlinks in the table of contents frame are directed to the main frame. The main frame does not direct its hyperlinks to another frame. Because this layout is so useful, we'll explore it further in the "Using the Navigation Bar with Internal Table of Contents Template" section.

Top-Down Three-Level Hierarchy

The wizard creates a frameset page with three rows of frames: top, middle, and bottom frames (see Figure 15.17b). This layout works the same way as the Banner with nested Table of Contents. The only difference is that the wizard rearranges the frames in three rows instead of a banner at the top of two columns, and uses different names for the frames (see the description above for more information). The hyperlinks in the top frame are directed to the middle frame, which directed its hyperlinks to the bottom frame. The bottom frame does not direct its hyperlinks to another frame.

FIGURE 15.17

The Navigation bars with internal Table of Contents template (a). The Top-down three level hierarchy template (b).

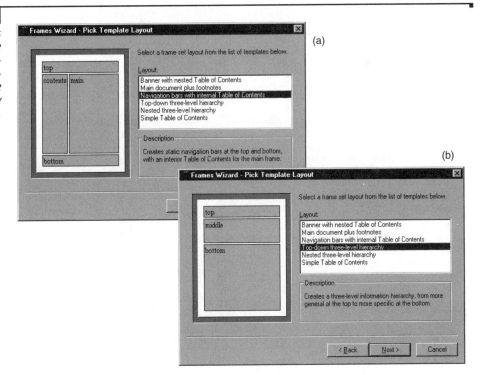

PART

III

Creating Web Pages

Nested Three-Level Hierarchy

The wizard creates a frameset page with a frame on the left, a top right frame, and a bottom right frame (see Figure 15.18a). This layout also works the same way as the Banner with nested Table of Contents. The only difference is that the wizard rearranges the frames, and changes the frame names, so that the navigation bar frame is at the left (named left), the table of contents frame is at the top right (named rtop), and the main frame is at the bottom right (named rbottom). The hyperlinks in the left frame are directed to the rtop frame, which directs its hyperlinks to the rbottom frame. The rbottom frame does not direct its hyperlinks to another frame. See the description above for more information.

Simple Table of Contents

The wizard creates a frameset with a table of contents frame on the left and a main frame on the right (see Figure 15.18b). This layout is useful when a topic in your web has a set of subtopics. The hyperlinks in the contents frame on the left are directed to the main frame on the right. The main frame does not direct its hyperlinks to another frame. We created this layout from scratch in the "Linking the Frames" section.

FIGURE 15.18

The Nested three-level hierarchy template (a). The Simple Table of Contents template (b).

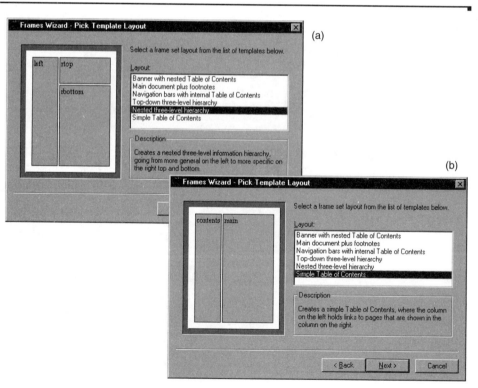

When you use a frames template, the Frames Wizard creates the frameset page and template pages as placeholders for each frame. For example, when you use the Nested Three-Level Hierarchy template, the wizard creates the frameset with frames named left, rtop, and rbottom, as shown in Figure 15.18a, and creates three template pages, as shown in Table 15.1.

TABLE 15.1: FRAMES AND TEMPLATE PAGES FOR THE NESTED THREE-LEVEL HIERARCHY TEMPLATE

Frame Name	Template Page URL	Default Target Frame
left	frleft.htm	rtop
rtop	frrtop.htm	rbottom
rbottom	frrbotto.htm	

Figure 15.19 shows the frameset in a browser. Each frame displays the template page created by the wizard. The targets of the hyperlinks in the left frame are displayed in the right top frame. The targets of the hyperlinks in the right top frame are displayed in the right bottom frame. The right bottom frame does not affect the other frames.

FIGURE 15.19

The template pages of the Nested three-level hierarchy frameset.

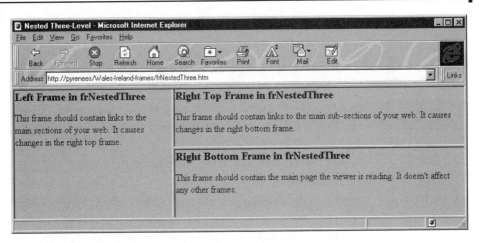

Figure 15.20 shows the hyperlink view of the frameset with internal links to the template pages of the three frames in the Explorer. You can edit a source template page by double-clicking a page icon to display the page in the Editor. Alternatively, you can replace a source template page with an existing page. To replace a source template page, double-click the frameset icon in the Explorer to start the Frames Wizard and change the source URL for a frame as described in the "Replacing the Default Pages" section.

PART

III

Creating Web Pages

FIGURE 15.20

*The hyperlink view
of the Nested
Three-Level
Hierarchy frameset*

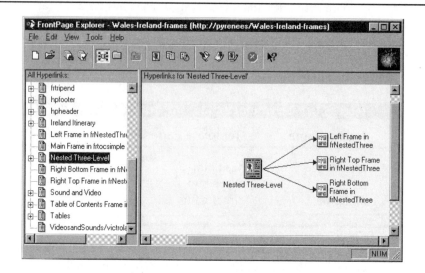

Using the Navigation Bar with Internal Table of Contents Template

To illustrate frameset templates, we'll use one of the templates to create a new frameset that could be used as a new home page for the Wales-Ireland web. We'll use the Navigation Bars with internal Table of Contents template shown in Figure 15.17a to create a frameset, and use the four frames as follows:

- **Top**   Let's use the top frame to display a header with the web's title and with hyperlinks to the itineraries for the Welsh and Irish portions of the tour. Figure 15.21a shows the header.htm page with text and image links to the Welsh and the Irish portions of the trip. Clicking a link in this frame will display the corresponding itinerary in the contents frame.

- **Bottom**   We'll use the bottom frame to display a footer with the webmaster's e-mail address and hyperlinks to the itinerary pages in the contents frame. Figure 15.21b shows the footer.htm page with text links to the Welsh and Irish portions of the trip. Clicking a hyperlink in the footer frame will also display the corresponding itinerary in the contents frame.

- **Contents**   The Wales-Ireland tour has an itinerary page for each of the two countries, with URLs itinwales.htm and itinireland.htm shown in Figure 15.22. We'll use each of these pages as a table of contents, and set each page's Default

Target Frame to main. Clicking a hyperlink on an itinerary page displays the corresponding day page in the main frame.

FIGURE 15.21

The header page displayed in the top frame has hyperlinks to two tables of contents (a). The footer page displayed in the bottom frame also has hyperlinks to two tables of contents (b).

(a)

(b)

FIGURE 15.22

The itinerary pages for the Wales section (a) and the Ireland section (b) displayed in the contents frame

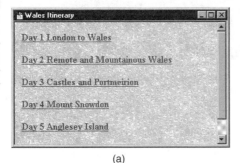

(a)

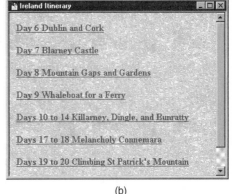

(b)

- **Main** We'll display the individual day pages in the main frame. However, when the frameset first opens, we'll display the maininit.htm page with photos of the trip shown in Figure 15.23. When the web user clicks on a text link in an itinerary page, the photo page is replaced with the day page.

The top and bottom frames do not change; both frames display pages containing hyperlinks that change the itinerary page displayed in the contents frame. The itinerary pages displayed in the contents frame contain hyperlinks that change the day page displayed in the main frame.

PART

III

Creating Web Pages

FIGURE 15.23

*The page initially
displayed in the
main frame when
the browser displays
the frameset*

Using a Frames Template

Let's see how the wizard uses a template:

1. Choose the New command from the File menu in the Editor, choose the Frames Wizard, and click Next. The Pick Template Layout dialog displays the available templates.

2. Choose the Navigation Bar with internal Table of Contents template. After you choose a template, you can resize the frames using the graphic on the left of the dialog.

3. Move the pointer to the lower boundary of the top frame. When the pointer changes to a double arrow, drag to increase the top frame to twice its height. Click Next. The wizard displays the Choose Alternate Contents screen in which you can specify a page for browsers that don't recognize frames. You can also resize the frames in this dialog using the graphic on the left.

4. Click Next. Type **Table of Contents with Navigation Bars** as the frameset Title and **frtocnavbar.htm** as the frameset URL, and then click Finish.

The wizard creates the new frameset, creates template pages for each of the frames, and sets the Default Target Frame property for the pages, as shown in Table 15.2.

TABLE 15.2: FRAMES AND PAGES FOR THE NAVIGATION BAR WITH INTERNAL TABLE OF CONTENTS TEMPLATE		
Frame Name	**Template Page URL**	**Default Target Frame**
top	frtop.htm	content
contents	frconten.htm	main
main	frmain.htm	
bottom	frbottom.htm	content

Figure 15.24 shows the new frameset with the default pages in a browser.

FIGURE 15.24

The Frames Wizard creates page templates to display in the frames.

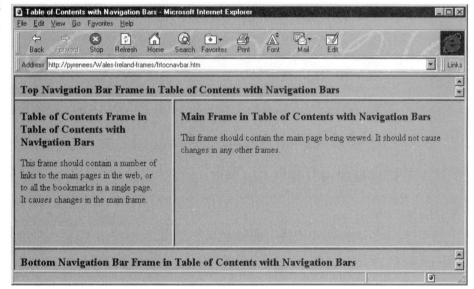

Replacing the Default Pages

The next step is to edit the frameset to replace the templates with the pages that already exist in the Web.

1. Choose File ➤ Open from the Editor menu bar or press Ctrl+O, choose the frtocnavbar.htm in the Open File dialog, and click OK. The Frames Wizard displays the Edit Frameset Grid dialog.

2. Click Next. We don't need to modify the grid.

PART
III

Creating Web Pages

3. Click in the frame at the top of the graphic, click the Browse button, select the header.htm page in the Choose Source URL dialog, and choose OK. Click the Not resizable check box and set Scrolling to No. The next step is to set the Default Target Frame for the page. We need to direct all hyperlinks in the header page to display their targets in the contents frame.

4. Click the Edit button. The Editor displays the header.htm page. Right-click and choose Properties from the shortcut menu. Type **contents** in the Default Target Frame text box and click OK.

5. Repeat Steps 3 and 4 to specify the source of the contents frame at the left as the itinwale.htm page, type **main** as the page's Default Target Frame, specify the source of the main frame at the right to be the maininit.htm page, specify the source of the frame at the bottom as the footer.htm page, and type **contents** as the page's Default Target Frame. With the bottom frame selected, click the Not resizable check box and set Scrolling to No.

6. Click Next and then click Finish. Click Yes when the wizard prompts you for confirmation that you want to overwrite the existing frameset with the same name. Now that we've replaced the page templates that the Frames Wizard created with other pages, we'll discard the page templates in the next step.

7. In the Explorer, click the Folder View button in the toolbar. Select the four template pages with URLs frtop.htm, frconten.htm, frmain.htm, and frbotto.htm and press Delete. Click the Yes to All button to delete all four pages.

Displaying the Frameset

We'll create a hyperlink to the new frameset from the Home Page as follows:

1. In the Editor, click the Open button in the toolbar and double-click the Home Page in the Open File dialog.

2. Click the frtocnavbar.htm page icon in the Explorer, drag to the bottom of the Home Page in the Editor, and drop the page icon to create a text hyperlink.

3. Click the Save button and then click the Preview in Browser button in the toolbar. Click the Table of Contents with Navigation Bars hyperlink. Figure 15.25 shows the frameset in the Internet Explorer 3.0 browser. Verify that you cannot resize the header and footer sections, but you can resize the content and main frames.

4. Click the Ireland text hyperlink or the Irish peace symbol in the top frame; the content frame displays the Irish itinerary. Click the Wales text link in the bottom frame to display the Welsh itinerary again. Click a text link in the itinerary; the main frame displays the corresponding day.

5. Minimize the browser.

FIGURE 15.25

The Table of
Contents with
Navigation Bar
frameset

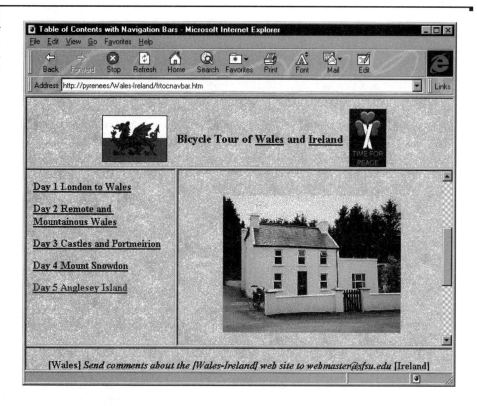

Nesting Framesets

You can nest one frameset within another by specifying the source of a frame to be another frameset. To explore nesting framesets, we'll create a new custom frameset with three frames. We'll display the header.htm page in the top frame and the footer.htm page in the bottom frame. In the middle frame, we'll nest the frtocsimple.htm frameset that we created earlier in the chapter.

Here are the steps for nesting a frameset inside another frameset:

1. Choose the File ➤ New command from the Editor menu bar, choose Frames Wizard in the New Page dialog, and click OK. Click the Make a custom grid option in the first wizard dialog and then choose Next.

2. Type **3** as the number of rows and **1** as the number of columns, and click Next. Resize the frames at the top and bottom so that the top frame is about 20% of the height and the bottom frame is about 15% of the total height.

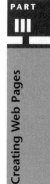

PART

III

Creating Web Pages

3. Click in the frame at the top of the graphic Type **top** as the Name, and **header .htm** as the Source URL. Click the Not resizable check box and set Scrolling to No.

4. Click in the middle frame, type **middle** as the Name and **frtocsimple.htm** as the Source URL.

5. Click in the frame at the bottom of the graphic, type **bottom** as the Name,and **footer.htm** as the Source URL.

6. Click Next and click Next again. Type **Nested Table of Contents with Navigation Bars** as the frameset title and **frtocnested.htm** as the URL. Click Finish.

Displaying the Nested Frameset

Let's create a hyperlink to the new frameset from the Home Page as follows:

1. If necessary, open the Home Page in the Editor by clicking the Open button in the toolbar and double-clicking the Home Page. If the Home Page is already open, click the Windows menu in the Editor menu bar and choose Home Page from the list of open pages.

2. Click the frtocnested.htm page icon in the Explorer, drag to the bottom of the Home Page in the Editor, and drop the page icon to create a text hyperlink.

3. Click the Save button and then click the Preview in Browser button in the toolbar.Click the Nested Table of Contents hyperlink. The Nested Table of Contents frameset looks nearly identical to the Table of Contents with Navigation Bars frameset. However, in the next section, you'll see that the behavior of the nested frameset is slightly different.

Predefined Frame Names

Browsers that recognize frames also recognize four predefined frame names. You use the predefined frame names to control the way the browser displays a target page as follows:

_blank	When you specify the target frame for a link as _blank, the browser displays the target page in a separate browser window.
_self	When you specify the target frame for a link as _self, the browser displays the target page in the same frame as the link.

_parent	When you specify the target frame for a link as _parent, the result depends on whether the current frame is a member of a nested frameset. If the current frame is not a member of a nested frameset, the browser displays the target page in the full browser window. If the current frame is a member of a nested frameset, the browser displays the target page in the frame that contains the nested frameset.
_top	When you specify the target frame for a link as _top, the browser displays the target page in the full browser window (but not a new browser window).

To explore predefined frame names, we'll modify the links in the Wales Itinerary page as follows:

1. In the Editor, click the Open button in the toolbar and double-click the Wales Itinerary page in the Open File dialog. We'll modify the first four links.

2. Click in the first link, and press Ctrl+K to display the Edit Hyperlink dialog. Type **_blank** in the Target Frame text box and press Enter to close the dialog.

3. Click in the second link, press Ctrl+K, type **_self** in the Target Frame text box, and press Enter.

4. Click in the third link, press Ctrl+K, type **_parent** in the Target Frame text box, and press Enter.

5. Click in the fourth link, press Ctrl+K, type **_top** in the Target Frame text box, and press Enter.

6. Press Ctrl+S to save the changes.

To see the effect of using the predefined frame names, do the following:

1. Press Ctrl+F6 repeatedly to cycle through the open pages in the Editor until the Home Page is displayed. Click the Preview in Browser button in the toolbar.

2. Click the Table of Contents with Navigation Bars text hyperlink.

3. Click the Day 1 text hyperlink. When the target frame is _blank, the browser opens a separate browser window and displays the Day 1 page (see Figure 15.26). Click the new window's Close button.

4. Click the Day 2 text hyperlink. When the target frame is _self, the browser displays the target page in the same frame as the hyperlink (see Figure 15.27). Click the browser's Back button.

PART

III

Creating Web Pages

FIGURE 15.26

When the Target Frame is _blank, the browser displays the target page in a separate browser window.

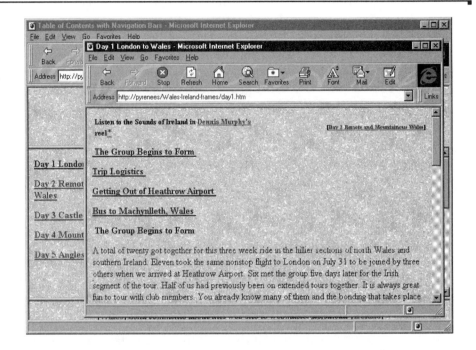

FIGURE 15.27

When the target frame is _self, the browser displays the target page in the same frame as the hyperlink.

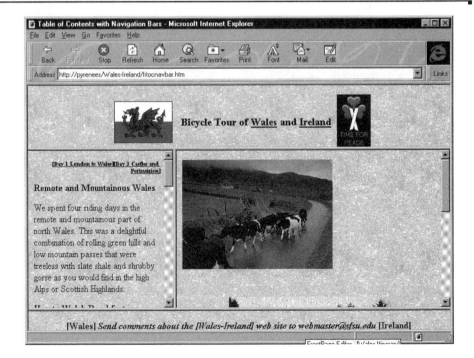

5. Click the Day 3 text hyperlink. The browser displays the target page in the full browser window (see Figure 15.28a).

FIGURE 15.28

When the target frame is _parent and the hyperlink is in a frame that is not a member of a nested frameset, the target page is displayed in the full browser window.

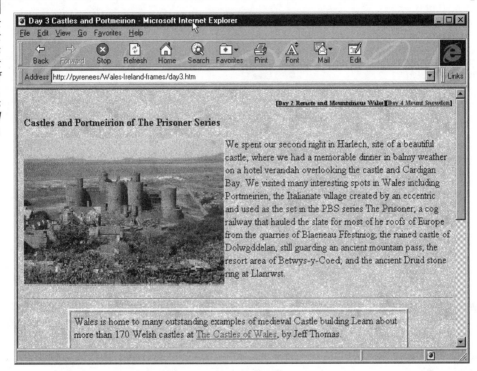

6. Click the browser's Back button twice to return to the Home Page. Click the Nested Table of Contents hyperlink in the Home Page, and then click the Day 3 text hyperlink. The browser displays the target page in the middle frame that holds the nested frameset (see Figure 15.29). Click the browser's Back button.

7. Click the Day 4 text hyperlink. When the target frame is _top, the browser displays the target page in the full browser window (see Figure 15.30).

8. Minimize the browser.

Now that you have seen the effect of the special frame names, you can delete the target frame settings for the individual links so that the frameset works as before.

1. In the Editor, press Ctrl+F6 repeatedly until the Wales Itinerary page is the active page. Click on each of the four links in the Wales Itinerary page, press Ctrl+K, delete the Target Frame setting, and press Enter.

2. Press Ctrl+S to save the page.

PART

III

Creating Web Pages

FIGURE 15.29

When the target frame is _parent and the hyperlink is in a frame that is a member of a nested frameset, the target page is displayed in the frame that contains the nested frameset.

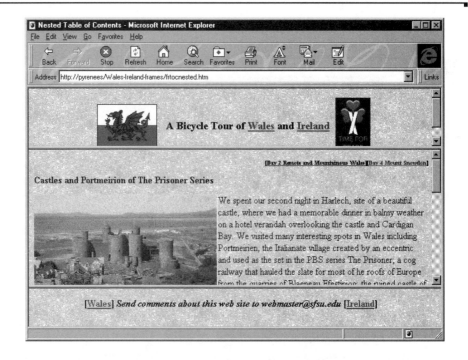

FIGURE 15.30

When the target frame is _top, the browser displays the target page in the full browser window.

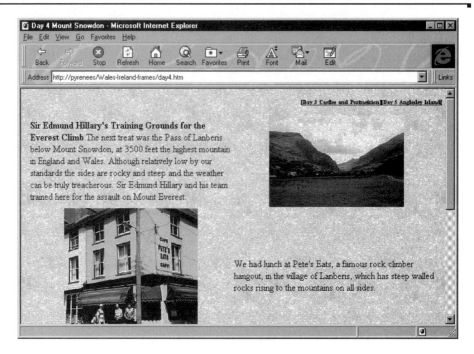

For More...

Using a frameset to divide the browser window into a set of subwindows is an excellent way to use the browser window more efficiently. The subwindows can display separate web pages simultaneously. Framesets can help your Web visitor understand the layout of your web if you use a frame to display the "big picture" at all times while other frames change to display content.

The following chapters provide more information on laying out the content of a page:

- Chapter 14: Adding Tables shows you how to use tables to lay out information on a page.

- Chapter 19: Understanding Discussion Group Webs explains how you can display the pages of an online discussion group using frames.

PART

III

Creating Web Pages

Chapter

16

Using WebBots in Page Design

Chapter 16

Using WebBots in Page Design

I n the last five chapters, you've learned how to insert the standard web objects into web pages, including text, horizontal lines, images, and tables, and how to use frames to enhance a page. We have been using the FrontPage Editor to insert and edit these objects. The results we've obtained can be achieved with any HTML editor and by starting from scratch and writing HTML codes in a text editor such as the Microsoft Notepad. This chapter is the first of four chapters that deal with inserting special FrontPage web objects called WebBot components, or simply, bots.

A *bot* is an object that that has a prewritten script attached to it. You insert a bot in a page in the same way you insert any web object.There are two fundamental categories of bots:

- A *page design bot* is executed by the FrontPage Explorer or Editor either when you insert the bot in a page or when you save or update the page in the Editor.

- A *form bot* is executed by a FrontPage-enabled Web server when the Web visitor enters information into a form and takes some action, such as clicking a button, to start running the script.

This chapter covers the page design bots and the next three chapters cover the form bots. Table 16.1 describes the page design bots.

WebBot	Description
TABLE 16.1: THE PAGE DESIGN WEBBOT COMPONENTS	
Comments	Use to display comments in the Editor and hide them when viewing the page in a browser.
HTML Markup	Use to insert HTML tags that FrontPage doesn't recognize.
Include	Use to merge another page into the current web page.
Scheduled Image	Use to display an image in the current web page for a specified period of time.
Scheduled Include	Use to merge another page into the current web page for a specified period of time.
Substitution	Use to display a specified piece of text in the current web page.
Table of Contents	Use to automatically build a table of contents based on links for a page or for the entire web.
Timestamp	Use to display the date and time that the current page was last saved or updated.

NOTE

The features that bots provide can be duplicated in a nonFrontPage web by writing the scripts yourself. FrontPage saves you from having to learn how to write the scripts.

NOTE

To work through the examples in this chapter, you'll need to replace the Wales-Ireland web you created in previous chapters with a modified version on the book's CD-ROM. Open your existing Wales-Ireland web and choose File ➤ Delete FrontPage Web from the Explorer menu bar to delete the web. Then choose File ➤ Import and use the Import Web Wizard to create a new web named Wales-Ireland and to import all the files from the web named Wales-Ireland-Ch15Ch16 stored in the Webs folder on the book's CD-ROM.

Inserting a Page Design Bot

Insert a page design bot in the active page in the Editor the same way you insert a standard web object. To insert a design bot:

1. Place the insertion point at the location where you want to place the bot. Choose Insert ➤WebBot Component from the Editor menu bar or click the Insert WebBot Component button in the Standard toolbar. The Insert Bot dialog shown in Figure 16.1a lists all but two of the page design bots and a few of the form bots. The list does not include the Comments and HTML Markup page design bots because these bots have commands on the Editor's Insert menu.

2. Choose the bot you want to insert and click OK. The Editor displays a property sheet for the type of bot you choose. For example, Figure 16.1b is the property sheet for the Table of Contents bot.

3. Specify the properties of the bot and click OK. Setting the bot's properties is also called *configuring* the bot.

FIGURE 16.1

Select the page design bot in the Insert WebBot Component dialog (a). Set the bot's properties in a properties dialog (b).

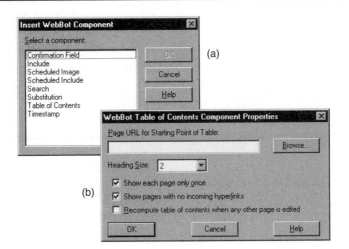

After you configure the bot and close the property sheet, FrontPage executes the script and the Editor displays its representation of the bot. (In a few cases described later, the FrontPage doesn't run the script until you save the page.) For most—but not all—page design bots, the Editor's representation of a bot is the same as a browser's representation.

PART

III

Creating Web Pages

You insert Comments and HTML Markup bots using their own menu commands. These bots are discussed in the "Adding Comments to a Page" and "Adding Other HTML Elements" sections.

Bot Mechanics

When you move the pointer over the region occupied by a bot, the pointer icon changes to the bot icon shown in Figure 16.2.

FIGURE 16.2

The pointer icon changes to the bot icon when you move the pointer over a bot in the Editor.

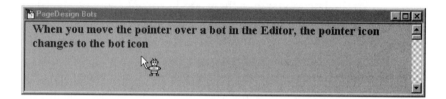

Select an existing bot by clicking anywhere in the bot. A selected bot is highlighted in the Editor. After selecting a bot, you can use drag and drop to move or copy a bot to another location on the same page or on another page by right-clicking the selected bot and dragging it to the new location. When you release the mouse button, the shortcut menu displays the choices. Select Move Here to remove the bot from its original location and paste the bot to the new location. Select Copy Here to paste a copy of the bot to the new location.

NOTE

For the Timestamp, Comment, and Substitution bots, the Link Here command is available so you can create a text hyperlink at the new location and set a bookmark for the text that the page design bot creates.

You can also copy and paste a selected bot the same way you copy and paste a standard web object using menu commands, toolbar buttons, and keyboard combinations (see the "Manipulating Page Elements" section in Chapter 10).

Editing a Bot

Display the property sheet for an inserted bot by doing any of the following:

- Double-click when the bot icon is visible
- Right-click the bot and choose WebBot Component Properties from the shortcut menu

- Click the bot and choose Edit ➤ WebBot Component Properties from the Editor menu bar
- Click the bot and press Alt+Enter

Change the bot's properties in the property sheet and click OK to close the dialog.

Including a Page in Another Page

One of the most useful page design bots is the Include Bot. You use the Include Bot when you want to include or merge another page within the current page. For example, when you have a header or footer that you want to use in several pages of your web, create a separate header page or footer page and use the Include Bot to merge the header or footer page into another page. Figure 16.3 shows the Include Bot Properties dialog. You enter the Page URL in the text box. You can type the URL or click the Browse button to display the list of pages in the current web (you can only include a page from the current web). When you click OK, FrontPage runs the script for the bot, retrieves the specified page, and generates a new version of the page that includes the retrieved page. FrontPage also creates an implicit link to the included page.

Using the Include WebBot

To explore including another page in the active page:

1. Click the Open button in the toolbar and double-click the Home Page in the Open File dialog. Click in the bottom of the page. Click the Insert WebBot Component button in the toolbar, choose Include bot and click OK.

2. Click the Browse button in the properties dialog, open the _private folder in the Current Web dialog and double-click footer.htm. Click OK to close the Properties dialog and run the script. The Editor briefly displays the message that the page is being retrieved and then displays the footer page merged into the home page (see Figure 16.4). The blinking bar in the left margin indicates the height of the included page. Click the Save button in the toolbar.

PART

III

Creating Web Pages

3. Switch to the Explorer and click the Hyperlink View button in the toolbar. The Hyperlinks pane displays the implicit link to the included page (see Figure 16.5).

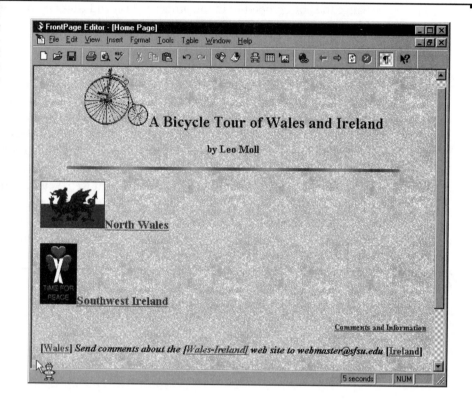

Opening an Included Page

You can open an included page as follows:

1. Right-click in the Include Bot that displays the included page. The shortcut menu displays the command Open followed by the absolute URL of the inserted page, such as http://pyrenees/Wales-Ireland/_private/footer.htm.

2. Choose the Open.... command. The Editor displays the included page.

FIGURE 16.5

When you use the Include bot to merge another page into the active page, FrontPage creates an implicit link to the merged page.

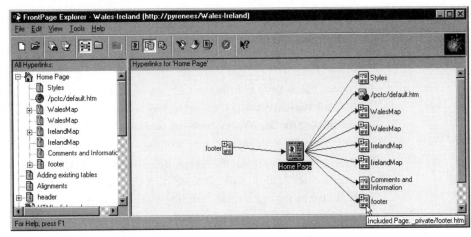

NOTE

When you use the Include Bot, the background image or color and the text and link colors of the included page are ignored. The included page inherits the styles of the parent page.

Hiding Included Files

Often the included pages are standard header and footer pages. Because these pages are not complete pages, they should not be accessible to the web visitor, you normally hide them. To hide included pages, move them to the _private folder.

Creating a Template Using Included Pages

Creating your own page templates can save you a lot of time. You can use the Include bot to merge pages into a page template. To explore, we'll create a new page template for the Wales-Ireland web.

1. Create a new page and set its properties so that the page borrows its styles from the styles.htm page in the _private folder.

2. Insert an Include bot and choose the header.htm page in the private folder.

3. Click in the next line, choose Insert ➤ Comment from the Editor menu bar, and type **Comment: Insert page contents here** in the Comment dialog and click OK.

4. Press Enter. Insert an Include bot and choose the footer.htm page in the private folder.

5. Choose File ➤ Save As from the Editor menu bar, type **Wales-Ireland** as the page title and **WalesIreland.htm** as the page name. Click As Template and type **Page template for the Wales-Ireland web** as the Description. Click OK. FrontPage stores the new template in a new template folder named walesireland.tem

6. Choose File ➤ New from the Editor menu bar. Scroll to the bottom to view the new template (see Figure 16.6a). Double-click the Wales-Ireland template. Figure 16.6b shows the new page created from the template. The error messages are temporary. When you save the page to the current web, the server retrieves the included pages.

7. Save the new page with the name Page From Template. Click the Refresh button in the toolbar to update the window (see Figure 16.7)

FIGURE 16.6

When you create a new page template (a) using Include bots, the Editor displays temporary error messages (b).

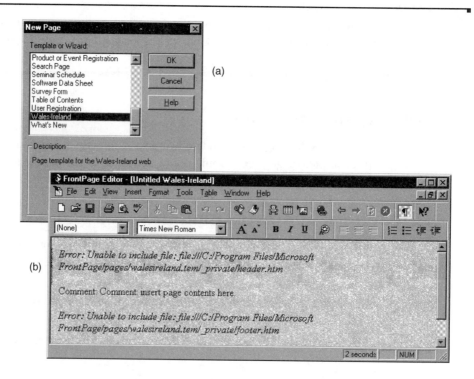

FIGURE 16.7

Save and refresh the page to eliminate the error messages.

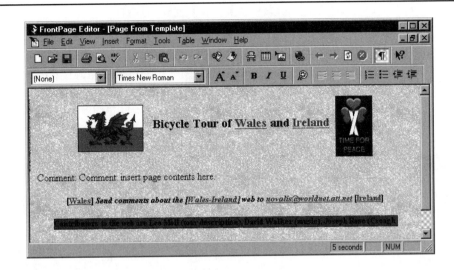

Avoiding the Temporary Error Messages   You can avoid the temporary error messages by storing copies of the included pages in the template folder. Also, store copies of any images, sound clips, or video clips that may be inserted in the included pages. Store the pages and files in the same folder structure in the template folder that they have in the web folder.

For practice, you'll create _private and images folders in the template folder and export the included pages and files.

1. Start the Windows Explorer. Locate and open the walesireland.tem folder (default path C:\Program Files\Microsoft FrontPage\pages\walesireland.tem).

2. Create new folders named _private and images. Close the Windows Explorer.

3. Export the header.htm and footer.htm pages to the new _private folder. Export the dragon.gif and peace.gif images to the new images folder. (See Chapter 6 for information on exporting files.)

4. Open a new page based on the Wales-Ireland template. The new page displays the included pages and images.

NOTE

If the current web has different versions of the included pages and files, the versions stored in the current web override the versions stored in the template folder.

PART

III

Creating Web Pages

Using the Scheduled Include Bot

You use the Scheduled Include Bot when you want to include a page for a specific time period. The Scheduled Include Bot Properties dialog is shown in Figure 16.8. You can specify any page in the current web and the time interval that you want to display the page. You can also specify a second page in the current web for display before the beginning and after the end of the specified time interval. You can type the Page URLs or click the Browse buttons to display a list of the pages in the current web.

FIGURE 16.8

Use the WebBot Scheduled Include Component Properties dialog to specify the time interval, the page to display during the time interval, and the page to display before and after the time interval.

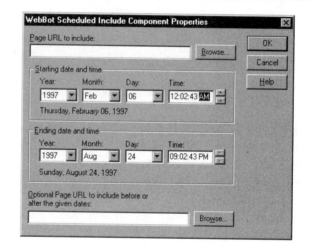

When you click OK, FrontPage runs the script for the bot and compares the current date to the specified time interval. If the current date is in the time interval you specified, FrontPage generates the page with the included page; otherwise, FrontPage generates the page and includes the alternate page if you specified an alternate page. If you don't specify an alternate page and the current date is not in the specified time interval, the Editor displays the message *[Expired Scheduled Include]* at the location of the bot and a browser displays nothing.

NOTE

If you specify a starting date that is after the ending date, the Editor displays the expired message and a browser does not display the included page.

FrontPage executes the script for a Scheduled Include bot only when you make a change to the web. Each time you make a change to the web, FrontPage looks for the Schedule Include bots on any pages in the web. When it finds a Scheduled Include bot, FrontPage executes the bot's script, checks the dates you specified for the bot, and generates a new page based on the dates. If you don't change the web, the scripts are not run and web pages with Scheduled Include Bots are not updated and continue to display the last version generated.

Using the Scheduled Image Bot

The Scheduled Image Bot works the same way as the Scheduled Include Bot. The only difference is that the bot displays an image instead of a page during the specified time interval and displays an optional alternate image before and after the specified time interval (see Figure 16.9). The Scheduled Image Bot is useful when you want to draw attention to a new item in your web by displaying a special image for a limited time.

FIGURE 16.9

Use the WebBot Scheduled Image Component Properties dialog to specify the time interval, the image to display during the time interval, and the image to display before and after the time interval.

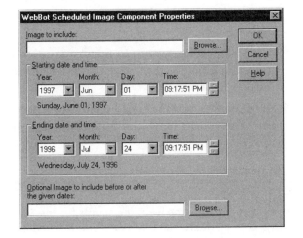

NOTE

To be sure that FrontPage runs the Scheduled Include and Scheduled Image bot scripts on a regular basis, you must make a change to your web on the same regular basis.

PART

III

Creating Web Pages

To explore using a scheduled image, we'll add an animated line to the page. The burstani.gif image file is an animated gif stored in the ClipArt gallery. You must add a copy of the file to the current web before you can insert the image on a page using the Scheduled Include bot. The easiest way to add a copy of the ClipArt image file to the web is to insert the image in a page and save the image to the web.

1. In the Home Page, delete the turquoise and gray line image. Choose Insert ➤ Image from the Editor menu bar and click the ClipArt tab in the Image dialog. Choose burstani.gif in the Animations category and click OK. Click the Save button in the toolbar to save the page. When the Editor prompts you to save the image, change the URL to images/burstani.gif and click Yes.

2. Click the image and press Delete.

3. Click the Insert WebBot Component button in the toolbar and double-click Scheduled Image in the Insert WebBot Component dialog. Click the Browse button in the properties dialog. Locate the burstani.gif file in the Current Web dialog and click OK.

4. By default, the Starting date and time is the current date and time. Set the Ending date and time to a future time, such as one hour from the current time and click OK.

5. Click the Browse button to select an optional image. Locate the turquoise _and_gray.gif file in the Current Web dialog and click OK. Click OK to close the Properties dialog.

6. Click the Save button and then click the Preview in Browser button in the toolbar. Figure 16.10 shows the animated image that will display for the specified time interval.

NOTE

If you don't change the web, the scripts for the Scheduled Include and Scheduled Image bots are not run and web pages with Scheduled Include and Scheduled Image bots are not updated. These pages continue to display the last version generated.

Adding a Table of Contents

The Table of Contents bot can be used to build a table of contents for your entire web or for only part of the web. When you run the script, the bot starts with the page you specify, examines its hyperlinks to other pages in the current web, and includes the

FIGURE 16.10

The animated gif image is displayed during the specified time interval.

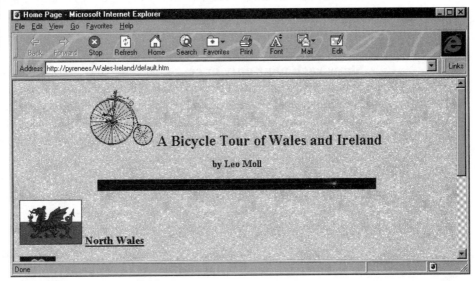

titles of these target pages as the first level of the table of contents for the start page. Next, the bot examines the set of hyperlinks on each first-level page and includes the titles of the targets of these hyperlinks as the page's second level in the table of contents. If the second-level pages have hyperlinks, the bot examines these to build a third level of target pages, and so on. When the bot is finished, the table of contents is a hierarchical list of hyperlinks to all the pages that can be reached by a sequence of hyperlinks beginning at the start page. You can also configure the bot to include pages that cannot be reached by any sequence of hyperlinks beginning at the start page.

NOTE

The Table of Contents bot examines only hyperlinks to other pages in the current web and does not consider external hyperlinks.

Use the WebBot Table of Contents Component Properties dialog to set several properties that control how the bot carries out the task (see Figure 16.11), as follows:

- **Page URL to Starting Point of Table**   Enter the Page URL of the page you want to start with. For example, to create a table of contents for an entire web, start with the home page.

- **Heading Size**   By default, the Table of Contents Bot displays the title of the starting page as the heading for the table of contents using a heading size of 2.

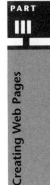

PART

III

Creating Web Pages

To omit the heading, choose (none), or to specify the heading size, choose a number from the list. Omitting the heading altogether or changing the heading size is the only formatting change you can make. You cannot change the format of individual items in the table of contents.

- **Show each page only once**   A page may have more than one incoming hyperlink from another page. Use this option to specify whether to include separate table items for each incoming link. Check this option to include the target page only once, regardless of the number of incoming hyperlinks that lead to the page. If you clear this check box, the target page will be listed separately for each incoming hyperlink that leads to the page.

- **Show pages with no incoming hyperlinks**   Clear this check box to include only the pages that can be reached by following a sequence of hyperlinks forward from the starting page. If you check this option, all the pages in the web will be listed.

- **Recompute table of contents when any other page is edited**   Check this option to run the script and update the table of contents automatically whenever any page in the web is edited. When you clear this option, the script runs only when you open and save a page with a Table of Contents bot.

FIGURE 16.11

The WebBot Table of Contents Component Properties dialog

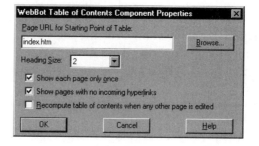

Automatic updating of a table of contents can be time consuming if the web has a large number of pages. In most cases, a better solution is to clear the Recompute check box and force the update of the table of contents by opening and saving the pages that contain the Table of Contents Bots.

The properties dialog in Figure 16.11 includes all of the properties you can set. Unfortunately, you cannot specify the number of levels to include and you cannot change the format of the table of contents, except the size of the table's heading.

When you save the page, FrontPage runs the script and creates the list of pages to be displayed. The Editor is not able to display the list and, instead, represents the bot with a dummy heading and three dummy items, as shown in Figure 16.12. You must load the page into a browser to view the table of contents.

FIGURE 16.12

The Editor displays a dummy heading and lists items for the table of contents.

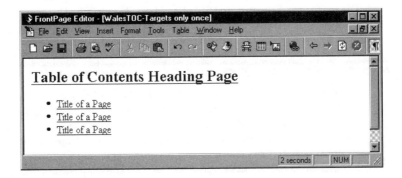

Figure 16.13a shows a portion of the WalesMap page in the Wales-Ireland web. The page has a set of text hyperlinks and a set of image hyperlinks to each day page. Each day page has text hyperlinks to the next day and the previous day in the upper-right corner of the page (see Figure 16.13b).

FIGURE 16.13

The WalesMap page has a text hyperlink and an image hyperlink to each day page (a). A day page has text hyperlinks to the next day page and the previous day page (b).

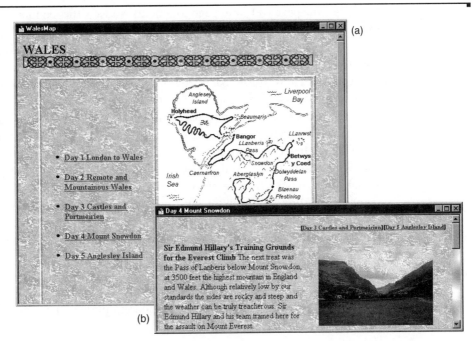

PART

III

Creating Web Pages

Figure 16.14a shows the table of contents created by the bot for the Wales-Ireland web using the WalesMap page as the starting page and selecting options to include only the pages you can reach from the WalesMap page and including pages only once. Figure 16.14b shows the table of contents based on options to include only the pages with direct hyperlinks from the WalesMap page but with pages listed separately for each incoming hyperlink. Each day page is listed twice in the first level: once for the text hyperlink and once for the image hyperlink. The second level for each page includes the text hyperlinks to the next day page and the previous day page.

NOTE

When building a table of contents, the Table of Contents bot ignores implicit links, including links to images, styles pages, and images merged into a page using an Include or a Scheduled Image bot. The bot also ignores hyperlinks to bookmarks. To create a table of contents for a page based on the page's bookmarks, see the "Using Bookmarks to Create a Table of Contents" section in Chapter 12.

Adding Web Parameters to a Page

In Chapter 5: Explorer Basics, you learned that each web page has a set of parameters. The standard web parameters include the name of the authors who created and modified the page, the page URL, and page comments. To view the Explorer's Properties dialog, right-click a page in the Explorer and choose Properties in the shortcut menu. You can also create custom parameters using the Web Settings dialog. To display the dialog, choose Tools ➤ Web Settings from the Explorer menu bar. You can display the values of standard and custom parameters on the web page using the Substitution Bot. FrontPage runs the script for each Substitution bot when you save a change to the web. FrontPage generates a new page, substituting the bot with the current value of the parameter. Substitution bots are extremely useful for the following reason. If the value of a web parameter changes, you only have to make the change in one place (in the Web Settings dialog), and FrontPage automatically udpates every page that uses a Substitution bot to display the value.

Figure 16.15a shows the WebBot Substitution Component Properties dialog.

The first four items in the Substitute drop-down menu are the standard page parameters and are followed by any custom parameters. Examples of Substitution bots in the Editor are shown in Figure 16.15b. A web browser and the Editor display the identical items.

Substitution bots are particularly useful for displaying custom web settings such as the webmaster's e-mail address, the company address, phone number, and fax number.

FIGURE 16.14

The tables of contents created by the bot when a page with incoming links is shown once (a) and more than once (b).

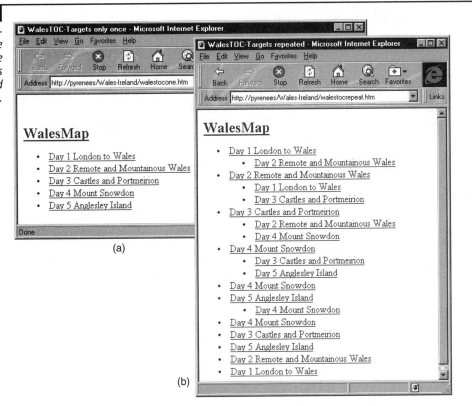

(a)

(b)

FIGURE 16.15

Select a web parameter in the WebBot Substitution Component Properties dialog (a). The Substitution bot displays the parameter values (b).

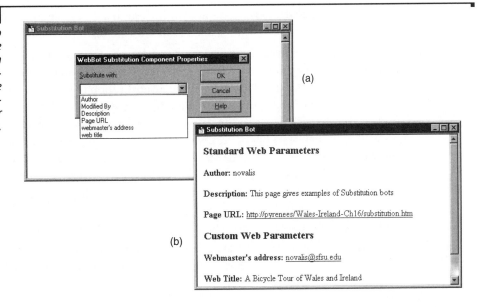

(a)

(b)

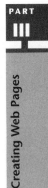

PART

III

Creating Web Pages

Timestamping a Page

Use the Timestamp bot to display the date and time that the page was last saved or updated. The Timestamp Bot Properties dialog is shown in Figure 16.16.

The Timestamp Bot Properties dialog

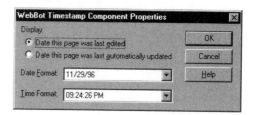

You can specify that the bot display either the date and time that you last saved the page in the Editor or the date and time that the page was last updated. A page is automatically updated by FrontPage whenever any action occurs that affects the page, including:

- Saving the page in the Editor
- Recalculating the web's links in the Explorer
- Saving another page or image that is included in the page using an Include or Scheduled Image bot
- Changing the pages that affect a Table of Contents bot in the page
- Changing a web parameter value in the FrontPage Web Settings dialog or a custom web parameter in the page's Properties dialog in the Explorer

When you save a page, the page is updated as well, however, a page can be updated by FrontPage without your saving the page. For example, changing the value of a web parameter that is displayed in a page using a Substitution bot updates the page automatically. Whether you configure the timestamp to display the last save or the last update, the changed date and time are displayed the next time you visit the page in a browser. Although the Editor and a web browser both display the date and time using the same format, the values they display are usually different. When you open the page in the Editor, the timestamp bot displays the current time and date. By contrast, when you visit the page in a browser, the timestamp bot displays the time and date of either the last save or the last update.

To explore the difference between the save and update timestamps:

1. Place the insertion point at the end of the Comments and Information line in the home page and press Enter. Click the Insert Table button in the toolbar and insert a table with one row and two columns. Click in the first cell, click the Insert WebBot Component button in the toolbar, choose the Timestamp bot, and click OK.

2. Select a time format and click OK.

3. Click in the second cell. Repeat Step 1, but choose the "Date this page was last automatically updated" option. Select a time format and click OK.

4. Click the Save button and then click the Preview in Browser button in the toolbar. Figure 16.17a shows the times when the two bots were created. Figure 16.17b shows the time that the page was last saved.

FIGURE 16.17

The Editor displays the times that the timestamp bots were created (a). The browser displays the time that the page was last saved (b).

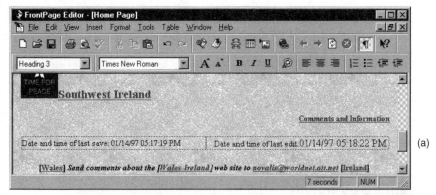

(a)

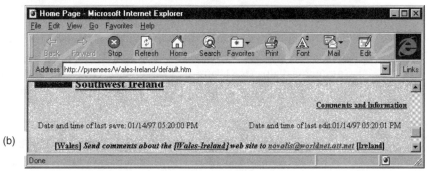

(b)

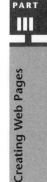

5. Right-click in the Include bot and choose the Open... command in the shortcut menu to open the merged footer page. Edit the footer page, click the Save button in the toolbar to save the change to the footer page, and close the footer page. When you save a page, FrontPage automatically looks for pages with an Include bot or a Scheduled Include bot and updates them.

6. Click the Refresh button in the toolbar to update the home page. Click the page's Close button. The Editor does not prompt you to save changes to the home page because you haven't made any changes to this page.

7. Switch to the browser and click the Refresh button in the browser's toolbar. The browser displays the home page with the change. The second timestamp displays the time of the edit of the included footer page. The first timestamp continues to display the time the home page was last saved (see Figure 16.18)

FIGURE 16.18

The first timestamp continues to display the time the page was last saved and the second time-stamp displays the time the change to the merged header page was saved.

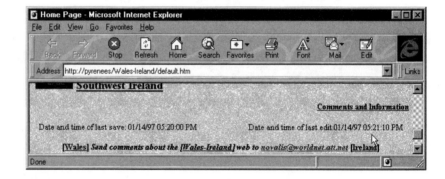

Adding a Comment

You use the Comment bot to make a note to yourself on a web page. The comment is displayed only by the Editor and not by a web browser. The Comment bot has its own menu command. Choose Insert ➤ Comment from the Editor menu bar to display the Comments dialog (see Figure 16.19). Type the comment in the box and press OK. Figure 16.20 shows the representation in the Editor (a) and in a browser(b).

FIGURE 16.19

The Comment dialog

FIGURE 16.20

The Comment bot in the Editor (a) and in a browser (b)

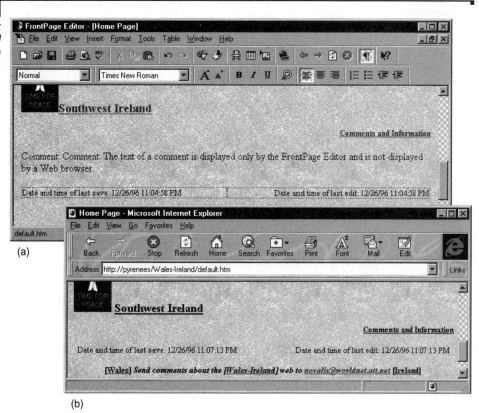

(a)

(b)

Adding Other HTML Elements

You can use the HTML Markup bot to add HTML elements that FrontPage doesn't recognize. The HTML Markup bot has its own menu command. Choose Insert ➤ HTML Markup to display the HTML Markup Bot dialog shown in Figure 16.21.

An *HTML element* consists of a start tag, and end tag and text between the two tags. The start tag is a code enclosed by the symbols < and > and the end tag is the same code enclosed by the symbols </ and >. Most HTML elements require both a start tag and an end tag. The start tag tells the browser to begin using the formatting element and the end tag tells the browser to stop. For example, the Bold element has the start tag <B> and the end tag </B>. A browser that recognizes the Bold element displays any text you place between the tags in bold font.

PART

III

Creating Web Pages

FIGURE 16.21

The HTML Markup
dialog

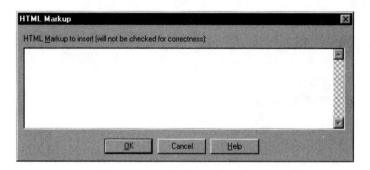

FrontPage 97 recognizes nearly all of the HTML elements that the Microsoft Internet Explorer 3.0 browser recognizes. However, new HTML elements are constantly being added. When you use the HTML Markup bot to add new HTML elements to a page, FrontPage does not review the HTML codes you enter in the dialog.

For example, there is an HTML element for creating styles that FrontPage 97 does not recognize. FrontPage allows you to create a styles page and assign the styles page to one or more pages in the web (see the "Basing a Page's Styles on Another Page" section in Chapter 10). The only properties you can specify for the styles page include the background color or image, text color, and hyperlink text colors. However, Microsoft Internet Explorer 3.0 has HTML elements that give additional flexibility. You can use the SPAN element to apply style information to a piece of text. For example, the following applies a font size and margin to the enclosed text:

> <SPAN STYLE="font-size: 24pt; margin-left: 1.0in"> This text
> has its own style </SPAN>

Because FrontPage 97 does not recognize the <SPAN> element, you use the HTML Markup bot to insert the new element.

1. Click the New button in the toolbar. Choose Insert ➤ HTML Markup in the Editor menu bar, type **<SPAN STYLE="font-size: 24pt; margin-left: 1.0in">** and click OK. The Editor inserts the HTML code and displays the HTML bot icon on the page.

2. Type **This text is in 24 point and has a 1 in margin** and then choose Insert ➤ HTML Markup in the Editor menu bar. Type **</SPAN>** and the ending tag and click OK. The Editor inserts a second HTML bot icon (see Figure 16.22a).

3. Click the Save button in the toolbar and save the page as HTML Markup. Click the Preview in Browser button. Figure 16.22b shows the page in the Microsoft

Internet Explorer 3.0 with the style applied. Figure 16.22c shows the page in the Netscape Navigator 3.0 which does not recognize the SPAN element.

HTML Markup bots in the Editor (a). The page displayed in Microsoft Internet Explorer 3.0 (b) which recognizes the SPAN element, and in the Netscape Navigator 3.0 (c), which does not.

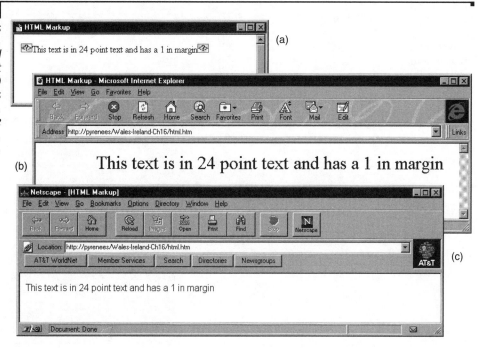

Viewing WebBot Errors

If you configure a bot incorrectly, the Explorer displays the error icon, a small red triangle to the left of the page icon in the All Hyperlinks pane of Hyperlink View (see Figure 16.23a). As an example, if you insert a Substitution bot and choose the Description parameter, but you haven't entered any text in the Comments text box in the Explorer's Properties dialog for the page, the bot generates an error. To view the error message, right-click the page icon in the Explorer and choose Properties in the shortcut menu. The dialog displays the error message in an Errors tab (see Figure 16.23b).

NOTE

If you know how to program you can use the FrontPage 97 Software Development Kit to create custom WebBot components.

PART

III

Creating Web Pages

FIGURE 16.23

If you configure a bot incorrectly, the Explorer displays the error icon (a). Right-click the page and choose Properties to display the error message (b).

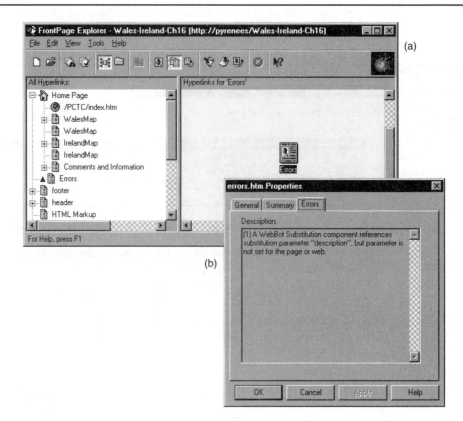

(a)

(b)

For More...

This chapter has shown you how to use page design bots to automate the creation and updating of pages. FrontPage runs these bots when you save changes to web pages or web parameters.

NOTE

You can use any Web server to publish pages that have page design bots because it is FrontPage and not the Web server that runs page design bots. However, if a page has form bots, you must publish the page using a FrontPage-enabled Web server because it is the FrontPage Server Extensions installed with the Web server that run form bots.

These chapters provide more information on the topics covered in this chapter:

- Chapter 17: Collecting Input Data shows you how to use the browse time bots to provide interactivity for a web page. The browse time bots are run by the FrontPage-enabled Web server.

- Chapter 20: Extending FrontPage with ActiveX, shows you how to insert ActiveX Controls into pages. ActiveX Controls also contain prewritten programs that provide additional features, however, the programs are run by the visitor's Web browser.

PART

III

Creating Web Pages

Chapter

17

Collecting
Input Data

Collecting Input Data

I n the previous chapters, you've learned techniques for creating interesting and informative web pages. Up to this point, however, the communication between you and your web visitors is one-way: your pages present the information but the visitor is not able give information back to you. The visitor has interacted with your site only by clicking hyperlinks to navigate around it. The next step in designing a web site is to provide ways for your visitors to give information back to you. This is the first of three chapters describing the FrontPage techniques for allowing visitors to participate in your web. This chapter shows you how to collect and store information from a visitor. The subsequent chapters cover ways to let the visitor search your web, register in it, and participate with other visitors in web discussion groups.

This chapter shows you how to create a web page that has a data entry form. The web visitor uses the form to type in text information, make choices, and submit the information back to you by clicking a button. You'll learn how to create a form using the Form Page Wizard and how to create a form from scratch. You'll learn how to manipulate and modify a form, and how the web server processes a form. The chapter describes the kinds of objects you can place inside a form and ends by describing how to create a page that confirms the submission.

Creating a Simple Data Entry Page

We'll start by creating a new page with a simple data entry form. A *form* is a set of data entry fields that gets processed by the web server when the web visitor submits the form. The FrontPage Editor displays the boundary of a form using dashed lines, which are invisible when you view the page in a browser. A *form field* is an object you insert inside the form boundary for collecting data or for submitting the form. There are five kinds of fields for entering information: check boxes, radio buttons, and drop-down menus for making selections; and single-line and scrolling text boxes for typing in text information. There are two kinds of fields for submitting the data: push buttons and images.

The easiest way to create a new form is to use the Form Page Wizard. To follow along, create a new Normal Web in the Explorer and name the new web Interactive.

Using the Form Page Wizard

The Form Page Wizard leads you through the process of creating a new page that contains a data entry form.

1. Choose File ➤ New from the Editor menu bar, choose Form Page Wizard in the New Page dialog, and click OK. The first screen explains what the wizard does (see Figure 17.1a).

2. Click Next. Type **formwiz.htm** as the Page URL and **Form Page Wizard** as the Page Title (see Figure 17.1b) and click Next. You use the next screen to develop a list of the questions you want to ask in the form. Only the Add button is available (see Figure 17.1c), but after you add the first request, the remaining buttons become available and you can use them to modify the list.

Creating Requests for Information

Use the wizard's next several dialogs to create requests for information.

1. Click the Add button. Choose the kind of input you want to collect in the list in the top of the next screen (see Figure 17.2a). The first five items are categories including contact, account, product, ordering, and personal information. When you select one of these items, the wizard inserts a group of data entry fields appropriate to your choice. For example, select contact information to collect data such as the visitor's name, title, phone, fax, and e-mail address as a group. Alternatively, you can select one of the last nine items to insert a specific type of data entry field. For example, select paragraph to insert a scrolling text box for collecting the visitor's comments.

FIGURE 17.1

The first screen of the Form Page Wizard describes what the wizard does (a). You enter the page URL and title in the next dialog (b). Click the Add button in the next dialog to begin adding requests for information to the form (c).

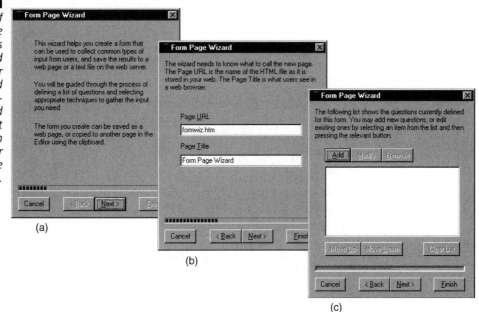

(a)

(b)

(c)

FIGURE 17.2

Choose the category of information you want to collect (a) and edit the request in the text box (b). In the next dialog, specify the kinds of information you want to collect and name the group (c).

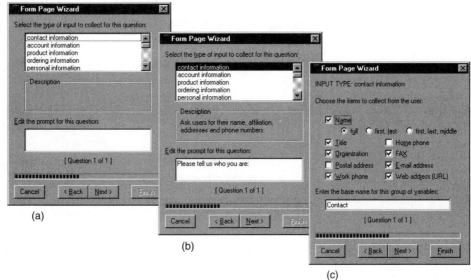

(a)

(b)

(c)

PART

III

Creating Web Pages

2. Select contact information. After you choose an item from the list box, the text box below the list changes to display the request that the wizard will enter in the form. You can type in the text box to modify the proposed request or replace it with a new one. You can also change the request after the wizard creates the page. Modify the request by typing **Please tell us who you are:** (see Figure 17.2b) and click Next. Use the next screen to specify the kinds of contact information (see Figure 17.2c) by clicking the check boxes and option buttons. The wizard proposes a set of fields and suggests Contact as the name for the set.

3. Click Next to accept the default choices. The wizard displays your first question in the question list (see Figure 17.3a). We'll add a second question that invites comments.

4. Click Add. The last nine items in the list let you choose a specific kind of field for answering a question. Table 17.1 shows the choices and the fields that the wizard uses.

TABLE 17.1: THE TYPES OF INPUT THE FORM WIZARD COLLECTS

Input Type	Fields Used	Comments
one of several options	drop-down menu, radio buttons, or list	
any of several options	check boxes	
boolean	check box, yes/no radio buttons, or true-false radio buttons	
date	text box	Can specify mm/dd/yy, dd/mm/yy, or free format
time	text box	Can specify hh:mm:ss-am/pm, hh:mm:ss - 24 hour clock, or free format
range	drop-down menu or radio buttons	Visitor can rate an opinion on a scale of 1 to 5, bad to good, or disagree strongly to agree strongly
number	text box	Can specify maximum length and currency format
string	single-line text box	Can specify maximum length up to 50 characters
paragraph	multi-line scrolling text box	No length restrictions

5. Choose "one of several options" as the input type so that you can provide a list of categories for the visitor's comments. Change the question by typing **Choose a topic for your comments:** and then click Next. You use the next screen to specify the choices in the text box and how you want the choices displayed: you can use a drop-down menu, a set of radio buttons, or a list. Use the text box at the bottom to name the field that holds the answer.

6. Type the following choices: **Our web site**, **The company**, and **Customer Support**, pressing Enter after typing each item to begin a new line. Choose drop-down menu, and then type **Category** as the name of the field (see Figure 17.3b).

7. Click Next to add the second request to the list and then click Add to design the final request. Choose "paragraph" as the input type, change the request by typing **Your comments please:** , and click Next. Type **Comments** as the name of the field (see Figure 17.3c) and click Next.

Figure 17.4 shows the list of requests for information. You can change any request in the list. After you click to select a request, the buttons become active. Click the Remove button to remove the request or click the Move Up or Move Down buttons to change the request's order in the list. After you click one of these buttons, the wizard automatically renumbers the requests. Click the Modify button to review the set of dialogs for modifying the request. Click the Clear List button to remove all of the requests and start again. When you are finished modifying the list, click the Next button.

Specifying the Layout and Handling of the Form

In the next few wizard dialogs, you'll specify the layout for the data entry form and how you want the web server to handle the information that the web visitor supplies.

1. Use the dialog shown in Figure 17.5a to select a format for the requests, and specify whether you want the page to start with a table of contents and whether the you want the wizard to use tables to align the form fields. Click Next to display the requests as paragraphs without a table of contents and to align the fields with tables.

2. Click Next. Use the next screen to specify how you want the server to handle the input and where to store the results (see Figure 17.5b). If you choose one of the first two options, FrontPage uses one of its own scripts (the Save Results bot) to store the results in either a web page (.htm) or a text file (.txt). Use the third option if you have a custom script that you want the server to run instead. The wizard suggests formrslt as the base name for the file that stores the results.

3. Click Next to store the results in a web page with the URL formrslt.htm and then click Finish to put the wizard to work.

4. Click the Save button in the toolbar and click OK to save the page.

PART

III

Creating Web Pages

FIGURE 17.3

The Wizard displays the first question (a). Specify choices for the drop-down menu (b). Specify the name for the scrolling text box (c).

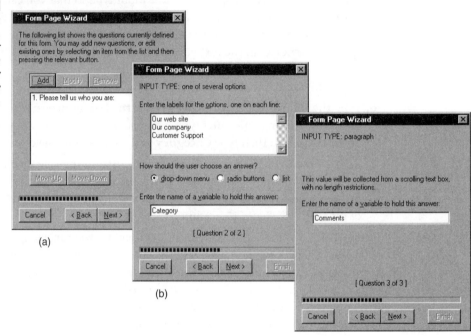

(a)

(b)

(c)

FIGURE 17.4

You can modify or remove a request item, rearrange the order of the list items, or you can clear the list and start over.

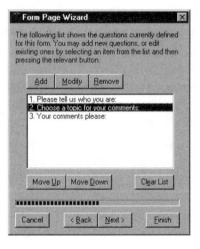

FIGURE 17.5

You can specify the presentation of the requests (a) and how the server handles the input (b).

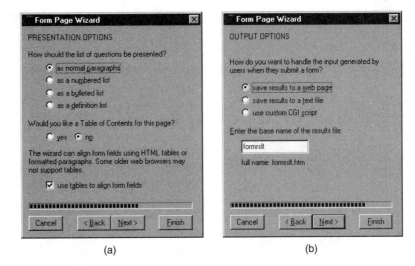

(a)   (b)

Parts of a Form

The wizard creates a new page containing the data entry form you specified. Figures 17.6a and 17.6b show the page in the Editor.

The Editor shows the boundaries of the form as dashed lines. The dashed lines are formatting marks and you can hide them by clicking the Format Marks button in the toolbar or by choosing View ➤ Format Marks from the Editor menu bar. When you view the page in a browser, the boundaries are not displayed. The form contains the following:

- The requests for information
- A label for each field that describes the kind of information to be entered
- Fields for typing in text or making selections
- A button for submitting the form to the server and a button for resetting the fields to their initial values
- A Timestamp bot displaying the date the page was last saved

The wizard also provides instructions to the web server for creating the file for storing the collected input. The storage file isn't created or added to the list of files and pages in the web until the first input is received from a visitor.

FIGURE 17.6

The Form Page
Wizard creates
a new page
containing a
data entry form.

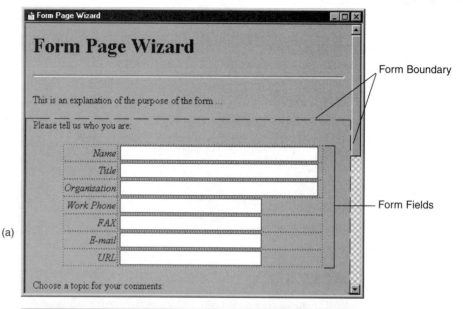

(a)

(b)

Entering Data in the Form

Let's view the page in a browser and enter some data.

1. Click the Preview in Browser button, enter some information in the form (see Figure 17.7a), and then click the Submit Form push button. The browser sends the data to the server. The web server creates and displays the form confirmation page shown in Figure 17.7b. The confirmation page includes a text hyperlink back to the data entry page. The server also creates the results page and adds the submitted information.

2. Point the browser to the storage page by typing the URL **http://localhost/interactive/formrslt.htm**. The browser displays the results page as shown in Figure 17.8.

FIGURE 17.7

Enter information in the data entry form (a). After you click the Submit Form push button, the server creates and displays the confirmation page (b).

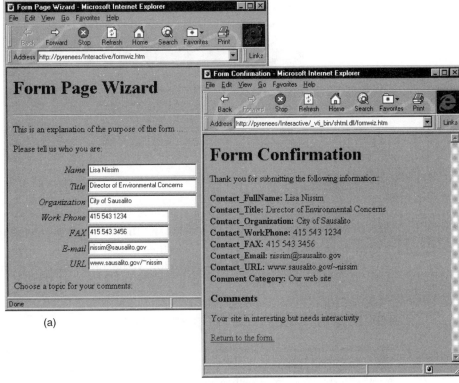

(a)

(b)

PART

III

Creating Web Pages

FIGURE 17.8

The input is added
to the results file.

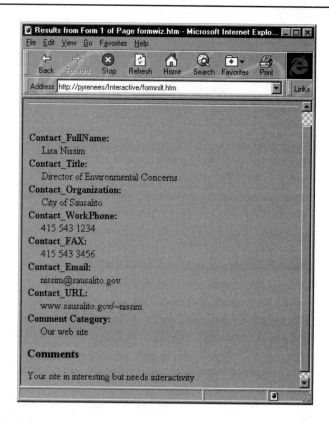

Form Mechanics

This section describes how to change the appearance of an existing form. You'll learn how to manipulate individual form fields and the form itself using many of the techniques you've learned for manipulating other objects. You'll learn two ways to display the results form in the same browser window as the form, and how to insert a new form into an existing page.

Changing the Form's Appearance

You can work inside the boundaries of the form to change the form's appearance. You can insert any web object inside the boundaries of a form except that you cannot insert another form. You can embellish a form with text, images, video clips, hyperlinks, lines, marquees, and so on. This section describes how to work with text and images inside a form's boundary and how to move the form fields to change the way the form looks.

Working with Text and Images

You can work with text and images inside the boundaries of a form using all the techniques you've learned for working with these objects.

Add, change, and delete text. Place the insertion point at the location where you want to make a change and then add or edit the text in the usual way. Change the paragraph and character formats. Embellish the form by inserting images. Use the familiar commands to cut, copy, and paste a selection of text and images to other pages and to other locations inside or outside a form boundary. Use drag-and-drop to move or copy a selection of text and images to a new location inside the form or to a location outside the form boundary.

Click in the selector bar of a line in the form—but not a line that is part of a table—to select all objects in the line, including the form fields. Selected objects are shown in reversed video. Click the align buttons in the Format toolbar to change the alignment of the selected objects.

Creating Hyperlinks inside a Form

You can define a bookmark for a text phrase inside the form boundary and use the bookmark as the target of a hyperlink. You can use a text phrase inside the form boundary to create a text hyperlink with a target to a bookmark, a page, or another file. You can also create image hyperlinks and hotspots.

Working with Fields

You can use most of the same techniques for fields that you've learned for other web objects. As an exception, you can't use a form field to create a hyperlink.

Selecting and Resizing a Field   There are two selection techniques for individual fields. Select a field by clicking to the right or left of the field and dragging the mouse to the opposite boundary; the selection is shown in reverse video. Alternatively, select a field by clicking anywhere inside the field's boundaries; in this case, FrontPage displays small squares at the corners and midpoints of the sides of the field. Use the second method when you want to resize a text box.

To resize a text box or a scrolling text box, move the pointer to one of the resizing squares; when the pointer icon changes to a double arrow, press the left mouse button and drag in the direction of one of the arrows. You can resize only one text box at a time and you can't resize combo boxes, check boxes, and option buttons. You can't resize push buttons using this method but you'll learn how to change a push button's size in the next section.

Deleting, Copying, Cutting, and Pasting a Field   Whether you select an individual field or include one or more fields as part of a larger selection of objects, you can use the familiar menu commands and keyboard shortcuts to delete a field selection and to cut, copy, and paste a field selection to another location inside or outside a form boundary. You can also use drag-and-drop to move or copy a field selection to another location inside the form boundary to a location inside the boundary of another form, or to a location outside any form boundary. However, a data entry field is associated with a form only as long as the field is inside the form's boundary—if you copy or move a data entry field outside the boundary of any form, the field is no longer associated with a form. When the web visitor submits the form, the data in a field outside the form's boundary is not submitted.

The association between a submit field and the form is a little trickier. You can copy or move the form's Submit button to a location on the page outside the form's boundary. As long as you paste the button below the form, and not inside the boundary of another form on the same page, clicking the button below the form submits the form to the server. However, if you paste the button to a location above the form boundary, there is no response to clicking the button.

In order to function properly, a form needs at least one data entry field inside its boundary, and a field—typically a push button—to submit the form to the server. You can remove all other items from inside the form boundary. If you try to submit a form without any data entry fields, the server sends a message to the browser that it can't carry out the request. Figure 17.9a shows the type of message the Microsoft Internet Explorer 3.0 displays and Figure 17.9b shows the Netscape Navigator 3.0 message.

FIGURE 17.9

The messages displayed by the Internet Explorer 3.0 (a) and Navigator 3.0 (b) when the web visitor submits a form that has no data fields.

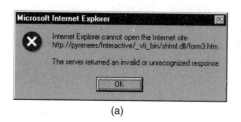

(a)

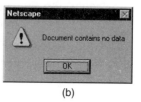

(b)

By copying and pasting fields, you can create a form that has duplicate data entry fields and duplicate Submit buttons. Clicking either of the duplicate Submit buttons submits the data to the server.

Using Tables to Lay Out a Form

When you use the Form Page Wizard to create a new form with groups of fields, such as the contact information fields, the wizard lays out the labels and the fields using either a table or the formatted text paragraph style. The easiest way to lay out the elements of a form is to use tables. Use the techniques described in Chapter 14: Adding Tables to insert, select, and modify tables and table cells.

You can modify the two-column tables that the wizard uses to add new columns and rearrange the labels and fields in a more compact layout. You can also insert new tables within the form boundaries and move fields and labels to table cells. Figure 17.10 shows a different layout for the form you created using the Form Page Wizard. The modified layout adds columns to the table that the wizard created and includes a new table for the comments categories, the comments text box, and the Submit and Reset buttons.

FIGURE 17.10

You can use tables to lay out the fields of the form.

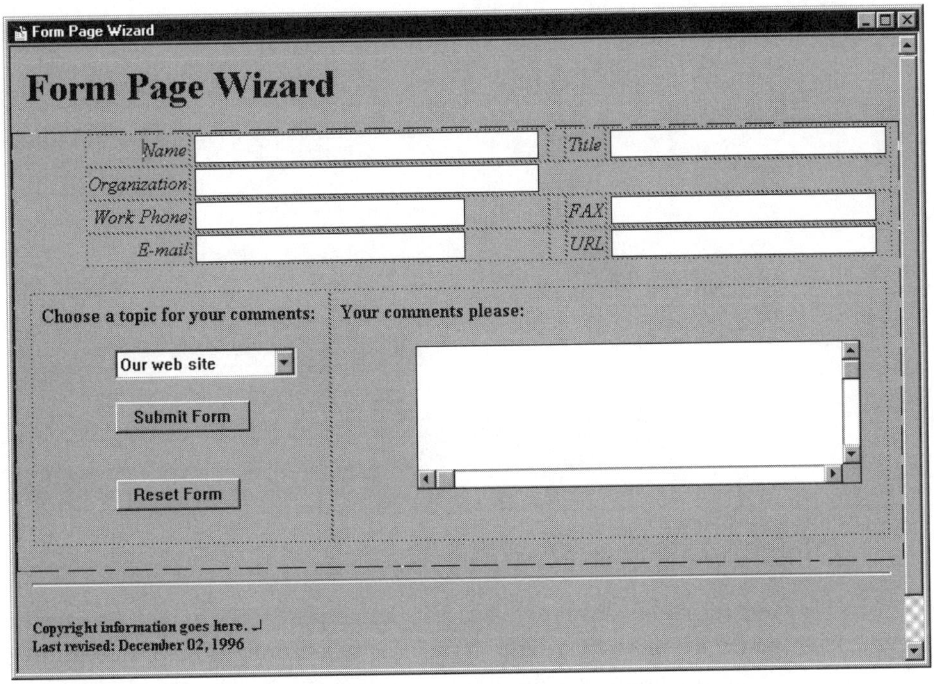

Manipulating the Form

You can manipulate the form together with its contents. Before you manipulate the form, you must select it.

Selecting a Form

To select a form, move the pointer inside the left boundary of the form and double-click when the pointer changes to an arrow pointing into the boundary (see Figure 17.11). The entire area within the form boundary is shown in reverse video when the form is selected.

Deleting, Copying, Cutting, and Pasting a Form

You can use the familiar menu commands and keyboard shortcuts to delete a selected form and to cut, copy, and paste a form to another location on the page or on another page. You can also use drag-and-drop to move or copy a selected form to another location. You can copy or move a form to a cell in an existing table. Figure 17.11 shows a form embedded in a table cell.

FIGURE 17.11

You can insert a form in a table cell.

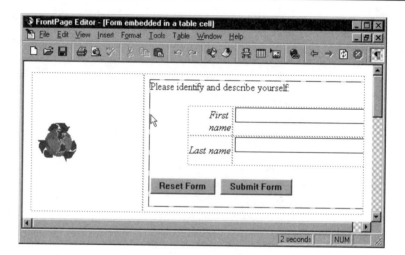

Displaying the Results

Sometimes you want to display the entire results file to the web visitor. For example, you may use a form to collect membership information for a club and want to make the information available to other club members. There are several ways you can display the results file to the user. This section describes three simple ways:

- Create a hyperlink to the results file.
- Merge the results page in the form page using an Include bot.
- Display the form page and the results page as frames.

Creating a Hyperlink to the Results File

You can create a hyperlink to the results file. If you store the results in a text file, the browser displays the results in the helper application that has been designated for displaying text files. If you store the results in a web page, the browser displays the results page in the browser.

Including the Results Page in the Form Page

When you store the results in a web page, you can use the Include bot to display the results in the same page that holds the form (see Chapter 16 for information on the Include bot). You need to include a message that tells the user to refresh the page in order to see the updated results page. The Guest Book page template uses this technique to display existing comments on the guest page. Figure 17.12 shows an example of including the results page.

FIGURE 17.12

Use an Include bot to include the results page in the same page that contains the form.

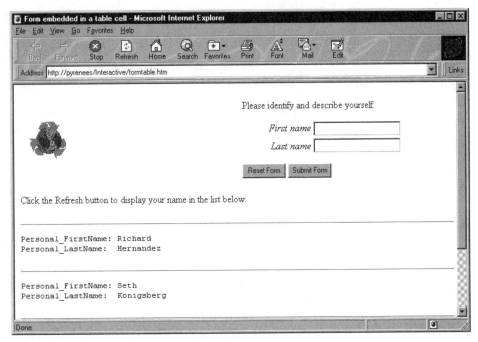

Displaying a Form Page and Results in Frames

When you store the results in a web page, you can create a frameset that displays the data entry page in one frame and the results page in another frame. This arrangement lets the user scroll the pages independently. See Chapter 15: Understanding Frames for more information on creating framed pages.

PART

III

Creating Web Pages

To explore creating a frameset to display a form and the form results:

1. Use the Form Page Wizard to create a new page with a data entry form to collect contact information including name, work phone, fax, and e-mail. Create the page with the page URL collect.htm and the title Collect Data. Specify that the server store the results in a web page with the base name collectrslt.

2. Modify the Collect Data page as shown in Figure 17.13, and then click the Save button in the toolbar to save the page.

FIGURE 17.13

Use the Form Page Wizard to create the Collect Data page.

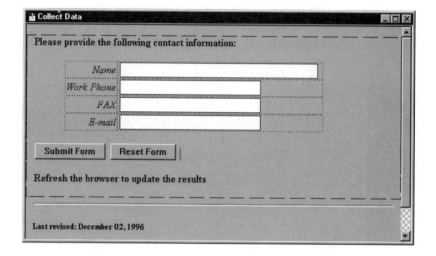

3. Use the Frames Wizard to create a frameset. Elect to create a custom grid with one row and two columns. In the Edit Frame Attributes dialog, click in the left frame in the graphic, type **formentry** as the name of the frame and type **collect .htm** as the source URL. Click in the right frame of the graphic, and type **formresults** as the name of the frame and **collectrslt.htm** as the source URL.

4. Save the frameset with the title Form in a Frame and the URL frameform.htm.

5. Start up a browser and type the URL **http://localhost/interactive/frameform.htm**. Figure 17.14 shows the frameset with the data entry page on the left. The right frame is blank because the results file hasn't been created yet. After you submit the first data, the server creates the results page. Thereafter, the entire results page is displayed in the right frame.

The first time you browse to the frameset, the right frame is empty because the results page hasn't been created.

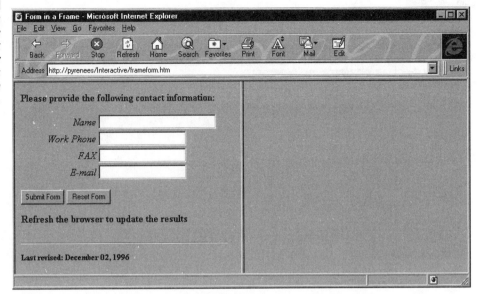

6. Enter some information and submit the form. The browser displays the default confirmation page in the left frame.(see Figure 17.15a). Click the hyperlink on the confirmation page to display the data entry page in the left frame.

7. Click the browser's Refresh button to update the results page. The browser displays the results page in the right frame (see Figure 17.15b).

Inserting a Form into an Existing Page

There are two ways to insert a new form into an existing page: you can use the Form Page Wizard or you can start from scratch.

Using the Form Page Wizard

The easiest way to create a new form for collecting data is to use the Form Page Wizard and then modify the results. The wizard won't let you insert the new form into an existing page. Instead, you use the wizard to create a new page containing the new form and then move the form to the existing page. Here are the steps.

1. Choose File ➤ New from the Editor menu bar, choose Form Page Wizard from the New Page dialog, and click OK.

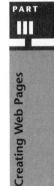

PART

III

Creating Web Pages

FIGURE 17.15

The confirmation page is displayed in the left frame (a). Refresh the browser to display the updated results file in the right frame (b).

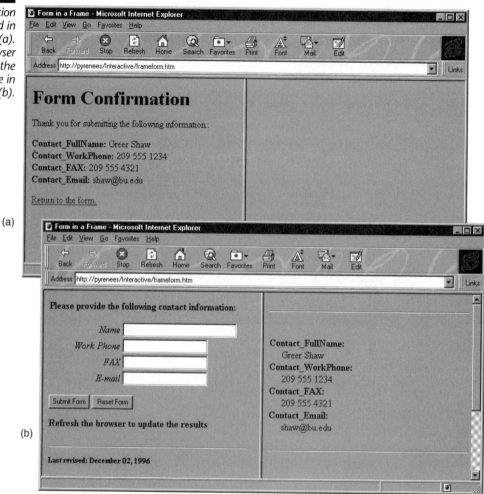

(a)

(b)

2. Use the dialogs of the wizard to design the data entry fields for the form. The wizard adds push buttons to submit the form to the server and to clear the data entry fields. By default, the wizard uses the Save Results bot as the form handler and you must specify the name of the file for storing the results. Alternatively, you can specify a Custom CGI script.

3. After the wizard creates the new page, select the form by double-clicking in its extreme upper-left corner. Right-click in the selected form and drag the form to its new location on an existing page.

4. Modify the form by changing its properties and its form handler as discussed in the "Setting Form Properties" section. Change fields and specify data validation rules as explained in the "Understanding Fields" section.

 WARNING

Do not use an Include bot to merge a page with a form into another page. Although the merged page can be created, trying to submit the form generates an error.

Creating a Form from Scratch

You can also create a new form in an existing page by starting from scratch. To create a new form, place the insertion point outside any existing forms in the page, click a field button in the Form Fields toolbar or choose Insert ➤ Form Field from the Editor menu bar, and then choose a field from the flyout menu. After you design the field using its properties dialog, the Editor creates a new form and inserts the field. The "Understanding Fields" section later in this chapter shows you how to design fields and insert additional fields in the form. When you create a new form from scratch, you must insert a push button or an image field for submitting the form to the server and you must specify the script that you want the server to use. If you choose the Save Results bot, you must specify the name of the file or page that you want to use for storing the results. The next section shows you how to set these properties.

 NOTE

You can create a new form in a cell of an existing table by placing the insertion point in the table cell and inserting a form field.

Setting Form Properties

Like all other web page objects, forms and fields have properties you can set. To view the property dialog for the form, do one of the following:

- Right-click anywhere in the form and choose Form Properties from the shortcut menu.

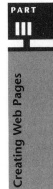

PART

III

Creating Web Pages

- Double-click in the extreme upper-left corner to select the form, and press Alt+Enter.

- Double-click a push button or an image form field and click the Form button on the field's properties dialog. (Figure 17.16 shows the Form button on the Push Button Properties dialog.)

Click the Form button on the Push Button Properties dialog to display the Form Properties dialog.

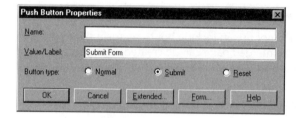

Figure 17.17 shows the Form Properties dialog. Use the Form Properties dialog to specify the name of the script, called the form handler, that you want the server to run when the web visitor submits the form; to specify where you want the output displayed (if the form is in a framed page); and to add hidden fields to the form. The next sections describe the form properties.

The Form Properties dialog

Assigning the Form Handler

When the web visitor clicks the form's submit button, the browser packages the data and sends the data package to the server along with the name of the script the server should use to process the data. The combo list at the top of the Form Properties dialog lists the choices as follows:

WebBot Save Results Component This is the form handler we have been using to process the collected data. This script instructs the server to create and display a form confirmation page—either the default page or a custom page that you specify—and to add the data to the results page or text file stored on the server. Select this choice only if the Web server has FrontPage Server Extensions installed.

WebBot Registration Component This is the form handler that you use to register a new visitor to your web. The data is the user's name and password and the additional information you want to collect. This script instructs the server to create and display a form confirmation page and to add the user's name and password to the list of registered users, called the authentication database. Chapter 18: Understanding Searches and Visitor Registration covers the Registration bot. Select this choice only for FrontPage-enabled Web servers that support this bot, such as the FrontPage Personal Web Server.

WebBot Discussion Component This is the form handler that you use to process a new submission—either a new article or a reply to an existing article—to an online discussion. The data is information about the user, whether the submission is a new article or a reply, and the text of the submission. This script instructs the server to create and display a form confirmation page, to create a new page to display the submission to other visitors, and to update the table of contents page and the text index that FrontPage uses to keep track of articles and replies. Chapter 19: Understanding Discussion Group Webscovers the Discussion bot. Select this choice only if the Web server has FrontPage Server Extensions installed.

Internet Database Connector This is the form handler that you use to send the collected data to an ODBC database, such as Microsoft Access. The script instructs the Web server to run a query based on the collected form data and generate a new page with the query results. Chapter 21: Creating Dynamic Database Pages with Microsoft Access describes the Internet Database Connector form handler. Select this choice only if the Web server has the FrontPage Server Extensions installed and only if the Web server has the Internet Database Connector server extensions, such as the Microsoft Personal Web Server (on Windows 95), the Microsoft Peer Web Server (on Windows NT Workstation), or the Microsoft Internet Information Server (on Windows NT Server).

Custom ISAPI, NSAPI, or CGI Script   You can create your own script to tell the server how you want the form data handled. You can create CGI scripts for any web server, ISAPI scripts for the Microsoft Internet Information Server, and NSAPI scripts for the Netscape web servers. If you are creating a form for a web that will be published by a Web server that doesn't have the FrontPage Server Extensions installed, you'll have to use a custom script.

NOTE

When you use the Form Page Wizard to create a form, the wizard automatically assigns the Save Results bot as the form handler. When you create a data entry form from scratch, FrontPage assigns the Custom ISAPI, NSAPI, or CGI Script by default.

Assigning a Form Name

Often a custom form handler needs to refer to the form. You can enter a name in the Form Name text box.

Assigning a Target Frame

If you use a frameset and display a page that contains a form in one of the frames, you can choose to have the output of the form displayed in another frame. You can specify the default target frame in which you want the browser to display the output, such as the confirmation page, an error page, and the results page.

Defining Hidden Fields

FrontPage lets you define hidden fields for a form and save the values along with the entered values. Hidden fields are useful when you are collecting data using several different forms and you save the data to the same file. For example, in the Corporate Presence web discussed in Chapter 4, each product has its own page containing the product description, and a form that the web visitor can use to request additional information. For efficient handling of the requests, you may decide to store all of the product information requests in the same file. You need a way to identify the product that a user wants to know about. You could ask the user to fill in a product name field in the form, but a better solution is to define a hidden field for each form that identifies the product. When the user submits the form on a product page, the value in the hidden field is packaged with the entered data and sent to the server. The server saves the product name along with the user's contact information.

The name of the field and the value you want to submit should be entered in the Hidden Fields text box. For example, if the product name field is ProductName, and you are creating the product information request form for the product named Elan, you would click the Add button and enter the information in the Name/Value Pair dialog, as shown in Figure 17.18a, and click OK to create the hidden field (see Figure 17.18b). After defining a hidden field, you can click the Modify button to review the Name/Value Pair dialog for the field, or you can click the Remove button if you want to delete the hidden field.

FIGURE 17.18

Use hidden fields to submit information that you specify along with the data that the web visitor supplies.

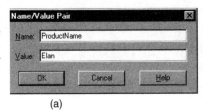

(a)

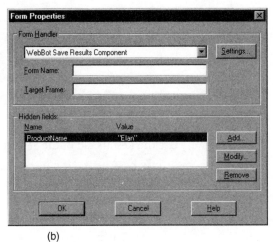

(b)

Form Handler Settings for the Save Results Bot

After you choose a form handler in the Form Properties dialog, you can specify additional information to tell the web server how to handle the data. Click the Settings button to the right of the form handler combo list to display the Settings dialog for the handler. Each type of handler has its own Settings dialog. This chapter describes the settings for the Save Results bot. (See Chapter 18 for information on the Registration bot settings, Chapter 19 for information on the Discussion bot settings, and Chapter 20 for information on the Internet Database Connector and Custom scripts handler settings.)

Setting Properties for the Results File

The settings for the Save Results bot are arranged in three tabs (see Figure 17.19).

PART

III

Creating Web Pages

FIGURE 17.19

Use the Results tab to set properties for the results file.

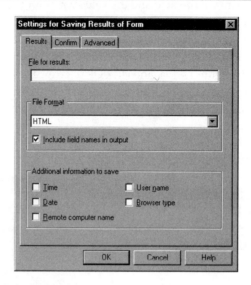

Use the Results tab of the Settings dialog to specify the following:

File for results   Enter the name of the file that you want to use for storing the results. If the file does not exist, the server creates it for you. To save the results to a page or file in the current web, enter the page URL; to save the results to a page or file anywhere in your server's file system, specify the absolute filename and folder. For example, to save a text file named collect.txt to the folder in your server's C: drive named Collection, enter **C:\Collection\collect.txt**.

File Format   You can specify the format for the storage file and whether you want to include the names of the fields or just the date that the user entered. The Form Page Wizard provides only two file formats, a web page and a text file, but you can specify any of four formats for a web page and four formats for the text file. Figure 17.20 shows the four HTML formats, as follows:

- HTML
- HTML definition list
- HTML bulleted list
- Formatted text within HTML

FIGURE 17.20

The HTML formats for storing data as a web page

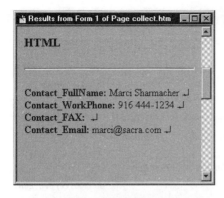
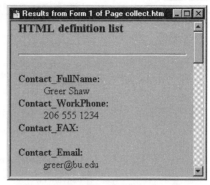
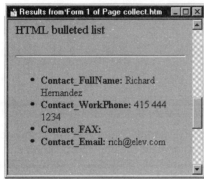

The HTML formats let you create a results page that is easy to read, however the server must create a new HTML results page each time the form is submitted. Generating the updated results page takes time, so unless you plan to display the results as part of your web, you should use one of the text file formats instead.

Figure 17.21 shows the four text file formats, as follows:

- Formatted text
- Text database using comma as a separator
- Text database using tab as a separator
- Text database using space as a separator

You can use the Formatted text format to create a results file that is easy to read. When you intend to use the text file as input to a database application such as Microsoft Access or a spreadsheet application such as Microsoft Excel, you should specify one of the text database formats.

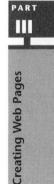

PART

III

Creating Web Pages

FIGURE 17.21

The text formats for storing data as a text file

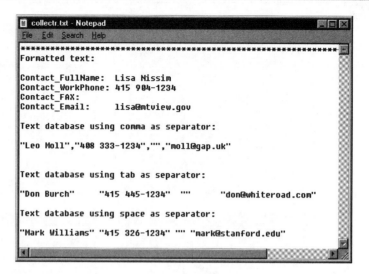

NOTE

In Chapter 21: Creating Dynamic Database Pages with Microsoft Access, you'll learn how to enter the results of a form directly into an Access database.

You can specify whether to include the names of the fields or just the data that the user entered. Clear the Include field names in output check box to omit the field names.

NOTE

The Form Page Wizard uses the HTML definition list format if you choose to store the results as a web page and the Text database using tab as a separator file format if you choose to save the results as a text file. In either case, the wizard includes the field names along with the data.

Additional information to save   You can save additional information with the submission, including the current time and date, and the web visitor's user name, browser type, and computer name. Check the options you want to include.

Specifying Custom Confirmation and Validation Failure Pages

Use the Confirm tab of the Settings dialog (see Figure 17.22a) to specify the page URL of a custom confirmation page that the server sends to the browser instead of the default confirmation page. Either type the URL directly or click the Browse button to create a link to the page in the current web.

You can also specify the page URL of a custom validation failure page that the server sends to the browser when any field in the form fails to satisfy the validation rule you set (validation rules are discussed in the "Field Properties" section). If you don't specify a page, the Save Results bot creates a default validation failure page. If validation rules have not been specified, the text box is grayed out, as shown in Figure 17.22a.

Setting Advanced Properties

FrontPage lets you create two files with different formats for storing the results so you can create one file that is easy to read and another file for importing to a database or spreadsheet application. You use the Advanced tab of the Settings dialog (see Figure 17.22b) to specify a second file and file format for storing results.

FIGURE 17.22

Use the Confirm tab to specify custom confirmation and validation failure pages (a). Use the Advanced tab to specify a second storage file and select the fields to submit to the server (b).

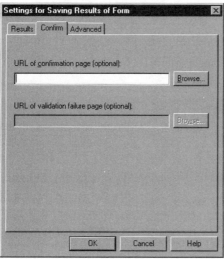

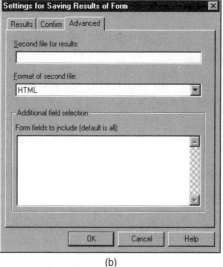

(a)   (b)

PART

III

Creating Web Pages

You use the Additional Field Selection text box to change the order that you want the fields saved to the results file. You can also select a subset of the fields. If you leave the text box blank, FrontPage stores all of the fields in the order in which they appear on the form. To change the order or the selection, enter the name of each field in the order you want it to be stored and separate the field names with commas.

Using a CGI Script to Send by E-Mail

You can use a custom CGI script to send the results of a form as an e-mail attachment instead of saving the results in a file. To submit results as an e-mail attachment, do the following:

1. Create the form. Right-click in the form and choose Form Properties in the shortcut menu.

2. Choose Custom ISAPI, NSAPI, or CGI Script in the Form Handler combo list and then click the Settings button. In the Action text box, type **mailto: *e-mail-address***, where e-mailaddress is the e-mail address to which you want the results sent. Make sure the Method combo box is set to POST.

3. Click OK twice and then click the Save button in the toolbar.

When the Web visitor clicks the Submit button, the visitor's browser sends the results as an e-mail attachment. For this process to work, the visitor's e-mail program and Web browser must support this action.

Netscape Navigator 3.0 supports this method of sending form results as an e-mail attachment but the Microsoft Internet Explorer 2.0 and 3.0 browsers do not.

Understanding Fields

This section shows you how to add a field to a form and set field properties. You'll learn how to use five kinds of data entry fields and two kinds of form submission fields.

Adding a Field

To insert a new field in a page, place the insertion point where you want the field, and do either of the following:

- Choose Insert ➤ Form Field from the Editor menu bar and then choose the type of field in the flyout menu.

- Click a field button in the Form Fields toolbar.

There are five kinds of form fields for data entry, including the one-line text box, scrolling text box, check box, radio button, and drop-down menu, and two form fields for submitting data, including the push button and the image form field. The Form Fields toolbar has buttons for the five data entry fields and the push button field (Figure 17.23). The image form field doesn't have a toolbar button, so you must use the menu command to inset it.

The Form Fields toolbar

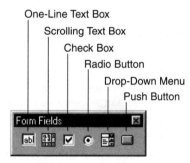

One-Line Text Box
Scrolling Text Box
Check Box
Radio Button
Drop-Down Menu
Push Button

If you placed the insertion point in an existing form, the new field is added to the form. Otherwise, FrontPage creates a new form and inserts the field.

Field Properties

After you insert a form field you can set its properties. Do any of the following to display the properties dialog for a field:

- Double-click the field.
- Right-click the field and choose Form Field Properties in the shortcut menu.
- Click the field and press Alt+Enter.
- Click the field and choose Edit ➤ Form Field Properties.

Each type of field has its own set of properties. However, all fields have a Name property. The browser and the server use the Name property to identify the field. The Name property is required for all fields. When you use the Form Page Wizard, the wizard may enter the Name property automatically. When you insert a field, the Editor assigns a default name. You can change the name in the fields properties dialog. The Name can't have spaces, but you can use an underscore (_) if you want to use two or more words. The Name of a field is not displayed in the web page in either the Editor or a browser. You must display the properties dialog to view or change the field's name.

PART

III

Creating Web Pages

All data entry fields have a second property, called Value. The Value property of a field is the text that the web visitor types or the choice that the visitor makes. You can specify an initial value in the Properties dialog; this is the value that the browser displays when the visitor browses to the page, clicks a reset button for the form, or refreshes the page in the browser. You can also display a *label* for the field by typing the label directly on the web page; the label identifies the field to the user. The label is not a field property and is ignored when the visitor submits the form to the server.

When the visitor enters data and choices in the data entry fields and clicks the submit button or image, the browser collects the name and the value in the field at the moment for each field in the form and sends the name-value pairs together with the name of the form handler to the server.

In addition to the Name, the properties dialog for each type of form field has several other properties that you use to design the field. A new feature of FrontPage 97 is that you can set a validation rule for testing the value that the visitor enters in a form field. For example, you can specify that the visitor must enter a value in a field and that the value must be text or a number that falls in a specified range. If the data does not satisfy the validation rule, the Web server sends a validation failure page and the form data is not accepted.

NOTE

Like other property sheets in the Editor, each form field properties dialog has an Extended button. You click this button to display a dialog for specifying attributes for the field that FrontPage doesn't recognize. See the "Understanding Extended Attributes" section in Chapter 10 for more information.

Data Entry Fields

Table 17.2 lists the five kinds of data entry fields.

TABLE 17.2: DATA ENTRY FORM FIELDS

Type	Description
One-Line text box	For entering one line of text. You can specify the maximum number of characters or display asterisks for a password. You can specify validation rules for the value.
Scrolling text box	For entering text entries of unlimited length. You can specify validation rules for the value.

Continued ▶

TABLE 17.2: DATA ENTRY FORM FIELDS (CONTINUED)

Type	Description
Check box	For making a single yes/no type choice, or for selecting one or more items in a group of check boxes.
Radio button	For selecting one item in a group of radio buttons. You can specify validation rules for the value.
Drop-down menu	For selecting one or more items in the menu list. You can specify validation rules for the choices.

One-Line Text Boxes

One-line text boxes are used to collect text. Although you can use this field to collect text of unlimited length, normally you use the one-line text box to collect a single piece of information and use the scrolling text box to collect long text entries, such as comments or e-mail messages. Use the Text Box Properties dialog (see Figure 17.24a) to set the following properties:

Name   The name must begin with a letter and can contain no spaces.

Initial Value   Enter the initial value.

Width in characters   Specify the width of the field by entering an integer for the number of characters in the Properties dialog; the default width is 20 characters. You can also change the width of the field by clicking on the field in the Editor and dragging one of the resizing squares at the corners and the sides of the field. Specify the maximum number of characters that the visitor can type in the field; the maximum is 256 characters. After the visitor has typed the maximum number of characters, the browser refuses to accept additional characters and may beep to indicate the limit has been reached. If the maximum number of allowed characters is greater than field size, the field scrolls horizontally as the visitor types; normally, the visitor can press arrow keys to view the characters that have scrolled out of view.

Password field   You can choose to use the field as a password field; when you choose the Yes option, the browser displays as asterisk for each character that the user types.

PART

III

Creating Web Pages

Setting Validation Rules   Click the Validation button to display the Text Box Validation dialog (see Figure 17.24b). The first property is the Display Name property. The Display Name is the name that validation failure messages use to identify the field. If you don't enter a Display name, the server uses the field's Name in the message. When the field's Name and label are different, the Web visitor may have difficulty determining which field failed the validation test. In this case, you can make the message easier to interpret by entering the field's label as the Display Name.

Use the dialog to set the following validation rules:

Data Type   You can specify that the field contain text, integers, or numbers, or choose not to constrain the data type.

Text Format   If you specify the text data type, the Text Format choices become available. Specify the types of characters that are permitted, including letters, numbers, white space (such as spaces and tabs), and other permissible characters.

Numeric Format   If you specify the number data type, the Numeric Format choices become available. Specify permissible grouping and decimal characters.

Data Length   For all data types, you can specify whether an entry is required. You can also specify the minimum and maximum length in characters of the entry.

Data Value   You can specify the limits of a permissible range of values for all data types. If the data type is text, or there are no data type constraints, the Web server uses alphabetical comparisons to test the value. If the data type is an integer or number, the server uses numerical comparisons. You can enter limiting values and use the following comparisons in defining the range: Less Than, Greater Than, Less Than Or Equal To, Greater Than Or Equal To, Equal to, and Not Equal To. For example, you can specify that a text value must be Less Than M and Greater Than D to require that the text value start with a letter between D and M.

When the visitor submits a form, the Web server tests the data submitted for each field, and displays a message when a value does not satisfy the validation rule set for the field (see Figure 17.24c).

FIGURE 17.24

Use the Text Box Properties (a) and the Text Box Validation (b) dialogs to design a text box field. When a submitted value fails the validation test for the field, the browser displays a message (c).

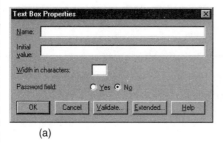

(a)

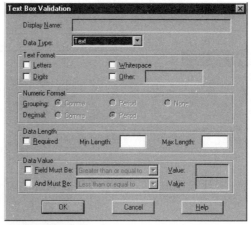

(b)

(c)

NOTE

The Web server tests the validation rules you set in the FrontPage Validation dialogs. Alternatively, you can use scripting languages such as VBScript or JavaScript to create validation rules that are tested by a Web browser that understands these scripting languages. See Chapter 20 for more information on scripting.

Scrolling Text Boxes

A scrolling text box is used to collect longer text input, such as comments or e-mail messages. Figure 17.25 shows the Scrolling Text Box Properties dialog. You enter the name in the Name text box and text you want to display initially in the Initial Value text box. You can set the dimensions of the text box by entering its width as a number of characters and its height as a number of lines; the default dimensions are 20 characters in width and two lines in height. You can also change the dimensions by clicking the text box in the Editor and dragging a resizing square at a corner or side of the text box.

PART

III

Creating Web Pages

Click the Validation button to display the Text Box Validation dialog (see Figure 17.24b). See the previous section for information on the validation rules you can set for text box fields.

FIGURE 17.25

Use the Scrolling Text Box Properties to set the name, an initial value, and the size for the text box.

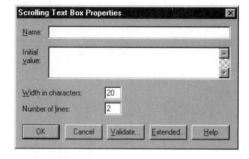

Check Boxes

A check box field has two states: either the box is checked or it isn't checked. You can use the check box field in two ways. Use a single check box field to give the user a choice of two options; for example, to answer a yes or no question. Or, use a group of check box fields to present a list of choices and let the user select any number of items. Figure 17.26 shows examples of the two ways to use check boxes.

FIGURE 17.26

Use a single check box to give two choices (a), or use a group of check boxes to allow the visitor to choose any number of options (b).

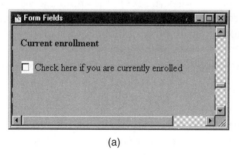

(a)

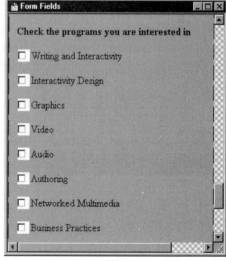

(b)

Figure 17.27 shows the Check Box Properties dialog. The settings depend on whether you are using a single check box or a group of check boxes.

FIGURE 17.27

*The Check Box
Properties dialog*

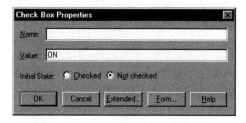

Single check box   When you are using a single check box, you can specify the Name of the check box to describe the information you are collecting, and set the Value as the text you want to submit if the user checks the box. If the user doesn't check the box, no value is sent. You can specify the initial state of the check box as checked or unchecked. For example, the single check box in Figure 17.26a is named Enrolled, the Value is Yes, and the Initial State is Unchecked.

Group of check boxes   When you are using a group of check boxes, you can use a different name for each check box and have the browser send separate name-value pairs for each check box. As an alternative, you can set the Name property for each check box to the same name and set the Value to a description of the choice. For example, for the group check box example in Figure 17.26b, the Name property is Program for all the check boxes to Program, the Initial State is Unchecked, and the Value property for each check box describes the choice, such as Writing for the check box that has the label Writing and Interactivity. When two or more check boxes have the same Name property, the server lists the values separated by commas.

Figure 17.28 shows the default confirmation page for the single check box and the group of check boxes for a user who is not enrolled.

Radio Buttons

A radio button field has two states: either the button is selected or it isn't selected. Although it is possible to use a single radio button for the answer to a "yes or no" question, normally you use a group of radio buttons to present a list of choices, and let the user select one of the items. The difference between a group of check boxes and a group of radio buttons is that the user can check any number of check boxes, but can select only one radio button in the group.

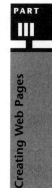

PART

III

Creating Web Pages

FIGURE 17.28

The confirmation form for the single check box and the group of checkboxes

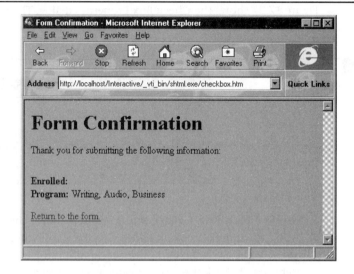

Figure 17.29a shows the Radio Button Properties dialog. You set the Name property for every radio button in the group to the same name and set the Value for each radio button to a description of the option. You can set the Initial State for one of the radio buttons to Selected; if you try to set the initial state of a second radio button to Selected, FrontPage automatically sets the initial state of the first radio button to Not selected. Click the Validate button to display the Radio Button Validation dialog (see Figure 17.29b). You can set the Display Name to the name you want the validation failure message to refer to. Check the Data Required check box to require that the web visitor select a choice.

FIGURE 17.29

The Radio Button Properties dialog (a) and the Radio Button Validation dialog (b)

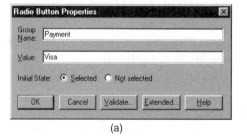

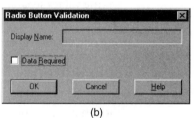

(a)   (b)

Figure 17.30a shows an example of using a group of radio buttons. The Name property is set to Payment for all the radio buttons, the Initial State is set to Not selected, and the Value property for each radio button describes the option, such as Visa for the radio button with the label Visa. Figure 17.30b shows the default confirmation page when the user elects to pay by check.

FIGURE 17.30

Use radio buttons to give the visitor a single choice (a). The default confirmation page displays the Name of the group and the Value of the selected option (b).

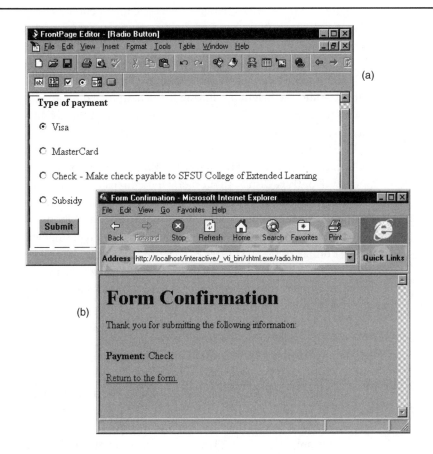

Drop-Down Menus

Use the drop-down menu field to display a list of choices. You can specify that the visitor may select a single item or a group of items. Figure 17.31a shows the Drop-Down Menu Properties dialog. You enter the name of the field in the Name text box. To specify a menu choice, click the Add button to display the Add Choice dialog shown in Figure 17.31b. Enter the text you want to display in the menu in the Choice text box. You can either send this value to the browser or you can specify that you want to send an alternate value by clicking the Specify Value box and entering a different value in the text box. For example, you can display Writing and Interactivity as a menu choice, but send Writing to the browser. You can specify whether the menu choice is initially selected or not.

After specifying menu choices, use the buttons at the right of the Properties dialog in Figure 17.31a to make changes. Select the menu choice you want to change, and click the Modify button—or double-click the menu item—to display the Modify Choice dialog, click Remove to delete the selected menu choice, and click the Move Up or Move Down buttons to change the position of the selected menu choice.

You can specify the height of the field by entering the number of rows you want to display. Adjust the height by clicking the field in the Editor and dragging any of the resize squares at the field's corners and sides. If you set the height to a number smaller than the number of menu choices, FrontPage displays a scrolling list. (Some browsers include the vertical scroll bar even if you set the height to the number of menu choices.) As an exception, if you set the Allow multiple selections option to No and the Height to one row, FrontPage displays a drop-down menu instead of a scrolling list.

You specify whether the visitor can select multiple items by choosing Yes for Allow multiple selection. When you allow multiple selections, FrontPage automatically displays the field as a scrolling list if you set the height to a smaller number than the actual number of menu choices (see Figure 17.31b). Each browser has its own way of allowing multiple selections; for example, with Microsoft Internet Explorer 3.0, you press the Ctrl key to make selections of discontiguous items and the Shift key to click and drag to select contiguous items.

Click the Validate button in the properties dialog to display the Drop-Down Menu Validation dialog (see Figure 17.31c). You can enter a Display Name to be used in place of the field name in validation failure messages, and you can specify that the visitor must make a selection.

FrontPage allows you to use the first menu item to provide instructions to visitors on how to use the menu. If you use the first menu item this way, check the Disallow First Item check box so that the first menu item cannot be sent as a choice.

As an example, Figure 17.32a shows a set of menu choices, none of which is selected initially, and the corresponding values that are sent to the server when the form is submitted. Figure 17.32b shows the field in a browser when the height is set to 6 and multiple selections are allowed.

FIGURE 17.31

The Drop-Down Menu dialogs to design the field (a), to add a menu item (b), and to set validation rules (c).

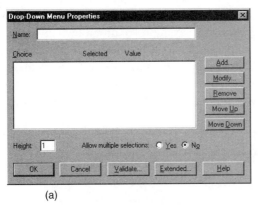

(a)

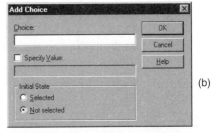

(b)

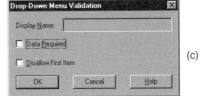

(c)

FIGURE 17.32

You can display one set of menu choices and send different values to the server (a). When you allow multiple choices, the field displays as a scrolling list instead of a drop-down menu (b).

(a)

(b)

PART III

Creating Web Pages

When you allow a single selection, you can display the field as a scrolling list by setting the height to an integer greater than one or as a drop-down menu by setting the height to one. Figure 17.33 shows two examples of drop-down menus. In the field on the left, the visitor is limited to a single selection and the number of rows is set to one to display the list when the visitor clicks the down arrow. In the field on the right, the visitor can make multiple selections and the number of rows is set to the number of menu choices so that the visitor doesn't have to scroll to view the choices.

FIGURE 17.33

You can use the drop-down menu field as a drop-down menu or as a list.

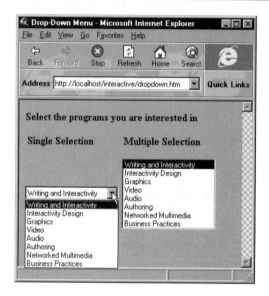

Form Submission Fields

You can use either a push button or an image field to submit the form to the server.

Push Buttons

FrontPage provides two types of push buttons: a submit button to send the form's data to the server, and a reset button to set the fields to the initial values you specified. Figure 17.34 shows the Push Button Properties dialog. Specify the type by choosing Submit or Reset and enter a label in the Value/Label text box. FrontPage submits the label as the Value property of the button. Click the Form button to display the Form Properties dialog when you can specify the form handler and the storage file.

If you are using one of the FrontPage bots as form handler, the Name property is optional. If you enter a value for the Name property, the browser submits the name along with the entry in the Value/Label text box; otherwise a name-value pair is not submitted for the button. You can include two or more submission fields. For example, you can have both a submit button and an image field; in this case, all the submission fields execute the same form handler and save the results to the same storage file, even if you specify different storage files for each submitting field. By contrast, if you create your own form handlers, you can place two or more buttons on a form, each button with a unique name, and use each button to run a different form handler.

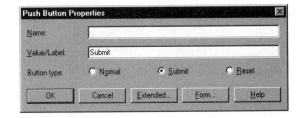

FIGURE 17.34

The Push Button Properties dialog

Image Fields

An image field can be used to submit a form. To insert an image field, place the insertion point where you want the image, choose Insert ➤ Form Field from the Editor menu bar, and choose Image from the flyout menu. Choose the image you want to display from the list in the Image dialog. Double-click the image field to display the Image Form Field Properties dialog (see Figure 17.35).

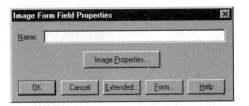

FIGURE 17.35

The Image Form Field Properties dialog

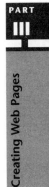

Enter the name for the field in the Name text box. You can change the properties of the image by clicking the Image Properties button (see Chapter 13 for information on setting image properties). Click the Form button to display the Form Properties dialog where you can set the form handler and specify the name of the storage file.

When a visitor clicks the image in the browser, the browser sends the image's Name property and the x and y coordinates of the point that you clicked (using the image's coordinate system). As an example, Figure 17.36 shows an image field as a Submit button and the default confirmation page after submitting the form. When you use a FrontPage bot as a form handler, the coordinate information is ignored. However, if you create a custom form handler, you can provide instructions that depend on the coordinates of the point you clicked.

When the visitor clicks an image form field (a), the coordinates of the clicked point are sent to the server (b).

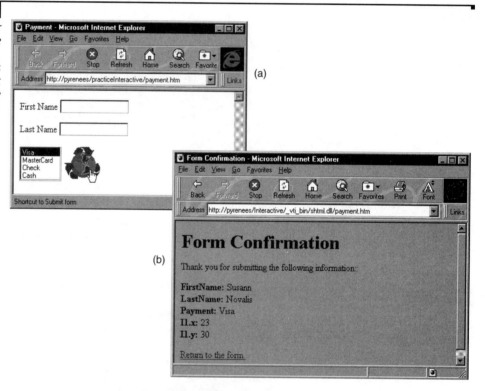

Creating a Custom Confirmation Page

When you use a FrontPage bot as a form handler, the server automatically creates a page to confirm all of the values submitted. You can also create a custom confirmation page and have the browser display your custom page instead. There are at least three reasons for creating a custom confirmation page:

- To create your own confirmation message that includes only some of the values entered instead of confirming all values

- To include a link to another page or include a navigation bar to the main pages in the web instead of the default link back to the form page
- To specify styles for the confirmation page to harmonize with the other pages in the web instead of the default style

Using the Confirmation Field Bot

To create a confirmation page, you start with a new page, add the explanatory text, and insert a Confirmation bot for each field that you want to confirm. When the browser displays the confirmation page, each Confirmation bot displays the contents of the field you specified. After creating the page, assign the confirmation page in the settings dialog of the form handler.

As an example, we'll create a confirmation form for the Collect Data page we created earlier in the chapter using the Form Page Wizard. We'll confirm only the name and the e-mail address, create a hyperlink to the web's home page, and specify that the confirmation page get its styles from the Collect Data page. First, we'll set a background color for the form and create a hyperlink from the web's Home Page.

1. Click the Open button in the toolbar, choose Collect Data in the Open File dialog, and click OK. Right-click and choose Page Properties from the shortcut menu. Click the Background tab, choose a background color, and click OK to close the dialog. Press Ctrl+S to save the page.

2. Click the Open button in the toolbar, choose the Home Page in the Open File dialog, and click OK. Create a text hyperlink to the Collect Data by clicking the Collect Data page icon in the Explorer and dropping the text hyperlink on the Home Page. Press Ctrl+S to save the page.

3. Click the New button in the Editor's toolbar to display a new blank page. Enter the explanatory text, including labels for the fields you want to confirm, and create a text hyperlink to the Home Page. In the next step, we'll set the styles for the confirmation page to match the styles for the data entry page.

4. Right-click and choose the Page Properties command from the shortcut menu. Click the Background tab, click the Get Background and Colors from Page option, click the Browse button, and double-click Collect Data. Click OK to close the dialog. Figure 17.37a shows the form.

5. Place the insertion point at the end of the second line, and click the Insert Web-Bot Component button in the toolbar. Choose Confirmation Field in the Insert WebBot Component dialog and click OK. Enter the name of the field you want to confirm. The Form Page Wizard used Contact_FullName for the name of the field with the Name label and Contact_Email for the name of the field with the E-Mail address label. Enter Contact_FullName to confirm the field with the Name label and click OK.

6. Repeat Step 5 to insert a Confirmation Field bot at the end of the third line to confirm the field named Contact_Email. Figure 17.37b shows the form with the two Confirmation Field bots.

7. Save the page as Collect Data Confirmation with the URL _private/confirm.htm. Normally, confirmation pages are private pages that you store in the _private directory.

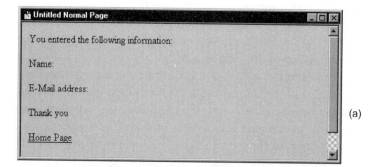

(a)

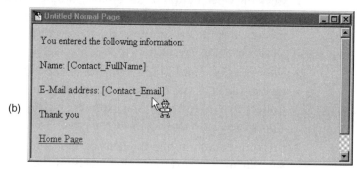

(b)

Assigning the Confirmation Page

Now that the custom confirmation page is complete, the next step is to tell the server to use the custom page instead of the default page.

1. Click the Window menu in the Editor menu bar and select Collect Data. Right-click anywhere in the form and choose the Form Properties command. Click the Settings button in the Form Properties dialog. Click the Confirm tab, click the Browse button, locate the confirm.htm page in the _private folder, and double-click. Click OK twice to close the Settings dialog and the Form Properties dialog.

2. Click the Save button in the toolbar.

3. Click the Window menu in the Editor menu bar and select Collect Data. Click the Preview in Browser button in the toolbar. Click the hyperlink in the Home Page to display the Collect Data form. Fill out the form and click the Submit button. Figure 17.38 shows the confirmation page.

FIGURE 17.38

The Web server sends back the custom confirmation page.

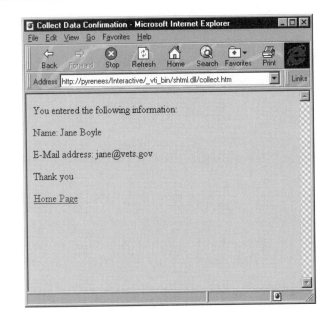

For More...

This chapter has shown you how to create data entry forms for collecting information from a Web visitor. You've seen how to use a CGI Script to send the form results as an e-mail attachment and how to save the results to a file using the Save Results form bot. For information on using other form handlers see the following:

- Chapter 18: Understanding Searches and Visitor Registration shows you how to use the Search and the Registration bots.
- Chapter 19: Understanding Discussion Group Webs shows you how to use the Discussion bot.
- Chapter 21: Creating Dynamic Database Pages with Microsoft Access shows you how to use the Internet Database Connector to send form results directly to an Access database.

PART

III

Creating Web Pages

Chapter

18

Understanding Searches and Visitor Registration

Understanding Searches and Visitor Registration

I n addition to allowing you to collect information from your Web visitors using forms, FrontPage provides other ways for the visitor to interact with your web site. This chapter describes two web features you can add to your web using FrontPage. The first feature is the text search, which allows a visitor to search the pages of your web to find all pages containing a specified text string. In large webs, this feature makes it much easier for the web visitor to locate information. You add a text search using the Search bot, officially called WebBot Search Component. The second feature is the ability to require that visitors register in your web. This feature does not work with many Web servers, however if you are using a web server that does allow user registration, such as the FrontPage Personal Web Server, you'll find this feature useful for tracking the visitors to your web. User registration depends on the Registration bot, officially called the WebBot Registration Component.

NOTE

To work through the examples in this chapter, you'll need to replace the Wales-Ireland web you created in previous chapters with a modified version on the book's CD-ROM. Open your existing Wales-Ireland web and choose File ➤ Delete FrontPage Web from the Explorer menu bar to delete the web. Then choose File ➤ Import and use the Import Web Wizard to create a new web named Wales-Ireland-Ch18 and to import all the files from the web named Wales-Ireland-Ch18 stored in the Webs folder on the book's CD-ROM.

Searching a Web

FrontPage includes a text search tool as part of the FrontPage Server Extensions. When you create a new web on a FrontPage-enabled Web server, FrontPage creates a text index for all words on every page in the web. When you save a page in the Editor or recalculate links in the Explorer, the Web server updates the text index. FrontPage uses the text index when you run the Find and Replace commands. When you are working on a page and run the Edit ➤ Find and Edit ➤ Replace commands from the Editor menu bar, the FrontPage search engine uses the text index to find the word or phrase you specify. When you run the Tools ➤ Find and Tools ➤ Replace commands from the Explorer menu bar, the search engine finds all pages that contain the specified word or phrase. The text index for a page includes only the words that that you can edit in place on the page.

NOTE

The text index for a page does not include any of the following: the page title (which you edit in the Page Properties dialog) or the page URL (which you edit in the Explorer); words on any included pages unless the words are also on the page itself; and words that you specify in a field property sheet, such as button labels, names of fields, initial values for fields, and drop-down menu choices. The text index of a page includes the words that you can edit in place.

FrontPage makes a search engine available for you to add a text search capability to your web. A *search engine* is the software that searches an index and returns a list of matching pages. To use the FrontPage search engine, you insert a search form in a page. When the Web visitor enters a word or combination of words in a search form and submits the form, the Web server searches through the text index and creates a modifed version of the search page that displays a list of links to pages that contain the search word or words. The list of found pages is displayed below the search form. By default, the server searches every public page in the web. The pages in the _private folder are not included in the search.

NOTE

When you create a disk-based web, FrontPage does not create text indexes. A disk-based web is identified by a drive letter and backslashes, as in the example D:\Webs\PCTC. A server-based web is identified by http: and forward slashes, as in the example http://pyrenees/PCTC.

NOTE

If the web contains a discussion group, the pages of the discussion group are stored in a separate hidden folder (see Chapter 19 for more information on discussion groups). The Frontpage-enabled Web server maintains a separate text index for a discussion group folder, and you can specify a separate search of the pages in a discussion group folder.

You should consider including the text search capability in your web site. Include a hyperlink to a search page or include a search form on every web page. Text searching is an essential navigational capability that busy web visitors expect. The FrontPage web wizards and web templates include search pages, and FrontPage makes it easy to add this valuable capability to your own web.

Creating a Search Form

There are two ways to create a search form: use the Search Page template to create a new page containing a search form or insert a Search bot in an existing page.

Using the Search Page Template

You can use the Search Page template to create a new page for the search. The Search Page template creates a new page with the search form as one section and a description of the ways to enter the words or parts of words that you want to search for (see Figure 18.1a). The description gives the web visitor instructions on how to design a search that includes or excludes pages using the keywords AND, OR, and NOT and combining parentheses with the keywords, and that uses the asterisk for wildcard searches. You should include this description of the query language in any search page you add to your web (see Figure 18.1b for a more compact version of the description).

FIGURE 18.1

The Search Page template creates a page with a search form (a) and instructions for creating searches (b)

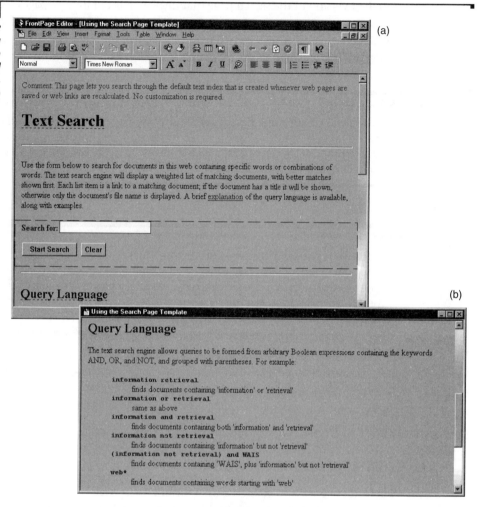

You can modify the search page to include the look and feel of your web by inserting text, images, and other web objects and by using your web's styles, headers, and footers. However, your ability to modify the search form is limited. The Search bot inserts a special kind of form that contains three fields: a single one-line text box with a label, a submit push button, and a reset push button. You cannot directly edit any part of this form—you cannot add additional fields or delete any of the three fields, and you cannot modify, label, or resize the text box. The only way to change the search form is to change properties in its properties dialog. To change how the bot is configured, double-click the search form and modify its properties, as explained in the next section.

Configuring the Search Bot

Insert the Search bot at the insertion point in an existing page by choosing Insert ➤ WebBot Component from the Editor menu bar and choosing Search from the list of bot components. You must set all of the field and search form properties using the WebBot Search Component Properties dialog (see Figure 18.2) as follows:

Label for Input   Enter the label you want to display.

Width in Characters   Specify the width of the search text box. The default width is 20 characters.

Label for Buttons   Specify the label for the Start Search button and the Clear button.

Word List to Search   Specify whether to search all the public pages of the web by typing All or to search the pages of a discussion group stored in the web by typing the name of the discussion group folder. The name of a discussion group folder starts with an underscore and is created automatically by FrontPage when you create the discussion group (see Chapter 19 for more information). The Search bot does not search the web's _private folder or a discussion group's _private folder.

Additional information to display in the search results list   You can elect to include any of the following information:

- Score is a number that that the Web server calculates based on the number of times the word appears on the page and on the target pages of links on the page. The higher the score, the more relevant the page is considered by the server. The pages are ordered in the list according to their scores whether or not you display the number.

- File Date is the date and time that the page was most recently modified.

- File Size is the size of the document in Kbytes.

FIGURE 18.2

The only way to change the search form is to change properties in the WebBot Search Component Properties dialog.

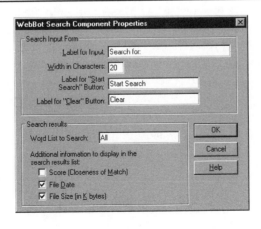

To explore creating a search, we'll use the Search Page template to add a search page to the Wales-Ireland web.

1. Choose File ➤ New from the Editor menu bar or press Ctrl+N, select Search Page in the New Page dialog, and click OK. Modify the search page by deleting blank lines, comments, horizontal lines, and the three lines of the footer. Modify the heading to **Text Search of the Wales-Ireland Web** and change the heading style to Heading 4. In the next two steps, you'll set the styles of the search page to match the web and merge the web's header and footer pages.

2. Right-click the page and choose Page Properties. Click the Background tab, click the Get background and Colors from Page option, and click the Browse button. Locate the styles.htm page in the _private folder and double-click. Click OK to close the Page Properties dialog.

3. Place the insertion point at the left of the heading and press Enter to insert a new line. Click the Insert WebBot Component button in the toolbar, and double-click Include. Click the Browse button in the properties dialog, locate the header.htm page in the _private folder, and double-click. Click OK to close the properties dialog. Place the insertion point at the bottom of the page, and take similar steps to insert an Include bot to merge the footer.htm page.

4. Double-click the search form to display the Search bot properties dialog. Change the width of the text box to 30, check the Score check box, and click OK.

5. Click the Save button in the toolbar, type **Search of the Wales-Ireland Web** as the Page Title, and type **searchweb.htm** as the file path.

6. In the Explorer, click the Folder View button in the toolbar, and double-click the default.htm page in the Contents pane to display the page in the Editor. Click the searchweb.htm page icon in the Explorer, drag the page icon to the Home Page and drop the icon to create a text hyperlink in the line below the Comments and Information hyperlink. Click the Save button in the toolbar.

7. Click the Preview in Browser button in the Editor toolbar. Click the new hyper-link. Type **Irish** in the search text box and click the Start Search push button. When you click the push button to start the search, the web server runs the Search bot program, and locates the public pages that contain the search word. The Web server generates a new page by inserting below the form a table with hyperlinks to each of the matching pages, the date and size of the matching page and the relevance score (see Figure 18.3).

8. Minimize the browser.

FIGURE 18.3

*When you start the
search, the Search
bot locates the
matching pages
and modifies the
search page by
inserting a table of
the search results.*

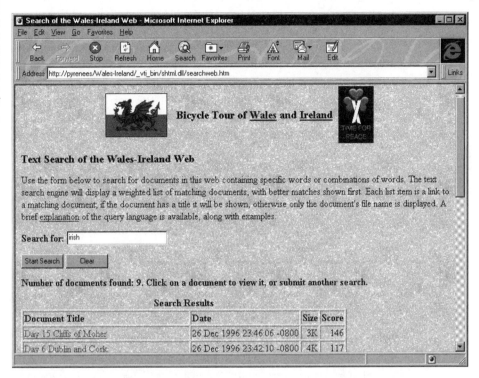

Inserting a Search Bot in an Existing Page

You can also insert a search form in an existing page. To insert a search form, place
the insertion point where you want the form, click the Insert WebBot Component
button in the Standard toolbar, and double-click Search. Configure the search by setting properties in the WebBot Search Component Properties dialog (see Figure 18.2
earlier in the chapter) and click OK. When you use the Search bot, the Editor inserts
only the form and does not insert directions for performing a search or the query language instructions.

Registering to Use a Web

There are two ways you can control access to a FrontPage web. In the first way, you
allow only visitors who have been registered by the web's administrator, as explained

in Chapter 9: Administering a Web. In this type of restriction, the administrator assigns one or more username- password combinations. Use this type of controlled access when your web contains information that you want to make available to a specified set of visitors. For example, you can give the same username and password to all purchasers of a product so that they can enter a restricted product-support web. The second way is to allow entry to all visitors who register for your web. In this case, access is controlled but virtually unlimited—the web is public to all visitors who are willing to register. Use this type of controlled access to track contact information for your visitors or to build a membership list of visitors.

NOTE

Not all web servers allow self-registration. The registration forms discussed in this section work on the FrontPage Personal Web Server, O'Reilly's WebSite and on other Web servers, but do not work on the Microsoft Personal Web Server or the Microsoft Internet Information Server.

Changing to the FrontPage Personal Web Server

If you installed only the Microsoft Personal Web Server and want to work through the rest of this chapter, you must first install the FrontPage Personal Web Server (see Appendix A for installation instructions). If you are currently working with Microsoft Personal Web Server (on Port 80), you must copy the Wales-Ireland-Ch18 web to the FrontPage Personal Web Server as follows:

1. Start up the FrontPage Personal Web Server by double-clicking vhttpd32.exe located in the C:\FrontPage Webs\Server folder (the default installation folder). You have to start the FrontPage Personal Web Server manually when another web server is your default server.

2. Choose File ➤ Publish FrontPage Web, select the FrontPage Personal Web Server (on Port 8080), clear the options, and click OK to copy the Wales-Ireland-Ch18 web to the FrontPage Personal Web Server.

3. Choose File ➤ Open FrontPage Web, choose the FrontPage Personal Web Server and click List Webs. Select Wales-Ireland-Ch18 and click OK.

The Wales-Ireland-Ch18 web is now open on the FrontPage Personal Web Server.

Protecting a Web

A web with either type of controlled access is called a protected web. To protect a web:

1. In the Explorer, open the web you want to protect and choose Tools ➤ Permissions from the Explorer menu bar. The Settings tab of the Permissions dialog (see Figure 18.4a) lets you specify that the current web uses the same permissions as the FrontPage root web or that the current web has its own permissions.

2. Click the Use unique permission for this web option.

3. Click the Users tab (see Figure 18.4b), click the Only registered users have browse access, and click Apply to activate the changes. The current web is now protected and only registered users can enter the web.

FIGURE 18.4

To protect a web, you choose the option to require unique permissions (a) and require that only registered users may enter the web (b).

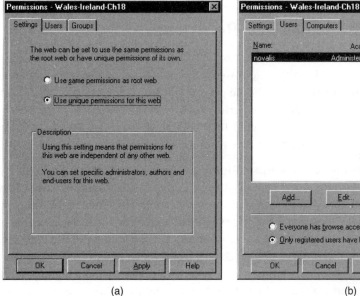

(a)   (b)

In a protected web, only registered users may enter. A registered user is a user whose name and password is recorded in the registration database that FrontPage maintains for each protected web. The two types of controlled access differ according to who registers users into the registration database. In an administrator-controlled

PART

III

Creating Web Pages

web, only the web administrator can add or remove registered users in the FrontPage Explorer as explained in Chapter 9. By contrast, in the second type of controlled access, you let your web visitors register themselves using a self-registration form that you have placed in the FrontPage root web.

NOTE

A hybrid of the two types of controlled access is to allow an open registration period during which any visitor can register for access to the web. At the end of the registration period, the web administrator reviews the registration database and modifies the list of registered users, if necessary. The web administrator removes the self-registration page from the root web and modifies the root web's home page to provide a hyperlink to the home page of the protected web. Thereafter, the protected web allows entry only to existing registered users.

Understanding Self Registration

Here is how the self registration process works. First, the Web visitor browses to your Web server's FrontPage root web. To simplify the process, we'll include two hyperlinks on the root web's home page: one hyperlink to the protected web's self registration page, and another hyperlink to the protected web's home page for previously registered visitors (see Figure 18.12 later in the chapter). Figure 18.5 depicts what happens when the visitor clicks one of the hyperlinks.

Hyperlink to the Registration Page   The new visitor follows the hyperlink to the self registration page, fills in the form's required information, and clicks the Register button. Clicking the registration push button starts the Registration bot. The bot tests the submitted username and password against the registration database stored in the protected web. If duplicate information already appears in the database, or if you require a secure password and the visitor types a password that is not secure (A *secure password* has six or more characters and does not partially match the username), the registration fails and the bot sends a registration failure page to the browser (see Figure 18.6).

The failure page has a hyperlink back to the registration page so the visitor can try again. If the registration is successful, the bot instructs the Web server to add the user name and password to the registration database of the protected web, add all the form's information to a results file stored in the root web, and send a registration confirmation page (see Figure 18.7a) to the browser. The visitor can click a hyperlink on the confirmation page to go to the protected web. At this point, the Registration bot has finished its work.

FIGURE 18.5

The self registration process

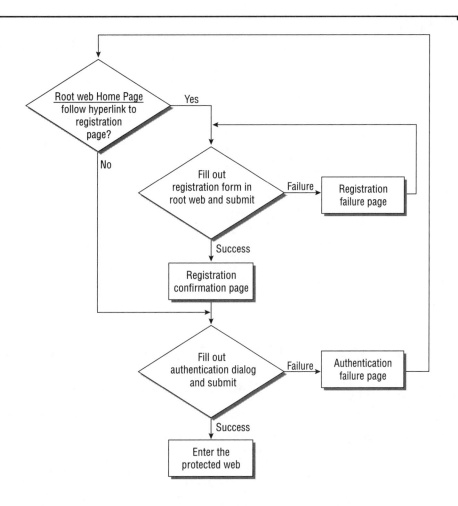

Because the web is protected, when a visitor tries to enter the web, the Web server uses its own authentication procedure and displays an authentication dialog (see Figure 18.7b) requesting a username and password. If the visitor enters a usename and password that is in the protected web's registration database, the visitor enters the web. Otherwise, the Web server sends an authentication failure page to the browser (see Figure 18.8). Clicking the browser's Back button returns the visitor to the home page of the root web to try again.

FIGURE 18.6

Registration may fail if you enter a username and password that is already in the registration database.

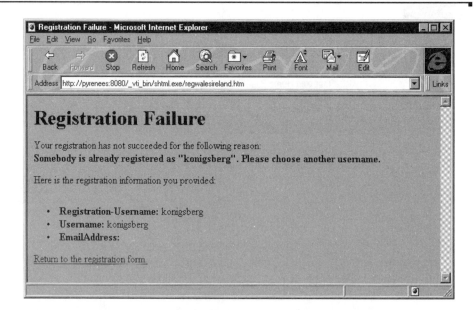

FIGURE 18.7

If registration is successful, the registration is confirmed (a). When you try to enter the protected web, the authentication dialog is displayed (b).

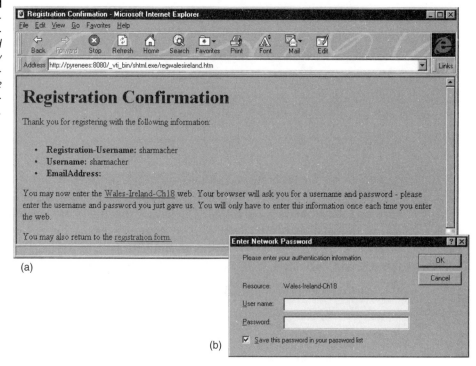

If the username and password you type in the authentication dialog are not in the registration database, the authentication fails.

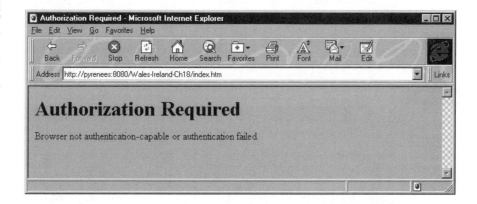

Hyperlink to the Protected Web   When a previously registered visitor browses to the root web's home page, the visitor can click the hyperlink to the protected web. The Web server displays the authentication dialog. If the visitor types a username and password in the registration database, the Web server allows the visitor to enter the protected web. Otherwise, the Web server sends an authentication failure page to the browser (see Figure 18.8). Clicking the browser's Back button returns the visitor to the home page of the root web to try again.

The User Registration Template

The easiest way to create a user registration form is to use the User Registration template. After creating the registration form page, you store it in the FrontPage root web. You can start with either the root web or the web you are protecting as the current web.

1. With Wales-Ireland-Ch18 as the current web, choose File ➤ New from the Editor menu bar, choose the User Registration template, and click OK. Figure 18.9a shows the registration instructions and Figure 18.9b shows the registration form. The form includes one-line text boxes for the user's name, password, password verification, and e-mail address, a register button, and a clear button. You can modify the page by inserting the usual page objects, such as images and text. You can also add or modify individual form fields. For example, you can insert additional fields to collect contact information.

2. Choose Edit ➤ Replace from the Editor toolbar. Type **[OtherWeb]** in the Find what text box, type **Wales-Ireland Web** in the Replace with text box, and click Replace All. After all replacements have been made, click Cancel to close the Replace dialog.

3. Click the form and choose Form Properties from the shortcut menu. The Form Properties dialog shows that the form handler is the WebBot Registration Component. Click Settings to display the Settings for the Registration Form Handler.

FIGURE 18.9

The User Registration template creates a page with registration instructions (a) and a registration form (b).

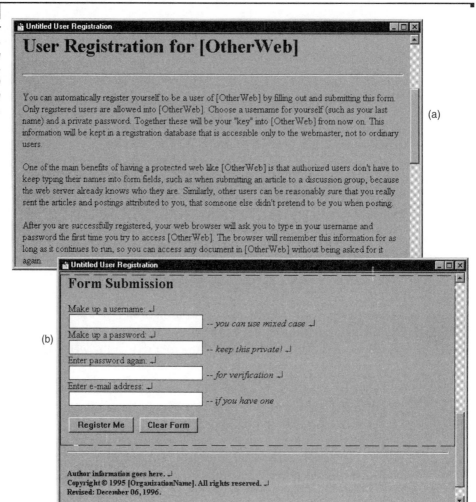

Configuring the Registration Bot

You configure the Registration bot by setting properties in the four tabs of the Settings dialog.

Use the Registration tab of the Settings dialog (see Figure 18.10a) to specify the following:

FrontPage web name   This is the name of the protected web, such as Wales-Ireland-Ch18.

User name and password   The User Registration template automatically inserts the names of the username, password, and password verification fields. Instead of a single username field, you can change the registration form and use two or more fields, and then type in the User name fields text box the names of the form fields separated by commas. The Registration bot creates the username based on the fields (omitting the commas between the field names). For example, suppose the form has separate fields named FirstName and LastName and you type **FirstName, LastName** in the User name fields text box; if a web visitor enters James in the FirstName field and Smith in the LastName field, the Registration bot creates the username JamesSmith.

Require secure password   If you check the Require secure password option, the server compares the proposed password to the username and rejects the proposed password if it is not a secure password.

Registration failure page   Enter the URL of a custom registration failure page that the server displays instead of the default. Enter either the relative URL or absolute URL. The registration fails if the visitor enters the username and password of someone already registered or the visitor did not enter a secure password after you specified the password must be secure.

Use the Results tab to specify the file for the results (see Figure 18.10b). The file must be stored in the FrontPage root web along with the registration page.

Use the Confirm tab of the Settings dialog (see Figure 18.11a) to specify the URL of a custom confirmation page stored in the FrontPage root web. If you specify validation rules for the fields of the registration form, you can specify the URL of a custom validation failure page that will be displayed if the entered values do not satisfy the validation rules (see Chapter 17 for more information on validation rules). If validation rules have not been specified, the text box is grayed out as shown in the figure.

Use the Advanced tab to specify a second results file and to specify the form fields to include in the file (see Figure 18.11b). For more information on using the Advanced tab, see Chapter 17.

FIGURE 18.10

Use the Registration tab to specify the name of the web for which the visitor is registering (a) and the Results tab to specify the name of the results file in the root web (b).

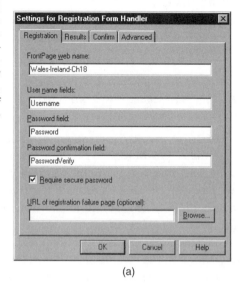

(a)

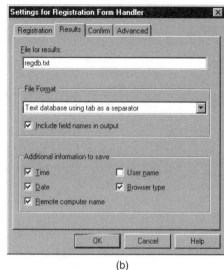

(b)

FIGURE 18.11

Use the Confirm tab to specify a custom confirmation page (a) and use the Advanced tab to specify a second results file (b).

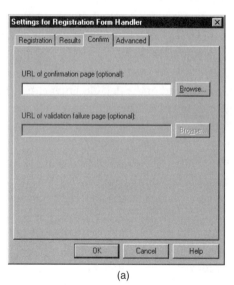

(a)

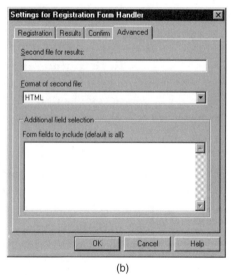

(b)

Adding User Registration to the Wales-Ireland Web

To explore user registration, do the following:

1. In the Registration tab, type **Wales-Ireland-Ch18** as the web name.

2. Click the Results tab, modify the filename to **regdb.txt,** and click OK to close the form handler dialog. The next step is to open the root web and save the registration page as a page in the root web.

3. In the Explorer, choose File ➤ Open FrontPage Web in the Explorer menu bar, click the List Webs button in the Open FrontPage Web dialog, and click OK to open the root web.

4. Switch to the Editor, choose File ➤ Save As in the Editor menu bar, type **Registration for Wales-Ireland** as the Page Title, and type **regwalesireland .htm** as the filename. Next you'll add hyperlinks on the home page, to the registration page, and to the protected web's home page.

5. Click the Open button in the Standard toolbar and choose default.htm in the Open File dialog. Insert a text hyperlink to the Registration for Wales-Ireland page and a second text hyperlink to the home page of the Wales-Ireland-Ch18 web (with the URL Wales-Ireland-Ch18/default.htm). Figure 18.12 shows the modified home page of the FrontPage Personal Web Server root web.

6. Click the Save button in the toolbar, and then click the Preview in Browser button.

7. Test the user registration process. Click the Registration for Wales-Ireland hyperlink. In the User Registration page, type a username and password. Confirm the password and submit the page. In the confirmation page, click the Wales-Ireland-Ch18 hyperlink to enter the web. In the authentication dialog, type the same username and password and then click OK to enter the web.

Viewing the Registration Database and the Results File

You can observe the registration database by opening the protected web and choosing Tools ➤ Permissions from the Explorer menu bar. Click the Users tab in the Permissions dialog to view the list of registered usernames (see Figure 18.13a). The Users tab includes the names of the visitors who have self-registered along with their Browse access rights. The Users tab also includes the names and access rights of the other users who are assigned permissions by the web's administrator (see Chapter 9 for more information on assigning permissions). The Users tab does not display passwords.

To observe the contents of the results file that stores the fields of the registration form, open the root web, and then open the results file. Figure 18.13b shows the regdb.txt file for the Wales-Ireland-Ch18 web. The results file includes the username and other values, except passwords, entered in the registration form. The results file also includes the date and time of the registration, the IP address of the visitor, and information regarding the visitor's browser and operating system.

FIGURE 18.12

Modify the home page of the root web to include hyperlinks to the protected web and to the registration page for the protected web.

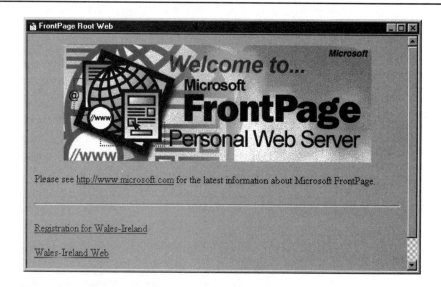

FIGURE 18.13

The registration database of a protected web lists the usernames of the registered users (a). The results file in the root web stores the information collected in the registration form except for passwords (b).

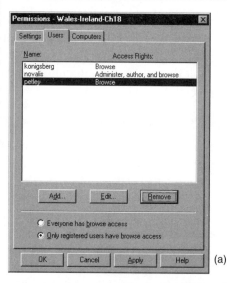

(a)

(b)

For More . . .

This chapter has shown you how to use the Search and Registration bots to add interactivity to a web. Although the Search bot works with any FrontPage-enabled Web server, the Registration bot works only with the FrontPage Personal Web Server and other Web servers that support the bot.

For information on other ways to add interactivity to a web, see the following chapters:

- Chapter 17: Collecting Input Data covers the Save Results bot for collecting and saving form results to a file.

- Chapter 19: Understanding Discussion Group Webs describes the Discussion bot that keeps track of topics and replies in an online discussion group.

- Chapter 21: Creating Dynamic Database Pages with Microsoft Access shows you how to use the Internet Database Connector server extension of the Microsoft Personal Web Server to query a database.

PART

III

Creating Web Pages

Chapter

19

Understanding
Discussion Group
Webs

Understanding Discussion Group Webs

n Chapter 17, you learned how to create forms for collecting information from your web visitors. Forms allow two-way communication between you and your visitors. FrontPage provides a way to allow your visitors to communicate with each other: You can create a special web called a discussion group that allows visitors to post articles that become part of your public web. A discussion group can be a valuable addition to most types of webs. For example, a customer support discussion group allows customers to share their experiences with a product, ask questions, and report problems to technical support personnel. Visitors to the web can benefit from both the replies of the support personnel who monitor the discussion group and from the insights and comments of other customers.

What Is a Discussion Group?

A discussion group is a web that allows web visitors to communicate with each other. A discussion group normally includes a welcome page that introduces the central discussion subject and explains the rules and etiquette that visitors are expected to follow. Visitors can post new discussion topics and reply to articles posted by others. A well-designed discussion group organizes the articles so that visitors can easily follow a series of related articles and replies and can easily find specific topics or replies.

Understanding the Features of a FrontPage Discussion Group

To create a discussion group, you use the FrontPage Discussion Web Wizard. The wizard guides you through a series of dialogs in which you can select the options you want to include in the web. The basic features that you can include are as follows:

Welcome page   Use a welcome page to introduce the discussion group and explain the rules.

Submission form page   A visitor submits an article, either a new topic or a reply to another article, by entering a subject and comments in a form and clicking a push button to submit the form to the web server. When the article is a reply to another article, FrontPage automatically enters the subject for the reply by placing Re: in front of the subject of the original article. The form handler for the submission form is the Discussion bot. When the visitor submits the form, the Discussion bot creates a new article/reply page in the web. The submission form page is a required element of a discussion web.

Confirmation page   After an article is submitted, the server uses the instructions in the Discussion bot to create a confirmation page that displays the information you choose to confirm. You can use the default confirmation page or create a custom confirmation page.

Threaded replies option   When you elect the threaded replies option, FrontPage creates threads to keep track of the replies to articles. A *thread* is a series of related articles. When a visitor posts a reply to an article, FrontPage appends the reply to the end of the thread. As more visitors submit replies to articles and submit replies to other replies, threads grow in length and may develop subthreads as discussion topics diverge. The articles and replies in each thread are grouped together. If you do not elect the threaded replies option, each article is added to a single list arranged in chronological order, and FrontPage doesn't keep track of relations between articles.

Table of contents page   Use a table of contents to organize and provide access to the articles. The table of contents is composed of hyperlinks to the articles. The text of a hyperlink is the article's subject. In a threaded discussion group, a table of contents displays threads and subthreads by indenting each reply article in a thread and using additional levels of indentation to display subsequent replies to other replies in the thread. Although a table of contents is optional, you should always include a table of contents in a threaded discussion group so that visitors can use the table as a map of the flow and evolution of each discussion. When you include a table of contents page, the Discussion bot creates and updates the page automatically after an article is posted.

Search page   Include a search form page to allow visitors to do a full-text search of the articles and replies submitted to the discussion group.

User Registration option   You can control the access to the discussion web by requiring each visitor to register and supply a user name and password before entering the protected web. Not all web servers allow the self-registration feature in FrontPage (see Chapter 18 for more information). Whether you include the self-registration feature, you can always restrict access to users registered by the web administrator, as explained in Chapter 9.

Frames option   You can elect to display the table of contents page as a frame in a frameset. When the visitor clicks an item in the table of contents, the selected article is displayed in another frame.

After you use the screens of the Dicusssion Web Wizard to design the discussion web, the Wizard creates a folder for all the subfolders and pages required for your options. You can either create a discussion group as a separate web or as a sub web of another web. If you intend to restrict a discussion group, you should create the discussion group as a separate web and include hyperlinks from the main web. You can then control access to the discussion group and leave the main web as a public, unprotected web.

Creating a Discussion Group

In this section, we'll explore using the Discussion Web Wizard to create a discussion group as a new web. We won't include the self-registration option, so you can use either the Microsoft Personal Web Server or the FrontPage Personal Web Server to work through the steps of the chapter.

Using the Discussion Web Wizard

Let's create a discussion group for the the Wales-Ireland bicycle tour. In Chapter 1, we created the PCTC web as a web site for a bicycle touring club, and announced the tour to Ireland and Wales as an upcoming event. We'll start a discussion group to provide a forum for interested club members to learn more about the tour, to provide feedback during the planning process, and to participate in group decisions involving the logistics of the tour.

We'll create the discussion web as a separate web that can be linked to the PCTC web while the trip is being planned. After the trip has taken place, the discussion web can be linked to the Wales-Ireland web to provide a forum for the comments of the trip participants and questions from other club members.

1. Choose File ➤ New ➤ FrontPage Web from the Explorer menu bar and double-click Discussion Web Wizard in the New FrontPage Web dialog. Type **Wales-Ireland-Discussion** as the name of the new web and click OK. The first screen introduces the wizard (see Figure 19.1a).

NOTE

To create a discussion group that is a subweb of the current web instead a separate web, click the Add to the current web check box on the New FrontPage Web dialog.

2. Click Next to display the available features (see Figure 19.1b). We'll include all of the options and create a web that has its articles and replies organized into threads, that has a table of contents and a search page, and that displays a confirmation of each submission.

FIGURE 19.1

The Discussion Web Wizard begins with an introduction (a). Use the next screen to select the features you want to include (b).

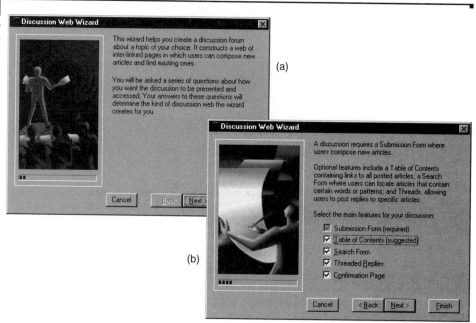

3. Click Next. Type **Discussion of Wales-Ireland Bicycle Tour** as the title and type **_discwalesireland** as the name of the discussion folder (see Figure 19.2a). The folder name must begin with an underscore. FrontPage uses a hidden folder in a discussion group web as a way to keep the discussion's article/reply pages separate from other pages in the web.

4. Click Next. Use the dialog shown in Figure 19.2b to specify the fields you want to include in the submission form. Choose Subject, Category, Comments. With this choice, the submission form includes a drop-down menu so that you can specify discussion categories. You can add other form fields later by modifying the submission form page in the Editor.

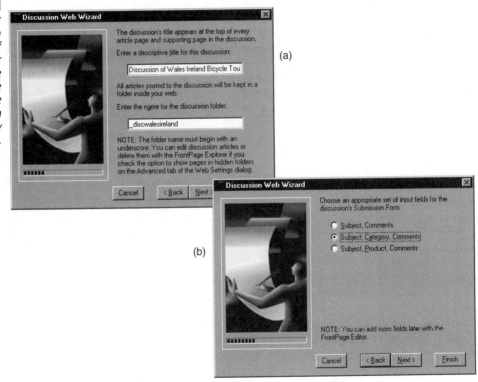

FIGURE 19.2

Specify a title for the discussion group and the name of the hidden folder that contains the articles (a). Choose the fields to include in the submission form and modify the form later (b).

5. Click Next. Use the dialog shown in Figure 19.3a to specify whether the web will be protected. If you choose Yes, you'll have to change the web permissions to protect the web when the wizard is finished (see Chapter 9 for information on protecting a web and setting user permissions). We'll leave the web unprotected.

6. Click Next. Use the dialog shown in Figure 19.3b to specify how you want the articles sorted in the table of contents. Click the Newest to Oldest option to display the newer articles at the top of the list.

FIGURE 19.3

You can require that visitors register before entering the discussion group (a). You specify the sort order of the articles in the Table of Contents (b).

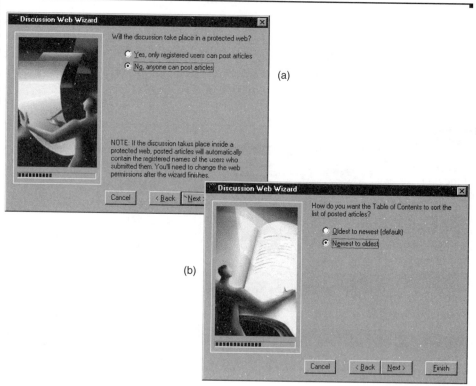

(a)

(b)

7. Click Next. Use the dialog shown in Figure 19.4a to specify whether you want to use the Table of Contents page as the home page of the web.

8. Click Next to accept the default Yes option. Use the dialog shown in Figure 19.4b to specify the information you want to display in the list of matching pages returned when the visitor uses the Search Form to do a text search.

9. Click Next to accept the default option to display the subject, file size, and date for each matching article/reply page returned by the search. Use the dialog shown in Figure 19.5 to specify the styles for the pages of the discussion. The wizard creates a styles page named Web Colors based on the choices you make, but you can modify the styles page later. Click the Custom option to change the background or the text colors. You can choose a background pattern (but not a custom image). To change the color of the text or the hyperlinks, click the color button to the

PART

III

Creating Web Pages

FIGURE 19.4

Choose options to design the styles page called Web Colors that all of the web's pages use.

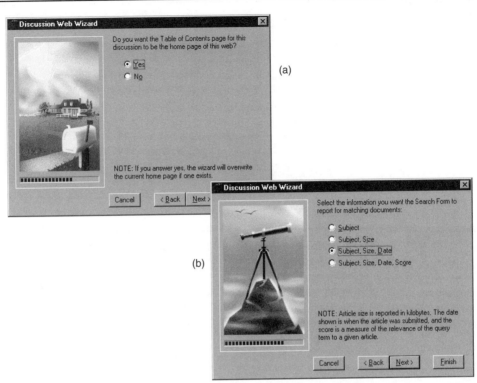

(a)

(b)

right of the property to display the Color dialog for selecting a different color. When you change the background or text colors, the graphic in the left of the dialog displays your choices. Choose White Texture 2 for the background color, and change the Link color to green and the Visited link color to purple.

10. Click Next. Use the dialog shown in Figure 19.6a to specify whether to use a frameset to display the discussion. We'll use the Dual interface default option. With this choice, the Wizard creates two sets of pages, including a set for browsers that support frames and another set for browsers that do not recognize frames. The first set includes a frameset with two frames: the table of contents page is displayed in the upper frame, and the lower frame changes as the visitor clicks hyperlinks to display the welcome page, submission page, the search page, and the article/reply page.

11. Click Next. The last screen lists the main pages the wizard creates (see Figure 19.6b). In our example, the wizard creates a submission page and the frameset for displaying the table of contents and the articles. Click Finish to put the wizard to work.

FIGURE 19.5

Choose options to design the styles page called Web Colors that all of the web's pages use.

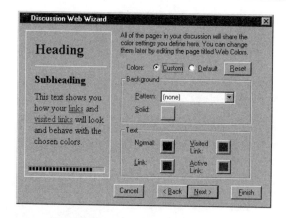

FIGURE 19.6

You can use a frameset to display the Table of Contents in the upper frame and a selected article in the same browser window (a). The last screen lists the main pages that the wizard creates (b).

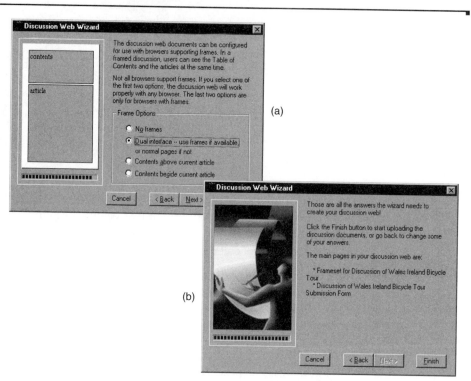

(a)

(b)

The Wizard has finished its work, but there is one more detail we need to take care of before examining the web. We'll modify the submission form page to specify the category items in the drop-down menu as follows:

1. In the Explorer, double-click the discwalesireland_post.htm page to display the submission form page in the Editor. Double-click the drop-down menu field and modify the menu choices shown in Figure 19.7 (see Chapter 17 for information on modifying form fields).

FIGURE 19.7

Enter the menu choices for the drop-down menu field.

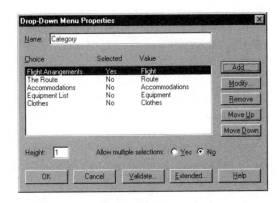

2. Click the Save button in the Editor toolbar to save the page (see Figure 19.8). Click the page's Close button.

FIGURE 19.8

The submission form page that visitors use to submit articles and replies to articles

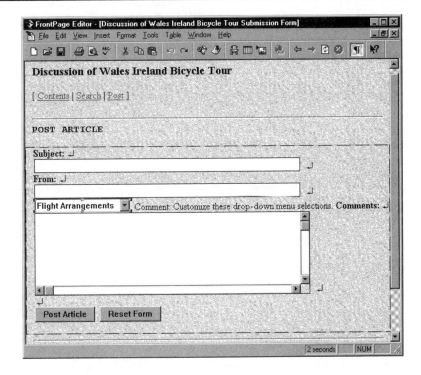

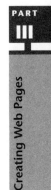

PART

III

Creating Web Pages

Viewing the Discussion Web in the Explorer

The discussion web is more complex than any web we've created so far. The wizard uses many of the FrontPage features that you've learned about in the previous chapters of Part III. We've seen the components separately, including data entry forms, search forms, confirmation pages, and framesets. The Discussion Web Wizard has put the components together and has added some advanced programming to create an elegant interactive web.

Let's take a look at the folders and pages the Wizard has created for the features we included and the options we chose. The Explorer displays the web folder containing three folders and seven web pages (see Figure 19.9).

FIGURE 19.9

The Discussion Web Wizard creates a web folder with three subfolders and seven web pages.

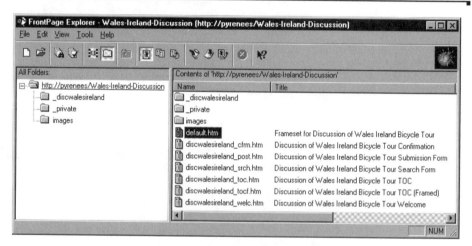

Understanding the Pages in the Main Web Folder

The main folder includes the pages shown in Table 19.1.

TABLE 19.1: THE PAGES STORED IN THE MAIN FOLDER OF THE DISCUSSION WEB

File name	Purpose
discwalesireland_welc.htm	This is the welcome page that introduces the discussion. This page is displayed in the lower frame of the frameset home page.
discwalesireland_post.htm	This is the submission form page. This page is required for any discussion group web. The submission page is displayed in the lower frame of the frameset home page.

Continued ▶

TABLE 19.1: THE PAGES STORED IN THE MAIN FOLDER OF THE DISCUSSION WEB (CONTINUED)	
File name	**Purpose**
discwalesireland_tocf.htm	This is the table of contents page that is displayed in the upper frame of the frameset home page.
discwalesireland_toc.htm	This the the table of contents page that is displayed by a browser that does not support frames.
default.htm	This the the home page for the web. With the Dual interface option, the home page is a frameset with two frames.
discwalesireland_cfrm.htm	This is the confirmation page. This page is not displayed in the frameset.
discwalesireland_srch.htm	This is the search page. This page is displayed in the lower frame of the frameset home page.

Understanding the Web's Subfolders

The three subfolders are as follows:

images   for storing the images including the whttxtr2.jpg file we selected for the background

_private   for storing a web's private pages, which include the styles page (discwalesireland_styl.htm); a header and footer for the submission page, the table of contents page, the search form page, and the confirmation page (discwalesireland_head.htm and discwalesireland_foot.htm); and a header and footer for the article page that the server creates when the submission form is posted (discwalesireland_ahdr.htm and discwalesireland_aftr.htm)

_discwalesireland   for storing the article/reply pages that the server creates. This hidden folder is empty until the first submission form is posted.

Viewing the Discussion Web in a Browser

To see how the pages of the web work together, open a browser and type **http://**servername/**Wales-Ireland-Discussion** in the browser's address text box. Figure 19.10 shows the web's home page (default.htm) with an empty table of contents (discwalesireland_tocf.htm) in the upper frame and a welcome page (discwalesireland_welc.htm) in the lower frame.

FIGURE 19.10

The home page of the discussion web displays the table of contents in the upper frame and the welcome page in the lower frame.

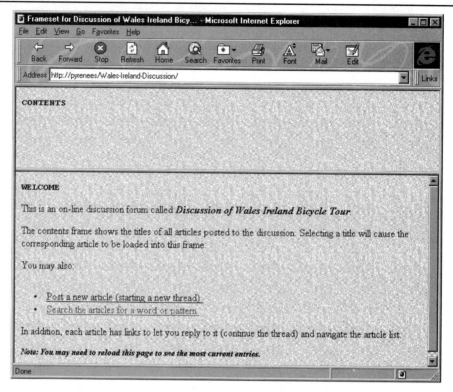

When you create a new discussion group, avoid an empty Table of Contents page by starting the discussion with at least one thread.

Let's post a few articles to understand how a thread is formed.

1. Click the Post a new article hyperlink. The lower frame changes to display the submission page, discwalesireland_post.htm. The navigation bar at the top of the submission page has hyperlinks to the table of contents, the search page, and the submission form page.

2. Enter the data shown in Figure 19.11, and click the Post Article button. The server runs the Discussion bot, creates a new web page using the submitted information, and sends a new confirmation page to the browser. The browser displays the confirmation page, discwalesireland_cfrm.htm.

FIGURE 19.11

When you click a Post hyperlink, the submission form page is displayed in the lower frame of the home page.

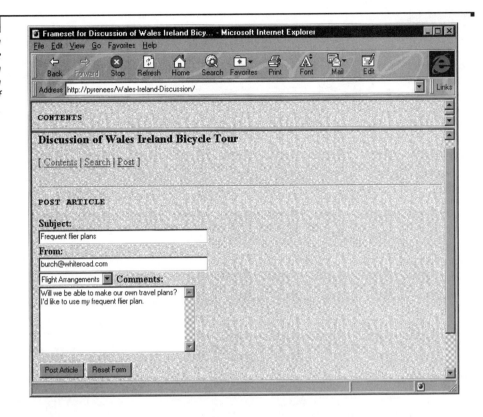

3. Click the <u>Refresh the main page</u> hyperlink in the confirmation page to refresh the browser. The browser displays the frameset. The upper frame lists the submitted article in the table of contents and the lower frame redisplays the welcome page (see Figure 19.12). You can enter a new article and start a new thread by clicking the <u>Post a new article</u> hyperlink again.

4. Click the hyperlink for the submitted article in the table of contents frame. The browser displays the selected article in the lower frame (see Figure 19.13). The article/ reply page has a navigation bar with four additional hyperlinks with link text <u>Reply</u>, <u>Next</u>, <u>Previous</u>, and <u>Up</u>.

5. Click the <u>Reply hyperlink</u> in the navigation bar to display a blank submission form ready for your replay to the article. Enter a reply message from Leo Moll, the trip leader,and click the Post Article button. The web server runs the Discussion bot, creates a new article/reply page, and sends a confirmation page to the browser. The browser displays the confirmation page (see Figure 19.14).

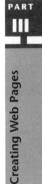

PART

III

Creating Web Pages

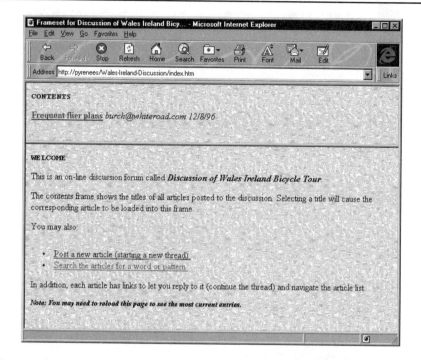

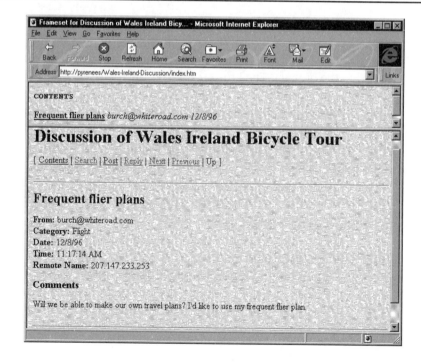

FIGURE 19.14

The confirmation page has hyperlinks back to the table of contents, to the search page, and to the submission form page.

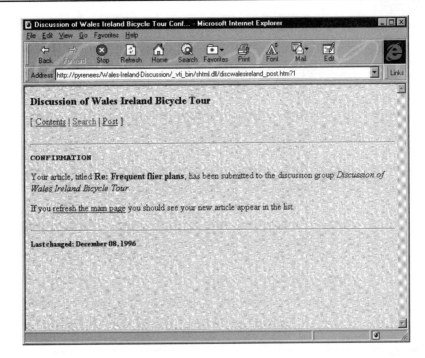

6. Click the <u>Contents</u> hyperlink in the navigation bar to return to the home page. The upper frame displays the two items of the thread.

7. Click Leo's reply in the table of contents to display Leo's reply in the lower frame. Click the <u>Reply</u> hyperlink in the navigation bar, enter a reply to Leo's reply, and post the article.

8. Click the <u>Post</u> hyperlink in the navigation bar of the confirmation page. Clicking <u>Post</u> displays a blank submission form and you can start a new thread. Enter a new subject and post the article.

9. Click the hyperlink in the confirmation page to refresh the browser. The table of contents lists the three articles of the first thread and the single article of the second thread (see Figure 19.15).

10. Click the <u>Search the articles...</u> hyperlink in the lower frame. The lower frame displays the search page (discwalesireland_srch.htm). Type **group** and click the start Search button. The results of the search are displayed in the lower frame (see Figure 19.16).

PART

III

Creating Web Pages

FIGURE 19.15

The articles of a thread are indicated by increasing indentations in the table of contents.

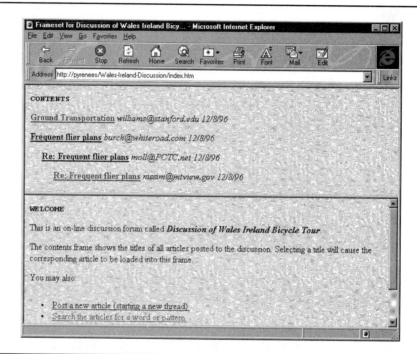

FIGURE 19.16

The search form page is displayed in the lower frame. After running the search, the results are listed below the search form.

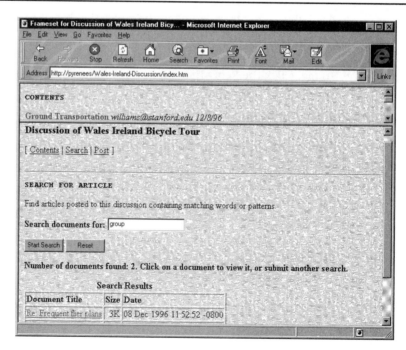

You can continue to explore the features of the discussion web. For example, the article/reply pages include hyperlinks to navigate within a thread. If you display a reply to an article, clicking the <u>Next</u> hyperlink in the article page's navigation bar takes you to the next article in the same thread. When you are at the last article in a thread, clicking the <u>Next</u> hyperlink has no effect. Click the <u>Previous</u> hyperlink to display the previous article in the same thread. When you are at the first article in a thread, clicking the <u>Previous</u> hyperlink has no effect.

Viewing the Article/Reply Pages in the Explorer

To see the article/reply pages that the Discussion bot has created, minimize or close the browser, and do the following:

1. In the Explorer's Folder View, click the _discwalesireland folder. The Contents pane is blank because the files in hidden discussion group folders remain hidden unless you unhide them.

2. Choose Tools ➤ Web Settings from the Explorer menu bar, click the Advanced tab, check the Show documents in hidden directories check box (see Figure 19.17), and click OK. Click Yes in the message to refresh the web.

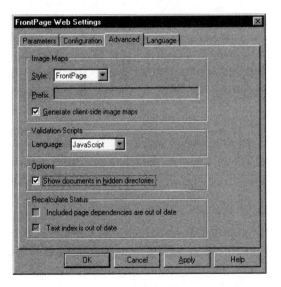

3. Click the _discwalesireland folder again. Now the folder displays a page for each submitted article. Each article is named using the format ########.htm, where # represents a digit, such as 00000003.htm. The folder also contains two other pages named toc.htm and tocproto.htm (see Figure 19.18). We'll take a look at each type of page in the discussion folder.

FIGURE 19.18

The discussion web uses a hidden folder to store the article pages and the two pages that FrontPage uses to keep track of the threads and update the table of contents.

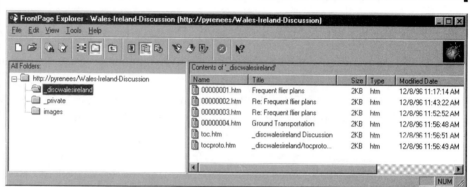

4. Double-click tocproto.htm to display the page in the Editor. This is the page that the server creates to keep track of the threads (see Figure 19.19a). Each under-lined item is a hyperlink to an article page. Between the references to the articles is the phrase *Form Results Inserted Here*. The phrase represents another bot called the Form Insert Here WebBot Component, which the server runs to insert the information the visitor typed in. The tocproto.htm page is included in the table of contents page using an Include bot. You can open the discwalesireland_tocf.htm page to view the current table of contents with the four articles. The server also uses the tocproto.htm page to generate the article/reply pages, as you'll see in the next step.

5. Click the Open button in the toolbar, choose toc.htm in the Open File dialog, and click OK. The server uses this page to create an article page: the top and bot-tom of the page use the Include bot to display the article header page and the article footer page. Between the header and footer, the page uses another Include bot to display the tocproto.htm page (see Figure 19.19b).

6. Click the Open button in the toolbar and double-click one of the article pages in the Open File dialog. Figure 19.20 shows the page which includes a Reply WebBot Component at the top of the page and a Form Results Inserted Here bot above the form results.

FIGURE 19.19

The Discussion bot uses the tocproto .htm page (a) to build the table of contents and the toc.htm page to create the article pages (b).

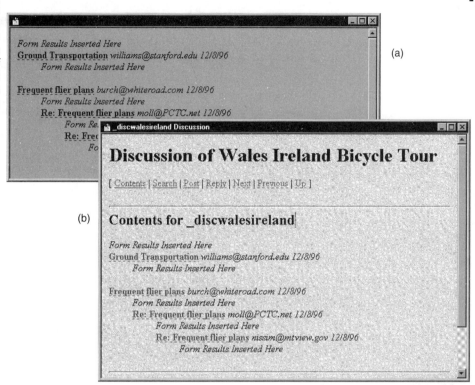

(a)

(b)

7. Right-click in the included header and choose Open... in the shortcut menu to display the header page (see Figure 19.21a). The first three hyperlinks in the navigation bar are directed to the table of contents, the search page, and the submission page respectively. The last four hyperlinks are displayed with dotted underlines. Click any of the last four hyperlinks and press Ctrl+K. The Edit Hyperlink dialog indicates the name of a script, such as --WebBot-Next--, as the target of the hyperlink (see Figure 19.21b).

Exploring an article page this way gives a glimpse into the additional programming that is required to make the discussion group function. FrontPage makes it easy to create a discussion group because all of the programming is done for you. In Part IV you'll see that FrontPage also allows you to include your own programs.

PART

III

Creating Web Pages

The server generates an article page including information submitted by the article's author and an included header page.

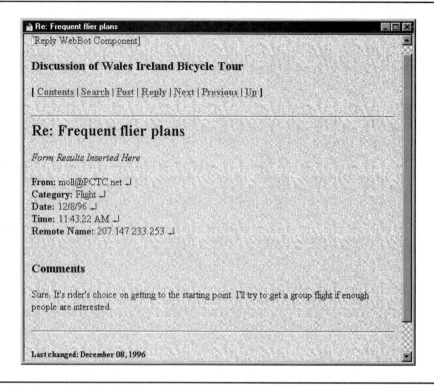

Four of the hyperlinks in the navigation bar of the article header page (a) have targets that are web bot scripts (b).

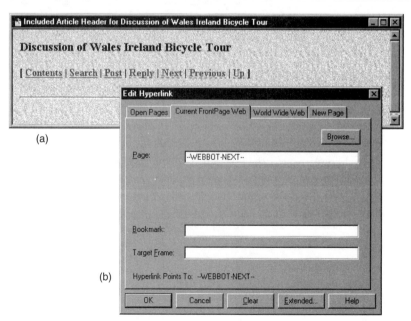

NOTE

As you explore the pages in the Editor, you'll discover that the Discussion bot calls on other bots to relate the web pages such as the Form Insert Here WebBot Component mentioned above and the Reply WebBot Component that is inserted at the top of each article page. In addition, there are bots that make the navigation hyperlinks for a thread work properly so that the Next hyperlink retrieves the next article in the thread, the Previous hyperlink retrieves the previous article, and the Up hyperlink retrieves the first article in the thread.

Moderating a Discussion Group

Although FrontPage doesn't provide any special tools for managing the discussion group, the web administrator has full access to the submitted articles. To review an article, open the discussion group's hidden article folder and double-click to display an article in the Editor. The web administrator can delete old or inappropriate articles. To delete article pages, select the article pages in the Explorer and press Delete. The pages are removed and the remaining links in the web are automatically updated. The Table of Contents page is updated and the Next and Previous hyperlinks in the navigation bars of the other pages in the thread are updated.

The web administrator can also edit existing articles. If you do plan to edit articles, you should include a statement of your intent to edit in the welcome page or on the submission page so that your visitors are aware that their comments may be changed.

Modifying a Discussion Group

After you create a discussion group using the Discussion Web Wizard, you can use the techniques you've learned in the previous chapters of Part III to modify the results. Here are some modifications you can make:

Modifications	Chapter
You can display the Web Colors page and change the styles, including using a custom background image.	Chapter 10
You can view the main pages in the Editor and modify pages by adding text, images, sounds, video clips, tables, and other web objects to embellish the pages.	Chapters 11, 13, and 14
You can add hyperlinks to the navigation bars in the header pages for the main pages and for the article pages.	Chapter 12

PART

III

Creating Web Pages

Modifications	Chapter
You can modify the frameset to display the pages in a different arrangement.	Chapter 15
You can insert additional confirmation fields using the Substitution bot in the confirmation page.	Chapter 16
You can insert additional fields for collecting information in the submission form page.	Chapter 17
You can reconfigure the Search bot to change the information displayed in the search results list.	Chapter 18

WARNING

Take care in modifying the hyperlinks that the wizard has created. Some of the hyperlinks, such as the Reply, Previous, Next, and Up hyperlinks on the article pages use special scripts and won't work properly if you change them.

For More...

This chapter has shown you how to use the Discussion Web Wizard to create a sophisticated interactive discussion group. The Wizard used the FrontPage features covered in the previous chapters of Part III and bound the features together with additional programming. This is the essence of Microsoft FrontPage—you can use FrontPage to create professional quality webs without having to write the programs yourself.

To explore some of the ways you can expand the awesome capabilities of FrontPage, continue on to Part IV.

PART IV

Advanced Topics

- *Working with ActiveX*
- *Making ActiveX Controls available to visitors*
- *Connecting a database to a web*
- *Letting visitors select data*

Chapter

20

Extending
FrontPage with
ActiveX

Chapter 20

Extending FrontPage with ActiveX

I n Part III, you learned how to use the built-in features of FrontPage to create compelling interactive Web pages. This chapter introduces you to one way of extending the capabilities of Front-Page by using the ActiveX technologies. You'll learn about the three main components of ActiveX: Documents, Controls, and Scripting. To explore ActiveX Controls and Scripting, we'll create an ActiveX version of the home page for the Wales-Ireland Web.

 NOTE

To work through the examples in this chapter, you must use the Microsoft Internet Explorer 3.0. If you didn't do a complete installation, you'll need to reinstall this browser, making sure to do the complete installation. You'll also need to replace your Wales-Ireland web with a modified version from the book's CD-ROM. Open your Wales-Ireland Web in the FrontPage Explorer and choose File ➤ Delete FrontPage Web to delete the Web. Then choose File ➤ Import to create a new Web named Wales-Ireland and import the files of the Wales-Ireland-Ch20 web in the Webs folder of the book's CD-ROM.

What Is ActiveX ?

ActiveX is a whole set of technologies that Microsoft has developed to enhance the Internet. Although most of the fundamentals were already in place, Microsoft extended and optimized the technologies for the Internet. The main components of ActiveX are:

ActiveX Documents   These are documents created in an application such as Microsoft Word that can be displayed in a browser window in their native formats by a Web browser that supports the technology. The Web browser calls on the application itself or a viewer application to display the document within the browser window.

ActiveX Controls   These are small software programs that you can embed in a web page or in any other document that supports the technology. Similar to the WebBot components of FrontPage, ActiveX controls can perform a variety of tasks, such as playing multimedia files, displaying data, providing timers, and doing calculations.

ActiveX Scripting   This allows simple programming scripts to be embedded in a web page. The scripts are used to link a page's components together and add interactivity to a web page. For example, with scripting, one component, such as a push button, can give instructions to another component, such as telling a label to change its font color whenever the Web visitor clicks the button. Scripts can be written in any scripting language. Normally, you write scripts for the Web browser to run, but you can also use the Active Page technology to write scripts for the Web server. (The ActivePage technology is not available in the Microsoft Personal Web Server 1.0 that ships with FrontPage 97.)

NOTE

The ActiveX standards are open and available for use by other software vendors and developers. At the time this book was written, only Microsoft Word, Excel, and Power-Point can create ActiveX documents, but look for other vendors to support the ActiveX Document technology. Hundreds of third-party developers are creating ActiveX controls. For more information on available controls, see the ActiveX Control Gallery at Microsoft's Web site.

Understanding ActiveX Documents

ActiveX documents are documents that can be displayed in their native formats in the browser windows of a Web browser that supports the ActiveX documents technology. At the time this book was written, the Web browsers that support the technology include Microsoft Internet Explorer 3.0 and Netscape Navigator 3.0 with the NCompass ActiveX plug-in installed, and the applications that create ActiveX documents include Microsoft Word, Excel, and PowerPoint. The Web visitor's computer must have either the parent appplication or an ActiveX document viewer in order to view the application. The Microsoft Word Viewer, Excel Viewer, and the Microsoft PowerPoint Animation Player can be downloaded from Microsoft's Web site.

NOTE

If you plan to include ActiveX documents in your Web site, you can use hyperlinks to direct your visitors to these Microsoft sites so that they can download and install the appropriate viewer.

When the Web visitor clicks a hyperlink whose target is an ActiveX document, what happens next depends on whether the visitor's computer has the corresponding parent application or viewer. If either of these applications is installed, the document opens in the browser window and the application's menus are grafted onto the browser's menus. Figure 20.1 shows the Day1.doc Word document opened as in the Microsoft Internet Explorer browser, and displaying the Insert menu. If the visitor has Word, the visitor can use the Word commands to edit the copy displayed by the browser and then save the copy to the local disk. If the visitor has only the Word Viewer, the document can be browsed but not edited.

To explore how FrontPage works with ActiveX Documents, do the following:

1. In the Editor, click the New button to display a new page.

2. In the FrontPage Explorer, click the day1.doc file icon, drag the icon to the new page in the Editor, and drop to create a text hyperlink.

3. Repeat Step 2 to create a text hyperlink to the tourinfo.xls file. To replace the text of the link to the Excel spreadsheet with the name of the file, select the characters between the first and last character and type **Manuscript/tourinfo.xls**. Then, delete the first and last character.

4. Click the Save button in the toolbar and save the page with the name Office Links and the filename officelinks.htm.

FIGURE 20.1

When a Web visitor who has Microsoft Word installed clicks a link to a Word document in the Web browser, the document is displayed in the browser window and Word's menus are grafted onto the browser's menus.

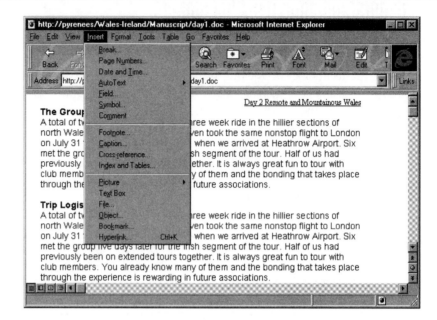

5. Click the Preview in Browser button in the toolbar and click the link to the Day1.doc Word document. If you have Word or the Word Viewer installed, the Day1.doc document is displayed in the browser window.

6. Click the hyperlink in the upper-right. The browser displays the Day2.doc Word document. Continue following the hyperlinks to the Day3.doc, Day4.doc, and then the Day5.doc. When you try to follow the link to the Day6.doc, the browser displays the 404 error because the Day6.doc is not in the Manuscript folder.

7. Click the browsers Back button five times to return to the Day 1 Word document. Scroll to the bottom of the page and follow the link back to the Office Links page. Click the link to the Excel document. If you have Excel or the Excel Viewer installed, the spreadsheet is displayed in the browser window (see Figure 20.2). The Excel spreadsheet has hyperlinks to the Word documents for the descriptions of each day of the Welsh section of the tour. There is also a hyperlink to the PCTC.mdb Access database.

8. Click one of the hyperlinks in the Description column to display the Word document in the browser window. Click the browser's Back button to return to the Excel spreadsheet.

9. Click the <u>Club Database</u> hyperlink. If you have Access installed on your computer, the browser opens Access as a helper application and displays the Database window for the pctc database (see Figure 20.3). Double-click the Tour Description table icon to display its contents. Click the <u>Day 1</u> hyperlink in the LinkToDocument column (see Figure 20.4). A new instance of Microsoft Word opens and displays the Day 1 document. Because Microsoft Access does not comply with the ActiveX Document technology, when an Access database is the target of a link, Access opens as a helper application and displays the database and when you follow a hyperlink stored in the database, the application opens in a separate window and displays the target even if the document is an ActiveX Document.

10. Close the instance of Word, close the instance of Access, and close the browser.

FIGURE 20.2

The tourinfo.xls spreadsheet has hyperlinks to Word documents and an Access database.

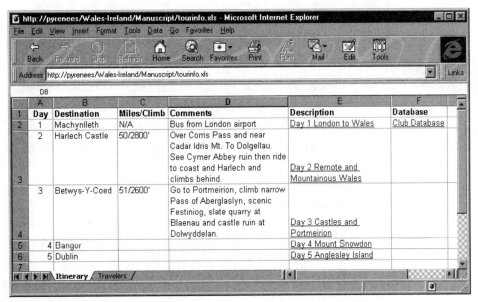

FIGURE 20.3

Clicking the link to the Access database starts Access in a separate window and displays the Database window for the pctc database.

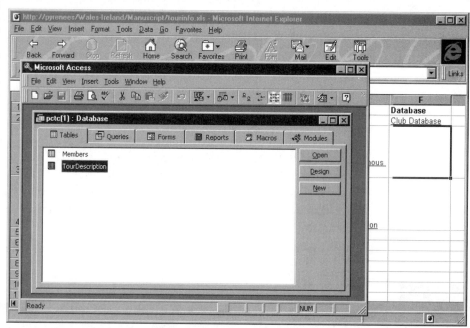

FIGURE 20.4

The data stored in the TourDescription table

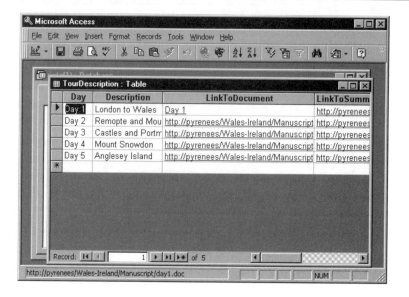

Viewing the Office Hyperlinks in the FrontPage Explorer

The FrontPage Explorer recognizes only some of the hyperlinks between the Microsoft Office documents. To explore, do the following:

1. Right-click the tourinfo.xls file icon in the FrontPage Explorer and choose Show Hyperlinks from the shortcut menu (see Figure 20.5a). The FrontPage Explorer detects the hyperlinks to the database file and to the Word documents.

2. In the All Hyperlinks pane, click the Manuscript/day2.doc file (see Figure 20.5b). The FrontPage Explorer does not detect either the incoming or the outgoing hyperlinks between the Word documents.

3. In the All Hyperlinks pane, click the Database/pctc.mdb database file. The FrontPage Explorer does not detect the outgoing hyperlinks to the Word documents or to the Excel spreadsheet.

FIGURE 20.5

The FrontPage Explorer recognizes outgoing links from a Microsoft Excel spreadsheet (a), but does not recognize links between Microsoft Word documents (b).

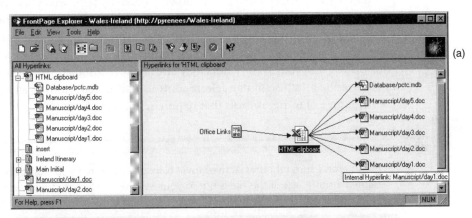

(a)

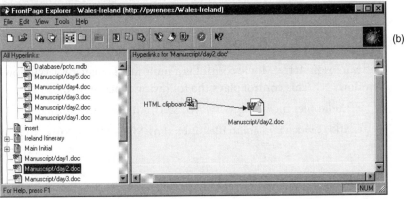

(b)

For a Microsoft Office document, the FrontPage Explorer recognizes incoming hyperlinks from Web pages and from Microsoft Excel ActiveX spreadsheets. The FrontPage Explorer also recognizes outgoing hyperlinks from a Microsoft Excel ActiveX spreadsheet to other Web pages and to other ActiveX documents.

NOTE

In the future, it is expected that FrontPage will detect the hyperlinks between any Microsoft Office documents.

Inserting ActiveX Controls

Inserting an ActiveX control in a Web page is similar to inserting a FrontPage Web-Bot Component: you insert the object and then set properties for the object. Some ActiveX controls are independent of other controls and setting their properties is all you need to do. Other controls don't do very much by themselves and are really useful only when you write scripts that allow controls to work together. When you do a complete installation of the Microsoft Internet Explorer 3.0, you install a small but extremely useful set of ActiveX controls. In this chapter, we'll examine a few of the controls you and your Web visitors may already have installed. We'll start by exploring one of the most useful standalone controls, called ActiveMovie, and then we'll take a glimpse of using controls that require scripting to be useful.

NOTE

If you aren't sure whether ActiveMovie is installed, search your hard disk for the file named amovie.ocx. If this file is not in your \Windows\System folder, you can download the control from the Internet Explorer section of the Microsoft web site.

Using the ActiveMovie Control

The Microsoft ActiveMovie control is a multimedia player for Windows 95 and Windows NT. This control plays the following types of media:

- Audio files including WAV, AU, SND, AIF, and AIFF formats
- MPEG video and audio files, including MPG, MPEG, MPV, MP2, and MPA formats

PART
IV

Advanced Topics

- AVI video, including AVI format
- QuickTime video, including MOV and QT formats

In this book, we've been using the ActiveMovie control to play sound files. The text hyperlinks to the sound files on several of the tour description pages in the Wales-Ireland Web. When the Web visitor clicks the hyperlink, the ActiveMovie control appears in a separate window (see Figure 20.6).

FIGURE 20.6

When the target of a hyperlink is a media file, the ActiveMovie control plays the file in a separate window.

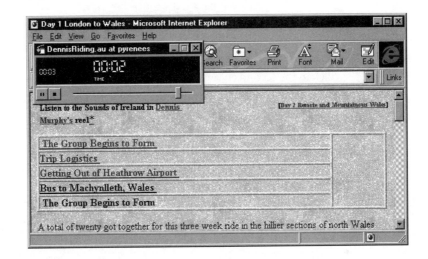

If you want to include the player as part of the Web page instead of in a separate window, you can insert the ActiveMovie control.

1. In the Editor, click the Open button in the toolbar and double-click day1.htm. Choose View Advanced Toolbar in the Editor menu bar to display the toolbar for inserting ActiveX controls and other advanced objects (see Figure 20.7). (The page table of contents has been rearranged as the first column of a table. The cells in the second column have been merged into a single cell. You'll insert the ActiveMovie player in the merged cell.)

FIGURE 20.7

The Advanced Toolbar

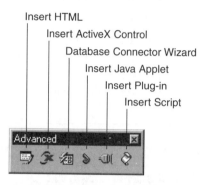

Insert HTML

Insert ActiveX Control

Database Connector Wizard

Insert Java Applet

Insert Plug-in

Insert Script

2. Click in the second column of the table and choose Insert ➤ Other Components ➤ ActiveX Control from the Editor menu bar, or click Insert ActiveXControl in the Advanced toolbar. Click the down arrow in the Pick a Control combo list to display a list of all the ActiveX controls currently installed on your computer. If you've done a complete installation of the Microsoft Internet Explorer 3.0, the ActiveMovie Control Object appears at the top of the list (see Figure 20.8).

FIGURE 20.8

Use the ActiveX Control Properties to select the control and set a few basic properties.

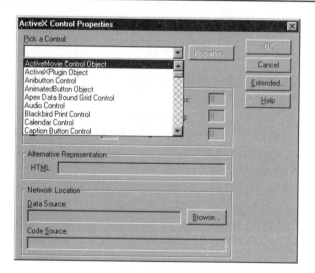

3. Click the ActiveMovie Control Object and type PlaySound as the name of the control. To play a file, you set the Filename property to the name and location of the file in the Web.

4. Click the Properties button to display the Object Parameters dialog (see Figure 20.9a). This dialog lists the properties you have set.

5. Click the Add button to display the Edit Object Parameter dialog. You use this dialog to specify the name of the property and the value you want to set. You have to study the documentation that comes with an ActiveX control to determine the names of the properties you can set. You can get more information about the ActiveMovie control at www.microsoft.com/mediadev/video/usingam.htm. Type Filename in the Name text box, click the Page option, click the Browse button, and locate the DennisRiding.au sound file in the Sounds and Video folder (see Figure 20.9b).

Use the Object Properties dialog (a) to add or edit additional properties (b).

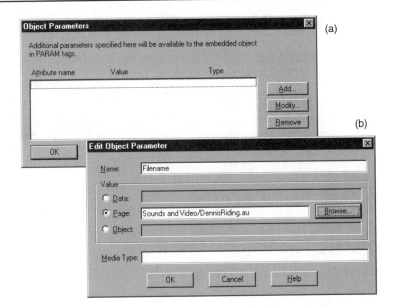

(a)

(b)

6. Click OK to close the dialog. There are two more properties that you must set to make the control work: _ExtentX and _ExtentY (The documentation for the control doesn't explain the purpose of these required properties, but they appear to be related to the size of the control). Repeat Step 5 to add these properties as shown in Figure 20.10a. Click OK two times to close the dialogs.

7. Click the Save button and then the Preview in browser button in the toolbar. Click the play button in the embedded ActiveMovie control to play the reel (see Figure 20.10b).

FIGURE 20.10

The additional properties of the ActiveMovie player required to play a sound file (a). The ActiveMovie control embedded in the page (b).

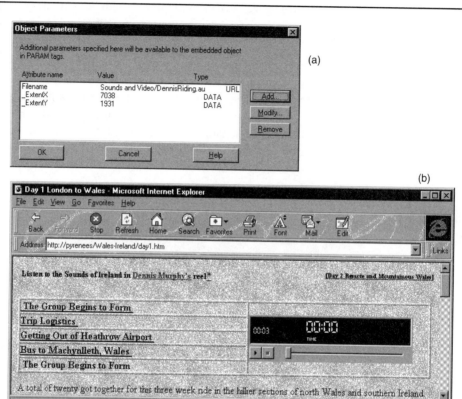

Inserting Forms 2.0 Controls

When you do a complete install of the Microsoft Internet Explorer 3.0, the ActiveX controls called the Microsoft Forms 2.0 are installed automatically. This set of controls includes ActiveX versions of the FrontPage form controls we worked with in Chapter 17, as well as the other controls listed in Table 20.1.

To explore how ActiveX controls work, we'll use a few of the Forms 2.0 controls to create an ActiveX version of the home page for the Wales-Ireland Web. The ActiveX version uses options buttons to provide a choice to go to the NorthWales or the Southwest Ireland sections of the tour (see Figure 20.11). When the Web visitor selects an option, the caption of the command button changes to reflect the choice. The visitor clicks the command button to jump to the page that lists the itinerary for the section.

1. In the FrontPage Editor, click the Open button in the toolbar and choose HomePage(ActiveX) in the Open File dialog (see Figure 20.12).

TABLE 20.1: THE MICROSOFT FORMS 2.0 ACTIVEX CONTROLS

Control	Purpose
Microsoft Forms 2.0 CheckBox	Allows the visitor to check a choice
Microsoft Forms 2.0 ComboBox	Allows the visitor to choose a single item from a list
Microsoft Forms 2.0 CommandButton	Allows the visitor to click a push button
Microsoft Forms 2.0 Frame	Allows you to group related controls together
Microsoft Forms 2.0 Image	Allows you to crop, size, and display an image
Microsoft Forms 2.0 Label	Creates a label
Microsoft Forms 2.0 ListBox	Allows the visitor to choose one or more items from a scrollable list
Microsoft Forms 2.0 MultiPage	Allows you to create a set of multiple pages
Microsoft Forms 2.0 OptionButton	Allows the visitor to choose one of several options
Microsoft Forms 2.0 ScrollBar	Creates a horizontal or a vertical scroll bar
Microsoft Forms 2.0 SpinButton	Creates a pair of up and down buttons
Microsoft Forms 2.0 TabStrip	Creates a set multiple pages with tabs. The visitor clicks a tab to display a page.
Microsoft Forms 2.0 TextBox	Creates a single or multiple line text box
Microsoft Forms 2.0 ToggleButton	Creates a button that can have two or three states

2. Place the insertion point in the empty line. Choose Insert ➤ Other Components ➤ ActiveX Control from the Editor menu bar, or click Insert ActiveXControl in the Advanced toolbar. Click the down arrow in the Pick a Control combo list to display a list of the Microsoft Forms 2.0 controls (see Figure 20.13a).

3. Choose Microsoft Forms 2.0 OptionButton from the Pick a Control: combo list and type **OptionWales** in the Name text box (see Figure 20.13b).

4. Click the Properties button on the dialog. This time, FrontPage gives you more help in setting the properties. The Microsoft Forms 2.0 controls and many other ActiveX controls display two windows when you click the Properties button. The Edit ActiveX Control window is a graphical representation of the control (see Figure 20.14a). You can resize or position the control in this window. The second window is the Properties dialog for the control (see Figure 20.14b). The Properties dialog is a list of the properties that you can change. We'll change the Caption, Font, and BackStyle properties.

FIGURE 20.11

When the Web visitor clicks an option button on the ActiveX version of the home page, the command button's caption changes. The visitor clicks the command button to jump to the selected section.

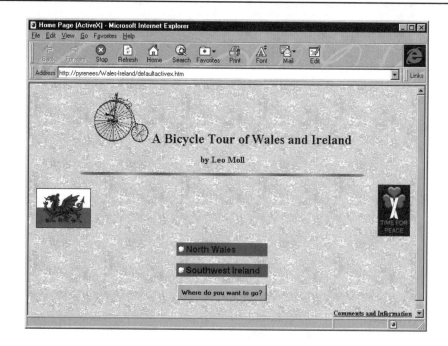

FIGURE 20.12

The modified home page uses a table to lay out the graphics.

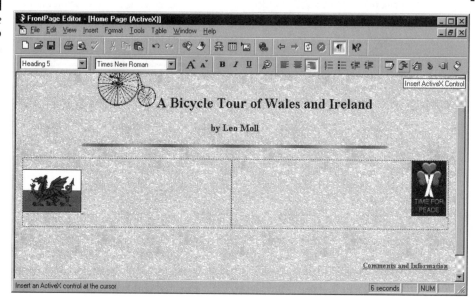

FIGURE 20.13

The combo box lists the Microsoft Forms 2.0 controls (a). Choose a control and enter a name (b).

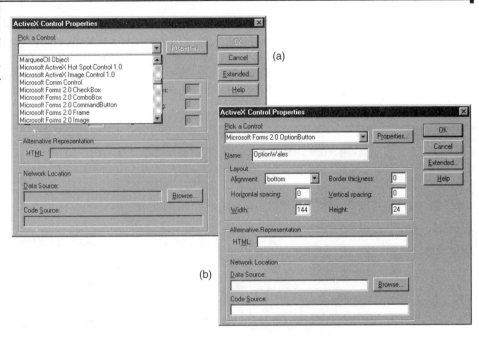

FIGURE 20.14

Use the Edit ActiveX Control window (a) to resize and move the control and use the Properties dialog to set property values (b).

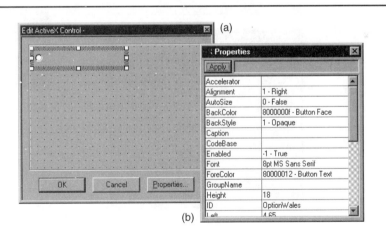

9. Click in the control in the Edit Active X Control window and type **North Wales**. As you type in the control, the Caption property in the Properties dialog displays the changes you type. Click Font and click the button with the ellipses (…)

in the upper-right corner of the Properties sheet to display the Font dialog (see Figure 20.15a). Choose Arial Font, Bold Font style, Size 12, and then click OK. Click BackColor and click the ellipsis button to display the Color dialog (see Figure 20.15b). Click the green square in the fourth row and fourth column in the Color dialog and click OK. The changes are displayed in the Edit ActiveX Control window (see Figure 20.15c).

FIGURE 20.15

Set the Font properties for the Caption (a), select the BackStyle color (b), and then view the changes in the Edit ActiveX Control window (c).

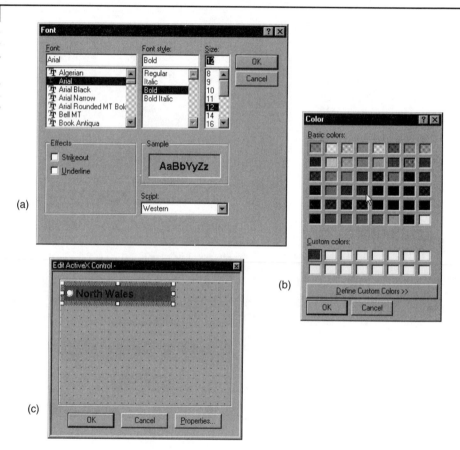

10. Click OK to close both windows. Set the Width to 170 (pixels) and click OK in the ActiveX Control Properties dialog. The Editor inserts the control on the page (see Figure 20.16).

FIGURE 20.16

The Microsoft Forms 2.0 OptionButton control inserted in the home page

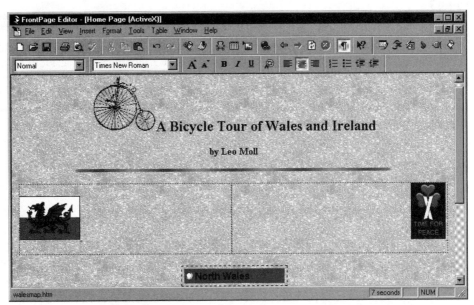

11. Press Enter to insert a new line. Repeat Steps 1 through 4 to insert a second ActiveX Control option button typing **OptionIreland** as the Name and **Southwest Ireland** as the Caption.

12. Press Enter. Click Insert ActiveX Control from the Advanced toolbar. Choose Microsoft Forms 2.0 CommandButton and type **Command** in the Name text box. Click in the button in the Edit ActiveX Control window. Click AutoSize and choose -1 True from the combo list. With the AutoSize property set to True, the command button changes its size automatically as the length of the caption changes. Type **Where do you want to go?.** Click Font, click the ellipsis button, and change the Font type to Bold.

13. Click the Save button and then click the Preview in Browser button in the Standard toolbar (see Figure 20.11 a few pages back).

At this point, the three controls have no intelligence. You can click the options buttons and the command button in the browser and there is no response. The next step is to write the scripts so that there will be a response when the visitor clicks a control.

NOTE

Many ActiveX controls do not have an Edit ActiveX Control window and a Property dialog that lists the properties you can set. In these cases, clicking the Properties button on the ActiveX Control Properties dialog displays the Object Parameters dialog instead (see Figure 20.9). You have to study the documentation for the ActiveX control to determine the properties you can set and add the property (attribute) name and your setting to the Object Parameters dialog.

Writing ActiveX Scripts

Here are the visitor actions that we are going to write scripts for:

North Wales option button: When the visitor clicks this option button, the caption of the command button changes to Come join us in Wales!

Southwest Ireland option button: When the visitor clicks this option button, the caption of the command button changes to Come join us in Ireland!

Command button: When the visitor clicks the command button, the response depends on which option the visitor selected. If the visitor didn't select either option, then clicking the command button gives no response. If the visitor clicked the North Wales option button, then clicking the command button jumps to the walesmap.htm page. If the visitor clicked the Southwest Ireland option button, then clicking the command button jumps to the eiremap.htm page.

Changing the caption of the command button is easy. The hard part is telling the command button which page to jump to. Here is how we'll pass the page information to the command button: we'll set up a storage container that we'll use to store the name of the target page. The storage container is called a global variable. A *variable* is a temporary storage location in the computer's memory. A *global variable* is a variable that can be used by any scripts that you write for objects on the page. By contrast, a *local variable* is a variable that can be used only in the script that sets up the storage container for the variable and cannot be used by other scripts.

We'll use Country as the name of the global variable. When the visitor clicks an option button, we'll store the name of the target page as the value of Country. Then, when the visitor clicks the command button, we'll just tell the command button to jump to whatever page name has been stored in Country.

Now that we've got the logic part done, it's time to write some scripts.

1. Choose Insert ➤ Script from the Editor menu bar or click Insert Script in the Advanced toolbar to display the Script dialog (see Figure 20.17). You can write scripts in VBScript or JavaScript. (The Other option is for additional scripting languages that become available in the future.) The default langauge is VBScript. If you know how to write scripts, you can type the script directly in the Script text box. Instead, we'll summon the Script Wizard to write the script for us.

2. Click the Script Wizard button to start the wizard.

FIGURE 20.17

Choose a scripting language in the Script dialog. You can also write the script in the text box.

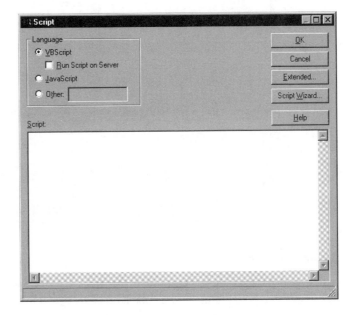

NOTE

VBScript is a simplified version of the Microsoft Visual Basic programming language. JavaScript is the scripting language created by Netscape with help from Sun Microsystems for the Netscape Navigator browser. The Microsoft Internet Explorer 3.0 supports both scripting languages. It is expected that by the time you read this book, the Netscape Navigator 3.0 will also support both languages.

Understanding the Script Wizard

The Script Wizard dialog has three panes (see Figure 20.18).

FIGURE 20.18

*Use the three panes
of the Script Wizard
to write scripts that
have sequential
single-line
instructions*

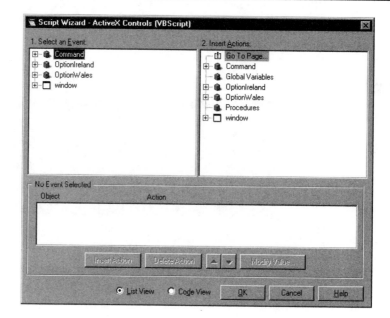

Events Pane

The Events pane in the upper-left lists the three ActiveX controls we inserted. Each object is listed by its name and a cube icon is displayed to the left of the name. The list also includes the window object that represents the browser window that displays the page. The window object has a window icon to the left.

Expanding an Object to View Its Events   Clicking the plus sign to the left of an object's icon expands the object and displays the events that the object recognizes. An *event* is a change that an object recognizes. For example, when the visitor clicks the command button, the button recognizes the change from being unclicked to being clicked. The change from unclicked to clicked is the button's Click event. Click the plus sign to the left of Command to display the list of events that the comand button recognizes (see Figure 20.19a).

An event is a scripting opportunity—you write a script for an event, then, when the event occurs, the browser executes the script. You click the event for which you want to write a script. After you write a script for an event, the diamond icon to the left of the event changes to a solid diamond.

Actions Pane

The Actions pane in the upper-right also lists the the three objects you inserted in the page and the windows object. Clicking the plus sign to the left of an object's icon expands the object and displays the object's properties (the same properties that were listed in the Properties dialog that was displayed when you inserted the ActiveX control). The list also includes instructions, called *actions*, that you can include in your script. Properties are indicated by the icon that has three blue lines, and actions are indicated by the icon with the exclamation point. Click the plus sign to the left of Command to display the list of properties that you can change and actions you can include in a script (see Figure 20.19b).

FIGURE 20.19

Expand an object in the Event pane to display the object's events (a). Expand an object in the Actions pane to display the object's properties and actions (b).

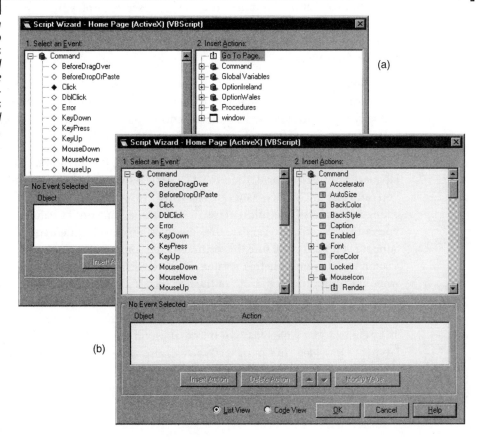

The Actions pane also lists three other items:

- The Go To Page action item at the top of the list is the action you include in a script to jump to another page. This action is available for any object, so it is listed only once in the Actions pane.
- Global Variables represents the list of the global variables you have defined for the page. These are the storage containers for values that can be used by all the scripts you write for the page. Clicking the plus sign to the left displays the list of global variables.
- Procedures represents the list of scripts you have written for the page.

Script Pane

The Script pane at the bottom of the dialog is used to display the scripts that you write. Because each script runs when an event is recognized, a script you create in the Script pane is also called an *event handler*. There are two views of the Script pane: Code View and List View.

List View   When you click the List View option, only a simplified version of scripting is available. In List View, each instruction is a single line that either changes a property of a control or runs a built-in action. You create a list of the single line instructions that are to be executed sequentially and assign the list to a specific event.

Code View   When you click the Code View option, the full power of the scripting language is available. In addition to writing the sequential single-line instructions that you can write in List View, you can also write instructions to test a value, and then change the order of execution of instructions depending on the value. For example, you can write a script to validate the data that the Web visitor enters in a text box. Suppose you want to be sure the visitor entered some value in a text box. You can write a script to determine whether a value was entered and have the browser run the script when the visitor tries to tab out of the text box. If a value was not entered, the browser runs an instruction to display a message to the visitor and place the insertion point back in the text box. If a value was entered, the insertion point moves to the next data entry control. (See Chapter 17 for information on the built-in data validation that FrontPage provides.) In Code View, you can also write instructions to repeat a set of instructions.

In this chapter, we'll use only List View to write simple sequential instructions.

Defining a Global Variable

We'll start by setting up the storage container for the name of the target page.

1. Right-click Global Variables in the Action pane and choose New Global Variable from the shortcut menu. Type Country in the New Global Variable dialog (see Figure 20.20a) and click OK. The storage container is created and named Country.

2. Click the plus sign to the left of Global Variables to view the new global variable (see Figure 20.20b).

Create a global variable (a) to store a value that all scripts on the page can use. Expand Global Variables in the Actions pane to display the list of global variables for the page (b).

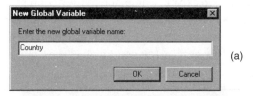

(a)

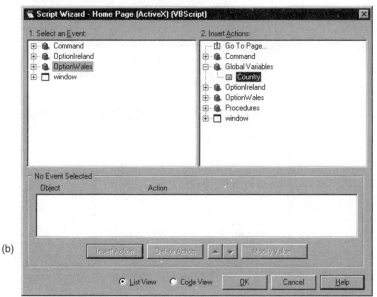

(b)

Creating the ActiveX Scripts

We'll write the script for the OptionWales option button. We want the browser to run the script when the visitor clicks the option button, so we script the Click event. The script needs to have two instructions: change the caption of the command button and store walesmap.htm in the country global variable.

To write an instruction, you choose an item in the Actions pane and click the Insert Action button. If additional information is required to carry out the action, the Script Wizard displays a dialog asking for the information.

1. Click the plus sign to the left of OptionWales in the Event pane, and click the Click event. The first instruction involves the command button.

2. Click the plus sign to expand Command in the Action pane. Click Caption and click the Insert Action button to display the Command Caption dialog. Type **Come join us in Wales!** in the dialog (see Figure 20.21a), and click OK. Figure 20.21b shows the instruction. The next instruction involves the Country global variable.

FIGURE 20.21

Enter the new text for the button's Caption (a). The Script Wizard creates the instruction (b).

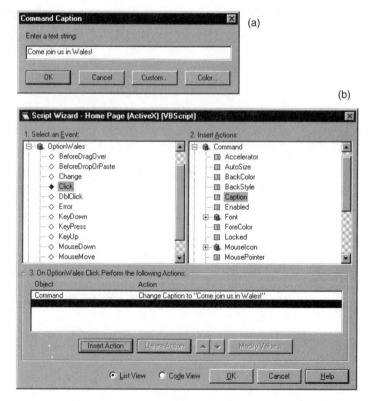

3. Click the plus sign to expand Global Variables in the Action pane. Click Country and click the Insert Action button. Type **"walesmap.htm"** in the Country dialog and click OK. You enclose the page name in double-quotes because the value is a text value (and not a number or a date value). Figure 20.22 shows the completed script.

The script for the Command button

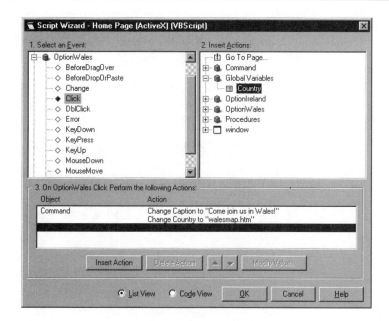

4. Repeat Steps 1 through 3 to create the script for the Click event of the OptionIreland option button that changes the Caption property of the command button to Come join us in Ireland! and changes the Country global variable to "eiremap.htm".

The last script is for the Click event of the command button. We want the script to instruct the browser to go to the page whose name is stored in the Country global variable.

1. Click the plus sign to the left of Command in the Event pane and click the Click event.

2. Click Go To Page in the Action pane and click Insert Action. The Go To Page dialog expects you to enter the name of a page. However, we want to enter the name of a global variable instead. To enter a global variable, click the Custom button on the dialog (see Figure 20.23a). Type **Country** in the Go To Page dialog (Figure 20.23b) and click OK. Figure 20.23c shows the completed script for the command button.

To enter a global variable instead of a page, click the Custom button (a) and enter the variable (b). The wizard writes the instruction (c)

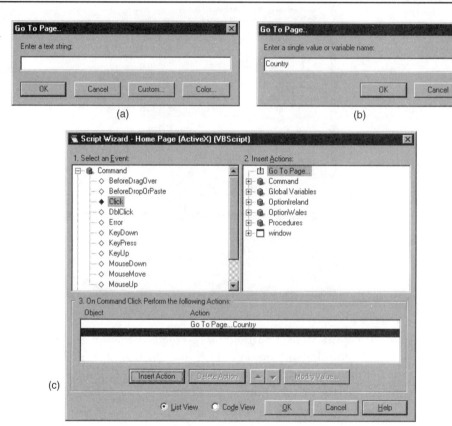

3. Click the plus sign to expand Procedures in the Actions pane. The list includes the three scripts. Each script is named using the object's name followed by an underscore followed by the event name: Command_Click, OptionIreland_Click, and OptionWales_Click.

4. Click OK to close the Script Wizard.

Viewing the Active Page in the Editor

Figure 20.24 shows the page. To the left of each ActiveX control is a script icon that indicates the control has at least one script attached to it. When you move the pointer to the script icon, the pointer changes to the bot icon.

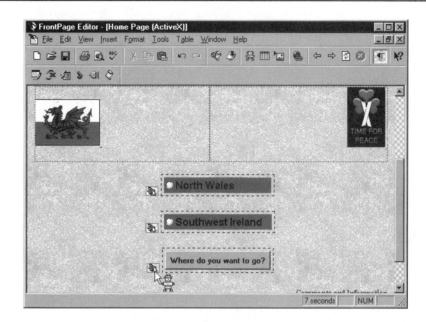

1. Double-click the script icon to the left of the North Wales option button. The Script dialog displays the script that the Script Wizard wrote using VBScript (see Figure 20.25). The first and last lines identify the beginning and end of the script. Click OK to close the dialog.

2. Click the Save button and then click the Preview in Browser button in the toolbar.

Previewing the ActiveX Enhanced Page in a Browser

Now you are ready to test the ActiveX version of the home page.

1. Click the command button. The page blinks as the browser refreshes.

2. Click the North Wales option button. The option button displays a solid dot to indicate the selection and caption of the command button changes (see Figure 20.26).

FIGURE 20.25

Double-click a script icon to view the event handler.

FIGURE 20.26

The ActiveX enhanced home page

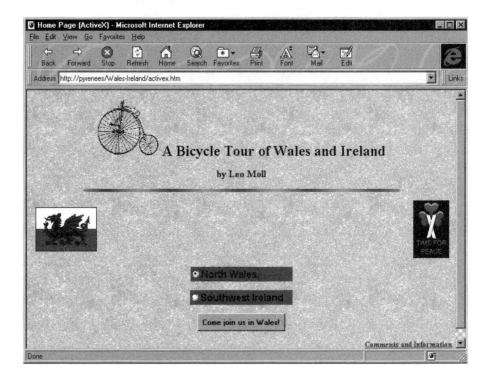

3. Click the command button. The browser jumps to the walesmap.htm page. Click the Back button in the browser.

4. Click the Southwest Ireland option button. The option button displays a solid dot to indicate the selection and caption of the command button changes. Click the command button. The browser jumps to the eiremap.htm page.

Viewing the ActiveX Enhanced Page in the FrontPage Explorer

When you insert an ActiveX control in a page, FrontPage creates a link to the control. Figure 20.27 shows the Hyperlink View of the ActiveX enhanced home page. There is a link to each of the controls. The links are implicit links to the ActiveX control programs stored on the visitor's computer.

FIGURE 20.27

The FrontPage Explorer shows an implicit link to each ActiveX control inserted in the page.

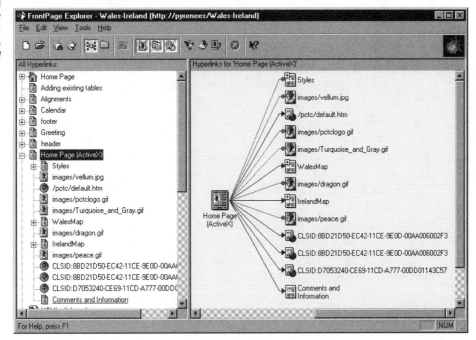

Each ActiveX control is uniquely identified by a 24-character identification string, called a CLSID. The ActiveX controls we used in the ActiveX version of the home page are installed automatically when you install the Microsoft Internet Explorer 3.0 browser. So any visitor to your web using the Internet Explorer 3.0 has these ActiveX controls installed and registered on their computer.

When the visitor goes to a page with ActiveX controls, the browser retrieves the corresponding ActiveX control from the visitor's computer and displays the representation of the control on the Web page (however, not all ActiveX controls have a visual representation). When the visitor takes an action to cause an event, for example, when the visitor clicks an option button or the command button in the page, the browser runs the script.

Making ActiveX Controls Available to Your Visitors

When you include ActiveX controls in a web page, you need to make a provision for your visitor to download the ActiveX controls if the controls don't already exist on the visitor's computer. You can arrange for automatic downloading to the visitor's computer by using the CodeBase property of the ActiveX control. You set the Code-Base property to the address of the file where the browser can locate the ActiveX control and automatically download the control.

When you use the ActiveX controls that are shipped with the Microsoft Internet Explorer 3.0, you can probably assume that your visitor has also done a complete install of the browser and has these controls already installed. When you use the Microsoft Forms 2.0 controls and a few other controls (including the HTML Layout Control, the ActiveX Image Control and the ActiveX Hotspot Control) and don't want to assume that your visitors have done a complete install, there are two ways you can provide controls to your visitors. In one method, you can provide access to the controls yourself. Download the file named Mspert10.cab from Microsoft's Web site at http://activex.microsoft.com/controls/mspert10.cab and copy this file to the Web server you are using to publish your webs. Set the CodeBase property to the address of this file on your Web server. In the second method, you can set the CodeBase to Microsoft's Web site. This method requires that the browser connect to Microsoft's Web server, which adds additional waiting time.

In addition to the ActiveX controls listed in Table 20.1 Microsoft provides other sets of ActiveX controls that you can download. Another set of Microsoft ActiveX controls can be downloaded from the ActiveX Controls Gallery at www.microsoft.com/intdev/controls/ctrlref.htm. as shown in Table 20.2.

TABLE 20.2: MICROSOFT ACTIVEX CONTROLS FROM THE ACTIVEX CONTROLS GALLERY	
Control	**Purpose**
Animated Button	Use to display sequences in an .AVI file
Chart	Use to draw and display different chart styles such as bar-chart and pie-chart
Gradient	Use to draw shaded regions between two colors
Label	Use to display text at different angles or along curves
Menu	Use to display a pull-down menu
Popup Window	Use to display a specified web page in a pop-up window
Preloader	Use to automatically download a file in the background and store the downloaded file in the browser's cache
Stock Ticker	Use to display changing data in text or .XRT format by downloading a specified file at regular intervals and displaying the data.
View Tracker	Use to generate events whenever a control leaves the viewing area

You can download these controls individually and add them to your Web pages. You can make the controls in Table 20.2 available to your visitors without having to obtain a license from Microsoft. Other third parties have created more than 1000 ActiveX controls that you can purchase and obtain licenses to make them available to your visitors. When you use the ActiveX controls in Table 20.2, other controls from the ActiveX Component Gallery, or any third party controls, you must specify the CodeBase property correctly or your visitors will not be able to view your page.

For More...

This chapter has introduced you to the basic concepts of the ActiveX technologies. You've learned how to insert ActiveX controls and how to write simple scripts to link two controls. The Script Wizard helps you to write only sequential single-line instructions using either VBScript or JavaScript. To create scripts that control which instructions are executes and which repeat instructions, you need to learn one of the scripting languages. There are many excellent tutorials available for both VBScript and JavaScript.

Chapter

21

Creating Dynamic Database Pages with Microsoft Access

Creating Dynamic Database Pages with Microsoft Access

Up until now, the text information you've been learning to publish in your FrontPage Web is in the form of documents that you've created directly by typing in a page in the FrontPage Editor, or documents that have been created in another application such as a word processor or spreadsheet program, brought into FrontPage, and converted into a web page. However, an essential type of information storage is not the text document—the fundamental type of storage for large quantities of information is the database. A database is any collection of information stored in a manner that allows you to retrieve the specific information you need for some purpose. Every business and organization of any size uses computer database management systems to organize, store, and manipulate the information it needs—customer information, product and sales data, supplier contact and ordering information, sales records, or club membership records. The Web as an essential communication channel would be extremely limited if there were no easy access to the information stored in databases. This chapter shows you how to connect your FrontPage Web to a database so that your Web visitors can retrieve data directly from the database.

What Is a Dynamic Database Web Page?

A web page can be based on the information in a database in two ways.

A *static* database page is based on a snapshot of the data as it exists at the time you publish your web. The static database web page contains a copy of the data. In Chapter 14, you created a static web page by copying and pasting an Access database table to a page. If the data in the database changes, a static web page doesn't reflect the changes. To update the static page, you have to retrieve an updated copy of the data from the database and create a new web page.

A *dynamic* database page is based on the data that is in the database at the moment the Web visitor requests the data. A dynamic database web page isn't even created until the visitor takes some action to request the data. After the data is retrieved, the Web server creates the new web page based on the fresh data and sends it to the browser.

How does the magic of a dynamic page happen? The details of the process are fairly complicated, but the overall idea is simple.

Connecting a Database to a Web

On one hand you have a Web visitor who sends a request for data to your Web server, and on the other hand, you have a computer database file with the information you'd like to make available to visitors on a direct and continuous basis. Here is a way to connect the two in a dynamic relationship. There are two components you must have:

- A Web server that has special software for connecting to data
- Data stored in one of the standard database file formats

Actually, there is a third component you must have because the Web server doesn't connect directly to the database file. There are so many database file formats in common use that it would probably not be possible to create the Web server software to connect to every type of data file format. To solve the data file format problem, Microsoft developed the *Open Database Connectivity* (*ODBC*) standards. A key element of the standards is that you can use a common language called *Structured Query Language*, or *SQL*, to write requests for data from any database in a file format that conforms to the ODBC standards. In addition to being a set of written standards, ODBC is a set of software programs that you install on your computer and use as the software interface between an application, such as a Web server, that wants to access data, and a database file that stores the data. The ODBC programs must be installed on the same computer that houses your Web server. Because the Web server communicates with the database through the ODBC programs, the third component required for the Web-database connection is the specific ODBC software, called the *ODBC driver*, for the database file format you want to use.

Figure 21.1 depicts the connection between a web and a database.

FIGURE 27.1

The Web-database connection

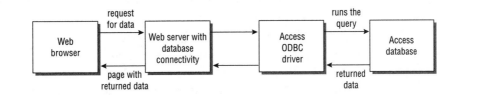

The Web visitor initiates a request for data by clicking a hyperlink or a push button. The Web server passes the request to its special data connection software, which in turn passes the request to the ODBC driver. The ODBC driver operates directly on the database and retrieves the requested data. Now the path is reversed and the data is channeled back to the browser. The ODBC driver sends the returned data to the Web server, which uses its data connection software to create a new page page based on the returned data. The Web server sends the new page back to the browser for display to the visitor.

NOTE

Figure 21.1 is a simple model of the Web-database connection for a Web server that has its own database connection software. Another model adds the database connection software as a separate software component in the chain. There are several database connection programs available for the popular Web servers. One of the best is Cold Fusion by Allaire corporation.

It's time to take inventory to determine whether you have the required components:

Database connection software   If you installed the Microsoft Personal Web Server, you've got the Web server requirement covered. This Web server, along with the Microsoft Peer Web Server (for Windows NT) and the Microsoft Internet Database Server (for Windows NT Server), contains special database connection software, called the Internet Database Connector (IDC), as a server extension.

ODBC database file   You'll need to determine if the database management system you are using has an ODBC driver. The common ODBC file formats are Microsoft Access, Microsoft Excel, Oracle, Microsoft SQL Server, and dBase. (See the Knowledge Base at the Microsoft Web site for article Q140548 listing the ODBC drivers by product.) In this chapter, we'll be using a Microsoft Access 97 database on the book's CD-ROM, so you've got the ODBC database file requirement taken care of.

ODBC driver You can determine which ODBC drivers are currently installed on your computer as follows:

1. Click the Windows Start button, choose Settings ➤ Control Panel to display the Control Panel, and then click the 32-bit ODBC icon.

2. Click the ODBC Drivers tab in the ODBC Data Source Administrator. The tab lists the ODBC drivers installed on your computer (see Figure 21.2). For working through this chapter, you'll need the Microsoft Access Driver. If you've installed Microsoft Access 97, you've automatically installed the Access ODBC driver.

FIGURE 21.2

The installed ODBC drivers are listed in the ODBC Data Source Administrator.

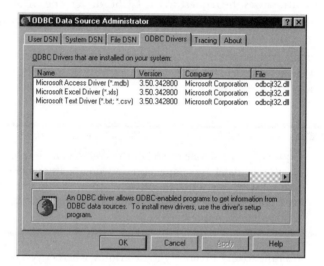

NOTE

To work through the examples in this chapter, you must have Microsoft Access 97 and the Access ODBC driver installed, and you must be running FrontPage with the Microsoft Personal Web Server for Windows 95, the Microsoft Peer Web Services for Windows NT Workstation 4.0, or the Microsoft Internet Information server for Windows NT Server. (See Appendix A for more information.) If you have the Access ODBC driver, but do not have Microsoft Access 97, you'll have to create the .idc and .htx files from scratch, as explained later in this chapter.

NOTE

If you don't have Microsoft Access 97, you won't be able to use the new Web-database connection features that are built into Access 97. However, you can still connect an Access database to your FrontPage Web as long as you have the Access ODBC driver installed on your computer because the Access ODBC driver retrieves data directly from an Access database without opening Access. If you have one of the following Microsoft products—Access, Excel, Word, Office, Project for Windows 95 or later, Visual Fox Pro 3.0 or later, Visual Basic 4.0 or later, or C++ 4.0 or later—you can download the ODBC drivers from Microsoft's Web site.

If you have all the components, you are ready to continue. Let's create a new web and import the book's Access database as follows:

1. In the FrontPage Explorer, choose File ➤ New FrontPage web and double-click Normal Web in the New Web dialog.

2. In the Normal Web Template dialog, choose the name for your Microsoft Web Server, type **Database** as the name of the new web, and click OK.

3. Choose File ➤ Import in the menu bar, click Add File in the Import File to FrontPage Web dialog, open the PCTC Information folder on the book's CD-ROM, and double-click the PCTC.mdb database file. Click OK to import the file.

Connecting the Access ODBC Driver to the Database

The Access ODBC driver can take requests for data from the Internet Database Connector and then operate directly on a specific Access database, but the driver needs to know which database to retrieve data from. In addition to the name and location of the database, the Access ODBC driver needs other connection information, such as the username and password if the database is password-protected. ODBC requires that you give a name called the *Data Source Name (DSN)* to the complete set of connection information. Normally, you use the database's filename as the Data Source Name, but you can use another name if you prefer. Connect the Access ODBC driver to the PCTC.mdb database as follows:

1. Display the ODBC Data Source Administrator by clicking the 32-bit ODBC icon in the Control Panel. The dialog has tabs for three kinds of DSNs. Each type of DSN has a different purpose. For example, you set up a User DSN when you

want to make the database available only to yourself. However, to make the Access database available to the Web server installed on the computer, you must set up a *System DSN*.

2. Click the System DSN tab. The System DSN tab displays a list of names of the data sources previously set up as System DSNs (see Figure 21.3).

FIGURE 21.3

To make a database file available to the Web server, set up a System DSN.

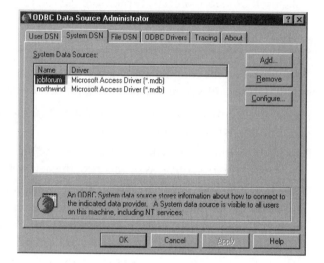

3. Click Add to display the Create New Data Source dialog, which lists the installed ODBC drivers (see Figure 21.4a). Click the Microsoft Access driver and then click Finish to display the ODBC Microsoft Access 97 Setup dialog (see Figure 21.4b). We'll use the database name as the name for the DSN.

4. Type **pctc** in the Data Source Name text box, type **The club's database** as the Description, and then click the Select button. Use the Select Database dialog to locate the Database folder (default path c:\Webshare\Wwwroot\Database). Double-click the Database folder in the list box on the right, select the pctc.mdb database in the list of files in the list box on the left, and then click OK (see Figure 21.5).

5. Click OK in the Setup dialog to create the System Data Source. The new data source is added to the list in the System DSN tab. Click OK to close the ODBC Data Source Administrator dialog.

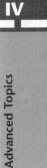

FIGURE 21.4

Select the ODBC driver you want to use (a), then name the data source and click the Select button (b).

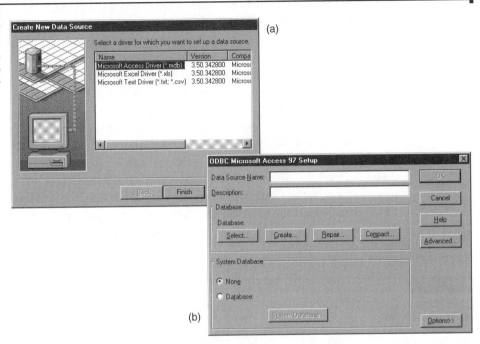

FIGURE 21.5

Locate the database file in your computer's file system.

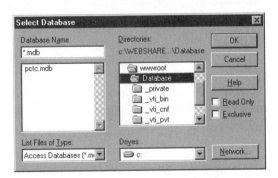

Understanding the Internet Database Connector

This is how the Internet Database Connector works: you formulate the request for data using the Structured Query Language—that is, you write an SQL statement that describes the data you want to retrieve from the database. You also design the page that the Internet Database Connector will generate to display the returned data. To design the results page, you create a set of formatting instructions in a file with the special .htx extension. The .htx file has formatting instructions, text, and images you plan to display, but no data. The file uses place holders to indicate where the returned data is to be located on the page. The final step is to package the three pieces of information: the SQL statement, the name of the data source, and the name of the .htx file, into a single file that has the special .idc extension.

When the Web visitor takes some action to submit the request for data to the Web server, the Internet Database Connector opens the .idc file and passes the name and location of the database and the SQL statement to the Access ODBC driver. The ODBC driver retrieves the data from the database and returns the data to the Internet Database Connector. The Connector opens the .htx file and uses its instructions to create a new web page with the retrieved data substituting for the placeholders. The Web server sends the generated page to the browser. Figure 21.6 depicts the process for the Microsoft Personal Web Server.

FIGURE 21.6

The Internet Database Connector requires an .idc file with the query and data source information, and an .htx file with formatting instructions for the returned data.

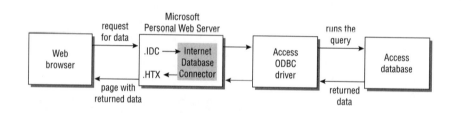

Because the Web server actually executes the instructions in the .idc and .htx files, you need to store these files in a separate folder and specify that the files in the folder are to be executed and are not to be displayed as ordinary web pages.

Prepare for the new files as follows:

1. In the FrontPage Explorer, choose File ➤ New ➤ Folder and name the folder Queries.

2. Right-click the Queries folder and choose Properties from the shortcut menu. Check the Allow scripts or programs to be run check box and click OK(see Figure 21.7a). Click OK in the message indicating that the Queries folder can not be browsed when you allow scripts to be run from the folder (see Figure 21.7b).

We are now ready to create the two files that the Internet Database Connector requires. It is possible to create both files using a text editor such as Notepad, but FrontPage has some tools to help.

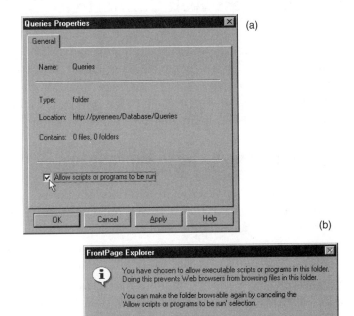

FIGURE 21.7

When you specify that the Queries folder contains programs to be run (a), the files in the folder are not available for browsing by the Web visitor (b).

Using the FrontPage Database Connectivity Tools

A new feature of FrontPage 97 is its ability to connect to ODBC databases using the Internet Database Connector. FrontPage provides a page wizard to assist in creating the .idc file and a page template for creating the .htx file. Unfortunately, neither of these tools provides the kind of help that would make connecting to a database as easy as everything else in FrontPage. The Internet Database Connector Wizard has a dialog for specifying the data source name and the .htx file for the results, but the wizard doesn't help with creating the SQL statement for the data request. The Database Results page template creates an empty page with the .htx format, but doesn't help you to write the formatting instructions. Later in the chapter, you'll learn how to use these tools to create .icd and .htx files from scratch, but for now, we'll turn to Microsoft Access 97 to give us more help in creating these files.

**NOTE**

If you don't have Microsoft Access, you can "dry-lab" the next few sections by reading along and viewing the results that Access creates. Then, you can duplicate the results by creating the .idc and .htx files yourself as explained in subsequent sections.

Using the Access Web Connectivity Tools

Fortunately, Microsoft Access 97 comes through with the help we need. Access 97 can create both the .idc file and a default.htx file for us. The key is to create the data request in Access 97, and then have Access create the SQL statement and the two files that the Internet Database Connector needs. If you've worked with Access, you know how easy it is to create simple data requests using the graphical query design window (*query* is the database terminology for a request for data).

Displaying a Database Table Dynamically

We'll start with a simple example to see how the process works. The pctc database has a table named Members that stores information about the club members, including name, city, the date that the member joined the club, and the number of miles logged for the year. In this example we'll retrieve the entire table and use Access's default formatting instructions to display the results.

1. Double-click the pctc.mdb file in the FrontPage Explorer. Access starts and displays the pctc Database window with the Members table (see Figure 21.8).

FIGURE 21.8

The pctc Database window in Microsoft Access lists the Members table in the Tables tab.

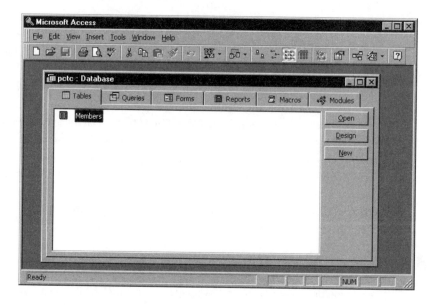

2. Double-click the Members table icon to display the data stored in the table (see Figure 21.9). Each horizontal row is called a *record,* and corresponds to a member in the club. Each vertical column is called a *field,* and corresponds to a type of information being stored. The fields in the members table are LastName, FirstName, City, JoinDate, and MilesYTD. You create the .htx and .idc files simply by exporting the table to the Queries folder and specifying these file formats.

FIGURE 21.9

Double-click the Members table icon to display the data in the table.

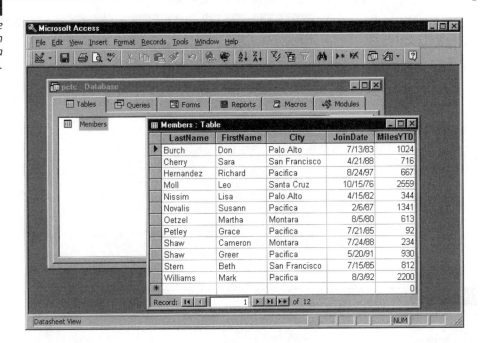

3. Choose File ➤ Save As/Export from the menu bar. Click OK in the Save As dialog to create an external file for the Members table (see Figure 21.10a).

4. In the Save Table 'Members' As dialog, locate the Queries folder in the Database Web (default path c:\Webshare\Wwwroot\Database\Queries). Note that the Queries folder icon has the hand indicating the folder is shared. Open the Queries folder and select Microsoft IIS 1-2 (*.htx; *.idc) in the Save as type combo list (see Figure 21.10b).

5. Click the Export button. Type **pctc** in the Data Source Name text box in the HTX/IDC Output Options dialog and click OK to have Access create a default template (see Figure 21.11). Access creates both files and stores them in the Queries folder.

FIGURE 21.10

Click the option to export the table to an external file (a). Locate the file and specify the .htx and .idc formats (b).

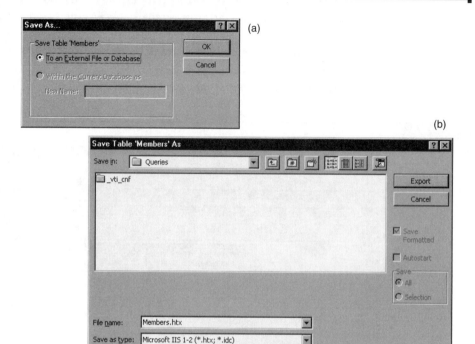

FIGURE 21.11

Specify the data source name and an optional template for the .htx file.

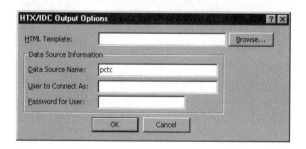

6. Click the Close button in the Access window. The changes are imported to the Web. In the FrontPage Explorer, choose View ➤ Refresh from the menu bar or press F5 to update the screen, and then click the Queries folder to display the list of the two new files.

Providing a Link to the Data Request

The .idc and .htx files are ready to go and we need only provide a way for the Web visitor to initiate the request for the current data in the Members table. We'll create a hyperlink from the home page to the .idc file. When the Web visitor clicks the link, the Internet Database Connector will execute the .idc file.

1. In the FrontPage Explorer, click the web folder to display the pages, and double-click the Home Page. Type **View the membership,** and create a text hyperlink to the Members.IDC file (see Chapter 12 for information on creating a link to a file).

2. Click the Save button and then the Preview in Browser button in the Editor toolbar. Click the hyperlink to have the Internet Database Connector run the query and create the dynamic database Web page shown in Figure 21.12.

FIGURE 21.12

The Internet Database Connector creates the dynamic page using the data retrieved from the database.

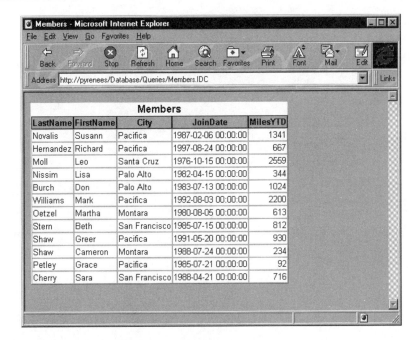

Viewing the IDC and HTX Files

Let's take a look at the files Access created.

1. In the FrontPage Explorer, double-click the Members.IDC file. The Internet Database Connector Wizard starts and displays its first screen (see Figure 21.13a).

PART

IV

Advanced Topics

The ODBC Data source is shown as pctc and the Query results template is shown as Members.htx.

2. Click Next to display the SQL statement (see Figure 21.13b). As is the case with most SQL statements, you can usually figure out what the statement means even if you don't know how to create the statement yourself. In this case, the statement SELECT * FROM [Members] means select all of the fields (the asterisk represents all the table fields) in the Members table.

3. Click Next and then Finish.

FIGURE 21.13

The first wizard screen shows the data source name and the name of the results file (a). The second wizard screen shows the SQL statement (b).

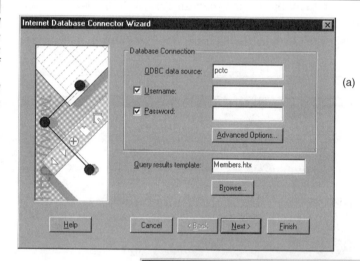

(a)

(b)

4. In the FrontPage Explorer, double-click the Members.htx file. The Editor displays the formatting instructions of the .htx file (see Figure 21.14).

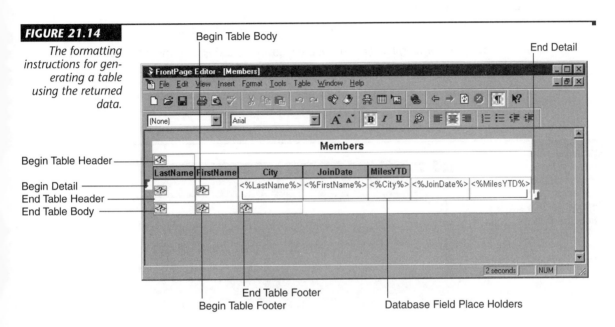

Begin Table Body

End Detail

Begin Table Header

Begin Detail
End Table Header
End Table Body

End Table Footer
Begin Table Footer

Database Field Place Holders

At the top of the table is a caption with the text Members. Below the caption cell is a row of header cells with the header labels LastName, FirstName, City, JoinDate, and MilesYTD. The formatting instructions for the table include six HTML Markup bots. When viewed in the FrontPage Editor, the bots are displayed using the syntax <?>, and are located in table cells. The two bots in the row below the header row occupy the first two cells of the row so the placeholders for the data are offset to the right by two cells. For example, the place holder for LastName, <%LastName%> appears to be in the "City" column. When the Web server generates the results page, the server uses the instructions in the HTML Markup bots to create the table, the <?> symbols do not appear in the generated page, and the data is correctly aligned with the corresponding header cell in the page that is sent to the browser. The next section describes the roles of the HTML Markup bots.

Understanding the Formatting Instructions for a Dynamic Database Table

In creating the formatting instructions for the table that displays the returned data, Access uses HTML elements to divide the table into header, body, and footer sections.

Because FrontPage does not recognize these elements, the Editor uses HTML Markup bots to represent them (see Figure 21.15). There is a pair of HTML Markup bots for each of the elements:

<THEAD> and </THEAD> mark the beginning and end of the table header cells

<TBODY> and </TBODY> mark the beginning and end of the table body cells

<TFOOT> and </TFOOT> mark the beginning and end of the table footer cells

In the table shown in Figure 21.13, there are no table footer cells, so there are no cells between the two HTML Markup bots for the footer section.

FIGURE 21.15

To create the table, Access uses HTML elements that FrontPage doesn't recognize to divide the table into header, body, and footer sections.

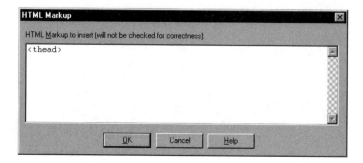

The rows of the returned data are displayed in the body of the table. FrontPage uses the red angle bracket symbols to mark the rows that will be created to hold the returned data. Corresponding to each field in the database table, the .htx table has a placeholder indicated by surrounding the field name with percent signs and then enclosing the result in angle brackets. For example, <%LastName%> is the .htx place holder for the LastName field. The red angle symbols indicate that a row is to be created for each record in the database table. The repeating section of the .htx page is called the *detail section*, the red angle bracket on the left is the *begin detail* symbol and the bracket on the right is the *end detail* symbol.

When the data is returned from the Access ODBC driver, the Internet Database Connector executes the instructions between the begin detail and end detail symbols for each returned row by replacing the place holders with the database table values. The Internet Database Connector repeats the instructions for each returned row and creates the detail section, or body, for the table as it generates the HTML page that is returned to the browser.

You can modify the .htx file using any of the techniques you've learned in the book. You can have the .htx page borrow its styles from another page, and you can insert additional text, images, video, and sound files. You can format the table cells with borders, fonts, and background colors. Do not move the database field place-holders and leave the HTML Markup bots undisturbed. Changing the location of the placeholders and bots will dramatically affect the results page. Figure 21.16 shows the.htx file modified to include an image, background styles, cell formatting, and a hyperlink back to the Home Page.

FIGURE 21.16

Use the familiar tools of the FrontPage Editor to modify the .htx file (a), and then display the modified page in a browser (b).

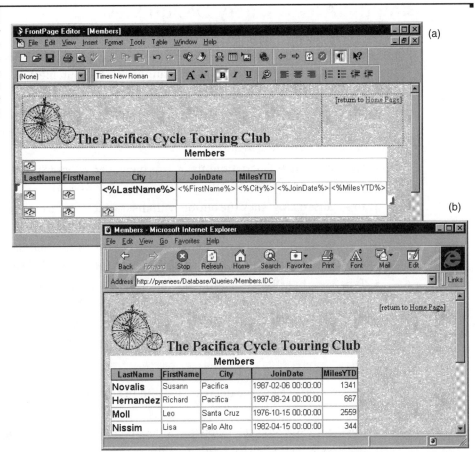

Letting the Visitor Select the Data

Suppose you want to allow the Web visitor to select the data that is returned instead of just returning the entire database table. For example, suppose the visitor just wants to view the "hard hitters"—that, is the club members who have logged lots of miles, or just the club members who live in Pacifica, or just the more recent members who joined since the beginning of 1995. To allow the Web visitor to select the data, we'll need to create a form to collect the visitor's selection criteria and pass the criteria along with the .idc file to the Internet Database Connector. Again, we can call on Microsoft Access to help in building the files.

Using the Access Query Design View

We'll use the graphical query design view to create a query that will allow the visitor to specify selection criteria. To illllustrate the technique, we'll create a query that uses the number of miles entered by the visitor and selects the club members who have exceeded this number.

1. In the FrontPage Explorer, double-click the pctc.mdb file. Access starts and displays the Database window as before. In the next step, we'll create a query to select data from the Members table.

2. Choose Insert ➤ Query from the Access menu bar, choose Simple Query Wizard in the New Query dialog, and click OK (see Figure 21.17a).

3. In the first dialog, click the button with the double arrow to include all the fields from the Members table (see Figure 21.17b), and click Next.

4. Click Next to accept the default of showing the individual database records (instead of creating a summary) and click Next (see Figure 21.18a).

5. Type **MembersByMiles** as the title of the query, click the option to modify the query design, and then click Finish (see Figure 21.18b).

Access creates the new query and displays the query window shown in Figure 21.19a. The grid in the lower pane has a column for each of the fields.

Creating the Parameter Query

You use the Criteria cell in the query design grid to enter selection criteria for a field as follows:

1. Click in the Criteria cell below the MilesYTD field and type > **[EnterMiles]** as the selection criteria (see Figure 21.19b). Access uses square brackets to indicate a value that the Web visitor supplies. The value that the visitor supplies is called a *parameter*. The Web visitor enters a number for the [EnterMiles] parameter, then when the query is executed, only the club members with miles greater than the number are returned.

FIGURE 21.17

Use the Simple Query Wizard (a) to create a query that includes all the fields from the Members table (b).

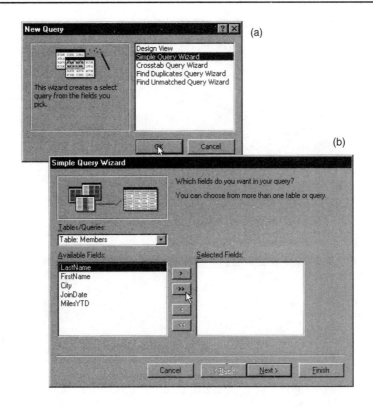

NOTE

A query that has a parameter that must be supplied before the query can run is called a parameter query.

2. Click the Save button in the Access toolbar. Choose File ➤ Save As/Export from the Access menu bar, click the option to save to an external file in the Save As dialog, and click OK. In the Save Query dialog, locate and open the Queries folder in the Database Web, select Microsoft IIS 1-2 (*.htx; *.idc) in the Save as Type combo list, and click Export. Click OK in the HTX/IDC Output Options dialog (Access remembers the Data Source Name for the previous export).

FIGURE 21.18

Choose the option to display the records (a) and name the query (b).

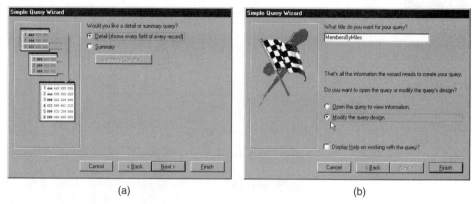

(a)   (b)

FIGURE 21.19

The Access query design grid (a). Enter the selection criteria in the Criteria cell below the field (b).

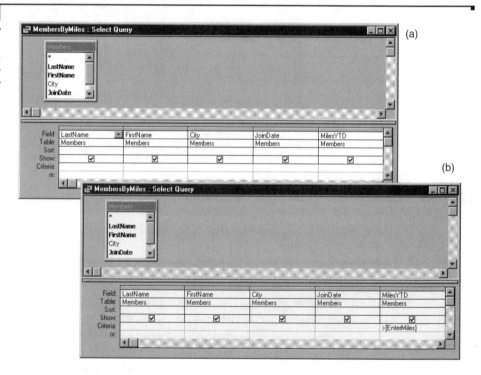

3. Click OK in the Enter Parameter Value dialog (see Figure 21.20). We leave this dialog blank because we want the Web visitor to enter the value for the parameter. Click the Close button in the Access window. FrontPage imports the changes to the database.

FIGURE 21.20

Leave the Enter Parameter Value blank, because the Web visitor will supply the value.

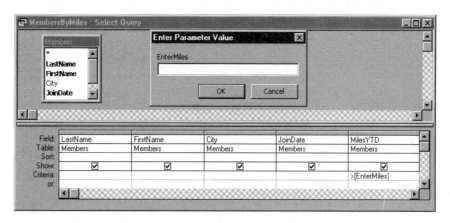

Viewing the Three Files That Access Creates

Let's take a look as the files that Access creates when you export a parameter query with the .htx and .idc formats.

1. Press F5 to refresh the web, and click to open the Queries folder in the FrontPage Explorer (see Figure 21.21). Access created .idc and .htx files for the new query, and also created an HTML file.

FIGURE 21.21

When you export a parameter query as .htx and .idc files, Access creates an .html file as well.

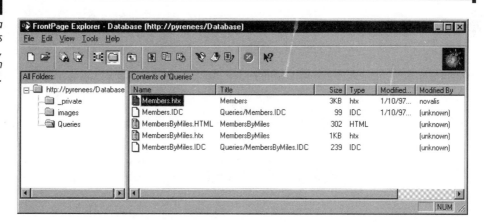

Understanding the Selection Criteria Form

The HTML file that Access creates is a page with a form that the Web visitor uses to enter the selection criteria.

1. Double-click the MembersByMiles.html file to view the page in the Editor (see Figure 21.22a). The page has a form with a single text box and a Run Query push button. Double-click the text box to view the Text Box Properties dialog (see Figure 21.22b). The text box has the same name as the query parameter. Click OK to close the dialog. Select the [EnterMiles] label, and type **Enter the number of miles,** and then click the Save button in the toolbar.

The selection criteria form (a). The text box has the same name as the query parameter (b).

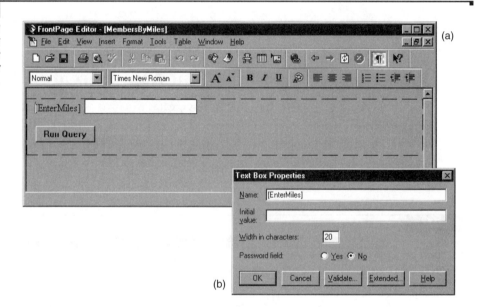

2. Right-click in the form and choose Form Properties from the shortcut menu. The Form Properties dialog shows that the Form Handler is an Internet Database Connector file (see Figure 21.23). Click the Settings button. The Settings for Database Connector dialog indicates that the MembersByMiles.IDC file is the handler for the form (see Figure 21.23). Click OK and then click OK again to close the form dialogs.

3. Because we are going to use this form to collect the visitor's selection criteria, we must make this page available for browsing. You can either move this page out of the Queries folder or just copy the form to an existing page and delete the MembersByMiles.html page. We'll copy the form in the next step.

FIGURE 21.23

The Form Handler is the Internet Database Connector, and the setting is the MembersByMiles .idc file.

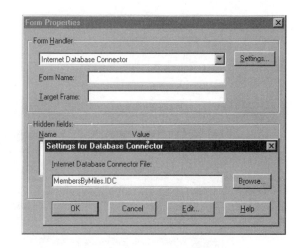

4. Move the insertion point to the left boundary of the form. When the pointer changes to a left-pointing arrow, double-click to select the form. Press Ctrl+C or choose Edit ➤ Copy from the Editor menu bar to copy the form. If necessary, open the Home Page, click in the page, and press Ctrl+V, or choose Edit ➤ Paste from the Editor menu bar to paste the form. Click the Save button to save the changes.

5. Click the Preview in Browser button in the toolbar. Type 1000 in the text box and click the Run Query button (see Figure 21.24a). The Internet Database Connector passes the value of the parameter along with the .idc file to the Access ODBC driver, which runs the query using the value, and returns only the records for the members with miles that exceed the value (see Figure 21.24b).

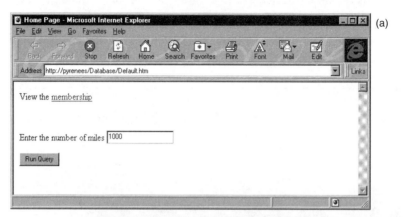

(a)

(b)

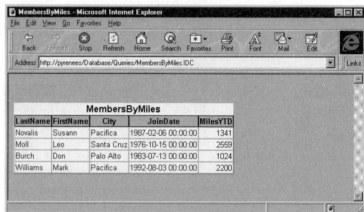

Understanding the .idc and .htx files

Let's take a look at the .idc and .htx files that Access created for the parameter query.

1. In the FrontPage Explorer, double-click the MembersByMiles.IDC file to start the Internet Database Connector Wizard. Click Next to display the second dialog with the SQL statement (see Figure 21.25). Here is the SQL statement that Access has created for the .idc file:

   SELECT Members.LastName, Members.FirstName, Members.City, Members.JoinDate, Members.MilesYTD

   FROM Members

   WHERE (((Members.MilesYTD)>%[EnterMiles]%));

This SQL statement selects the database fields from the Members table (this time the database fields are listed instead of using an asterisk to represent all the fields). The third line limits the data returned to the records for members whose miles to date exceed the number entered in the form field. The Internet Database Connector encloses the name of the form field in the percent signs. Copy the entire SQL statement to the Clipboard (we'll use it later). Click Finish to close the wizard.

FIGURE 21.25

The SQL statement for the parameter query limits the data returned.

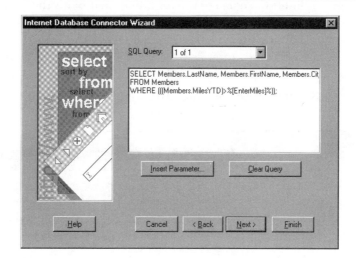

2. Double-click the MembersByMiles.htx file to view the formatting instructions in the Editor. The page looks just like the formatting instructions for the Members .htx file, except the table heading is changed to MembersByMiles.

In this simple example, you are allowing the Web visitor to enter a single selection criteria. Suppose you wanted to provide additional selection criteria. For example, you might want to allow the visitor to specify a mileage range by typing in the lower and upper bounds in separate text boxes and then selecting only the members whose mileage is greater than the lower bound and less than the upper bound. Or, you may want to allow the visitor to select members who joined after a specified date and who live in a specified city. You can use the Access query design grid to design parameter queries with several selection criteria and then have Access create the criteria selection form with text boxes for each criteria and the corresponding .idc and .htx files.

Displaying the Visitor's Selection Criteria in the Results Page

Let's modify the .htx file to display the value that the visitor entered for the query parameter.

1. Press Ctrl+Enter to insert a new first line above the table. Type **Here are the members who rode more than**

2. Choose Edit ➤ Database ➤ IDC Parameter Value from the Editor menu bar. Enter the name of the form field that holds the query parameter in the IDC Parameter Value dialog. Type **[EnterMiles]** and click OK (see Figure 21.26). The Editor represents the form field using the syntax <%idc.[EnterMiles]%>. The syntax for a form field place holder is similar to the syntax for a database field place holder except that idc. precedes the form field name.

3. Press Space and type **miles:** and then click the Save button in the toolbar.

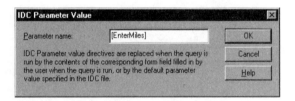

FIGURE 21.26

Enter the name of the form field in the IDC Parameter Value dialog.

To view the modified results page, display the Home Page in the Editor, click the Preview in Browser button in the toolbar, type **1000** in the text box, and click the Run Query push button. Figure 21.27 shows the modified results page in the browser.

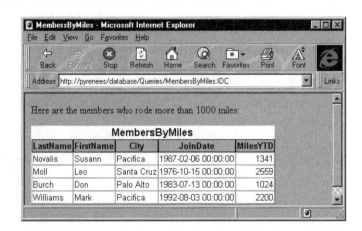

FIGURE 21.27

You can display the selection value on the results page.

Creating the Files from Scratch

Now that Access has shown us how to create the .idc, .htx, and selection criteria form for a simple request, let's create a set of files from scratch.

Specifying Data Types for Query Parameters

Unfortunately, the Internet Database Connector does not automatically recognize the different formats that data may have. Database management programs such as Microsoft Access store data in different formats. For example, in the Members table, the LastName, FirstName, and City fields all have the Text data format, the JoinDate field has the Date/Time format, and the MilesYTD field has the Number format. When you create a parameter query, the Internet Database Connector expects the parameter to have the Number data type. If the parameter has another data type, you have to tell the Internet Database Connector the parameter's data format by modifying the SQL statement, as follows:

- **Text data** If the parameter has the Text data format, enclose the query parameter with single quotes (').

- **Number data** If the parameter has the Date/Time format, enclose the query parameter with the number symbol (#).

Creating an .idc File from Scratch

To illustrate, we'll create an .idc file from scratch for a new parameter query that the visitor can use to select members from a city.

1. In the Editor, choose File ➤ New from the menu bar, and double-click the Database Connector Wizard in the New Page dialog. Type **pctc** in the ODBC data source text box, and type **MembersByCity** in the query results template (we haven't created this file yet).

2. Click Next, and paste the SQL statement you copied to the Clipboard in the last example. Change the third line of the SQL statement to

   WHERE (((Members.City)='%[EnterCity]%'));

   and be careful not to make any other changes. (SQL statements are quite delicate and an extra space in the wrong location or a missing parenthesis can cause an error.)

3. Click Finish to create the file. Open the Queries folder in the Current Web dialog, type **MembersByCity** in the Save As dialog, and click OK (see Figure 21.28).

FIGURE 21.28

When you create an IDC file from scratch, you use the Current Web dialog to specify the file-name and location.

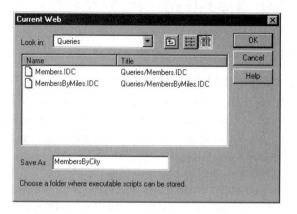

Creating the .htx File

Next, we'll create an .htx file to display the results. We'll create the new file by copying and then modifying the MembersByMiles.htm file.

1. In the FrontPage Explorer, right-click the MembersByMiles.htx file, drag the file icon to the bottom of the list, drop the file icon, and choose Copy Here from the shortcut menu. Change the filename to MembersByCity.htx.

2. Double-click the MembersByCity.htx file to display the file in the Editor. Modify the text in the first line to **Here are the members who live in**, change the table heading to **Members By City**, and change the Page Title to **Members By City**.

3. Click the form field place holder (when the pointer icon changes to the bot icon) and press Delete. Choose Edit ➤ Database ➤ IDC Parameter Value from the Editor menu bar, type **[EnterCity]** in the dialog, and click OK. Click the form field placeholder and then click the Bold button in the toolbar. Click the Save button in the toolbar.

You can also create an .htx file from scratch using the Edit ➤ Database commands as follows:

1. Choose File ➤ New from the Editor menu bar and double-click Database Results in the New Page dialog. You can choose whether to lay out the results in a table. To lay out the results without using a table, skip to Step 3.

2. To use a table to lay out the detail section, choose Table ➤ Insert Table from the menu bar and insert a table with one row and with the number of columns from the database query that you want to display (see Chapter 14 for information on formatting tables). Choose Table ➤ Select Row to select the row.

3. Create a detail section by choosing Edit ➤ Database ➤ Detail Section. If you are using a table, the Editor encloses the selected table row with the detail symbols (see Figure 21.29a). Otherwise, the Editor displays the detail symbols (see Figure 21.29b). The next step is to insert placeholders between the detail symbols for each of the database fields that you want to display.

FIGURE 21.29

To use a table in the detail section, insert and select a one-row table, and then insert detail symbols (a). To lay out the detail section without using a table, insert detail symbols (b).

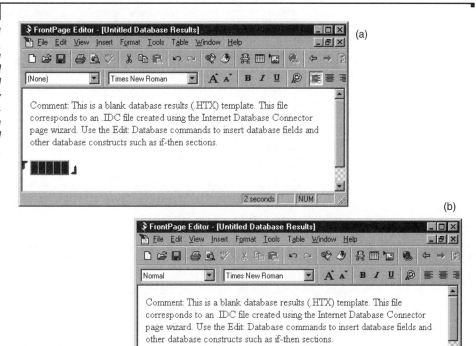

4. Place the insertion point in the first table cell (or between the detail symbols if you are not using a table), and choose Edit ➤ Database ➤ Database Column Value from the Editor menu. Type the name of the database field in the Database Column Name dialog and click OK (see Figure 21.30a). The Editor inserts a place holder for the database field (see Figure 21.30b).

5. Continue to insert placeholders for the database fields. After laying out the database fields and modifying the file to include the text and images you want to display, save the file to the Queries folder.

Type the name of the database field (a) and click OK to insert a placeholder for the field at the insertion point (b).

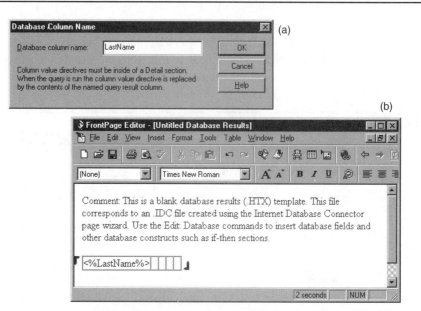

NOTE

You can also include conditional sections in the .htx file using the If-Then Conditional Section and the Else Conditional Section commands. See online help for more information.

Creating the Selection Criteria Form

Finally, we'll create the data entry form to collect the visitor's choice.

1. Display the Home Page in the Editor. Click the bottom of the page, type **Enter the name of a city**, insert a one-one text box and type **[EnterCity]** as the name of the text box. Insert a push button, change its caption to Run Query, and assign the MembersByCity.idc file as the form handler.

2. Click the Save button and then click the Preview in Browser button in the toolbar. Type **Pacifica** in the text box (see Figure 21.31a) and click the Run Query push button. Figure 21.31b shows the results.

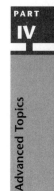

FIGURE 21.31

The selection criteria is a text value (a). The query results (b).

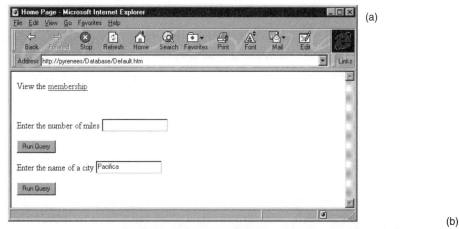

(a)

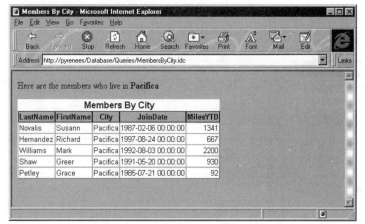

(b)

Entering a New Record in the Database

As a final example, we'll create a data entry form for entering a new member in the Members table in the pctc.mdb Access database. This time, we'll have to create the SQL statement ourselves, because Access can't create the .idc and .htx files for the type of SQL statement required to add a new record.

Creating the Data Entry Form

First we'll create the data entry form:

1. Display the Home Page in the Editor. Click in the bottom of the Home Page and type **Enter data for a new members.**

2. Use a table to lay out the form fields, insert one-line text boxes for each of the database fields, and name each form field using the corresponding table name. Use exactly the same name, for example the form field for the LastName database field has the name LastName. Type labels for the text boxes as shown in Figure 21.32.

3. Insert a push button and change the caption to Run Query. Click the Form button on the Push Button Properties dialog, set the form handler to Internet Database Connector, click the Settings button, and type **Queries/ AddMember.idc** in the Settings for Database Connector dialog. Because the file doesn't exist yet, FrontPage asks if you want to create a link to the file anyway. Click Yes to create the link.

FIGURE 21.32

The data entry form to add a new record to the Members table

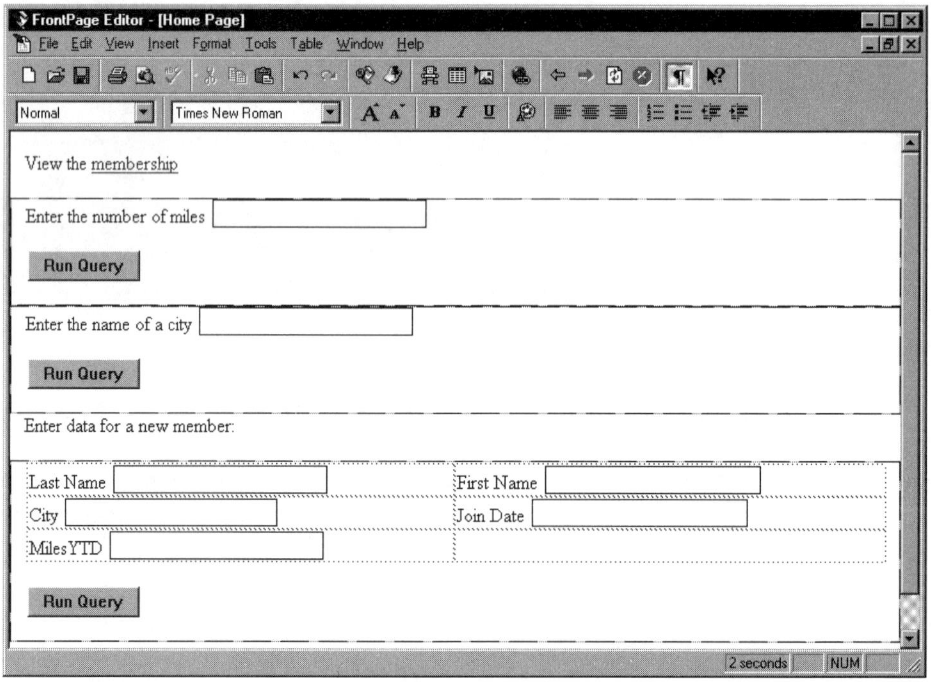

Creating the Results File

Now let's create the AddMember.htx results file. When you add a new record to a database you are entering data into the database and are not retrieving data. We'll create an .htx file to display the values from the data entry form that are entered into the database.

1. Choose File ➤ New in the Editor menu bar, and double-click Database Results in the NewPage dialog. Click in the bottom of the page and type **Here is the new member information that has been entered:**

2. We'll insert a form field placeholder for each of the data entry fields in the form. For each form field, type a label, choose Edit ➤ Database ➤ IDC Parameter Value, type the name of the form field in the IDC Parameter Value dialog, and click OK. Figure 21.33 shows the dialog for the MilesYTD form field.

FIGURE 21.33

Use the IDC Parameter Value command to create the data entry results file.

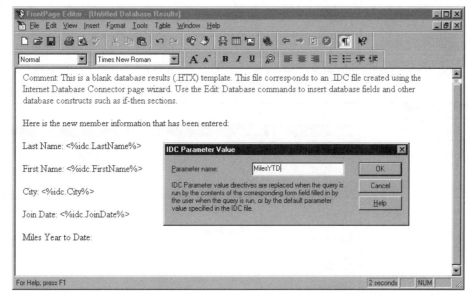

3. Click the Save button in the toolbar. Save the page with the title New Member Information and type the file path **Queries/AddMember.htx**

Creating the .idc File to Add a New Record

Finally, we'll create the .idc file. We'll need to create the SQL statement to add a new record to the Members table.

1. Choose File ➤ New in the Editor menu bar and double-click Database Connector Wizard.

2. Type **pctc** as the ODBC data source, type **AddMember.htx** as the results template, and click Next.

3. Type the following SQL statement in the next dialog:

> INSERT INTO Members (LastName, FirstName, City, JoinDate, MilesYTD)
>
> VALUES ('%LastName%', '%FirstName%', '%City%', #%JoinDate%#, MilesYTD);

This SQL statement creates a new row in the Members table and inserts the values that the Web visitor enters in the form fields in the data entry form into the corresponding database fields.

4. Click Finish to create the file. Save the file in the Queries folder and type **AddMember** as the name of the file.

Let's test the new files by adding a new member:

1. Display the Home Page in the Editor and click the Preview in Browser button.

2. Enter the data for the new member as shown in Figure 21.34, and click the Run Query button. Figure 21.35 reports that James Kelley has been added to the Members table.

FIGURE 21.35

The results file for the query that adds a new record displays the information entered in the data entry form.

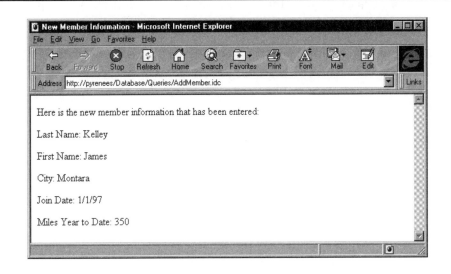

End Note . . .

This chapter has introduced you to using the Internet Database Connector server extension software in the Microsoft Personal Web Server to retrieve live data from an Access database. You've learned how to create the .idc file that contains the data source information, the request for data, and the name of the .htx file with the formatting instructions for the results, and how to create the .htx file. You also learned how to create a form that passes information entered by the Web visitor along with the idc file. You used this technique to create forms and queries that allow the Web visitor to select which data to display. You also learned how to add a new record to a table.

Congratulations! You've come to the end of Mastering FrontPage 97. You've learned how to create Web pages that are alive with multimedia effects such as sounds, animated text, images and animated images, and video clips. Your web pages include interactive features such as information collection forms, text searches, and online discussion groups. You can manage your web using the FrontPage Explorer to trace out all the links to be sure the targets exist. You can create the web pages and manage the web using the built-in features of FrontPage 97 without writing any programs yourself. Part IV introduced two of the advanced features that require simple programming. You learned how to insert ActiveX Controls in a page and write simple scripts to connect the controls. Finally, you learned how to display dynamic data from an Access database and write simple requests for data.

It's time now to put this book aside and create webs with interesting interactive pages that provide the information you want to publish, and collect information from your Web visitors. See you on the Web!

Appendix

A

Installing FrontPage 97 and the Personal Web Servers

INSTALLING FRONTPAGE 97 AND THE PERSONAL WEB SERVERS

This appendix shows you how to install Microsoft FrontPage 97 using the Microsoft Personal Web Server for Windows 95 as the default Web server and the FrontPage Personal Web Server as a secondary Web server.

NOTE

The Microsoft Personal Web Server for Windows 95 works only with the Windows 95 operating system. If you are using Windows NT, skip the "Installing the Microsoft Personal Web Server" section. Instead, follow the directions for your operating system to install the Microsoft Peer Web Services for NT 4.0 Workstation or the Microsoft Internet Information Server for NT Server 3.51 with Service Pack 5 or later. Then continue with the installation of FrontPage 97 and the FrontPage Personal Web Server.

You'll also learn how to do the following:

- Change the default page name
- Modify the Windows Start Menu to display the FrontPage program components
- Use the FrontPage Server Administrator
- Change a Web server's port number
- Test the connection between FrontPage and a Web server

Each of the Personal Web Servers has capabilities that the other doesn't have, and both Web servers are needed to work through the chapters of this book, as follows:

FrontPage Personal Web Server

Chapter 9: Administering a Web

Chapter 18: Understanding Searches and Visitor Registration

Appendix D: Creating Web Templates with the FrontPage 97 SDK

Microsoft Personal Web Server for Windows 95 (or Microsoft Peer Web Services for Windows NT or Microsoft Internet Information Server for Windows NT Server)

Chapter 21: Creating Dynamic Database Pages with Access

When you are finished with the book, you can continue to use both Personal Web Servers, uninstall one, or use another Web server. These instructions assume that you do not have any other Web servers installed on your computer. It is recommended that you follow the installation steps below:

- Install FrontPage 97 with Personal Web Servers

  1. Uninstall previous versions of Microsoft FrontPage and the FrontPage Personal Web Server.

  2. Install the Microsoft Personal Web Server for Windows 95, the Microsoft Peer Web Services for Windows NT Workstation, or the Microsoft Internet Information Server for Windows NT Server.

  3. Install the FrontPage 97, FrontPage Personal Web Server, and FrontPage Server Extensions to both Personal Web Servers.

- Install or upgrade to Microsoft Internet Explorer 3.0

- optional installations

  - Install Microsoft Image Composer

  - Install Microsoft Web Publishing Wizard

If you've already installed FrontPage 97 with only one of the Personal Web Servers or with another Web server, and want to set up your computer to follow along with the step by step instructions in this book, see the "Adding the FrontPage Personal Web Server" section or the "Adding the Microsoft Personal Web Server" section later in this appendix.

NOTE

If you have installed FrontPage 97 with another Web server, such as O'Reilly Website, and prefer not to install the Microsoft Web servers, you can still follow along with the book. Depending on your Web server, you may not be able to complete some of the chapters listed above.

Getting Ready to Install

Before installing, make sure your computer is able to run FrontPage 97, and uninstall previous versions of FrontPage.

APDX

A

Installing FrontPage 97 and the Web Servers

System Requirements for Microsoft FrontPage 97

You must have the following system requirements before you can run Microsoft FrontPage 97:

- A computer with a 486 or higher processor, sound card, and speakers
- Microsoft Windows 95 or Microsoft Windows NT Workstation 3.51 with Service pack 5 or later
- 8MB RAM for Windows 95 using FrontPage Personal Web Server (16MB recommended for use with Microsoft Personal Web Server); 16MB for Windows NT Workstation
- 30MB available hard-disk space
- CD-ROM drive
- VGA or higher resolution (Super VGA, 256 color recommended)
- Pointing device, such as Microsoft Mouse
- Internet access is required to use Internet features

Requirements for Bonus Pack components:

- 11-MB hard-disk space for Microsoft Internet Explorer 3.0
- 1MB hard-disk space for Microsoft Personal Web Server
- 1MB hard-disk space for Microsoft Web Publishing Wizard
- 2MB for Internet Mail and News add-ins for Internet Explorer 3.0
- 16MB RAM for Microsoft Image Composer (32MB recommended)
- VGA, 256 color (2MB video memory recommended)

Uninstalling Previous Versions of FrontPage

While is it possible to run previous versions of FrontPage on the same computer as FrontPage 97, you'll probably prefer to uninstall the previous versions and start with a fresh installation. To uninstall a previous version:

1. Click the Start button in the Windows taskbar and choose Settings ➤ Control Panel.

2. Click the Add Remove Programs icon. Locate the previous version of Microsoft FrontPage, and click OK to remove the application.

The uninstaller program removes the FrontPage programs and the FrontPage Personal Web Server, but does not remove all of the files and folders. The Microsoft

FrontPage program folder remains, and includes several subfolders, such as the sub-folders that contain the page and web templates. If you want to continue using any custom templates created previously, don't delete this folder. The FrontPage Webs folder remains, and includes the Contents subfolder with the webs you've created previously. Don't delete this folder unless you want to discard the FrontPage webs you created previously. The webs you created in FrontPage 1.1 will be updated when you install FrontPage 97.

Web server port numbers

Each type of server application that you install on your computer must be assigned a number for identification. This number is called the *port* number. Web servers typically use port 80. The first Web server you install on your computer will probably assign itself port number 80. Additional web servers must be assigned different numbers. You can assign any number greater than 1024 that is not already in use (numbers less than 1024 are reserved). Normally, the installation program for the second Web server detects the first Web server on port 80 and installs the second Web server to port 8080.

Installing the Microsoft Personal Web Server

Close all other applications to avoid conflicts with the updating of files that may be shared. Insert the Microsoft FrontPage 97 with Bonus Pack CD-ROM. The setup program starts automatically. The installation dialog displays buttons for FrontPage 97 and the four applications in the Bonus Pack (see Figure A.1).

NOTE

If you are using Windows NT, the Microsoft Personal Web Server for Windows 95 button is grayed out and unavailable. You should install the Microsoft Internet Information Server for NT Server or the Microsoft Peer Web Services if you are using NT Workstation. If you are using a Web server other than the Microsoft Personal Web Server for Windows 95, the installation steps for FrontPage 97 are similar to the steps described here.

*The FrontPage 97
setup dialog*

1. Click the button to install the Microsoft Personal Web Server for Windows 95.

2. If requested, insert your Windows 95 CD-ROM. The installation program may need to copy several files. Reinsert the FrontPage 97 CD-ROM.

3. Click Yes to restart the computer (see Figure A.2). You must restart your computer to complete the installation.

*After installing the
Microsoft Personal
Web Server, you
must restart your
computer.*

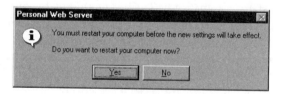

After restarting Windows 95 , the Microsoft Personal Web Server starts automatically, and displays its icon in the right end of the Windows status bar (see Figure A.3a). The icon is also displayed in the Control Panel (see Figure A.3b). The Microsoft Personal

Web Server is installed to the new Websvr folder (default path c:\Program Files\Websvr). A content folder named WebShare is created with a subfolder named Wwwroot, which is the default folder (the root web) for the Web server. The webs you create in FrontPage and store on the Microsoft Personal Web Server are stored in the Wwwroot folder (default path c:\Webshare\Wwwroot).

FIGURE A.3

When the Microsoft Personal Web Server is running, its icon is displayed in the Windows status bar (a) The icon is displayed in the Windows Control Panel (b).

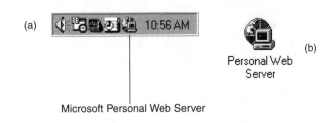

(a)

Microsoft Personal Web Server

(b)

Personal Web Server

Installing Microsoft FrontPage 97 and the FrontPage Personal Web Server

After installing the Microsoft Personal Web Server for Windows 95 (or another Web server if you are using Windows NT), insert the Microsoft FrontPage 97 with Bonus Pack CD-ROM.

1. Click the first button to install Microsoft FrontPage 97. Setup detects the presence of the Microsoft Personal Web Server (see Figure A.4). Click Yes to temporarily stop the server and continue the installation.

FIGURE A.4

To install FrontPage 97, you must temporarily shut down the Microsoft Personal Web Server.

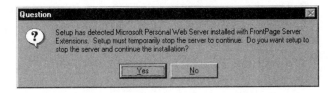

Question

Setup has detected Microsoft Personal Web Server installed with FrontPage Server Extensions. Setup must temporarily stop the server to continue. Do you want setup to stop the server and continue the installation?

Yes   No

2. Click Next to close the welcome screen (see Figure A.5a). Type your name and company (optional) in the Registration screen (see Figure A.5b), and click Next.

FIGURE A.5

The setup welcome screen (a) and the registration dialog (b)

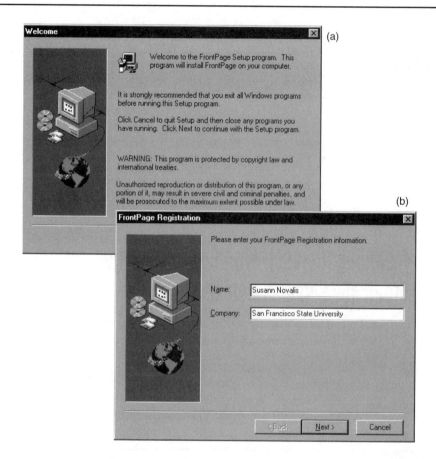

3. The next screen confirms your registration information. If the information is incorrect, click No to return to the previous screen. Otherwise, click Yes and enter the CD Key in the next screen (see Figure A.6a).

4. Click OK to display the Destination Path dialog (see Figure A.6b). Click Next to accept the default folder for installing FrontPage 97 to c:\Program Files\

Microsoft FrontPage, or click the Browse button and locate another folder. If you specify a folder that doesn't exist, the installation program offers to create it. After specifying the destination folder, click Next to display the Setup Type dialog (see Figure A.7a).

FIGURE A.6

The CD Key dialog (a) and the Destination Path dialog (b)

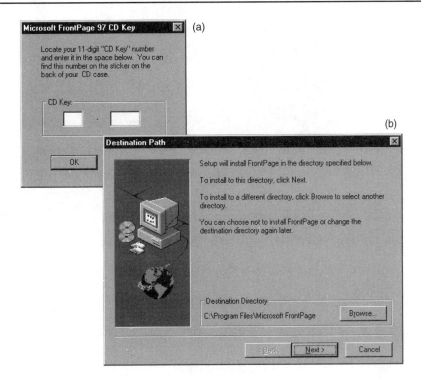

5. Click Custom so that you can specify which components to install and click Next. In the Select Components dialog, click the Microsoft FrontPage Personal Web Server check box and click Next (see Figure A.7b). (If you checked the Typical installation, the FrontPage Personal Web Server would not be installed).

6. Use this dialog to specify the folder in which you want to install the FrontPage Personal Web Server. Click Browse to specify a folder other than the default (see Figure A.8a). Click Next.

Choose the Custom installation (a) and select the FrontPage Personal Web Server (b).

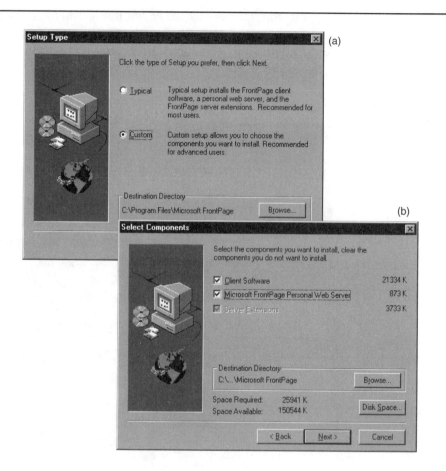

7. This screen informs you that because you already have a Web server on the default port (port 80), the FrontPage Personal Web Server will be installed on port 8080, and that to access the webs stored by this server, you and Web visitors will have to append :8080 to the server name (see Figure A.8b).

8. Click Next to display the Installed Servers Detected dialog indicating that the Microsoft Personal Web Server has been detected (see Figure A.9a).

FIGURE A.8

Select a destination folder for the FrontPage Personal Web Server (a). Setup detects the Microsoft Personal Web Server on the default port (b).

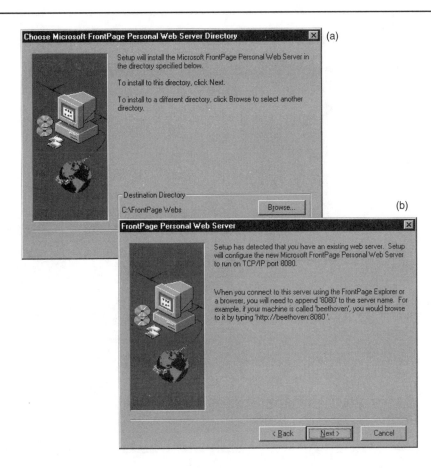

(a)

Choose Microsoft FrontPage Personal Web Server Directory

Setup will install the Microsoft FrontPage Personal Web Server in the directory specified below.

To install to this directory, click Next.

To install to a different directory, click Browse to select another directory.

Destination Directory

C:\FrontPage Webs   Browse...

(b)

FrontPage Personal Web Server

Setup has detected that you have an existing web server. Setup will configure the new Microsoft FrontPage Personal Web Server to run on TCP/IP port 8080.

When you connect to this server using the FrontPage Explorer or a browser, you will need to append '8080' to the server name. For example, if your machine is called 'beethoven', you would browse to it by typing 'http://beethoven:8080 '.

< Back   Next >   Cancel

APDX

A

Installing FrontPage 97 and the Web Servers

NOTE

The list in the Installed Servers Selected dialog will include any other Web servers you may have installed. You can select the Web servers for which you want to install FrontPage Server Extensions.

9. Click Next to display the Start Copying Files dialog, which indicates that FrontPage Client Software, the FrontPage Personal Web Server, and Server Extensions will be installed (see Figure A.9b).

FIGURE A.9

Setup detects other Web servers you've installed (a). Before installing, you can view the list of tems that will be installed (b).

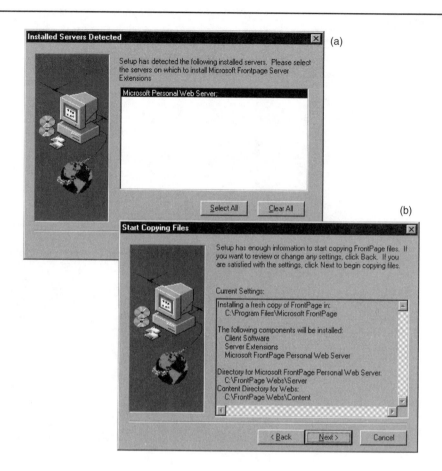

10. Click Next to begin the installation. Status bars update to show the progress of the installation (see Figure A.10). After installing the FrontPage 97 programs, the FrontPage Server Administrator runs once for each Web server, starting with the FrontPage Personal Web Server, and displays a pair of screens for each server. In the first screen of the pair, you establish yourself as the FrontPage administrator for the server. The second screen indicates that the Server Administrator is installing the Server Extensions and updating the server's content. (If you created webs previously in FrontPage 1.1, they are updated in this step). The

FrontPage Server Extensions are the software programs that will be installed with the specified Web servers, so that they will be able to run the programs that your FrontPage Webs require.

FIGURE A.10

As installation proceeds, setup indicates the files being copied.

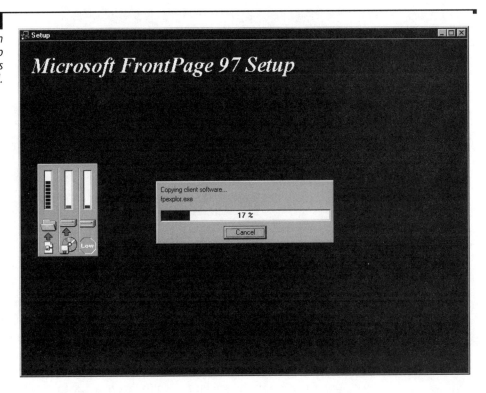

11. Type the name and password you want to use as the administrator for the FrontPage Personal Web Server (see Figure A.11a). Retype to confirm the password, and click OK to display the installation message (see Figure A.11b).

NOTE

You'll need to supply the name and the password using the same capitalization that you enter in the Administrator Setup for FrontPage Personal Web Server dialog whenever you create a new web or open an existing web stored by the FrontPage Personal Web Server.

Authorize yourself as the administrator of the FrontPage Personal Web Server (a). Setup installs the Server Extensions on port 8080.

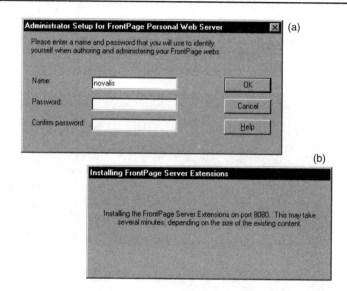

12. Type the name you want to use as the administrator for the Microsoft Personal Web Server, and click OK to display the installation message (see Figure A.11). The Microsoft Personal Web Server uses a security system that is more complex than the FrontPage Personal Web Server. However, when you have the Microsoft Personal Web Server and FrontPage installed on the same computer, security is disabled: When you open a web stored by the Microsoft Personal Web Server on the same computer as FrontPage, the server does not prompt you for a user name and password. (See Appendix C for information on this server's security features). Click Yes in the screen shown in Figure A.12c to complete the installation of the Server Extensions on this Web server.

13. Click Finish to complete the installation (see Figure A.13). The FrontPage Explorer window opens, but you are not quite through. The installation of FrontPage 97 is complete. FrontPage 97 is installed and the FrontPage Server Extensions are installed on port 80 to the Microsoft Personal Web Server and on port 8080 to the FrontPage Personal Web Server. The final step is to check the connection between FrontPage and the Web servers (you'll learn more about the TCP/IP connection in Chapter 2). Click OK to begin the test (see Figure A.14a). If the connection is OK, click OK in the screen shown in Figure A.14b). If another message is displayed, you'll have to check your TCP/IP installation; refer to the documentation for Windows 95 or Windows NT to resolve any problems, and then perform the TCP/IP test as described in the "TCP/IP Test" section.

FIGURE A.12

Authorize yourself as the administrator of the Microsoft Personal Web Server (a). Setup installs the Server Extensions on port 80 (b) and then restarts this server (c).

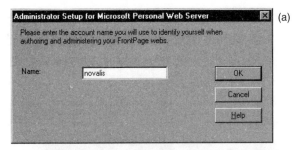

(a)

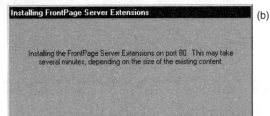

(b)

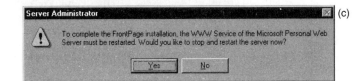

(c)

FIGURE A.13

The last setup dialog

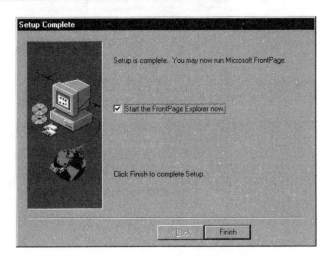

APDX

A

Installing FrontPage 97
and the Web Servers

FIGURE A.14

The final step is to check the connection between FrontPage and the Web servers (a). If the connection is OK (b), you can begin using FrontPage.

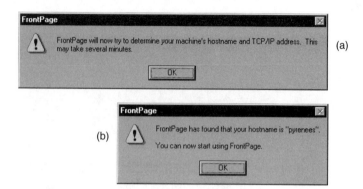

(a)

(b)

NOTE

The name identified as the hostname is the name you'll use as the Web server name when you create or open webs on the default Web server. To create or open webs on the FrontPage Personal Web Server, you'll use *hostname*:8080 instead.

14. You are now ready to start creating Webs with FrontPage (see Figure A.15)

FIGURE A.15

The Getting Started with Microsoft FrontPage dialog

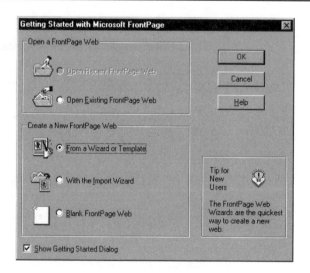

When the FrontPage Personal Web Server is running, the Windows task bar displays the icon shown in Figure A.16. Both Personal Web Servers can be running at the same time. In Chapter 5, you'll learn how to move webs from one server to another.

FIGURE A.16

When the FrontPage Personal Web Server is running, its icon is displayed in the Windows task bar.

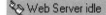

Changing the Name of the Default Page

When you browse to a web without specifying a page, the Web server that stores the Web looks for a default page to send to the browser. Web servers use different names for the default page. For example, the FrontPage Personal Web Server uses index.htm and the Microsoft Personal Web Server uses default.htm. You can change the name that the Web server uses for the default page. This section shows you how to change the default page name for the FrontPage Personal Web Server; Appendix B deals with the Microsoft Personal Web Server.

The FrontPage Personal Web Server stores its configuration settings in a subfolder named Conf. The file that defines the name of the default page has the name srm.cnf. You change the default page name by modifying this file in Notepad as follows:

1. Start the Windows Explorer, expand the FrontPage Webs folder, expand the Server folder, and open the Conf subfolder (see Figure A.17a).

2. Double-click the srm.cnf file to open the file in the Notepad. Scroll to locate the comment line #DirectoryIndex index.htm. (Any line that starts with # in the FrontPage configuration files is a comment.) In the next step you'll change the name of the default page to default.htm.

3. Insert a new line, type **DirectoryIndex default.htm,** and save the change to the file (see Figure A.17b).

4. Close Notepad.

If the FrontPage Personal Web Server is running, shut down and restart the server. The next time you browse to a web on this server without specifying a page, the server will load the default.htm page, if there is one. If there is no such page in the web, the server creates an index page for the web and sends it to the browser (see Chapter 4 for more information).

FIGURE A.17

The FrontPage Personal Web Server stores configuration information in a subfolder named conf (a). Change the name of the default page by modifying the srm.cnf file (b).

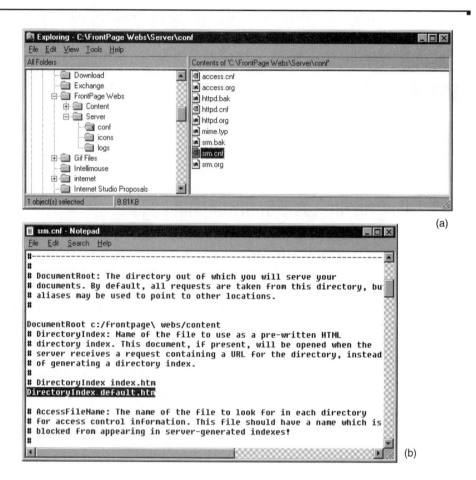

(a)

(b)

Modifying the Windows Start Menu

By default, the Start Menu in Windows 95 and Windows NT 4.0 lists Microsoft FrontPage as a single item. Choosing this item opens the FrontPage Explorer. You can modify the Start menu to include items for the FrontPage Editor, the TCP/IP Test, the FrontPage Server Administrator, and the FrontPage Personal Web Server as follows:

1. Click the Start button and choose Settings ➤ Taskbar. Click the Start Menu Programs tab in the Taskbar Properties dialog (see Figure A.18).

APDX

A

Installing FrontPage 97
and the Web Servers

FIGURE A.18

You can create new FrontPage Start Menu items using the Taskbar Properties dialog.

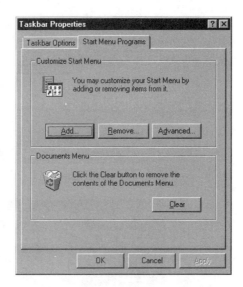

2. Click the Remove button, select Microsoft FrontPage in the Remove Shortcuts/Folder dialog and click Remove. Then click Close.

3. Click the Add button and then the Browse button. In the Browse dialog, locate and open the Microsoft FrontPage folder (default location C:\Program Files\Microsoft FrontPage).

4. Double-click the FrontPage Explorer shortcut icon (see Figure A.19a). Click Next in the Create Shortcut dialog. Click New Folder in the Select Program Folder dialog (see Figure A.19b). Type **Microsoft FrontPage** as the name of the new folder and then click Next. Click Finish to create the new startup program group and the FrontPage Editor item.

5. Repeat Steps 3 and 4 to add items for the FrontPage Editor and FrontPage Server Administrator to the Microsoft FrontPage program group.

6. Click the Add button, click the Browse button, and locate and open the bin folder in the Microsoft FrontPage folder. Double-click tcptest.exe and click Next. Select the Microsoft FrontPage folder in the Select Program Folder dialog, and click Next. Type **FrontPage TCP-IP Test** as the name for the shortcut, and then click Finish. (The slash is not allowed in the name of a shortcut, so we'll use a hyphen instead.)

Locate the program or the program shortcut (a) and click the New Folder button to create a new Start Menu program folder (b).

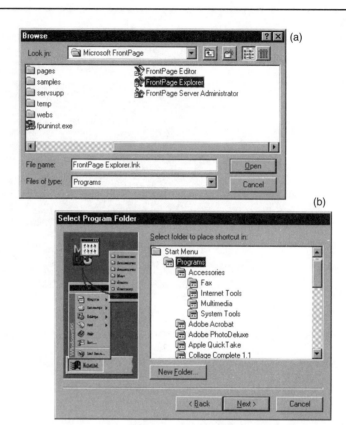

7. Repeat Step 6 to locate the vhttp32.exe program in the FrontPage Webs\Server folder and type **FrontPage Personal Web Server** as the name for the shortcut.

8. Click OK to close the Taskbar Properties dialog.

Figure A.20 shows the modified Start Menu.

NOTE

If you had a previous version of FrontPage installed, most of the Start Menu items already exist and it is not necessary to recreate them.

FIGURE A.20

*The customized
Start menu*

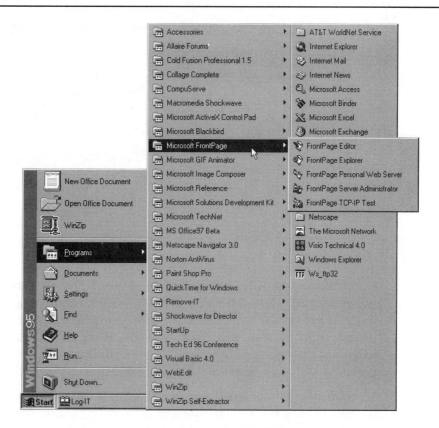

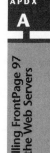

Understanding the FrontPage Server Administrator

This section describes the function of the FrontPage Server Administrator. It assumes you have modified the Windows Start Menu as described in the previous section. You use the FrontPage Server Administrator to manage the FrontPage Server Extensions for the Web servers installed on the same computer that is running the Web server. The Web server software doesn't have to be running when you use the Server Administrator.

To start the Server Administrator, click the Windows Start button and choose Programs ➤ Microsoft FrontPage ➤ FrontPage Server Administrator. The Server Administrator dialog displays the features (see Figure A.21).

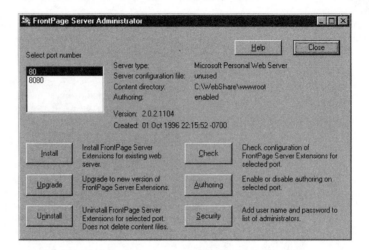

The Select port number list box lists the ports on which you currently have Web servers installed. When you select a port number, the dialog displays the server type, the file used to configure the server, the path for the server's content folder, and whether authoring is enabled. (When authoring is enabled, you can open the server's webs using the FrontPage Explorer and Editor.) The dialog displays buttons for the operations you can perform on the server at the selected port number, as follows:

Install   Click this button to install the FrontPage Server Extensions. You use the configure Server Type dialog to specify the type of the server installed on the selected port (see Figure A.22a). The Server type list displays the servers for which you can install Server Extensions. The list includes the servers for which the Server Extensions are included on the FrontPage 97 installation CD-ROM (see the list below), and any other servers for which you have downloaded Server Extensions from the FrontPage web site. Select the server type and click OK. Depending on the server, you may need to supply additional information.

Upgrade   Click this button to upgrade the webs stored by the server on the selected port using the FrontPage Server Extension software.

Uninstall   Click this button to remove the FrontPage Server Extensions from the server on the selected port. This operation does not affect the webs stored by the server. When you uninstall the Server Extensions, you remove certain files from the FrontPage webs stored by the server, but the web's content files are not disturbed. (The subfolders named _vti_bin and _vti_txt are removed from each FrontPage web.)

Check   Click this button to verify that the FrontPage Server Extensions are correctly installed on the server and the selected port.

Authoring   Click this button to display the dialog shown in Figure A.22b. Click the Enable button to allow the server's FrontPage webs to be opened using the FrontPage Explorer and Editor. If you click the Disable button, you can't open any of the server's webs from the FrontPage Explorer and Editor. If the server supports SSL (Secure Sockets Layer), you can check this option to require that the user connect to the server using the SSL protocol whenever creating, opening, or copying a web in the FrontPage Explorer.

Security   Click this button to display the Administrator name and password dialog (see Figure A.22c). You use this dialog to add new administrators for the Web server on the selected port. You can also use this dialog to add new administrators for an individual sub-Web stored by the server.

NOTE

Keep in mind that the security you set using the FrontPage Server Administrator applies only to the FrontPage application and that anyone with file system rights has direct access to the web files.

The FrontPage 97 installation CD-ROM includes FrontPage Server Extensions for the following Web servers:

FrontPage Personal Web Server

Microsoft Personal Web Server

O'Reilly WebSite and WebSite Professional

Microsoft Internet Information Server 1.0 and 2.0

Netscape Communication Server 1.1

Netscape Commerce Server 1.1 (Windows NT)

Netscapge Enterprise Server 2.0

Netscape FastTrack 2.0

FIGURE A.22

You can install FrontPage Server Extensions to a server type listed (a), enable or disable authoring (b), and create new administrators for a Web (c).

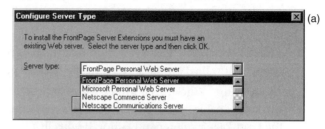

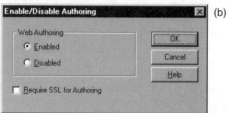

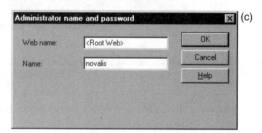

Adding the Microsoft Personal Web Server for Windows 95

This book assumes that you are running the Microsoft Personal Web Server on port 80 and the FrontPage Personal Web Server on port 8080. If you've already installed FrontPage 97 with the FrontPage Personal Web Server as the default server on port 80, and want to set up your computer to follow the book exactly, you'll need to move the FrontPage Personal Web Server to port 8080 and then install the Microsoft Personal Web Server to port 8080.

Changing a Server's Port Number

The first step is to move the FrontPage Personal Web Server from port 80 to port 8080. To change a server's port number, you uninstall the FrontPage Server Extensions from the server on its original port, and then install the FrontPage Server Extensions to the server on the new port. For the FrontPage Personal Web Server, you must manually configure the server to the new port before you can install Server Extensions. Here are the steps:

1. If necessary, shut down the FrontPage Personal Web Server by clicking the icon in the Windows task bar and then choosing File ➤ Exit from the server's menu bar.

2. Start the FrontPage Server Administrator. Click 80 in the Select port number text box and note the path to the server's configuration file. (The default path is C:\FrontPage Webs\Server\conf\httpd.cnf.) Click the Uninstall button. Click OK in the dialog to remove the server extensions from the server's root web and from each FrontPage web stored by the server. The port is no longer listed in the Select port number list box. In the next step, you modify the server's configuration file so that the server will be configured to port 8080.

3. In the Windows Explorer, locate the configuration file and open the file in Notepad. Locate the line that reads Port 80 and change it to Port 8080 (see Figure A.23). Save the change and close the configuration file.

APDX

A

Installing FrontPage 97 and the Web Servers

FIGURE A.23

You can modify the httpd.cnf file to change the port number for the FrontPage Personal Web Server.

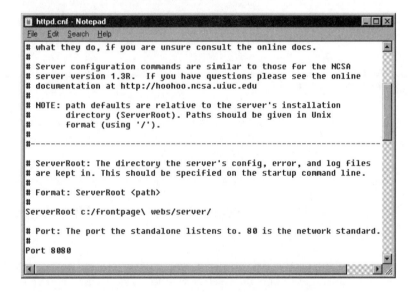

4. Click the Install button in the Server Administrator and click OK in the Configure Server Type dialog to specify that the server is the FrontPage Personal Web Server. When you install Server Extensions to the FrontPage Personal Web

Server, you must specify the path to the configuration file. Click Browse, locate the configuration file and click Open. Click OK to start the process. Click OK in the Confirmation Dialog (see Figure A.24). Type the name and password you want to use as the server's FrontPage administrator in the Administrator Setup dialog (see Figure A.11a earlier in the appendix) and click OK. The server extension software is installed in the server's root web and in the subwebs.

FIGURE A.24

Confirmation dialog to install Server Extensions on port 8080

NOTE

When you change the port number of a Web server other than the FrontPage Personal Web Server, it is not usually necessary to manually reconfigure the server to the new port. For most other Web servers, you enter the new port number in a dialog that is displayed after you click the Install button.

Installing the Microsoft Personal Web Server for Windows 95

1. Install the Microsoft Personal Web Server as described in the "Installing the Microsoft Personal Web Server" section. Because you've removed the FrontPage Personal Web Server from port 80, this port is now available for the installation.

2. Start the FrontPage Server Administrator and click the Install button. Choose Microsoft Personal Web Server in the Configure Server Type dialog and click OK.

Click OK in the Confirmation Dialog (see Figure A.25). The server extensions are installed to the server.

Confirmation dialog to install Server Extensions on port 80

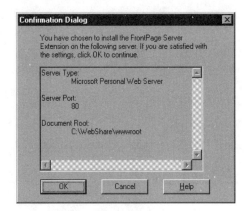

Adding the FrontPage Personal Web Server

If you've already installed FrontPage 97 with the Microsoft Personal Web Server or another Web server as the default server on port 80, and want to set up your computer to follow the book exactly, you'll need install the FrontPage Personal Web Server to port 8080. The installation process automatically detects another server on port 80 and installs the FrontPage Personal Web Server to port 8080.

1. Insert the FrontPage 97 CD-ROM and click the first button to start the FrontPage installation.

2. Click Yes in the Question dialog to stop the Microsoft Personal Web Server and continue the installation.

3. Click Next to close the welcome screen, and again to close the registration screen, and then click Yes to confirm registration. Type the CD Key and click OK to display the Destination Path screen (see Figure A.26a). Click Next.

4. Click Custom in the Setup Type dialog, and click Next to display the Select Components dialog. Uncheck the Client Software check box and check the Microsoft FrontPage Personal Web Server check box. The Server Extension check box is checked automatically (see Figure A.26b).

FIGURE A.26

To install the FrontPage Personal Web Server (a), select the server (b).

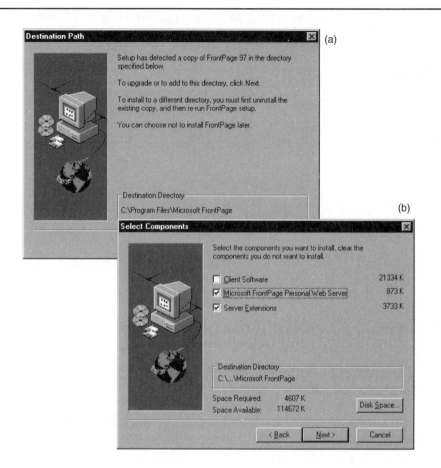

(a)

(b)

5. Click Next. You use the next dialog to specify the folder for the FrontPage Personal Web Server (see Figure A.8a). Click the Browse button to select another folder, or click Next to accept c:\FrontPage Webs as the default folder.

6. The next dialog explains that the FrontPage Personal Web Server will be configured to run on port 8080, and that you'll need to append 8080 to your computer's name to connect to this server (see Figure A.8b). Click Next.

7. Deselect the Microsoft Personal Web Server in the Installed Servers Detected dialog (we've already installed the Server Extensions on this server) and click Next. The Start Copying Files dialog (see Figure A.9b) indicates that the FrontPage Personal Web Server will be installed to the default directory c:\FrontPage Webs\Server, and that the content directory for this server's webs is c:\FrontPage Webs\Content.

8. Click Next to begin installation.

9. Type a name and password and then retype the password in the Administrator Setup dialog, and then click OK (see Figure A.11a).

NOTE

You'll need to supply the name and the password with the same capitalization that you enter in the Administrator Setup for FrontPage Personal Web Server dialog whenever you create a new web or open an existing web in the FrontPage Explorer.

10. The FrontPage Server Extensions are installed on port 8080. Click Finish to complete the installation.

TCP/IP Test Utility

The FrontPage TCP/IP Test program tests the status of your TCP/IP connection. If you modified the Windows Start Menu as described above, you can start the test program by clicking the Windows Start button and choosing Programs ➤ Microsoft FrontPage ➤ Microsoft TCP-IP Test. You can also start the test from the FrontPage Explorer by choosing Help ➤ About Microsoft FrontPage Explorer from the Explorer menu bar and then clicking the Network Test button (see Figure A.27a). Click the Start Test button to begin the test (see Figure A.27b). The results of the test indicate the host name and IP address (see Figure A.27c). If your computer does not have a direct connection to the Internet, it won't have its own IP address. In this case, your computer uses 127.0.0.1 as its IP address while you are working without an open network connection.

FIGURE A.27

You can start the TCP/IP test from the Windows Start Menu or from the FrontPage Explorer (a). Click Start Test to begin (b) and then view the results (c).

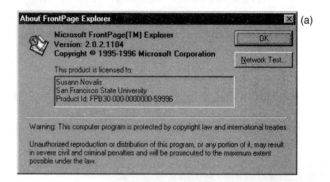

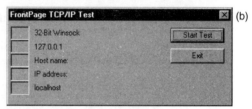

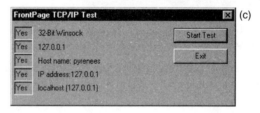

Appendix

B

Bonus Pack

Bonus Pack

The Bonus Pack that comes with FrontPage 97 contains four Microsoft applications that you can use to enhance FrontPage 97. This appendix gives a brief description of the applications. Additional updated information can be obtained from the Microsoft web site.

Microsoft Personal Web Server

The Microsoft Personal Web Server for Windows 95 is designed for use by workgroups in corporations sharing information on private intranets and by small businesses, community and religious organizations, schools, and individuals publishing information on the World Wide Web. The Microsoft Personal Web Server supports sharing of both HTTP and FTP files. It is more powerful than the FrontPage Personal Web Server and has many of the features of the more powerful Microsoft Internet Information Server for Windows NT 4.0, including support for CGI scripts and ISAPI server extensions (see Chapter 2 for more information on server extensions). The Microsoft Personal Web Server 1.0 provides the ability to connect to ODBC databases through the Internet Database Connector server extension (see Chapter 21 for more information). The next version is expected to support the Active Server Page technology that allows the server to execute scripts included on web pages. The Microsoft Personal Web Server does not support the Secure Sockets Layer (SSL) security protocol.

NOTE

Secure Sockets Layer is an enhanced security protocol developed by Netscape Communications Corporation that provides a security layer between application protocols such as HTTP and the TCP/IP networking protocol. This layer establishes a secure connection between the network and the data on your Web server using public key cryptography and digital certificates, and then encrypts and decrypts information as it is sent and received. Both the web server and the browser must support SSL.

Installing the Microsoft Personal Web Server is easy (see Appendix A for details). The server software is installed by default to the C:\Program Files\Websvr folder, and the content folders are installed as subfolders of the C:\Webshare folder. The Webshare folder contains these subfolders:

Content folders	Purpose
ftproot	For storing the files for others to download and the files that others copy to your computer using the ftp protocol
scripts	For storing the programs that you want to make available to all files stored by the server
wwwroot	For storing the individual web folders that you are making available using the HTTP protocol

Viewing and Changing Server Properties

The Microsoft Personal Web Server is integrated into the Windows 95 taskbar and the Control Panel. The easiest way to display the properties dialog for the server is to double-click its icon in the Windows 95 taskbar. The properties you can view and change are organized in four tabs (see Figure B.1a).

General Tab   The General tab displays the following information:

Internet address of the server   If your computer doesn't have a full-time Internet connection and an IP address, the Internet address includes the name of your computer. If your computer has an IP address, the Internet address uses the name assigned to your computer by your network administrator.

Default home page   This is the path and filename of the home page of the server—that is, the home page of the root web. Click the Display Home Page button to view this page in a browser.

Click the More Details button on the General tab to display the online documentation for both the Personal Web Server and the FTP Server.

Startup Tab   Use the Startup tab to control when the server starts up (see Figure B.1b). Click the Start or Stop buttons to manually start or stop the server. You can choose options to start the server automatically when you start the computer, and to show or hide the server icon in the toolbar.

APDX

B

Bonus Pack

The General tab (a) and the Startup tab (b) of the Personal Web Server Properties dialog

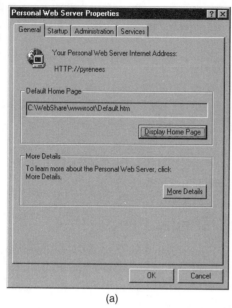
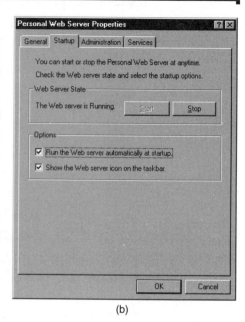

(a)   (b)

Administration Tab   Click the Administration button on the Administration tab to display the application, called the Internet Services Administrator, that you use to administer the Personal Web Server (see Figure B.2). The Internet Services Administrator is a web-based application and opens in your Web browser (see Figure B.3).

> **WWW Administration**   Click the WWW Administration hyperlink to display the Service page of the WWW Administrator (see Figure B.4).
>
> **Service page**   Use this page to change the number of seconds to wait before the attempt to connect to the server times out, and the maximum number of connections. Use the Password authentication section to allow anonymous access or to require users to supply a username and password using basic authentication, which does not encrypt the username and password before sending the information from the browser or Windows NT Challenge/Response authentication which encrypts the user name and password.

NOTE

Windows NT Challenge/Response authentication is supported only by the Microsoft Internet Explorer 3.0 browser and only over a local area network that has at least one Windows NT domain.

FIGURE B.2

Click the Administration button to start the Internet Services Administrator.

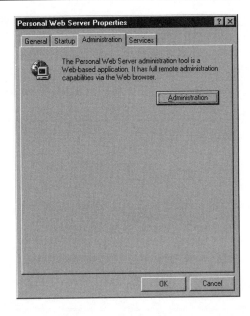

FIGURE B.3

Use The Administrator to administer the Web and FTP services

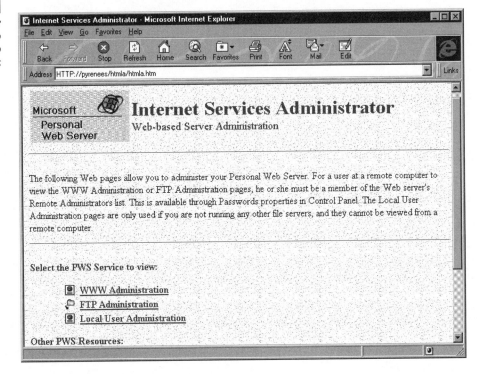

FIGURE B.4

The Administration page for the Web service

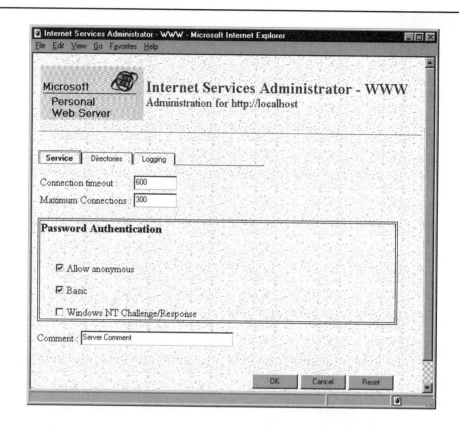

Directories page Click the Directories tab to display the Directory page (see Figure B.5). This page lists the _vti_ folders for the root web and for each web stored by the server. The list also displays all the shared folders including the individual web subfolders that contain programs and scripts. To edit or delete a folder, click the folder's <u>Edit</u> or <u>Delete</u> hyperlink. To add a new folder, click the <u>Add</u> hyperlink at the bottom of the list. You can use the Edit and Add pages to assign read and execute permissions to a folder. You can also specify an alias for a folder that is located elsewhere on your computer or on another server.

NOTE

An *alias* is the name that the Web visitor uses to access the folder without needing to specify the folder's real location. If a directory named Bicycle Outfitter is located somewhere other than in the wwwroot folder and has the alias /Bicycles, then the visitor can specify http://servername/Bicycles to access the folder.

The top (a) and bottom (b) of the Directories tab of the Web service administrator

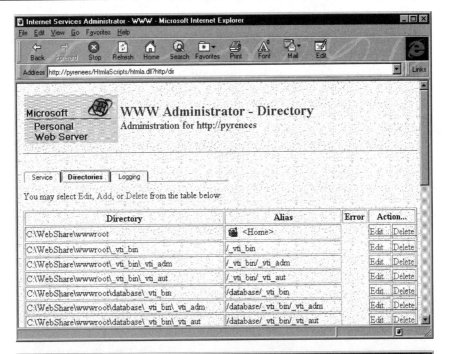

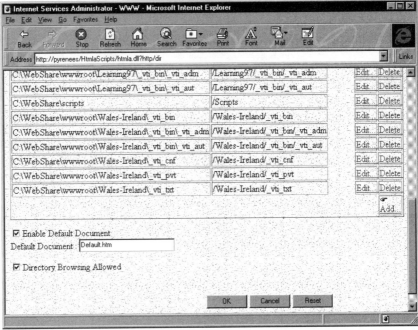

APDX

B

Bonus Pack

By default, the webs you store on the Microsoft Personal Web Server are stored in the C:\Webshare\Wwwroot folder. However, you can store webs in another folder and make it the server's root folder. Click the Edit hyperlink on the first line in the list (the line with <Home> in the alias column). In the Directory Edit page, type the full path of the folder you want to be the home root folder in the Directory box, or click the Browse button to locate the folder, and click OK (see Figure B.6).

FIGURE B.6

Enter the path and name of the new home root folder for the server.

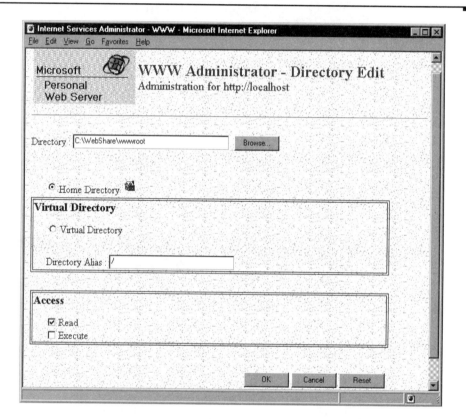

Do not change the alias for the home root folder. Changing the alias for the home root folder can lead to unpredictable results, and you may have to reinstall the Personal Web Server.

To change the name of the default page that the server displays when the visitor doesn't specify the name of a page in the web, scroll to the bottom of the Directory page and type the new name in the Default Document text box (see Figure B.5b). Click the OK button to save the change.

To prevent browsing of all folders stored by the server, uncheck the Directory Browsing Allowed option at the bottom of the Directory page. You may want to prevent any browsing while you are setting up or making major changes to your server.

Logging page   Click the Logging tab of the WWW Administrator to display the Logging Page (see Figure B.7). Use this page to enable logging and to specify when and where a new log file is created. The Personal Web Server creates an activity log of every request it handles, and keeps track of information including the IP address of the requesting computer, the date and time of the request, and the relative URL of each file requested. Figure B.8 shows the six log entries for the opening of the home page of the Wales-Ireland web, including the request for the home page and the five images used on the page.

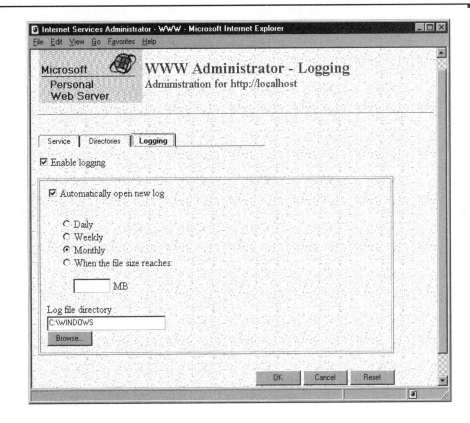

FIGURE B.7

Use the Logging tab to enable logging and to specify when and where the log file is created.

Log file entries for opening the home page of the Wales-Ireland web.

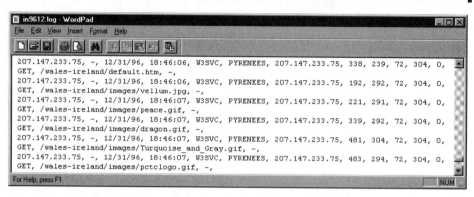

Local User Administration   Click the Local User Administration text link on the main page of the Internet Services Administrator to view the Local User Administrator page. If your computer is not set up to use user-level access control, you can control access to the webs stored by the Personal Web Server with the Local User Administrator. Use the tabs of the Local User Administrator to define new Users or new Groups and to assign users to groups. To learn how to enable user-level access control instead, see Windows 95 or Windows NT documentation.

Services Tab   The Services tab of the Personal Web Server Properties displays the current status of the HTTP and the FTP services that the Personal Web Server provides (see Figure B.9a). Change the running status of a service by selecting it and clicking the Start or Stop button. To view the properties of a service, select the service and then click Properties. The Properties dialog for the selected service provides startup options to toggle the startup between automatic and manual (see Figures B.9b and B.9c). The Properties dialog displays the name and path of the content folder for the service (home root folder). Click the Change Home Root button to display the Administrator and change the content folder as described in the previous section. The HTTP Properties dialog also displays the name and path of the home page for the root web. Click the Change Home Page button to display the WWW Administrator and change the name of the default page as described in the previous section.

FIGURE B.9

Click the Services tab to view and change the running status of the FTP and HTTP services (a). Click the Properties button to display the FTP Properties dialog (b) or the HTTP properties dialog (c).

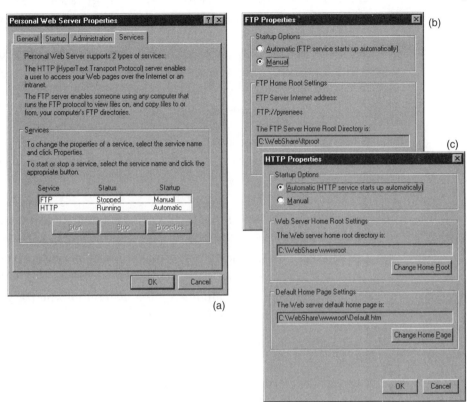

(a)

(b)

(c)

Microsoft Web Publishing Wizard

If the Web server you are planning to use for publishing your webs is not installed on your own computer, you can post your web to a FrontPage-enabled Web server by choosing File ➤ Publish FrontPage Web in the FrontPage Explorer menu bar (see the "Publishing a Web to a Web Server" section in Chapter 5 for more information). If the Web server does not have FrontPage Server Extensions installed, you may be able to post a modified version of your web to the Web server using the Microsoft Web Publishing Wizard. The wizard is not designed to determine whether your web uses the browse time bots or the FrontPage Server-side Image Maps. Before posting to a Web server without the FrontPage Server Extensions, modify the web as follows:

1. Remove or modify pages that use the Confirmation, Discussion, Registration, Save Results, and Search bots.

Bonus Pack

2. If your Web server can create NCSA, CERN, or Netscape image maps, specify the corresponding server-side image maps in the FrontPage Explorer (see Chapter 13 for more information).

This wizard can post to many of the popular Web servers, including Microsoft's Internet Information Server, APACHE Web server, and the National Center for Supercomputing Applications (NSCA) HTTPD server. The wizard can post to several Internet Service Providers, such as Compuserve, Sprynet, AOL, and GNN, and other ISPs running any of the standard Web servers installed with the default configuration and running the FTP protocol.

Whether you use the File ➤ Publish FrontPage Web command in the FrontPage Explorer or the Web Publishing Wizard, the hardest part is preparing to make the connection to the Web server.

Corporate Environment   If you are in a corporate environment and plan to use the company Web server, do the following:

1. If you access the Internet through a proxy server, contact your intranet administrator to determine how to configure your browser for posting to the Web server.

2. Contact your intranet administrator to determine whether you have write access to the Web server's content directory.

Internet Service Provider   If you plan to use an Internet Service Provider, do the following:

1. If you can not connect to the ISP with your browser, contact the ISP administrator for help in configuring your browser. Continue to Step 2a or 2b, depending on your ISP.

2a. If your ISP supports Dial-up Networking, make sure Dial-Up Networking is installed and create a connection icon to access your ISP. Contact your ISP administrator to determine whether you need a Dial-Up Networking script to automate the connection.

NOTE

The Dial-Up Networking software is on the Windows 95 CD. You can also download the software from http://www.microsoft.com/windows/software/admintools.htm.

2b. If your ISP does not support Dial-up Networking, contact your ISP to obtain the software dialer that the ISP provides. For example, AOL and GNN provide software dialers at http://www.aol.com and http://www.gnn.com, respectively. Install the software dialer.

Posting a Web with the Web Publishing Wizard

After preparing to make the connection, you are ready to post a web. To illustrate, this section steps through the process of posting a web to an ISP using the Web Publishing Wizard.

If necessary, open your Internet connection and then start the Web Publishing Wizard by clicking the Windows Start button and choosing Programs ➤ Accessories ➤ Internet Tools ➤ Web Publishing Wizard.

1. The first screen introduces the wizard. Click Next. Use the next dialog to select the file or folder you want to publish (see Figure B.10a). Type the full path to the web folder or click the Browse Folders button and locate the web folder.

2. Click Next. Use the next dialog to select the name of the Web server to which you are posting the web. If you are posting to an ISP that isn't in the list, click New to display a list of other Internet Service Providers (see Figure B.10b). The next screens depend on the ISP you choose. If your ISP isn't in the list, you are prompted to enter the ISP's Internet address and your username and password. To illustrate the process for an ISP in the list, the next steps assume you are posting to Compuserve.

FIGURE B.10

Use the Web Publishing Wizard to post a web in your computer's file system (a) to a Web server that does not have FrontPage Server Extensions installed (b).

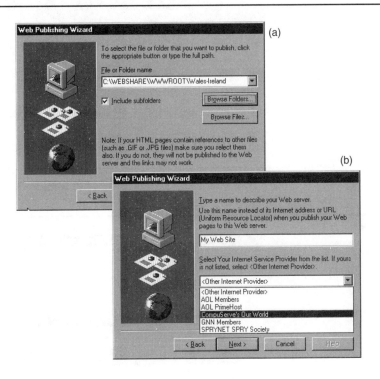

3. Click Next. Type the requested personal information in the next dialog and click Next (see Figure B.11a). Type your Compuserve UserID and Password in the next dialog and click Next (see Figure B.11b). Click Finish in the next dialog to begin the upload.

4. Select the default home page from the Select a Home Page dialog (see Figure B.12) and click OK. The files are uploaded to your account. Depending on your ISP, you may be able to view your web immediately.

The dialogs for Compuserve request personal information (a) and your Compuserve UserID and Password (b).

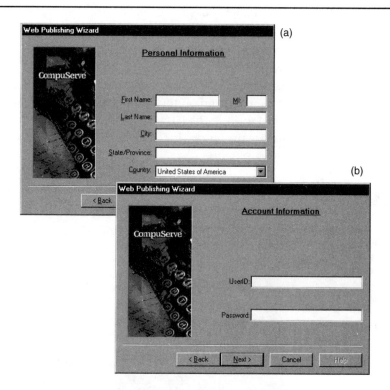

Select a home page and click OK to upload the web.

Microsoft Image Composer

The Microsoft Image Composer is an image creation and editing tool provided in the Bonus Pack. The Image Composer is integrated into FrontPage as the editor application assigned to handle images. When you double-click an inserted image or when you select an image and click the Edit button in the Edit ➤ Edit Properties dialog in the FrontPage Editor, the Image Composer starts up and displays the image.

Including the usual image editing tools, the Image Composer has a total of more than 500 tools and special effects, such as patterns and fills, warps and filters, and paint, sketch, graphic, exotic, and utility art effects. An important difference between the traditional image editing application and the Image Composer is that when you use the Image Composer, transparency information is built in and you can use the shape of the object to define the shape of the image. The image that uses the shape of the object as its boundary is called a *sprite*. By contrast, in traditional image editing you have to use a rectangular image regardless of the shape of the object. Sprites are easy to move, arrange, size, and transform with special effects. You can also vary the transparency within the sprite to compose images with see-through sprites.

You can use the editing tools to create new images from scratch, however, the real advantage of the Image Composer is that you can easily create new images by modifying and combining parts of existing images. The Image Composer comes with more than 700 royalty-free images, including 500 professionally prepared photographic images.

GIF Animator

Use the Microsoft GIF Animator to create animated GIF images. An animated GIF image gives the illusion of an animation by displaying a sequence of images stored together with timing information in a single file. Most browsers recognize the GIF89a file format used for animated GIF images and play the animation automatically without the need for a helper application or an add-in. In addition, the browser displays the frames of an animated GIF image as soon as they are downloaded instead of waiting until the file is completely downloaded.

Unfortunately, it is not possible to describe these excellent graphic tools in this book. The Microsoft Image Composer needs a separate book to describe its features. However, you can take guided tours of both tools and download the Microsoft GIF Animator and sample images at http://www.microsoft.com/imagecomposer/.

APDX

B

Bonus Pack

Microsoft Internet Explorer 3.0

The Bonus Pack includes the Microsoft Internet Explorer 3.0 browser. You can use this browser to preview your FrontPage webs. If you don't have a direct Internet connection, you may want to configure the browser so starting the browser does not also initiate your connection to your ISP.

1. Start the Internet Explorer 3.0 and choose View ➤ Options from the menu bar.

2. Click the Connection tab and uncheck Connect to the Internet as needed. When you preview a page by clicking the Preview in Browser button in the Editor toolbar (and the Internet Explorer 3.0 is set as the default browser in FrontPage), the Internet Explorer opens without triggering your ISP login dialog.

NOTE

Obtain comprehensive information about the features and technical aspects of the Microsoft Internet Explorer 3.0 browser at the Microsoft web site at www.microsoft.com.

Appendix

C

Creating Web Templates with the FrontPage 97 SDK

CREATING WEB TEMPLATES WITH THE FRONTPAGE 97 SDK

I t is easy to create your own web templates using the FrontPage Web Template Maker. This utility program is one of the components of the FrontPage 97 Software Developer's Kit. Don't let the name put you off—you don't need to be a developer and you don't have to know how to program to use the Web Template Maker. This appendix shows you how to install and use the utility.

NOTE

You can use the Web Template Maker to create a web template based only on a web stored by the FrontPage Personal Web Server. However, after creating the new web template, you can use it to create a new web on any Web server.

Installing the Web Template Maker

The SDK is the self-expanding fp97sdk.exe file located in the FrontPage 97 SDK folder on the book's CD-ROM. This section shows you how to expand the file and create a Start menu shortcut for the Web Template Maker.

1. Copy the folder named FrontPage SDK from the book's CD-ROM to your computer's file system.

2. Click the Windows Start button and choose Run. Click the Browse button in the Run dialog and locate the fr97sdk.exe file in the FrontPage SDK folder on your computer. This compressed file contains both folders and files. To instruct Windows to create the folders and place files in appropriate folders, you must modify the expression in the Run dialog by appending the flag -d.

3. Place the insertion point at the end of the expression, press Space, type **-d,** and click OK. The file expands to create the six folders and files of the FrontPage Software Developer's Kit. For more information about how to extend the capabilities of FrontPage, read the fpdevkit.doc Word document. This document explains how to use the SDK to create custom wizards, WebBot components, and menu commands, and how to use an extension to the WebBot HTML Markup component called Designer HTML. The Web Template Maker is in the Utility folder.

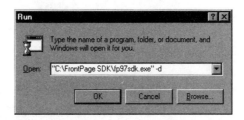

4. Open the Windows Explorer, locate and double-click the Utility folder in the FrontPage SDK folder on your computer, and double-click the Webtmpl folder. The Webtmpl.exe file is the Web Template Maker utility program.

5. Right-click on the Webtmpl.exe file, choose Create Shortcut from the shortcut menu, and type **FrontPage Web Template Maker** as the name of the shortcut. Drag the shortcut to the Windows\StartMenu\Programs\Microsoft FrontPage folder.

Creating a New Web Template

You can use the Web Template Maker to create a new web template based on any web stored by the FrontPage Personal Web Server. If the web you want to use for the web template is stored by another Web server, first copy the web to the FrontPage Personal Web Server. See Chapter 5 for information on copying a web to another Web server.

When you create a new web template, the Web Template Maker creates a new folder in the Webs folder that FrontPage uses to store web templates (default path C:\Program Files\Microsoft FrontPage\Webs) and copies all the selected web's content folders and files. (If the web contains discussion groups, the article pages are not copied as part of the template.) The web parameters set in the Parameters tab of the Tools ➤ Web Settings dialog and the To Do List tasks are copied as well. Afterwards, the new web template appears in the New Web dialog.

1. Click the Windows Start button and choose Programs ➤ Microsoft FrontPage ➤ FrontPage Web Template Maker. The utility starts and displays the dialog shown

in Figure C.1. The list box on the left displays the webs stored by the FrontPage Personal Web Server.

FIGURE C.1

The FrontPage Web Template Maker

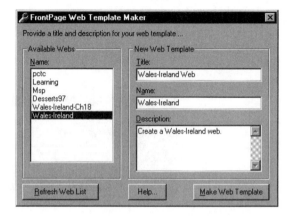

2. Click the web you want to use for the new template. The utility automatically fills in a title, name, and description for the template. The title and description will be displayed in the New Web dialog. The name is the base name of the folder that will be used to store the template files (the Web Template Maker appends .tem as the template extension). You can modify the title, name, or description. The base name must follow the rules for naming webs (see Chapter 5 for more information).

3. Click the Make Web Template button to create the new web template. After the new template is created, you can use it the same way you use a built-in web template.

To modify an existing template, create a modified version of the web on the FrontPage Personal Web Server. The Web Template Maker cannot update an existing template, and you must delete the template folder from the Webs folder. After manually deleting the existing web template folder, run the FrontPage Web Template Maker to create the new web template based on the modified web.

Index

Note to the Reader: Throughout this index page numbers in **boldface** indicate primary discussions of a topic. Page numbers in *italics* indicate illustrations.

D

F

—**W**—

X

What's on the Companion CD-ROM?

As you work through *Mastering FrontPage 97*, you'll participate in building example webs. The book's companion CD-ROM includes the following files needed to work through the examples:

- Files that you'll import into webs as you work are stored in the Images, PCTC Information, Sounds and Video, Wales-Ireland Manuscript and Wales-Ireland Maps, and Wales-Ireland Photos folders.

- The Webs folder includes the versions of webs that you'll copy at the beginning of a chapter. For example, at the beginning of Chapter 13, you'll create a copy of the Wales-Ireland-Ch13 web. The Webs folder also includes several "answer webs"—that is, webs as they exist at the end of a chapter. For example, the answer web named Interactive is the web you create in Chapter 17.

The Microsoft FrontPage 97 Software Development Kit is also included.